Lecture Notes in Computer Science 7199

Commenced Publication in 1973
Founding and Former Series Editors:
Gerhard Goos, Juris Hartmanis, and Jan van Leeuwen

Oliver C.S. Choy   Ray C. C. Cheung
Peter Athanas   Kentaro Sano (Eds.)

Reconfigurable Computing: Architectures, Tools and Applications

8th International Symposium, ARC 2012
Hong Kong, China, March 19-23, 2012
Proceedings

 Springer

Volume Editors

Oliver C.S. Choy
The Chinese University of Hong Kong
Department of Electronic Engineering
Shatin, N.T., Hong Kong, China
E-mail: cschoy@ee.cuhk.edu.hk

Ray C. C. Cheung
City University of Hong Kong
Department of Electronic Engineering
Kowloon Tong, Hong Kong, China
E-mail: r.cheung@cityu.edu.hk

Peter Athanas
Virginia Tech, Department of ECE
302 Whittemore Hall
Blacksburg, VA 24061, USA
E-mail: athanas@vt.edu

Kentaro Sano
Tohoku University
6-6-01 Aramaki Aza Aoba, Aobaku
Sendai, Miyagi, 981-8579, Japan
E-mail: kentah@caero.mech.tohoku.ac.jp

ISSN 0302-9743   e-ISSN 1611-3349
ISBN 978-3-642-28364-2   e-ISBN 978-3-642-28365-9
DOI 10.1007/978-3-642-28365-9
Springer Heidelberg Dordrecht London New York

Library of Congress Control Number: 2012931224

CR Subject Classification (1998): C.2, D.2, I.4, H.3, F.1, I.6, D.3

LNCS Sublibrary: SL 1 – Theoretical Computer Science and General Issues

Typesetting: Camera-ready by author, data conversion by Scientific Publishing Services, Chennai, India

Printed on acid-free paper

Springer is part of Springer Science+Business Media (www.springer.com)

Preface

The 8th International Symposium on Applied Reconfigurable Computing (ARC 2012) was held at the Chinese University of Hong Kong (CUHK), Shatin, Hong Kong during March 21–23, 2011. The symposium also included industrial workshops provided by Xilinx and Altera in CUHK and the City University of Hong Kong during March 19–20, 2011. The symposium and workshop were sponsored by Xilinx Inc., Altera Corp., and CPO Technologies Corporation.

ARC 2012 received 44 submissions from 17 countries all over the world. Each paper was reviewed by at least four committee members, involving nearly 200 reviews. More than 80 committee members were invited to form the Program Committee according to their particular areas of expertise. The Program Committee selected 25 papers for oral presentation, and 10 poster papers for the proceedings. The main theme this year was "ARC for better living". The program was completed with five excellent invited talks given by Michael J. Flynn (Stanford University), Sorin A. Huss (Technische Universitaet Darmstadt), Cetin Kaya Koc (UCSE), Wayne Luk (Imperial College London), and Grant Martin (Tensilica Inc.).

Many people contributed to the success of ARC 2012. First, we would like to thank all the authors who submitted their excellent research results to ARC. Second, we would like to thank all of the 80 Program Committee members, as well as the external reviewers, who volunteered to read the papers. We are greatly indebted to the Proceedings Chair, Yuet Ming Lam, for his relentless efforts in compiling the proceedings. We would like to thank the local Organizing Committee Chairs, Evan Young, Hayden So, and their team for all the hotel and local arrangements. We would like to thank all the great efforts of the ARC 2012 Organizing Committee team, and the Conference Secretariat, Momentous Asia, Hong Kong. Finally, we want to express our gratitude to our generous sponsors: Xilinx Inc., Altera Corp., CPO Technologies Corporation, and the support from the local Hong Kong universities and the IEEE Hong Kong Section Computer Society Chapter and CAS/COM Chapter.

December 2011

Oliver Choy
Ray Cheung
Peter Athanas
Kentaro Sano

Organization

ARC 2012 was organized by the Department of Electronic Engineering, the Chinese University of Hong Kong and the Department of Electronic Engineering, City University of Hong Kong.

Organising Committee

General Chair

Oliver Choy	The Chinese University of Hong Kong, Hong Kong
Ray Cheung	City University of Hong Kong, Hong Kong

Program Chair

Peter Athanas	Virginia Tech, USA
Kentaro Sano	Tohoku University, Japan

Local Arrangements Chair

Hayden So	University of Hong Kong, Hong Kong
Evan Young	The Chinese University of Hong Kong, Hong Kong

Publicity Chair

Suhaib Fahmy	Nanyang Technological University, Singapore
Bryan Hu	University of Alberta, Canada

Proceedings Chair

Yuet Ming Lam	Macau University of Science and Technology, Macau

Finance Chair

Chiwai Yu	City University of Hong Kong, Hong Kong

Registration Chair

Bruce Sham	The Hong Kong Polytechnic University, Hong Kong

Banquet Chair

Patrick Hung	CPO Technologies Corporation, USA

Sponsorship Chair

Wei Zhang   Nanyang Technological University, Singapore

Webmaster

Cedric Yiu   The Hong Kong Polytechnic University,
                                       Hong Kong

Secretariat

Laurie Lau   Momentous Asia, Hong Kong

Program Committee

Jeff Arnold	Strech Inc., USA
Peter Athanas	Virginia Tech, USA
Michael Attig	Xilinx Research Labs, San Jose, USA
Jürgen Becker	Universität Karlsruhe (TH), Germany
Khaled Benkrid	University of Edinburgh, UK
Mladen Berekovic	Braunschweig University of Technology, Germany
Neil Bergmann	University of Queensland, Australia
Koen Bertels	Delft University of Technology, The Netherlands
Christos-Savvas Bouganis	Imperial College London, UK
Stephen Brown	Altera Corp., University of Toronto, Canada
João M.P. Cardoso	University of Porto/INESC-ID, Portugal
Ray Cheung	City University of Hong Kong, Hong Kong
Oliver Choy	The Chinese University of Hong Kong, Hong Kong
Albert Chung	The Hong Kong University of Science and Technology, Hong Kong
Katherine Compton	University of Wisconsin-Madison, USA
George Constantinides	Imperial College London, UK
Florent de Dinechin	Ecole Normale Superieure de Lyon, France
Pedro C. Diniz	Technical University of Lisbon (IST) / INESC-ID, Portugal
Tarek El-Ghazawi	George Washington University, USA
Robert Esser	Apple Inc., USA
Suhaib Fahmy	Nanyang Technological University, Singapore
António Ferrari	University of Aveiro, Portugal
Kris Gaj	George Mason University, USA
Guy Gognia	Université de Bretagne Sud, France
Yajun Ha	National University of Singapore
Jim Harkin	University of Ulster, Magee, UK
Reiner Hartenstein	University of Kaiserslautern, Germany
Roman Hermida	Universidad Complutense, Madrid, Spain

Lesley Shannon   Simon Fraser University, Canada
Yuchiro Shibata   Nagasaki University, Japan
Hayden So   University of Hong Kong, Hong Kong
Pedro Trancoso   University of Cyprus, Cyprus
Markus Weinhardt   Osnabrück University of Applied Sciences,
                           Germany
Stephan Wong   Delft University of Technology,
                           The Netherlands
Roger Woods   The Queen's University of Belfast, UK
Yoshiki Yamaguchi   Tsukuba University, Japan
Cedric Yiu   The Hong Kong Polytechnic University,
                           Hong Kong
Evan Young   The Chinese University of Hong Kong,
                           Hong Kong
Chiwai Yu   City University of Hong Kong, Hong Kong
Wei Zhang   Nanyang Technological University, Singapore
Peter Zipf   University of Kassel, Germany

Sponsoring Organizations

Gold sponsorship   Xilinx Inc
Silver sponsorship   Altera Corporation
Bronze sponsorship   CPO Technology Corporation

Table of Contents

Applied RC Design Methods and Tools

Applied RC Architectures

Applied RC Applications

Critical Issues in Applied RC

Posters

Automating Reconfiguration Chain Generation for SRL-Based Run-Time Reconfiguration

Karel Heyse* Brahim Al Farisi, Karel Bruneel, and Dirk Stroobandt

Ghent University, ELIS Department
Sint-Pietersnieuwstraat 41, 9000 Gent, Belgium
{Karel.Heyse,Brahim.AlFarisi,Karel.Bruneel,Dirk.Stroobandt}@UGent.be

Abstract. Run-time reconfiguration (RTR) of FPGAs is mainly done using the configuration interface. However, for a certain group of designs, RTR using the shift register functionality of the LUTs is a much faster alternative than conventional RTR using the ICAP. This method requires the creation of reconfiguration chains connecting the run-time reconfigurable LUTs (SRL). In this paper, we develop and evaluate a method to generate these reconfiguration chains in an automated way so that their influence on the RTR design is minimised and the reconfiguration time is optimised. We do this by solving a constrained multiple travelling salesman problem (mTSP) based on the placement information of the run-time reconfigurable LUTs. An algorithm based on simulated annealing was developed to solve this new constrained mTSP. We show that using the proposed method, reconfiguration chains can be added with minimal influence on the clock frequency of the original design.

Keywords: FPGA, Run-Time Reconfiguration, Tuneable LUT Circuit, Shift-Register-LUT, SRL, Multiple Travelling Salesman Problem, Simulated Annealing.

1   Introduction

Run-time reconfiguration (RTR) allows for more efficient utilisation of Field Programmable Gate Arrays (FPGA). Indeed, RTR enables us to specialise an FPGA's functionality for the current problem situation. This is called dynamic circuit specialisation (DCS) [1]. DCS can be done by simply writing a specialised configuration in the FPGA's configuration memory. A specialised configuration uses fewer resources and can attain higher clock speeds than a generic implementation and thus uses the FPGA resources more efficiently. The downside is that the gain in efficiency can be nullified by the reconfiguration overhead – the time needed to rewrite the configuration. Whether the dynamic circuit specialisation is useful depends on the problem itself, the rate at which the problem situation changes and the size of the reconfiguration overhead.

The reconfiguration overhead is greatly reduced when the TLUT method [1] is used to implement dynamic specialisation, because it only requires that some of

---

* Supported by a Ph.D. grant of the Flemish Fund for Scientific Research (FWO).

O.C.S. Choy et al. (Eds.): ARC 2012, LNCS 7199, pp. 1–12, 2012.

the FPGA's LUTs, called the TLUTs, are reconfigured in order to specialise the configuration of the FPGA and because the LUT truth tables constitute only ca. 4% (Virtex 2 Pro) of the complete configuration memory. Moreover, since only LUTs need to be reconfigured and not the routing, FPGAs that contain LUTs with shift register functionality (SRLs) offer the opportunity to perform even faster reconfiguration. Indeed, when a conventional reconfiguration port, like the ICAP, is used, many static configuration bits are rewritten because the ports require the reconfiguration of a full frame which contains many truth tables, some of which don't require reconfiguration. On the other hand, when using SRL reconfiguration [2], every LUT can be accessed individually which reduces the size of the configuration data that needs to be sent. Further, when using SRLs, all the LUTs can be reconfigured in parallel, while the reconfiguration ports of the FPGA have a restricted bandwidth. When this maximum reconfiguration bandwidth is not needed, the bandwidth can be customised to the design by arranging the SRLs as large shift registers, which we call reconfiguration chains.

The problem we address in this paper is how to introduce the reconfiguration chains so that their influence on the design is minimised. The only requirement is that each of the TLUTs is part of one of the reconfiguration chains in order to enable its reconfiguration. Which chain it is part of and where it is positioned in that chain are two degrees of freedom that can be used to minimise the impact the introduction of the chains has on the original design, and to optimise the reconfiguration time.

Our goal is to create an automatic and generic method to enable more widespread use of SRL reconfiguration, in particular in combination with the TLUT method but not restricted to it. This in contrast to previous work, which has mainly focussed on implementing individual problems using SRL reconfiguration.

We model the problem of generating these reconfiguration chains as a constrained multiple travelling salesman problem (mTSP) based on the placement information of the TLUTs after placement. A solution method based on simulated annealing is presented to solve this mTSP. We evaluated the proposed method by introducing reconfiguration chains into several dynamically specialisable FIR filter and TCAM designs, and found that for most problems the influence on the clock frequency of the design is limited to 5%, while allowing for extremely fast reconfiguration.

The paper is organised as follows. Section 2 gives a more profound introduction to the TLUT method and SRL reconfiguration. In Section 3 the problem is formulated as an mTSP and our proposed algorithm is described. Section 4 contains the experimental results. Finally, we draw conclusions in Section 5.

2   RTR Background

2.1   TLUT Method

A conventional FPGA tool flow transforms an HDL description of a design into an FPGA configuration. The TLUT method [1], on the other hand, is able to construct a parameterised FPGA configuration, i.e. a dynamically specialisable configuration where some of the bits are expressed as Boolean functions of the parameters, from a parameterised HDL description. Particularly for the TLUT method, only the truth table bits of some of the LUTs are expressed in function of the parameters. All the routing, and thus the timing-information, of the design is fixed. The LUTs that have a parameterised truth table are called TLUTs.

Every time one of the parameters changes value, the new truth tables for the TLUTs are generated by evaluating the Boolean functions. The evaluation of these functions is performed by the configuration manager, which is generally implemented as software running on a (softcore) microprocessor [3]. Note that evaluating these Boolean functions is multiple orders of magnitude faster than generating the specialised configuration using a conventional FPGA tool flow.

2.2   SRL Reconfiguration

An efficient way to reconfigure the truth tables of the TLUTs is using SRLs (Shift Register LUTs) [2]. SRLs are LUTs whose truth table memory elements are also organised as a shift register (Fig. 1). Consequently, the truth table of an SRL can be changed by shifting data into the SRL. By repeatedly connecting the shift output of an SRL to the shift input of another SRL we can create longer shift registers (Fig. 2), which we call reconfiguration chains. When the reconfiguration chains are added to the design, the configuration manager can easily reconfigure all the TLUTs in the design by shifting the truth tables it has generated in the reconfiguration chains.[1]

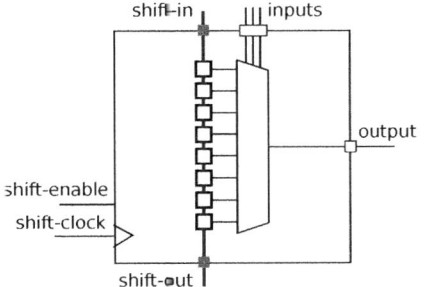
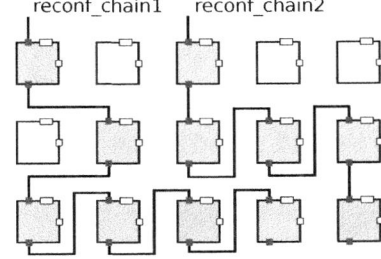

Fig. 1. A shift register LUT (SRL)   **Fig. 2.** Two reconfiguration chains connecting SRLs/TLUTs

Reconfiguration using SRLs is more efficient than using the ICAP for two reasons. First, using SRLs, only the truth tables of the TLUTs need to be written, while the ICAP always needs to rewrite a full frame.[2] A frame contains several truth tables, many of which are actually static. The bandwidth of the ICAP is

---

[1] A reconfiguration clock tree and clock enable signal connecting all TLUTs are also added. They are controlled by the configuration manager.

[2] A frame is the atom of reconfiguration when the ICAP is used.

thus used inefficiently. Second, when using SRL reconfiguration, the reconfiguration bandwidth can be adapted to the requirements of the system at hand, by choosing the number of reconfiguration chains. It has been shown in [4] that SRL reconfiguration can be up to two orders of magnitude faster than ICAP reconfiguration.

3 Automatic Linking of SRLs into Reconfiguration Chains

3.1 Problem Definition

In this paper, we automate the process of organising the TLUTs of an RTR design as a number of reconfiguration chains[3] so that their influence on the design is as low as possible and the reconfiguration speed is as high as possible.

Influence on the Design. The order of the TLUTs in the reconfiguration chains and the distribution of all the TLUTs among the chains has an import influence on the total wire length of the extra connections required for the reconfiguration chains. Because they make use of the same programmable routing resources as regular connections, they influence the routability of the original design, and thus its clock frequency.

Reconfiguration Speed. The reconfiguration time is defined as the product of the required number of clock cycles and the clock period of the reconfiguration clock. The number of reconfiguration clock cycles needed to reconfigure all the TLUTs is determined by the number of SRLs in the longest reconfiguration chain. This is because one clock cycle is needed for each configuration bit in a chain. Therefore, we need to minimise the number of SRLs in the longest chain. Since the total number of TLUTs is fixed and the number of chains is defined by the user, the lengths of the chains thus need to be balanced.

   The clock period of the reconfiguration clock is approximately proportional to the length of the longest wire needed in the reconfiguration chains. We thus need to minimise the longest connection used to build the reconfiguration chains.

   Optimising both the routability of the original design and the reconfiguration speed at the same time isn't always possible and sometimes requires a trade-off. Although in most situations minimising the total wire length will favour short connections, sometimes it is necessary to allow the total wire length to slightly increase to remove another long connection.

Modelling as a Multiple Travelling Salesman Problem. The reconfiguration chains can be introduced at three points in the FPGA tool flow: before, during and after placement. We choose to add the reconfiguration chains after placement. At that point in the tool flow the position of every TLUT is known. This allows us to model the introduction of reconfiguration chains as a constrained mTSP

---

[3] The number of chains is defined by the user.

problem,[4] where not only the total traveling distance is minimised, but also the longest distance travelled between two cities and where the number of cities per salesman is balanced.

3.2   Previous Work on the Multiple Travelling Salesman Problem

The multiple travelling salesman problem has been extensively studied because of its many occurrences in real world problems. The main goal of all solution methods is to minimise the total path length. However, no previous research was found that also takes into account both the balancing requirement and minimisation of the longest connection.

k-opt. k-opt is the name of a group of iterative solution methods for TSP, that was also adapted for mTSP [5]. The method does not take into account the balancing requirement or the length of the longest connection.

In each iteration of k-opt, k randomly chosen connections of a valid solution are broken and replaced with the k connections that minimise the total wire length. For small k, an exhaustive search for the new connections can be performed.

Solving a Balanced mTSP by Partitioning. For the sake of testability, the flip-flops and registers in large ASIC designs are often organised in large shift registers, called scan chains. In [6] and [7] a method is proposed to introduce scan chains in two steps. In the first step the flip-flops are evenly partitioned based on their position relative to the position of the in and output pins of the scan chains. In the second step, each of the scan chains is interconnected using a regular travelling salesman solver.

We have considered this solution method for our work because of its straight-forwardness and the similarity of the problem, but rejected it because of several reasons. First, the method of separating the partitioning and the solving of the individual TSP is not easily adaptable to take into account the longest connection. Depending on the design it might introduce unnecessary and very long connections. Secondly, the geometrical guidance used in these methods, the location of in and output pins, is not available to partition the TLUTs; only one common starting point, the configuration manager, and no endpoints are defined.

Solving an mTSP Using Simulated Annealing. Simulated annealing is a heuristic that has been applied successfully to many problems in different domains, e.g. the placement problem in the FPGA tool flow. In [8] a theoretical justification is given for applying the simulated annealing method (SA) to the mTSP problem. More useful information on the application of SA to the TSP problem can be found in [9].

---

[4] The mTSP can be defined as follows: Given a collection of cities (the TLUTs) and a number of salesmen (the reconfiguration chains), find for each salesman a traveling route so that the combined traveling distance of all salesmen is minimised and each city is visited exactly once.

The algorithm leaves a lot of freedom to the developer in defining the cost function to optimise. This is an advantage that distinguishes this method from those previously described, and it is the main reason we have chosen this technique for the proposed method.

3.3 Proposed Method for Solving the Constrained mTSP

The proposed solution method is based on simulated annealing. In our solution method, many SA implementation details are inspired by VPR's placement algorithm [10]. Some elements of the algorithm are based on 2-opt.

Simulated Annealing. Simulated annealing is a heuristic to find the global minimum of a cost function inspired by the physical annealing of metals. It is an iterative algorithm in which a solution is repeatedly randomly altered and evaluated (Fig. 3). If a proposed alteration causes the cost of the solution to drop, the newly altered solution is accepted and used for further alterations in the next iterations. To avoid getting stuck in local minima, sometimes a solution with a higher cost is accepted as well. The probability of such a solution to get accepted depends on how much worse the solution is, and the value of the temperature (T) at the current iteration. The algorithm starts with a high temperature (high probability of acceptance) to allow exploration of the solution space. The temperature will then gradually decrease to make the solution converge to a minimum. The algorithm stops when the solution doesn't improve anymore. The temperature curve or annealing schedule is an important element of a simulated annealing based algorithm [10].

$$
\begin{aligned}
&\textbf{function } simulatedAnnealing(): \\
&\quad s = s_0,\ T = T_0 \\
&\quad \textbf{while not } stopCondition \\
&\quad\quad \textbf{repeat } n \textbf{ times}: \\
&\quad\quad\quad c_{previous} = cost(s) \\
&\quad\quad\quad s_{proposed} = randomAlteration(s) \\
&\quad\quad\quad c_{proposed} = cost(s_{proposed}) \\
&\quad\quad\quad \Delta c = c_{proposed} - c_{previous} \\
&\quad\quad\quad \textbf{if } \Delta c < 0 \textbf{ or } e^{-\frac{\Delta c}{T}} > random([0,1]) \\
&\quad\quad\quad\quad s = s_{proposed} \\
&\quad\quad T = nextTemperature(T) \\
&\quad \textbf{return } s
\end{aligned}
$$

Fig. 3. Pseudo code for a simulated annealing algorithm

Solution Space and Random Alterations. Every TLUT was assigned a physical position on the FPGA during the placement step. We now define a second notion of position for the TLUTs, namely their position in the reconfiguration chains; each TLUT is assigned to one reconfiguration chain and has an index in this chain. When searching for efficient reconfiguration chains we will only change the positions of the TLUTs in the reconfiguration chains.

We start by randomly giving every TLUT a position in the reconfiguration chains. We only require that every reconfiguration chain has about the same number of TLUTs (at most 1 TLUT difference between the longest and shortest chain). In this way, the number of clock cycles to reconfigure all TLUTs is minimal. A single common starting point, the configuration manager, is set for all the reconfiguration chains but the end points are not fixed.

Two alterations of a solution are possible. The first alteration (Fig. 4(a)) is based on 2-opt and was proposed in [9]. Two connections of a single reconfiguration chain are replaced in such a way that the new solution remains valid. The second alteration (Fig. 4(b)) is specific for the multiple travelling salesman problem and allows the interchange of TLUTs between the different reconfiguration chains. In this alteration two groups of TLUTs of equal size and from different reconfiguration chains are swapped.

Because both the alteration types will never change the number of TLUTs in a reconfiguration chain and the initial solution was balanced, the final solution will also be balanced.

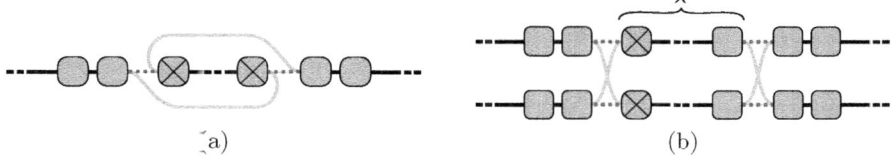

(a)   (b)

Fig. 4. Alterations of a solution. The dotted (red) lines are removed and replaced by the solid grey (green) lines. The rounded squares represent the TLUTs.

An alteration happens by randomly selecting a TLUT, and then selecting a second TLUT so that the Manhattan distance between the physical locations of the two TLUTs is not more than R. The variable R is used to keep the fraction of accepted solutions, β, close to $\beta_{target} = 35\%$ in order to speed up convergence [10]. R is adapted at each temperature iteration using the following equation:

$$R'_{new} = (1 - \beta_{target} + \beta) \cdot R_{old} \tag{1}$$
$$R_{new} = \max(R_{min}, \min(R'_{new}, R_{max})) \tag{2}$$

If the two randomly selected TLUTs (crossed squares in Fig. 4) already are on the same reconfiguration chain, then an alteration of type 1 is performed. If not, an alteration of the second type is used. The remaining degree of freedom, the length of the group of TLUTs to exchange (represented by x in Fig. 4), is solved by exhaustively calculating the alteration with the lowest cost.

Cost Function. The cost function used in the proposed algorithm is presented in Equation (3), where L represents a set of connections which form a valid solution for the reconfiguration chains, and l_i is the Manhattan distance between the physical positions on the FPGA of the TLUTs connected by i.

The first term of the cost function represents the total wire length of the reconfiguration chains. The second term is used to minimise the longest connection of the reconfiguration chains. The parameter α is introduced to make a trade-off between the two parts of the function possible.

Because of the restrictions on the initial solution and alterations, the solution will always be balanced and this requirement does not have to be included in the cost function; the number of clock cycles will always be minimal.

$$C_{SA} = \alpha \sum_{i \in L} l_i + (1 - \alpha) \cdot \sum_{i \in L} f(l_i) \tag{3}$$

$$f(l) = \begin{cases} l - 0.95 \cdot l_{max}, & \text{if } l > 0.95 \cdot l_{max} \\ 0, & \text{otherwise} \end{cases} \tag{4}$$

$$l_{max} = \max_{i \in L} l_i \tag{5}$$

The second term is an approximation of the real cost of the longest connection to speed up convergence to a solution with minimal longest connection length. We take a weighted sum of the lengths of all connections, where only the longest connections, $l > 0.95 \cdot l_{max}$, are given a penalty. This penalty is proportional to the length. An alteration that creates a connection that is longer than the currently longest wire will be penalised, while an incentive exists to replace existing long wires with shorter ones, even if they aren't the longest one.

At the end of the algorithm the weight function $f(l)$ is replaced by $f_{final}(l)$ (6). This removes the bias that is caused by penalising long connections which are not the longest connection ($0.95 \cdot l_{max} < l < l_{max}$). Those connections will have no influence on the longest connection so they can be used without a problem. The reason to apply this weight function only for finalisation is that it does not include an incentive to remove long connections, which is necessary to quickly reduce the length of the longest connection and make the solution converge.

$$f_{final}(l) = \begin{cases} \infty, & \text{if } l > l_{max} \\ 0, & \text{otherwise} \end{cases} \tag{6}$$

Annealing Schedule. An annealing schedule (Equation (7)), based on [10] with some minor experimentally determined differences, was chosen with exponential cooling using a variable parameter γ in function of the fraction of accepted alterations, β. The goal of the variable parameter $\gamma(\beta)$ is to make the algorithm spend more time in the stage where the algorithm makes the most improvement, namely when β is between 5% and 96%.

$$T_{new} = \gamma(\beta) \cdot T_{old} \tag{7}$$

$$\gamma(\beta) = \begin{cases} 0.8, & \text{if } \beta \leq 5\% \\ 0.95, & \text{if } 5\% < \beta \leq 80\% \\ 0.9, & \text{if } 80\% < \beta \leq 96\% \\ 0.5, & \text{if } 96\% < \beta \end{cases} \tag{8}$$

4   Experimental Results

The proposed method was evaluated using two designs: a FIR filter (Finite Impulse Response filter) and a TCAM (Ternary Content Addressable Memory). The FIR filter has about 37% TLUTs while 60% of the TCAM's LUTs are TLUTs. For each design several instances of different sizes were used.

4.1   Results Using the VPR Tools

A first set of experiments evaluates the impact of the introduction of reconfiguration chains on the clock frequency of the design and was conducted with the commonly used academic VPR (Versatile Place and Route) tool version 5.02 [10]. The reconfiguration chains are generated based on the information from the VPR placer. Afterwards, when the reconfiguration chains have been added, routing is performed.

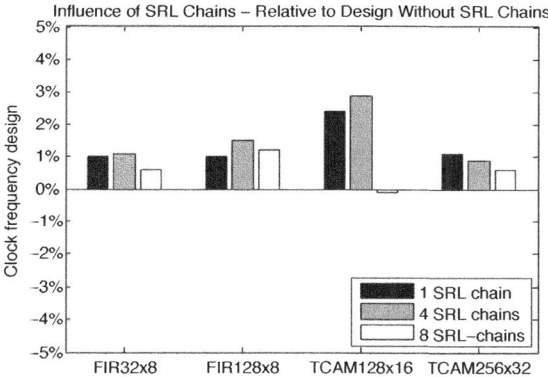

Fig. 5. Influence of the reconfiguration chains on the design's clock frequency using the VPR tool flow

From these experiments (Fig. 5) we conclude that, within the VPR tool flow and for the evaluated designs, it is possible to add up to (at least) 8 reconfiguration chains with minimal negative influence on the design's clock frequency (less than 0.2%). In most cases we even notice a small improvement of up to 3%. This improvement is most likely caused by the addition of the reconfiguration clock tree, which influences placement. The frequency of the reconfiguration clock is between 4 and 24 times higher than the design's clock frequency.

4.2   Results Using the Xilinx Tools

A second set of experiments to evaluate the impact of the reconfiguration chains was performed with the commercial tools from Xilinx, primarily using the Virtex 2 Pro architecture. For these tests, the placement step was performed a second time after adding the reconfiguration chains. The reason for this is that the Xilinx tools do not easily allow editing a design after placement while retaining that placement. This might become possible in the future using recently developed tools such as Torc (`http://torc-isi.sourceforge.net`) or Rapid-Smith (`http://rapidsmith.sourceforge.net`).

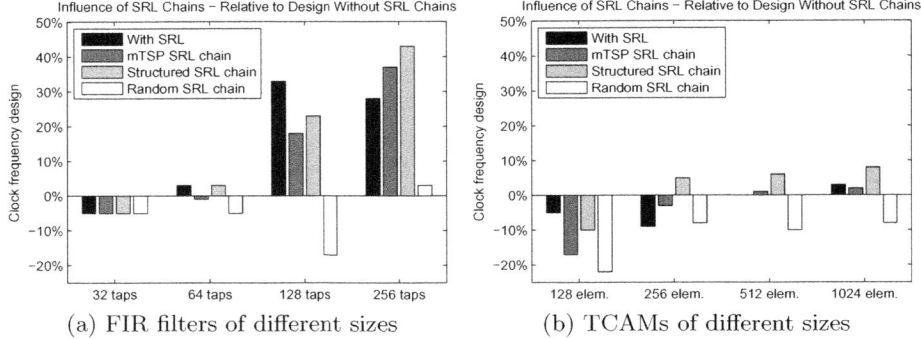

(a) FIR filters of different sizes   (b) TCAMs of different sizes

Fig. 6. Influence of the reconfiguration chains on the design's clock frequency using the Xilinx tool flow, averaged over experiments with 1, 4, 16 and 32 chains

Clock Frequency of the Design. In Fig. 6 we see that for all but one problem instance (TCAM, 128 elem.), the clock frequency of the design, with the configuration chains added according to the proposed method, is at most 5% worse than the clock frequency of the design without reconfiguration chains, while in many cases we even notice an improvement. In comparison, when using randomly generated reconfiguration chains, the RTR design has a clock frequency that is up to 30% worse than the proposed method (FIR, 256 taps).

The improvement caused by adding the reconfiguration chains is mostly caused by the addition of the reconfiguration clock tree and reconfiguration enable signal and the conversion of regular LUTs into SRLs. This influences packing and placement of the TLUTs. The data labeled *"With SRL"* in Fig. 6 represents the clock speed of the design after adding just the reconfiguration clock and reconfiguration enable signals, but no reconfiguration chains. We see that this influences the clock frequency significantly.

In some designs, a regular structure can be found, such as the memory elements of the TCAM or the taps of the FIR filter. In those designs, this structure can be used to (manually) determine an order of the TLUTs in the reconfiguration chains. It was found that this method (labeled *"Structured SRL chain"*) performed in some cases up to 10% better than the proposed method. This method however is not universally applicable.

Second Placement Step. To determine the influence of the second placement step, which we are forced to do when using the Xilinx tools, we performed the experiment in VPR again using an additional placement step after adding the reconfiguration chains. The clock frequency of the design was 4% to 28% lower

using this method. This is mainly because the replacement step shuffles the
TLUTs which causes the mTSP problem to change and renders the previously
calculated solution suboptimal. This may be counterintuitive because one ex-
pects the placer to place connected (T)LUTs closer together.

To illustrate this: we found that for the TCAM design, using the Xilinx tools,
the total estimated wire length of the reconfiguration chains generated using
the proposed method is on average 130% longer after the second placement step
than before.

Number of Reconfiguration Chains. The influence of the number of reconfiguration chains (not in the figures) on the design's clock is negligible for up to 32
chains, while the influence on the reconfiguration clock is small enough to allow
faster RTR by using parallel reconfiguration. The frequency of the reconfiguration clock ranges from 1x to 2x the frequency of the design's clock.

FPGA Family. Additional experiments were performed on the Virtex 4 and
Virtex 5 families (Fig. 7). For large designs with large numbers of TLUTs a
significant degradation of the design's clock frequency was noticed using the
Virtex 5. The reason for this is that in the Virtex 5 only 25% of all LUTs can
be configured as SRLs, and therefore the placement of the design can be worse.
A similar deterioration can be found for the Virtex 4, which has 50% SRLs, but
only for the TCAM design which has 60% TLUTs and not for the FIR filter
with only 37% TLUTs. The limited number of SRLs can make it impossible
to implement large designs with a high fraction of TLUTs on these families of
FPGAs.

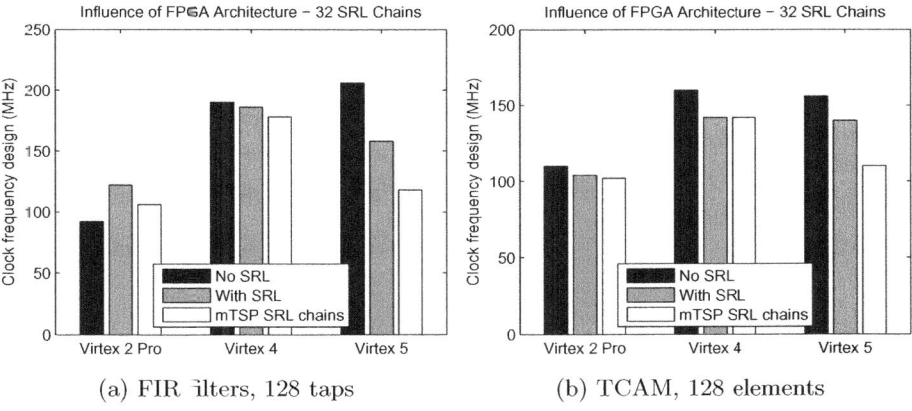

(a) FIR filters, 128 taps   (b) TCAM, 128 elements

Fig. 7. Influence of the FPGA family on the design's clock frequency when using 32
reconfiguration chains

5   Conclusion

An automated solution method based on simulated annealing was proposed to generate reconfiguration chains, which are needed to perform SRL reconfiguration.

When generating the reconfiguration chains, our method takes into account the routability of the original design and the reconfiguration time.

Experiments using the VPR and Xilinx tool flows show that, when adding up to 32 reconfiguration chains using the proposed method, the influence on the design's clock speed is in most cases limited to 5%. The quality of the reconfiguration chains generated by the proposed method approaches that of a hand made solution and is significantly better than that of a random solution.

Currently the Xilinx tools force us to perform a second placement step after adding the reconfiguration chains. Experiments show that our results could still be improved if a technique was implemented to avoid this.

References

1. Bruneel, K., Heirman, W., Stroobandt, D.: Dynamic Data Folding with Parametrizable FPGA Configurations. ACM TODAES 16, 43:1–43:29 (2011)
2. Dynamic Constant Coefficient Multiplier v2.0. Xilinx (2000)
3. Abouelella, F., Bruneel, K., Stroobandt, D.: Towards a More Efficient Run-Time FPGA Configuration Generation. In: Proceedings of ParCo 2009, pp. 113–116 (2009)
4. Al Farisi, B., Bruneel, K., Devos, H., Stroobandt, D.: Automatic Tool Flow for Shift-Register-LUT Reconfiguration. In: Proceedings of the 18th Annual ACM/SIGDA International Symposium on Field Programmable Gate Arrays, p. 287 (2010)
5. Potvin, J., Lapalme, G., Rousseau, J.: A Generalized K-Opt Exchange Procedure for the mTSP. INFOR 27, 474–481 (1989)
6. Kobayashi, S., Edahiro, M., Kubo, M.: A VLSI Scan-Chain Optimization Algorithm for Multiple Scan-Paths. IEICE Trans. Fund. E82-A, 2499–2504 (1999)
7. Rahimi, K., Soma, M.: Layout Driven Synthesis of Multiple Scan Chains. IEEE TCAD 22, 317–326 (2003)
8. Song, C., Lee, K., Lee, W.D.: Extended Simulated Annealing for Augmented TSP and Multi-salesmen TSP. In: Proceedings of IJCNN 2003, vol. 3, pp. 2340–2343 (2003)
9. Kirkpatrick, S.: Optimization by Simulated Annealing: Quantitative Studies. Journal of Statistical Physics 34, 975–986 (1984)
10. Betz, V., Rose, J., Marquardt, A.: Architecture and CAD for Deep-Submicron FPGAs. Kluwer Academic Publishers, Norwell (1999)

Architecture-Aware Reconfiguration-Centric Floorplanning for Partial Reconfiguration

Kizheppatt Vipin and Suhaib A. Fahmy

School of Computer Engineering, Nanyang Technological University,
Nanyang Avenue, Singapore
{vipin2,sfahmy}@ntu.edu.sg

Abstract. Partial reconfiguration (PR) has enabled the adoption of FP-GAs in state of the art adaptive applications. Current PR tools require the designer to perform manual floorplanning, which requires knowledge of the physical architecture of FPGAs and an understanding of how to floorplan for optimal performance and area. This has lead to PR remaining a specialist skill and made it less attractive to high level system designers. In this paper we introduce a technique which can be incorporated into the existing tool flow that overcomes the need for manual floorplanning for PR designs. It takes into account overheads generated due to PR as well as the architecture of the latest FPGAs. This results in a floorplan that is efficient for PR systems, where reconfiguration time and area should be minimised.

1 Introduction

Partial reconfiguration (PR) makes use of the fact that the functionality implemented in an FPGA can be altered by selectively modifying the contents of part of the configuration memory, while the remaining portions continue to operate. Although PR has several advantages, it also entails a number of design challenges. One of these is the floorplanning of reconfigurable regions.

For standard static FPGA design, floorplanning is generally only of interest to expert designers trying to highly optimise a design. The tools available from vendors are sufficiently versatile to perform area-constrained placement and routing, while achieving timing closure. Current PR tools do not perform floorplanning automatically, and require considerable input from the designer. The designer is expected to have knowledge about the physical architecture of the target FPGA, as well as the details of the PR process and the run-time costs associated with it, if they are to come up with an efficient floorplan. Manual floorplanning based on these factors is cumbersome and often leads to sub-optimal results and consumes a large amount of design time. This floorplanning requirement has made PR less attractive to adaptive system designers.

In this paper we propose methods, which can help system engineers adopt PR without the need for manual floorplanning. The tool we propose can be integrated into the existing FPGA tool chain. We are interested primarily in adaptive applications where reconfiguration occurs at the module level, and the

O.C.S. Choy et al. (Eds.): ARC 2012, LNCS 7199, pp. 13–25, 2012.

sequence of configurations is unknown up front. We consider the overheads associated with PR as well as the characteristics of target devices. We are interested in recent families of FPGAs such as the Xilinx Virtex-5 and Virtex-6, which are highly heterogeneous in nature, include embedded processors and transceivers, and comprise an irregular arrangement of DSP and Block RAM columns. For PR applications, we are typically concerned with reducing reconfiguration time and area. An intelligent arrangement and allocation of PR regions can result in reduced area and hence allow designs to fit on smaller devices. Cost functions are used that take into account several factors such as resource wastage and reconfiguration time, rather than ASIC floorplanning metrics.

The remainder of the paper is organised as follows: Section 2 discusses related work, Section 3 presents background on the PR process, Section 4 introduces the proposed floorplanning approach, Section 5 presents experimental results and Section 6 concludes the paper.

2   Related Work

Several approaches to FPGA floorplanning have been published, although work related to floorplanning for PR is less abundant. Traditionally, FPGA floorplanning is considered as a fixed-outline floorplanning problem, as introduced in [1] and further extended in [3]. The authors present a resource-aware fixed-outline simulated-annealing and constrained floorplanning technique. Their formulation can be applied to heterogeneous FPGAs but the resulting floorplan may contain irregular shapes, which are not allowed in current PR designs. Another interesting study is presented in [9], which presents an algorithm called "Less Flexible First (LFF)". In order to perform placement, the authors define the flexibility of the placement space as well as the modules to be placed. A cost function is derived in terms of flexibility and a greedy algorithm is used to place modules. The generated floorplan will have only rectangular shapes, but the approach only addresses older-generation FPGAs and is unsuitable for recent families due to their heterogeneous resources.

Findings in [2] are based on slicing trees. Using this method it can be ensured that the floorplan contains only rectangular shapes. Here, the authors assume that the entire FPGA fabric is composed of a repeating basic tile, which contains all types of FPGA resources including Configurable Logic Blocks (CLBs), Block RAMs and DSP slices. Although this assumption is valid for older-generation FPGAs, such as the Xilinx Spartan-3, more recent FPGAs such as the Xilinx Virtex-5 family, do not have such a repeated tile architecture.

Yuh et al. have published two methods for performing floorplanning for PR. One method is based on using a T-tree formulation [10] and the other is based on a 3D-sub-Transitive Closure Graph (3D-subTCG) [11]. Using T-trees, each reconfigurable operation is represented as a 3D-box, with its width and depth representing the physical dimensions and its height being the execution time required for the operation. Here the reconfiguration operations are at task level rather than functional level and the authors consider older-generation Virtex FPGAs, which require columnar reconfiguration.

Montone et al. present a reconfiguration-aware "floorplacer" in [4]. They consider the latest architecture of Virtex-5 FPGAs. Initially the design is divided into reconfiguration areas based on the minimisation of temporal variance of the resource requirement. Then a floorplacer tries to minimise the area slack using simulated-annealing. In [5] a floorplanning method based on sequence pairs is presented. In this work, authors have shown how sequence pairs can be used to represent multiple designs together. Here, designs are the circuitry present in the FPGA at different instances. An objective function tries to maximise the common areas between designs and simulated-annealing is used for optimisation. Although simulated-annealing-based floorplanners have been developed, for soft modules, which are common in PR designs, the results are not satisfactory [12].

All existing work we have found focuses on the static properties of a particular placement. Hence the placement is not optimised for the dynamic behaviour of a partially reconfigurable system. Other work relies on fixed task-graphs and hence only optimises for a fixed sequence of configurations. This paper presents an approach that optimises the runtime properties by finding a placement that results in the lowest possible reconfiguration time, considering the lowest level granularity of heterogeneous resources on modern FPGAs, for designs where the adaptation is at a functional level and hence unpredictable.

3   PR Floorplanning Considerations

In this section we develop a device model and explore the factors to be considered while designing an efficient floorplanner for PR. The limitations of several existing methods will be also explained.

3.1   Architecture Considerations

For efficient floorplanning, the tool should be aware of the FPGA architecture and special requirements arising due to PR. Xilinx Virtex-5 FPGAs are divided into rows and columns. The number of rows in a device depends upon the size of the device. The smallest configurable unit is a *frame*. A *frame* is one bit wide and spans an entire device row [8]. Resources such as CLBs, Block RAMs etc. are arranged in a columnar fashion extending the full height of the device and are referred to as *blocks*. A tile is one row high and one block wide, and contains a single type of resource, as shown in Fig. 1. One CLB tile contains 20 CLBs, one DSP tile contains 8 DSP Slices, and one BRAM tile contains 4 Block RAMs arranged vertically. A CLB tile contains 36 *frames*, a DSP tile 28 and a Block RAM tile 30 *frames* arranged side by side. The data size of a *frame* is 164 bytes. Embedded processors and transceivers are arranged along device row boundaries, but they obstruct the continuity of DSP and BRAM columns. Most existing floor-planners have not taken this device architecture into account, claiming only to use regular grid structures.

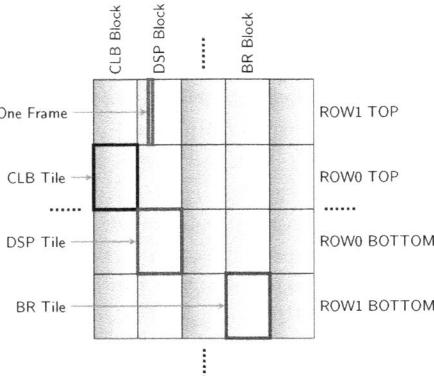

Fig. 1. Virtex 5 FPGA architecture

3.2   PR Operation

Partial reconfiguration is performed by modifying the circuitry implemented in the PR regions. Any modification in a region requires the full reconfiguration of the corresponding region. For accurate calculation of efficient PR schemes, the reconfigurable regions should be considered in terms of tiles since configuration must occur on a per tile basis. To use regions with incomplete tile boundaries, extra circuitry is required to read, modify, and write configuration information, resulting in increased area and latency. Reconfigurable regions must always be rectangular in shape. Since each tile is one device row high, the height of reconfigurable regions is an integer multiple of device rows. Partial bitstreams are loaded into the FPGA with the help of an Internal Configuration Access Port (ICAP), which is usually controlled by an embedded processor. The size of the bitstream, and hence the reconfiguration time of a region, is directly proportional to the total area of the region, irrespective of how many resources present in the region are actually utilised.

3.3   Required Reconfigurable Area

An important factor in floorplanning a reconfigurable region is its area. At run-time, reconfigurable regions implement different functional instances at various points in time. These functional instances are called *modes*. The required area (A_{ra}), in frames, for a PR region is the net area required for implementing all the modes assigned to it. This area is calculated by taking the maximal resource requirement for each resource type, in tiles, and multiplying by the number of frames needed for each tile of that type: Note that there is some overhead in this resource requirement due to it being based on whole tiles.

$$A_{ra} = \sum_{j} W_j * N_j, \quad j \in CLB, DSP, BlockRAM. \tag{1}$$

where W_j is the number of *frames* per type of tile j and N_j is the number of tiles of type j needed.

3.4   Actual Reconfigurable Area

When a design is placed, the actual area may differ from the initial requirement due to the rectangular shape requirement for PR regions or the disparate arrangement of resources on the FPGA fabric. Mathematically, the actual area (A_{aa}) of a region is calculated as

$$A_{aa} = \sum_i W_i * N_i, \quad i \in CLB, DSP, BlockRAM. \tag{2}$$

where W_i is the number of *frames* per tile of type i and N_i is the number of tiles of type i allocated in the region. The result is the number of frames to configure the placed region.

3.5   Resource Wastage

The resource wastage for a particular placement of a reconfigurable region (A_{rw}) is the difference between the actual area and the required area of that region, in frames. The total resource wastage of a full floorplan (A_{tw}) is the sum of resource wastage among all the regions.

$$A_{rw} = A_{aa} - A_{ra}. \tag{3}$$

$$A_{tw} = \sum_r A_{rw}. \tag{4}$$

While floorplanning partial regions, the floorplanner should try to minimise the total resource wastage in order to minimise reconfiguration time and maximise the resources available for implementing static logic.

3.6   Wirelength

Total wirelength is an important parameter in determining the effectiveness of floorplanning. Here we consider the Manhattan distance between regions and the total wirelength between two regions is calculated as the product of the Manhattan distance between them and the number of wires connecting them. Several previous researches consider total Half Perimeter Wire Length (HPWL) as the minimisation objective function for their floorplanner. Practically, HPWL has very little impact in FPGA floorplanning. In ASIC floorplanning, HPWL gives a figure of compactness of cells and hence the best timing achievable, but in FPGAs, where all resources as well as routing between them are fixed, HPWL does not give an accurate measure of timing performance.

3.7   Static Logic

Static logic is the area of the FPGA with fixed functionality. I/O pins are always assigned to the static region, since assigning I/O pins to reconfigurable regions may cause undesirable switching during reconfiguration. There is no restriction on the shape of static logic. To make optimal use of FPGA resources, and achieve timing closure, it is better not to restrict the shape of static logic or allocate a special location for it. The reconfigurable regions should be floorplanned in such a way that, the area available for the implementation of static logic is maximised, and it should be floorplanned after the PR regions.

4   Proposed Floorplanner

The input to our proposed floorplanner is the partition information of reconfigurable regions and their connectivity information. A connectivity matrix is used, whose element (i, j) represents the number of nets between region i and region j. The output of the floorplanner is a set of area constraints, which specify the coordinates of the bottom left and top right corners of each region. These constraints can be used for generating the *user constraints* file, which will be used by the vendor specific place and route tool for generating the final configuration bitstreams. The floorplanning problem can be formulated as follows:
   Given:

- M regions with resource requirement 3-tuple, (n_{CLB}, n_{BR} and n_{DSP}) for each region,
- an FPGA of width W and height H,
- with N_{CLB}, N_{BR} and N_{DSP} resources available,
- and R device rows,

partition the FPGA into M rectangles, so that:

- each region can be mapped into a rectangle, which contains sufficient resources,
- rectangle height being an integer multiple of device row,
- no rectangles overlapping,
- minimising the cost function.

The outputs are the (x_{min}, y_{min}) and (x_{max}, y_{max}) coordinates of each rectangle so that $0 \leq x_{min} \leq x_{max} \leq W$ and $0 \leq y_{min} \leq y_{max} \leq H$.

4.1   Columnar Kernel Tessellation

Mapping an area directly using FPGA primitives is not practical, due to number of factors such as the large search space, limited number of available primitives in the FPGA, fixed primitive locations, rectangular shape region constraint, etc. Hence we adopt a new method called Columnar Kernel Tessellation. A kernel is a structure one device row high, containing FPGA primitives, which can be repeated in the vertical direction to satisfy a region's resource requirements. The availability of kernels for floorplanning a region changes based on the floorplanning of previous regions. The smallest kernel is a single tile. Each tile can be clustered with nearby tiles and can form new kernels.
   The first step of floorplanning is to calculate the resource usage of each region in terms of reconfigurable tiles. For this purpose, the input resource utilisation

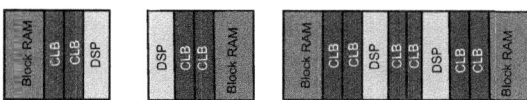

Fig. 2. Two Block RAM-DSP kernels and a merged kernel

values are divided by the corresponding number of resources available in a tile. This may result in some overhead if the resources needed do not use a whole tile. For example in Virtex-5 FPGAs, the required number of CLBs will be divided by 20, DSPs by 8, and Block RAMs by 4. The floorplanner maintains a database of FPGA architectures that contains information about the resource type of each device column. The different types of columns are mapped to a single co-ordinate system for better management. Each tile in the FPGA is encoded using a data-structure with information including location, resource type, used or not, and availability. Once a tile is used to floorplan a region, its *use field* is set to true. The tiles belonging to the locations of hard processors and transceivers are set to be unavailable.

In order to perform floorplanning, the regions are initially sorted according to descending resource requirements, into a floorplanning schedule. Regions are selected based on the following ordered criteria.

1. Require both DSP as well as Block RAM tiles,
2. Require DSP and CLB tiles,
3. Require Block RAM and CLB tiles,
4. Require CLBs tiles alone.

This classification is based on the fact that DSP tiles are the least available and hence the most precious FPGA resource. Block RAM tiles are weighted next and CLB tiles are the most abundant resource available, and so given the least weighting. Regions belonging to each group are sorted in descending order of DSP, Block RAM and CLB tiles required. Regions are selected from the scheduling list in sequential order and packed.

The floorplanner starts with regions which use both DSP tiles and Block RAM tiles. The floorplanner selects a kernel, which contains both DSP and Block RAM tiles. To generate kernels, the resource column information from the database is utilised. For each DSP column, the nearest Block RAM column location is calculated. The nearest tiles of DSP and Block RAM along with the tiles between them are merged to create kernels. These kernels are merged again and larger kernels are created. This operation is illustrated in Fig. 2 in the case of a Virtex-5 FX70T FPGA. It is to note that when kernels are merged, the CLB tiles in between them are also included in the resulting kernel. All kernels are one device row high. From the set of available kernels, the kernel with smallest size is chosen and used for packing. Example calculation of kernel size is shown in Fig. 3. Kernels are repeated in a columnar direction to meet the region's resource requirements. The minimum number of kernels required for packing is equal to the number of DSP tiles required divided by the number of DSP tiles in the

Kernel	#DSP tiles	#BR tiles	#CLB tiles	#Frames	#Bytes
	1	1	2	28 + 30 + 36 = 94	94 * 164 = 15416
	2	2	6	2*28 + 2*30 + 6*36 = 332	332 * 164 = 54448

Fig. 3. Example calculation of the size of kernel

kernel. The maximum number of kernels that can be used to satisfy the DSP resource requirement is equal to the number of device rows, i.e. the full device height, since the height of a kernel is one device row. If the arrangement of a kernel cannot meet the required number of DSP tiles, that kernel is discarded and the kernel with next lowest resource requirement is selected and used for packing.

Once the DSP-BR kernels are packed, the remaining BR and CLB resources required for that region are calculated. If more Block RAMs are needed, the nearest Block RAM column is selected from the database and used. Preference is given to columns towards the right and left edges of the FPGA in order to maximise free space available towards the centre of the FPGA. If more CLB tiles need to be allocated, CLB columns towards the device edge are selected and allocated. Once the allocation is performed, the tiles which are used are marked in the database as *used*.

Now the regions which use only DSP and CLB tiles are packed. For this purpose, the kernels considered contain only DSP tiles and CLB tiles. The minimum number of kernels required for packing will be equal to the number of DSP tiles required divided by the number of DSP tiles in the kernel. Tiles which are not marked as *used* or *not available* are used to generate the new set of kernels. This same process is followed once more for regions containing Block RAMs. Finally, regions containing only CLB tiles are packed.

The inherent rectangular shape of kernels and the columnar repetition guarantees that the allocated area for each region will be of rectangular shape and region height will be an integer multiple of device rows. The floorplanner follows a divide and conquer method. The packing of each region reduces the search space for implementing subsequent regions as well as the number of kernels available. The algorithm runs a number of times, each time starting with a different kernel for packing. The number of iterations can be specified or can be stopped when a required cost objective is met. At the end of each complete packing, a cost function is evaluated for the floorplan . The cost function is defined as

$$CF = \alpha * A_{tw} + \beta * WL. \tag{5}$$

where A_{tw} is the total resource wastage and WL is the total wirelength between regions. α and β are weight factors with $\alpha > \beta$. For designs where reconfiguration time is highly critical compared to speed of operation, the value of β can be set to zero and for applications where timing is highly critical rather than

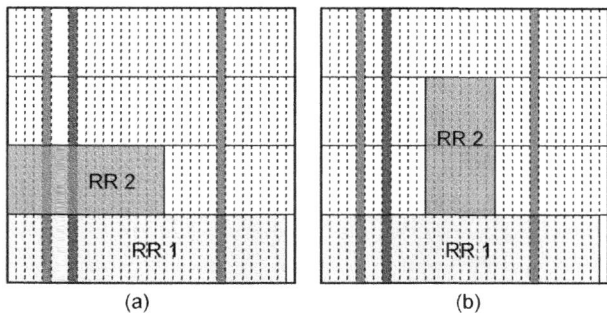

Fig. 4. (a) Resulting floorplan from [4], (b) Resulting floorplan from our method

reconfiguration time α can be set to zero. For other applications, the value of α and β are weighted accordingly.

At the end of each complete floorplan generation, a post processing step is performed, in which the regions are moved along the columnar direction towards the middle of the columns. If this movement improves wirelength, the movement is accepted otherwise it is rejected. Also, regions that occupy the same columns are swapped and wirelength is recalculated. This move is also accepted only if it improves wirelength. These moves are a type of pseudo-simulated-annealing. This is possible due to the fact that the resources are arranged in columnar fashion in the FPGA, and moving a region along its columns does not affect resource availability, provided there are no unavailable tiles in the direction of movement.

5   Case Study

A direct comparison of our method with existing methods is not possible due to the unavailability of other floorplanning tools and uniform benchmark circuits. Hence, we use a reported case study, taken from [4], and compared the results using our method. The system implemented consists of a CAN controller, Floating Point Unit (FPU) FIR filter, CRC controller and an Ethernet controller. Based on the partitioning algorithm, modules are partitioned into two reconfigurable regions. The CAN controller, FPU and CRC are implemented in reconfigurable region 1 (RR 1) and FIR filter and Ethernet controller are implemented in region 2 (RR2), as per [4]. The design is implemented in a Virtex-5 LX30T device. Region 1 requires 24% of the available CLB and 5 Block RAMs and region 2 requires 13% of CLBs. The static region requires 61% of CLBs and 40 Block RAMs. The resulting floorplan reported in the paper is given in Fig. 4.a. It is clear that although region 2 does not require Block RAMs or DSP slices, the resulting floorplan includes these resources. This leads to increased region size. higher configuration time and additional storage requirement. Furthermore, these resources cannot be used elsewhere in the design. This floorplan uses a total of 1766 frames.

A floorplan determined by our method is shown in Fig. 4.b. Region 2 is floorplanned in such a way that no DSP slices and Block RAMs are used. Hence our method uses 58 fewer frames and reserves more resources for static logic implementation. The smaller size of the region also contributes to 18.4 KB (9.2×2 since there are two partial bitstreams for that region) less storage requirement and a corresponding improvement in reconfiguration time.

For a more complex investigation, we could find no existing work to compare to, nor standard tools to use, so we floorplanned an in-house design using our proposed method and compared it to an ad-hoc floorplan based on previous experience with some optimisation effort. The ad-hoc floorplanning is done as per Xilinx PR floorplanning guidelines, with the help of the PlanAhead software. The selected design is a software defined radio (SDR) targeted for Xilinx Virtex-5 FX70T FPGA. The SDR chain consists of a matched filter, carrier recovery circuit, demodulator, signal decoder and video decoder. Each module has a number of *modes* with different resource requirements. *Modes* are mutually exclusive implementations of the module with the same set of inputs and outputs. Partitioning of *modes* into regions is beyond the scope of this paper, but is explained in our previous work [6]. Here we assume each module is assigned to a single region, and hence the resource requirement of each region is the requirement of the largest *mode* of the module assigned to it. Here, all modules are connected in sequential order with a 64 bit wide bus. The static logic contains a PowerPC-440 embedded processor, external memory interface and an ICAP controller. The different regions and associated resource requirements are given in Table 1. The $rq'd$ field indicates the exact number of resources required, the *tiles* field indicates the required number of tiles needed to satisfy the resource requirement and the *waste* field indicates the resources wasted due to rounding the resources to tiles. The total number of frames wasted due to the tiling operation is roughly 115 frames.

Table 1. Resource utilisation for reconfigurable regions

Region	CLBs			BRs			DSPs			No. of Frames
	Rq'd	Tiles	Waste	Rq'd	Tiles	Waste	Rq'd	Tiles	Waste	
Matched Filter	500	25	0	0	0	0	34	5	6	1040
Carrier Recovery	123	7	17	0	0	0	8	1	0	280
Demodulator	97	5	3	8	2	0	0	0	0	240
Decoder	234	12	6	2	1	2	0	0	0	462
Video Decoder	1100	55	0	6	2	2	34	5	6	2180
Total	2054	104	26	16	5	4	76	11	12	4202

As per the description in Section 4.1, the order for floorplanning regions is the video decoder first, followed by the matched filter, carrier recovery, demodulator and finally the decoder. The result of the ad-hoc floorplanning and 5 of the best floorplans using our method are given in Table 2.

Table 2. Resource wastage and total wirelength for different floorplans

Plan No.	Wastage, A_{tw} (frames)	Wirelength, WL (Normalised)
Adhoc	956	7420
Plan1	466	8640
Plan2	486	9056
Plan3	592	11776
Plan4	516	7392
Plan5	556	9120

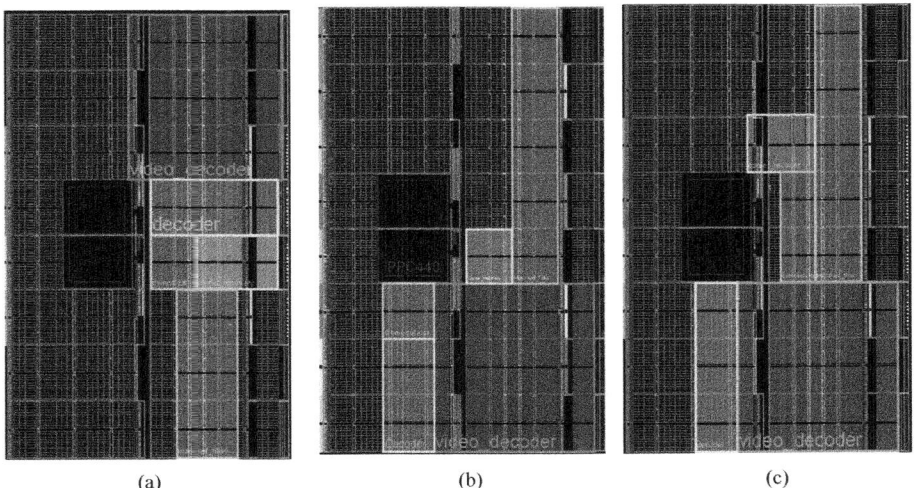

(a)   (b)   (c)

Fig. 5. Floorplans using (a) An ad-hoc approach, (b) proposed method with minimum resource wastage, (c) with minimum wirelength

There is no fixed relationship between the resource wastage and wirelength, owing to the rectangular shape requirement of the reconfigurable regions as well as the disparate arrangement of resources. The ad-hoc plan, the plan which produces minimum resource wastage (Plan1) and the plan which gives minimum wirelength (Plan4) are shown in Fig. 5. When the value of α is set to zero in the cost function, Plan 4 is the preferred floorplan, and when β is set to zero, Plan 1 gives the best results. We can see that the proposed floorplanner performs well on area: all the floorplans have lower resource wastage from 38% to 51%, which corresponds to a decrease in reconfiguration from 7% to 9.5% compared to the ad-hoc plan. Since the modules of the regions are in a continuous chain, the ad-hoc method is able to achieve good total wirelength. In usual FPGA floorplanning without PR, the ad-hoc floorplan is fairly acceptable, since all the resource requirements are satisfied and wirelength is minimised. But for PR designs, the resource wastage creates a considerable overhead in terms of reconfiguration time. Moreover, storing 956 frames of configuration frames requires 153 KB extra storage memory for each system configuration.

These results demonstrate the advantage of considering the required implementation metrics in floorplanning. While static designs only require the floorplan to fit and achieve timing, a PR design's reconfiguration time is also affected by the floorplan. Our approach ensures this is factored into the floorplanning process, and results in savings as shown.

6   Conclusion

In this paper we introduced a novel method for PR design floorplaning. The method described is fully compatible with the latest vendor-supported PR toolflows. The heterogeneous and irregular architecture of modern FPGA families are considered and floorplanning cost functions tailored for PR are introduced. Our floorplanning method is portable to older FPGAs by considering them as having a single device row. Our study proves that it is possible to optimise the area requirement considering the tile constraint. We have also found that a significant area overhead is generated due to the tiling requirement of reconfigurable regions. Hence, considering tiling at the partitioning stage, prior to floorplanning may yield more efficient designs. We intend to integrate this floorplanner with our previous work on efficiently partitioning modules into reconfigurable regions. The partitioning tool and floorplanner along with the vendor supplied synthesis and place and route tools can essentially automate most of the PR design flow, which is our long term goal. [7] This will lead to wider adoption of partial reconfiguration and development of more efficient and effective adaptive systems.

References

1. Adya, S., Markov, I.: Fixed-outline floorplanning through better local search. In: Proceedings of ACM/IEEE International Conference on Computer Design (2001)
2. Banerjee, P., Sangtani, M., Sur-Kolay, S.: Floorplanning for partially reconfigurable FPGAs. IEEE Transactions on Computer-Aided Design of Integrated Circuits and Systems 30(1), 8–17 (2011)
3. Feng, Y., Mehta, D.: Heterogeneous floorplanning for FPGAs. In: Proceedings of International Conference on VLSI Design (2006)
4. Montone, A., Santambrogio, M., Sciuto, D., Memik, S.: Placement and floorplanning in dynamically reconfigurable FPGAs. ACM Transactions on Reconfigurable Technology and Systems 3(4), 24:11–24:34 (2010)
5. Singhal, L., Bozorgzadeh, E.: Multi-layer floorplanning for reconfigurable designs. IET Computers & Digital Techniques 1(4), 276–294 (2007)
6. Vipin, K., Fahmy, S.: Efficient region allocation for adaptive partial reconfiguration. In: Proceedings of the International Conference on Field Programmable Technology, FPT (2011)
7. Vipin, K., Fahmy, S.: Enabling high level design of adaptive systems with partial reconfiguration. In: Proceedings of the International Conference on Field Programmable Technology, FPT (2011)

8. Xilinx Inc.: UG191: Virtex-5 FPGA Configuration User Guide (2010)
9. Yuan, J., Dong, S., Hong, X., Wu, Y.: LFF algorithm for heterogeneous FPGA floorplanning. In: Proceedings of Asia and South Pacific Design Automation Conference, ASP-DAC (2005)
10. Yuh, P., Yang, C., Chang, Y.: Temporal floorplanning using the T-tree formulation. In: Proceedings of IEEE/ACM International Conference on Computer Aided Design, ICCAD (2004)
11. Yuh, P., Yang, C., Chang, Y., Chen, H.: Temporal floorplanning using 3D-subTCG. In: Proceedings of Asia and South Pacific Design Automation Conference, ASP-DAC (2004)
12. Zhan, Y., Feng, Y., Sapatnekar, S.: A fixed-die floorplanning algorithm using an analytical approach. In: Proceedings of Asia and South Pacific Design Automation Conference, ASP-DAC (2006)

Domain-Specific Language and Compiler for Stencil Computation on FPGA-Based Systolic Computational-Memory Array

Wang Luzhou, Kentaro Sano[*], and Satoru Yamamoto

Graduate School of Information Sciences, Tohoku University
6-6-01 Aramaki Aza Aoba, Aoba-ku, Sendai 980-8579, Japan
{limgys,kentah,yamamoto}@caero.mech.tohoku.ac.jp

Abstract. This paper presents a domain-specific language for stencil computation (DSLSC) and its compiler for our FPGA-based systolic computational-memory array (SCMA). In DSLSC, we can program
stencil computations by describing their mathematical form instead of
writing explicit procedure optimally. The compiler automatically parallelizes stencil computations for processing elements (PEs) of SCMA, and
schedules multiply-and-add operations for PEs considering data-reference
delay via a local memory or communication FIFOs between PEs. For arbitrary grid-sizes of 2D Jacobi compilation with 3x3 and 5x5 stencils,
the compiler achieves high utilization of PEs, 85.6 % and 92.18 %, which
are close to 87.5 % and 93.75 % for ideal cases, respectively.

Keywords: stencil computation, compiler, domain-specific language,
systolic computational-memory architecture.

1 Introduction

Stencil computation [3] is one of the typical high-performance scientific computing kernels in such numerical simulations as thermal propagation, fluid dynamics
and electromagnetic computations [5]. These scientific applications are based on
finite difference methods to numerically solve the partial differential equations
(PDEs) constructing the governing equations of physics. The difference methods
approximate PDEs with discrete values defined at 2D or 3D grid points. The
values at each grid-point are updated to obtain a solution for successive time-
steps by locally computing some functions with the values in *a stencil*, which is
a region of neighbor grid-points. A stencil-function is usually simple, being of
multiply-and-add operations. Consequently, the number of required operations
per memory-read is small, so that stencil computation is memory-intensive. The
many-core approach of recent general-purpose microprocessors and accelerators
is not suitable for such memory-intensive computations, because their sustained
performance depends on the insufficient off-chip memory bandwidth, rather than

---

[*] Corresponding author.

O.C.S. Choy et al. (Eds.): ARC 2012, LNCS 7199, pp. 26–39, 2012.
© Springer-Verlag Berlin Heidelberg 2012

the peak arithmetic performance of the cores[15]. To efficiently scale the sustained performance of stencil computation, we need increase both arithmetic-performance and memory-bandwidth.

The inefficiency of microprocessors and accelerators is caused by their fixed structure. So far we have been focusing on custom computing machines (CCMs) on field-programmable gate arrays (FPGAs) for efficient computation with balanced and scalable arithmetic-performance and memory-bandwidth. Thanks to the remarkably advanced FPGA technology, state-of-the-art FPGAs are having floating-point performance competitive with or more than that of microprocessors [14], and therefore very attractive to implement high-performance CCMs.

We proposed the systolic-computational memory (SCM) architecture [8, 10, 11] for scalable stencil computation on FPGAs. We demonstrated that the extensible design of an SCM array (SCMA) on multiple FPGAs achieves higher performance and scalability than those of microprocessors with high utilization of processing elements (PEs). SCMA is composed of decentralized memories locally coupled with programmable PEs of a 2D systolic array. This architecture makes both entire bandwidth of local memories and arithmetic performance completely scalable to the array size. However, we still have a problem with SCMA: it is difficult to optimally program PEs. SCMA has several sequencers to control SIMD groups of PEs with their sequences of microprograms. We have to schedule multiply-and-add operations for PEs of different SIMD groups so that inter-PE data reference is made via communication FIFOs with as less no-operation cycles as possible for required data-transfer delay. Since optimal scheduling requires expert's skill, we need a compiler that allows users to easily program various stencil computations for SCMA.

In this paper, we propose a domain-specific language for stencil computation (DSLSC) and its compiler for SCMA. In DSLSC, we can intuitively describe n-dimensional stencil computations without explicit and optimal procedure. The compiler automatically parallelizes the computations by partitioning and allocating them for PEs in an array, and schedules operations of stencil computations considering data-dependence of grid points. The parallelization and scheduling are performed with a data-dependency graph (DDG) of grid points and a data-flow graph (DFG) whose vertices are stencil computations. For various sizes of SCMA, the implemented compiler achieves high utilization of computing units close to ideal cases for 3x3 or 5x5 stencil computations.

This paper is organized as follows. Section 2 describes related work. Section 3 explains stencil computation and SCM architecture, and then Section 4 presents DSLSC and its compiler. Section 5 discusses implementation results and performance evaluation. Finally, Section 6 gives conclusions and future work.

2   Related Work

A number of domain-specific languages (DSLs) and their compilers have been proposed and developed for stencil computations. Dominic et al. proposed DSL Ypnos, which is embedded in Haskell [9]. Programs in Ypnos express abstract,

```
1: for (n=0; n<N; n++)
2:   for (j=0; j<J; j++)
3:     for (i=0; i<I; i++)
4:       v[i,j,n+1]
5:         = f({v[x,y,n] | (x,y) in S(i,j)});
6: // S(i,j) is a stencil.
```

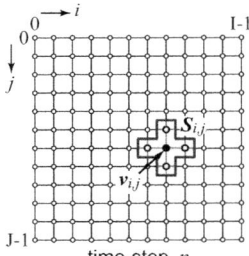

Fig. 1. Pseudo code of 2D stencil computation   **Fig. 2.** Stencil computation

declarative specifications of stencil computations which are guaranteed free from out-of-bounds array access. Yuan et al. proposed the Pochoir stencil compiler and its DSL embedded in C++ [12]. The Pochoir compiler translates a DSL code into high-performing Cilk code which employs an efficient parallel cache-oblivious algorithm for general-purpose microprocessors. Pochoir supports general d-dimensional stencils and periodic and aperiodic boundary conditions. Bradford et al. proposed an advanced version of their array-based parallel programming language, ZPL, for sparse computations including stencil computations to be executed such parallel machines as T3E [2]. This language allows users to express their sparse computation using dense array syntax, making the code easier for readers to understand and for compilers to parallelize and optimize. These DSLs are all designed for describing procedure of computations. Our DSLSC is totally different from them due to its programming style without explicitly describing procedures.

Parallelization techniques for regular computations with dependences have been studied [13, 16]. Wolf et al. proposed an approach to transform general loop-nests and an algorithm to apply the transformation to loop parallelization for maximizing the degree of coarse- or fine-grain parallelism [16]. Teich et al. proposed an integer linear programming model to schedule and map the partitioned computations to a processor array under resource constrains such as communication resources and memory resources [13]. Our DSLSC complier partitions regular stencil computations defined by DSLSC without explicit loop representation by analyzing their data dependence. After the partitioned computations are mapped onto PEs, the compiler schedules operations of stencil computation under constrains of a multiplication-and-accumulation unit of a PE and data-arrival delays via a local memory or communication FIFOs.

3   Systolic Computational-Memory Architecture

3.1   Stencil Computation

In typical scientific computing, such iterative computations are often seen that update a data set on a grid at iteration n to obtain those of the next iteration. This kind of iterative computation is described as nested loops with inner loops for grid traverse and an outer loop for their repetition. Here we focus on a 2D case of a $I \times J$ rectangular grid for simplicity, where each grid-point (i, j) has datum $v_{i,j}^n (0 \leq i < I, 0 \leq j < J)$ for iteration or time-step n. Figure 1 shows a pseudo code of the iterative computation on a 2D grid, where $f()$ shows a function to update $v_{i,j}^n$ to $v_{i,j}^{n+1}$ for all grid points.

In most cases, the function is of *stencil computation* [3], which gives the updated result at (i, j) only using the data of adjacent grid-points as shown in Fig.2. The region of the adjacent grid-points is referred to as *stencil*, which is generally unchanged for grid positions. Let $S_{i,j}$ denote the stencil at (i, j) so that stencil computation is written as $v_{i,j}^{n+1} = f(\{v_{x,y}^n | (x, y) \in S_{i,j}\})$. Particularly, the 2D case of the Jacobi method [6], which is the simplest iterative linear-equation solver, has the following stencil function:

$$v_{i,j}^{n+1} = c_W v_{i-1,j}^n + c_S v_{i,j+1}^n + c_N v_{i,j-1}^n + c_E v_{i+1,j}^n . \tag{1}$$

where c_W, c_S, c_N and c_E are constants. Here we mathematically describe a stencil computation for d-dimensional grid-space in preparation for DSL explanation of the next Section. We deal with an axis of iterations/time-steps as well as spatial axes like i and j. When we consider a single axis, t, for a time-step, we need a grid in $(d + 1)$-D computational space for a stencil computation. A coordinate of a grid point is given as $\boldsymbol{p} \in \boldsymbol{Z}^{(d+1)}$. For example, $\boldsymbol{p} = (i_1, i_2, ..., i_d, t)$ where i_* and t are integers. We define some quantities as vector $\boldsymbol{v_p}$ for each grid point at $\boldsymbol{p}$, where $\boldsymbol{v} \in \boldsymbol{R}^n$. n is the number of elements in $\boldsymbol{v}$. Let S denote a stencil so that $S \subset \boldsymbol{Z}^{(d+1)}$. Stencil computation is written as

$$\boldsymbol{v_{p+t}} = f_{\boldsymbol{p}} \left(\{\boldsymbol{v_{p+s}} | \boldsymbol{s} \in S\} \right), \tag{2}$$

where $(\boldsymbol{p} + \boldsymbol{t})$ means the next time-step of $\boldsymbol{p}$, and $\boldsymbol{s} \in S$ shows a relative position to the central grid-point. For example, $\boldsymbol{p} = (i_1, i_2, t)$, $(\boldsymbol{p} + \boldsymbol{t}) = (i_1, i_2, t + 1)$, and $(\boldsymbol{p} + \boldsymbol{s}) = (i_1 + 1, i_2, t)$ in the case of $d = 2$. As Eq.(2) shows, a stencil function requires only data of the local grid-points in a stencil. Computations of the function for grid points are independent, so that they can be performed in parallel. Moreover, all the grid-points are usually updated with the same stencil function. Thus, stencil computation has *locality*, *parallelism* and *homogeneity*.

3.2   Systolic Computational-Memory Architecture

So far, we have proposed SCM architecture as shown in Fig.3 to achieve scalable stencil computation by exploiting its locality, parallelism and homogeneity [8, 10, 11]. SCM architecture is the combination of the systolic architecture [7] and the computational memory approach [4], which is designed for pipelining and spatially-parallel processing with sufficient memory-bandwidth of PEs, making both computing performance and aggregate bandwidth scalable to the array size.

As Fig.3 shows, SCMA is composed of an 2D array of PEs connected by a 2D mesh network. We designed a PE as a programmable simple-processor with a local memory and a floating-point unit. It's data-path is controlled by *a sequencer*

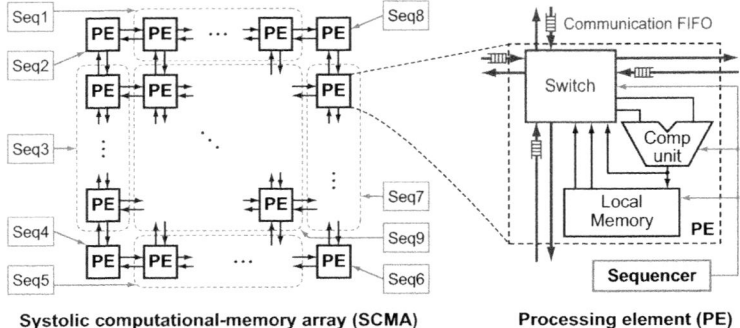

Fig. 3. Systolic computational-memory array (SCMA) and processing element (PE)

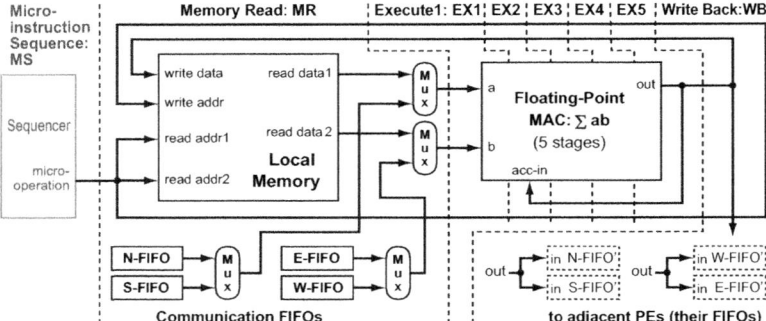

Fig. 4. Pipelined data-path of PE

with a micro-program stored in the sequencer. Although the instruction set is not almighty but limited for stencil computation, the programmability provides SCMA computational versatility and facility, so that we can perform various stencil computations without re-designing and re-implementing the hardware. It also provides high-utilization of computing units by allowing the same units to be used for various computations including boundary computations.

3.3   Processing Elements

Fig.4 shows the data-path of the PE, which is designed to efficiently perform Eq.(1). The local memory stores all the data of the sub-gird allocated to the PE. The sequencer, which is implemented actually out of PEs, has a sequence memory, a program counter and loop-control modules for a loop instruction [11]. Basically, an SCMA has less sequencers than PEs. Each sequencer takes charge of an SIMD group of PEs. In the case of 2D stencil computations, we usually use nine sequencers for the nine SIMD groups of Fig.3, which are of PEs in the internal region, in the four edges and at the four-corners of a grid.

```
1:  /***** Jacobi : F[i,j] to T[i,j]  *****/
2:  for (j=0; j<2; j++)
3:    for (i=0; i<3; i++)
4:      T[i,j] := c1*F[i,j-1] + c2*F[i-1,j]
5:               + c3*F[i,j+1] + c4*F[i+1,j];

6:  /***** Jacobi : T[i,j] to F[i,j]  *****/
7:  for (j=0; j<2; j++)
8:    for (i=0; i<3; i++)
9:      F[i,j] := c1*T[i,j-1] + c2*T[i-1,j]
10:              + c3*T[i,j+1] + c4*T[i+1,j];
```

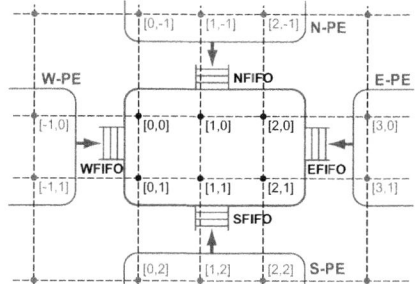

Fig. 5. Pseudo code of Jacobi computation on a 3x2 grid with double-buffering

Fig. 6. 3x2 Grid of Jacobi computaion

The data-path is pipelined with eight stages: *MS stage, MR stage, five EX stages* and *WB stage*. The multiplication-and-accumulation (MAC) unit computes weighted sums of single precision floating-point numbers in the five EX stages. In the accumulation mode, the MAC unit computes $a \times b$ with the two inputs of a and b, and then adds or subtracts ab with its output. The MAC unit has a forwarding path from EX5 to EX2 for accumulation. This three-stage forwarding forces inputs to be fed for each accumulation every three cycles. This means that three concurrent accumulations of Eq.(1) are necessary to fully utilize the multiplier and the adder of the MAC unit. The output of the MAC unit is written into the local memory, and/or sent to the four adjacent PEs of *north(N)*, *south(S)*, *west(W)* and *east(E)* by writing it to their communication FIFOs. The FIFOs mitigate timing requirement for sending and receiving data.

3.4   Execution Model of PE

Here we describe how PEs execute stencil computation with three concurrent accumulations by exchanging boundary data to each other. The details including the instruction set are written in [11]. We assume that PEs each perform the same stencil computation on a different 3x2 grid as shown in Fig.6. Figure 5 is a pseudo code of the Jacobi computation.Note that the computation is performed by double buffering with F[i,j] and T[i,j]. The first loop writes the results of the stencil computation to T[i,j], a temporal grid, so that F[i,j] is not broken. The second loop writes the results of the next stencil-computation to F[i,j].

Figure 7 shows the PE's execution slots with hand-scheduled operations of Fig.5. Column "accumulation by MAC unit" has the accumulation chains 1 to 3, which show operations at each cycle for the three concurrent accumulations, respectively. Column "outputs of MAC unit" shows the availability of the output data in the local memory and the communication FIFOs of the adjacent PEs: N-, S-, W- and E-PEs. In Fig.7, the stencil computation for T[0,0] is performed in the accumulation chain1 from cycle 1 to cycle 10, writing the result to the local memory for T[0,0] and the FIFOs of the N- and W-PEs. Since WB stage is 7th stage from MR stage, the datum is actually written to the local memory at cycle 16, and gets able to be read out at cycle 17. The communication FIFOs

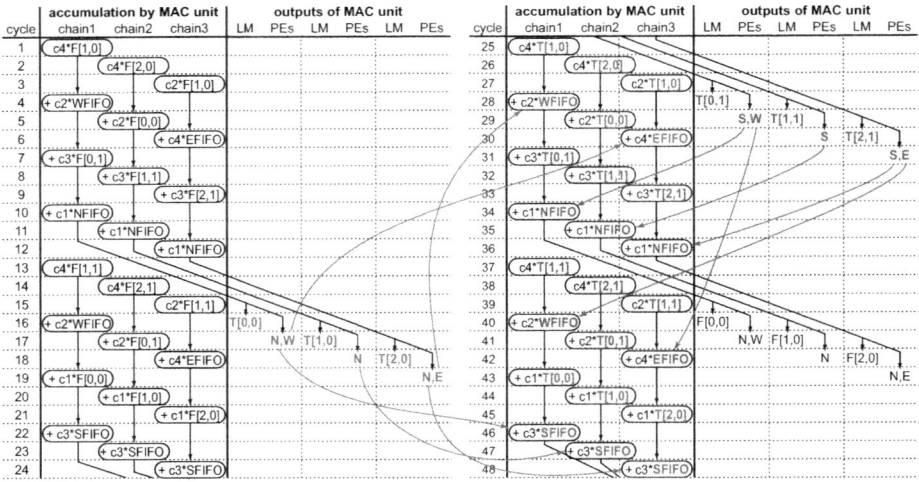

Fig. 7. PE's execution slots for 3x2 Jacobi computation

require one more cycle, and therefore the datum becomes available in the SFIFO
of N-PE and the EFIFO of W-PE at cycle 18, respectively. We refer to these
delay cycles for data to be available as *data-reference delay*.

The arrows from the MAC outputs show the data-dependence of the operations. All the operations must be scheduled in cycles where their inputs are
available. Since the adjacent PEs also synchronously execute the same sequence
of operations in this case, the datum read from WFIFO at cycle 28 is of the
output to E-PE written by the W-PE at cycle 12. That is, we have to consider
periodic connections with FIFOs among PEs executing the same computations.

Since the scheduled operations of Fig.7 do not have no-operation (nop) cycles
at all, it is optimal. Larger and 3D grids require longer time for hand-scheduling.
Moreover, since SCMA actually has multiple sequencers, PEs have to satisfy the
timing requirements for data-dependence among different SIMD sequences for
irregular boundary-computations. In the next section, we present a compiler for
SCMA, which parallelizes stencil computation in our domain-specific language
and schedules operations for all the sequencers.

4   Domain-Specific Language and Compiler

4.1   Domain-Specific Language for Stencil Computation

We present our domain-specific language for stencil computation (DSLSC) for
SCMA compiler. For computations to be executed on actual hardware, we lastly
need sequences of operations, and therefore procedure description is preferred
for most of existing languages including C and other DSLs [2, 9, 12]. However,
procedural languages require optimization in writing codes which depends on
the hardware structure, while programmers are not always skilled in optimizing

```
 1: int I = 6, J = 4, T = 100;  // integer constants
 2: float C = 1/4.0;            // float constant
 3: float [1::I,1::J,0::T] F;   // grid F[i1,i2,i3]
 4:
 5: scan F {                    // stencil computation
 6:   F[0,0,0] = C * F[ 1, 0, -1] + C * F[-1, 0, -1]
 7:            + C * F[ 0, 1, -1] + C * F[ 0,-1, -1];
 8: }                           // relative reference
 9:
10: scan F in [*,*,0] { F[0,0,0] = 0; } // for i3 = 0
11: scan F in [1,*,*] { F[0,0,0] = 1; } // for i1 = 1
12: scan F in [I,*,*] { F[0,0,0] = 0; } // for i1 = I
13: scan F in [*,1,*] { F[0,0,0] = 0; } // for i2 = 1
14: scan F in [*,J,*] { F[0,0,0] = 0; } // for i2 = J
```

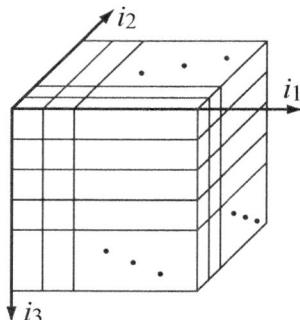

Fig. 8. Example code in DSLSC for the Jacobi stencil computation of Fig. 5

Fig. 9. 3D Computational grid

codes. On the other hand, our DSLSC is designed so that codes for stencil computation in any dimensions are written intuitively by describing their mathematical equations without procedure. Optimized procedure is found by a compiler to generate a sequence of instructions to be executed by PEs of SCMA.

Figure 8 shows an example code in DSLSC, which is for 2D Jacobi computation on a 6x4 grid for 100 time-steps. DSLSC describes dependence of grid points with functions, instead of procedure. This limits all assignments "=" to *static single assignment forms*, making compilation simple. Lines 1 to 2 are for declaration of integer and floating-point constants: I,J,T and C. Line 3 declares a 3D computational grid, $F[i_1, i_2, i_3]$ for $1 \leq i_1 \leq I$, $1 \leq i_2 \leq J$ and $0 \leq i_3 \leq T$, shown in Fig.9. The i_1, i_2 and i_3 axes of the grid space are not distinguished between spatial and temporal ones in the code while a programmer intends to use i_3 for time-steps in this case. This manner is similar to the mathematical description written in Section 3.1.

The "scan" statement of line 5 applies the stencil function defined in the statement's body to all the positions (i_1, i_2, i_3) by scanning the grid F. The stencil computation is written to homogeneously give both a stencil and a function with relative reference of grid positions. For example, "F[1, 0, −1]" is interpreted as "F[$i_1 + 1, i_2, i_3 − 1$]" for position $\boldsymbol{p} = (i_1, i_2, i_3)$. To set initial values and boundary conditions, we provide *override feature* to the scan statement, which is used in Lines 10 to 14. For example, line 11 overrides the stencil computation of "F[$i_1, i_2, 0$]" with the constant assignment. Here "in [*,*,0]" specifies the scanning range. This is the same descriptor as written in line 3, where "0" means "0::0" and asterisk "*" denotes the entire range defined for each axis. Lines 11 to 14 similarly override the computations on the four boundary surfaces of the grid. Thus, this feature replaces a former assignment with a new one. Such a style as separates common and special cases leads up to easily-readable codes.

4.2 Overview of Compiler for DSLSC

We developed a compiler for DSLSC which parallelizes the computation written in DSLSC and schedules operations to be executed by PEs in as less nop cycles

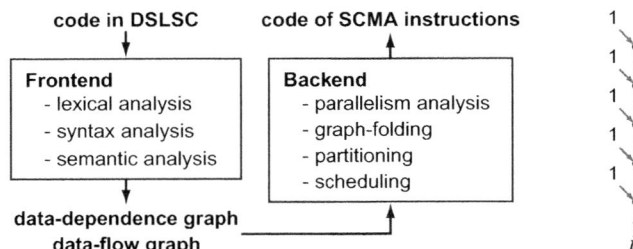

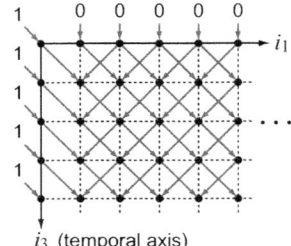

Fig. 10. Overview of DSLSC compiler

Fig. 11. Data-dependence graph on the i_1-i_3 plane of Fig.9

as possible. Figure 10 shows the overview of the compiler, which consists of the frontend and the backend. The frontend performs the lexical analysis, the syntax analysis and the semantic analysis to generate a data-dependency graph (DDG) and a data-flow graph (DFG) as an intermediate representation of the input code in DSLSC. DDG represents dependence of the grid points with edges and vertices. DFG represents stencil computations with vertices and their data-dependence with edges. The backend consists of *the parallelism analysis stage*, *the graph-folding stage*, *the partitioning stage*, and *the scheduling stage*.

4.3   Parallelism Analysis Stage

Since a code in DSLSC describes data dependence of grid points without explicit description of procedure, axes of the grid are indistinctive for spatial and temporal ones. However, we have to know which axis should be used to partition the computations for parallelization and to sequence them. By analyzing data-dependence of grid points, this stage distinguishes between *a temporal axis* and *parallel axes*. A temporal axis is an axis where stencil computations have to be executed sequentially due to data-dependence. Fig.11 is the DDG on the i_1-i_3 plane. In this case, i_3 is a temporal axis because all the dependence arrows have the same direction along this axis. Then, each of the remaining axes is recognized as a parallel axis only if it has no dependence arrow along the axis, because stencil computations for grid points on such a axis can be performed in parallel at each temporal position. In Fig.11, i_1 is a parallel axis. Similarly i_2 of Fig.9 is also a parallel axis.

4.4   Graph-Folding Stage

This stage folds DDG and DFG so that stencil computations are performed by iterating operations with a loop instruction, and minimizing the size of memory to store grid data. Figures 12a and 12b show examples of DDG and DFG before and after folding. Since i_3 is a temporal axis, the grid points of rows ($i_3 = t, t + 1, ...$) are computed sequentially. For the unfolded graphs of Fig.12a, we need a too big memory if we assign different memory addresses to all the vertices

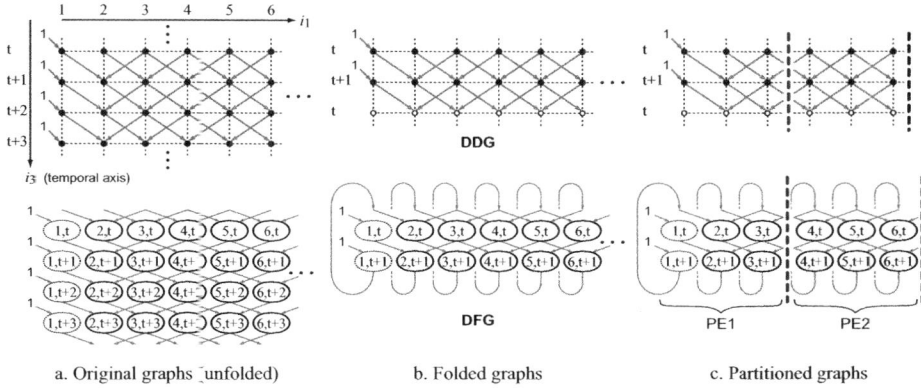

a. Original graphs (unfolded)   b. Folded graphs   c. Partitioned graphs

Fig. 12. Folding and partitioning DDG and DFG

in the DDG. However, multiple vertices can share the same address because a datum that is not referred further does not have to be stored in a memory.

Since the graph has regularity for i_3, we can fold the DDG to reduce the memory usage. Figure 12b shows the folded DDG, which has only the vertices for $i_3 = t$ and $t + 1$. The vertices for $i_3 = t$ have data-dependence from those for $i_3 = t + 1$. This folded DDG requires memory addresses only for the vertices of $i_3 = t$ and $t + 1$. Actually, two memory regions to be assigned for $i_3 = t$ and $t + 1$ are used for double-buffering of the grid. The folded DFG represents stencil computations to be iterated. Since SCMA has a loop instruction, we will use the folded DFG to generate instructions of a loop body in the scheduling stage.

4.5   Partitioning Stage

This stage parallelizes the entire computation by partitioning the DFG into sub-DFGs, and allocating them to PEs. Since PEs are connected to form a 2D array, the partitioning is performed by dividing two axes. In the case of Fig.11 where i_1 and i_2 are parallel axes, both axes are divided to generate sub-DFGs. Note that PEs of each SIMD group need to have such sub-DFGs that have the same number of vertices and the same topology for the common instruction sequence. Figure 12c shows partitioning of i_1. This generates the left and right sub-DFGs, which are allocated to PE1 and PE2, respectively. Since the vertices of "1,t" and "1,t+1" represent constant substitution instead of accumulation with four terms, these sub-DFGs will be converted to different instruction-sequences. This means that these sub-DFGs require two different sequencers.

4.6   Scheduling Stage

In this stage, multiply-and-add operations of each stencil computation are scheduled for sequencers. Then instructions are generated with the scheduled operations. Figure 13 shows several steps in scheduling the partitioned sub-DFGs of Fig.12c. Before scheduling, we give *data-reference delay* to all the edges in the

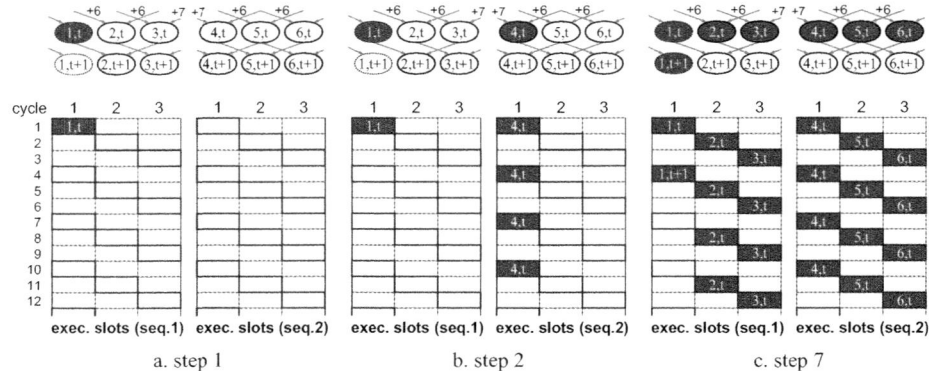

Fig. 13. Scheduling operations with execution slots

sub-DFG, which is 6 and 7 cycles for the local memory and the communication FIFOs of the adjacent PEs, respectively. Figure 14 also shows the execution slots for the three accumulation-chains of Fig.7. Here we assume that we have only the two sequencers for PE1 and PE2. The operations of the sub-DFGs are scheduled by assigning them to the empty slots as follows:

1. For each sequencer, find executable vertices from non-assigned ones. A vertex is executable when all the input edges are connected to executed vertices.
2. From the executable vertices, select the vertex whose output edges have the maximum data-reference delay.
3. Find the earliest slots where all the operations of the vertex can be assigned with their input data available. In step 1 of Fig.13, the vertex of "1,t" is selected and written to the slots at cycles 1 because the vertex contains only one operation for constant substitution. If the selected vertex contains four operations, it occupies four slots in the same accumulation-chain as shown in step 2 of Fig.13.
4. Perform 1 to 3 for the next sequencer. Thus the vertices of the sub-DFGs are assigned to the slots one by one in a round-robin order for multiple sequencers.
5. Scheduling finishes when all the vertices are assigned.

In step 7 of Fig.13, vertex "1,t+1" is selected and written to the slot in the accumulation chain 1 of sequencer 1 at cycle 4.

5   Implementation and Results

We implemented the compiler for DSLSC in C++. We used Boost library version 1.44.0 [1] especially to implement the frontend. Such a code as Fig.8 is compiled with different stencils: 3x3 and 5x5. The 5x5 stencil function is given:

```
F[0,0,0] = C*F[1,0, -1] + C*F[-1,0, -1] + C*F[0,1, -1] + C*F[0,-1, -1]
         + C*F[2,0, -1] + C*F[-2,0, -1] + C*F[0,2, -1] + C*F[0,-2, -1];
```

For experiments, we changed the grid size and the total time-steps, I,J and T in Fig.8. For different sizes of a PE array, we obtained the utilization of MAC units in all the PEs, which is given by $\frac{\text{(total cycles)} - \text{(total nop cycles)}}{\text{(total cycles)}}$.

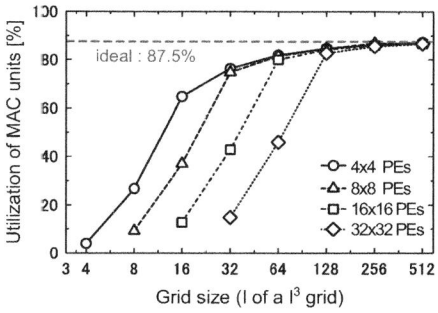
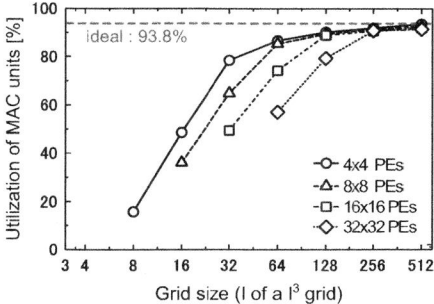

Fig. 14. MAC utilization for a 3x3 stencil   **Fig. 15.** MAC utilization for a 5x5 stencil

Figure 14 shows the utilization of MAC units for different grid sizes with the 3x3 stencil function. For small grids, the utilization is very low because the latency of data reference cannot be hidden by computations. The sufficient size of a sub-grid is necessary for each PE to hide the latency. As the grid size increases, the utilization becomes higher, getting up to 85.6 % for I=J=T=512. Since the the 3x3 stencil function requires four multiplications and only three additions, the ideal utilization is 7/8, which is 87.5 %. This means that our compiler generates a sequence of instructions close to ideal one.

The SCMA size also influences the utilization. As Fig.3 shows, current SCMA has eight SIMD groups for boundary computations and one group for internal ones. The PEs of boundary groups tend to have lower utilization than the internal PEs because of constant-substitution operations for boundary grid-points. Since the boundary PEs have a big ratio to all the PEs in a small SCMA, the smaller SCMA has lower utilization than the larger SCMA. The same tendency was observed for the 5x5 stencil function as shown in Figure 15, resulting in the high utilization of 92.18 %. This is close to the ideal utilization of 93.75 % (=15/16).

We executed the compiled sequences of 3x3 stencil computation on a 8x12-PE SCMA implemented on ALTERA Stratix III EP3SL150 FPGA of Terasic DE3 board [8]. Since the local memory of each PE has the size of 512 words, we computed a grid of 64x72 and 64x92 for 1000 time-steps so that each PE has a sub-grid of 8x6 and 8x8, respectively. The 8x6 sub-grid is easy to manually schedule three concurrent accumulations while the 8x8 one is not. As a result, our compiler achieved the utilization of 87.4% and 86.9% for computing the 8x6 and 8x8 sub-grid with the internal PEs, while hand-scheduling gave 87.4% to the 8x6 sub-grid computation.

6   Conclusions

In this paper, we have proposed DSLSC and its compiler for SCMA. In DSLSC, we can program stencil computations by describing their mathematical form instead of writing explicit procedure. The backend of the compiler finds a loop body, parallelizes it for PEs by folding and partitioning DDG and DFG of the input code. Finally operations in a sub-DFG are scheduled each sequencer so that we have as less nop cycles as possible. We evaluated the compiler with codes of 2D Jacobi compilation with 3x3 and 5x5 stencils. For sufficiently large grids, high utilization of PEs, up to 85.6% and 92.18%, is achieved for the 3x3 and 5x5 stencils, respectively, which are very close to their ideal utilization. In the future work, we will evaluate utilization of PEs with more complex stencil computations, e.g., with multiple stencil functions or 3D stencil functions. Although the structure of SCMA is given before compilation currently, we will develop a framework to generate HDL codes for appropriate SCMA structure with the DSLSC compiler.

Acknowledgments. This research was supported by Grant-in-Aid for Scientific Research (B) 23300012 and Grant-in-Aid for Challenging Exploratory Research 23650021 from the Ministry of Education, Culture, Sports, Science and Technology, Japan.

References

1. Boost C++ Library, http://www.boost.org
2. Chamberlain, B.L., Snyder, L.: Array language support for parallel sparse computation. In: Proceedings of the 15th International Conference on Supercomputing, pp. 133–145 (June 2001)
3. Datta, K., Murphy, M., Volkov, V., Williams, S., Carter, J., Oliker, L., Patterson, D., Shalf, J., Yelick, K.: Stencil computation optimization and auto-tuning on state-of-the-art multicore architectures. In: Proceedings of the 2008 ACM/IEEE Conference on Supercomputing, pp. 1–12 (November 2008)
4. Elliott, D.G., Stumm, M., Snelgrove, W., Cojocaru, C., Mckenzie, R.: Computational ram: Implementing processors in memory. Design & Test of Computers 16(1), 32–41 (1999)
5. Ferziger, J.H., Perić, M.: Computational Methods for Fluid Dynamics. Springer, Heidelberg (1996)
6. Hageman, L.A., Young, D.M.: Applied Iterative Methods. Academic Press (1981)
7. Kung, H.T.: Why systolic architecture? Computer 15(1), 37–46 (1982)
8. Luzhou, W., Sano, K., Yamamoto, S.: Local-and-global stall mechanism for systolic computational-memory array on extensible multi-fpga system. In: Proceedings of the International Conference on Field-Programmable Technology (FPT 2010), pp. 102–109 (December 2010)
9. Mycroft, D.O.A.: Efficient and correct stencil computation via pattern matching and static typing. In: Proceedings of IFIP Working Conference on Domain-Specific Languages (September 2011) (to appear)
10. Sano, K., Iizuka, T., Yamamoto, S.: Systolic architecture for computational fluid dynamics on FPGAs. In: Proceedings of the 15th Annual IEEE Symposium on Field-Programmable Custom Computing Machines (FCCM), pp. 107–116 (April 2007)
11. Sano, K., Luzhou, W., Hatsuda, Y., Iizuka, T., Yamamoto, S.: FPGA-array with bandwidth-reduction mechanism for scalable and power-efficient numerical simulations based on finite difference methods. ACM Transactions on Reconfigurable Technology and Systems 3(4) (November 2010), doi:10.1145/1862648.1862651

12. Tang, Y., Chowdhury, R., Kuszmaul, B.C., Luk, C.K., Leiserson, C.E.: The pochoir stencil compiler. In: Proceedings of the 23th ACM Symposium on Parallelism in Algorithms and Architectures (June 2011)
13. Teich, J., Thiele, L.: Partitioning processor arrays under resource constrains. Journal of VLSI Signal Processing 17, 5–20 (1997)
14. Underwood, K.D., Hemmert, K.S.: Closing the gap: CPU and FPGA trends in sustainable floating-point blas performance. In: Proceedings of the IEEE Symposium on Field-Programmable Custom Computing Machines, pp. 219–228 (2004)
15. Williams, S., Waterman, A., Patterson, D.: Roofline: an insightful visual performance model for multicore architectures. Communications of the ACM 52(4), 65–76 (2009)
16. Wolf, M.E., Lam, M.S.: A loop transformation theory and an algorithm to maximize parallelism. IEEE Transactions on Parallel and Distributed Systems 2(4), 452–471 (1991)

Exploiting Both Pipelining and Data Parallelism with SIMD Reconfigurable Architecture[★]

Yongjoo Kim[1], Jongeun Lee[2,★★], Jinyong Lee[1], Toan X. Mai[2],
Ingoo Heo[1], and Yunheung Paek[1]

[1] School of EECS, Seoul National University, Seoul, Korea
[2] School of ECE, Ulsan National Institute of Science and Technology, Ulsan, Korea
jlee@unist.ac.kr

Abstract. Reconfigurable Architecture (RA), which provides extremely high energy efficiency for certain domains of applications, have one problem that current mapping algorithms for it do not scale well with the number of cores. One approach to this problem is using SIMD (Single Instruction Multiple Data) paradigm. However, SIMD can complicate the mapping problem by adding an additional dimension, i.e., *iteration mapping*, to the already inter-dependent problems of data mapping and operation mapping, and can significantly affect performance through memory bank conflicts. In this paper we introduce *SIMD reconfigurable architecture*, which allows for SIMD mapping at multiple levels of granularity, and investigate ways to minimize bank conflicts in a SIMD reconfigurable architecture with the related sub-problems taken into consideration. We further present *data tiling* and evaluate a conflict-free scheduling algorithm as a way to eliminate bank conflicts for a certain class of iteration and data mapping.

Keywords: Coarse-grained reconfigurable architecture, Application mapping, Sequential, Interleaving, Memory bank conflict.

1 Introduction

Reconfigurable architectures feature extreme parallelism, very simple compute units, and programming without instructions, thereby achieving the highest energy efficiency only next to ASIC while maintaining programmability. Programming, however, is one of the biggest challenges for reconfigurable architectures. Fine-grained ones such as FPGAs are typically "designed" in hardware description languages. Coarse-Grained Reconfigurable Architectures (CGRAs) often support compilation from high level languages such as C, but even the best known algorithms [1] do not scale well, for reasons that also impede compilation for large VLIW processors, i.e., limited ILP (Instruction

---

[★] This work was supported in part by the Korea Science and Engineering Foundation(KOSEF) NRL Program grant funded by the Korea government(MEST) (No. 2011-0018609), the Engineering Research Center of Excellence Program of Korea Ministry of Education, Science and Technology(MEST) / Korea Science and Engineering Foundation(KOSEF) (Grant 2011-0000975), IDEC, and in part by Basic Science Research Program through the National Research Foundation of Korea (NRF) funded by MEST, under grant 2010-0011534.
[★★] Corresponding author.

O.C.S. Choy et al. (Eds.): ARC 2012, LNCS 7199, pp. 40–52, 2012.

Level Parallelism) and rapidly increasing search space. As a result, target architecture sizes for CGRA mapping have not increased much during the last decade, and still remain at 4x4 or 8x8 at the most.

While one can avoid the compiler scalability issue on larger CGRAs by executing multiple, unrelated threads/applications simultaneously [2, 3, 4], a more preferable solution would be a scalable framework that allows not only a large CGRA to be used at its entirety but also the size of CGRA mapping target to be changed depending on the workload or application requirements. Despite its apparent challenge, it can be done easily, by exploiting SIMD (Single Instruction Multiple Data) or data parallelism existing in many multimedia and graphics applications. Similarly to GPGPU (General Purpose Graphics Processing Unit) computing, we can map independent iterations of a loop to different subsets of a CGRA, which we call *cores*. (We call a CGRA consisting of multiple identical cores *SIMD reconfigurable architecture*.) This way we can ensure that the entire CGRA is utilized without necessarily burdening the scheduler—the scheduler only needs to generate code for a single core of a CGRA, which can be done efficiently even with existing algorithms.

However, this adds an additional dimension to the application mapping problem; the iteration mapping, or which iteration should be mapped to which core, needs to be addressed in addition to operation mapping and data mapping. As it turns out, there is a strong dependence between iteration mapping and data mapping, both of which can significantly affect the number of bank conflicts in the CGRA's multi-banked local memory. To maximize performance and energy efficiency we investigate ways to minimize bank conflicts with all related sub-problems of application mapping taken into account. The scalability of our SIMD reconfigurable architecture goes beyond distributing independent iterations over multiple cores, but we can gang multiple cores to create larger ones, called *macrocores*, to be used as scheduling targets. In macrocore mapping the problem of minimizing bank conflicts becomes much more complicated even for a simple SIMD reconfigurable architecture, for which we present an algorithm to minimize bank conflicts through better compilation.

Our experimental results using important kernels from OpenCV computer vision library, multimedia, and SPEC 2000 benchmark demonstrate that our SIMD compilation is not only more scalable but also can generate mappings that, depending on the CGRA size, are 20~30% faster and require 61~79% less configuration memory on average compared to traditional non-SIMD mappings.

2   Related Work

The two most related fields to our work are reconfigurable architecture and SIMD or vector (array) processing. Reconfigurable architectures, especially coarse-grained ones became an active research field recently due to their flexibility and superior energy efficiency. While earlier architectures were programmed at the assembly level, compilation for high level languages have started emerging since early 2000s. Compilation algorithms vary depending on the constraints of the target architecture. For reconfigurable architectures that allow one cycle context switch such as ADRES [5], a variant of modulo scheduling can be used to find quality mappings within reasonable time. Subsequently memory issues are recognized as a dominant problem, making it necessary to consider data mapping in addition to compute-operation mapping during scheduling [6, 7]. Data distribution and mapping in the context of the RAW machine is considered in [8].

Nowadays SIMD typically refers to MMX or SSE instructions [9] in the x86 architecture, but its original meaning is Single Instruction Multiple Data, which includes vector or array processors. CGRAs can be used as SIMD machines, and in fact some [10] report the result of mapping a cryptography kernel to a CGRA using a SIMD style. However, how to map loops optimally to a CGRA using a SIMD style and what are the issues are largely unexplored. Moreover, there is a difference in granularity between vector processors and CGRAs used as SIMD. The former has micro-operation granularity such as VADD (vector add) and VMUL (vector multiply) instructions, whereas the latter has loop granularity as it applies the whole body of a loop to different iterations. SIMD processors are particularly popular and effective [11, 12, 13] for signal processing applications such as wireless communications and software-defined radio, and some of them [12, 13] even support MIMD (Multiple Instruction Multiple Data) in addition to SIMD; however, they are all based on micro-operation granularity SIMD.

There are a few approaches in the literature containing both a SIMD aspect and a reconfiguration aspect. The IMAPCAR architecture [14] from NEC combines reconfigurable architecture with SIMD processing. The architecture, however, is restrictive in that the communication between processing elements and memory banks is one-to-one, which ensures scalability of the communication architecture but compilation is also restricted and simple. On the other hand, Fatemi et al. [15] considers the communication problem of adding a SIMD feature to an image processor, and proposes a cost-effective architecture, RC-SIMD, that can provide nearly the performance of a fully connected interconnect at a significantly lower cost. While the communication architecture of RC-SIMD could be applied to CGRAs, RC-SIMD does not consider reconfigurable architectures or mapping issues thereof.

3   SIMD Reconfigurable Architecture

3.1   Architecture

The main part of a CGRA consists of a PE (Processing Element) array and a local memory, which is typically a multi-bank scratchpad memory. A CGRA is responsible for executing loops, and therefore a loop's compute-operations are mapped to the PE array while the data arrays used by the loop are placed in the local scratchpad memory for fast access. The PE array is a 2D array of PEs with local (e.g., mesh) interconnects between them. All PEs can perform arithmetic operations while some can do memory operations (i.e., load/store) or expensive operations (i.e., division) as well. The result of one PE can be used by another PE in the next cycle; thus, every PE has at least one register at its output. In addition, a PE may contain a small set of private registers for constants and temporary variables. The absence of global register file is one of the biggest differences from VLIW processors, and hinders direct application of VLIW compilation techniques.

We define SIMD Reconfigurable Architecture (SIMD RA) as a CGRA that consists of multiple identical parts, called cores. Fig. 1(a) illustrates a SIMD RA with four cores,

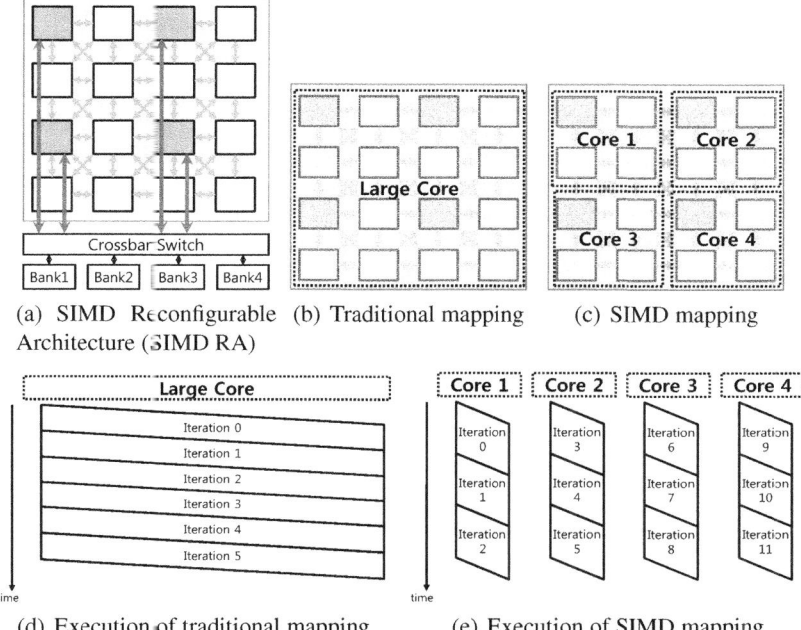

(a) SIMD Reconfigurable   (b) Traditional mapping   (c) SIMD mapping
Architecture (SIMD RA)

(d) Execution of traditional mapping   (e) Execution of SIMD mapping

Fig. 1. SIMD reconfigurable architecture allows both traditional mapping (Using the entire PE array for a single pipelining) and SIMD mapping (Intra-core pipelining plus inter-core parallelism)

with each core being a 2x2 PE array that includes one load-store PE. Every core must be identical to each other to allow for the reuse of configurations between them. This implies that every core must have at least one load-store PE. There is no restriction on the topology of interconnect between the PE array and the local scratchpad memory, except that every core must have the same view of the memory. Examples include one-to-one connection (one load-store PE to one memory bank) as in the IMAPCAR architecture, and the full crossbar switch. In the latter case, the number of cores does not have to be the same as the number of banks, though fewer banks can increase the possibility of bank conflicts.[1]

3.2 Compilation

The behavior of PEs and how data move among them are dictated by configuration, which is analogous to the instructions of a microprocessor. For CGRAs supporting one-cycle configuration change, the best known mapping algorithms are based on modulo scheduling, which generates schedules with modulo constraints taken into account, so

---

[1] In this paper we assume that each bank has a small queue [16] at its port to handle temporary surge of requests to the same bank. While this queue can spread out simultaneous requests over multiple cycles, it adds to the latency of a load operation by load-store PE. The latency increase, or equivalently the depth of the queue, is assumed to be four in our experiments.

that schedules for consecutive iterations can be overlapped at a certain distance, called *Initiation Interval (II)*, to create a steady-state one. The difference from traditional modulo scheduling (e.g., for VLIW processors) is that since there is no global register file in CGRAs, the data flow between PEs must be implemented with operand routing using existing interconnect resources, which can hinder direct application of VLIW compilation algorithms. Fig. 1(d) illustrates loop pipelining using the entire PE array.

While modulo scheduling can find quality mappings within reasonable time, it has to search a very large mapping space for placement and routing because it handles all PEs independently of each other. Consequently, modulo scheduling-based mapping algorithms suffer from skyrocketing compilation time as the number of PEs increases. Moreover, modulo scheduling exploits Loop-Level Parallelism (LLP) only in a limited way; the number of iterations it can execute concurrently is only a few, and does not scale with the number of PEs available.

Our SIMD reconfigurable architecture can greatly alleviate these problems by facilitating SIMD mapping. Our SIMD RA is divided into N cores, each of which can work on different iterations using the same configuration, thus effectively increasing throughput by N times (*parallelism between cores*). At the same time, each core can do pipelining to execute multiple iterations concurrently (*pipelining within a core*). Therefore by using SIMD, the number of loop iterations executed in parallel can increase greatly, and scale with the PE array size, as illustrated in Fig. 1(e). Moreover by keeping the core size small, the mapping space can remain small, leading to short compilation time. A side benefit of SIMD mapping is that the generated schedules tend to be denser compared to non-SIMD mapping for the same modulo scheduling algorithm, which can contribute to higher utilization and performance.

However, not every loop can benefit from SIMD mapping, since SIMD requires that there be no loop-carried dependence. Also for large loops with many operations in the loop body, our small core might not be a good match. In the latter case we can gang multiple cores to create a larger one (e.g., 2x4, 4x2, or 4x4), which is called *macrocore*. Henceforth a core is also called *microcore* when emphasizing that it is not a macrocore. Note that whether to use a microcore, a macrocore, or the entire PE array for mapping is purely a software decision, and does not involve hardware modification in a SIMD RA.

4   Minimizing Bank Conflicts in SIMD Mapping

Compared to the traditional mapping, SIMD mapping involves an additional problem of assigning iterations to cores, which has to be considered along with other mapping problems such as operation mapping (which operation to which PE) and data mapping (which data array to which memory bank). The iteration-to-core mapping is closely related to data mapping, and can significantly affect the number of bank conflicts, and consequently performance. In addition, depending on whether to use a microcore or a macrocore, mapping feasibility and results may vary. In this section we first consider the effect of iteration mapping and data mapping on the number of bank conflicts for microcore-grained SIMD mapping. We then consider macrocore-grained SIMD mapping.

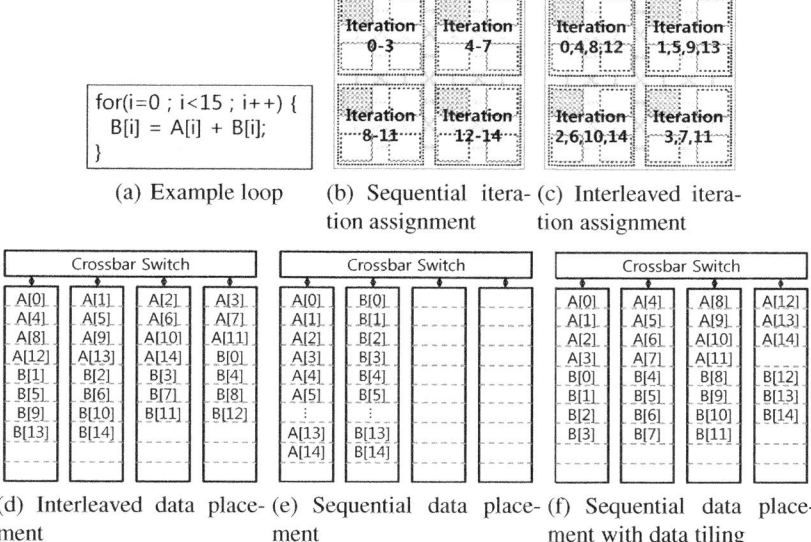

```
for(i=0 ; i<15 ; i++) {
    B[i] = A[i] + B[i];
}
```

(a) Example loop   (b) Sequential iteration assignment   (c) Interleaved iteration assignment

(d) Interleaved data placement   (e) Sequential data placement   (f) Sequential data placement with data tiling

Fig. 2. Different iteration mapping and data mapping examples

4.1 Microcore Mapping

Though any partitioning of loop iterations into cores can be a valid iteration mapping, for ease of code generation and data management let us consider two simplest schemes: sequential and interleaved. Sequential iteration assignment is to assign a sequence of iterations to each core whereas interleaved is to assign iterations to cores in a round-robin fashion, as illustrated in Fig. 2(b) and (c). Similarly for data mapping, there are two most straightforward schemes, i.e., sequential and interleaved. These iteration and data mapping schemes create four possible combinations.

Interleaved Data Placement. Interleaved data placement, where the next address is in the next bank as illustrated in Fig. 2(d), has some good qualities, such as balanced bank usage, simplicity (no need to decide which bank to place arrays in), and robustness to architecture parameters (e.g., number of banks). It is easy to see that with interleaved data placement, interleaved iteration assignment is better than sequential. For example, consider the loop in Fig. 2(a) with sequential vs. interleaved iteration assignment, given that array $A[i]$ is placed as shown in Fig. 2(d). With interleaved iteration assignment, the four cores will first access $A[0]$, $A[1]$, $A[2]$, and $A[3]$, which are all in different banks, thus no bank conflict. However, with sequential iteration assignment, the cores will first access $A[0]$, $A[4]$, $A[8]$, and $A[12]$, which are all in the same bank, thus generating many bank conflicts.[2] If the stride of array access expression is greater than one (e.g., $A[2i]$), only some banks may have all the array elements ever accessed; others have

---

[2] Whether bank conflicts will occur in the sequential-iteration interleaved-data case depends in general on the relationship between the number of banks, the number of iterations, and the number of cores.

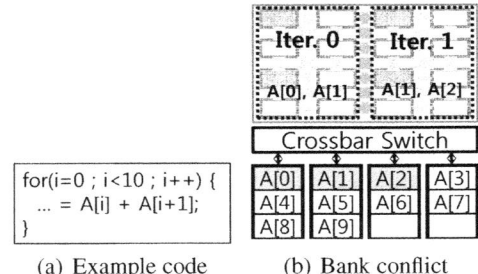

(a) Example code   (b) Bank conflict

Fig. 3. In macrocore mapping with *interleaving*, bank conflicts can be inevitable

array elements that are never accessed. This will effectively reduce the number of banks, and increase bank conflicts. This problem is common to both the cases using interleaved data placement. Thus we see that with interleaved data placement, interleaved iteration assignment is better than or equal to sequential iteration assignment in terms of the number of bank conflicts.

Sequential Data Placement. In sequential data placement, address spans one bank completely before covering the next one, as illustrated in Fig. 2(e). While sequential data placement can work well with traditional non-SIMD mapping, with SIMD mapping it can cause extremely frequent bank conflicts if all cores simultaneously access nearby data elements, as in the case with interleaved iteration assignment. This is because nearby data elements are almost always in the same bank in sequential data placement. Therefore interleaved iteration assignment is a poor choice if sequential data placement is in use.

In the case of sequential iteration assignment, we can nearly eliminate bank conflicts by rearranging data elements, as illustrated in Fig. 2(f). This data arrangement, which we call *data tiling*, involves two things: i) code modification so that each core will access arrays from a different base address, and ii) actually rearranging data on the CGRA local memory. Due to the second issue, data tiling does not encourage data reuse between different loops executed on a CGRA; however, its data arrangement overhead can be (partially) hidden if CGRA-executed loops do not appear back-to-back, by issuing DMA (Direct Memory Access) data transfers early. The exact layout for data tiling can be determined only after iteration mapping and operation mapping are done, but since it sorts out the data according to each core's usage, data tiling can eliminate bank conflicts completely for predictable (e.g., linear or affine) memory access patterns. If there are reused data (e.g., $A[i]$ and $A[i+1]$) in a loop, data tiling duplicates some array elements into multiple banks. While this may cause a problem in a recurrent loop (e.g., if a *write* array is duplicated), recurrent loops cannot be SIMD-mapped anyway. Thus with sequential data placement, sequential iteration assignment is better than or equal to interleaved iteration assignment in terms of the number of bank conflicts, and can be much better if data tiling is used.

In summary, our analysis finds that from the bank conflict point of view, two out of the four combinations have strong advantages. We next investigate how to extend the two combinations for macrocore-grained SIMD mapping.

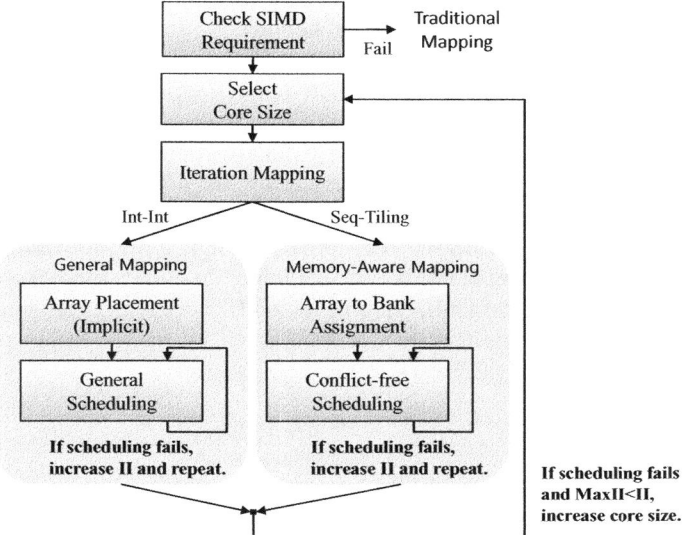

Fig. 4. Our SIMD RA mapping flow

4.2   Macrocore Mapping

The best two combinations for microcore mapping are i) interleaved-iteration, interleaved-data mapping and ii) sequential-iteration, sequential-data mapping with data tiling, which are shortened in this subsection to interleaving and sequential, respectively.

Macrocore mapping is fundamentally no different from microcore mapping. The only difference is that since a macrocore must have at least two load-store PEs,[3] bank conflicts are more likely to occur, and preventing bank conflicts becomes more complicated.

In the case of the *interleaving* combination, bank conflicts are sometimes inevitable. Fig. 3(b) illustrates an example where two macrocores are each accessing two memory elements at the same cycle ($A[0]$ and $A[1]$ by one macrocore, $A[1]$ and $A[2]$ by another). Since $A[1]$ is requested by both macrocores, there is no way to avoid a bank conflict, unless we duplicate $A[1]$ in multiple banks as is done in our data tiling. Note however that if the same loop is mapped to microcores, there will be no bank conflict at all, since all four microcores will access four different banks every cycle.

In the case of the *sequential* combination, we can eliminate bank conflicts completely for affine memory access patterns, by using our data tiling and a conflict-free scheduling algorithm [7]. The existing conflict-free scheduling algorithm can be applied here without modification, observing that since data tiling essentially manages all the data for one macrocore, we only need to take care of one macrocore and its associated memory banks. In other words there can't bank conflicts between multiple macrocores, if there is no bank conflict within a macrocore—in which the latter is guaranteed by conflict-free scheduling. The main idea in conflict-free scheduling is to keep track of memory banks as well as PEs in the reservation table when performing modulo scheduling, in

---

[3] A microcore must have at least one load-store PE.

order to ensure that at any cycle there is no more than one access to the same memory bank. This requires that the array-to-bank assignment be determined beforehand, which is done using a heuristic algorithm.

Fig. 4 illustrates our overall mapping flow for a SIMD RA. After first checking if the loop can be mapped using SIMD, we begin with the smallest core size, or micro-core mapping. The iteration mapping step is straightforward, which is followed by data and operation mapping. In the case of interleaving, the array placement step is trivial and implicitly done independently of operation mapping, which is a variant of modulo scheduling. For the sequential case, arrays are first assigned to banks, after which operation mapping is done using conflict-free scheduling. In either case, scheduling failure incurs an increment in the target II, but if the target II exceeds a certain limit, we regard that as indicating the lack of registers for temporary live variables, and increase the core granularity.

5   Experiments

To evaluate the effectiveness of our approach, we use five kernels (Harris edge detection, color conversion, dot product, Gaussian filter, erode) from OpenCV computer vision library, as well as kernels from multimedia and SPEC 2000 benchmarks (Laplace transform, wavelet, swim kernels). We use two CGRA sizes, 4x4 and 8x4, with a microcore being a 2x2 PE array that includes a load-store PE and a multiplier PE. Each PE has four registers, and connected to its 8 neighbors (mesh + diagonal) except the ones on boundary. The CGRA local memory consists of as many banks as the number of microcores, and is connected to load-store PEs via full crossbar switch. We use the EMS algorithm [1] as the baseline modulo scheduling algorithm, where we try 50 times before incrementing the target II. To measure the system-level performance, we use the Gem5 simulator [17] with DRAMsim [18], modeling a system with an ARM9 processor and a CGRA connected via AMBA AHB system bus.

5.1   Effect of SIMD Mapping: Performance and Configuration Size

We first compare SIMD vs. non-SIMD mapping in terms of performance and configuration size. The traditional non-SIMD mapping (denoted by Original in figures) exploits pipelining on the full CGRA level only, whereas our SIMD can exploit both pipelining and parallelism on the microcore level.

Fig. 5 compares the CGRA runtimes by the two mapping methods for 4x4 and 8x4 CGRA architectures. For the SIMD mapping we use the interleaving combination, and the CGRA runtimes here do not include DMA time, which is the same regardless of whether it is SIMD or non-SIMD. In the non-SIMD case we unroll the loop sufficiently to achieve high utilization of PEs; the unrolling factors are shown in parentheses on the x-axis.

From the results we first note that as the CGRA size increases, the runtimes generally decrease, to about 50% on average, which is expected. The results also suggest that our SIMD mapping can achieve much higher performance than non-SIMD mapping, reducing CGRA runtimes by 29% and 32% on average for 4x4 and 8x4 CGRAs, respectively.

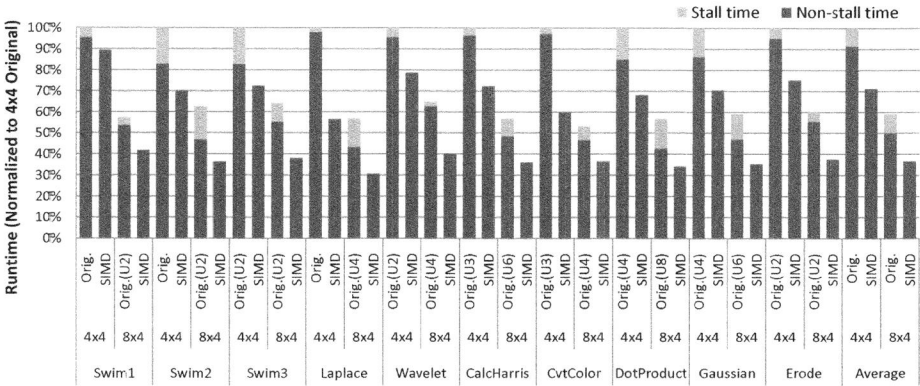

Fig. 5. CGRA runtimes (Orig. means non-SIMD). Numbers in parentheses are unrolling factors.

Table 1. Configuration size comparison

UF: Loop unrolling factor, Size: Configuration size in bytes

| | 4x4 | | | | | 8x4 | | | | |
| | Original | | SIMD | | % | Original | | SIMD | | % |
	UF	Size	UF	Size		UF	Size	UF	Size	
Swim 1	1	512	1	480	−6%	2	1152	1	448	−61%
Swim 2	1	512	1	432	−16%	2	1152	1	448	−61%
Swim 3	2	768	1	336	−56%	2	1024	1	352	−66%
Laplace	1	320	1	192	−40%	4	1152	1	208	−82%
Wavelet	2	448	1	192	−57%	4	1152	1	192	−83%
CalcHarris	3	512	1	128	−75%	6	1024	1	128	−88%
CvtColor	3	704	1	144	−80%	4	896	1	176	−80%
Dot Product	4	320	1	64	−80%	8	640	1	64	−90%
Gaussian	4	320	1	64	−80%	6	512	1	64	−88%
Erode	2	768	1	304	−60%	2	896	1	304	−66%

Shorter runtime by our SIMD mapping is partly due to higher PE utilization, which can be caused by less *routing PEs*, or PEs used solely for data routing—this is understandable as there is denser interconnection on the microcore level than on the CGRA level. Another factor contributing to the difference is the stalls due to memory bank conflict, which account for 8∼9% of the runtime on average in the non-SIMD mapping.

While we assume in this experiment that configuration memory and configuration cache sizes are unlimited, they have to be limited in practice, giving incentive to minimize the configuration size. Table 1 lists configuration sizes for various cases, and indicates that our SIMD mapping can also reduce configuration sizes often greatly. On average configuration sizes are reduced by 61% and 79% for 4x4 and 8x4 CGRAs, respectively, if our SIMD mapping is used instead of non-SIMD mapping. The impressive configuration size reduction is partly due to the loop unrolling that we perform to maximize the performance of non-SIMD mapping.

5.2 Macrocore Mapping Comparisons

Though all the kernels used in our experiments can be mapped on the microcore, to evaluate macrocore mapping we select five kernels that are the largest in terms of

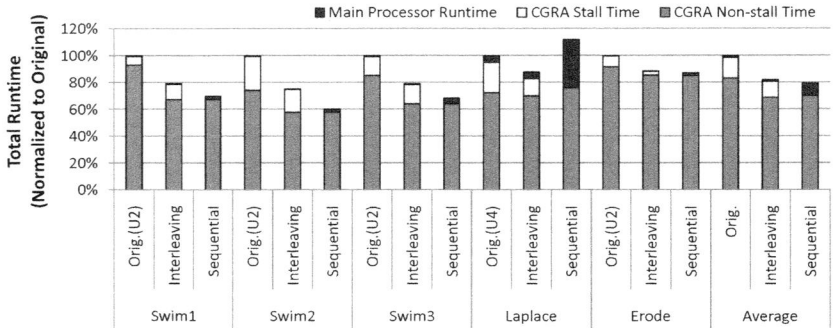

Fig. 6. Macrocore mapping results (unrolling factors are shown in parentheses)

number of operations. We use 2x4 macrocores and 8x4 CGRA for this experiment. We compare three cases, non-SIMD (=Original), interleaving, and sequential. To make a fair comparison between interleaving and sequential we compare total runtime that includes main processor runtime spent for DMA code execution. The DMA data transfer time itself is assumed to be hidden and not included.

Fig. 6 summarizes the runtime results, which indicate that our SIMD mapping outperforms the non-SIMD mapping in most cases, even though loop unrolling optimization is applied to non-SIMD mapping. On average runtime is reduced by about 20% compared to non-SIMD mapping, which is again due to increased PE utilization and reduced bank conflicts. Between our SIMD mappings, sequential shows better performance than interleaving in most cases, which is due to the elimination of stall time by data tiling and conflict-free scheduling. Though not shown here, the amount of duplicate data in sequential SIMD mapping is marginal, being only 1.6%, on average, of the loop's total data size, which is another reason why sequential performs well compared to interleaving. There is one noticeable exception however. In the Laplace kernel the main processor runtime for DMA is increased disproportionately in the sequential case. This is because the loop has a very small trip count (thus small runtime) and the data tiling pattern for the loop is relatively complicated, which makes the DMA overhead a relatively large fraction of the total runtime.

5.3   Compilation Time

Fig. 7 shows, on a log scale, the compilation times of the non-SIMD mapping algorithm for different CGRA sizes. For 4x4 and 8x4 CGRA sizes the loops are unrolled by the factors listed in Table 1, and for 8x8 CGRA we unroll the loops by twice the factor of 8x4 CGRA. From the graph we can see that as the size of the CGRA increases the mapping time increases at least exponentially. Unsurprisingly our SIMD mapping using 2x2 microcores takes less than one second for every kernel (not shown in the graph). This demonstrates that our SIMD mapping is scalable and suited to many-core CGRAs.

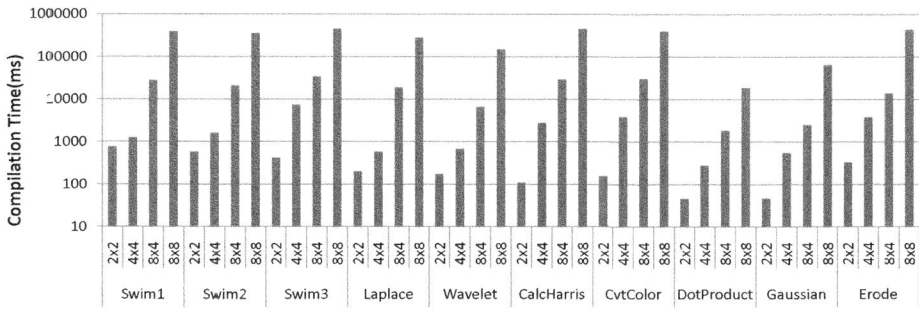

Fig. 7. Compilation time of non-SIMD mapping algorithm increases exponentially in the CGRA size

6 Conclusion

In this paper we introduced SIMD reconfigurable architecture to address the problem of exponentially increasing compilation time of existing CGRA mapping algorithms. SIMD mapping can be more complicated due to the nontrivial combination of iteration mapping, data mapping, and operation mapping, which are all related to each other and can affect performance through memory bank conflict. To minimize bank conflicts we presented data tiling and evaluated conflict-free scheduling for sequential mapping. Our experimental results demonstrate that our SIMD mapping is not only more scalable but also can generate mappings that are 20~30% faster and require 61~79% less configuration memory on average compared to traditional non-SIMD mappings.

References

1. Park, H., Fan, K., Mahlke, S.A., Oh, T., Kim, H., Kim, H.-S.: Edge-centric modulo scheduling for coarse-grained reconfigurable architectures. In: PACT 2008, pp. 166–176. ACM, New York (2008)
2. Wu, K., Kanstein, A., Madsen, J., Bereković, M.: MT-ADRES: Multithreading on Coarse-Grained Reconfigurable Architecture. In: Diniz, P.C., Marques, E., Bertels, K., Fernandes, M.M., Cardoso, J.M.P. (eds.) ARCS 2007. LNCS, vol. 4419, pp. 26–38. Springer, Heidelberg (2007)
3. Park, H., Park, Y., Mahlke, S.: Polymorphic pipeline array: A flexible multicore accelerator with virtualized execution for mobile multimedia applications. In: MICRO-42, pp. 370–380 (December 2009)
4. Kim, Y., Lee, J., Mai, T.X., Paek, Y.: Improving performance of nested loops on reconfigurable array processors. ACM Transactions on Architecture and Code Optimization (2012)
5. Mei, B., Vernalde, S., Verkest, D., De Man, H., Lauwereins, R.: ADRES: An Architecture with Tightly Coupled VLIW Processor and Coarse-Grained Reconfigurable Matrix. In: Cheung, P.Y.K., Constantinides, G.A. (eds.) FPL 2003. LNCS, vol. 2778, pp. 61–70. Springer, Heidelberg (2003)
6. Kim, Y., Lee, J., Shrivastava, A., Yoon, J., Paek, Y.: Memory-Aware Application Mapping on Coarse-Grained Reconfigurable Arrays. In: Patt, Y.N., Foglia, P., Duesterwald, E., Faraboschi, P., Martorell, X. (eds.) HiPEAC 2010. LNCS, vol. 5952, pp. 171–185. Springer, Heidelberg (2010)

7. Kim, Y., Lee, J., Shrivastava, A., Paek, Y.: Operation and data mapping for cgras with multibank memory. SIGPLAN Not. 45(4), 17–26 (2010)
8. Barua, R., Lee, W., Amarasinghe, S., Agarawal, A.: Compiler support for scalable and efficient memory systems. IEEE Trans. Comput. 50, 1234–1247 (2001)
9. Peleg, A., Weiser, U.: MMX technology extension to the intel architecture. IEEE Micro 16(4), 42–50 (1996)
10. Singh, H., Lee, M.-H., Lu, G., Kurdahi, F.J., Bagherzadeh, N., Chaves Filho, E.M.: MorphoSys: an integrated reconfigurable system for data-parallel and computation-intensive applications. IEEE Trans. Comput. 49(5), 465–481 (2000)
11. Lin, Y., Lee, H., Woh, M., Harel, Y., Mahlke, S., Mudge, T., Chakrabarti, C., Flautner, K.: Soda: A high-performance dsp architecture for software-defined radio. IEEE Micro 27(1), 114–123 (2007)
12. Woh, M., Seo, S., Mahlke, S., Mudge, T., Chakrabarti, C., Flautner, K.: Anysp: anytime anywhere anyway signal processing. In: Proceedings of the 36th Annual International Symposium on Computer Architecture, pp. 128–139. ACM (2009)
13. Dasika, G., Woh, M., Seo, S., Clark, N., Mudge, T., Mahlke, S.: Mighty-morphing power-SIMD. In: Proceedings of the 2010 International Conference on Compilers, Architectures and Synthesis for Embedded Systems, pp. 67–76. ACM (2010)
14. Kyo, S., Okazaki, S.: IMAPCAR: A 100 gops in-vehicle vision processor based on 128 ring connected four-way VLIW processing elements. J. Signal Process. Syst. 62, 5–16 (2011)
15. Fatemi, H., Mesman, B., Corporaal, H., Jonker, P.: RC-SIMD: Reconfigurable communication SIMD architecture for image processing applications. Journal of Embedded Computing 2, 167–179 (2006)
16. Bougard, B., De Sutter, B., Verkest, D., Van der Perre, L., Lauwereins, R.: A coarse-grained array accelerator for software-defined radio baseband processing. IEEE Micro 28, 41–50 (2008)
17. Binkert, N., Beckmann, B., Black, G., Reinhardt, S.K., Saidi, A., Basu, A., Hestness, J., Hower, D.R., Krishna, T., Sardashti, S., Sen, R., Sewell, K., Shoaib, M., Vaish, N., Hill, M.D., Wood, D.A.: The gem5 simulator. SIGARCH Comput. Archit. News 39, 1–7 (2011)
18. Wang, D., Ganesh, B., Tuaycharoen, N., Baynes, K., Jaleel, A., Jacob, B.: Dramsim: a memory system simulator. SIGARCH Comput. Archit. News 33, 100–107 (2005)

Table-Based Division by Small Integer Constants

Florent de Dinechin[1] and Laurent-Stéphane Didier[2]

[1] LIP, Université de Lyon (ENS-Lyon/CNRS/INRIA/UCBL)
46, allée d'Italie, 69364 Lyon Cedex 07
`Florent.de.Dinechin@ens-lyon.fr`
[2] LIP6, Université Pierre et Marie Curie (UPMC/CNRS)
4 place Jussieu, 75252 Paris Cedex 05
`Laurent-Stephane.Didier@upmc.fr`

Abstract. Computing cores to be implemented on FPGAs may involve divisions by small integer constants in fixed or floating point. This article presents a family of architectures addressing this need. They are derived from a simple recurrence whose body can be implemented very efficiently as a look-up table that matches the hardware resources of the target FPGA. For instance, division of a 32-bit integer by the constant 3 may be implemented by a combinatorial circuit of 48 LUT6 on a Virtex-5. Other options are studied, including iterative implementations, and architectures based on embedded memory blocks. This technique also computes the remainder. An efficient implementation of the correctly rounded division of a floating-point constant by such a small integer is also presented.

1 Introduction

When porting applications to FPGAs, arithmetic operations should be optimized in an application-specific way whenever possible. This is the goal of the FloPoCo project [1]. This article considers division by a small integer constant, and demonstrates operators for it that are more efficient than approaches based on standard division [2] or on multiplication by the inverse [3,4].

Division by a small integer constant is an operation that occurs often enough to justify investigating a specific operator for it. This work, for instance, was motivated by the Jacobi stencil algorithm, whose core computes the average of 3 values: this involves a division by 3. Small integer constants are quite common in such situations. Division by 5 also occurs in decimal / binary conversions. The proposed approach could also be used to interleave memory banks in numbers that are not powers of two: if we have d memory banks, an address A must be translated to address A/d in bank $A \mod d$.

Division by a constant in a hardware context has actually been studied quite extensively [3,5,4], with good surveys in [6,7]. There are two main families of techniques: those based on additions and subtractions, and those based on multiplication by the inverse. In this article we introduce a technique that has, to our knowledge, only been described in lecture notes as a general combinational

O.C.S. Choy et al. (Eds.): ARC 2012, LNCS 7199, pp. 53–63, 2012.

circuit example [8]. It is in essence a straightforward adaptation of the paper-and-pencil division algorithm in the case of small divisors. The reason why this technique is not mentioned in the literature is probably that the core of its iteration itself computes a (smaller) division: it doesn't reduce to either additions, or multiplications. However, it is very well suited to FPGAs, whose logic is based on look-up tables (LUTs): they may implement such complex operations very efficiently, provided the size in bits of the input numbers matches the number of inputs to the hardware LUTs.

Let us introduce this technique with the help of usual decimal arithmetic. Suppose we want to divide an arbitrary number, say 776, by 3. Figure 1 describes the paper-and-pencil algorithm in this case.

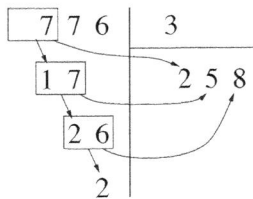

We first computes the Euclidean division of 7 by 3. This gives the first digit of the quotient, here 2, and the remainder is 1. We now have to divide 176 by 3. In the second iteration, we divide 17 by 3: the second quotient digit is 5, and the remainder is 2. The third iteration divides 26 by 3: the third quotient digit is 8 and the remainder is 2, and this is also the remainder of the division of 776 by 3.

Fig. 1. Division by 3 in decimal

The key observation is that in this example, the iteration body consists in the Euclidean division of a 2-digit decimal number by 3. The first of these two digits is a remainder from previous iteration: its value is 0, 1 or 2. We may therefore implement this iteration with a look-up table that, for each value from 00 to 29, gives the quotient and the remainder of its division by 3. This small look-up table will allow us to divide by 3 numbers of arbitrary size.

In Section 2 we adapt this radix-10 algorithm to a radix that is a power of two, then chose this radix so that the look-up table matches well the fine structure of the target FPGA. We study the case of floating-point inputs in Section 3: it is possible to ensure correct rounding to the nearest for free. Section 4 provides a few results and comparisons.

2   Euclidean Division of an Integer by a Small Constant

2.1   Notations

Let d be the constant divisor, and let α be a small integer. We will use the representation of x in radix $\beta = 2^\alpha$, which may also be considered as breaking down the binary decomposition of x into k chunks of α bits (see Figure 3):

$$x = \sum_{i=0}^{k-1} x_i.2^{-\alpha i} \quad \text{where} \quad x_i \in \{0, ..., 2^\alpha - 1\}$$

In all this section, we assume that d is not a multiple of 2, as division by 2 resumes to a constant shift which is for free in FPGAs.

2.2   Algorithm

The following algorithm computes the quotient q and the remainder r_0 of the high radix euclidean division of x by the constant d. At each step of this algorithm, the partial dividend y_i, the partial remainder r_i and one radix-2^α digit of the quotient are computed.

Algorithm 1. LUT-based computation of x/d

1: **procedure** CONSTANTDIV(x, d)
2:     $r_k \leftarrow 0$
3:     **for** $i = k - 1$ **down to** 0 **do**
4:         $y_i \leftarrow x_i + 2^\alpha r_{i+1}$ (this + is a concatenation)
5:         $(q_i, r_i) \leftarrow (\lfloor y_i/d \rfloor,\ y_i \mod d)$ (read from a table)
6:     **end for**
7:     **return** $q = \sum_{i=0}^{k} q_i.2^{-\alpha i}$, r_0
8: **end procedure**

Theorem 1. *Algorithm 1 computes the Euclidean division of x by d. It outputs the quotient $q = \sum_{i=0}^{k} q_i.2^{-\alpha i}$ and the remainder r_0 so that $x = q \times d + r_0$. The radix-2^α representation of the quotient q is also a binary representation, each iteration producing α bits of this quotient.*

The proof of this theorem is in the appendix. The line $y_i \leftarrow x_i + 2^\alpha r_{i+1}$ is simply the concatenation of a remainder and a radix-2^α digit. Let us define γ as the size in bits of the largest possible remainder: $\gamma = \lceil \log_2(d-1) \rceil$ – this is also the size of d as d is not a power of two. Then, y_i is of size $\alpha + \gamma$ bits. The second line of the loop body, $(q_i, r_i) \leftarrow (\lfloor y_i/d \rfloor,\ y_i \mod d)$, computes a radix-$2^\alpha$ digit and a remainder: it may be implemented as a look-up table with $\alpha + \gamma$ bits of input and $\alpha + \gamma$ bits of output (Fig. 2). Here, α is a parameter which may be chosen to match the target FPGA architecture, as we show below. The algorithm computes α bits of the quotient in one iteration: the larger α, the fewer iterations are needed for a given input number size n.

The iteration may be implemented sequentially as depicted in Fig. 2, although in all the following we will focus on the fully unrolled architecture depicted in Fig. 3, which enables high-throughput pipelined implementations.

It should be noted that, for a given d, the architecture grows linearly with the input size n, where general division or multiplication architectures grow quadratically.

2.3   Memory Structures in Current FPGAs

Current FPGAs offer two main memory structures. The first is the 4- to 6- input LUT used in the logic fabric. In the following we note LUTk a k-bit input, 1-bit

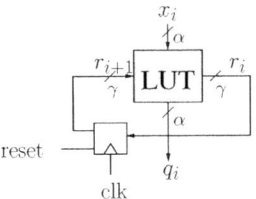

Fig. 2. LUT-based sequential division by a constant of a radix-2^α digit extended by a remainder

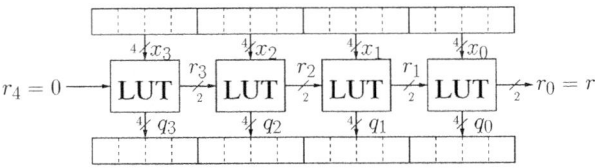

Fig. 3. LUT-based division by 3 of a 16-bit number written in radix 2^4 ($\alpha = 4$, $\gamma = 2$)

output LUT. In each FPGA family, there are restrictions on LUT utilization. Let us review recent FPGAs with the motivation to build k-input, k-output LUTs.

The Altera Stratix IV Adaptive Logic Module (ALM) can be used as two arbitrary LUT4, but may also implement two LUT5 or two LUT6 under the condition that they share some of their inputs. This is the case for our architectures: a 6-input, 6-output LUT may be built as 3 ALMs.

In Xilinx Virtex-5 and Virtex-6, the logic slice includes 4 registers and 4 LUT6, each of which is fractionable as two LUT5 with independent outputs. The sweet spot here is therefore to build 5-input tables, unless we need to register all the outputs, in which case 6-input tables should be preferred.

We may use, for instance, 6-input LUTs to implement division by 3 ($\gamma = 2$) in radix 16 ($\alpha = 4$). Implementing the core loop costs 6 LUTs (for a 6 bits in, 6 bits out table). The cost for a fully combinatorial (or unrolled) divider by 3 on n bits is $\lceil n/4 \rceil \times 6$ LUT6s, for instance 36 LUT6s for 24 bits (single precision), or 78 LUTs for 53 bits (double precision). The best shift-and-add algorithm to date needs respectively 118 and 317 full-adders (FA), each FA consuming one LUT both in Xilinx and in Altera devices. The approach proposed here is four times as efficient on division by 3. The larger d, the more inefficient this approach becomes, as we need more bits to represent the r_i.

For larger constants, a second option is the embedded memory block, from 9Kbits to 144 Kbits depending on the architecture. We will use them as $2^9 \times 9$ (9Kbits), $2^{10} \times 10$ (18Kbits or 36KBits) or $2^{13} \times 13$ (144 KBits). For division by 3, we may now use $\alpha = 7$ to $\alpha = 11$, but these larger memories also push the relevance of this technique to larger constants.

These memories are not combinatorial, their inputs must be registered: they are best suited to either sequential, or unrolled but pipelined implementation.

In the latter case, we may exploit the fact that all these embedded memories are dual-ported: two iterations may be unrolled in one single memory block as depicted in Figure 4. Again for division by 3, exploiting the M9K blocks of a Stratix IV (using $\alpha = 7$), a fully pipelined single-precision divider by 3 could be impemented in 2 M9K only (2*2*7=28 bits) and run in 4 cycles at the maximal practical speed supported by these devices. We have no experimental data to support these claims as we implemented only the logic-based dividers so far. Indeed, results in Section 4 suggest that architectures based on embedded RAMs would not be very competitive.

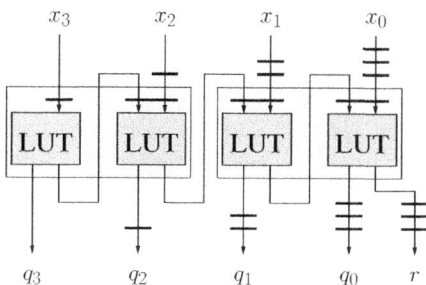

Fig. 4. A pipelined divider using two dual-ported embedded RAMs

3   Division of a Floating-Point Number by a Small Integer Constant

A floating-point input X is given by its mantissa m and exponent e:

$$x = 2^e m \quad \text{with } m \in [1, 2).$$

Similarly, the floating-point representation of our integer divisor d is:

$$d = 2^s d' \quad \text{with } d' \in [1, 2)$$

with $s = \gamma - 1$ if d is not a power of two.

As the mantissa has a fixed number of bits, its normalization and rounding have to be performed for almost each floating-point operation [9].

3.1   Normalization

Let us write the division

$$\frac{x}{d} = \frac{m.2^e}{d} = \frac{2^s m}{d} 2^{e-s}.$$

As $\frac{2^s m}{d} = \frac{m}{d'} \in [0.5, 2)$, this is almost the normalized mantissa of the floating-point representation of the result:

– if $m \geq d'$, then $\frac{m}{d'} \in [1, 2)$, the mantissa is correctly normalized and the floating-point number to be returned is

$$y = \circ \left(\frac{2^s m}{d} \right) 2^{e-s}$$

where $\circ(z)$ denotes the IEEE-standard rounding to nearest even of a real z.

– if $m < d'$, then $\frac{m}{d'} \in [0.5, 1)$, the mantissa has to be shifted left by one. Thus, the floating-point number to be returned is

$$y = \circ \left(\frac{2^{s+1} m}{d} \right) 2^{e-s-1} \quad .$$

It can be observed that the comparison between m and d' is extremely cheap for small integers because d' has only γ non-zero bits. Thus, the comparison is reduced to the comparison of these γ bits to the leading γ bits of m. As both m and d' have a leading one, we need a comparator on $\gamma - 1$ bits. In terms of latency, this is a very small delay using fast-carry propagation.

3.2 Rounding

Let us now address the issue of correctly rounding the mantissa fraction. If we ignore the remainder, the obtained result is the rounding towards zero of the floating-point division.

To obtain correct rounding to the nearest, a first idea is to consider the final remainder. If it is larger than $d/2$, we should round up, *i.e.* increment the mantissa. The comparison to $d/2$ would cost nothing (actually the last table would hold the result of this comparison instead of the remainder value), but this would mean an addition of the full mantissa size, which would consume some logic and have a latency comparable to the division itself, due to carry propagation.

A better idea is to use the identity $\circ(z) = \lfloor z + \frac{1}{2} \rfloor$, which in our case becomes

$$\circ \left(\frac{2^{s+\epsilon} m}{d} \right) = \left\lfloor \frac{2^{s+\epsilon} m}{d} + \frac{1}{2} \right\rfloor = \left\lfloor \frac{2^{s+\epsilon} m + d/2}{d} \right\rfloor$$

with ϵ being 0 if $m \geq d'$, and 1 otherwise. In the floating-point context we may assume that d is odd, since powers of two are managed as exponents. Let us write $d = 2h + 1$. We obtain

$$\circ \left(\frac{2^{s+\epsilon} m}{d} \right) = \left\lfloor \frac{2^{s+\epsilon} m + h}{d} + \frac{1}{2d} \right\rfloor = \left\lfloor \frac{2^{s+\epsilon} m + h}{d} \right\rfloor$$

so instead of adding a round bit to the result, we may add h to the dividend before its input into the integer divisor. It seems we haven't won much, but this pre-addition is actually for free: the addend $h = \frac{d-1}{2}$ is an s-bit number, and we have to add it to the mantissa of x that is shifted left by $s + \epsilon$ bits, so it is a mere concatenation. Thus, we save the adder area and the carry propagation latency.

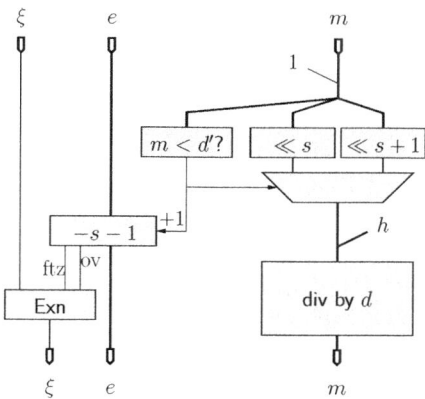

Fig. 5. Floating-point division by a small constant

To sum up, the management of a floating-point input adds to the area and latency of the mantissa divider those of one (small) exponent adder, and of one (large) mantissa multiplexer, as illustrated by Figure 5. On this figure, ξ is a 2-bit exception vector used to represent 0, $\pm\infty$ and NaN (Not a Number).

The implementation in FloPoCo manages divisions by small integer constants and all their powers of two. The only additional issues are in the overflow/underflow logic (the Exn box on Figure 5), but they are too straightforward to be detailed here.

4   Results and Comparison

All the results in this section are obtained for architectures generated by FloPoCo 2.3.0, using ISE 12.1 for an FPGA with 6-input LUTs (Virtex-5). These are synthesis results before place and route, which is perfectly meaningful for such tiny operators.

Table 1 provides some results for Euclidean division (integer division with remainder). We only report the architecture obtained with the optimal value of α.

4.1   Integer Division

One would believe that for such simple architectures, we can predict the synthesis results, at least with respect to LUT count. However, there are still some surprises, which we are currently investigating.

The first surprise is that the synthesis tools perform further optimization out of our designs: the LUT numbers are not always those predicted (they are always better). For instance, for the 64-bit divider by 3, we predict simply 96 LUT6, but the tool reports 15 LUT3, 18 LUT4, 16 LUT5, and only 45 LUT6, then merges that into 95 LUTs. One of the reasons could be that some remainder values never occur, which means that there are "don't care" in the logic tables that enable further optimizations. This would explain that the results are better for division by 5 than for division by 7 although they have the same α and β: there are more "don't care" in the table for 5. Such improvements should be studied systematically.

Also, we have mentioned earlier that the sweet spot on Virtex-5 should be to use 5-input LUTs, but the synthesis tools seem to decide otherwise: architectures designed for 5-input LUTs actually consume more than those designed for 6-input LUTs. This could come from a coding style issue, or from a misunderstanding of the intricate details of the Virtex-5 logic block.

Table 2 provides some synthesis results for pipelined dividers by 3. Each line is a different frequency/area tradeoff (incidentally, thanks to FloPoCo's pipelining framework [1], this flexible pipeline took less than ten minutes to implement out of the combinatorial design). Here we have to investigate why the LUT number is larger than the predicted size.

Table 1. Synthesis results for combinatorial Euclidean division on Virtex-5

	$n = 32$ bits			$n = 64$ bits		
constant	LUT6	(predicted)	latency	LUT6	(predicted)	latency
$d = 3$ ($\alpha = 4, \gamma = 2$)	47	(6*8=48)	7.14ns	95	(6*16=96)	14.8ns
$d = 5$ ($\alpha = 3, \gamma = 3$)	60	(6*11=66)	6.79ns	125	(6*22=132)	13.8ns
$d = 7$ ($\alpha = 3, \gamma = 3$)	60	(6*11=66)	7.30ns	125	(6*22=132)	15.0ns

Table 2. Synthesis results for pipelined Euclidean division by 3 on Virtex-5

$n = 32$ bits		$n = 64$ bits	
FF + LUT6	performance	FF + LUT6	performance
33 Reg + 47 LUT	1 cycle @ 230 MHz	122 Reg + 112 LUT	2 cycles @ 217 MHz
58 Reg + 62 LUT	2 cycles @ 410 MHz	168 Reg + 198 LUT	5 cycles @ 410 MHz
68 Reg + 72 LUT	3 cycles @ 527 MHz	172 Reg + 188 LUT	7 cycles @ 527 MHz

4.2   Floating-Point Division

Table 3 shows results for floating-point division by 3. The behaviour of these operators, including the fact that they return correctly rounded results, has been verified by simulation against millions of test vectors generated by an independent floating-point division by 3 [1].

Table 3. Synthesis results for pipelined floating-point division by 3 on Virtex-5

single precision		double precision	
FF + LUT6	performance	FF + LUT6	performance
35 Reg + 69 LUT	1 cycle @ 217 MHz	122 Reg + 166 LUT	2 cycles @ 217 MHz
105 Reg + 83 LUT	3 cycles @ 411 MHz	245 Reg + 250 LUT	6 cycles @ 410 MHz

For comparison, a single precision standard (non-constant) floating-point divider consumes 1122 reg and 945 LUT and needs 17 cycles @ 290 MHz.

4.3   Comparison with Previous Work

A review of several algorithms for division by a constant is available in [6]. Many of these algorithms require the division to be exact (null remainder) and return wrong results otherwise. We will not consider them. Among the remaining techniques, the most relevant is method 6 in [6].

In this method, the divisor has the form $2^t \pm 1$, which corresponds to most of the small divisors we are targeting. The quotient and the remainder are obtained through $\lceil \frac{n}{\gamma} \rceil - 1$ additions and substractions involving n-bit numbers.

Table 4 summarizes the comparison of the size of our implementation and an estimation of the area of an FPGA implementation of this previous technique. It can be observed that in this implementation, the larger d, the fewer required additions, therefore the smaller the implementation. This means that this method is increasingly relevant for larger constants $2^t \pm 1$, and this is a method to investigate in the future. Our proposition remains very significantly smaller for the small divisors that it targets. Besides, it doesn't involve any carry propagation, so its latency should also be better, but this remains to be quantified experimentally.

Table 4. Comparison of the size in LUT between the implementation of our divider and [6] on Virtex 5

	$n = 16$ bits		$n = 32$ bits		$n = 64$ bits	
Constant	Our	[6]	Our	[6]	Our	[6]
3	23	80	47	320	95	1344
5	29	48	60	192	125	768
7	29	32	60	128	125	640

The presented floating-point division by a small constant also largely outperforms the best technique used so far, which are based on multiplication by the constant $1/d$ using shift-and-add algorithm [4]. For instance, using this technique, a double-precision multiplication by $1/3$, in the conditions of Table 3, consumes 282 reg + 470 LUT and runs in 5 cycles @ 307 MHz.

5   Conclusion

This article adds division by a small integer constant such as 3 or 10 to the bestiary of arithmetic operators that C-to-hardware compilers can use when they target FPGAs. This operation can be implemented very efficiently, be it for integer inputs, or for floating-point inputs. It is now part of the open-source FloPoCo generator.

Some synthesis results suggest that a careful study of the tables could lead to further optimizations. In addition, we should try to reformulate our tables so that the propagation of the r_i uses the fast-carry lines available on all modern FPGAs: this would reduce the latency dramatically.

Another issue worth of interest is the case of larger constants that are product of smaller constants, for which a cascaded implementation could be studied.

Due to routing pressure, the number of inputs to the FPGA LUTs keeps increasing as technology progresses. This should make this technique increasingly relevant in the future.

References

1. de Dinechin, F., Pasca, B.: Designing custom arithmetic data paths with FloPoCo. IEEE Design & Test of Computers 28(4) (August 2011)
2. Ercegovac, M.D., Lang, T.: Digital Arithmetic. Morgan Kaufmann (2003)
3. Artzy, E., Hinds, J.A., Saal, H.J.: A fast division technique for constant divisors. Communications of the ACM 19, 98–101 (1976)
4. de Dinechin, F.: Multiplication by rational constants. IEEE Transactions on Circuits and Systems II (to appear, 2012)
5. Li, S.-Y.R.: Fast constant division routines. IEEE Transactions on Computers C-34(9), 866–869 (1985)
6. Srinivasan, P., Petry, F.: Constant-division algorithms. IEE Proc. Computers and Digital Techniques 141(6), 334–340 (1994)
7. Doran, R.W.: Special cases of division. Journal of Universal Computer Science 1(3), 67–82 (1995)
8. Paplinski, A.: CSE2306/1308 Digital Logic Lecture Note, Lecture 8. Clayton School of Information Technology Monash University, Australia (2006)
9. Muller, J.-M., Brisebarre, N., de Dinechin, F., Jeannerod, C.-P., Lefèvre, V., Melquiond, G., Revol, N., Stehlé, D., Torres, S.: Handbook of Floating-Point Arithmetic. Birkhauser, Boston (2009)

A   Proof of Correctness of Algorithm 1

The proof proceeds in two steps. First, we establish that $x = d\sum_{i=0}^{k} q_i.2^{-\alpha i} + r_0$ in lemma 1 below. This shows tha we compute some kind of Euclidean division, but it is not enough: we also need to show that the q_i form a binary representation of the result. For this it is enough to show that they are radix-2^α digits, which is established thanks to lemma 2 below.

Lemma 1

$$x = d\sum_{i=0}^{k} q_i.2^{-\alpha i} + r_0$$

Proof. To show this lemma, we use the definition of the Euclidean division of y_i by d: $y_i = dq_i + r_i$.

$$
\begin{aligned}
x &= \sum_{i=0}^{k-1} x_i.2^{-\alpha i} \\
&= \sum_{i=0}^{k-1} (x_i + 2^\alpha r_{i+1}).2^{-\alpha i} - \sum_{i=0}^{k-1} (2^\alpha r_{i+1}).2^{-\alpha i} \quad \text{and } r_k = 0. \\
&= \sum_{i=0}^{k-1} (dq_i + r_i).2^{-\alpha i} - \sum_{i=1}^{k} r_i.2^{-\alpha i} \\
&= d\sum_{i=0}^{k-1} q_i.2^{-\alpha i} + r_0 - r_k.2^{-\alpha k}
\end{aligned}
$$

Lemma 2. $\forall i \quad 0 \leq y_i \leq 2^\alpha d - 1$

Proof. The digit x_i verifies by definition $0 \leq x_i \leq 2^\alpha - 1$; r_{i+1} is either 0 (initialization) or the remainder of a division by d, therefore $0 \leq r_i \leq d - 1$. Therefore $y_i = x_i + 2^\alpha r_{i+1}$ verifies $0 \leq y_i \leq 2^\alpha - 1 + 2^\alpha(d-1)$, or $0 \leq y_i \leq 2^\alpha d - 1$.

We deduce from the previous lemma and the definition of q_i as quotient of y_i by d that

$$\forall i \quad 0 \leq q_i \leq 2^\alpha - 1$$

which shows that the q_i are indeed radix-2^α digits. Thanks to Lemma 1, they are the digits of the quotient.

Heterogeneous Systems for Energy Efficient Scientific Computing

Qiang Liu[1] and Wayne Luk[2]

[1] School of Electronic Information Engineering, Tianjin University,
300072 Tianjin, China
[2] Department of Computing, Imperial College London,
SW7 2AZ London, UK

Abstract. This paper introduces a novel approach for exploring heterogeneous computing engines which include GPUs and FPGAs as accelerators. Our goal is to systematically automate finding solutions for such engines that maximize energy efficiency while meeting requirements in throughput and in resource constraints. The proposed approach, based on a linear programming model, enables optimization of system throughput and energy efficiency, and analysis of energy efficiency sensitivity and power consumption issues. It can be used in evaluating current and future computing hardware and interfaces to identify appropriate combinations. A heterogeneous system containing a CPU, a GPU and an FPGA with a PCI Express interface is studied based on the High Performance Linpack application. Results indicate that such a heterogeneous computing system is able to provide energy-efficient solutions to scientific computing with various performance demands. The improvement of system energy efficiency is more sensitive to some of the system components, for example in the studied system concurrently improving the energy efficiency of the interface and the GPU by 10 times could lead to over 10 times improvement of the system energy efficiency.

1 Introduction

Scientific computing applications, such as dense linear algebra and N-body simulation, require powerful computing engines to perform huge amounts of arithmetic operations [1]. This work explores heterogeneous computing hardware for scientific computing, aiming at relieving the increased energy demand of traditional high performance computers [2] and providing computing performance in between desktops and supercomputers. With reasonable trade-off between performance and energy and affordable price, the heterogeneous computing systems can be owned and used by organizations requiring local scientific computing.

The target heterogeneous computing systems integrate CPUs, GPUs and FPGAs, built based on a widely used host-accelerator structure. We study the heterogeneous systems' throughput, energy efficiency and energy efficiency sensitivity. These will help designers to make decisions on building heterogeneous computing systems, such as selecting devices and interconnect interfaces. The

O.C.S. Choy et al. (Eds.): ARC 2012, LNCS 7199, pp. 64–75, 2012.

aim is to design a heterogeneous platform which is able to provide a high energy-efficient solution to scientific computing with various performance demands.

Several homogeneous and heterogeneous systems have been developed for scientific applications. Ding *et al.* [3] study energy efficiency and scaling efficiency issues when many low power processors (PowerPC440) are connected. The impact of interconnect interfaces and memory accesses together with voltage and frequency scaling (DVFS) is taken into account. Wang *et al.* [4] develop an algorithm for determining workload allocation and DVFS on a system with a CPU and a GPU for scientific computation. Turkington *et al.* [5] accelerate Linpack 1000 on a platform with a CPU and an FPGA, by implementing a time-consuming subroute of Linpack 1000 on the FPGA. Fatica [6] uses a cluster, where each node has a CPU and a GPU, to speed up High Performance Linpack. A linear programming model is used in [7] to distribute workload between a CPU and a GPU, leading to accelerated FFT implementation. Tse *et al.* [8] propose a framework for accelerating financial applications on a cluster with CPUs, GPUs and FPGAs. A parallel programming approach combining OpenMP, OpenCL and C++ is proposed in [9] to facilitate the management of CPU–GPU clusters.

This paper explores adding recent GPUs and FPGAs into traditional high performance computing systems for improving system energy efficiency. A linear programming (LP) model [10] is used for computational workload allocation in such systems. This paper builds on this model and provides, for the first time, two novel results: (a) a design exploration flow for energy efficient scientific computing, and (b) detailed analysis about energy efficiency of various heterogeneous systems including FPGAs and GPUs, the sensitivity of system energy efficiency to individual system components, and energy efficiency versus power consumption.

The main contributions of this work are:

- A novel approach based on a linear programming model for exploring heterogeneous computing engines which include GPUs and FPGAs as accelerators, helping designers to find the right combinations of various computing devices and interconnections;
- Analysis of energy efficiency sensitivity and the derivative of energy efficiency with respect to power consumption, finding the system bottleneck and being aware of system power consumption when trying to scale systems; and
- Evaluation of the proposed approach on a heterogeneous system with a CPU, a GPU and an FPGA, showing that the heterogeneous computing system provides an energy-efficient solution to High Performance Linpack (HPL) and the system is more sensitive to some of the system components, *e.g.* by estimation concurrently improving the energy efficiency of the interface and the GPU by 10 times could lead to over 10 times improvement of the system energy efficiency.

The rest of this paper is organized as follows. A linear programming model for workload allocation is present in Section 2. The design exploration methodology is proposed in Section 3. The evaluation setup of the proposed approach is described in Section 4 and results are shown in Section 5. Section 6 concludes the paper with future work.

2 Workload Allocation Formulation

In this section, we will briefly present an LP model, which was used in [10] to study different workload allocation problems with regards to throughput, energy efficiency and temperature. We adopt this model to facilitate our exploration of heterogeneous systems.

Given a heterogeneous system containing H hardware computing devices, the throughput and run-time power consumption of device i are R_{di} and P_{di}, respectively, and the throughput and run-time power consumption of the communication channel between devices i and j are R_{cij} and P_{cij}, respectively. x_i is a percentage of computation workload W assigned to device i.

The execution time t_{di} of device i for performing x_i of W is

$$t_{di} = \frac{x_i \times W}{R_{di}}, 1 \leq i \leq H. \tag{1}$$

It is assumed that the host is device 1 and all data reside at the host memories. t_{d1} is the execution time of the host for computation workload x_1.

When x_i workload is allocated to device i, the host will send data to device i and receive resultant data back from it upon finishing. The amount of data involved in these transfers is $D(x_i)$, usually a linear function because the larger workload is associated with the more data transfers. As a result, the time spent on data transfers between the host and device i is

$$t_{c1i} = \frac{D(x_i)}{R_{c1i}}, 2 \leq i \leq H. \tag{2}$$

Eq.(3) shows the execution time of the heterogeneous computing system, which include computation time and data transfer time and should not be larger than the requirement execution time T.

$$t = \max(t_{d1}, \max_{i=2,H} \{t_{di} + t_{c1i}\}) \leq T \tag{3}$$

The system energy consumption e is

$$e = \sum_{i=1,H} (t_{di} \times P_{di}) + \sum_{i=2,H} (t_{c1i} \times P_{c1i}) \tag{4}$$

The first sum is the run-time energy consumption of all devices, including static and dynamic power. The second one is the energy consumed on data transfers between the host and accelerators.

The variables in this workload allocation formulation are $x_i \in [0,1]$ ($1 \leq i \leq H$), and are added to one, $\sum_{i=1}^{H} x_i = 1$.

The main purpose of [10] is to find the right workload allocation x_i, such that the system execution time t or the system energy consumption e is minimized, while meeting user constraints. This paper has a different focus: to exploit the insights derived from the linear programming model in exploring and optimizing system architectures, given various devices and interfaces with different throughput and power consumption parameters. In particular, based on formulae for t and e, we propose a design exploration approach for heterogeneous systems in the next section.

3   Exploration Approach

This section introduces a design exploration flow for heterogeneous systems. Let us first describe system metrics for our approach.

3.1   System Metrics

A *workload* is a set of arithmetical calculations, particularly floating point operations (FLOP).

A widely used metric for computer performance is *throughput*, which is

$$\text{throughput} = \frac{\text{number of floating point operations (FLOP)}}{\text{execution time}},$$

measured in FLOPS (Floating Point Operations Per Second).

Energy efficiency is defined below:

$$\text{energy efficiency} = \frac{\text{throughput}}{\text{power}} = \frac{\text{FLOP}}{\text{execution time} \times \text{power}} = \frac{\text{FLOP}}{\text{energy}},$$

which is measured in FLOPS/Watt or FLOP/Joule. This metric evaluates the computation rate per unit power of a computing engine. Obviously, the higher the energy efficiency is, the more promising a computing engine is. However, energy efficiency may hide one fact that a high energy efficiency computing engine has high power consumption, leading to high device temperature and thus degraded reliability.

Therefore, we study another metric in which power is paid more attention when improving system energy efficiency. The metric is the derivative of energy efficiency with respect to power (DEEP), defined as below:

$$\text{DEEP} = \frac{\Delta \text{energy efficiency}}{\Delta \text{power}}.$$

The unit of measurement is FLOPS/Watt^2. It is desirable to increase energy efficiency, but without increasing power consumption sharply.

In addition, we investigate how significant the effect of improving energy efficiency of each individual device and interface is on the heterogeneous system energy efficiency, *i.e.* sensitivity analysis. This is desirable due to the fact that

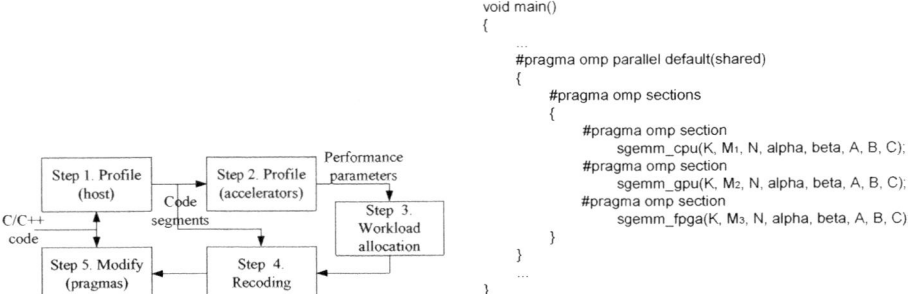

Fig. 1. Design exploration flow

Fig. 2. The main program performing SGEMM on the three devices

improving energy efficiency of a heterogeneous system is possibly blocked by some of the system components, such as the interface bandwidth. By identifying the bottleneck, the system energy efficiency can be further improved, or the other parts of the system could be downgraded to reduce costs.

3.2   Design Exploration Flow

The design exploration flow of the heterogeneous systems is shown in Fig. 1 and summarized as follows.

Step 1. Profile the original program of a scientific computing application in C/C++, by means of tools such as *gprof* on the host, to identify the time-consuming segments (workload W) of the program. Usually these segments contain loop nested arithmetic operations.

Step 2. Profile each of the time-consuming segments on different accelerator devices to obtain parameters, such as R_{di}, P_{di}, R_{cij} and P_{cij}. There are two methods to perform this profiling: a) using mathematical formulations of throughput and power consumption of each device and interconnection; and b) executing the code segments on each device to measure these parameters, respectively. From the designers' point of view, the former is more promising, because rewriting and executing the codes on devices which may not be used in the final system is avoided. However, it is not always easy to precisely formulate the performance metrics of different devices. Speed and power consumption of FPGA-based systems with various optimizations have been formulated in [11] and an analytical GPU performance model can be seen in [12]. In this paper, we focus on system exploration, and thus use the second method.

Step 3. Allocate workloads over different devices. This step can be performed at compile time if the workloads are *a priori* known and can be performed at run-time otherwise. We use the LP model described in the previous section.

Step 4. Rewrite those code segments, which will be executed on accelerator devices, considering various necessary optimizations based on hardware device properties. For example, kernel functions are written as regards register and shared memory sizes for GPUs. A code transformation approach from C to a C-like hardware description for FPGA has been proposed previously in [13].

Step 5. Modify the original program, including adding codes for data transfers between the host and accelerators and inserting OpenMP *pragmas* at where the time-consuming code segments originally execute to invoke the parallel executions of them on multiple devices, following the workload allocation determined at Step 3. An example is shown in Fig. 2.

In our future work, the above flow will be gradually automated. In the scope of this paper, as regards the purpose of exploring system designs, we follow this flow to carry out experiments manually with a typical benchmark of dense linear algebra applications in the next section.

4   Experiment Setup

Benchmark. In this work, High Performance Linpack (HPL) [14] is used as a benchmark to evaluate the proposed design exploration approach. Linpack solves a dense system of linear equations and is widely used to evaluate high performance computers. In this paper, we look at the function SGEMM in HPL, which performs the following computation:

$$C = \alpha AB + \beta C,$$

where $A \in \mathbb{R}^{M \times K}$, $B \in \mathbb{R}^{K \times N}$, $C \in \mathbb{R}^{M \times N}$ and $\alpha, \beta \in \mathbb{R}$. All data are in the single-precision floating point format. The number of float point operations (FLOP) in SGEMM is $MN + 2MKN + MK$ ($O(N^3)$). This function is the most time-consuming part in HPL [6].

In our experiments, we partition matrices A and C horizontally, $C_j = \alpha A_j B + \beta C_j$, and assign different sizes of workload $M_i(N + 2KN + K)$ ($M_i = x_i M$) to different computing devices i, and on each device we also parallelize the computation of rows of $C_{M_i \times N}$ based on the number of parallel processing units available.

Here the number of data transferred $O(N^2)$ between host device 1 and accelerator device i is

$$D(x_i) = x_i MK + x_i' KN + x_i MN + x_i MN, \tag{5}$$

where x_i' is a Boolean variable which is zero if $x_i = 0$; otherwise 1.

Heterogeneous System. The heterogenous system used in our experiments contains a CPU, a GPU and an FPGA, whose parameters are shown in Table 1. The GPU card is connected to the CPU host system using PCIe, while the FPGA card (ADM-XRC-5T2 [15]) uses the PCIx interface and has a converter from PCIx to PCIe to connect to the host. The parameters of the two kinds of PCI interface, measured on the platform, are also shown in Table 1.

The CPU runs 64-bit Linux OS. With 2 threads the CPU performs SGEMM using the same code as the function HPL_dgemm() in Intel MKL 10.3.3, but in the single-precision data format. For GPU, we call the function `cublasSgemm()` from the CUBLAS library in the CUDA SDK, which can automatically tune the number of threads and the number of thread blocks based on input matrix sizes.

We implement the SGEMM function using Verilog for FPGA. The FPGA card has four SDRAM banks, each at the bandwidth of 256Mb/s, and three of them are used to store the input matrices and the fourth stores the results. On the target FPGA device, 32 parallel processing units are realized to perform the SGEMM computation in parallel. Resource utilization is shown in Table 1, where the number of DSP blocks embedded on-chip and slices are the constraints that limit the number of processing units running at 100 MHz to 32. In other words, using a larger FPGA could realize more parallel processing units.

The execution mode of SGEMM on the heterogeneous platform is shown in Fig. 2, where three devices with different workloads (M_1, M_2, M_3) are triggered at the same time to perform SGEMM by using openMP directives. The data transfers between CPU and GPU and between CPU and FPGA are included in the corresponding functions.

The throughput and power results for each individual device, shown in Table 1, are measured separately, when the SGEMM function is executed on the hardware platform. The results are measured several times when all devices and interfaces run in the steady state, *i.e.* running at the highest speed for a period of time, and reported as average values. The throughput of the CPU, the GPU and the FPGA is the computation rate, without considering data I/O of the devices. The power consumption of the FPGA card is obtained by monitoring the current flowing over a current sense resistor on the card [15]. The power consumption of the GPU card and the CPU system is measured by placing a AC/DC current clamp at the corresponding power supplies, respectively. The power consumption for the CPU is in fact the power consumed on the whole PC system, when removing the FPGA and GPU cards. The power consumption of the PCI interfaces are obtained by subtracting the system idle power from the power measured when data are being transferred between CPU and FPGA or between CPU and GPU, without executing computation on any of the devices.

The energy efficiency values in Table 1 are derived from the throughput and power results. All results present in the next section are calculated based on these results, using the formulations in Section 2.

5   Experimental Results

In our experiments, we vary M to change the size of input matrices of the SGEMM function, while $K = 400$ and $N = 1000$. The results from various K and N can be obtained similarly by simply partitioning the matrices.

From Table 1, it is clear that the GPU has the highest throughput in the target system, compared to the CPU and the FPGA, because the GPU has 448 processing cores for floating point operations and the SGEMM function is well matched to the GPU system structure. We could use more powerful CPUs and larger FPGAs to reduce the performance gap. For example, by estimation, a

Table 1. Hardware platform characteristics. *These are measured based on SGEMM.

Device	Intel CPU (Xeon w3505)	nVidia GPU (Tesla c2070)	Xilinx FPGA (Virtex5-vlx330t)	PCIx	PCIe
#Cores	2	448	32 (100% DSP, 78% slices, 79% RAMs)	n/a	n/a
Clock Freq	2.53 GHz	1.15 GHz	100 MHz	n/a	n/a
Lithography	45 nm	40 nm	65 nm	n/a	n/a
Throughput*	12.83 GFLOPs	558.94 GFLOPs	13.90 GFLOPs	0.21 GBs	5.79 GBs
Power*	151.0 W	164.4 W	3.87 W	4.4 W	33 W
Energy efficiency*	0.085 GFLOPs/W	3.47 GFLOPs/W	3.66 GFLOPs/W	47.7 MBs/W	175.5 MBs/W

Virtex6-vsx475t FPGA could accommodate 133 parallel processing units, and thus the throughput of the FPGA implementation could be increased by about 4 times, respectively. However, our aim here is to exploit the strengths of different devices within a system. Specifically, in the following it is shown that in the target heterogeneous system the CPU is suitable to the scenarios where significant communication is involved, and the FPGA is more promising for the scenarios with concerns about power and temperature.

As known, in the host-accelerator systems, when communication is taken into account, accelerators' nominal performance usually suffers a discount. Two main factors need consideration. The first one, from the algorithm perspective, is computation per data transfer. In SGEMM, this factor is $O(N)$, while the factor of another function SGER from Linpack, involving $O(N^2)$ floating point operations and $O(N^2)$ data transfers, is $O(1)$. We use the LP model in Section 2 to determine the workload allocation of these two functions on the three devices to maximize throughput. Results are shown in Figs. 3 and 4, where x_c, x_g and x_f are the percentages of workloads assigned to CPU, GPU and FPGA, respectively. We can observe that most of the SGER's workload is assigned to the CPU, while the SGEMM's workload is distributed and the faster device receives more.

The second one, from the hardware perspective, is communication channel bandwidth. For SGEMM shown in Fig. 4, with the fast interface PCIe, a large portion of the workload is assigned to the fast devices, regardless of the matrix size; with the slow interface PCIx, the allocation depends on the matrix size M.

It is clearly shown that the workload allocation scheme varies, according to different scenarios. The heterogeneous system is able to provide such variety. In the rest of this section, results are calculated based on the PCIe interface which connects the host and accelerators.

In addition, as shown in Table 1, although in the target heterogenous system the GPU has the highest throughput, the FPGA has the highest energy efficiency, which is 44.9 times over CPU and 1.2 times over GPU. This illustrates the strength of the FPGA in the heterogeneous system, and the impact will be more significant if a latest large FPGA is used. For example, by estimation, a Virtex6-vsx475t FPGA could provide energy efficiency in about 14 GFLOPS/W.

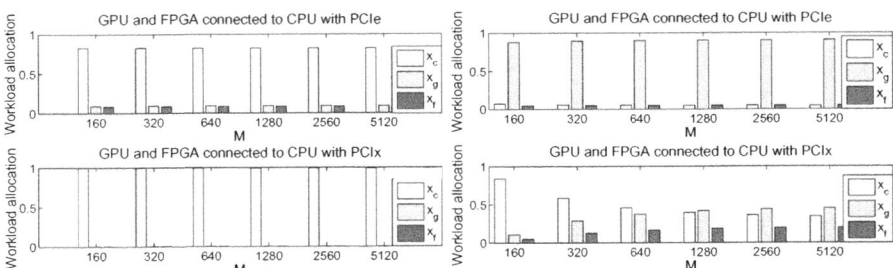

Fig. 3. SGER workload allocation   **Fig. 4.** SGEMM workload allocation

Table 2. Energy efficiency of heterogeneous systems for SGEMM with $M = 20480$

	CPU	CPU+FPGA	CPU+GPU	CPU+GPU+FPGA
Energy efficiency	0.06	0.12	1.08	1.11
GFLOPS/W	(1x)	(2x)	(18x)	(18.6x)

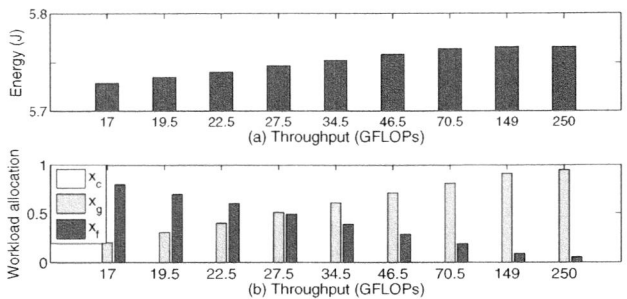

Fig. 5. SGEMM $(M=20480)$ (a) energy consumption of the CPU+GPU+FPGA system and (b) corresponding workload allocation $(x_c = 0)$, given throughput requirements

Given the different combinations of the three devices, the energy efficiency of various heterogeneous systems is shown in Table 2. The throughput and power consumption of the whole systems are measured. Note that the energy efficiency is the whole system's energy efficiency, including all kinds of overheads, such as data transfers and software protocol. Compared to the single CPU system, the heterogeneous systems improve system energy efficiency. As a point of reference, the number one in the world Green500 energy-efficient supercomputer list is 1.68 GFLOPS/W as reported in 2010 [16]. Note that the peak performance 1.11 GFLOPS/W shown in this paper is just for the function SGEMM.

Moreover, the heterogeneous system, containing CPU, GPU and FPGA, could potentially provide a high energy-efficient solution to scientific computing with various performance demands. Fig. 5 illustrates energy consumption of the heterogenous system and the corresponding workload allocation targeting at

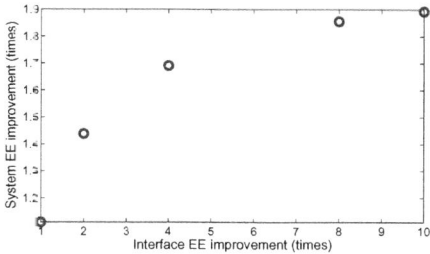

Fig. 6. System energy efficiency (EE) sensitivity to interface

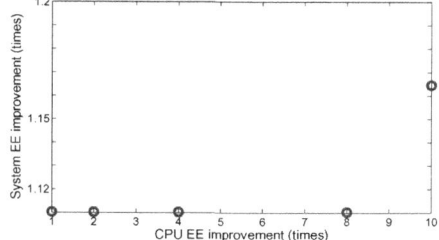

Fig. 7. System energy efficiency (EE) sensitivity to CPU

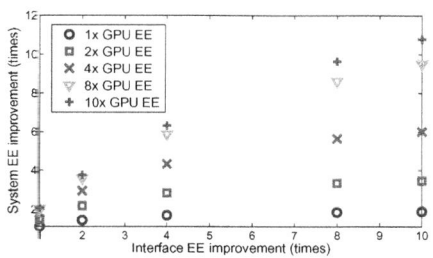

Fig. 8. System energy efficiency (EE) sensitivity to GPU

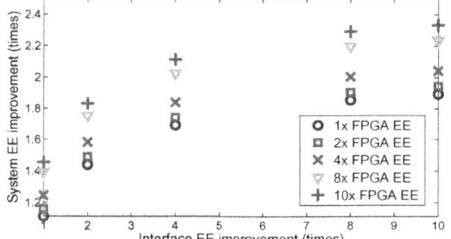

Fig. 9. System energy efficiency (EE) sensitivity to FPGA

minimizing run-time energy, given different throughput requirements for performing SGEMM. In Fig. 5 (a) we can see that the system (CPU+GPU+FPGA) has a varied energy consumption as the throughput requirement varies. The variation could be explained by the fact shown in Fig. 5 (b). The majority of the workload is assigned to the FPGA in the early stage, and then as the throughput requirement increases the workload starts to be allocated to GPU and the system energy consumption increases, and when more and more workloads are allocated to GPU the system energy consumption is dominated by the GPU.

Furthermore, we investigate how effective improving energy efficiency of each device and the interface individually is on the whole system energy efficiency. By simulation, we increase the energy efficiency of CPU, GPU, FPGA and the interface between them by 2, 4, 8, 10 times, respectively. Results are estimated and shown in Figs 6–9. For example, in Fig. 6 improving the energy efficiency of the interface alone by 10 times leads to 1.9 times improvement of the system energy efficiency. In Fig. 7, CPU's energy efficiency is increased alone and only after 8 times improvement applied the system energy efficiency starts to show very limited improvement. This is because in the target platform the CPU's energy efficiency is 40 times lower than the other two devices, as shown in Table 1. In Fig. 8, the energy efficiency of the interface and GPU is increased at the same time. It can be seen that the impact of increasing GPU's energy efficiency is more significant with the high energy efficiency interface. Similar results can be observed in Fig. 9 as well for FPGA. Overall, it is clearly shown that the energy

Table 3. Energy efficiency and power consumption of heterogeneous systems for SGEMM with $M = 20480$

	CPU+GPU+FPGA+FPGA	CPU+GPU+FPGA+GPU
Energy efficiency	1.14 GFLOPS/W	1.45 GFLOPS/W
Power	477.28 W	632.96 W

efficiency of the utilized heterogeneous computing system is more sensitive to the concurrent improvement of the interface and the GPU, 10 times improvement in the interface and the GPU leading to over 10 times improvement of the system energy efficiency. Of course, feasibility and difficulty of achieving these improvements should be taken into account. Although the results are estimated, this sensitivity analysis indicates the direction, in which system requirements could be met.

Finally, based on the previous results we experiment with adding one more GPU and one more FPGA to the current heterogeneous platform. The estimated results are reported in Table 3. It can be seen that the energy efficiency by adding a GPU is 1.27 times higher than by adding an FPGA in the target system. However, the power consumption of the system after adding a GPU is very high and the system requires a powerful power supply over 800 W. The energy efficiency derivative with respect to power (DEEP) for adding one GPU is 0.0016 GFLOPs/W^2 and is 0.0037 GFLOPs/W^2 for adding one FPGA. Therefore, devices with higher DEEP factors are more promising when system energy efficiency is expected to improve within certain power constraints, such as power supply and cooling system limitation.

Overall, designers of heterogeneous systems should carefully choose computing engines and interfaces to achieve required performance with respect to applications, cost and power consumption budgets. The approach proposed in this paper provides designers with such an exploration tool.

6   Conclusion

This paper explores heterogeneous computing hardware, including CPUs, GPUs and FPGAs, for scientific computing to maximize system energy efficiency while considering system performance and power consumption. The sensitivity of the system energy efficiency to individual system components is also studied. The approach presented could help system designers to evaluate and choose the right combinations of high energy-efficient devices and interfaces, when designing energy efficient scientific computing systems.

Our design exploration approach is evaluated using Linpack on a hardware platform containing a CPU, a GPU and an FPGA, and results show that the heterogeneous computing system could provide a high energy-efficient solution to scientific computing with various performance demands.

In the future, we will extend our design exploration approach to cover applications which have a mixture of diverse computation and communication behavior.

Such applications have potential to benefit significantly from appropriate optimization of heterogeneous computing systems.

Acknowledgment. This work was supported in part by UK EPSRC, by the European Union Seventh Framework Programme under Grant agreement number 248976 and 257906, by the HiPEAC NoE, by Alpha Data, by Celoxica, by nVidia, and by Xilinx.

References

1. Eijkhout, V., et al.: Introduction to high-performance scientific computing (May 2011), http://www.tacc.utexas.edu/eijkhout/istc/istc.html
2. Feng, W.-C.: The importance of being low power in high performance computing. Cyberinfrastructure Technology Watch Quarterly 1 (2005)
3. Ding, Y., et al.: Towards energy efficient scaling of scientific codes. In: IPDPS, pp. 1–8 (April 2008)
4. Wang, G., Ren, X.: Power-efficient work distribution method for CPU-GPU heterogeneous system. In: ISPA, pp. 122–129 (September 2010)
5. Turkington, K., et al.: FPGA based acceleration of the linpack benchmark: A high level code transformation approach. In: FPL, pp. 1–6 (August 2006)
6. Fatica, M.: Accelerating linpack with CUDA on heterogenous clusters. In: GPGPU-2, pp. 46–51 (March 2009)
7. Ogata, Y., et al.: An efficient, model-based CPU-GPU heterogeneous FFT library, pp. 1–10 (April 2008)
8. Tse, A., et al.: Dynamic scheduling Monte-Carlo framework for multi-accelerator heterogeneous clusters. In: FPT, pp. 233–240 (December 2010)
9. Barak, A., et al.: A package for openCL based heterogeneous computing on clusters with many GPU devices. In: Int. Conf. on Cluster Computing Workshops and Posters, pp. 1–7 (September 2010)
10. Liu, Q., Luk, W.: Objective-driven workload allocation in heterogeneous computing systems. In: FPT (December 2011)
11. Liu, Q., et al.: Combining optimizations in automated low power design. In: DATE, pp. 1791–1796 (2010)
12. Hong, S., Kim, H.: An analytical model for a GPU architecture with memory-level and thread-level parallelism awareness. In: ISCA, pp. 152–163 (2009)
13. Liu, Q., et al.: Optimising designs by combining model-based and pattern-based transformations. In: FPL, pp. 308–313 (2009)
14. Petitet, A., et al.: HPL - a portable implementation of the high-performance linpack benchmark for distributed-memory computers, version 2.0, http://www.netlib.org/benchmark/hpl/
15. Adm-xrc-5t2 data sheet, http://www.alpha-data.com/pdfs/adm-xrc-5t2.pdf
16. The green 500, http://www.green500.org/

The Q² Profiling Framework: Driving Application Mapping for Heterogeneous Reconfigurable Platforms

S. Arash Ostadzadeh, Roel Meeuws, Imran Ashraf,
Carlo Galuzzi, and Koen Bertels*

Computer Science and Engineering
Department of Software and Computer Technology
Delft University of Technology, Delft, The Netherlands
{S.A.Ostadzadeh,R.J.Meeuws,I.Ashraf,C.Galuzzi,K.L.M.Bertels}@tudelft.nl

Abstract. Heterogeneous multicore architectures pose specific challenges regarding their programmability and they require smart mapping schemes to make efficient use of different processing elements. Various criteria can drive this mapping, such as computational intensity, memory requirements, and area consumption. In order to facilitate this complex mapping task, there is a clear need for tools that investigate the use of such critical resources, like memory and hardware area. For this purpose, we developed the Q^2 *profiling framework*. It consists of two main parts: an advanced memory access profiling toolset, which provides detailed information on the runtime memory access patterns of an application and a statistical modeling component, which makes hardware area predictions early in the design phase based on software metrics. These tools are integrated using a partitioning methodology. We demonstrate the effectiveness of our framework using three applications in our experiments. One application is further detailed in a case study to illustrate the use of our methodology. Experimental results show application speedup of up to $2.92\times$.

1 Introduction

Multicore architectures, especially when containing heterogeneous processing elements, pose specific challenges regarding their programmability. Programming such platforms implies, among other things, determining what parts of the application should be mapped on what processing elements. Various criteria can drive this mapping, such as the nature of the computation or the number of cycles required by individual tasks. However, in multicore platforms, data communication is often the primary bottleneck in achieving the anticipated speedups. This is especially true for legacy applications, which have to be ported to such platforms. Furthermore, in the case of reconfigurable architectures, the application development process involves building and synthesizing hardware blocks, which is quite time-consuming. As a consequence, there is a need for fast and early predictions of the hardware costs of the different parts of an application.

---

* This research is partially supported by the Artemisia iFEST project (grant 100203), the Artemisia SMECY project (grant 100230), and the FP7 Reflect project (grant 248976).

O.C.S. Choy et al. (Eds.): ARC 2012, LNCS 7199, pp. 76–88, 2012.

Efficient mapping of the application is the main concern of the Q^2 *profiling frame-work*. Q^2 is part of a semi-automatic tool platform for integrated HW/SW co-design, targeting heterogeneous computing systems containing reconfigurable components. The profiling framework focuses on the data communication that occurs inside the application and on the estimation of reconfigurable resource consumption expected for each part of the application. The ultimate goal is to efficiently partition the application into hardware and software. The profiling data is utilized to guide developers in reducing the data communication between the hardware and the software components so as to maximize the potential speedup, while satisfying resource constraints.

HW/SW partitioning has been an active field of research in the last decade. Many approaches have been proposed, which address the problem in diverse ways. Generally, the process can be carried out based on various levels of granularity, ranging from fine-grained basic blocks or loops [11,2] to coarse-grained functions [15,8]. Apart from the traditional partitioning methods, different heuristic and evolutionary approaches have also been investigated to address this problem [16].

Our partitioning methodology is similar to the one presented in [8], which supports the partitioning of an application between several processing elements (SW/SW partitioning) at the function-level, as well as HW/SW partitioning utilizing some profiling information. However, in [8], as in most other approaches, partitioning is performed based on the call graph, whereas we utilize the Quantitative Data Usage (QDU) graph [14], annotated with *Quipu* area estimates [13] as the main reference. The data communication between functions in the application is extracted automatically by our advanced profiling toolset. In this way, complex data-flows between functions can be made clear, enabling developers to find better partitions compared to the ones obtained using only the call graph and general execution time profiling data.

As the available area in contemporary FPGAs continues to increase, the size of the code segments that are mapped into the hardware is no longer a restriction. In fact, it is often more efficient to map larger sections of the code into the hardware. Consequently, the utilization of HW/SW partitioning at fine granularities will diminish in future reconfigurable systems, while coarser grained approaches will gain in relevance. As a result, we believe that mapping a rather large function or, in general, a combination of several coupled functions, will not be elusive anymore. To the best of our knowledge, the work presented in this paper is the only approach which proposes such merging of functions based on accurate profiling information. Merging tightly communicating functions not only presents a comprehensive view on the whole task, but also allows developers to perform optimizations, particularly for memory requirements, in a feasible and efficient way. In this paper, we show the need for and the usage of the proposed profiling framework by mapping three real applications onto the Molen reconfigurable architecture [5].

The main contributions of this paper can be summarized as follows:

- the presentation of the Q^2 profiling framework;
- the introduction of a HW/SW partitioning methodology based on detailed dynamic and static profiling data;
- the utilization of dynamic profiling information for reducing the data communication between hardware and software partitions;
- the presentation of experimental results on three well-known applications.

The rest of this paper is structured as follows. Section 2 briefly describes the research context of the work presented in this paper. In Section 3, we describe the Q^2 profiling framework. Subsequently, a detailed case study of an image processing application is presented in Section 4. After that, the experimental results on two other applications are presented in Section 5. Finally, Section 6 concludes the paper.

2   Research Context

The work presented in this paper, although not restricted to any specific platform, has been developed in the context of the Delft WorkBench (DWB). The DWB addresses the entire design cycle from profiling and partitioning to synthesis and compilation of an application. It focuses on four main steps within the entire heterogeneous system design. The first step is related to application profiling. In the second step, code partitioning is investigated along with possible code segments parallelization. Following the decision to map particular code segments onto the hardware, a *retargetable compiler* generates new object code, which contains calls to reconfigurable hardware blocks for selected segments of the code. Finally, in the last step, *VHDL generation*, the identified code segments are translated into HW blocks.

The Molen polymorphic processor has been used for the experiments in the work presented in this paper. The Molen architecture is based on the co-processor architectural paradigm. It couples a General Purpose Processor (GPP) and a reconfigurable co-processor (RP). The GPP controls the execution and (re)configuration of the RP. An instruction fetched from memory goes to the arbiter, which partially decodes the instruction and issues the instruction to either processors. One of the advantages of the Molen paradigm is that it can be easily ported to various platforms. In our case, we have used the Xilinx *XC5VFX200T* Virtex5 FPGA as a platform. The PowerPC on this FPGA is used as the GPP and the rest of the $30K$ slices is available for (re)configuration. The advancement in technology will lead to FPGAs with even larger sizes. This, in turn, will increase the possibility of mapping larger code segments on hardware.

3 Q^2 Profiling Framework

Fig. 1 depicts the two pillars of the Q^2 *profiling framework*. The static profiling part extracts code characteristics from the application source code. These characteristics are used by a linear model to make fast and early predictions of hardware implementation details, such as FPGA area estimates. The dynamic profiling part focuses on extracting data communication information by examining the runtime behavior of the application and, therefore, is not as fast as the static part.

3.1   Quipu Modeling Approach

With the growing adoption of heterogeneous and reconfigurable computing platforms, it has become important to have efficient prediction models to drive early HW/SW partitioning. Therefore, we incorporate the *Quipu* high level quantitative prediction modeling approach [13] in the Q^2 framework. This approach accurately

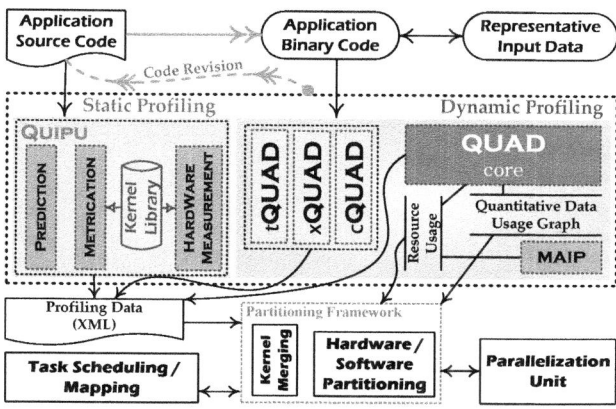

Fig. 1. The Q^2 Profiling framework within the DWB

models the relation between hardware and source code related software metrics using several statistical techniques. The proposed approach generates models that predict hardware-related indicators for reconfigurable components, such as the number of slices, the number of flip-flops, and the number of wires. It employs automatic model selection, artificial neural networks, (logistic) regression, and data transformations. These models take a high-level language description as input, enabling hardware prediction in the early design stages. In this paper, we focus only on using *Quipu* area estimation models for the combination of the DWARV C-to-VHDL compiler and the Xilinx FPGA toolchain, although different combinations can be considered as well.

The approach is generic and not limited to any particular platform or toolchain by allowing the generated models to be recalibrated for different tools and platforms, contrary to the majority of existing techniques. Furthermore, a major strength of *Quipu* models is their linear nature. Although the statistical techniques used to create the models may be very time-consuming, the resulting prediction models require only a few multiplications in addition to parsing the source code. This allows for the integration of *Quipu* models in highly iterative design processes, where new estimates are required many times in a short period of time. Additionally, as *Quipu* models are based on measurements from C code, very early predictions become possible, allowing designers to make important decisions on hardware mapping at an early stage.

In order to characterize the software complexity as it relates to hardware, *Quipu* utilizes Software Complexity Metrics (SCMs) [12]. Currently, we use 92 SCMs as a base for our model. Most of these metrics are counts of different operators, but other metrics, such as the Cyclomatic complexity, the number of definition-use pairs, or more complex data-flow metrics, are also included. *Quipu* consists of a set of tools and a kernel library. In the modeling flow, *Quipu* extracts SCMs and hardware-related indicators from a kernel library. The library contains 235 kernels from a wide variety of application domains, contrary to many existing techniques, which use libraries of tens of kernels at most. This allows us to build models that are generally applicable. It is also possible to build domain-specific models by using, for example, only the 54 cryptography-related kernels out of the 235 kernels considered. An overview of the

Table 1. Overview of the kernel library, the number of kernels and their main algorithmic characteristics in each application domain

Domain	Kernels	Floating Point	Bit-based	Streaming	Control
Bioinformatics	6	0			×
Compression	9	0	×		×
Cryptography	54	0	×	×	some
DataProcessing	9	0			×
DSP	24	10	×	×	some
ECC	15	0	×	×	×
Mathematics	49	21			
Multimedia	58	20	some	×	×
Physics	11	11			
Total	235	62			

kernels in this library is provided in Table 1. The *Quipu* modeling approach consists of the following tools:

- **The Metrication tool** - This tool extracts the software complexity metrics from C kernels in the library or from a different application. The tool is implemented in the CoSy compiler system [7] and, as such, can adopt some of the more high-level optimizations and transformations that are used in the modeled toolchain, such as common subexpression elimination or dead code elimination.
- **The Hardware Measurement tool** - This tool processes the log files of the hardware toolchain and parses the netlists, in order to obtain hardware characteristics. These include, for example, the number of slices, the number of wires, and the clock period.
- **The Modeling Scripts and the Prediction tool** - *Quipu* automatically evaluates different statistical modeling techniques and generates an optimized model instance for a particular toolchain. This model can later be used by the *Prediction tool* to make predictions for examined kernels.

3.2   QUAD Dynamic Memory Profiling Toolset

Traditionally, a general profiler, such as *gprof* [9], is utilized to identify application hotspots at the function-level in terms of the execution time. *gprof* provides sample-based execution timing estimates, in addition to an accurate call graph. On the other hand, MAIP, its counterpart in our Q^2 profiling framework, provides *accurate* measurements for the contribution percentage of individual functions with respect to the whole execution time of an application. Furthermore, MAIP distinguishes between memory access related and computation related operations.

The QUAD toolset[1] consists of several tools developed to provide a comprehensive overview of the memory access behavior of an application, as well as, to extract fine-grained detailed memory access related statistics. The QUAD [14] core module

---

[1] The QUAD toolset is available at http://sourceforge.net/projects/quadtoolset/

primarily detects the *actual* data dependencies at the function-level. QUAD measures data dependency as producer/consumer bindings. More precisely, actual data dependency arises when a function consumes data that was produced earlier by another function. It should be noted that the conventional argument passing by the caller function to the callee does not necessarily imply that the data will be used later by the called function. Furthermore, QUAD does not rely on the common approach of data dependency detection based on hierarchies of function calls (conventionally depicted with a call graph), as it merely traces byte transfers between the functions via memory accesses without any connection to the control dependencies of functions. The exact amount of byte transfers and the number of *Unique Memory Addresses* (UnMAs) used in the transfer process are also measured. Based on the efficient *Memory Access Tracing* (MAT) module implemented in QUAD, which tracks every single access (read/write) to a memory location, a variety of statistics related to the memory access behavior of an application can be calculated. This includes, for example, the ratio of local to global memory accesses in a particular function call. In addition to the QUAD core module, there are several other tools available in the QUAD toolset. Anyhow, they are not in the focus of this work. All the tools in the dynamic profiling part of Q^2 are implemented utilizing the Pin [3] Dynamic Binary Instrumentation (DBI) platform.

3.3 Partitioning Methodology

The outputs of both profiling parts are used to derive a suitable HW/SW partitioning of the application. For this purpose, we follow these steps:

- *Execution Time Profiling* - *MAIP* determines the computational hotspots.
- *Hardware Estimation* - All functions in the application are annotated with FPGA hardware area estimates, as predicted by the respective *Quipu* models.
- *Initial Partitioning* - With the knowledge of the computational hotspots and the respective area predictions, an initial partitioning is determined. In this respect, as many computation-intensive kernels as possible are moved to the hardware, so as to speed up their execution, while satisfying the area constraints.
- *Data Communication Analysis* - The data communication of the kernels in the initial partitioning set is then analyzed using QUAD. Because the set of functions that is analyzed has been reduced, QUAD can run much faster. Additionally, it helps the developer to focus on the main data communication bottlenecks.
- *Final Partitioning* - Certain kernels in the initial partitioning can still heavily communicate with other functions in software, implying a heavy communication overhead. Therefore, an additional set of kernels may be moved to hardware, if possible, so as to reduce the amount of data communicated between hardware and software.

4 Case Study

In this section, we present a concise analysis of an image processing application, Canny Edge Detection (*CED*), to illustrate the Q^2 *methodology* and the added value of the Q^2 *profiling framework*. Canny [6] is a well-known edge detection algorithm, which outperforms other edge detection methods. Given an image, the algorithm first eliminates any noise. It then finds the image gradient to highlight regions with high spatial derivatives. The next step is to track along these regions and suppress any pixel that is not at the maximum. The gradient array is further reduced by hysteresis. We have used the implementation provided by the CVL at the University of South Florida [1]. The performed procedure can be clearly divided into the following four main steps: 1) *the use of a Gaussian filter to remove the noise,* 2) *the determination of the edge strength,* 3) *the application of Non-Maximal Suppression,* and 4) *the application of hysteresis.*

We examine the memory access behavior of the application to spot the main flow of the data along the top contributing kernels and further utilize the profiling data in HW/SW partitioning. The profiling data is also used to spot deficiencies related to the application memory usage, resulting in some code optimizations to improve the performance of the application mapped onto the Molen reconfigurable architecture. In this case study, we specifically show the following qualities related to the Q^2 framework:

- the analysis of the data communication between the kernels in the application;
- the prediction of hardware resource utilization for the different kernels;
- the detailed analysis of the application to decide on HW/SW partitioning;
- the introduction of some manual application source code optimizations derived by the inspection of the extracted profiling data;
- the preparation of an executable version of the application that can run on the Molen machine respecting the restrictions previously mentioned.

The *CED* implementation consists of three source files containing 12 functions. For the experiments, we used a sample grayscale *PGM* image with a resolution of 800×600 pixels and 8 bpp. The standard deviation of the Gaussian filter was set to 2.0. The values of low and high thresholds for hysteresis were both set to 0.5.

All experiments were performed on two different platforms. We used the QUAD toolset on an Intel 32-bit Core2 Duo E8500 @3.16 GHz, running Linux kernel v2.6.34. The source code was compiled with *gcc* v4.5.0 using level two optimizations and without function inlining. An embedded PPC 440 @400 MHz is integrated in a Xilinx Virtex5 FX 200T with 2.0 MB BRAM FPGA. The utilized *Quipu* prediction models were generated for the DWARV C-to-VHDL compiler and the Xilinx ISE 13.2 synthesis tools targeting the same Virtex5 FPGA containing a Molen machine implementation. The implementation requires 7283 slices, leaving 23437 slices available for accelerating application kernels. Simulations were performed using *Modelsim 6.5f.*

Quipu Profiling. We modified the *CED* application, where necessary, so that the kernels could be mapped to hardware. The modification involves moving dynamic memory allocations and recursive function calls to function stubs, which call the actual kernels. Of course, these changes required new profiling results. In Table 2, the top five kernels with their associated new time contributions are listed. We also performed an investigation of the size of potential hardware designs. The results of the area predictions are also presented in Table 2. The table lists the predicted number of slices, as well as the percentage of that area with respect to the available area in

Table 2. The Area predictions and theoretical speedups for the kernels in *CED*

Kernel	Area^a		% Exec.	speedup^b	
	Slices	% of area	time	single kernel	cum.
hw_gaussian_smooth	1951	8.3%	70.59%	3.40×	3.40×
hw_derrivative_x_y	510	2.2%	2.49%	1.03×	3.71×
hw_magnitude_x_y	1442	6.2%	5.14%	1.05×	4.59×
non_max_supp	2132	9.1%	14.36%	1.17×	13.48×
hw_apply_hysteresis	765209	3265%	2.68%	1.03×	21.10×

^{a} Area predicted by a *Quipu* prediction model for the Virtex 5 FX 200T.
^{b} Theoretical application speedup, assuming 0s execution time for each kernel.

the Molen implementation. The kernels in the table are in the order of execution in the *CED* application. Note that the *apply_hysteresis* kernel is exceedingly resource-intensive, requiring 3265.0% of the target FPGA area. This big requirement can be traced back to a local array of 32K 32-bit integers. The used *Quipu* model was generated for *DWARV*, which generates registers for such local arrays, requiring 1024K flip-flops with additional logic and wiring. When we consider to merge several kernels together, the predictions suggest that the first four kernels will easily fit together on the target FPGA, requiring a total of 19.6% of the FPGA area.

In addition to the area predictions, the theoretical application speedups are also reported in Table 2. These speedups are calculated using Amdahl's law, assuming an unlimited speedup for the kernel(s) in question, as follows:

$$\lim_{p\to\infty} \frac{p}{1 - f(p - 1)} = \frac{1}{f} = \frac{1}{1 - s}, \qquad (1)$$

where p is the speedup factor of the accelerated part, f is the percentual contribution of the sequential part, and s is the original percentual contribution of the accelerated part. Note that these speedups are not predictions made by *Quipu*. Table 2 lists both the speedup, when one kernel is accelerated, and the cumulative speedup, where each kernel is accelerated together with the previous ones. Observe that, as large parts of the application are accelerated, the contributions of the remaining kernels become more significant. For example, *apply_hysteresis* has a contribution of 2.68%, but, with much of the application already accelerated, the difference in theoretical speedup is 56.8%.

As mentioned earlier, merging the first four kernels in Table 2 would yield a hardware block that would fit on the target FPGA. The maximum speedup of the application using that block would be 13.48×. Of course, the efficiency of accelerating this block will never be 100% and the actual speedup will be lower.

QUAD Profiling. We utilized QUAD to reveal the data communication between different functions of the *CED* application. Due to space limitations, only a part of the resulting Quantitative Data Usage (QDU) graph is depicted in Fig. 2(a). It contains the functions in the critical data path of the application. The graph allows to trace, at runtime, what is happening to the input image. Furthermore, the extracted quantitative values help to understand what are the memory requirements for each function to accomplish its task.

Data Communication Bottlenecks. Modifying the *CED* application to comply with the hardware mapping restrictions, in turn, causes some changes in the data communication patterns of the application. As an obvious result, new data communication channels are formed between the introduced function stubs and the corresponding hardware-compliant kernels. However, this characteristic will not reinforce the data communication problem, as the connections between the stubs and their corresponding kernels are limited to providing the starting address of allocated memory blocks and some related basic data elements. There is only one exception in the case of *apply_hysteresis*, whose body can not be moved entirely to hardware, due to the invocation of a recursive function, *follow_edges*. Therefore, a considerable amount of data transfer is established between the extracted *hw_apply_hysteresis* and the corresponding function stub, *apply_hysteresis* (850kb using 425k UnMAs). The newly formed communication channel may be considered as a source of potential memory bottleneck and needs proper handling. Primarily, *apply_hysteresis* is dependent on the data that is provided by the *nms* and *magnitude* arrays. The data-flow originating from *magnitude_x_y* is now divided into separate flows for *apply_hysteresis* and *hw_apply_hysteresis*. From the total amount of 225k memory accesses, approximately 70% is accounted for *hw_apply_hysteresis* and the rest for *apply_hysteresis*. Nevertheless, both functions strictly access a whole part of the *magnitude* array. In essence, *magnitude* should be made available for both functions as a whole, regardless of the number of accesses carried out on the data residing in the array.

Not every heavy data communication yields a potential memory bottleneck. A more detailed investigation is required to pinpoint problems related to memory accesses. Special attention has to be given to the size of the accessed memory blocks, the locality, the reusability and, most significantly, to the placement of the data (on-/off-chip data allocation), where applicable. For our experiments, there was no off-chip data allocation due to the Molen restrictions. However, this property must be considered in the general case. A review of the critical data path reveals several potential problematic memory access bottlenecks, which limit the performance of the application. Loading the image from an external source is the first obstacle.

Beginning with *hw_derrivative_x_y*, there is a series of data communication via different memory blocks, which is responsible for the main performance bottleneck of the application. In each (sub)phase, one or more memory blocks are used as input to produce an output block. The data movement is performed through *hw_magnitude_x_y*, *non_max_supp*, *hw_apply_hysteresis*, *apply_hysteresis*, and *follow_edges*. Optimizing the *CED* application should be centered around the block processing. This, in a subsequent analysis, requires thorough examination of the exact life span of each block, the data dependencies between them, and the possible merging/reusing of the relevant data.

Optimization. After a careful analysis of the results, we observed that all hardware-compliant kernels up to *hw_apply_hysteresis* fit together on the reconfigurable fabric. Furthermore, together, they would exhibit a significant potential speedup of $13.46\times$.

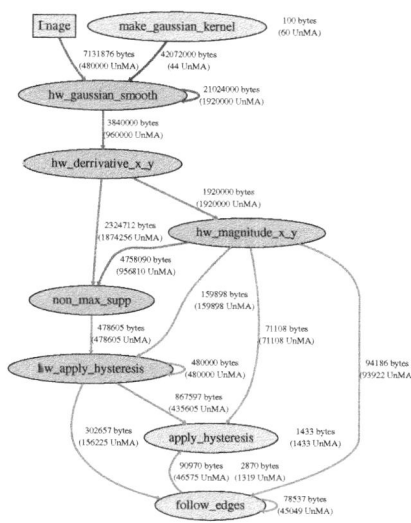

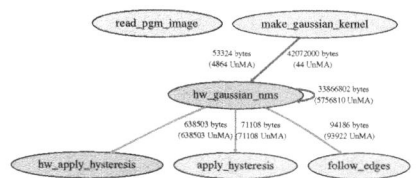

Instance	Area	MAIP %time	speedup	
cumulative	7711	92.58%	13.48×	
merged	5874	92.58%	13.48×	Theoretical
optimized	5808	92.57%	13.46×	

Instance	Area	Time (ms)	speedup	
simulation	n/a	88.5	2.92×	Real

(b) Area predictions and theoretical speedups for the kernels in *CED*

(a) The Partial QDU graph for the hardware version of *CED*

(c) Partial QDU graph for the hardware version of *CED* after merging

Fig. 2. Merging identified kernels. (a) QDU before merging, (b) Area predictions and speedups, (c) QDU after merging.

Finally, the bulk of the communication occurred in this group of functions. In the following, we continue our evaluation by merging these kernels, providing additional profiling results, and implementing certain optimizations that the results suggest.

The initial merging process consisted of the concatenation of the subsequent function calls. In the case of *CED*, this process was trivial. However, in case the to-be-merged functions have no direct connections in the call graph, the process may become more complex. In the table in Fig. 2(b), we observe that, prior to the merging, the predicted area consumption was 7711 slices with a theoretical speedup of 13.48×. After the merging, the potential speedup remains the same, but the predicted area decreases to 5874 slices. The reason for this behavior is very likely the increased reuse of calculations and variables. The used *Quipu* model was generated for the *DWARV* compiler and Xilinx ISE synthesizer, which use common compiler front-end optimizations and resource sharing, which can significantly reduce the required area.

Now that we have a merged kernel, the QUAD results also change accordingly. In Fig. 2(c), we see that most of the memory locations and accesses are now internal to the merged *hw_gaussian_nms* kernel. When we carefully investigate these new results, we see that the number of UnMAs is roughly 12 times as large as our input image ($800 \times 600 \times 12 \times 1$ byte = 5760000 bytes). As subsequent phases of *CED* use different temporary data objects, we analyzed how the corresponding memory blocks might be reused. By determining the live ranges of different memory regions, we observed that the maximum amount of memory needed at the same time is 7 times the size of one image block. Therefore, we optimized the merged kernel to reuse memory blocks when they are no longer needed. The table in Fig. 2(b) indicates that this optimization does not influence the potential speedup, but the required amount of memory is reduced significantly. Furthermore, the required area remains effectively the same at 5808 slices.

In order to evaluate the proposed adjustments, VHDL code was generated for the merged *hw_gaussian_nms* kernel and simulated for the target platform using *Modelsim 6.5f*. Using exactly the same kernel input data as the one used on the PPC, the simulation took 177 million cycles. The synthesis of the kernel suggested a maximum clock speed of 235 MHz. Assuming a conservative 200 MHz results in an execution time of 88.5 ms. On the PPC, the execution took 292 ms, accounting for a kernel speedup of 3.44× and an application speedup of 2.92×. Because of the merging we performed, the kernel speedup has a big impact on the application speedup, as the merged kernel represents most of the computational work.

5   Experimental Results

Table 3 provides a summary of the results for three well-known applications. The first application is the *MELP vocoder* [4], used mainly for secure voice in radio devices. *MELP* uses extensive look-up tables and models of the human voice to extract and re-generate speech and, as such, it is a computation intensive application. *CED* has been discussed in detail in Section 4. *N-Body* [10] is a widely used technique to investigate the evolution of particles in various fields of science, such as physics or astronomy. The *N-Body* simulation proceeds over time steps, each time computing the net force on every body and thereby updating its position and other attributes. The system is then updated by moving each body to its new position. The simulation is performance hungry, because of the large number of particles involved in such application.

Table 3 shows that four kernels for each application have been selected in the final partitioning as potential candidates to be mapped onto the hardware. For each application, the total execution time of the merged kernel containing the selected candidates is reported in Table 3. In case of *MELP*, *Quipu* predictions have an error of 8%, whereas in case of *N-Body* this error is about 30%. According to QUAD, data communication between the HW and SW parts is reduced considerably as a result of the selected partitioning. The data reduction is measured by comparing two scenarios

Table 3. Summary of the Q^2 profiling results and the partitioning based on those results

App.[a]	Number of kernels		Exec. time[b]	Area (slices)			Comm. Red.[c]	Speedup	
	Tot.	Map.		Pred.	Act.	Err.(%)		Theor.	Act.
MELP	59	4	51.8%	6534	6043	8.1%	57.1%	1.80×	1.30×
Canny	12	4	92.6%	5381	7307	26.4%	22.7%	13.48×	2.92×
N-Body	10	4	99.7%	11730	8209	30.0%	42.9%	136.99×	n/a

[a] Application(App.), Execution(Exec.), Total(Tot.), Mapped(Map.), Predicted(Pred.), Actual(Act.), Error(Err.)

[b] Percentage contribution reported by the MAIP profiler for all the mapped kernels together.

[c] The communication reduction as reported by QUAD.

where, in one, only the top contributing kernel is mapped to the hardware and, in the other, the merged kernel is mapped to the hardware. The overall theoretical speedup for *MELP* is 1.8×, although the actual speedup is 1.3×. For *CED*, the actual speedup is 2.92×. The actual speedup could not be reported for *N-Body* because the simulation scripts of our framework do not support the automatic generation of test benches for multidimensional arrays.

6 Conclusions

Efficient application partitioning for heterogeneous architectures is a difficult task. There are multiple factors to take into account, such as application speedup, area constraints, and memory bottlenecks. In this paper, we introduced the Q^2 *profiling framework* that addresses this problem by providing a detailed insight into the mentioned aspects at early design stages. We have demonstrated how this profiling data can drive partitioning using three different applications, exhibiting speedups of up to 2.92×. In the future, we plan to investigate speedup estimation and power issues, as well as, to examine additional applications for mapping onto our target platform.

References

1. Canny Edge Detector, Image Analysis Research Lab., USF,
   http://marathon.csee.usf.edu/edge/edge_detection.html
2. Baleani, M., et al.: HW/SW partitioning and code generation of embedded control applications on a reconfigurable architecture platform. In: CODES 2002, pp. 151–156 (2002)
3. Luk, C., et al.: Pin: building customized program analysis tools with dynamic instrumentation. In: PLDI 2005, pp. 190–200 (2005)
4. Supplee, L.M., et al.: MELP: the new federal standard at 2400 bps. In: IEEE International Conference on Acoustics Speech and Signal Processing, pp. 1591–1594 (1997)
5. Vassiliadis, S., et al.: The Molen polymorphic processor. IEEE Transactions on Computers 53(11), 1363–1375 (2004)
6. Canny, J.: A computational approach to edge detection. IEEE Trans. Pattern Anal. Mach. Intell. 8, 679–698 (1986)
7. Experts, A.A.C.: Cosy: Compiler system, http://www.ace.nl/
8. Gohringer, D., et al.: A design methodology for application partitioning and architecture development of reconfigurable multiprocessor systems-on-chip. In: FCCM 2010, pp. 259–262 (2010)
9. Graham, S.L., Kessler, P.B., Mckusick, M.K.: Gprof: A call graph execution profiler. SIGPLAN Not. 17(6), 120–126 (1982)
10. Hut, P., Makino, J., McMillan, S.: Building a better leapfrog. The Astrophysical Journal 443(2), L93–L96 (1995)
11. Li, Y., Callahan, T., Darnell, E., Harr, R., Kurkure, U., Stockwood, J.: Hardware-software co-design of embedded reconfigurable architectures. In: DAC 2000, pp. 507–512 (2000)
12. Meeuws, R.J.: A Quantitative Model for Hardware/Software Partitioning. Master's thesis, Delft University of Technology, Delft, Netherlands (2007)

13. Meeuws, R.J., Galuzzi, C., Bertels, K.: High level quantitative hardware prediction modeling using statistical methods. In: SAMOS 2011, pp. 140–149 (2011)
14. Ostadzadeh, S.A., Meeuws, R.J., Galuzzi, C., Bertels, K.: QUAD – A Memory Access Pattern Analyser. In: Sirisuk, P., Morgan, F., El-Ghazawi, T., Amano, H. (eds.) ARC 2010. LNCS, vol. 5992, pp. 269–281. Springer, Heidelberg (2010)
15. Santambrogio, M., et al.: A novel SoC design methodology combining adaptive software and reconfigurable hardware. In: ICCAD 2007, pp. 303–308 (2007)
16. Wang, G., Gong, W., Kastner, R.: Application partitioning on programmable platforms using the ant colony optimization. Journal of Embedded Computing 2(1), 119–136 (2006)

PPMC: A Programmable Pattern Based Memory Controller

Tassadaq Hussain[1], Muhammad Shafiq[1], Miquel Pericàs[1],
Nacho Navarro[2], and Eduard Ayguadé[1,2]

[1] Barcelona Supercomputing Center
[2] Universitat Politecnica de Catalunya
{thussain,mshafiq,miquel.pericas,eduard.ayguade}@bsc.es,
nacho@ac.upc.edu

Abstract. One of the main challenges in the design of hardware accelerators is the efficient access of data from the external memory. Improving and optimizing the functionality of the memory controller between the external memory and the accelerators is therefore critical. In this paper, we advance toward this goal by proposing PPMC, the Programmable Pattern-based Memory Controller. This controller supports scatter-gather and strided 1D, 2D and 3D accesses with programmable tiling. Compared to existing solutions, the proposed system provides better performance, simplifies programming access patterns and eases software integration by interfacing to high-level programming languages. In addition, the controller offers an interface for automating domain decomposition via tiling. We implemented and tested PPMC on a Xilinx ML505 evaluation board using a MicroBlaze soft-core as the host processor. The evaluation uses six memory intensive application kernels: Laplacian solver, FIR, FFT, Thresholding, Matrix Multiplication, and 3D-Stencil. The results show that the PPMC-enhanced system achieves at least 10x speed-ups for 1D, 2D and 3D memory accesses as compared to a non-PPMC based setup.

1 Introduction

The current trend in the design of HPC systems is shifting towards the integration of microprocessors with accelerators in order to achieve the increasing performance targets. However, high-performance microprocessor/accelerator systems are of little use if the memory hierarchy is unable to provide the necessary data bandwidth. The efficient management of memory accesses by timely prefetching across the set of accelerators and microprocessors in such a scenario is critical for performance. However, it is also very challenging.

A lot of research has been conducted in the past to build efficient prefetchers. Basic patterns that have been exploited include vectors with constant strides or linked lists [1]. Dynamic prefetching [8,11] is useful for microprocessors designed for general purpose. On the software side, blocking (tiling) algorithms [13] are used extensively to improve cache efficiency by partitioning the working set to the characteristics of cache memories. Software managed caches or scratchpad memories [4] are used when stricter control of data locality is desired. However, it also increases the programming complexity, particularly when data layouts are complex.

O.C.S. Choy et al. (Eds.): ARC 2012, LNCS 7199, pp. 89–101, 2012.

This paper introduces a memory controller based on high-level data patterns ensuring high performance and high efficiency while providing simplified programming of SoC applications. The main contribution of this paper is the description of the hardware implementation of a Pattern-based Programable Memory Controller (PPMC) which takes a data access description (descriptor blocks) and provides 1D, 2D and 3D data in streaming mode. The PPMC system provides the following novel features to the computing system:

- *Concurrency*: To expose maximum parallelism, the PPMC system fetches complex streams in parallel to be processed by the compute engine(s).
- *Programmability*: Standard C/C++ language calls are used to schedule the access patterns.
- *Simplicity*: The PPMC design offers simplicity in the management of different complex (strided) data access patterns in hardware by allowing users to program them.

This paper discusses the architecture of the memory controller and its implementation on a Xilinx Virtex 5 FPGA (ML505 development board), including its integration with a Xilinx MicroBlaze processor. We also show how PPMC can be attached to reconfigurable accelerators. We use reconfigurable accelerators for the Laplacian solver, FFT, FIR filters and 3D-Stencil kernel. Thresholding and Matrix Multiplication kernels are executed on a MicroBlaze processor. We evaluate these application kernels on a MicroBlaze-based SoC Architecture using PPMC. This shows that the PPMC system is equally usable as a stand alone component within a reconfigurable system, and also as a slave in a system with a general purpose processor. The results are compared with a system that lacks the pattern based controller, showing great benefits from the usage of PPMC.

2   Programmable Pattern Based Memory Controller (PPMC)

In general, a conventional Direct Memory Access (DMA) controller's data access pattern consists of source, destination addresses and size of the transfer with unit stride. This scheme is not efficient to access complex/irregular memory patterns. In such cases, the task of DMA becomes significantly more complicated. Delays while computing addresses are generated when non-contiguous memory locations are being accessed.

One of the main characteristic of the proposed PPMC is its efficiency in managing more complex address patterns by combining scatter/gather and strided vector accesses, while generic DMA controllers can only support simple address patterns due to scatter/gather access. Another important feature of the proposed controller is its capability to work standalone as well as in SoC environment, which enables it to operate in parallel with/without a microprocessor unit while previous state of the art DMA controllers have to follow microprocessor instructions and bus protocols to perform the same operation. When dealing with volumes of large size in high performance computing applications, the address generation and volume decomposition are done by a host unit which puts additional pressure on the computing unit. This shortcoming has been overcome in the proposed controller by remapping and generating physical addresses without delay in the hardware unit.

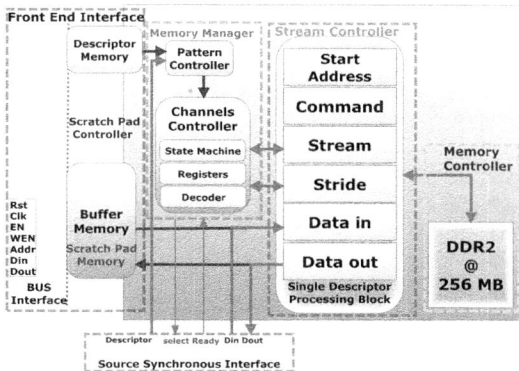

Fig. 1. PPMC Internal Architecture

The PPMC unit efficiently accesses complex data patterns (either as *Array of Structure (AoS), Structure of Array (SoA) or Tiled*) with the help of a single or multiple descriptor blocks. The minimum set of parameters for a single descriptor block includes *command, source address, destination address, stride* and *stream*. *Command* specifies whether to read or write a single element or a stream of data. The address parameters specify the starting addresses of the source and destination locations. *Stride* indicates the distance between two consecutive physical memory addresses of a stream. All of this helps data being transferred from a non-contiguous memory to a contiguous address space, and vice versa.

2.1   PPMC Architecture

To demonstrate the operation of PPMC, we first depict its internal architecture in Figure 1, which also briefly shows the interconnection with the external processing units. The PPMC system is comprised of four units which are *the front-end interface, the memory manager, the stream controller* and *the memory controller.*

2.1.1   The Front-End Interface

The Front-End interface includes two separate interfaces, the *Scratchpad Controller Interface* and the *High-Speed Source Synchronous Interface*, to link with the microprocessor unit (master) and the hardware accelerator unit (slave), respectively.

Scratchpad Controller Interface. The Scratchpad Controller Interface as shown in Figure 2 (a) provides a bus interface between the master unit (microprocessor) and the scratchpad memory (Block RAM). Currently the bus interface is compliant with the *Xilinx* Local Memory Bus (LMB) unit. The scratchpad memory subsystem consists of the *Descriptor Memory* along with the *Buffer Memory*. The descriptor blocks are placed in *Descriptor memory* in priority order. The Memory Manager (see Section 2.1.2) accesses these descriptor blocks without any delay, thus reducing the additional synchronization

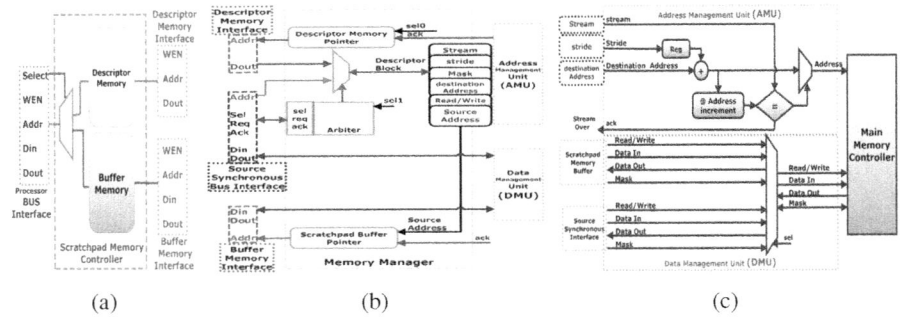

Fig. 2. PPMC Architecture: (a) PPMC Scratchpad Controller Interface (b) PPMC Memory Manager (c) PPMC Stream Controller

time required to access non-contiguous memories. Each descriptor block contains information of source unit and destination unit that eliminates request/grant time. The Bus interface is used to initialize the descriptor memory with the support of C/C++ calls such as send(), receive(), send_tile() and receive_tile(). send() and receive() occupy a single descriptor memory block, whereas send_tile and receive_tile reserve descriptor blocks according to the volume of the tile. The *Buffer memory* is used to hold data temporarily while it is being moved to/from physical memory. Depending on the system architecture and applications access pattern the *Buffer memory* can be partitioned.

High-Speed Source Synchronous Interface. The Source Synchronous Interface as shown in Figure 1 is used to supply high-speed data to reconfigurable accelerators. To *request* and *grant* data for multiple accelerators, a handshaking protocol is applied to the bus arbiter. Transfer of data is accomplished according to the physical memory clock.

2.1.2 Memory Manager
In a PPMC system having a scratchpad memory and multiple hardware accelerators, several requests can occur concurrently. The PPMC has to select one source from multiple requesting sources. PPMC manages concurrent access by implementing scheduling policies for both hardware accelerators and the scratchpad read/write access. The memory manager is composed of two modules: *the Arbiter* and *the Address Manager*.

Arbitration. PPMC applies an arbitration policy that is processed by the bus arbiter. The current bus arbiter handles 32 hardware accelerators. It manages the distribution of streams to the appropriate hardware accelerator. A round-robin token passing protocol is implemented in the arbiter. For each descriptor access cycle, one of the hardware accelerators has the highest priority (token). If the token-holding master does not need the resource in this turn, the master with the next highest priority (sending a request) is granted the resource, and the highest priority master later passes the token to the next master in round-robin order.

Address Manager. The address manager controls the addresses of the scratchpad memory (descriptor block, scratchpad buffer). It handles a Descriptor Memory Pointer (DMP) and a Scratchpad Buffer Pointer (SBP) as shown in Figure 2 (b). The DMP holds the address for the next descriptor block and provides this address to the descriptor memory to fetch a descriptor block. After completion of target data access, the address manager sends an `ack` signal to the DMP that requests the next descriptor block. The SBP is responsible to generate addresses for the scratchpad memory. Depending on the application (multi-threaded) or hardware architecture (multi-accelerator), the scratchpad memory is divided into multiple buffers. The SBP takes the source address (*Base Address*) from the descriptor controller and with single cycle latency starts incrementing in it. The SBP stops incrementing addresses, when the `ack` signal is granted by the *Stream Controller* (see Section 2.1.3).

2.1.3   Stream Controller

The stream controller, shown in Figure 2 (c), takes memory transaction descriptions from the Memory Manager. This unit is responsible for transferring data between the Memory Controller and the Front-End Interface depending on the programmed descriptor. The stream controller is comprised of the *Data Management Unit (DMU)* and the *Address Management Unit (AMU)*.

Data Management Unit (DMU). The DMU manages data lines labeled as *Data In* and *Data Out* shown in Figure 2 (c). It enables the *data stream* to be written at the appropriate location of the physical memory by generating the write–enable along with the write–data and mask–data control signals. The source of the *data stream* can be a contiguous buffer memory or a streaming accelerator unit. The DMU unit supports 64-bit data bus and 8-bits mask bus. For every 8 bits of data bus, there is a mask bit.

Address Management Unit (AMU). The AMU deals with the *Address*, *Stream* and *Stride* units. Strides between two consecutive accesses are handled by the AMU without generating delay. For each stream, the first data transfer uses an address taken by the descriptor unit and for the rest of the transfers, the address is equal to the address of the previous transfer plus the size of the stride. The AMU supports a stream size of up to 1024 contiguous memory elements with one descriptor. Supported strides need to be multiple of 4.

2.1.4   Memory Controller

A modular DDR2 SDRAM [16] controller is used to access data from physical memory. The DDR2 SDRAM controller provides a high-speed source-synchronous interface and transfers data on both edges of the clock cycle.

3   Data Access Pattern

In order to elaborate the functionality of PPMC two types of data access patterns are discussed in this section: Vector Access Pattern (AoS or SoA) and Tiling Access Pattern.

3.1 Vector Access Pattern (AoS or SoA)

Gou et. al observed that most HPC applications are in favor of operating on SoA format [5]. The PPMC system allows to access a SoA in AoS format without generating any delay. AoS or SoA data access is performed by the `send()` and `receive()` calls. Each call is associated to a single descriptor block which needs to be initialized for each transfer. SoA data access requires unit-stride, whereas the AoS requires strided access. The stride is determined by the size of the working set. Figure 3 (a) presents three different vector accesses ($x[n][0]$, $y[0][n]$ and $z[n][n]$) for a n×n matrix where *vector x* corresponds to the contiguous row having *unit stride*, *vector y* belongs to column access with stride equal to *row length* and *vector z* is a diagonal SoA pattern. Stride of $z[n][n]$ access is the addition of *row length* and *unit stride*.

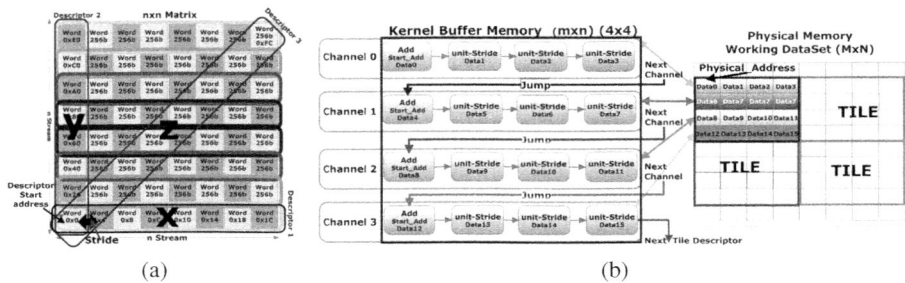

(a)   (b)

Fig. 3. Two PPMC Patterns: (a) AoS and SoA access pattern (b) PPMC tiling example

3.2 Tiling Access

The tiling technique is employed to improve system performance. It is widely used for exploiting data locality and improving parallelism.

Single Tile Access. To access a single tile, the PPMC uses multiple descriptors. By combining these descriptors, the PPMC exchanges tiled data between physical memory and scratch pad memory buffer. To read/write a single tile, the `send_tile()` and `receive_tile()` *calls* are used to initialize the descriptor memory blocks. Each *call* requires two input parameters *Buffer_#* and *Physical_Address*. Parameter *Buffer_#* indicates the starting address of the buffer where the tile is read/written. *Physical_Address* holds start address of the working dataset.

Multi-Tiling Access. The PPMC multi-tiling method attempts to derive an effective tiling scheme. It requires information about the *Physical Memory Tiled Dataset* (M^N) and the *Buffer's Tile size* (m^n) of the computing engine. Where *(M,m)* represents width and *(N,n)* represents dimension of each tile. Depending on the structure of the buffer memory, the PPMC partitions Physical memory into multiple tiles. The *number of tiles* for the even multidimensional memory access is given by Equation 1.

$$Number\ of\ Tiles = \left\lceil \frac{M^N}{m^n} \right\rceil = \left\lceil \frac{DataSet\ Width^{Dimension}}{LocalBuffer\ Width^{Dimension}} \right\rceil \quad (1)$$

An example of PPMC (4×4) 2D-tile access is shown in Figure 3 (b). The PPMC uses 4 descriptors to access a single tile. Channel 0 takes *descriptor 0* from descriptor memory and accesses data starting at location *Physical_Address* with unit-stride and n-stream (row width) size. Depending on the size of the main memory dataset (M^N), different strides (address) are used between channels. The *starting address* of the next channels is dependent on Equation 2. Channel 1 starts right after the completion of Channel 0. Channel 3 is the last channel. After completion of channel 3, PPMC generates an interrupt signal indicating to the external source that the tile data transfer has finished. The PPMC will move ahead to the next tile and restart processing.

$$Start\ Address = Dataset\_Base\_Address_{Tile} + Buffer\_Width_{Tile} * channel\ number \quad (2)$$

4   Evaluations of PPMC

In this section, we describe and evaluate the PPMC-based SoC architecture for the FIR, Thresholding, FFT, Laplacian solver, Matrix Multiplication and 3D-Stencils application kernels. In order to evaluate the performance of the PPMC System, the results are compared with a similar system that does not feature a PPMC unit.

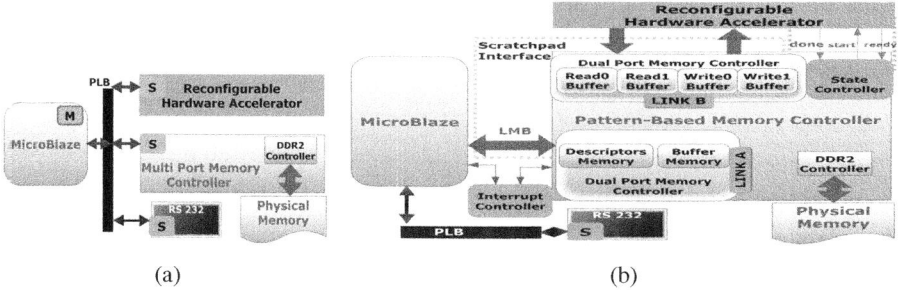

(a)   (b)

Fig. 4. Test Environment: (a) MPMC based SoC with Reconfigurable Hardware Accelerator (b) PPMC based SoC with Reconfigurable Hardware Accelerator

4.1   The System Architecture

In our evaluations, we used two types of systems: one system is based on MicroBlaze and the other system is based on a reconfigurable accelerator. The former system is used to test Matrix Multiplication and Thresholding while the later one is used to test the FFT, FIR, Laplacian solver and 3D-stencil application kernels. Both systems are configured with and without support of PPMC.

4.1.1   MPMC Based SoC

A generic Multi-Port Memory Controller (MPMC) with a hardware accelerator based SoC architecture is proposed in Figure 4 (a). The MPMC is employed as it provides an efficient means of interfacing the processor to SDRAM. MicroBlaze soft-core processor is used to control the system. The target architecture has a Single Precision Floating Point Unit, 16 KB of each instruction and data cache. The design uses 9612 flip-flops, 9388 LUTs and 14 BRAMs in a Xilinx V5-Lx110T device.

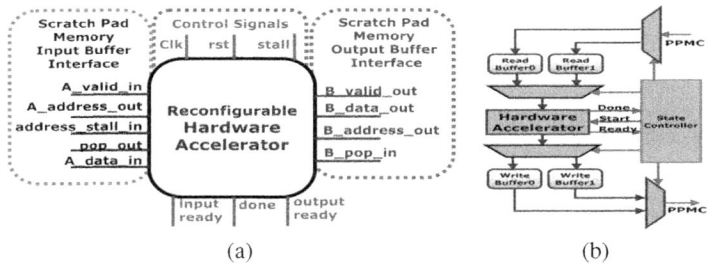

Fig. 5. (a) ROCCC-based Hardware Accelerator (b) PPMC State Controller for Hardware Accelerator

Table 1. Brief description of application kernels

Application Kernel	Description	Access Pattern	Executed By
Thresholding	An application of image segmentation, which takes streaming 8-bit pixel data and generates binary output.	Streaming	MicroBlaze
Finite Impulse Response	Calculates the weighted sum of the current and past inputs.	Streaming	ROCCC IP
Fast Fourier Transform	Used for transferring a time-domain signal into corresponding frequency-domain signal.	1D Block	ROCCC IP
Laplacian solver	Applies discrete convolution filter that can approximate the second order derivatives.	2D Tiling	ROCCC IP
Matrix Multiplication	$X = Y \times Z$	2D Tiling	MicroBlaze
3D-Stencil Decomposition [10]	An algorithm that averages nearest neighbor points (size 8x9x8) in 3D.	3D-Tiling	MicroBlaze

4.1.2 PPMC Based SoC

The PPMC based system is shown in Figure 4 (b). In this architecture, dual-port memory controllers are used to share the descriptor memory between the Microblaze and the PPMC. The MicroBlaze is connected with the PPMC for programming PPMC's descriptor memory, to execute applications (more information in Table 1) and to display results using a serial link. The PPMC is connected to the reconfigurable hardware accelerator using PPMC's source synchronous interface and a state controller. The PPMC state controller, shown in Figure 5 (b), is used to control the hardware accelerator and the buffer memory. Four memory buffers (two read and two write) are specified to accesses tiled data to/from main memory. The system consumes 6280 flip-flops, 5581 LUTs and 24 BRAMs on a V5-Lx110T device. Due to the light weight of PPMC, the proposed architecture consumes 38% less slices than the generic MicroBlaze SoC.

4.2 Test Applications

The application kernels used to validate the design are shown in Table 1. These kernels are chosen to characterize different data access patterns. The results are validated by comparing the execution time of these kernels on a MicroBlaze system with PPMC and without PPMC support. To execute FIR, FFT and Laplacian kernels separate hardware IP cores are used. The hardware (shown in Figure 5 (a)) is generated by the ROCCC [12] compiler as IPs for the evaluated application kernels. The IPs are compliant with the

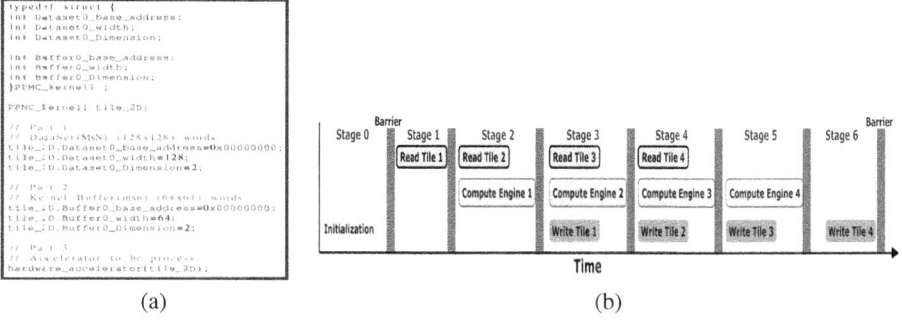

(a)   (b)

Fig. 6. PPMC: (a) 2D-Tiling Program Example (b) Scheduling of the Tiling program

scratchpad memory interface which makes it feasible to be integrated into the MPMC and PPMC based systems. In order to give a standard interface to ROCCC IPs with the PPMC system, a state controller is designed (see Figure 5 (b)).

4.2.1   PPMC Programming

The proposed system provides comprehensive support for the C and C++ languages. The functionality of the PPMC is managed by C based device drivers. An example code segment that is used to initialize and run PPMC by an accelerator program is shown in Figure 6 (a). The accelerator program uses this structure to communicate with the PPMC for handling a 2D tiling pattern. The first part of the structure specifies physical memory parameters. The PPMC will automatically adjust the dataset into appropriate tile sizes, to be processed by the hardware accelerator. The second part defines the size of the accelerator's buffer memory, the maximum tile size depends on the buffer size. The third part contains the name of a hardware accelerator and passing structure which is used during the execution of the kernel. If more than one hardware accelerator is connected to the PPMC system, then the above information is required for each kernel. The MicroBlaze is used to program the PPMC by using an API. The API takes the code (shown in Figure 6 (a)), pipelines and overlaps the PPMC operations shown in Figure 6 (b), and then programs the *Descriptor Memory*.

5   Results and Discussion

Figure 7 shows a plot with Read/Write data accesses for MPMC and PPMC based systems. The X-axis presents 1D/2D/3D datasets that are read and written from/to the main memory and the scratchpad memory. The Y-axis of the plot represents the number of clock cycles consumed, while accessing the tiled dataset. The MicroBlaze with MPMC has load/store data access patterns, whereas PPMC based access patterns contain multiple noncontiguous streams. The results show that PPMC memory access times are 10 times faster than a generic memory controller.

Figure 8 shows the execution time (clock cycles) for the application kernels, executed on MPMC and PPMC based systems. The X and Y axis represent application kernels and number of clock cycles, respectively. By using our PPMC system, the results show that the Thresholding and FIR application kernels respectively achieve 32x

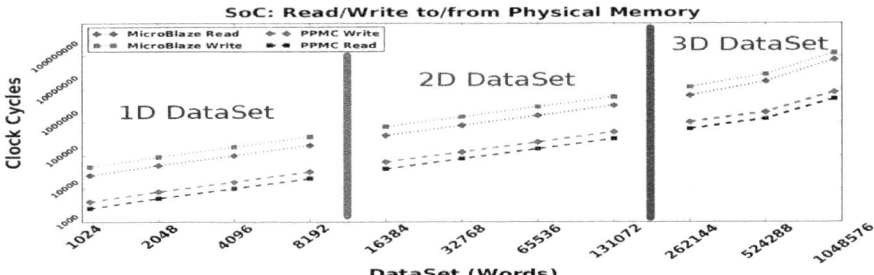

Fig. 7. Clock Cycles : PPMC and MicroBlaze Read/Write data to/from Main Memory

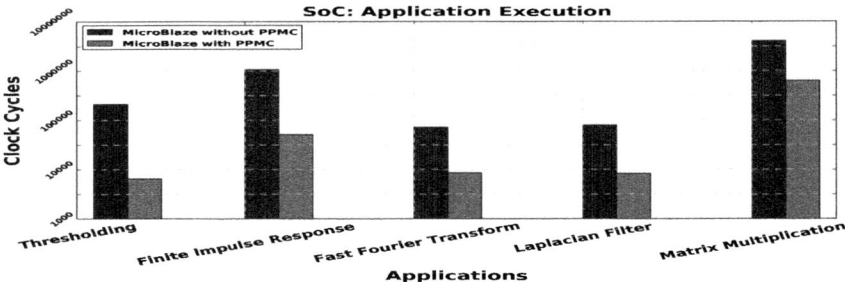

Fig. 8. Execution time (clock cycles) of the applications for different volume sizes

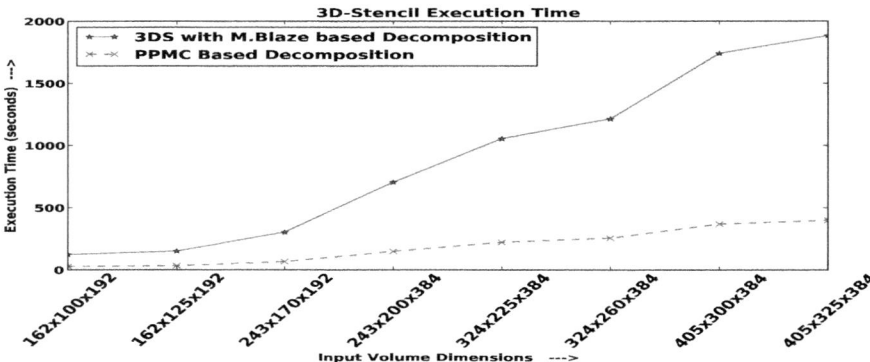

Fig. 9. Execution time for various volume sizes with domain decomposition done by the host processor and tiling done by the PPMC for the 3D-Stencil

and 22x speed-ups. Both applications kernels have streaming data access pattern. The results confirm that PPMC reduces physical memory data access delay and that it decreases memory request/grant time by overlapping it with application execution time. The FFT application kernel reads a 1D block of data, processes it and then writes it back to physical memory. This application observes a 8.2x speed-up. The Matrix Multiplication and Laplacian applications respectively achieve speed-ups of 6.4x and 9.6x. Both applications have 2D-Data access and both use data tiling. Figure 9 shows the execution time for the 3D-Stencil for various sizes of large input volumes. The stencil is run for 500 time steps. The usage of PPMC for directly handling the tiling for 3D volumes improves around 5x the performance of the stencil kernel as compared to software based volume decomposition. In our evaluations for the 3D-stencil, the accelerator directly writes the tiling commands to the PPMC.

6   Related Work

A number of DMA Memory Controllers have been proposed in literature and developed commercially. The Xilinx XPS Channelized DMA Controller [15] provides simple DMA services to peripherals and memory devices on the Processor Local Bus (PLB). Lattice Semiconductor's Scatter-Gather Direct Memory Access Controller IP [9] and Altera's Scatter-Gather DMA Controller core [3] provide data transfers from non-contiguous blocks of memory by means of a series of smaller contiguous transfers. Both scatter-gather cores read a series of descriptors that specify the data to be transferred. However, the transfer of data uses unit-stride which is not suitable to access complex memory patterns. These DMA controllers are forced to follow microprocessor instructions and bus protocol. PPMC extends this model by enabling the memory controller to work standalone as well as in SoC environment.

Chai et. al proposed a configurable stream unit for the memory hierarchy [2]. This unit takes descriptor blocks from the on-chip bus system. Based on these descriptor blocks it prefetches and aligns streaming data. As with the aforementioned controllers, the configurable stream unit does not have the ability to operate independently from a microprocessor, which is one of the main features provided by PPMC and which allows hardware accelerators to directly fetch data patterns from memory without processor intervention. The Impulse memory controller [7] supports application-specific optimizations through configurable physical address remapping. By remapping the physical addresses, applications can control the data to be accessed and cached. The Impulse controller works under the control of the operating system and manages physical address remapping in software, which may not always be appropriate for hardware accelerators. PPMC remaps and generates physical addresses in the hardware unit without producing delay. Based on its C/C++ language support, PPMC can be integrated with any operating system that supports a the C/C++ stack. A study on FPGA based implementation of the N-Body (Barnes-Hut) algorithm introduced the design of traversal caches [14,6] for traversing tree data, in particular the Barnes-Hut octree. Initially traversal caches were presented by Stitt et. al [14] based on exploiting the opportunity of repeated traversals for a branch of a tree. The traversal cache fetches a branch of data into FPGA and if the algorithm needs the same branch data it can be accessed from the local memory of FPGA. Otherwise a new branch needs to be fetched from main memory. Coole et al. extended the idea by prefetching multiple branches into the FPGA and keeping them accessible by the compute block, thus enabling repeated traversals and parallel execution of multiple traversals whenever possible [6].

7   Conclusion

In this work, we propose a Programmable Pattern-based Memory Controller (PPMC). The PPMC improves the memory-processor data access bottlenecks by allowing to fetch *complex patterns* without processor intervention. Further, to improve the on chip bandwidth, this work proposes hardware tiling based on programmable domain decomposition. The proposed controller can be programmed by a microprocessor using HLL or directly from an accelerator using a special command interface. The experimental evaluations based on the Xilinx MicroBlaze accelerator system demonstrate that the PPMC based approach improves utilization of hardware resources and efficiently accesses physical data. In the future, we plan to embed a selective set of data access patterns inside PPMC that would effectively eliminate the requirement of programming PPMC by the user for a range of applications.

Acknowledgments. This work has been supported by the Ministry of Science and Innovation of Spain (CICYT) under contract TIN–2007–60625 and by the European Union Framework Program 7 HiPEAC2 Network of Excellence. The authors would like to thank the Barcelona Supercomputing Center and the Universitat Politecnica de Catalunya (UPC) for their support. The authors also wish to thank the reviewers for their insightful comments.

References

1. Roth, A., Sohi, G.S.: Effective jump-pointer prefetching for linked data structures. In: ISCA 1999 Proceedings of the 26th Annual International Symposium on Computer Architecture (May 1999)
2. Chai, S.M., Bellas, N., Dwyer, M., Linzmeier, D.: Stream Memory Subsystem in Reconfigurable Platforms (2006)
3. Altera Corporation: Scatter-Gather DMA Controller Core, Quartus II 9.1 (November 2009)
4. Gannon, D., Jalby, W., Gallivan, K.: Strategies for Cache and Local Memory Management by Global Program Rransformation. Journal of Parallel and Distributed Computing
5. Gou, C., Kuzmanov, G., Gaydadjiev, G.N.: SAMS multi-layout memory: providing multiple views of data to boost SIMD performance (2010)
6. Coole, J., Wernsing, J., Stitt, G.: A Traversal Cache Framework for FPGA Acceleration of Pointer Data Structures: A Case Study on Barnes-Hut N-body Simulation. In: International Conference on Reconfigurable Computing and FPGAs (2009)
7. Carter, J., Hsieh, W., Stoller, L., Swanson, M., Zhang, L., Brunvand, E., Davis, A., Kuo, C.-C., Kuramkote, R., Parker, M., Schaelicke, L., Tateyama, T.: Impulse: Building a Smarter Memory Controller. In: Fifth International Symposium on High Performance Computer Architecture, HPCA-5 (January 1999)
8. Farkas, K.I., Jouppi, N.P., Chow, P.: How Useful Are Non-blocking Loads, Stream Buffers, and Speculative Execution in Multiple Issue Processors? (1995)
9. Lattice Semiconductor Corporation: Scatter-Gather Direct Memory Access Controller IP Core Users Guide (October 2010)
10. Shafiq, M., Pericas, M., de la Cruz, R., Araya-Polo, M., Navarro, N., Ayguade, E.: Exploiting Memory Customization in FPGA for 3D Stencil Computations (2009)

11. Jouppi, N.: Improving Direct-Mapped Cache Performance by the Addition of a Small Fully-Associative Cache and Prefetch Buffers (1990)
12. Riverside Optimizing Compiler for Configurable Computing (ROCCC),
    `http://www.jacquardcomputing.com/roccc/`
13. Derrien, S., Rajopadhye, S.: Loop Tiling for Reconfigurable Accelerators. In: Brebner, G., Woods, R. (eds.) FPL 2001. LNCS, vol. 2147, pp. 398–408. Springer, Heidelberg (2001)
14. Stitt, G., Chaudhari, G., Coole, J.: Traversal Caches: A First Step Towards FPGA Acceleration of Pointer-Based Data Structures (2008)
15. Xilinx: Channelized Direct Memory Access and Scatter Gather (February 2010)
16. Xilinx: Memory Interface Solutions (December 2009)

A Run-Time Task Migration Scheme for an Adjustable Issue-Slots Multi-core Processor

Fakhar Anjam, Quan Kong, Roel Seedorf, and Stephan Wong

Computer Engineering Laboratory,
Delft University of Technology,
Mekelweg 4, 2628 CD, Delft, The Netherlands
{F.Anjam,R.A.E.Seedorf,J.S.S.M.Wong}@tudelft.nl, kongquanquan@hotmail.com

Abstract. In this paper, we present a run-time task migration scheme for an adjustable/reconfigurable issue-slots very long instruction word (VLIW) multi-core processor. The processor has four 2-issue ρ-VEX VLIW cores that can be merged together to form larger issue-width cores. With a task migration scheme, a code running on a core can be shifted to a larger or a smaller issue-width core for increasing the performance or reducing the power consumption of the whole system, respectively. All the cores can be utilized in an efficient manner, as a core needed for a specific job can be freed at run-time by shifting its running code to another core. The task migration scheme is realized with the implementation of interrupts on the ρ-VEX cores. The design is implemented in a Xilinx Virtex-6 FPGA. With different benchmarks, we demonstrate that migrating a task running on a smaller issue-width core to a larger issue-width core at run-time results in a considerable performance gain (up to 3.6x). Similarly, gating off one, two, three, or four cores can reduce the dynamic power consumption of the whole system by 24%, 42%, 61%, or 81%, respectively.

Keywords: Softcore, VLIW processor, Interrupts, Multi-core, Task migration.

1 Introduction

Reconfigurable processors have filled the gap between general-purpose (GP) cores and application-specific integrated circuits (ASICs) in such a way that higher performance can be achieved without losing flexibility. A softcore processor is a processor that can be parameterized at design time and/or reconfigured at run-time when implemented in a field-programmable gate array (FPGA). It provides an efficient way to adapt to large number of applications.

The ρ-VEX [24] is a reconfigurable and extensible softcore very long instruction word (VLIW) processor. The processor can be adapted to different applications. The entire or partial datapath of the processor can be reconfigured. Multiple smaller issue-width cores can be combined to create a larger issue-width

O.C.S. Choy et al. (Eds.): ARC 2012, LNCS 7199, pp. 102–113, 2012.

core to exploit the instruction level parallelism (ILP) available in an application
and improve the performance [3].

Task migration among different cores has been studied in the context of multi-
core architectures. There could be different reasons for task migration. For example, the task migration is used for balancing workload, power, and thermal
characteristics [21][17][13][5][4]. A fair task distribution results in lower power
consumption in all cores, lower network and memory traffic, and lower heating of
the overall system. In case of a fault at a core, its running code can be migrated
to another core as well. We utilize the task migration for possible improvement
in performance, workload balancing, and power reduction.

Figure 1 depicts the timeline for a task migration example. At a time instance,
core1, a 2-issue core is running *task1* and requires time *t1* to finish the task.
Core2, which is a 4-issue core is running *task2* and requires time *t2* to finish the
task. At *t2*, core2 is free, and in a time *Δt*, *task1* can be migrated from *core1* to
core2. Since core2 is a larger issue-width core, it can boost the performance and
hence finishes *task1* at *t3 < t1*. Similarly, shifting from a larger issue-width core
to a smaller issue-width core at run-time and turning off the larger issue-width
core can reduce the power consumption of the overall system.

We first present the design and implementation of the interrupts system. The
interrupts system is parameterized to support different applications. Parameters
include the number of interrupt vectors, the interrupt priority for each vector,
and the interrupt service routine (ISR) location address in the instruction memory. We implemented the interrupts in an reconfigurable issue-slots multi-core
processor [3]. The processor has four 2-issue cores. Each core can be run independently. Multiple 2-issue cores can be combined to make a larger issue-width core.
Building on the interrupts system, we developed a mechanism for task switching
or task migration between different cores when these cores are combined or split
for increasing the performance or reducing the dynamic power of the system. Because different issue-width VLIW cores require different codes, we assume that
different code versions are available with defined switching points.

The contribution of the paper is summarized as follows:

- design and implementation of the interrupts system tailored for the ρ-VEX
  VLIW processor;
- setting run-time adaptation of the issue-slots by utilizing the ρ-VEX processors with interrupts in a reconfigurable issue-slots multi-core processor;

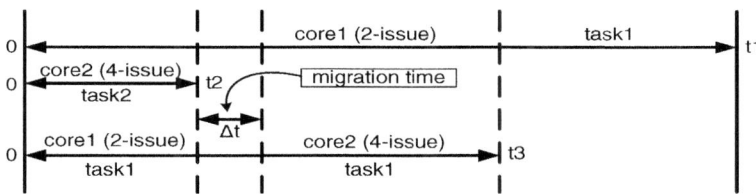

Fig. 1. A task migration example

– design and implementation of a task migration scheme targeting performance improvement, power reduction, and workload balancing.

The remainder of the paper is organized as follows. Section 2 presents some related work. The ρ-VEX processor and the related toolchain are briefly discussed in Section 3. The proposed task migration scheme for the ρ-VEX based adjustable/reconfigurable issue-slots multi-core processor is presented in Section 4. Experimental results are discussed in Section 5. Finally, Section 6 presents the conclusions.

2   Related Work

There are several softcore VLIW processors discussed in literature. Spyder [10] appeared as the first softcore VLIW processor. The toolchain was not complete and there was no interrupts system on the processor. An FPGA-based design of a softcore VLIW processor based on the ISA of the Nios-II soft processor is presented in [12]. Due to the licensed Nios-II, this VLIW design is not much flexible and not open-source. The design can use the interrupts system of the Nios-II architecture. In [18], the micro-architecture of a customizable softcore VLIW processor is presented. The limitation is the absence of a compiler. The processor does not have an interrupts system. All of these processors cannot adjust their issue-slots at run-time to exploit the available ILP.

Several interrupts handling schemes to reduce the size of contexts to be switched to minimize the interrupt latency for VLIW and DSP processors are presented in [15][9][22]. All these mechanisms need the support of a relative compiler and even processor architecture. The ρ-VEX softcore is a parameterized open-source softcore VLIW processor and can be adapted to different applications [23]. In this paper, we implemented the interrupts system on the ρ-VEX processor to further enhance its capabilities, and use it for task migration.

Task migration is used in multi-core architecture to balance the workload and network congestion. An unbalanced workload may result in excessive power consumption and thermal hot-spots and unbalanced network congestion may result in missed deadlines. [21] and [17] present different task or process migration mechanisms and algorithms. The authors in [13] discuss different policies for real-time task migration in embedded multi-core architectures. [2] assesses the impact of task migration on embedded soft real-time streaming multimedia applications. Here, a middleware infrastructure at operating system (OS) level supporting dynamic task allocation for non-uniform memory architectures (NUMA) is presented. [11] presents a context-aware run-time adaptive task migration mechanism to reduce the task migration latency in multi-core architectures. A task migration between two cores results in cache warm-up overheads on the target core, which can result in missed deadlines for tight real-time schedules. [19] proposes a micro-architectural support for migrating cache lines that enables real-time tasks to meet their deadlines in the presence of task migration.

[5] and [8] present policies for task migration to control the thermal characteristics in multi-core systems. Energy-efficient real-time task scheduling and

migration in multiprocessor systems is discussed in [25] and [20]. In [4], the authors discuss the impact of task migration in network-on-chip based MPSoCs for soft real-time systems. [16] presents techniques to selectively migrate the code/data to reduce communication energy in embedded MPSoCs. [14] presents a fault-and-migrate mechanism for asymmetric multi-core architectures which traps a fault when a core executes an unsupported instruction, migrates the faulting thread to a core that supports the instruction, and allows the OS to migrate it back when load balancing is necessary.

We implemented a run-time task migration scheme for a reconfigurable and adjustable issue-slots VLIW multi-core processor. This processor has four 2-issue ρ-VEX cores. An interrupts system has been implemented for these cores, and hence a running core can be interrupted, its state saved, and can be transferred to another core. Multiple cores can be merged at run-time to increase the performance. We do not utilize caches rather we implement local memories. We utilize task migration for improving the performance or reducing the power consumption.

3   The ρ-VEX VLIW Processor

The VEX instruction set architecture (ISA) is a 32-bit clustered VLIW ISA that is scalable and customizable to individual application domains. The VEX ISA is loosely modeled on the ISA of the HP/ST Lx (ST200) family of VLIW embedded cores [6]. Based on trace scheduling, the VEX C compiler is a parameterized ISO/C89 compiler. A flexible programmable machine model determines the target architecture, which is provided as input to the compiler. A VEX software toolchain including the VEX C compiler and the VEX simulator is made freely available by the Hewlett Packard Laboratories [1].

The ρ-VEX is a configurable (design-time) open-source softcore VLIW processor [23]. The ISA is based on the VEX ISA [7]. Different parameters of the ρ-VEX processor, such as the number and type of functional units (FUs), number of multiported registers (size of register file), number and type of accessible FUs per syllable, width of memory buses, and different latencies can be changed at design time. Figure 2 depicts the organization of a 32-bit, 2-issue ρ-VEX VLIW processor implemented in an FPGA. The ρ-VEX processor is a 5-stage pipelined processor consisting of fetch, decode, execute 0, execute 1/memory, and writeback stages. There are two arithmetic logic units (ALUs), two multiplication units (MUL), a control/branch unit (CTRL), and a load/store (LS) or memory unit (MEM). There are two multiported register files: a 64×32-bit general-purpose register (GR) file and an 8×1-bit branch register (BR) file. The instruction and data memories for the processor are implemented with block RAMs (BRAMs). The data memory is also utilized for storing the state or context of a program when an interrupt is serviced. The ρ-VEX processor supports reconfigurable operations, as the VEX compiler supports the use of custom operations via pragmas inside the application code.

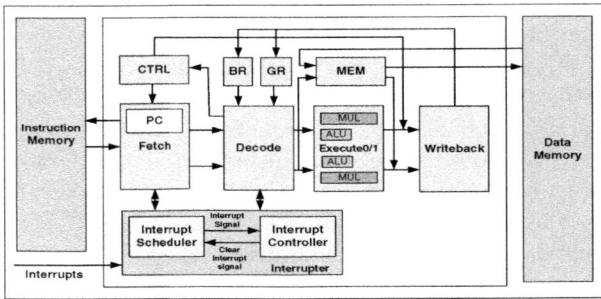

Fig. 2. A 2-issue ρ-VEX processor with the Interrupter

4   Task Migration Scheme

In this section, we first discuss the interrupts system for the ρ-VEX processor. Subsequently, we explain how we utilize the interrupts system in a ρ-VEX based multi-core system for task migration among different cores.

4.1   Interrupts System

Figure 2 depicts our interrupts system called the *interrupter* embedded into the ρ-VEX processor. It can be easily plugged in or out of the ρ-VEX core. The interrupter receives input signals from interrupt pins and then generates control signals to the fetch stage to reschedule instructions such that an ISR could be executed. At the same time, the necessary context is stored. When a *return from interrupt (RFI)* instruction is decoded, a signal is passed to the interrupter to indicate the end of an ISR. After that the context is restored back to the core and the core resumes the original execution. The interrupter has two sub modules: *interrupt scheduler* and *interrupt controller*.

Interrupt Scheduler. The interrupt scheduler has the knowledge of the task that is being executed and the requests that are issued to the ρ-VEX processor. The interrupt scheduler is responsible for (1) receiving the interrupt input signals from different interrupt sources, (2) scheduling different tasks into the task queue, and (3) enabling interrupt requests to the interrupt controller when the priority of the requested task is higher than the current task. There are two inputs for the interrupt scheduler: external *interrupt in* signals from the outside world and the internal *clear* interrupt-flag signal from the interrupt controller. The *interrupt in* signal adds tasks to the task queue and the *clear* signal removes it from the task queue. Only if an interrupt with a higher priority enters, or a higher priority task is finished, a waiting task can become active. The interrupt vector table records information such as the interrupt vectors (type of interrupts) and their priorities, interrupt flags which show the status of each interrupt request, ISR addresses, and the interrupt enable bits to mask the interrupts.

Interrupt Controller. The interrupt controller's main jobs are (1) receiving interrupt request signals from the interrupt scheduler, (2) storing the context, (3) loading the ISR address, (4) restoring the context, and (5) resuming the main program again from the point where it was left before the interrupt. The interrupt controller is designed as a finite state machine (FSM). An interrupt queue is implemented to record information of ISR addresses, return addresses, and interrupt vectors received from the interrupt scheduler along with the interrupt request signal. We utilize the pipeline of the processor to perform the context storing and restoring and the instructions for storing and restoring the context are generated in the software.

ISA Support Software Interrupt and Interrupt Enable/Disable. Since in the original VEX ISA there is no instruction that can generate an interrupt, consequently, we extended the instruction set to support this functionality. We designed and implemented a custom instruction for the ρ-VEX processor called *INT_SOFT*. With this instruction, a software code can interrupt the core.

We extended the instruction set of the ρ-VEX processor with two more instructions, one for enabling and one for disabling the interrupts. When these instructions are decoded, enable/disable signals are sent to the interrupts system, and hence the interrupts can be masked.

4.2 Run-Time Task Migration for VLIW Multi-core Processor

In [3], the authors presented an architecture where a group of small 2-issue VLIW cores can be combined to make a larger issue-width core to exploit the available ILP in an application. Figure 3 depicts the general view of this adjustable issue-slots processor. A group consists of four 2-issue cores. Each core can be run independently. Multiple 2-issue cores can be combined or split at run-time. Within a group of four 2-issue cores, following are the possible configurations of VLIW cores:

1. four 2-issue cores;
2. one 4-issue and two 2-issue cores;
3. two 4-issue cores;
4. one 8-issue core.

When multiple cores are configured, some of them can be gated off and thereby adding more configurations and flexibility to the system. The issue-width of the cores is reconfigured by writing to a configuration register, and it takes only one cycle to configure/adjust the issue-width of the cores. The methodology utilized in [3] was that the cores could only be combined or split when these were idle (i.e., had finished their current execution). In this paper, we enhanced that architecture. We provided another level of control to that multi-core architecture with the development of the interrupts system. Each core is now able to pass on its environment (execution state) to another core of the same or different type in order to manage the cores utilization at run-time. We can now combine

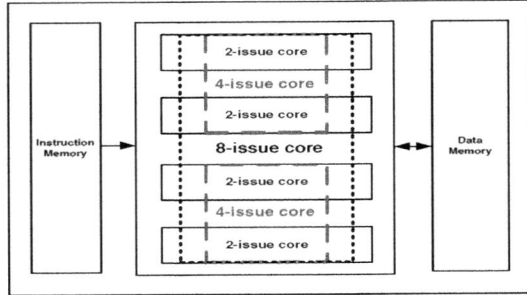

Fig. 3. The adjustable issue-slots VLIW Multi-core processor

or split cores that are even not idle. We implemented an environment shifting or task migration mechanism for the cores utilizing the interrupts system. The environment shifting is needed in different situations. For example, if a larger issue-width core becomes available, it might be needed to switch an application running on a smaller issue-width core to the larger issue-width core for performance reasons. Similarly, one might need to switch a code running on a larger issue-width core to a smaller issue-width core and turn the larger issue-width core off to reduce the dynamic power consumption of the whole system at run-time. We assume here that different code versions of the same application are accessible and there are defined switching points available in the codes. These code versions are manually generated at the assembler level.

Figure 4 depicts the mechanism for migrating a task from ρ-VEX1 to ρ-VEX2. Here ρ-VEX1 and ρ-VEX2 could be any issue-width cores (2-issue, 4-issue, or 8-issue). A scheduler (currently implemented in a hardware, but in future may be a process of an operating system running on a certain core) controls the task migration. When an application is running on a certain issue-width core and a request to migrate to another core (a request to change the issue-width) is received, the application is first allowed to execute through to the switching point on the current core, and then the process for migrating the task to the

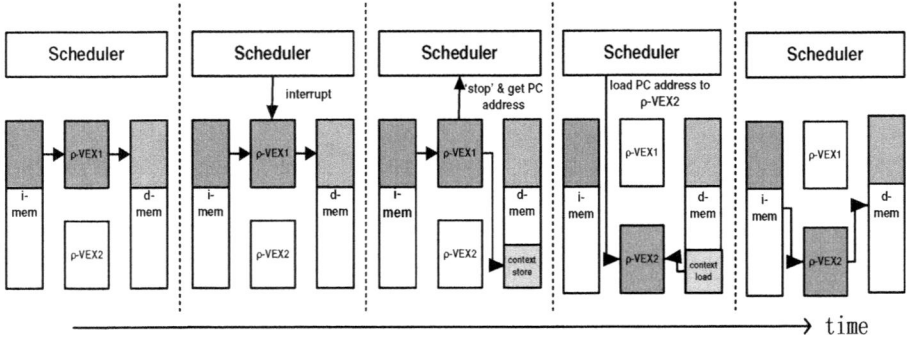

Fig. 4. Mechanism for task migration

new core is started. When shifting a code running on ρ-VEX1 to ρ-VEX2, the following steps are performed by the scheduler as depicted in Fig. 4:

- generate an interrupt on ρ-VEX1 core
- a special ISR is called on ρ-VEX1 which stores the context into the data memory (shared memory accessible to all cores) and the program counter (PC) address with respect to a defined switching point where the currently running program was stopped is recorded
- reconfigure the issue-width of the core (now called ρ-VEX2) by changing the configuration register values [3]
- generate an interrupt on ρ-VEX2 core
- a special ISR is called on ρ-VEX2 that restores the context from the data memory
- load the PC address into ρ-VEX2
- start ρ-VEX2 to resume execution of the remaining code

Here, we only store the general-purpose registers and the branch registers. We implement the stack in the data memory accessible to both cores and hence, we do not store and restore the stack while moving the task from one core to another. The new and the previous cores should know the address where the stack is implemented, and it is done at compile/assemble time. This reduces the migration time among different cores.

5   Experimental Results

Table 1 presents the hardware resource utilization for the adjustable issue-slots processor with the interrupts system. There is a marginal increase in the hardware resources and the critical path remains the same. The processor has four 2-issue cores, each having 2 ALUs, 2 multipliers, 1 load/store (LS) unit, a 64×32-bit general-purpose register file and an 8×1-bit branch register file. These cores can be run independently or combined at run-time to make larger issue-width cores. We utilized the Xilinx ISE release version 12.4 for synthesis and implementation and the target FPGA device is Virtex-6 *XC6VLX240T-1-FF1156* available on the *ML605* development board. The blockRAMs (BRAMs) utilized are 36 kbits BRAMs.

In the ρ-VEX architecture, the general-purpose register number 0 ($\$r0.0$) is hardwired to value zero, and cannot be written. When read, it will always return value zero. Therefore, it is not stored during context store. The interrupt response time for our interrupter is 76 cycles. It includes 4 cycles for completing

Table 1. Hardware resource utilization and maximum frequency for the adjustable issue-slots VLIW multi-core processor with the interrupts system

Processor	Registers	LUTs	DSPs	BRAMs	Max. Frequency
Original adjustable processor	2880	15600	128	64	110 MHz
New adjustable processor	4528	16281	128	64	110 MHz

the currently fetched instruction and stopping the pipeline, 1 cycle for scheduling the interrupt, 63 cycles for moving the general-purpose registers and 8 cycles for moving the branch registers to the memory.

In our case, task migration from one core to another requires a total of 155 cycles. Out of these 155 cycles, 76 cycles are required for storing the context of the first core, 1 cycle for accessing the program counter of the first core, 1 cycle for reconfiguring the issue-width, 76 cycles for restoring the context on the newly configured core, and 1 cycle for loading program counter of that core. This means that switching a running application from one type of core to another core consumes 155 additional cycles, but then the execution time for the remaining part of the application could be reduced much.

We considered the following benchmark applications/kernels: advanced encryption standard (AES) encode and decode, inverse discrete cosine transform (IDCT), matrix multiplication, finite impulse response (FIR) filter, Hamming distance, secure hash algorithm (SHA), Huffman compression, data encryption standard (DES), and Sobel filter. Generally, these applications/kernels are part of some large applications such as H.264, and are repeated continuously or at least many times. Normally, these applications/kernels are implemented in the form of functions operating on a subset of data continuously; hence, the call to these functions within the code can be marked as a switching point. For example, the AES encode/decode takes 16 bytes input at a time and encrypt/decrypt them to generate 16 bytes output. When an application is running on a specific issue-width core, the application repeatedly call the kernel functions each time with different data set. The request for the change of the issue-width of a core can only be fulfilled when the current execution on that core has reached to a switching point in the code.

Figure 5 depicts the speedup for different benchmarks when the applications are migrated from a 2-issue core with 1 load/store (LS) unit to a larger issue-width core. As depicted in the figure, the compiler is able to extract more ILP, and hence the execution time is reduced. In our multi-core system, each of the four 2-issue cores has 1 LS unit. When multiple 2-issue cores are merged, the resulting larger issue-width core can also utilize the additional LS units to increase the data input (provided the data memory has multiple ports) and hence can further increase the performance for different applications. Figure 5 depicts the speedup for the benchmarks when the applications are migrated from a 2-issue core with 1 LS unit (2-issue-1-LS) to 4-issue-1-LS, 8-issue-1-LS, 4-issue-2-LS, and 8-issue-4-LS cores at different percentage of the total execution cycles for the 2-issue-1-LS core. The maximum speedup is at 0%, i.e., when the application has just started on the 2-issue-1-LS core. Hence, the speedup is more when the migration is done at the earlier stages of execution.

Similarly, when a code running on a larger issue-width core is shifted to a smaller issue-width core (e.g., from an 8-issue to a 2-issue), the unused issue-slots or 2-issue cores can be gated off to reduce the power consumption of the system. We present the power consumption results for ASIC instead of FPGAs because clock gating is not effective in the current state of the art FPGAs, and techniques like

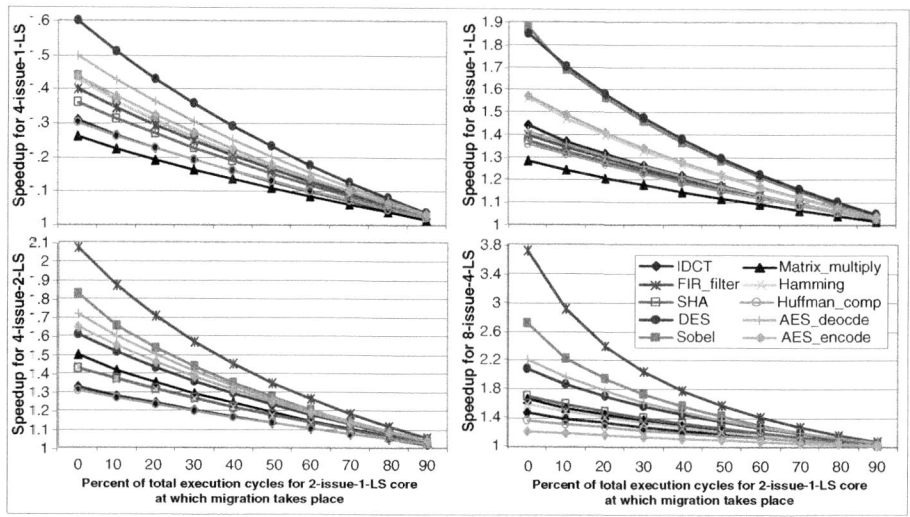

Fig. 5. Speedup compared to a 2-issue core with 1 load/store (LS) unit

gated-Vdd or power gating to reduce the leakage/static power cannot be applied. In the case of ASIC, all these techniques are possible and hence, task migration from a larger to a smaller issue-width core can reduce the power consumption. We implemented clock gating in our multi-core processor. When a core is not in use, it can be gated off to reduce the dynamic power consumption. Figure 6 presents the dynamic power consumption for our multi-core processor. We utilized the Synopsis Design Compiler and 90nm ASIC technology. From Fig. 6, it can be observed that gating off one, two, three, or four cores can reduce the dynamic power consumption of the whole system by 24%, 42%, 61%, or 81%, respectively.

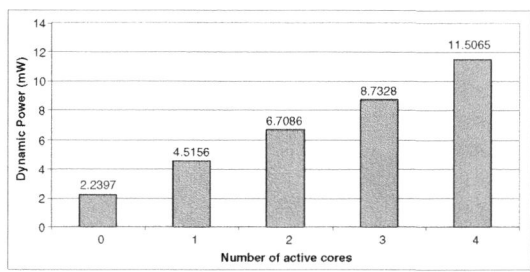

Fig. 6. Dynamic power consumption for the adjustable issue-slots processor with 90nm ASIC technology

6   Conclusions

In this paper, we presented a task migration scheme for a reconfigurable issue-slots VLIW multi-core processor having four 2-issue ρ-VEX cores. With the capability of task migration, the cores can be utilized more efficiently. A task running on a core can be migrated to a larger or a smaller issue-width core to increase the performance or reduce the power consumption, respectively. To realize the task migration scheme, a parameterized interrupts system is implemented for the processor. The design is implemented in a Xilinx Virtex-6 FPGA. There is a marginal increase in resources compared to the original processor. With different benchmarks, we demonstrated that migration from a smaller issue-width core to a larger issue-width core could result in considerable performance improvements (up to 3.6x). Additionally, we demonstrated that gating off one, two, three, or four cores in our multi-core processor could reduce the dynamic power consumption of the whole system by 24%, 42%, 61%, or 81%, respectively. For future work, we are considering the implementation of different migration policies for the scheduler.

Acknowledgment. This work is supported by the European Commission in the context of the ERA (Embedded Reconfigurable Architectures) collaborative project #249059 (FP7). The opinions expressed in this paper are of the authors only and in no way reflect the European Commissions opinions.

References

1. H. P. Labs. VEX Toolchain, http://www.hpl.hp.com/downloads/vex/
2. Acquaviva, A., Alimonda, A., Carta, S., Pittau, M.: Assessing Task Migration Impact on Embedded Soft Real-Time Streaming Multimedia Applications. EURASIP Journal on Embedded Systems, 1–15 (2008)
3. Anjam, F., Nadeem, M., Wong, S.: Targeting Code Diversity with Run-time Adjustable Issue-slots in a Chip Multiprocessor. In: Design, Automation, and Test in Europe Conference, pp. 1358–1363 (2011)
4. Briao, E.W., Barcelos, D., Wronski, F., Wagner, F.R.: Impact of Task Migration in NoC-based MPSoCs for Soft Real-time Applications. In: International Conference on VLSI-SoC, pp. 296–299 (2007)
5. Cuesta, D., Ayala, J.L., Hidalgo, J.I., Atienza, D., Acquaviva, A., Macii, E.: Adaptive Task Migration Policies for Thermal Control in MPSoCs. In: International Symposium on VLSI, pp. 110–115 (2010)
6. Faraboschi, P., Brown, G., Fisher, J.A., Desoli, G., Homewood, F.: Lx: A Technology Platform for Customizable VLIW Embedded Processing. In: International Symposium on Computer Architecture, pp. 203–213 (2000)
7. Fisher, J.A., Faraboschi, P., Young, C.: Embedded Computing: A VLIW Approach to Architecture, Compilers and Tools. Morgan Kaufmann (2005)
8. Ge, Y., Malani, P., Qiu, Q.: Distributed Task Migration for Thermal Management in Many-Core Systems. In: Design Automation Conference, pp. 579–584 (2010)
9. Hsieh, K.Y., Lin, Y.C., Huang, C.C., Lee, J.K.: Enhancing Microkernel Performance on VLIW DSP Processors via Multiset Context Switch. Journal of Signal Processing Systems 51, 257–268 (2008)
10. Iseli, C., Sanchez, E.: Spyder: A Reconfigurable VLIW Processor using FPGAs. In: FPGAs for Custom Computing Machines, pp. 17–24 (1993)
11. Jahn, J., Faruque, M.A.A., Henkel, J.: CARAT: Context-Aware Runtime Adaptive Task Migration for Multi Core Architectures. In: Design, Automation, and Test in Europe Conference, pp. 1–6 (2011)

12. Jones, A.K., Hoare, R., Kusic, D., Fazekas, J., Foster, J.: An FPGA-based VLIW Processor with Custom Hardware Execution. In: International Symposium on Field Programmable Gate Arrays, pp. 107–117 (2005)
13. Katre, K.M., Ramaprasad, H., Sarkar, A., Mueller, F.: Policies for Migration of Real-Time Tasks in Embedded Multi-Core Systems. In: Real-Time Systems Symposium, pp. 17–20 (2009)
14. Li, T., Brett, P., Hohlt, B., Knauerhase, R., McElderry, S., Hahn, S.: Operating System Support for Shared-ISA Asymmetric Multi-core Architectures. In: Workshop on the Interaction between Operating Systems and Computer Architecture, pp. 19–26 (2008)
15. Ozer, E., Sathaye, S.W., Menezes, K.N., Banerjia, S., Jennings, M.D., Conte, T.M.: A Fast Interrupt Handling Scheme for VLIW Processors. In: International Conference on Parallel Architectures and Compilation Techniques, pp. 136–141 (1998)
16. Ozturk, O., Kandemir, M., Son, S.W., Karakoy, M.: Selective Code/Data Migration for Reducing Communication Energy in Embedded MpSoC Architectures. In: Great Lakes Symposium on VLSI, pp. 386–391 (2006)
17. Richmond, M., Hitchens, M.: A New Process Migration Algorithm. ACM SIGOPS Operating Systems Review 31(1), 31–42 (1997)
18. Saghir, M.A.R., El-Majzoub, M., Akl, P.: Customizing the Datapath and ISA of Soft VLIW Processors. In: De Bosschere, K., Kaeli, D., Stenström, P., Whalley, D., Ungerer, T. (eds.) HiPEAC 2007. LNCS, vol. 4367, pp. 276–290. Springer, Heidelberg (2007)
19. Sarkar, A., Mueller, F., Ramaprasad, H., Mohan, S.: Push-Assisted Migration of Real-Time Tasks in Multi-Core Processors. In: Conference on Languages, Compilers, and Tools for Embedded Systems, pp. 80–89 (2009)
20. Seo, E., Jeong, J., Park, S., Lee, J.: Energy Efficient Scheduling of Real-Time Tasks on Multicore Processors. IEEE Transactions on Parallel and Distributed Systems 19(11), 1540–1552 (2008)
21. Smith, J.M.: A Survey of Process Migration Mechanisms. ACM SIGOPS Operating Systems Review 22(3), 29–40 (1988)
22. Snyder, J.S., Whalley, D.B., Baker, T.P.: Fast Context Switches: Compiler and Architectural Support for Preemptive Scheduling. Microprocessors and Microsystems 19, 35–42 (2000)
23. Wong, S., Anjam, F.: The Delft Reconfigurable VLIW Processor. In: International Conference on Advanced Computing and Communications, pp. 242–251 (2009)
24. Wong, S., van As, T., Brown, G.: ρ-VEX: A Reconfigurable and Extensible Softcore VLIW Processor. In: International Conference on Field-Programmable Technologies, pp. 369–372 (2008)
25. Zheng, L.: A Task Migration Constrained Energy-Efficient Scheduling Algorithm for Multiprocessor Real-time Systems. In: International Conference on Wireless Communications, Networking and Mobile Computing, pp. 3055–3058 (2007)

Boosting Single Thread Performance in Mobile Processors via Reconfigurable Acceleration

Geoffrey Ndu and Jim Garside

The APT Group
School of Computer Science,
The University of Manchester,
Oxford Road, Manchester
United Kingdom
{g.ndu,jdg}@cs.man.ac.uk
http://apt.cs.man.ac.uk

Abstract. Mobile processors, a subclass of embedded processors, are increasingly employing multicore designs to improve performance. This often requires sacrificing resources in each CPU, degrading single thread performance which is still important according to Amdahl's law. The traditional technique for efficiently boosting serial performance in embedded processors, dedicated hardware acceleration, is unsuitable for modern mobile processors because of the heterogeneity and the diversity of applications they run. This paper proposes 'general purpose' accelerators, reconfigured on an application-by-application basis, as a means of increasing single thread performance. These accelerators are placed within the datapath of CPUs and support dynamic compilation. This paper presents the design of an architecture with such accelerators and evaluates the cost/performance implications of the design.

Keywords: reconfigurable, dynamic compilation, multicore, accelerator, JIT.

1 Introduction

Mobile processors, a subclass of embedded processors, are General Purpose Processors (GPPs) designed primarily for small, fan-less, battery powered, mobile computing devices such as smart-phones. They are characterised by high performance, low energy consumption, small area and low cost. Mobile processors are increasingly moving to multicore designs to improve performance.

Multicore processors, multiple Central Processing Units (CPUs) on a die, improve performance by handling more work in parallel. Increasing the number of CPUs often requires sacrificing resources in each CPU which degrades single thread performance. Single thread performance is still important as some key applications have limited Thread-level Parallelism (TLP). Further, according to Amdahl's law [6], serial sections within a massively parallel application with lots of TLP are performance constraints. A current (and future) challenge for mobile processors vendors is how to efficiently increase single thread performance in these resource-constrained processors.

O.C.S. Choy et al. (Eds.): ARC 2012, LNCS 7199, pp. 114–125, 2012.

Unfortunately, the time-tested approach for serial performance improvement in embedded processors – accelerating compute intensive parts of applications using dedicated hardware – is unsuitable for modern mobile processors because of the heterogeneity and diversity of applications. The next best alternative is having 'general purpose' hardware, reconfigured on an application-by-application basis to realise frequently occurring functions. This is less efficient in terms of area, cost and power than fixed hardware but allows a GPP to be specialised based on the application it's currently running.

Reconfigurable hardware has been used successfully to accelerate single threads in experimental and commercial processors. However, employing it in multicore mobile processors poses two unique challenges.

A typical Reconfigurable Architecture (RA) is composed of several memory elements, programmable interconnect and an array of many Processing Elements (PEs) making its deployment prohibitive due to its significant area and power consumption. Further, mobile processors rely extensively on dynamic compilation, which is not yet common on RAs, to improve portability. Dynamic compilation is important as an increasing number of parallel programming systems rely on it to provide forward scaling [13]: applications that effectively scale with new core counts as well as the unavoidable augmentation and evolution of the instruction set. For instance, kernels (critical parallel functions) in Intel ® Array Building Blocks (IABB) [13] are first compiled to a platform independent Intermediate Representation (IR) then dynamically compiled to binary via a Virtual Machine (VM) at run-time.

This paper presents the VIrtual REconfigurable Micro-ENgine for Translation (VIREMENT) , a mobile multicore processor employing general purpose accelerators to improve single thread performance. The general purpose accelerator is a Reconfigurable Functional Unit (RFU) placed within the datapath of each CPU. VIrtual REconfigurable Micro-ENgine for Translation (VIREMENT) supports dynamic compilation by providing a run-time library for generating reconfigurable instructions on-the-fly. Experiments show an average performance improvement of 133% (2.33×) with area overhead of 34% per CPU.

2 Related Work

Over the years, architectures that dynamically translate code to run on reconfigurable hardware have been developed. Such architectures eliminate dependencies on hardware features, letting hardware vendors significantly change features from one hardware generation to the next without breaking binary portability.

Warp [17] is a family of processors that automatically extracts and compiles kernels to Field-Programmable Gate Array (FPGA). A typical Warp processor is a System on Chip (SoC) with a main processor for executing applications, a less powerful processor on which a lean FPGA compiler runs, a profiler and a custom FPGA. It translates binary sequences to hardware transparently by profiling executing binary program, detecting critical regions, decompiling them, synthesising them to hardware, placing and routing them onto a custom on-chip FPGA, and updating the binary to call the hardware next time. However, its CAD algorithms, which run on a separate microprocessor, require significant resources as well as time to execute. The use of an FPGA limits it to a few loops and consequently to applications where a few loops dominate because of the large memory required to save FPGA configurations.

The Configurable Compute Array (CCA) [11] is a matrix of simple, coarse-grained functional units coupled to a host CPU. Accelerating applications on the CCA involves two steps: the discovery/delineation of suitable, critical sub-graphs within the Directed Flow Graphs (DFGs) for the CCA and the replacement of such sub-graphs with micro-operations that configure the CCA. Static and dynamic approaches for sub-graphs selection were presented. Dynamic discovery involves a trace cache and its associated hardware optimiser which is rare in mobile processors because of cost and energy issues. Static discovery finds suitable code sequences for mapping onto the CCA at compile time using traditional compiler-based techniques for instruction set customisation.

CCA offered performance improvements to a variety of applications but no area, power nor latency measurements were provided making it difficult to evaluate the overall effectiveness of the approach. Further, CCA does not support shifts nor memory operations and handles only four inputs and two outputs thus limiting its application.

Dynamic Instruction Merging (DIM) [7] dynamically translates binaries to coarse-grained hardware using a hardware based translator. Translation is simultaneous with instruction fetch and translated sequences are cached on-chip. The next time a cached sequence is fetched the saved translation is executed atomically and the processor's Program Counter (PC) updated to allow software execution to continue. Custom Reconfigurable Arrays for Multiprocessor System (CReAMS) [18] is based on DIM but has a pipelined translator.

The translation algorithm is simple and fast as it is implemented in hardware but opportunities for optimising the many micro-operations produced by the translation process are missed. Further, energy is spent translating cold instruction sequences that contribute little to performance as DIM attempts to translate all instructions.

Another project [19] is based on a heterogeneous multicore processor where, cores being either Reconfigurable Hardware Unit (RHU)-cores or Reconfiguration Instruction Generation (RIG)-cores. An RHU-core is a superscalar CPU augmented with an RFU. The RIG-core is based on the same CPU as the RHU-core but with a hardware reconfigurable instruction generator. Each RIG-core services a number of RHU-cores and has no reconfigurable fabric. Each RHU-core collects traces of committed instructions and dispatches them to a RIG-core for translation. When the configuration is returned, it is stored in the RHU-core thread's address space. When next the start of a trace is detected the associated configuration(s) is fetched, decoded and processed by the RFU instead.

Despite its performance improvements this architecture may be too 'complex' for mobile processors as it uses trace caches with the consequent cost and energy penalties.

3   System Architecture

VIREMENT could be described as a multicore dynamic Application Specific Instruction-set Processor (ASIP) [14] that uses reconfigurable functional unit(s) instead of custom functional unit(s) to reduce power consumption and boost processing speed. It consists of a host CPU extended with reconfigurable hardware. Non-critical parts of an application are implemented using the standard instruction set (and run on standard functional units) while kernels are implemented using a reconfigurable instruction set (micro-ops) which run on the reconfigurable functional unit(s). VIREMENT, unlike traditional stream oriented systems, takes small amounts of data at a time from the host's register file and produces another small amount of output. This imposes fewer restrictions on the characteristics of the application, allowing acceleration in most cases.

VIREMENT provides a compiler, the Dynamic Compilation Engine (DCE), to support dynamic compilation in VMs. In addition to its use in traditional 'write-once-run-anywhere' language VMs dynamic compilation is increasingly being employed in parallel programing systems to allow applications to 'forward scale' [13] as well as to support dynamic mapping [16]. DCE, based on Low Level Virtual Machine (LLVM) [15], provides dynamic code generation on VIREMENT and C/C++ APIs to enable integration into VMs. The code generation process is quite simple and is illustrated at a high level in Figure 1a. Initially, kernels in an application are identified and translated into a suitable IR. Each basic block from the critical functions is then translated into micro-ops by the DCE. The original basic block is extracted from the function and replaced by a single instruction which serves as a pointer to the memory location of the micro-ops for that particular basic block. Each of the original basic block, now replaced by a special instruction pointing to its configuration, executes as an atomic unit on the reconfigurable functional unit(s) (Figure 1b). Essentially the DCE synthesises an application specific instruction, on-the-fly, to replace each basic block in a kernel. Large basic blocks may map into more than one group of micro-ops.

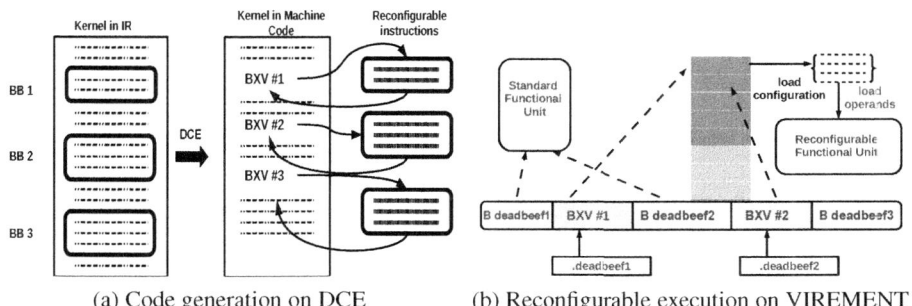

(a) Code generation on DCE   (b) Reconfigurable execution on VIREMENT

Fig. 1. Overview of compilation and execution on VIREMENT

4 Microarchitecture

VIREMENT is simply a 4-core processor with each CPU augmented with an RFU. Logically each core can be divided into the CPU and the VIREMENT Reconfigurable Functional Unit (VRFU).

4.1 CPU

The CPU is comparable to the ARM926EJ-S and runs at 200 MHz. It has a simple, in-order, 5-stage pipeline, Harvard architecture, RISC core which is replicated four times.

Each VIREMENT core has separate L1 data and instruction caches. The data cache is two-way banked allowing two simultaneous cache accesses per cycle if the two cache accesses are to different banks.

Each CPU supports three types of instruction sets: ARM, Thumb and VIREMENT Execution Environment (VEE). ARM is the 32-bit main instruction set while Thumb is the 16-bit subset of ARM. VEE is the reconfigurable instruction set, micro-ops, but can only be accessed by executing a special 'ARM' instruction "Branch-to-Virement"(BXV). Decoding micro-ops is the responsibility of the VRFU. Therefore, each BXV serves only as a pointer to a single context of micro-ops, uniquely identified by the address encoded in the BXV.

Figure 2a shows how the RFU is integrated into the CPU. The decode stage is modi-fied to stall the pipeline once it recognises a BXV. The decoder simply forwards the ad-dress portion of the BXV to the VRFU and awaits for the completion signal from VRFU to remove the stall signal. The VRFU itself consists of an array of PEs, the VIREMENT Reconfigurable Datapath (VRD) and the VIREMENT Control Unit (VCU). The VCU is mainly responsible for managing reconfiguration.

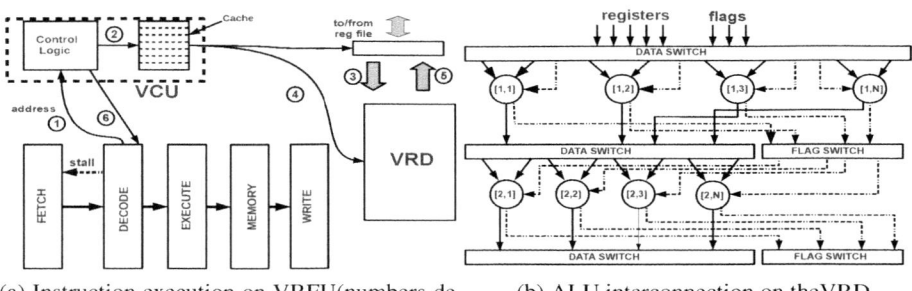

(a) Instruction execution on VRFU(numbers de-note sequence)   (b) ALU interconnection on theVRD

Fig. 2. Overview of compilation and execution on VIREMENT

4.2   VIREMENT Reconfigurable Datapath

The VRD comprises an array of interconnected PEs with data routed using multiplexers. It is purely combinational to reduce its complexity, latency and energy consumption. The PEs are arranged into rows, with each row connected to the next through a switch box. Computation flows from top to bottom with each switch box capable of connect-ing any of the previous row output to any of the next row PE input. This restrictive interconnection simplifies P&R facilitating dynamic compilation on the RFU.

The fundamental processing element in the VRD is the Arithmetic and Logic Unit (ALU). The ALUs are simple to reduce latency, cost and energy consumption. Currently only integer operations are supported. Each operation has three operands, two 32-bit values and a 1-bit flag. Operations generate a four flag bits: a *sign flag*, a *zero flag*, an *overflow flag* and a *carry out flag*. These are similar to the host CPU's allowing the core and the VRFU to exchange flags. Figure 2b shows how the ALUs are interconnected.

In addition to ALU operations, a few PEs per row are capable of loads/stores through the multi-banked L1 data cache. The address of each load/store must be calculated in an ALU in the previous row. All data accesses are through the L1 cache and the VCU stalls the VRD in the case of a miss. Channelling all memory accesses through the L1 cache allows the VRFU to out-source cache coherency management to the CPU. This keeps the VRFU design and programming simple.

4.3 VIREMENT Control Unit

The VCU's primary responsibility is to manage reconfiguration. It has a small SRAM for caching configuration contexts fetched from the main memory. Contexts are supplied almost instantaneously to VRD from the local cache. The VCU fetches configuration contexts directly from the main memory, via the DMA. Configuration contexts are all the same size making cache management simple and eliminating cache fragmentation. The cache employs a LRU replacement policy.

5 Structure of the Dynamic Compiler Engine (DCE)

The DCE generates code on the fly for the VRFU, starting from LLVM IR [15]. As with time- and resource-limited run-time compilers used on mobile processors, emphasis is on speed, small memory footprint and energy efficiency rather than code quality. The DCE relies heavily on the LLVM compiler framework [15] for transformations and analysis.

Dynamic compilation incurs substantial overhead. Further, quality may suffer in the quest to generate code within a limited time budget. However, overheads are largely amortised in the typical DCE usage model: compiling relatively small, critical sections in a long running application. Quality issues could be tackled with split compilation, performing time-consuming analysis offline and saving the results for run-time use.

LLVM's Static Single Assignment (SSA) IR offers a number of advantages to DCE. It can serve both as a persistent, offline code representation and as a compiler internal representation, with no semantic conversions needed between the two [15]. It is increasingly being used in parallel compilation systems targetted by DCE. For instance, AMD embeds LLVM IR source for kernels in its OpenCL Binary Image Format (BIF) 2.0 [5].

5.1 Code Generation Process

The generation of reconfigurable instruction is basically a post-pass optimisation within the CPU code generator. CPU instructions are first generated and then translated into micro-ops. This allows for the seamless intermixing of standard and reconfigurable instructions since not all operations can be performed on the VRFU. The pass is fast and lean (it is slightly more complex than the code generators in software binary translators) allowing its use in mobile devices with constrained processing power and storage. However, it has advantages over present hardware reconfigurable translators as more sophisticated optimisations and post-fabrication modifications are enabled.

Code generation can be logically divided into nine distinct steps which are:

1. **DAG Formation:** The first step is the expansion of the LLVM input into a Direct Acyclic Graph (DAG) of LLVM instructions.
2. **Instruction Selection:** This step converts the DAG of LLVM instructions into a DAG of native CPU instructions using a pattern-matching instruction selector.
3. **Scheduling and Formation:** In this pass, a scheduler assigns a linear order to the DAG from the previous stage. The DAG is now converted to a sequential list of *MachineInstrs* [4] and destroyed. *MachineInstr* is an abstract way of representing machine instructions in LLVM. It represents a machine instruction as an op-code number and a set of operands.
4. **Register Allocation & SSA Deconstruction:** Virtual registers are eliminated from instructions and replaced with physical registers.
5. **Reconfigurable Instruction Generation:** This is the pass that extracts and converts CPU instructions into micro-ops with each set of extracted CPU instructions being replaced by a single BXV instruction. The pass is a functional level pass i.e. it executes on each function in the program independent of all of the other functions.

   (a) **Instruction Translation:** This stage identifies and translates supported *MachineInstrs* to micro-ops. Here, instructions are extracted, sequentially, from the list of *MachineInstrs* and translated into micro-ops represented using VIREMENT Intermediate Representation (VIR). A micro-op in VIR is an n-tuple consisting of an operator and operands. Each instruction is given a unique number, called an *ID*, as it is translated. *ID*s help in tracking dependencies between micro-ops.

   Translation starts from the beginning of a basic block and ends when an unsupported instruction or the end of the basic block is encountered. Listing 1 shows an example translation. If the number of translated *MachineInstrs* is above a certain threshold compilation proceeds to item 5b else the translated micro-ops are discarded and translation restarts at the next instruction beyond the unsupported one (see pseudo code in algorithm 1).

   (b) **Micro-ops optimisation:** A number of optimisations could be applied to the micro-ops at this stage. Presently, the main one is the removal of copy instructions. Copy (register-to-register move) instructions, are redundant on VRFU as operands can be moved directly from producers to consumers.

   (c) **Micro-ops Placement and Routing:** This stage involves the simultaneous placement and routing of micro-ops on the VRFU. The output of this stage is pseudo-assembly code for the VRFU. Placement and Routing (PR) of the micro-ops uses a simple, single-pass greedy algorithm (subsection P and R Algorithm) to keep resource consumption and time overhead to a minimum. The algorithm simply takes a micro-op from the linear VIR and determines, based on data dependencies and resource availability, where to place it on the VRD.

   (d) **Micro-ops Code Emission:** Binary code is generated for the VRFU along with 'glue' code needed for loading operands and writing results back to the CPU. This happens during code emission for the CPU.

6. **Code Emission:** The completed machine code is emitted into memory ready for execution. Each BXV in the machine code points to a corresponding configuration.

```
Input: MBB /* Basic block of MachineInstrs from step 4
       */
Output: MBB_BXV /* Basic block of MachineInstrs with BXV
       instructions                                         */
Output: Configs_{1,2,...,n} /* VIREMENT configurations       */
1  while MachineInstr in MBB do
2      Translation_Buffer ← initialise_translation_buffer(void);
3      while MachineInstr is supported do
4          Micro-op ← translate_to_microop(MachineInstr);
5          save_microop_in_translation_buffer(Microops);
6      end
7      if number_translated_MachineInstr < threshold then continue;
8      Translation_Buffer_opt ← optimize_microops(Translation_Buffer);
9      Translation_Buffer_pr ← place_&_route(Translation_Buffer_opt);
10     if P_&_R fails —— P_&_R unbeneficial then continue;
11     MBB_BXV ← replace_successfully_routed_machineinstr_with_bxv(MBB);
12     Configs_{1,2,...,n} ← emit_microop_to_memory(Translation_Buffer_pr);
13 end
```

Algorithm 1. Pseudo code for the Reconfigurable Instruction Generation pass

P and R Algorithm. The algorithm is quite simple: the first step is to retrieve the next unscheduled micro-op in the VIR. The operands (including flags) are read to verify dependencies. Dependencies are tracked using a small data structure called the *Dependency table* which shows the row and column on the VRD where each operand was last defined. The columns are numbered from left to right while the rows are numbered from top to bottom. The row numbers of all the source operands are compared and the operand with the highest row number determines where the micro-op is to be placed.

The next step is to search for a free PE on the VRD to place the micro-op in. Resource usage is modelled with a matrix-like structure, *PE Table*, which has the same dimensions as the VRD. Each element represents a PE and contains information such as resource availability. Each row in the PE Table is scanned from left to right, starting from the row determined by the *Dependency table*, until a free unit is found. The *Dependency table* is then updated if the micro-op just place defines a value(s). The configuration for the multiplexers are generated from information stored in the *PE Table*.

If the VRFU size is 4x4 and the first micro-op from Listing 1.2 is already placed in PE_{00}. A query to the *Dependency table* for the second instruction will return row 1 as $\%r5$ and $\%f1$ are defined (have entries in the *Dependency table*) by the first instruction in row 0. The other source operands do not have entries in the *Dependency table* and need to be fetched from the register file, so they have no influence on the placement. The *PE Table* is then scanned from left to right starting from row 1. PE_{01} is empty so the micro-op is placed on it and the *Dependency table* table updated to reflect that $\%r3$ is now defined by PE_{10}. The next use of $\%r3$ (third instruction) must now be placed in a row higher than 1.

Listing 1. Example translation MachineInstrs to micro-ops. The subscript numbers in Listing 1.2 are the IDs. $\%f,\%i,\%r,\%t$ denote flag, register,immediate and temporary operands. $\%f1$ means that flag is supplied by instruction with ID 1 and $\%i8$ is an immediate of size 8 bits. The PC relative branch in Listing 1.1 stops translation.

```
bb12:
%r5  =  adds  %r4,%r3
%r3  =  adc   %r2,%r5
%r4  =  ldr   [%r3,-%r0]
br  %i8
```

Listing 1.1 Translation: MachineInstrs

```
%r5  =  add₁   %r4,%r3
%r3  =  adc₂   %r2,%r5,%f1
%t1  =  sub₃   %r3,%r0
%r4  =  ldr₄   [t1]
```

Listing 1.2 Translation: Micro-ops

---

6 Evaluation

6.1 Performance Evaluation

To evaluate the performance the architecture a cycle approximate simulation model of VIREMENT based on GEM5 [9] was developed. The parameters used in the model were derived by describing VIREMENT in Verilog and synthesising the description using the Synposys DC compiler [3] with the Nangate 45 nm cell library [2]. The initial development of the DCE was done on Open Virtual Platform (OVP) CPIntegratorPlatform [1] (a virtual platform). The simulator runs under Linux with a memory of 256 MB and no swap space. This is similar to the execution environment in a typical modern smart-phone. The size of the VRD is 4X4 with two PEs per row capable of performing loads and stores using address calculated in the previous row.

Table 1. Description of benchmarks

Program	Benchmark Suite	Application Domain	Parallelization Model	Implementation	Total Instructions (Billions)
fib	BOTS	integer	tasks	OpenMP	7.02
sort	BOTS	integer sorting	tasks	OpenMP	6.34
bfs	Rodinia	graph	tasks	OpenMP	16.69
freqmine	Parsec	data mining	data-parallel	OpenMP	43.90
nqueens	BOTS	games	tasks	OpenMP	61.31

Benchmarks from Parsec [8], Rodinia [10] and Bots [12] were compared (the benchmark suite is described in Table 1) running on VIREMENT and using DCE for code generation against statically complied versions running on a baseline. The baseline is exactly like VIREMENT less the VRFU. The benchmarks are largely integer benchmarks as VRFU does not yet support floating point operations. We modified benchmarks for VIREMENT to mimic parallel systems that dynamically compile kernels by compiling kernels to LLVM IR and embedding them in the native binary. The compilation of kernels to LLVM IR does not require special preparation and was done with a standard compiler. The host code was then modified to trigger a DCE based VM when a kernel was called for the first time. The VM's input was LLVM IR with code cache for storing generated code. We only measured performance (speedup) over the parallel region(s) of each benchmark.

Figure 3 shows speedup, the ratio of execution time on VIREMENT to the execution time on baseline, for each benchmark described in Table 1. *nqueens* gained most running on VIREMENT with a speedup of 2.7 against *sort* with only 1.4. On average, VIREMENT is faster than the baseline by 2.3×. This is largely attributable to the increased Instruction Level Parallelism (ILP) offered by VRD. This, combined with the relatively small overhead of DCE (on average about 2% of the execution time on VIREMENT) and the small number of compilations, only a few functions need to be compiled for VIREMENT to outperform the baseline.

The benchmarks that experienced significant boost in performance, such as *nqueens* and *freqmine* all have dominant kernels with significant ILP. However, ILP is limited within basic blocks especially non-numeric programs. This suggests that enabling DCE to compile across basic block boundaries would improve performance further. Presently, we are enhancing DCE to support PR across basic block boundaries. We are also developing a pass that allows the DCE code generator to quickly estimate the benefits of compiling a piece of code. This will save energy and time compared to the present approach where DCE has to translate and PR code before finding out if the code sequence will benefit from running on VIREMENT.

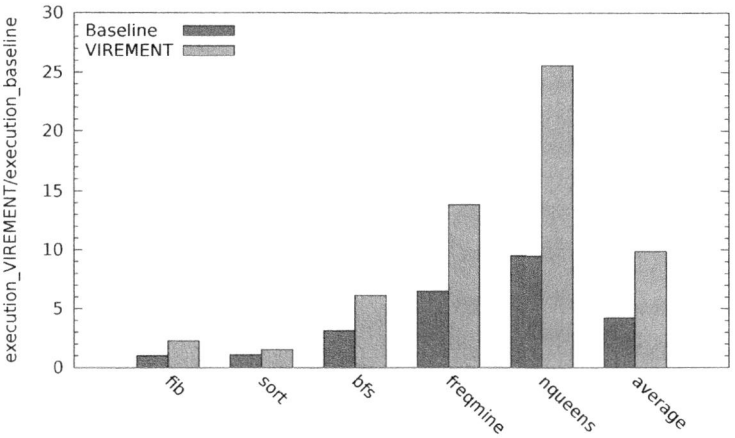

Fig. 3. Results of performance evaluation

Figure 4 shows the percentage of execution time spent compiling and the number of kernels (critical functions) complied by DCE for each application. Table 2 shows for each benchmark the number of LLVM instructions complied and the compilation overhead in cycles.

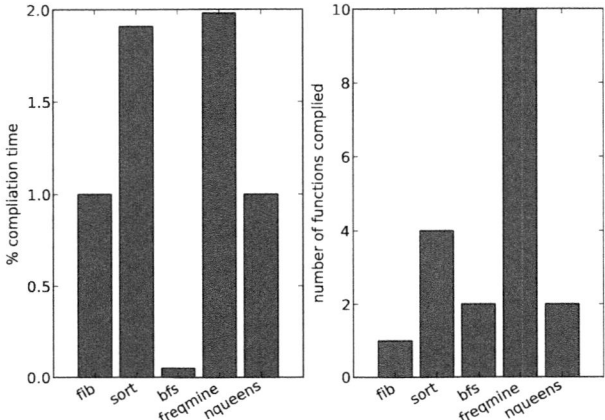

Fig. 4. Compilation Statics

Table 2. Compilation Overhead

Program	Num. LLVM Instructions	Compilation Overhead (Millions Cycles)
fib	9	31.16
sort	324	58.27
bfs	280	52.37
nqueens	89	49.27
freqmine	2194	352.86

Table 3. Area breakdown

Component	Gate Equivalents
CPU	226,000
VRD	66,808
VCU	51,612

6.2   Area Evaluation

Estimates from synthesis show that VRFU is only 34% of each VIREMENT CPU because of simplicity of the design, (Table 3). The addition of the VRFU increases the size of the CPU by half with majority of the area of the VRFU occupied by the VRD. We believe that the size of the VRFU could be reduced significantly with design and synthesis optimizations. Assuming each gate is a NAND gate (4 transistors) each VRFU requires about 473,000 transistors.

7   Conclusions

This work demonstrates that it is possible to use a reconfigurable hardware to improve single thread performance on resource constrained mobile processors in a cost effective manner. It also showed how dynamic compilation could be provided on such an architecture. We obtained mean speedup of up $2.33\times$ over five diverse programs while increasing the area of each CPU by only 52%.

Acknowledgements. The authors would like to thank Imperas Software Limited for supporting this research through tool provision.

References

1. Open Virtual Platform ^{TM}, http://www.ovpworld.org
2. Si2, http://www.si2.org

3. Synopsys Inc., http://www.synopsys.com
4. The LLVM Target-Independent Code Generator,
   http://llvm.org/docs/CodeGenerator.html
5. AMD Accelerated Parallel Processing OpenCL®. Advanced Micro Devices, Inc., Sunny-
   vale, CA, USA (August 2011),
   http://developer.amd.com/sdks/amdappsdk/assets/
   AMD_Accelerated_Parallel_Processing_OpenCL_Programming_Guide.pdf
6. Amdahl, G.M.: Validity of the single processor approach to achieving large scale computing
   capabilities. In: Proc. of the Spring Joint Comp. Conf., AFIPS 1967, April 18-20, pp. 483–
   485. ACM, New York (Spring 1967)
7. Beck, A.C.S., et al.: Transparent reconfigurable acceleration for heterogeneous embedded
   applications. In: Proc. of the Conf. on Design, Automation and Test in Europe, DATE 2008,
   pp. 1208–1213. ACM, New York (2008)
8. Bienia, C., et al.: The PARSEC benchmark suite: characterization and architectural implications. In: Proc. of the 17th Int. Conf. on Parallel Arch. and Compilation Techniques, PACT
   2008, pp. 72–81. ACM, New York (2008)
9. Binkert, N.L., et al.: The M5 simulator: Modeling networked systems. In: IEEE Micro, vol.
   26, pp. 52–60 (July 2006)
10. Che, S., et al.: Rodinia: A benchmark suite for heterogeneous computing. In: Proc. of the
    2009 IEEE Int. Symp. on Workload Characterization, IISWC 2009, pp. 44–54. IEEE Comp.
    Society, Washington, USA (2009)
11. Clark, N., et al.: Processor acceleration through automated instruction set customization. In:
    Proc. of the 36th Annual IEEE/ACM Int. Symp. on Microarchitecture, MICRO, vol. 36, p.
    129. IEEE Comp. Society, Washington, USA (2003)
12. Duran, A., et al.: Barcelona OpenMP Tasks Suite: A set of benchmarks targeting the exploita-
    tion of task parallelism in OpenMP. In: Proc. of the 2009 Int. Conf. on Parallel Processing,
    ICPP 2009, pp. 124–131. IEEE Comp. Society, Washington, USA (2009)
13. Ghuloum, A., et al.: Future-Proof Data Parallel Algorithms and Software on Intel^{TM} for
    Multi-Core Architecture. Intel Technology Journal 11(4), 333–347 (2007)
14. Keutzer, K., et al.: From ASIC to ASIP: the next design discontinuity. In: Proc. 2002 IEEE
    Int. Conf. on Comp. Design: VLSI in Comp.s and Processors, pp. 84–90 (2002)
15. Lattner, C., Adve, V.: LLVM: A compilation framework for lifelong program analysis &
    transformation. In: Proc. of the Int. Symp. on Code Generation and Optimization, CGO 2004,
    pp. 75–86. IEEE Comp. Society, Washington, USA (2004)
16. Luk, C.K., et al.: Qilin: exploiting parallelism on heterogeneous multiprocessors with adap-
    tive mapping. In: Proc. of the 42nd Annual IEEE/ACM Int. Symp. on Microarchitecture,
    MICRO, vol. 42, pp. 45–55. ACM, New York (2009)
17. Lysecky, R., et al.: Warp processors. In: Proc. of the 41st Annual Design Automation Conf.,
    DAC 2004, pp. 659–681. ACM, New York (2004)
18. Rutzig, M.B., Beck, A.C.S., Carro, L.: CReAMS: an Embedded Multiprocessor Platform. In:
    Koch, A., Krishnamurthy, R., McAllister, J., Woods, R., El-Ghazawi, T. (eds.) ARC 2011.
    LNCS, vol. 6578, pp. 118–124. Springer, Heidelberg (2011)
19. Suri, T., Aggarwal, A.: Improving scalability and per-core performance in multi-cores
    through resource sharing and reconfiguration. In: 2009 22nd Int. Conf. on VLSI Design,
    pp. 145–150 (2009)

Complexity Analysis of Finite Field Digit Serial Multipliers on FPGAs

Gang Zhou, Li Li, and Harald Michalik

Institute of Computer and Network Engineering,
Technical University of Braunschweig, Germany
{zhou,li,michalik}@ida.ing.tu-bs.de

Abstract. This paper presents the complexity analysis of digit serial finite field multipliers over $GF(2^m)$ on FPGAs. Instead of discussing the complexity by using AND and XOR gates as primitives, we present the complexity analysis directly based on FPGA primitives, e.g., Look-Up-Tables (LUTs). Given digit size d, the number of LUTs and the level of LUT delay are estimated. The previous ASIC based complexity analysis shows the optimum digit size (for Area-Time-Product) is $2^l - 1$. We show in this work that the optimum digit sizes are different on FPGAs. They are those digits ds which satisfy $\lceil \frac{m}{d-1} \rceil \neq \lceil \frac{m}{d} \rceil$. We also validate our analysis with experimental results on $GF(2^{163})$ and $GF(2^{233})$.

Keywords: digit serial multiplier, finite field, elliptic curve cryptography, FPGAs.

1 Introduction

Cryptographic systems are present in all aspects of our lives. The cryptographic functions are usually parts of an embedded system, which can be low-end systems (e.g. RFID) or high-end communication systems (e.g. routers). Each part of the designs and implementations has to be studied with respect to different requirements on power, cost and performance. This applies also for the Finite Field Multiplier (FFM), which plays an important role in modern cryptographic systems, e.g. the popular elliptic curve based public key cryptography.

The finite field over $GF(2^m)$ is especially interesting for hardware implementations because of its carry-free property. The addition is simple XOR operation. The FFM can be implemented bit serial wise, bit parallel wise or digit serial wise. The bit serial multiplier requires m clock cycles to generate one output and has the area complexity $\mathcal{O}(m)$. It is therefore suitable for area constrained applications. The bit parallel multiplier generates one output in every clock cycle but has the area complexity $\mathcal{O}(m^2)$ or $\mathcal{O}(m^{\frac{3}{2}})$ with Karatsuba algorithm. It is often used for high performance applications. The digit serial multiplier offers compromising options. It generates each output every $\lceil m/d \rceil$ clock cycles and has the area complexity $\mathcal{O}(md)$.

The systolic digit serial multiplier architectures [1] [2] and the special T-type register based architectures [3] [4] are more suitable for ASIC implementations. In [5], Kumar et al. present the optimum digit serial multiplier in ASICs. The optimum digit size for

O.C.S. Choy et al. (Eds.): ARC 2012, LNCS 7199, pp. 126–137, 2012.

Area-Time-Product (ATP) is $2^l - 1$. However, the optimum designs in ASICs may not be optimum on FPGAs. The modern FPGAs are Look-Up-Table (LUT) based, e.g. 4-input LUT in Xilinx Virtex-4 FPGAs [6] and 6-input LUT in Xilinx Virtex-5 [7], Virtex-6 and 7 serials FPGAs. As shown in [8], Guo et al. chose the digit size d, which satisfies $\lceil \frac{m}{d-1} \rceil \neq \lceil \frac{m}{d} \rceil$, for optimum ECC co-processors on FPGAs. Based on the place and route results on different digit sizes, Guo et al. had chosen the optimum digit sizes. In this paper, we will show the complexity analysis both for the LUT consumption and LUT delay. The optimum designs with better ATP can be systematically chosen.

The involved irreducible polynomial is assumed to be fixed in this paper. The studies on generic irreducible polynomials are more interesting for ASIC implementations because of the relatively high Non-Recurring-Engineering cost. Once the polynomial changes, the chip has to be manufactured, verified and tested again. The re-programmability of FPGAs or even FPGA based dynamic reconfigurable techniques enable us to update the designs easily without any extra cost.

This paper is organized as follows: The bit parallel multiplier, especially the reduction matrix Q, is reviewed in next section. Section 3 reviews the Least Significant Digit (LSD) first multiplier. Section 4 presents the LUT based complexity for LSD multiplier. Section 5 evaluates the analysis by comparing with different synthesis tools. Finally, section 6 concludes this paper.

2   Bit Parallel Multiplier

Suppose two operands of the multiplier are $A(x) = \sum_{i=0}^{m-1} a_i x^i$ and $B(x) = \sum_{i=0}^{m-1} b_i x^i$. The multiplier calculates $C(x) = A(x)B(x) \ mod \ F(x)$, where $F(x) = x^m + R(x)$ is an irreducible polynomial of degree m.

The straightforward multiplication includes two steps, first the classic polynomial multiplication and then a modular reduction. The classic polynomial multiplication calculates the $2m - 1$ terms polynomial

$$D(x) = \sum_{i=0}^{2m-2} d_i x^i \tag{1}$$

where

$$d_k = \sum_{i+j=k} a_i b_j, \qquad 0 \leq i, j \leq m - 1$$

The $m - 1$ most high degree terms of $D(x)$ are then iteratively reduced to polynomials with degree less than m by using the irreducible polynomial $F(x)$. The reduction can be described by an $(m - 1) \times m$ matrix Q [1], which satisfies

$$[x^m, .., x^{2m-2}]^T = Q \cdot [1, x, .., x^{m-1}]^T \tag{2}$$

For a given $F(x)$, the matrix Q is unique [9] and is usually a sparse matrix for the recommend domain parameters in [10]. The matrix Q depends only on $F(x)$ and can be iteratively calculated as

---

[1] The matrix is described in Matlab conventions, i.e. $Q(i, :)$, $Q(:, j)$ and $Q(i, j)$ represent the i-th row vector, the j-th column vector and the entry with position (i, j) in matrix Q, respectively.

$$Q(1,:) = R(0:m-1)$$
$$Q(i,:) = Q(i-1,m)R(0:m-1) + [0, Q(i-1, 1:m-1)]$$

If we denote $[d_0, d_1, \cdots, d_{m-1}]$ as D_l, the final output $C(x)$ can be expressed as

$$C = D_l + \sum_{i=m}^{2m-2} d_i Q(i-m+1, :) \tag{3}$$

3 Digit Serial Multiplier

In digit serial multipliers, one operand is divided into several digits. Assume the digit size is d. Let $t = \lceil m/d \rceil$ represents the number of digits. The operand $B(x)$ can be written as (4). If $d \cdot j + k \geq m-1$, the coefficients are padded with zeros. The digit serial multiplier is described in equation (5). The corresponding Least Significant Digit first serial Multiplier algorithm is described in Algorithm 1. The multiplication is achieved by t steps operations. Each digit $B(x)_j$ is multiplied with $A(x)$ and accumulated in $T(x)$. The operand $B(x)_j$ has only degree $d-1$ so that $A(x)B(x)_j$ can be performed in parallel circuit with less gate consumption compared with bit parallel multipliers.

$$B(x) = \sum_{i=0}^{m-1} b_i x^i = \sum_{j=0}^{t-1} B(x)_j x^{D \cdot j} = \sum_{j=0}^{t-1} (\sum_{k=0}^{D-1} b_{D \cdot j+k} x^k) x^{D \cdot j} \tag{4}$$

$$C(x) = A(x) \cdot B(x) = \sum_{j=0}^{t-1} B(x)_j ((A(x) x^{D \cdot j}) \tag{5}$$

Algorithm 1: LSD-first serial/parallel multiplier

---

    input : $A(x), B(x), F(x)$
    output: $C(x) = A(x)B(x) \bmod F(x)$
1 $T(x) = 0$;
2 **for** $j = 0; j \leq t-1; j++$ **do**
3     $T(x) = T(x) + A(x)B(x)_j$;
4     $A(x) = x^D A(x) \bmod F(x)$;
5 C(x)= T(x) mod F(x) ;

---

4 LUT Based Complexity Analysis for LSD Multiplier

In this section, the LUT based complexity analysis is discussed in detail. We assume the number of LUT inputs is ϕ, where ϕ is either 4 or 6. The LUT consumption and the level of LUT delay is denoted by $\mathcal{L}$ and $\mathcal{T}_{\mathcal{L}}$, respectively.

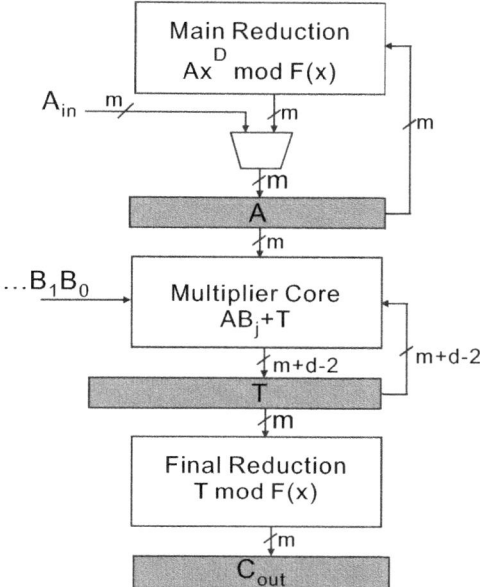

Fig. 1. LSD multiplier architecture

4.1 Hardware Architecture

The hardware architecture for LSD-first multiplier is very straightforward and is shown in Fig. 1, which has been discussed in [11] by Song et. al and in [5] by Kumar. et al. The architecture includes three registers, m-bit A to store either A_{in} or Ax^d, $m + d - 2$-bit accumulator T and m-bit output register C_{out}. Other parts of the architecture are pure combinatorial logics:

- m-bit multiplexer to select A_{in} and Ax^d. Either on 4-input or 6-input LUT FPGAs, the multiplexer can be achieved by m LUT with 1 level LUT delay.
- The *multiplier core* (MC) module calculates $AB_j + T$. The LUT consumption and LUT delay are denoted by $\mathcal{L}_{MC}$ and $\mathcal{T}_{\mathcal{L}MC}$, respectively.
- The *main reduction* (MR) module calculates $Ax^d \bmod F(x)$. The m-bit register A is left shifted d-bit and then reduced to an m-bit polynomial by using $F(X)$. The LUT consumption and LUT delay are denoted by $\mathcal{L}_{MR}$ and $\mathcal{T}_{\mathcal{L}MR}$, respectively.
- The *final reduction* (FR) module returns the final output C_{out} by reducing the $m + d - 2$-bit register T to an m-bit polynomial by using $F(x)$. The LUT consumption and LUT delay are denoted by $\mathcal{L}_{FR}$ and $\mathcal{T}_{\mathcal{L}FR}$, respectively.

The total LUT of the multiplier can be calculated as (6). The LUT delay is described as (7), which is the maximal delay of three paths: A to A, A to T and T to C_{out}.

$$\mathcal{L}_{total} = m + \mathcal{L}_{MC} + \mathcal{L}_{MR} + \mathcal{L}_{FR} \tag{6}$$

$$max(\mathcal{T}_{\mathcal{L}MC}, \mathcal{T}_{\mathcal{L}MR} + 1, \mathcal{T}_{\mathcal{L}FR}) \tag{7}$$

4.2 Multiplier Core (MC) Module

The multiplier core calculates $AB_j + T$ in one clock cycle. The combinatorial logic is shown in Fig. 2. Similar with (1), the $m + d - 2$-bit register/polynomial T' can be described by (8).

$$T'(x) = \sum_{i=0}^{m+d-2} d_i x^i \tag{8}$$

where

$$t'_k = \sum_{i+j=k} (a_i b_j) + t_k, \qquad 0 \le i \le m-1, 0 \le j \le d-1$$

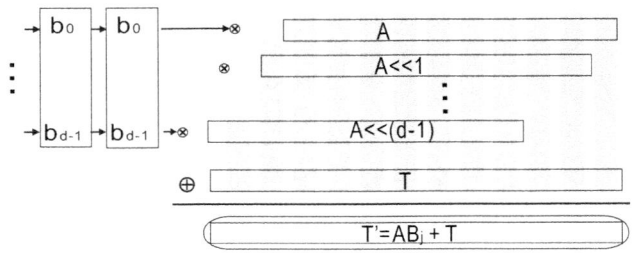

Fig. 2. LSD multiplier core

The calculation can be described by a tree architecture as the example shown in Fig. 3. The tree architecture is slightly different as the tree architecture presented in [12]. Fortunately, the technology mapping scheme shown in [12] can still be applied. When the tree is converted into ϕ-input LUT oriented schematics, $\phi - 1$ gates can be replaced by one LUT for ideal cases. If the number of gates is not a multiple of $\phi - 1$, the inputs of some LUTs may not be fully used. As shown in Fig. 3, the calculation of t'_4 requires 10 gates. On 4-input LUT FPGAs, $\lceil 10/(4-1) \rceil = 4$ LUTs are needed. On 6-input FPGAs, $\lceil 10/(6-1) \rceil = 2$ LUTs are needed. The number of gates for each t_k can be derived as (9) according to (8). The total number of LUTs is summarized by (10). The critical delay occurs at terms t_k when $d - 1 \le k \le m - 1$. If binary tree method for concatenating the LUTs is used, the delay is calculated by (11).

$$Gates_{t'_k} = \begin{cases} 1 + 2(k+1), 0 \le k \le d-2 \\ 1 + 2d, d-1 \le k \le m-1 \\ 1 + 2((m+d-2)-k+1), m \le k \le m+d-2 \end{cases} \tag{9}$$

$$\mathcal{L}_{MC} = \sum_{k=0}^{m+d-2} \mathcal{L}(t'_k), \; with \; \mathcal{L}(t'_k) = \lceil \frac{Gates_{t'_k}}{\phi - 1} \rceil \tag{10}$$

$$\mathcal{T}_{\mathcal{L}MC} = \lceil log_\phi 2d + 1 \rceil \tag{11}$$

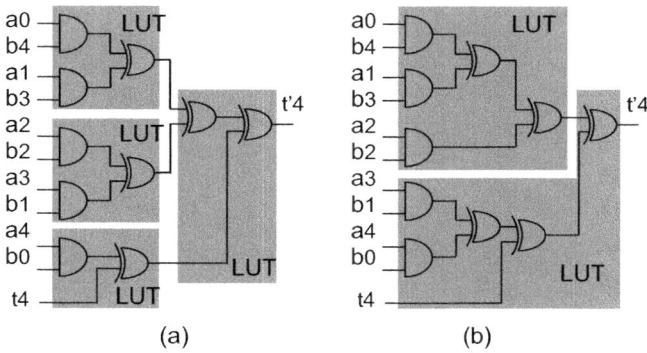

Fig. 3. Technology mapping of t_4 on (a) 4-input LUT FPGAs and (b) 6-input LUT FPGAs

4.3   Main Reduction (MR) Module

The MR module can be achieved in the same manner as the reduction of $D(x)$ shown in (2) and (3). The $Ax^d \bmod F(x)$ can be explicitly described with matrix Q as shown in (12), where A_l is the $d-1$-bit left shifted A or $A_l = [a_{m-d-1}\, a_{m-d-2} \cdots, a_0, 0, \cdots, 0]$. Each term of a'_k can be calculated as (13). The architecture is shown in Fig. 4.

$$A' = Ax^d \bmod F(x) = A_l + \sum_{i=m-d}^{m-1} a_i Q(i - (m-d), :) \tag{12}$$

$$a'_k = \begin{cases} \sum\limits_{i=m-d}^{m-1} a_i Q(i - (m-d), k), 0 \le k \le d-1 \\ a_{k-d} + \sum\limits_{i=m-d}^{m-1} a_i Q(i - (m-d), k), d \le k \le m-1 \end{cases} \tag{13}$$

The elements in Q are either '0' or '1', therefore the MR module requires only XOR gates. The number of XOR gates of each a'_k depends on the Hamming Weight (HW) of the column vector $Q(0 : d-1, k)$. $HW(Q(0 : d-1, k)) - 1$ XOR gates are required if $0 \le k \le d-1$. $HW(Q(0 : d-1, k))$ XOR gates are required if $d \le k \le m-1$ because the term a_{k-d} is always XORed. The total number of XOR gates for each a'_k is given in (14). The LUT consumption of the MR module is summarized in (15). The critical delay can be described as (16), where θ_1 and θ_2 is the maximum HW of the column vectors in sub-matrix $Q(0 : d-1, 0 : d-1)$ and $Q(0 : d-1, d : m-1)$, respectively.

$$Gates_{a'_k} = \begin{cases} HW(Q(0 : d-1, k)) - 1, 0 \le k \le d-1 \\ HW(Q(0 : d-1, k)), d \le k \le m-1 \end{cases} \tag{14}$$

$$\mathcal{L}(MR) = \sum_{k=0}^{m-1} \mathcal{L}(a'_k), \text{ with } \mathcal{L}(a'_k) = \lceil \frac{Gates_{a'_k}}{\phi - 1} \rceil \tag{15}$$

$$\mathcal{T}_{\mathcal{L}MR} = max(\lceil log_\phi \theta_1 \rceil), \lceil log_\phi \theta_2 + 1 \rceil) \tag{16}$$

Main Reduction

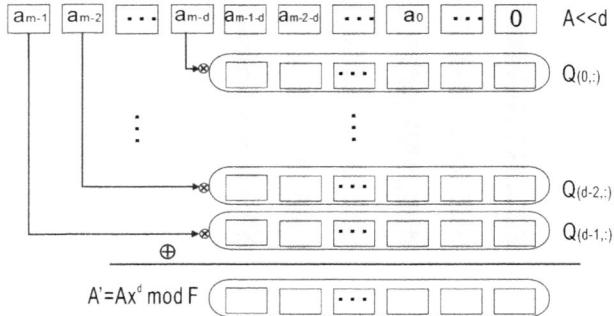

Fig. 4. LSD multiplier main reduction

4.4 Final Reduction (FR) Module

Similar to the analysis for the MR module, the architecture for the the FR module is presented in Fig. 5. The degree of $T(x)$ is 1-bit less than Ax^d, therefore only the sub-matrix $Q(0 : d - 2, :)$ is involved. The number of XOR gates for each $Cout_k$ is given in (17). The LUT consumption for the FR module is summarized in (18). The delay can be described by (19), where θ is the maximum HW of the column vector in matrix $Q(0 : d - 2, 0 : m - 1)$.

$$Gates_{Cout_k} = HW(Q(0 : d - 2, k)) \tag{17}$$

$$\mathcal{L}(FR) = \sum_{k=0}^{m-1} \mathcal{L}(Cout_k), \ with \ \mathcal{L}(Cout_k) = \lceil \frac{Gates_{Cout_k}}{\phi - 1} \rceil \tag{18}$$

$$\mathcal{T}_{\mathcal{L}FR} = \lceil log_\phi \theta + 1 \rceil) \tag{19}$$

5   Complexity Summary and Evaluation

With the complexity analysis given in equations (6), (7), (10), (11), (15), (16), (18) and (19), the number of LUTs and LUT level can be derived. This section summarizes the complexity for both 4-input and 6-input LUT based FPGAs and evaluates the results by comparing with different tools, i.e., Synopsys Synplify Pro 9.6.2 and Xilinx ISE 13.1. The targeted devices are Xilinx Virtex-4 XC4VLX40ff-11 and Virtex-5 XC5VLX85-1. Firstly, the area/LUT consumption is compared. Then, the variation on the critical delay is discussed. Finally, the optimum choices of d with better ATP are shown. Since the multiplier is often used as an internal module of the cryptographic processor, the IO delay is excluded by the synthesis tools. Other tool settings are kept with their default values. The irreducible polynomials involved are the NIST recommended finite fields with $F(x)_{163} = x^{163} + x^7 + x^6 + x^3 + 1$ and $F(x) = x^{233} + x^{74} + 1$ in [10].

Final Reduction

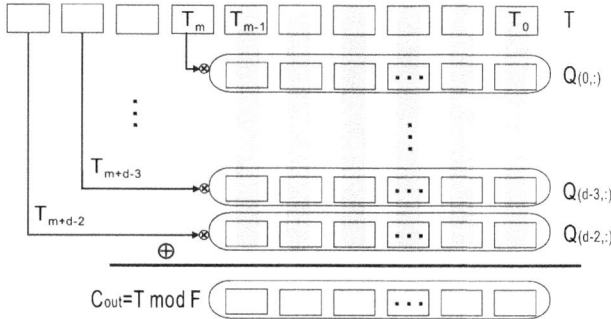

Fig. 5. LSD multiplier final reduction

5.1   LUT Consumption Comparison

Fig. 6 (a) and (b) show the estimated LUT consumption for $m = 163$ on Virtex-4 and Virtex-5 FPGAs, respectively. The results on $F(x)_{233}$ show nearly same diagrams and are not shown here to avoid the tediousness. The percentages of the LUT consumption for the sub-modules, i.e., MC, MR and FR, and the multiplexer are shown. The total number of LUTs monotonically increases along the digit size. Due to the fixed pentanomial ($F(x)_{163}$) and trinomial ($F(x)_{233}$), the MR module and FR module consume only small portion of the whole resources. The multiplexer consumes always m LUTs. Therefore the number of LUTs consumed by the multiplexer are up to 50% on 4-input LUT based FPGAs and up to 30% on 6-input LUT based FPGAs for smaller digit sizes. However it becomes not so notable for bigger digit sizes, for which the most LUTs are consumed by the MC module.

We should notice that LUT-based analysis is **not** the exact area consumption. The different synthesis tools/algorithms will generates different results. For example, The crossing boundary optimization and common expression sharing might further reduce the area consumptions. One could achieve exactly the same number of area consumption by using manual technology mapping, however it would be very time consuming. Nevertheless, the estimated LUT consumption can be used as an upper bound for the FPGA implementations. Fig. 6 (c) and (d) compare the estimated resources and the synthesis results with Synplify and ISE, respectively. The synthesis results with both tools match the presented analysis. The synthesis results with Synplify are closer to the estimated resources than those of ISE. However, the synthesis results are often a little higher than the estimated resources, which is supposed to be the upper bound. We have looked into the verbose resource report files. It was found that both tools do not return the smallest area for each term of t'_k in (8) in the MR module. One or two more LUTs are consumed by the synthesis tools.

5.2   Critical Delay Comparison

Fig. 6 (c) and (d) also compare the delay variations along the digit sizes on the second y-axis. The estimated delay is the number of LUT logic levels, therefore only the logic

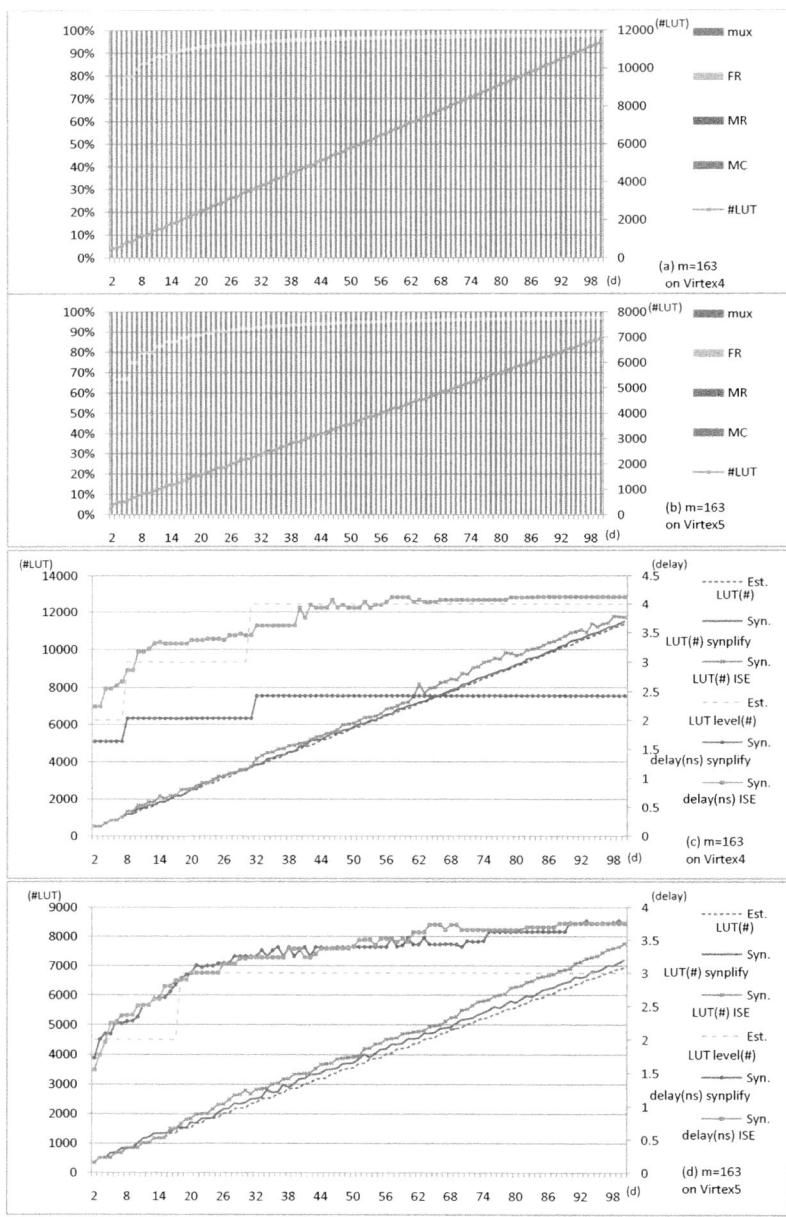

Fig. 6. (a) Estimated LUT consumption on 4-input LUT based FPGAs for $F(x)_{163}$, (b) Estimated LUT consumption on 6-input based FGPGAs for $F(x)_{163}$, (c) LUT and delay comparison on Virtex-4 device for $F(x)_{163}$ and (d) LUT and delay comparison on Virtex-5 device for $F(x)_{163}$

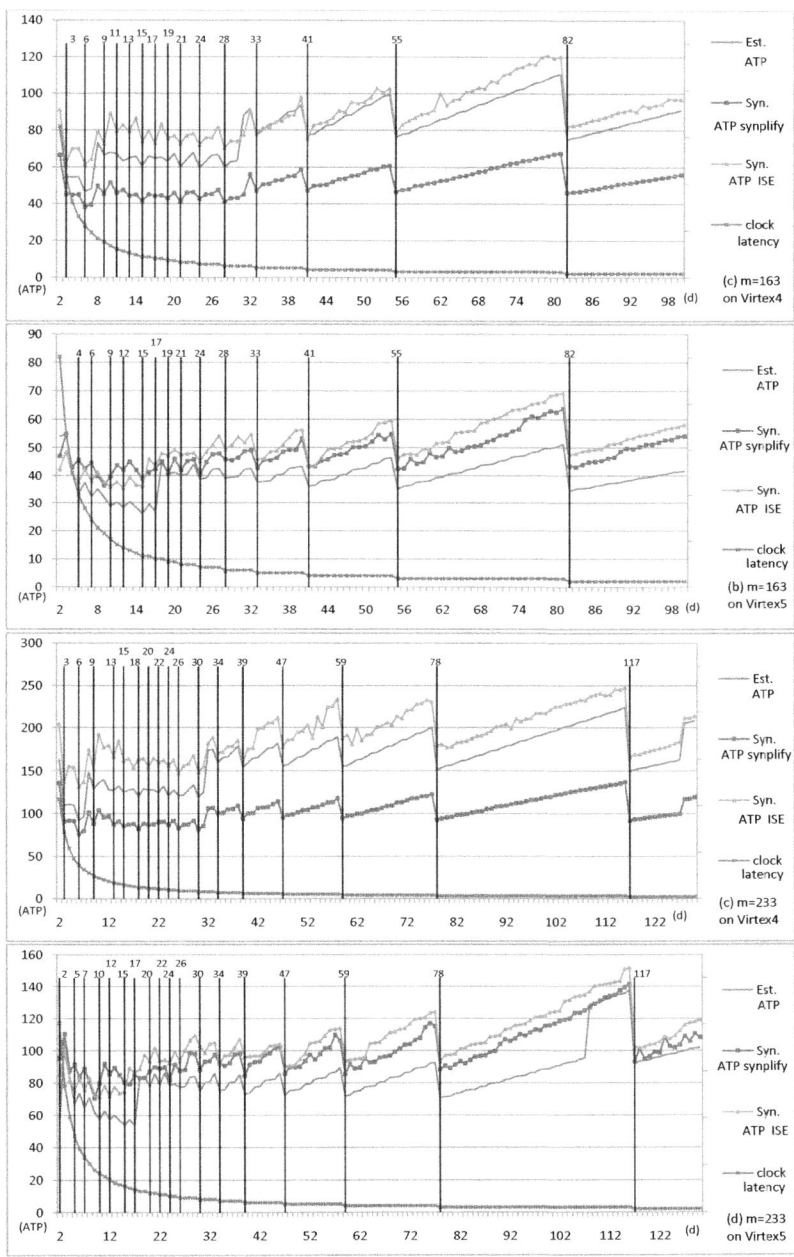

Fig. 7. The optimum digit sizes on Virtex-4 FPGA for $F(x)_{163}$ (a), on Virtex-5 FPGA for $F(x)_{163}$ (b), on Virtex-4 FPGA for $F(x)_{233}$ (c) and on Virtex-5 FPGA for $F(x)_{233}$ (d)

delay is included. The critical delay provided by the synthesis tools is the critical period in nanoseconds, which includes both the logic delay and the routing delay. The routing delay depends not only on the design density, but also on many other factors, e.g., the FPGA routing architecture, the placement, the fan-out and the number of wiring in the design, etc. The more complex the design is, the more difficult the routing will be. Nevertheless, the routing delay is expected to be proportional to the logic delay for most designs with moderate resource consumptions and normal routability.

As shown in Fig. 6 (c) and (d), the estimated number of LUT logic levels is a step function because of the combination of logarithm and ceiling operations in (11). E.g., the number of logic levels is 2 when $2 \leq d \leq 7$, 3 when $8 \leq d \leq 30$ and 4 when $31 \leq d \leq 100$ on Virtex-4 FPGAs; the number of logic levels is 2 when $2 \leq d \leq 17$ and 3 when $18 \leq d \leq 100$ on Virtex-5 FPGAs. The synthesized delay with Synplify on Virtex-4 is exactly a step function while the delay with ISE on Virtex-4 is an approximate step function. Only at the beginning the delay increases very fast when $d \leq 13$. On Virtex-5, the critical delay is linearly increasing with high slope for $d \leq 17$ but becomes much stable for $d \geq 18$. The detailed timing reports show that the logic delay level satisfies the estimation. However, the small increase on the routing delay, which is caused by the increasing fan-out in the multipliers, is a non-neglectable part especially for the multipliers with smaller digit sizes.

5.3   Optimum Digit Size on FPGAs

Fig. 7 shows the optimum digit sizes of Area-Time-Product (ATP) on both Virtex-4 and Virtex-5 FPGAs, for both $F(x)_{163}$ and $F(x)_{233}$. The area is the number of LUTs while the time is the calculation time of one multiplication operation, i.e., $critical\_delay \times clock\_latency$. The number of logic levels is used for the estimated ATP. Even thought the estimated ATP does not include the routing delay, the optimum digit sizes are revealed quite well both on Virtex-4 and Virtex-5 FPGAs.

In most cases, if a digit size is shown to be optimum by the estimated ATP, it is also shown to be optimum by both synthesis tools. There are only a few exceptions especially for smaller digit sizes. E.g., $d = 6$ over $F(x)_{163}$ on Virtex-5 is an optimum digit size revealed by the estimation and by ISE, but not by Synplify. However, for bigger digit sizes, the variation of ATP by the estimation and the synthesis tools are consistent with each other. For $F(x)_{163}$, the common optimum digit sizes are $15, 17, 19, 21, 24, 28, 33, 41, 55, 82$ returned by the estimation, Synplify and ISE. For $F(x)_{233}$, the common optimum digit sizes are $20, 22, 24, 26, 30, 34, 39, 47, 78, 117$. These digits are the digits ds which satisfy $\lceil \frac{m}{d-1} \rceil \neq \lceil \frac{m}{d} \rceil$.

In the previous ASIC based analysis in [5], the optimum digit size is $d = 2^l - 1$ for better and faster gate-based implementations. The FPGA based implementations in [8] did have chosen the right digit sizes based on the synthesis results. However, it would be very cumbersome to implement the multiplies of all the digit sizes and compare them, if a new irreducible polynomial is required. With the presented complexity analysis, one could select the correct digit size and perform good resource estimation at the very early design stages.

6   Conclusion

This paper presents the complexity analysis of LSD multipliers over finite field $GF(2^m)$ on FPGAs. Instead of using AND and XOR gates as primitives, the LUT is assumed to be the primitive in the analysis. The area consumption, the logic level as well as the ATP can be well estimated for the fixed irreducible polynomials. The fixed polynomial based analysis is not suitable for ASIC implementations, but is very interesting for FPGA implementations. The reconfigurability of FPGAs enables the update of design easily if the domain parameters change. We have validated the analysis on both Virtex-4 and Virtex-5 FPGAs, for both $F(x)_{163}$ and $F(x)_{233}$. The optimum digit sizes of ATP differ with the previous ASIC based analysis. The optimum digit sizes are $2^l - 1$ in ASICs while the optimum digit sizes are those digits ds which satisfy $\lceil \frac{m}{d-1} \rceil \neq \lceil \frac{m}{d} \rceil$ on FPGAs.

References

1. Meher, P.K.: Systolic and Non-Systolic Scalable Modular Designs of Finite Field Multipliers for Reed-Solomon Codec. IEEE Transaction on VLSI 17(6), 747–757 (2009)
2. Talapatra, S., Rahaman, H., Mathew, J.: Low Complexity Digit Serial Systolic Montgomery Multipliers for Special Class of $GF(2^m)$. IEEE Transaction on VLSI 18(5), 847–852 (2010)
3. Meher, P.K.: High-throughput hardware-efficient digit-serial architecture for field multiplication over $GF(2^m)$. In: International Conference on Information, Communications and Signal Processing (December 2007)
4. Meher, P.K.: On Efficient Implementation of Accumulation in Finite Field Over $GF(2^m)$ and its Applications. IEEE Transaction on VLSI 17(4), 541–550 (2009)
5. Kumar, S., Wollinger, T., Paar, C.: Optimum Digit Serial $GF(2^m)$ Multipliers for Curve-Based Cryptography. IEEE Transactions on Computers 55(10), 1306–1311 (2006)
6. Xilinx: Virtex-4 User Guide, V2.3 (August 2007), http://www.xilinx.com
7. Xilinx: Virtex-5 User Guide, V3.3 (February 2008), http://www.xilinx.com
8. Guo, X., Schaumont, P.: Optimized System-on-Chip Integration of a Programmable ECC Coprocessor. ACM Transactions on Reconfigurable Technology and Systems 4(1) (2010)
9. Reyhani-Masoleh, A., Hasan, A.: Low Complexity Bit Parallel Architecture for Polynomial Basis Multiplication Over GF(2^m). IEEE Transaction on Computers 53(8), 945–995 (2004)
10. NIST, Digital Signature Standard (DSS), FIPS PUB 186-3 (June 2009)
11. Song, L., Parhi, K.K.: Low-Energy Digit-Serial/Parallel Finite Field Multipliers. Journal of VLSI Signal Processing 19, 149–166 (1998)
12. Zhou, G., Michalik, H., Hinsenkamp, L.: Complexity Analysis and Efficient Implementations of Bit Parallel Finite Field Multipliers Based on Karatsuba-Ofman Algorithm on FPGAs. IEEE Transaction on VLSI 18(7), 1057–1066 (2010)

ScalableCore System: A Scalable Many-Core Simulator by Employing over 100 FPGAs

Shinya Takamaeda-Yamazaki[1,2], Shintaro Sano[1], Yoshito Sakaguchi[1],
Naoki Fujieda[1], and Kenji Kise[1,*]

[1] Graduate School of Information Science and Engineering,
Tokyo Institute of Technology,
2-12-1, Ookayama, Meguro-ward, Tokyo, Japan
[2] JSPS Research Fellow, Japan
{takamaeda,sanos,yoshito,fujieda,kise}@arch.cs.titech.ac.jp
http://www.arch.cs.titech.ac.jp/index-e.html

Abstract. FPGA-based processor prototyping system can fast simulate processor behavior and enables longer time simulations to obtain useful evaluation information. In this paper we present ScalableCore system 3.3, which is an FPGA-based simulator of NoC-based tile architectures by employing multiple Xilinx Spartan-6 FPGAs. Two key techniques enable the system to achieve scalable speed of simulations by using corresponding amount of FPGAs to the target number of processor cores. We evaluated behavior of a processor consisting of 100 cores and a mesh NoC by using our developed system. The simulation speed is 129 times faster than the one of a software-based simulator running on a standard computer of Core i7 processor.

Keywords: Processor Prototyping, Many-core Processor, Multiple FPGAs.

1 Introduction

In processor architecture research, various software-based processor simulators have been widely used to evaluate architectures or proposed schemes. These software-based simulators are very useful due to their customizability, however, they simulate in extremely slower simulation speed than actual processors, so it is difficult to evaluate in longer simulation time. The processor trend goes toward "many-core" for power efficiency and high performance. Therefore larger simulation is required to observe the cross-interactions among software, processor cores and on-chip networks. To accelerate the simulations, several FPGA-based simulators employing a single large FPGA have been developed. They achieved significant faster simulation speed than the software-based simulators' ones. However the previous FPGA-based simulators have less scalability to deal the increasing processor cores. It means that the simulation speed degrade by increasing the core counts in the target processor.

---

* This work is supported in part by Core Research for Evolutional Science and Technology (CREST), JST.

O.C.S. Choy et al. (Eds.): ARC 2012, LNCS 7199, pp. 138–150, 2012.

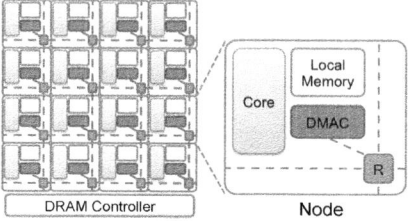

Fig. 1. M-Core: Target Many-core Architecture (configuration of 16 Nodes)

In this paper we present ScalableCore system 3.3, which is a scalable cycle-accurate FPGA-based simulator to accelerate simulations of a tile architecture with mesh NoC (Network on Chip). In this study we used M-Core[11] shown in Fig.1, but not limited for M-Core. The system employs the multiple low-end FPGAs (Xilinx Spartan-6 XC6SLX16) to construct a simulation environment of a tile architecture. It increases the simulated step count (the number of simulated cycles per Node × the number of cores) par unit time with keeping its cycle-accuracy by increasing the number of used FPGA units. In other words, even increasing the number of cores in the target processor does not change the simulated cycle rate of chip per unit time.

The main contributions of this paper are:

- A description of two key schemes to achieve the scalable simulation speed and the abstraction of hardware functions of target architecture: 1) Local Barrier Synchronization and 2) Virtual Cycle.
- Evaluation and analysis of ScalableCore system versus a software-based simulator and existing FPGA platforms.
- A case study of a novel task allocation scheme on a tile architecture by using ScalableCore system.

2 Related Work

Accelerating processor simulations is a hot research topic for many-core processor eras. ISSGPU[6] is a parallelized software simulator to accelerate instruction set simulations (ISS) by leveraging inherent parallelisms of GPGPU; it achieved 100 fold speedup than standard software-based sequential simulators. Matteo[3] presented a methodology to efficiently simulate shared-memory many-core processors by separating a processor simulator into the instruction simulator and a timing simulator of many-cores. It demonstrated that the simulator achieved higher scalability of simulations in up to 1024 cores with some simulation speed degradation, a 30% drop. These simulators accomplished efficient simulations, but do not support important hardware components in processors such as NoC.

Additionally, several FPGA-based environments accelerating many-core (or multicore) simulations are proposed. Nehir[8] proposed an FPGA-based multi-core emulation system that supports run-time and compiler infrastructure by

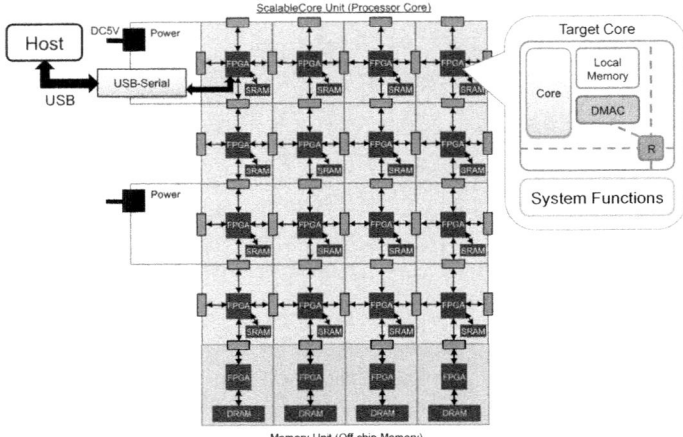

Fig. 2. Concept of ScalableCore system. Whole the FPGAs constitute a target processor (in this case, M-Core of 16 cores and 4 DRAM interfaces).

using open-source uniprocessor soft-core, which achieved about 3 fold speedup of simulations than M5 simulator[2]. As a major research that is employing a single large FPGA, RAMP Gold[10] simulates a many-core processor consisting of 64 cores with shared caches. In RAMP Gold, the simulation engine is separated into a functional model and a timing model for cache memory and off-chip memory, and each simulation unit is utilized in "host-multithreading" scheme for better function unit utilization. HASim[4] is able to model a shared memory multicore with 16 cores including core pipelines and cache hierarchy, and network on chip, using a single FPGA. HASim employs "time-multiplexing" scheme to scale the simulations and to emulate complex hardware function units taking multiple FPGA clock cycles.

These FPGA-based simulators are able to simulate faster and have better scalability of simulation speed than the software-based ones, however, they still have a simulation speed problem. In case increasing the number of cores in the simulation target, some overheads, such as a simulating thread synchronization and a cache memory pressure, bring on the degradation of simulation speeds. Additionally the simulated step count per core in unit time (or clock frequency of the simulation) degrades by increasing the core count. In order to keep the simulated step count per core in the target, we adopt corresponding amount FPGAs to the core count in the target processor for scalability of simulation speed.

3   ScalableCore System

3.1   Overall Concept and Architecture

We developed ScalableCore system 3.3 to emulate M-Core architecture shown in Fig.1 based on the concept to develop a scalable environment for tile architecture simulation[9]. Like Cell/B.E[1], M-Core is DMA-based tile architecture, but does

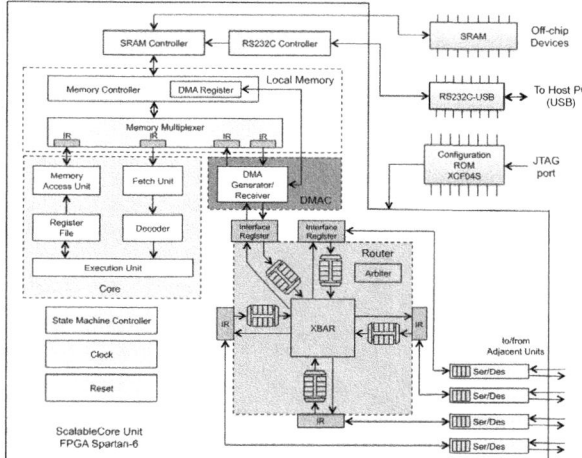

Fig. 3. Architecture of ScalableCore Unit. Target processor functions and some system functions are implemented on FPGA of each ScalableCore Unit.

not have caches. Every core communicates with the other cores and the off-chip memory via DMA transfers, but unlike Cell/B.E, interconnection on chip is a mesh NoC (network on chip). M-Core has a number of Nodes that is a set of Core (processor core), Router (on-chip router), DMAC (DMA controller) and Local Memory (core-local scratchpad memory). In the figure the number of Nodes is 16 but it is not restricted by the architecture, hence the other number is available.

Fig.2 shows an example structure of ScalableCore system to simulate a many-core processor with 16 processor cores and 4 off-chip memory interfaces. Whole the ScalableCore system emulate the many-core processor. In this case, the system consists of 16 ScalableCore Units (FPGA board with a Spartan-6 FPGA corresponding to a processor core, and an SRAM chip for core-local memory emulation) and 4 Memory Units (FPGA board with a Spartan-6 FPGA corresponding to a off-chip DRAM memory interface, and a DRAM chip). When simulating a processor consisting of 64 (8×8) cores with 4 DRAM controllers, for example, 64 (8×8) ScalableCore Units and 4 Memory Units are utilized.

One of key points of ScalableCore system is its connectivity: every ScalableCore Unit is connected to 4 neighbor ScalableCore Units (Up, Down, Left, Right), and communicate via bi-directional serial I/O ports of FPGA. ScalableCore system has no global signals through whole the system, and each ScalableCore Unit works under its own clock signal by own clock oscillator. Therefore the system is extendable for the target core count by increasing the number of ScalableCore Units with keeping the stability of system.

Applications running on the simulated processor are loaded via the USB-Serial controller from a host PC to the ScalableCore Unit in upper left in the figure, and simulation results are transferred to the host from the ScalableCore Unit. Power to drive the system is supplied from the edge on the system and is shared by the some rows of ScalableCore Units.

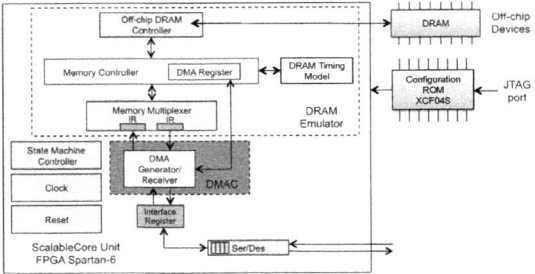

Fig. 4. Architecture of Memory Unit to emulate an off-chip DRAM controller

3.2   Architectures of ScalableCore Unit and Memory Unit

ScalableCore system consists of multiple ScalableCore Unit (FPGA node) with
processor core functions and some system level functions to control the system.
Fig.3 shows the architecture of ScalableCore Unit. Since our simulation target
in this study is M-Core which is a homogeneous many-core architecture, every
ScalableCore Unit uses the same FPGA circuit image (configuration file or bit
file). In this study, each ScalableCore Unit has 4 emulated functions of Node
in M-Core, Core, Router, DMAC and Local Memory. System functions in ScalableCore Unit support the system to emulate in cycle-accurate manner. As we
describe in the following sections, each FPGA emulate behavior of the target
core while taking synchronizations of simulation status with its 4 neighbor ScalableCore Units (Local Barrier Synchronization) via the Ser/Des components
with NRZI encoding and parity code. Since Ser/Des run faster than the other
components, asynchronous FIFOs are used in the boundaries between clock domains. Memory Multiplexer and State machine controller are important system
functions to virtualize the limited FPGA resources in time-multiplexing manner,
like A-Ports [5] (in this study we call it Virtual Cycle). SRAM controller, Clock
and Reset are basic functions of system.

In order to emulate off-chip memory, Memory Unit consisting of a DRAM emulation component instead of several processor core components in ScalableCore
Unit is used. Fig.4 shows the architecture of Memory Unit. Memory Unit has an
off-chip DRAM on the board, and uses a primitive DRAM controller of Spartan-6
hard macro. In order to provide adequate access latency of DRAM in the simulation world, this primitive DRAM controller is wrapped with a DRAM timing
model. DRAM timing model generate stall signal to control the Memory Controller for access latency emulation.

Following sections describes detailed rolls of the system functions.

3.3   System Level Functions

To satisfy the scalability and the cycle-accuracy of simulation, we present two
key schemes: Local Barrier Synchronization and Virtual Cycle.

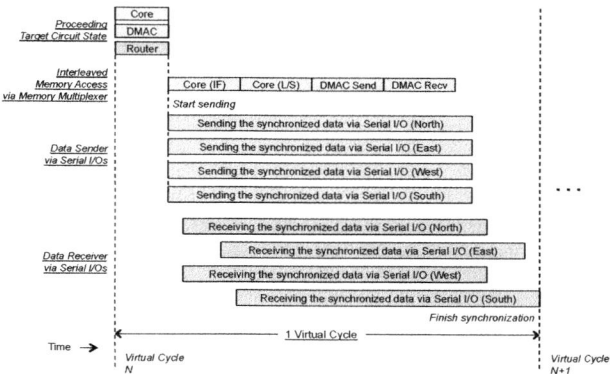

Fig. 5. Virtual Cycle. Behavior of target processor per cycle is emulated by comprising multiple FPGA clocks.

```
always @(posedge CLK or negedge RST_X) begin
    if(!RST_X) begin
        if_id_invalid <= 1;        When (EN == 1),
        if_id_pc <= 0;             update all flip-flops
    end else if(EN) begin
        if(!if_id_stall) begin
            if_id_invalid <= if_id_flush;
            if_id_pc <= icache_addr;
        end
    end
end
```

Fig. 6. Sample Code for target implementation. In order to control the update timing of flip-flops in the target, "EN" signal is inserted by user.

Local Barrier Synchronization. In order to obtain cycle-accurate simulation result, ScalableCore Unit needs to use the progressing newest simulation status to generate inter-Node dependent signals, such as output of on-chip routers. A simple way to make this is to take an all-to-all barrier operation with respect to each emulated cycle is proceeded on each ScalableCore Unit. However, to take an all-to-all operation is not realistic due to very large overhead to interfere the system scalability.

We decided to use a sophisticated way. Now we again consider the target architecture. The current ScalableCore system focuses on M-Core, tile architectures with mesh NoC. Therefore, to satisfy the cycle-accuracy, each ScalableCore Unit has to have newest simulation status of only its neighbor ScalableCore Units. Newest signal state of a simulated component generated at cycle N can propagate up to only its neighbors till the next cycle, cycle N+1. Therefore each ScalableCore Unit has to share among only its neighbor 4 ScalableCore Units (up, down, right, left) to satisfy the cycle accuracy. We named "Local Barrier Synchronization" for this minimum status synchronization scheme that enables to increase the number of target core count by increasing used ScalableCore Units without synchronization overhead increasing.

Virtual Cycle. Direct implementation of processor component is not easy due to FPGA resource characteristics and limitations [5]. As existing works, a clock cycle on FPGA does not correspond to a clock cycle on the target in ScalableCore system. To emulate a clock cycle of the target takes multiple clock cycle on FPGA in order to emulate complex hardware of the target like multi-port RAM. Additionally each ScalableCore Unit takes local barrier synchronization for each target clock cycle progression, and it takes some communication latency via Ser/Des components. We well scheduled these multi-cycle circuit emulations and the synchronizations for overwrapping these operations for the better simulation performance. We named "Virtual Cycle" for this time-multiplexed and well-scheduled emulation scheme. It makes easy to implement complex functions on an FPGA with keeping the simulation scalability. Fig.5 shows an example for timing chart of virtual cycle in ScalableCore Unit.

State machine controller in Fig.3 controls the emulated components in adequate timings (when and which). In the beginning of virtual cycle, the status of internal registers and output signals in target are emulated. Memory multiplexer, then, accesses to the memory controller by using the latest status in the target in order to emulate memory operations. We would like to emulate 4-port (Core instruction fetch, Core load/store, DMAC read, DMAC write) local memory, however, actual implemented functions for local memory is 1-port memory controller with DMA control registers and memory-mapped registers by using off-chip SRAM. Hence the memory multiplexer has 4 accessing ports, and processes their requests in time-division multiplex manner to functionally expand the memory port. At the same time, the latest simulation data is delivered to the neighbors in local barrier synchronization. Every ScalableCore Unit runs under its own clock signal, hence the timings of data transfers have some variability for each transfer. In the end of a virtual cycle, state machine controller wait for all simulation data transfers and memory accessing to be done. At this time, the ScalableCore Unit can use the newest simulation data of the neighbors. Finally, it goes to the next cycle in the target. In this way, emulated hardware can use correct information to satisfy the cycle-accuracy.

Simulation state is defined as output of emulated hardware, such as flip-flops and wires. To update at the certain timing using correct simulation state, an emulated component has a special input signal. Fig.6 shows a sample code of emulated component in Verilog HDL. Update statements for flip-flops (always statement in Verilog HDL) have an "if(EN)" rule. "EN" is an input signal to drive the update statements by state machine controller at the beginning of a virtual cycle. Additionally, to avoid propagating newest output state of emulated hardware to the other hardware components before the next virtual cycle, interface registers (IR in Fig.3) are inserted in boundaries of hardware components. Then values of them are updated at the end of a virtual cycle.

3.4   System Behavior

Users can control and read the output of the ScalableCore system by homemade Python script from a host Linux computer via USB-serial IC. An application

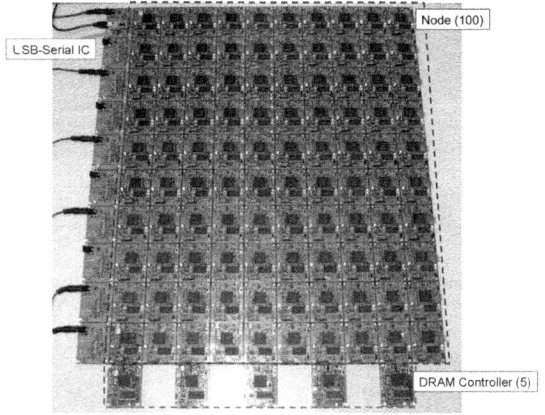

(b) ScalableCore Unit (Left)
and Memory Unit (Right)

(a) Snapshot of ScalableCore System 3.3 with 100
Spartan-6 FPGAs

Fig. 7. Snapshot of ScalableCore System 3.3 with 100 Spartan-6 FPGAs, ScalableCore Unit and Memory Unit. The system simulate M-Core processor consisting of 100 Nodes and 5 off-chip memory controllers.

program running on emulated hardware is loaded from the host to the SRAM on upper left ScalableCore Unit in the system. After the program loading, each ScalableCore Unit in the system begins detecting dynamically the existence of its neighbor ScalableCore Units. Every ScalableCore Unit sends certain amount of special bit streams by driving Ser/Des outputs. When it received a special bit stream, the receiving port is registered as a living port, which is used for local barrier synchronization in every virtual cycle. This flow brings the flexibility of the system size. After the detection of existence, upper left ScalableCore Unit delivers memory image to be executed on each ScalableCore Unit to others, and sends a start signal of simulation to them.

3.5   Implementation of ScalableCore System with 100 FPGAs

Fig.7 (a) shows a snapshot of ScalableCore system 3.3 consisting of 100 ScalableCore Units. The overall size of the system employing 100 ScalableCore Units is 46.7cm × 60cm. A ScalableCore Unit is a card-sized, 4.67cm × 6.0cm, FPGA board with Xilinx Spartan-6 XC6SLX16 (Speed Grade -2), a 512KB (1-port, 8 bit × 512K entry) SRAM and a configuration ROM Xilinx XCF04S shown in left of Fig.7 (b). A ScalableCore Unit also has a JTAG port to write circuit information for FPGA and configuration ROM. Several FPGA's I/O ports are assigned to external I/O pins in edge of board to communicate the neighbors. To drive the system of 100 units uses five DC 5V power supplies.

We used Xilinx ISE 12.4 for development. The main clock rate is 40MHz and the Ser/Des clock rate is 80MHz. Table.1 describes the micro architecture of the target processor, M-Core. Core is a simple single-issue pipeline core without

Table 1. Micro Architecture of Simulation Target

Core	MIPS32 ISA, 5-stage, Single-issue, Memory access port: 2 (Fetch, Load/Store)
DMA Controller	Memory access port: 2 (32-bit DMA Read, 32-bit DMA Write)
Router	5-input/output (North, East, West, South, Core), 4-stage
	(NRC and VA: Next Routing Computation and Virtual Channel Allocation,
	SA: Switch Allocation, ST: Switch Traversal, LT: Link Traversal),
	2-Virtual-Channel, FIFO depth: 4, Credit-base flow control
Local Memory	Access Latency: 1, 512KB, 32-bit 4-port
	(Core Fetch, Core Load/Store, DMA Read, DMA Write)
# Node	Variable
# Memory Interface	Variable

floating point units (it's future work). Router has advanced micro architecture, 4-stage and 2-VC, for use in NoC-oriented research. DMA Controller has 2-port for DMA read and DMA write to local memory.

4   Evaluation

4.1   Resource Usage

Fig.8 depicts the Spatan-6 XC6SLX16 floor plan of post place-and-route of ScalableCore Unit that target processor core components (Core, DMAC, Router, Local Memory) are implemented. Table.2 shows the detailed breakdown of resource usage. Note that the resource usage of Local Memory is comprised in the Memory Controller and the system functions, because the local memory is mapped to the off-chip SRAM. 84% of LUTs and 29% registers of Spartan-6 XC6SLX16 FPGA are utilized for the target implementation and the system functions. The target functions use 5429 LUTs and 2585 registers; LUTs are consumed than registers due to direct implementation of target functions. Router consumes especially uses LUTs more than registers because on-chip router contains a lot of wires for arbitration of switch and channel. The system functions use 1700 LUTs and 2693 registers; registers are used than LUTs due to memory multiplexer and interface registers to separate the emulated components. 20% of LUTs and 15% registers of entire Spartan-6 XC6SLX16 FPGA are used for the system functions. This resource usage is not so serious.

4.2   Simulation Speed

We evaluated the simulation speed of ScalableCore system 3.3 by compared to SimMc, the corresponding cycle-accurate software simulator for M-Core. SimMc we used models the same detailed micro-architecture of M-Core as we described above, excepting the flow-control of Router; SimMc's flow-control is Xon/Xoff. We measured the simulation speed of SimMc running on a standard computer of Intel Core i7 870 and 4GB memory, which is compiled by gcc 4.5.2 (optimization option: -O3) on Ubuntu server 11.04.

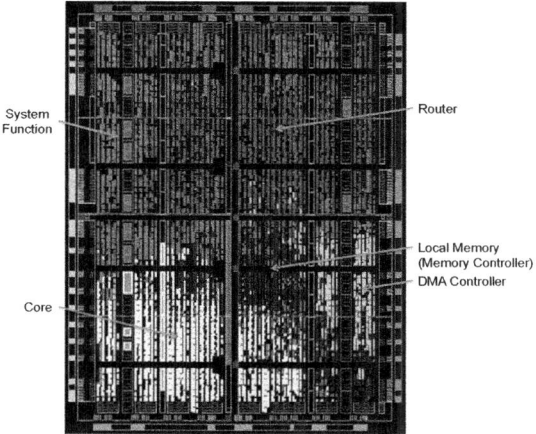

System
Function

Router

Local Memory
(Memory Controller)
DMA Controller

Core

Fig. 8. ScalableCore Unit floorplan on Spartan-6 XC6SLX16 device

Table 2. ScalableCore Unit resource utilization

Module	LUT	Register	BRAM	LUTRAM	DSP
System Function	1700	2693	16	0	0
Core	1910	713	3	0	6
DMA Controller	444	378	0	0	0
Memory Controller	590	535	0	0	0
Router	2475	959	0	280	0
Target Total	5429	2585	3	280	6
Total	7129	5278	19	280	6
Percent Utilization	84%	29%	31%	Nan	6%

We tested two benchmarks for M-Core: N-Queen (NQ) and Matrix Multiply (MM). N-Queen is a highly parallelized application of master-worker model with a few DMA communications. Matrix Multiply has a lot of DMA communications among the Nodes than N-Queen. Fig.9 (a) shows the simulation speeds of SimMc and ScalableCore system 3.3. Simulation speed is represented in simulation step count proceed in unit time [KHz]. Increasing the Node count in the target processor decreases the speed of SimMc because SimMc is not parallelized for its readability and customizability (even if parallelized, barrier for cycle-accuracy brings big overhead); SimMc achieved 90 KHz in 16-Nodes simulation of N-Queen, but decreases to 8.9 KHz in 100-Nodes simulation of N-Queen. In contrast, the result of ScalableCore system shows the key characteristic, scalability to the core count. It achieved constant simulation speed, 1142 KHz in the all cases without effects of application behaviors. To give emulation result of 1 cycle in the target processor, it takes about 35 FPGA clock cycles for update of target circuit state, memory emulation and synchronization of simulation status.

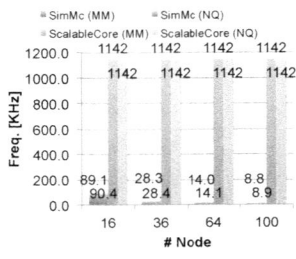 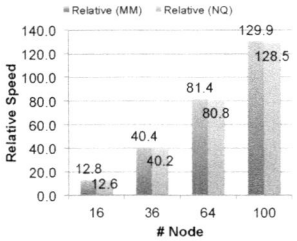

(a) Simulation Frequency [KHz]   (b) Relative Speed

Fig. 9. Simulation speed comparison. MM: Matrix Multiply (containing much commu-niactions), NQ: N-Queen (containing a few communications).

It does not depend the application behaviors and the core count, by adoption of local barrier synchronization and virtual cycle.

Fig.9 (b) shows the relative speed of the ScalableCore system to the SimMc. Increasing the number of cores in the target super-linearly decreases the simu-lation frequency of SimMc, however, the simulation frequency of ScalableCore system is not changed. In 16-Nodes simulation, the ScalableCore system runs at 12.6 fold faster than the SimMc, and the relative speed increases with the core count increases. In 100-Nodes simulation, the system peaks 129 fold simulation speed of SimMc. It enables a longer simulation.

In respect of absolute simulation speed, ScalableCore system has an advan-tage. HASim[4], FPGA-based multicore simulator employing fine-grain time-multiplexing scheme, achieves up to 3.2 MHz at the maximum, 160KHz at the minimum and 625KHz on the average in 16-cores simulation. Although not ac-curate due to some differences in processor architecture, micro-architecture, and complexity of processor core, the result shows that ScalableCore system achieves higher simulation rate on the average.

5   Case Study: Task Allocation on Tile Architecture

Since task allocation (or thread allocation) is one of distinct factors to affect application performance and processor throughput. However, to determine a task mapping for better performance on the many-core processor is not easy due to its large exploration field. We have proposed a pattern-based lightweight scheme of task allocation to improve the performance; RMAP[7]. We evaluated the impact of RMAP scheme for M-Core by running larger applications on the ScalableCore system of 100-Nodes. This simulation takes about 20 minutes. If it is simulated on the SimMc, it takes about 43 hours.

Parallel applications have some fragments of network traffic along of appli-cation behavior; at one phase, the application has low network usage, but at other phase, it has high network usage. Key idea of RMAP to improve the per-formance is to reduce self-contention of network (additional network contention

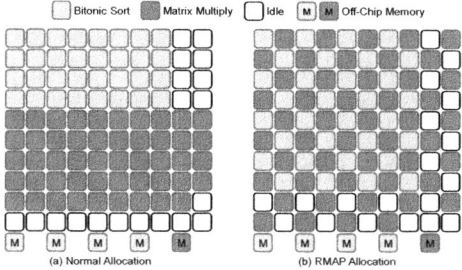

Fig. 10. Case Study: Task Allocation of Paraallel Application. (a) Noarmal Allocation, (b) Pattern Based Task Allocation (RMAP).

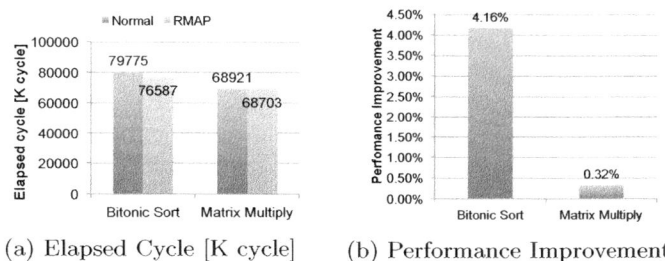

(a) Elapsed Cycle [K cycle]   (b) Performance Improvement

Fig. 11. Application Performance and Performance Improvement

by communications traffic of own application) by allocating together with other applications with different network behaviors. Fig.10 shows a normal task allocation (a) and a RMAP allocation (b) we used for this case study. We used two parallel applications: Bitonic sort and Matrix Multiply. Bitonic sort is network-intensive workload, heavier than matrix multiply. In normal task allocation, threads of each application are mapped separately to each group of Nodes. In contrast, in RMAP task allocation, threads of two applications are mixed and mapped. Location of each application forms one solution of N-Rook problem, as shown in Fig.10 (b). When one application consumes network bandwidth a lot and the other does not, the bi-section bandwidth for the network-consuming application is temporally increased by RMAP mapping.

Fig.11 shows (a) the application performances of each application in two task allocations and (b) the performance improvement by RMAP. The performance of bitonic sort is improved at 4% by RMAP because the serious self-contention of bitonic sort is eliminated in RMAP allocation. In contrast, the performance of matrix multiply is improved at 0.32% because matrix multiply does not originally have such serious self-contention.

6   Conclusion

In this paper we described ScalableCore system 3.3, a scalable cycle-accurate FPGA-based simulator for a tile architecture with mesh NoC. The system employs the multiple low-end FPGAs to construct a simulation environment of tile architectures. We presented two key schemes to achieve the scalable simulation speed and the abstraction of hardware functions of target architecture. We showed the simulation performance of the ScalableCore system. In 100-Node simulation, the ScalableCore system achieved 129 times faster simulation rate than the software simulator, which enables longer simulation than the software simulator.

Finally, we describe the future works. In order to efficiently simulate in different configurations of architecture, we want to consider a scheme to easily configure the parameters of architecture in the initialization of simulations. In order to handle a much greater number of cores, we want to consider time-multiplex techniques similar to those used in other studies.

References

1. Cell broadband engine, http://cell.scei.co.jp/
2. Binkert, N.L., Dreslinski, R.G., Hsu, L.R., Lim, K.T., Saidi, A.G., Reinhardt, S.K.: The M5 Simulator: Modeling Networked Systems. IEEE Micro 26, 52–60 (2006)
3. Monchiero, M.: How to simulate 1000 cores. SIGARCH Comput. Archit. News 37, 10–19 (2009)
4. Pellauer, M., Adler, M., Kinsy, M., Parashar, A., Emer, J.: Hasim: Fpga-based high-detail multicore simulation using time-division multiplexing. In: 2011 IEEE 17th International Symposium on High Performance Computer Architecture (HPCA), pp. 406–417 (February 2011)
5. Pellauer, M., Vijayaraghavan, M., Adler, M., Arvind, Emer, J.: A-ports: an efficient abstraction for cycle-accurate performance models on fpgas. In: Proceedings of the 16th International ACM/SIGDA Symposium on Field Programmable Gate Arrays, FPGA 2008, pp. 87–96. ACM, New York (2008)
6. Raghav, S., Ruggiero, M., Atienza, D., Pinto, C., Marongiu, A., Benini, L.: Scalable instruction set simulator for thousand-core architectures running on gpgpus. In: 2010 International Conference on High Performance Computing and Simulation (HPCS), pp. 459–466 (2010)
7. Sano, S., Sano, M., Sato, S., Miyoshi, T., Kise, K.: Pattern-based systematic task mapping for many-core processors. In: 2010 First International Conference on Networking and Computing (ICNC), pp. 173–178 (November 2010)
8. Sonmez, N., Arcas, O., Sayilar, G., Unsal, O., Cristal, A., Hur, I., Singh, S., Valero, M.: From Plasma to BeeFarm: Design Experience of an FPGA-Based Multicore Prototype. In: Koch, A., Krishnamurthy, R., McAllister, J., Woods, R., El-Ghazawi, T. (eds.) ARC 2011. LNCS, vol. 6578, pp. 350–362. Springer, Heidelberg (2011)
9. Takamaeda-Yamazaki, S., Sasakawa, R., Sakaguchi, Y., Kise, K.: An FPGA-based scalable simulation accelerator for tile architectures. SIGARCH Comput. Archit. News 39, 38–43 (2011)
10. Tan, Z., Waterman, A., Avizienis, R., Lee, Y., Cook, H., Patterson, D., Asanović, K.: RAMP gold: an FPGA-based architecture simulator for multiprocessors. In: DAC 2010: Proceedings of the 47th Design Automation Conference, pp. 463–468. ACM, New York (2010)
11. Uehara, K., Sato, S., Miyoshi, T., Kise, K.: A Study of an Infrastructure for Research and Development of Many-Core Processors. In: Workshop on Ultra Performance and Dependable Acceleration Systems Held in Conjunction with PDCAT 2009, pp. 414–419 (2009)

Scalable Memory Hierarchies for Embedded Manycore Systems

Sen Ma, Miaoqing Huang, Eugene Cartwright, and David Andrews

Department of Computer Science and Computer Engineering
University of Arkansas
{senma,mqhuang,eugene,dandrews}@uark.edu

Abstract. As the size of FPGA devices grows following Moore's law, it becomes possible to put a complete manycore system onto a single FPGA chip. The centralized memory hierarchy on typical embedded systems in which both data and instructions are stored in the off-chip global memory will introduce the bus contention problem as the number of processing cores increases. In this work, we present our exploration into how distributed multi-tiered memory hierarchies can effect the scalability of manycore systems. We use the Xilinx Virtex FPGA devices as the testing platforms and the buses as the interconnect. Several variances of the centralized memory hierarchy and the distributed memory hierarchy are compared by running various benchmarks, including matrix multiplication, IDEA encryption and 3D FFT. The results demonstrate the good scalability of the distributed memory hierarchy for systems up to 32 MicroBlaze processors, which is constrained by the FPGA resources on the Virtex-6LX240T device.

Keywords: Distributed memory hierarchy, manycore architecture, embedded system.

1 Introduction

Current FPGA densities have reached the Million LUT level, allowing a complete multiprocessor system on programmable chip (MPSoPC) to be configured within a single device. While FPGA density still lags CMOS ASIC's, the malleability of the FPGA fabric provides system designers the flexibility in mixing and matching different types of processors and computational components, tailored to the requirements of each individual application. The use of FPGA's as programmable multiprocessor systems on programmable chips instead of point design custom accelerators has been further enabled by the availability of necessary soft IP system components such as standard busses, soft processors with caches, and multi-port memory controllers. As an example, Xilinx's Microblaze soft processor hosts several standard bus interconnections such as the Processor Local Bus (PLB), XCL bus, Local Memory Bus (LMB), and a Multi-Port Memory Controller (MPMC). The MPMC enables the creation of a Symmetric Multiprocessor (SMP) shared memory architecture for up to 7 processors plus

O.C.S. Choy et al. (Eds.): ARC 2012, LNCS 7199, pp. 151–162, 2012.

standard bus interconnection. FPGA fabrication technology continues to follow Moore's law and vendors are promoting next generation devices where the number of processors along with transistors will double every 18 months. This fabrication capability promises future systems with 100's to 1,000's of processors integrated within a single chip. This capability promises significant advancements in scalability, portability, and design reuse. Scalable performance can be achieved through the use of parallel programming models and software design flows instead of more tedious and time consuming custom circuit designs. Design space exploration can occur through re-compilation instead of re-synthesis. Importantly MPSoPC's composed of standard bus and memory hierarchies and programmable processors will bring significant increases in design portability between logic families and across chip generations.

A key aspect of enabling this vision is the ability to support the new class of programming models emerging for manycore chips with scalable numbers of processors. Historically, programming models evolved as abstractions for existing architectures. The asynchronous multithreaded programming model has become popular for shared memory parallel machines. The multithreaded programming model is a suitable abstraction for multiprocessor systems with linear global address spaces, or systems in which all processors have visibility and access to the complete memory system. While models based on linear global address spaces are adequate for SMP architectures, the SMP architectures themselves have known scalability issues. Recently, interest has once again peaked in traditional non-uniform distributed memory hierarchies due to their ability to eliminate the classic SMP bottleneck associated with a global bus and single shared global memory. Unfortunately newly emerging multi-tiered memory hierarchies break the linear global address space assumption upon which many of our historic programming models are based. New programming models such as OpenCL are beginning to emerge as more suitable abstractions for the multi-tiered distributed memory hierarchies anticipated for manycores with 100's to 1,000's of processors. Within this new class of programming models, processors do not have visibility or access to all memory locations. In a significant departure with prior models, the memory hierarchy is no longer hidden under layers of abstractions and instead is now explicitly exposed to the programmer. Program execution times can depend on how well programmers understand and manage marshaling of data between memory tiers and address ranges. Explicit movement of program instructions between memory tiers also unfortunately eliminates the benefits of implicit transfer of instructions between memory and traditional cache organizations that occurred transparently under the global linear address abstractions. Still, the multi-tiered distributed memory hierarchies show promise for scalability and increased processor-memory bandwidth type metrics over much "flatter" SMP systems with caches. The challenge in enabling these next generation programming models for MPSoPC's is to provide necessary run time system services, processing resources, and multi-tiered memory hierarchy structures upon which the models rely.

Table 1. Characteristics of 5 Memory Hierarchies

Memory Hierarchies	Instructions	Data	Test Outcomes
1	SMP	No cache	No cache	Base case
2		Cached		Caching instructions
3	Hybrid			Distributed data access
4	Distributed	Distributed (PLB bus)		Bus latency
5	2-tiered	Distributed (LMB bus)		

In this paper, we present our exploration into how multi-tiered memory hierarchies can effect the scalability of systems with 100's to 1,000's of processors. New programming models such as OpenCL introduce new sets of system service calls layered on top of existing asynchronous multithreaded programming model infrastructure such as pthreads. For our explorations we take the same approach and build additional system service calls on top of our hthreads microkernel [6]. Hthreads was developed as a unifying abstraction within which designers could develop threads that run as custom hardware accelerators and software threads, as well as software threads running across heterogenous mixes of processors within an SMP model. Hthreads provides a full set of pthreads compliant run time system services for thread synchronization, management, and scheduling operations. Hthreads is structured as a hardware/software co-designed microkernel, and has been implemented on Xilinx family FPGA's. A detailed description of hthreads and it's prior uses can be found in [6]. For this work, hthreads allows direct comparison of a high level application running on SMP+cache based systems and with additional system service wrappers, distributed multi-tiered memory hierarchies with explicit data marshaling. We provide direct comparisons for systems with up to 6 slave processors, the limit of current MPMC components. We then provide evaluations for the same applications and system services running on different multi-tiered memory hierarchy configurations with up to 32 processors, the limit of our current FPGA components. An important outcome of our work is an analysis of how different configurations of multi-tiered memory hierarchies effect overall application run time performance, and an analysis on the effects of both weak and strong scalability. Our results represent actual run times of the applications and our system services, and not theoretical results predicated with simplifying assumptions.

2   Memory Hierarchies

We are interested in the five memory hierarchies listed in Table 1 and shown in Fig. 1. The first two memory hierarchies 1,2 represent traditional centralized global memories from our SMP architectures. The last two hierarchies 4,5 are distributed memory hierarchies. Memory hierarchy 3 is a hybrid, with instructions being centralized in the global memory and data being distributed within local memories. All five memory hierarchies are implemented on Xilinx FPGA

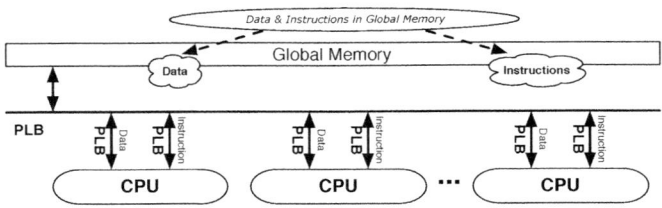

(a) Memory hierarchy 1: shared memory for both data and instructions

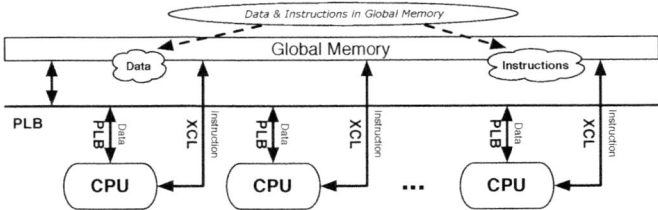

(b) Memory hierarchy 2: shared memory for both data and instructions with i-cache

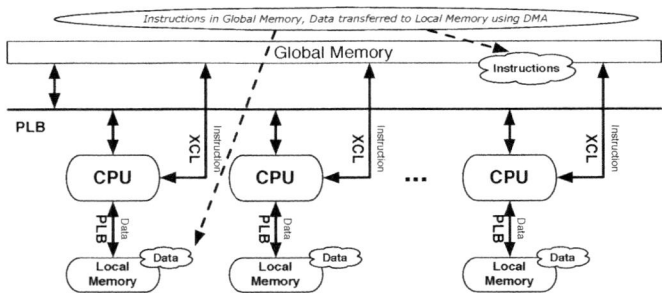

(c) Memory hierarchy 3: distributed memory for data and shared memory for instructions

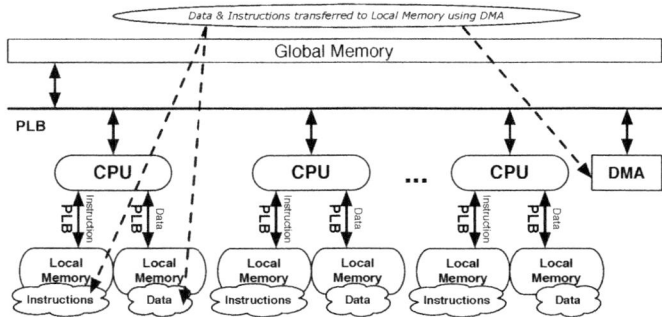

(d) Memory hierarchy 4: distributed memory for both data and instructions with slow local bus

Fig. 1. Various memory hierarchies

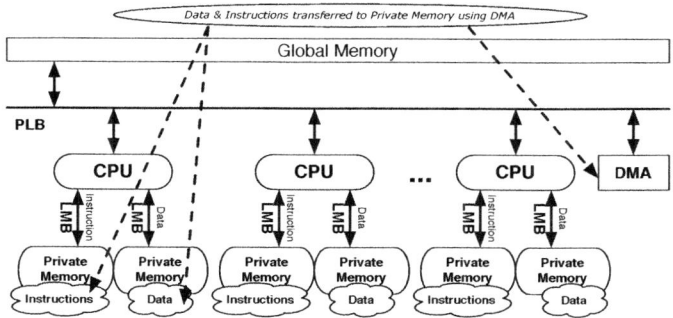

(e) Memory hierarchy 5: distributed memory for both data and instructions with fast local bus.

Fig. 1. (*Continued*)

ML-507 or ML605 boards, with off-chip DRAM used for global main memory. Local memories are implemented using distributed BRAMs. In all cases, data and instructions are originally stored in the main memory. Final results are saved in the main memory as well. In all memory hierarchies the off-chip main memory is connected to the main PLB bus through one MPMC port.

- In Memory Hierarchy 1 (Fig. 1(a)) both instruction port and data port of each MicroBlaze processor are connected to the PLB bus.
- In Memory Hierarchy 2 (Fig. 1(b)) the instruction port of each Microblaze is connected directly to one MPMC port. Processor data ports are connected to the PLB bus. The instruction cache uses the Xilinx CachLink (XCL).
- In Memory Hierarchy 3 (Fig. 1(c)) each instruction port is still connected to the off-chip main memory through an MPMC port. The instruction cache uses XCL. However, the data port is connected to a local memory module (through a local PLB connection). Before processing occurs, data are transferred using DMA from the main memory to the local memory. Final result data are transferred back to the off-chip memory later using DMA.
- In Memory Hierarchy 4 (Fig. 1(d)) both instruction port and data port of each MicroBlaze processor are connected to a local memory through separate PLB busses. Before processing occurs, data and instructions are transferred from the off-chip memory to local memory modules using DMA. Final result data are transferred back to the off-chip memory using DMA after the computation finishes.
- Memory Hierarchy 5 (Fig. 1(e)) is similar to memory hierarchy 4 with the exception that LMB busses replace PLB busses as connections between local memories and MicroBlaze processors.

Note that within the current EDK tools used, caches for each Microblaze require the use of XCL links connected directly to the MPMC port. Therefore, the data caches were turned off in Memory Hierarchies 1,2.

3   Experiments and Results

3.1   Experimental Setup

All application programs were configured to operate in a master-slave mode. A main program runs on the master processor and distributes work loads to slave, or worker processors. The PowerPC on the ML507 and a MicroBlaze on the ML605 serve as the master processors, respectively. Each master processor has a direct connection to one of the MPMC ports with instruction cache enabled. The data port of the master processor is connected to the main PLB bus. Work loads are distributed to each worker processor as a single thread kernel function. Each thread kernel function is compiled into a thread ELF (Executable and Linkable Format) file. This ELF file is stored in the main memory before execution. The start address and the size of the ELF file are given to the DMA engine that transfers kernel functions into local memory. The master processor is only responsible for creating the worker threads and initiating DMA transfers between the main memory and local memories.

3.2   Weak Scalability Analysis

Our first analysis concerns how the memory hierarchy effects the notion of weak scalability. Weak scaling defines how execution time varies when the computational load is linearly increased with the number of processors. In the ideal case, given a work load W on one processor, the work load for N processors should be NW, which is evenly divided in N processors. We chose matrix multiplication and IDEA (International Data Encryption Algorithm) encryption as representative applications to evaluate weak scalability. We implemented both matrix multiplication and IDEA encryption on a Xilinx ML507 board containing a Virtex-5FX70T device. Matrix multiplication is the representative of applications in which memory is frequently accessed for input data. Conversely, IDEA encryption is a more instruction-intensive application in which a series of eight identical transformations and an output transformation are performed for each 64-bit plaintext input, resulting in the generation of a 64-bit ciphertext. We use both benchmarks to comprehensively test the 5 different memory hierarchies for up to 6 worker threads, the limit of the MPMC for memory hierarchies 2,3. Fig. 2 shows the run time results.

In the matrix multiplication application, each node is given two 20×20 matrices, A and B, in which each element is a 32-bit integer. The computation involves $C = A \times B$ and $D = B \times A$. For distributed memory configurations A and B data arrays are transferred from the main memory to the local memory using DMA. Correspondingly, the C and D arrays are transferred back to the main memory. The volume of each DMA transfer is 3,200 bytes with a latency of approximately 50 μs. The kernel size of matrix multiplication is 2,520 bytes with a transfer latency of approximately 40 μs. For IDEA encryption, the size of both the plaintext and ciphertext is 3,200 bytes. The data transfer latencies are the same as in matrix multiplication. The kernel size of IDEA is 3,468 bytes with a DMA transfer latency of approximately 55 μs.

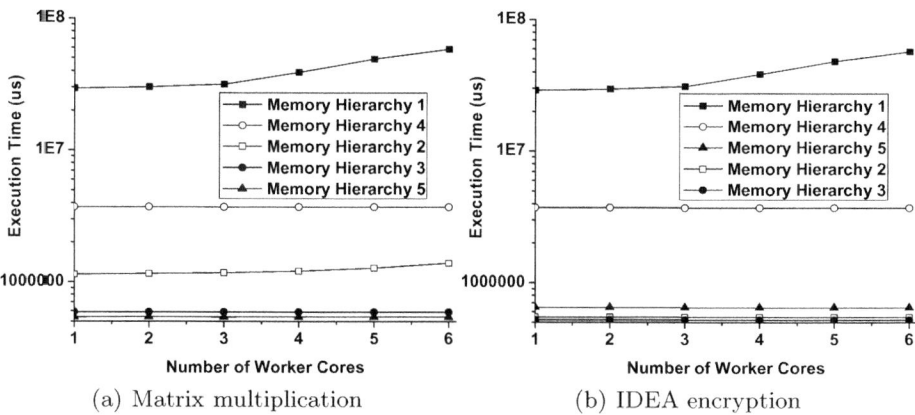

(a) Matrix multiplication   (b) IDEA encryption

Fig. 2. Performance comparison of benchmarks on 5 memory hierarchies (Note: (1) Instruction cache size: 8KB, local memory size: 8KB; (2) Matrix multiplication kernel size: 2,520 bytes, IDEA kernel size: 3,468 bytes; (3) DMA transfer time: data in $\rightarrow$ 50 μs, data out $\rightarrow$ 50 μs, instructions $\rightarrow$ 40 μs (matrix multiplication) / 55 μs (IDEA)).

Memory Hierarchy 1. For scalable systems, the end-to-end computation time should be approximately the same when the number of cores grows. In Fig. 2, Memory Hierarchy 1 exhibits the worst scalability. This is expected for SMP systems with no data or instruction caches. All memory requests are through a common bus. A system with a single worker core takes 29 seconds to finish the computation for both applications. The computation time then grows nonlinearly as more cores are added into the system. The computation time almost doubles for the 6-core system. Clearly traffic contention on the main PLB bus, and the contention for the centralized memory contributes to the nonscalability of this memory architecture.

Memory Hierarchy 2. In Memory Architecture 2, the instruction cache is enabled and connected to the global memory through the MPMC. A cache size of 8 KB is sufficient to accommodate all instructions of both applications. Thus only compulsory and conflict cache misses occur but no misses due to capacity. Bus contention on the main PLB bus is now only due to data requests. For both applications, the computation time is dramatically reduced compared with the first architecture. However, the matrix multiplication and IDEA applications demonstrate different performance trends. For matrix multiplication, the computation time continues to grow as the number of cores increases, with the growth at times exhibiting nonlinearity. Matrix multiplication is a data-intensive application in which the computation of one element in the result matrix involves reading one row and one column from the two source matrices. Thus the nonlinearity can be primarily attributed to the increased contention on the main PLB bus. On the other hand, the IDEA is a computation-intensive application. Since there are only 400 64-bit plaintexts, each processor generates 400 memory read and 400 memory write requests each of which is of 8 bytes. This represents a low volume

Table 2. Performance Comparison of Various Instruction Cache Sizes on Memory Architecture 3 (unit: μs)

Number of Worker Core	Matrix Multiplication*			IDEA**		
	Instruction Cache Size (byte)			Instruction Cache Size (byte)		
	256	1024	8192	256	1024	8192
1	1,602,136	589,413	589,405	2,493,714	825,241	520,919
6	2,062,022	1,474,003	590,093	3,680,123	1,164,336	521,660

* Matrix multiplication kernel size: 2,520 bytes.
** IDEA kernel size: 3,468 bytes.

of data transfer and will not result in any significant bus contention. For Memory Hierarchy 2 instructions are stored in the off-chip memory and are transferred into the cache largely due to compulsory misses during startup. The small size of the IDEA program will fit entirely into the cache. With minimal data contention and the use of the instruction cache, the IDEA encryption application demonstrates good scalability on Memory Architecture 2. The combined results show how even moderate contention across a single bus effects scalability.

Memory Hierarchy 3. In Memory Hierarchy 3, each worker core is equipped with an 8 KB local memory connected across a PLB bus. The instruction port of each core is connected to a cache and global memory through the MPMC. The results shown in Fig. 2 indicate good performance scalability for both applications. The total execution time increases by approximately 100 μs for each additional core. The 100 μs increases are contributed to the data transfer latencies between off-chip global memory and the local memory. Although this memory hierarchy is still centralized from the point of view of the instructions, it is distributed during the runtime. The 8KB cache is bigger than both application kernels. Therefore, all instruction accesses take place locally once the entire kernel is loaded into the cache. However, in normal cases, the cache is typically smaller than an application so that frequent memory access would be required during runtime. Table 2 shows the performance results for both applications for different cache sizes. The results show how execution time increases when the cache size decreases. This increase is more evident for the computation-intensive IDEA application. For both the matrix multiplication and IDEA encryption applications, Memory Hierarchy 3 loses the scalability when the cache size is reduced below what is necessary to eliminate capacity misses. As an example the execution time for the 6-core system running IDEA is 50% more than the 1-core system.

Memory Hierarchies 4,5. Both Memory Hierarchies 4,5 are distributed 2-tiered memory architectures in which both data and instructions are DMA'ed to local memories. The only difference between the two hierarchies is the type of local bus used to connect the processor to the local memory. Both the LMB-based and PLB-based architectures exhibit good scalability with the LMB slightly better. The slight increase in execution times for increased numbers of cores

Table 3. Performance Comparison of Various Options of Local Busses on a 1-core System (unit: μs)

Application	Data local bus - Instruction local bus			
	PLB-PLB	LMB-PLB	PLB-LMB	LMB-LMB
Matrix Multiplication	3,730,825	3,725,673	614,080	541,154
IDEA	3,745,240	3,744,717	653,599	648,696

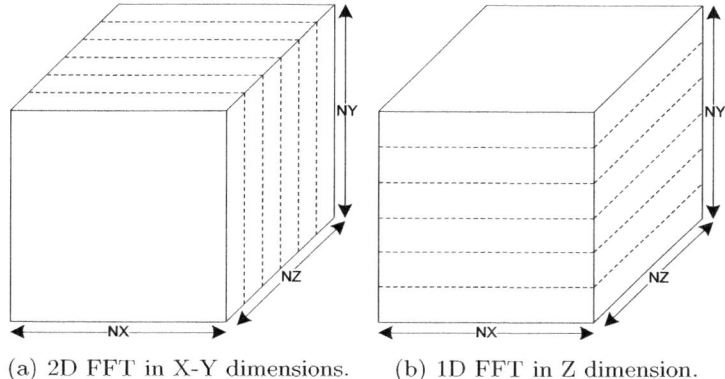

(a) 2D FFT in X-Y dimensions.   (b) 1D FFT in Z dimension.

Fig. 3. Two steps in 3D FFT

is mainly attributed to the additional data and instruction transfer latencies. Table 3 shows the timing results for the four different configurations of busses between local memory and the data and instruction ports of the MicroBlaze processor. First, no significant difference is observed between using a PLB or LMB bus configuration to the data port. For both applications, the difference is very small when different data bus is used while the instruction bus is the same. Conversely, the use of LMB in place of a PLB for the instruction bus shows significantly reduced execution times. Overall, Memory Hierarchy 5 demonstrates the best performance and scalability for all 5 hierarchies listed in Table 1. Particularly, the MPMC cannot support a system in which the number of worker nodes is bigger than 6. Therefore, Memory Hierarchy 5 is adopted in the study of strong scalability in which a 3D FFT is carried out on system up to 32 cores. Due to the limited resource on Virtex-5FX70T device, the 3D FFT is implemented on a Virtex-6LX240T device on the Xilinx ML605 board.

3.3   Strong Scalability Analysis

As shown in Fig. 3, the computation of 3D FFT can be performed in two steps. In the first step, the FFT along X and Y dimensions are carried out. The data are distributed to individual processors along the Z dimension. Once the computation of the first step finishes, an all-to-all data transpose are carried out to re-distribute the data along the Y dimension. In a typical case, this all-to-all

Table 4. Performance Results of 3D FFT on 3 Different Platforms of Memory Hierarchy 5 (unit: μs)

Number of Worker Cores	Performance Breakdown in 7 Stages						
	DMA_D(ata) D(ram)2B(ram)	DMA_I(str.) D2B	Kernel 2D	DMA_D B2D	DMA_D D2B	Kernel 1D	DMA_D B2D
4	3,822	557	1,944,370	4,101	3,690	771,932	4,108
16	4,388	1,898	486,651	4,813	4,385	178,565	4,818
32	4,501	3,653	247,842	4,987	4,525	93,848	5,004

	Total Execution time*	Data Size for Each Core	Kernel Size
4	2,987,148	65,788 bytes	8,124 bytes
16	963,412	16,636 bytes	7,056 bytes
32	693,361	8,444 bytes	6,836 bytes

* The matrix initialization time and the global data transpose time are not listed in the breakdown, but are counted in the total execution time. Both operations are carried out by the master processor.

transpose should be carried out in all threads in which one thread sends the proper data to other $N - 1$ threads and receives the data from them as well. In our case, the all-to-all transpose is carried out by the master node. The whole computation can be divided into the following stages:

(1) The data of X-Y plane(s) are sent to worker processors;
(2) The kernel instructions are sent to worker processors;
(3) The worker processors compute the 2D FFT separately;
(4) The results of 2D FFT are transferred back to the off-chip memory;
(5) The data along the Y dimension are sent to the worker processors;
(6) The worker processors compute the 1D FFT separately;
(7) The results of 1D FFT are sent back to the main memory.

The same kernel can compute both 2D FFT and 1D FFT. In order to reduce the kernel size, the computation of sin and cos functions is realized using lookup tables.

The size of the 3D matrix is fixed at $32 \times 32 \times 32$. Each element consists of the real part and the imaginary part, each of which is presented in the single precision floating-point precision. Three different manycore systems of Memory Hierarchy 5 are implemented and the performances are summarized in Table 4. As shown in the table, the kernel execution times for both 2D FFT and 1D FFT are linearly reduced as the number of worker cores increases, demonstrating an excellent strong scalability. Since the problem size is fixed in this case, the transfer volume of data stays the same as the number of cores varies. Therefore, the DMA transfer time is almost the same for different manycore systems, although the transfer time slightly increases when the same amount of data is divided into smaller pieces as more cores are added into the system. The only time that linearly grows is the instruction transfer time. The size of the instructions does not change much for different manycore systems. Since the instructions need to be sent to each individual worker node, the total time for transferring instructions is directly related to the number of cores.

4   Related Work

Most our previous manycore systems designed with hthreads [6] used the Memory Hierarchy 2 if the number of cores was ≤ 6. For systems more than 6 cores, Memory Hierarchy 1 was adopted, which demonstrated poor scalability. The local memory indeed is the scratchpad memory mentioned in many previous work. In [5, 7, 3, 9] several algorithms were proposed to partition instructions or data into the scratchpad memory for reducing the cache miss rate and the energy consumption. However, most of them assumed a fixed-size cache and scratchpad memory in the memory hierarchy. In [1] a reconfigurable instruction memory hierarchy for embedded system was proposed in which instructions were assigned to scratchpad memory and cache to maximize the performance. Their work was extended in [2] so that the configuration between the scratchpad memory and the cache can be changed during the different phases of an application. However, these previous work focused only on a single-node platform and did not address the scalability of manycore systems. Scalable memory hierarchy has been investigated in the field of general purpose chip multiprocessor (CMP) as well. Most of previous work in this field focused on the distributed cache and highly-efficient interconnect [4]. In [8], a cache hierarchy including L1, L2, and the last level cache was studied focusing on the design tradeoff of the last level cache. A two-level cache architecture was proposed in [10] consisting of private L1/L2 cache and shared L3 cache. The private cache is next to each processing core and only stores the private data. The L3 cache is a central one and saves the data shared by all cores. Our results already show that a distributed cache architecture alone can not provide the scalability for applications as the number of cores grows.

5   Conclusions

As the number of cores on embedded systems keeps growing as predicted by Moore's law, the original centralized memory hierarchy needs to be re-designed to provide the performance scalability. In this work, we evaluate the performance scalability of distributed multi-tiered memory hierarchies in which the data and the instructions are transferred to local memory next to the worker processor. Five different memory hierarchies, 2 centralized, 1 hybrid, and 2 distributed, are compared and analyzed on Xilinx FPGA devices. Through a detailed benchmarking using real-life applications such as matrix multiplication, IDEA, and 3D FFT, it is shown that the distributed memory hierarchy, in which the local memory can provide a access latency comparable to the cache, demonstrates an excellent performance scalability for embedded manycore systems up to 32 cores on a Virtex-6LX240T device.

Currently, the local memory sizes for both data and instructions are fixed and pre-decided. One size may not fit well for all applications. Therefore, one of the future work is to analyze the application source code to figure out the size for local memory accordingly, i.e., the size is application-specific. Other future work include the design of scalable interconnect to provide efficient cross-node communication during runtime.

References

1. Ge, Z., Lim, H.B., Wong, W.F.: A reconfigurable instruction memory hierarchy for embedded systems. In: Proc. 15th International Conference on Field Programmable Logic and Applications (FPL 2005), pp. 7–12 (August 2005)
2. Ge, Z., Wong, W.F., Lim, H.B.: DRIM: A low power dynamically reconfigurable instruction memory hierarchy for embedded systems. In: Proc. Conference on Design, Automation and Test in Europe (DATE 2007), pp. 1–6 (April 2007)
3. Kandemir, M., Choudhary, A.: Compiler-directed scratch pad memory hierarchy design and management. In: Proc. 39th Annual Design Automation Conference (DAC 2002), pp. 628–633 (June 2002)
4. Kumar, A., Peh, L.S., Kundu, P., Jha, N.K.: Express virtual channels: towards the ideal interconnection fabric. In: Proc. 34th Annual International Symposium on Computer Architecture (ISCA 2007), pp. 150–161 (June 2007)
5. Panda, P.R., Dutt, N.D., Nicolau, A.: On-chip vs. off-chip memory: the data partitioning problem in embedded processor-based systems. ACM Trans. Des. Autom. Electron. Syst. 5(3), 682–704 (2000)
6. Peck, W., Anderson, E., Agron, J., Stevens, J., Baijot, F., Andrews, D.: Hthreads: A computational model for reconfigurable devices. In: Proc. 16th International Conference on Field Programmable Logic and Applications (FPL 2006), pp. 885–888 (August 2006)
7. Steinke, S., Wehmeyer, L., Lee, B.S., Marwedel, P.: Assigning program and data objects to scratchpad for energy reduction. In: Proc. Conference on Design, Automation and Test in Europe (DATE 2002), pp. 409–415 (March 2002)
8. Thoziyoor, S., Ahn, J.H., Monchiero, M., Brockman, J.B., Jouppi, N.P.: A comprehensive memory modeling tool and its application to the design and analysis of future memory hierarchies. In: Proc. 35th Annual International Symposium on Computer Architecture (ISCA 2008), pp. 51–62 (June 2008)
9. Verma, M., Wehmeyer, L., Marwedel, P.: Cache-aware scratchpad allocation algorithm. In: Proc. Conference on Design, automation and test in Europe (DATE 2004), pp. 1264–1269 (February 2004)
10. Yan, S., Zhou, X., Gao, Y., Chen, H., Luo, S., Zhang, P., Cherukuri, N., Ronen, R., Saha, B.: Terascale chip multiprocessor memory hierarchy and programming model. In: Proc. 2009 International Conference on High Performance Computing (HiPC 2009), pp. 150–159 (December 2009)

Triple Module Redundancy of a Laser Array Driver Circuit for Optically Reconfigurable Gate Arrays

Takahiro Watanabe and Minoru Watanabe

Electrical and Electronic Engineering
Shizuoka University
3-5-1 Johoku, Hamamatsu, Shizuoka 432-8561, Japan
tmwatan@ipc.shizuoka.ac.jp

Abstract. Demand is increasing daily for a robust field programmable gate array that is useful for operations performed in a radiation-rich space environment, such as those of spacecraft, space satellites, and space stations. Optically reconfigurable gate arrays (ORGAs) are under development as robust field programmable gate arrays. Their holographic memories can generate correct configuration contexts at any time, even if up to 20 % of the holographic memory data are damaged. However, up to now, a soft error effect for a laser array on ORGA devices has never been discussed. Therefore, this paper first presents a proposal of a method to find an unexpected configuration procedure caused by a laser array driver circuit facing a soft error on conventional ORGA architectures and to recover from such a procedure. Then this paper presents a proposal of a new robust laser array driver circuit that is applicable for any ORGA architecture, which can perfectly remove the unexpected configuration procedure itself.

1 Introduction

Demand is increasing daily for a robust field programmable gate array (FPGA) that is useful for operations conducted in radiation-rich space environments, such as those of spacecraft, space satellites, and space stations [1]–[4]. However, embedded devices used for spacecraft, satellites, and space stations are vulnerable to the effects of high-energy charged particles [5][6]. They can cause a single-event upset (SEU) or a single-event transient (SET) in a device if such a particle is incident to the device [7]-[11]. Therefore, triple-module redundancy (TMR) is always used for implementations on FPGAs as well as those of application-specific integrated circuits (ASICs) to correct SEUs occurring on flip-flops, latches, and memory, or the SET on operations of logic circuits [12][13].

As a robust FPGA, optically reconfigurable gate arrays (ORGAs), which have a fine-grained gate array similar to those of FPGAs, were developed [14]–[16]. An ORGA comprises a holographic memory, a laser array, and a gate-array VLSI as shown in Fig. 1. Although the ORGA construction is slightly more complex than that of currently available FPGAs, the parallel programmable gate array VLSI supports high-speed recovery and perfect avoidance of its faulty areas; it uses the remaining area instead. Moreover, a holographic memory can supply correct configuration contexts at any time, even if up to 20 % of the holographic memory data are damaged [15]. A gate array, a holographic memory, and a laser array inside an ORGA can accept many failure modes

O.C.S. Choy et al. (Eds.): ARC 2012, LNCS 7199, pp. 163–173, 2012.

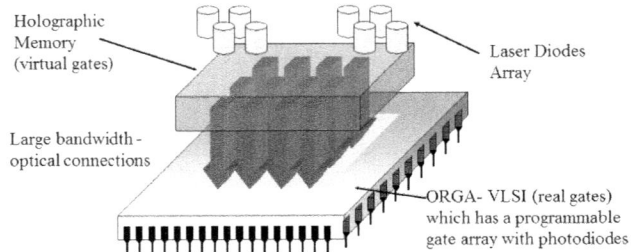

Fig. 1. Overview of an optically reconfigurable gate array (ORGA)

[17]. For that reason, the ORGA is a very robust device. Moreover, in addition to the robust ability, in ORGAs, many configuration contexts can be stored on a holographic memory so that the architecture realizes large virtual gates over physical gates. Therefore, the ORGA architecture can realize extremely high-gate-count VLSIs and can support a large-scale parallel computation.

However, the soft error effect for a laser array on ORGA devices has never been discussed in the relevant literature. If a high-energy charged particle is incident to a buffer controlling a driver circuit of a laser on a laser array, then the laser might turn on. In this case, an unexpected configuration context is programmed onto the ORGA-VLSI's programmable gate array so that an operation of the correct circuit working on the gate array might be broken.

Therefore, this paper first presents a proposal of a method to identify an unexpected configuration procedure caused by a laser array driver circuit facing a soft error and then presents a method to recover from it on conventional ORGA architectures. Furthermore, this paper presents a proposal of a new robust laser array driver circuit that is applicable for any ORGA architecture, which can perfectly remove the unexpected configuration procedure itself.

2   Triple Module Redundancy (TMR) on Conventional ORGA Architectures

2.1   Robust Ability of Conventional ORGA Architectures

An overview of an Optically Reconfigurable Gate Array (ORGA) is portrayed in Fig. 1. An ORGA comprises a programmable gate-array VLSI (ORGA-VLSI), a holographic memory, and a laser diode array. Many configuration contexts are programmed onto the holographic memory in advance. Such information is dynamically programmed onto the ORGA-VLSI's programmable gate array while the programmable gate array functions. The parallel optical connection between an ORGA-VLSI and a holographic memory allows a nanosecond-order high-speed reconfiguration [16]. Moreover, since the storage capacity of a holographic memory is extremely high, numerous configuration contexts can be implemented. Such an ORGA also presents advantages of high fault-tolerance because holographic memories are well known to have high defect-tolerance [18][19]. Since each bit of a reconfiguration context can be generated from the entire

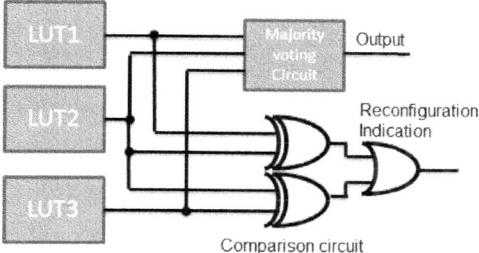

Fig. 2. Triple module redundancy with a majority voting and a reconfiguration indication circuits

holographic memory, the damage of some fraction rarely affects its diffraction pattern or its reconfiguration context. Even if a holographic memory device includes invalid data, holographic memories can generate configuration contexts correctly. Such mechanisms can be regarded as those for which majority voting for each configuration bit is executed from an infinite number of diffraction beams. In a semiconductor memory, single-bit information is stored in a single-bit memory circuit. Therefore, in the semiconductor memory, a defect or a soft error on a transistor always erases information of a single bit. In contrast, in a holographic memory, a single bit of a reconfiguration context is stored in the entire holographic memory. Therefore, the holographic memory's information is robust. The ORGA's robust ability is higher than that of FPGAs.

2.2   Triple Module Redundancy (TMR)

As explained above, in an ORGA device, optical configuration data can be regarded as constantly valid because an ORGA can use 20 % of the damaged configuration context data for a configuration procedure. However, if a high-energy charged particle is incident to a photodiode on an ORGA's gate array at the moment during which a configuration procedure is executed or while the configuration data is stored on the photodiode memory of an ORGA gate array, then a circuit constructed on the programmable gate array might be damaged, as they are in cases of FPGAs. However, an ORGA can repair it in nanosecond-order. As conventional space systems do, an ORGA also uses triple-module redundancy (TMR), so that three circuits are implemented onto the ORGA's gate array, as shown in Fig. 2. In this case, the configuration damage is identifiable by checking the outputs of three circuits. In Fig. 2, two exclusive OR operations are executed based on outputs of three Look-Up Tables (LUTs). One output among the three circuits' outputs differs from the others when the configuration data on the gate array are damaged. Finally, the two outputs of the two exclusive OR operations are connected to the inputs of an OR circuit. The output of the OR circuit becomes a reconfiguration indication signal. Therefore, when one or two outputs of the exclusive OR circuits become high, a repair reconfiguration procedure is executed. Since an ORGA can allow nanosecond-order reconfiguration, even if configuration damage trouble arises, the gate array can be repaired in less than 10 ns [16]. Therefore, although the gate array

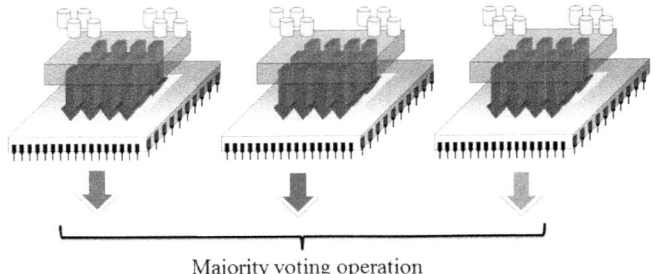

Majority voting operation

Fig. 3. Triple module redundancy on an ORGA architecture

structure and function are identical to those of FPGAs, an ORGA's rapid reconfiguration capability and an ORGA's capability of using invalid configuration data can realize a constantly working gate array that is equivalent to robust gate arrays on ASICs and anti-fuse FPGAs [3].

3   Unexpected Reconfiguration Procedure Detection and Recovery Methods

This paper first proposes the following two soft error improvement methods for a laser array driver circuit. The methods are applicable for conventional ORGA architectures with no modification.

3.1   Three-ORGA Implementation Method (1)

If a high-energy charged particle is incident to a buffer controlling a driver circuit of a laser on a laser array, then the laser might turn on. In this case, an unexpected configuration context is programmed onto the ORGA-VLSI's programmable gate array automatically. As a result, an operation of the correct circuit working on the gate array might be broken. The situation in which an unexpected configuration procedure is caused by a laser array driver circuit facing a soft error can be ascertained easily using a three-ORGA based system, as shown in Fig. 3. In this case, three ORGA devices, majority voting circuits, and reconfiguration indication circuits, shown in Fig. 2, are implemented onto a system. The majority voting circuits and reconfiguration indication circuits are connected to the three ORGAs' outputs. Using this system, even if a laser driver array of an ORGA receives a high-energy charged particle so that an unexpected configuration procedure arises on the ORGA, the unexpected configuration procedure can be detected by the reconfiguration indication circuit, which constantly monitors differences among the three ORGAs' operations. After finding the difference that includes any soft error for a laser driver circuit and a programmable gate array, the same reconfiguration circuit as that of a circuit currently working on a programmable gate array can be programmed onto a damaged ORGA or onto all ORGAs. Since the ORGA's reconfiguration time is less than 10 ns, quick recovery is possible. Therefore, this method presents the advantage that it can easily use conventional ORGA architectures with no modification. However, this method's shortcoming is that the architecture becomes larger and more complicated than a single ORGA system.

3.2   Reconfiguration Area Limitation Method (2)

Construction of a robust system using TMR on a single ORGA requires the use of the second reconfiguration area limitation method. Using this method, the reconfiguration area of each configuration procedure must be limited to 1/3 area of its programmable gate array and each circuit of TMR must be reconfigured individually. If a laser array driver circuit can not remove its soft error effect, three circuits must not be reconfigured simultaneously when TMR circuits are used. Otherwise, three circuits are reconfigured simultaneously by a soft error and the reconfiguration indication circuit can not find the difference between three circuits so that the unexpected reconfiguration circuit might work on ORGA. Here, any ORGA can support a partial reconfiguration. Therefore, three configuration contexts must be prepared for three circuits of a TMR circuit implementation, although the entire gate array can be reconfigured with one configuration context at once. Using this method, a single-ORGA TMR system can be achieved using a conventional ORGA which can not remove a soft error inside a laser array driver circuit. Although the method resolves the soft error issue inside a laser array driver circuit, there is an important shortcoming: three-times more numerous configuration contexts than those of common implementation must be stored on a holographic memory of an ORGA.

4   Robust TMR Laser Driver Circuit

In addition to the two methods explained above, this paper presents a proposal of a new robust laser array driver circuit that is applicable for any ORGA architecture. If the laser driver circuit can perfectly remove the unexpected configuration procedure that is caused by a soft error inside a laser array driver circuit, then three circuits of TMR can be reconfigured simultaneously using a single configuration context. Consequently, the number of TMR reconfiguration circuits recorded on a holographic memory can be increased drastically. The proposed robust laser array driver circuit allows such use. The circuit diagram is shown in Fig. 4. The circuit consists of a laser, a current-limitation register, and six transistors. The single laser is driven by a TMR series transistor array. The TMR transistor array consists of three-transistor passes. Such two three-transistor passes are cascaded for the x-direction and y-direction of a matrix, as portrayed in Fig. 5. Each cross point has a single laser and its driver circuit, as shown in Fig. 4. In each pass, the laser's current flows if two signals are activated. For example, if the XA signal, XB signal, YA signal, and YB signal are activated, then the laser diode turns on. Therefore, if two or three signals take a common activation condition, then the laser turns on, and so on. The XA, XB, XC, YA, YB, and YC are driven by a TMR circuit on a programmable gate array. Always, since an SEU or SET can only change the state of one signal, the voting driver circuit can remove a soft error effect perfectly around the laser driver circuit. This method is useful to avoid soft errors.

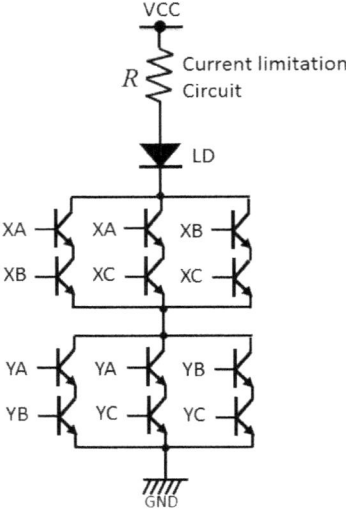

Fig. 4. Circuit diagram of a laser driver circuit

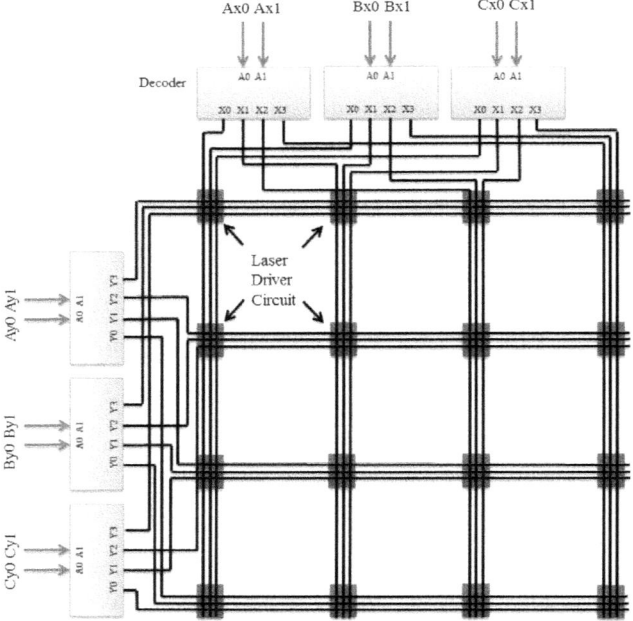

Fig. 5. A 4 × 4 laser array driver's matrix

Fig. 6. Laser module with a one-directional TMR driver circuit

5 Experiments

5.1 Prototype VLSI Chip

For this experiment, a 0.35 μm triple-metal CMOS process ORGA-VLSI chip was used. The ORGA-VLSI chip consists of 4 logic blocks, 5 switching matrices, and 12 I/O bits. The functionality of the VLSI chip is fundamentally equivalent to that of typical FPGAs. However, each programming element of all blocks of the ORGA-VLSI is connected to an optical reconfiguration circuit including a photodiode. An optical reconfiguration circuit serves roles of detecting an optically applied configuration context and maintaining it temporarily. A logic block consists of a four-input – one-output lookup table (LUT), six multiplexers, transmission gates, and a delay flip-flop with a reset function. These functions are optically reconfigurable using 40 optical reconfiguration circuits. Similarly, switching matrices are optically reconfigurable. One four-directional and four three-directional switching matrices were implemented in the gate array. The four-direction and three-direction switching matrices respectively include 24 and 12 optical connections. All programming elements can be optically reconfigured simultaneously. Each I/O block is also controlled using nine optical connections. For this fabrication, we designed the distance between each of the 340 photodiodes as 90 μm; the photodiode is 25.5×25.5 μm^2 to ease optical alignment. The gate array's gate count is 68. The ORGA-VLSI can be reconfigured within 10 ns.

5.2 Hologram Calculation Method

Here, a hologram calculation method for ORGAs is described. A laser aperture plane, a holographic plane, and an ORGA-VLSI plane are parallelized. The laser beam is expanded. The aperture size is assumed to be sufficiently wide for the holographic medium. Consequently, the laser beam can be regarded as a plane wave. The reference

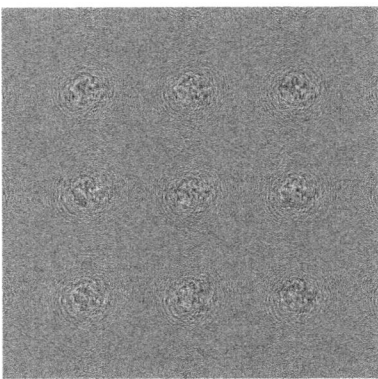

Fig. 7. Holographic memory pattern

wave from the laser propagates into the holographic plane. The holographic medium comprises rectangular pixels on the $x_1 - y_1$ holographic plane. The pixels are assumed to be analog values. The input object comprises rectangular pixels, which can be modulated to be either on or off, on the $x_2 - y_2$ object plane. The intensity distribution of a holographic medium is calculable using the following equation.

$$H(x_1, y_1) \propto \int_{-\infty}^{\infty} \int_{-\infty}^{\infty} O(x_2, y_2) \sin(kr) dx_2 dy_2,$$
$$r = \sqrt{Z_L^2 + (x_1 - x_2)^2 + (y_1 - y_2)^2}.$$

(1)

In that equation, $O(x_2, y_2)$ is a binary value of a reconfiguration context, k signifies the wave number, and Z_L represents the distance between the holographic plane and the object plane. The value $H(x_1, y_1)$ is normalized as 0–1 for minimum intensity H_{min} and maximum intensity H_{max}, as shown below.

$$H'(x_1, y_1) = \frac{H(x_1, y_1) - H_{min}}{H_{max} - H_{min}}.$$

(2)

Finally, the normalized image H' is used for implementing the holographic memory. Other areas on the holographic plane are opaque to the illumination.

5.3 Hologram Generation

Figure 7 portrays a holographic memory pattern calculated using Eqs. 1 and 2. Each parameter was selected to fit the experimental system, as explained in later sections. The target device is a liquid crystal spatial light modulator (LC–SLM) with 256 gradations. The resolution of the target LC–SLM is $14 \times 14 \ \mu m^2$. The number of pixels of the holographic memory is 700×700. The holographic memory pattern presented in Fig. 7 was used in later experiments.

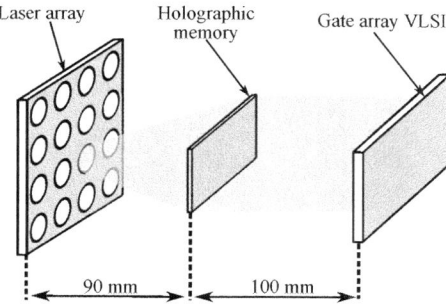

Fig. 8. Block diagram of a demonstration system including a 16-laser array

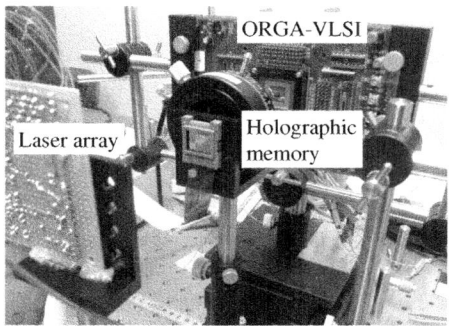

Fig. 9. Photograph of the experimental system

5.4   Experimental System and Results

Figure 8 presents an ORGA system. Photographs are also presented in Fig. 9. The ORGA system was constructed using 16 100-mW, 808-nm semiconductor lasers, an LC–SLM as a holographic memory, and an ORGA-VLSI. The LC–SLM is a projection TV panel. It is a 90° twisted nematic device with a thin film transistor. The panel has $1,024 \times 768$ pixels, each of 14×14 μm^2. The LC–SLM is connected to an evaluation board. The board's video input is connected to the external display terminal of a personal computer. Programming for the LC–SLM is executed by displaying a holographic memory pattern with 256 gradation levels on the personal computer display. The holographic pattern shown in Fig. 7 was displayed on the LC–SLM. The ORGA-VLSI was placed 100 mm distant from the LC–SLM. The robust TMR laser driver circuit was demonstrated. The circuit correctly blocks any soft error effect so that the ORGA can perfectly block any unexpected reconfiguration procedure. Therefore, an extremely robust ORGA was achieved.

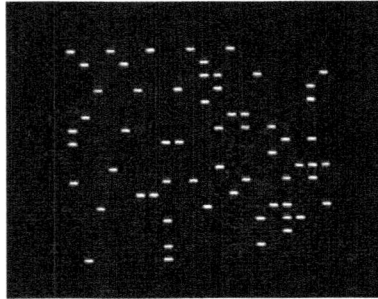

Fig. 10. CCD-captured configuration context pattern

6   Conclusion

This paper has proposed a method to find an unexpected configuration procedure caused by a laser array driver circuit facing a soft error and to recover from it on conventional ORGA architectures. In addition, this paper has proposed a new robust laser array driver circuit that is applicable for any ORGA architecture. It can perfectly remove the unexpected configuration procedure itself.

Acknowledgments. This research was supported by the Ministry of Education, Science, Sports and Culture, Grant-in-Aid for challenging Exploratory Research, No. 23650087. The VLSI chip in this study was fabricated in the chip fabrication program of VLSI Design and Education Center (VDEC), the University of Tokyo in collaboration with Rohm Co. Ltd. and Toppan Printing Co. Ltd.

References

1. Visser, S.J., Dawood, A.S., Williams, J.A.: FPGA based real-time adaptive filtering for space applications. In: IEEE International Conference on Field-Programmable Technology, pp. 322–326 (2002)
2. Miller, G., Carmichael, C.: Single-Event Upset Mitigation for Xilinx FPGA Block Memories, XILINX Application Note, Virtex-II FPGAs (2007)
3. Nejad, R.J., Rickey, P.A., Konadu, K., Stapor, W.J., McDonald, P.T., Heidergott, W.: Radiation Characterization of a Hardened 0.22 μ m Anti-Fuse Field Programmable Gate Array. IEEE Transactions on Nuclear Science 53(6), Part I, 3525–3531
4. Fay, D., Shye, A., Bhattacharya, S., Connors, D.A.D., Wichmann, S.: An Adaptive Fault-Tolerant Memory System for FPGA-based Architectures in the Space Environment. In: NASA/ESA Conference on Adaptive Hardware and Systems, pp. 250–257 (2007)
5. Redant, S., Marec, R., Baguena, L., Liegeon, E., Soucarre, J., Van Thielen, B., Beeckman, G., Ribeiro, P., Fernandez-Leon, A., Glass, B.: Radiation Test Results on First Silicon in the Design Against Radiation Effects (DARE) Library. IEEE Trans. on Nuclear Science 52(5), 1550–1554 (2005)
6. Schwank, J.R., Shaneyfelt, M.R., Fleetwood, D.M., Felix, J.A., Dodd, P.E., Paillet, P., Ferlet-Cavrois, V.: Radiation Effects in MOS Oxides. IEEE Transactions on Nuclear Science 55(4), 1833–1853 (2008)

7. Redant, S., Marec, R., Baguena, L., Liegeon, E., Soucarre, J., Van Thielen, B., Beeckman, G., Ribeiro, P., Fernandez-Leon, A., Glass, B.: Radiation Test Results on First Silicon in the Design Against Radiation Effects (DARE) Library. IEEE Trans. on Nuclear Science 52(5), 1550–1554 (2005)
8. Makihara, A., Sakaide, Y., Tsuchiya, Y., Arimitsu, T., Asai, H., Iide, Y., Shindou, H., Kuboyama, S., Matsuda, S.: Single-Event Effects in 0.18 um CMOS Commercial Processes. IEEE Trans. on Nuclear Science 50(6), 2135–2138 (2003)
9. Ikeda, N., Shindou, H., Iide, Y., Asai, H., Kubo, S., Matsuda, S.: Evaluation of the Errors of Commercial Semiconductor Devices in a Space Radiation Environment. Trans. of the Institute of Electronics, Information and Communication Engineers. B J88-B(1), 108–116 (2005)
10. Lin, Y., He, L.: Devices and architecture concurrent optimization for FPGA transient soft error rate. In: International Conference on Computer Aided Design (2007)
11. Lin, Y., He, L.: Device and architecture concurrent optimization for FPGA transient soft error rate. In: International Conference on Computer-Aided Design, pp. 194–198 (2007)
12. Stroud, C.E.: Reliability of Majority Voting Based VLSI Fault-Tolerant Circuits. IEEE Trans. on VLSI Systems 2(4), 516–521 (1994)
13. Radu, M., Pitica, D., Posteuca, C.: Reliability and failure analysis of voting circuits in hardware redundant design. In: International Symposium on Electronic Materials and Packaging, pp. 421–423 (2000)
14. Seto, D., Watanabe, M.: A dynamic optically reconfigurable gate array - perfect emulation. IEEE Journal of Quantum Electronics 44(5), 493–500 (2008)
15. Nakajima, M., Watanabe, M.: Optical buffering technique under space radiation environment. Optics Letters 34(23), 3719–3721 (2009)
16. Nakajima, M., Watanabe, M.: A four-context optically differential reconfigurable gate array. IEEE/OSA Journal of Lightwave Technology 27(24) (2009)
17. Seto, D., Watanabe, M.: Recovery method for a turn-off failure mode of a laser array on an ORGA. In: NASA/ESA Conference on Adaptive Hardware and Systems, pp. 242–247 (2010)
18. Toishi, M., Okamoto, A., Honma, S., Bunsen, M.: Fault-tolerant holographic memory with two photrefractive crystals. In: Pacific Rim Conference on Lasers and Electro-Optics, vol. 2, pp. 160–161 (2001)
19. Coufal, H.J., Psaltis, D., Sincerbox, G.T.: Holographic Data Storage. Springer, Heidelberg (2000)

A Routing Architecture for FPGAs
with Dual-VT Switch Box and Logic Clusters

Wei Ting Loke[1] and Yajun Ha[2]

[1] Xilinx Asia Pacific
5 Changi Business Park Vista, Singapore 486040
weitingl@xilinx.com
[2] ECE Department, Faculty of Engineering
4 Engineering Drive 3, Singapore 117576
elehy@nus.edu.sg

Abstract. In this paper, we present a novel routing architecture for FP-GAs with dual-V_T LUT and switch box architectures. The use of reverse back bias (RBB) is one strategy for mitigating leakage power, a critical issue as process technologies shrink relentlessly towards sub-nano proportions. FPGAs with the ability to adjust fabric V_T at configuration time offer leakage power reduction without sacrificing circuit speed. Most of the related works today investigate dual-V_T optimizations at the logic cluster level; Altera's Stratix-III/IV line of FPGAs already demonstrate the feasibility of a similar architecture. In this work, we present a further advancement to the dual-V_T architecture - the switch box, and a routing architecture that demonstrates the effectiveness of this true dual-V_T fabric architecture. Our switch box advancement alone yields an average of 17.44% in leakage power savings, and with the full EDA flow an average 29.65% in total power savings is observed.

Keywords: Programmable-V_T, Reverse Back Bias, Switch Box, FPGA.

1 Introduction

The management of power consumption has become an imperative for semiconductor vendors and customers. Despite efforts at multiple levels [1], the trend of ever-increasing leakage power does not appear to be letting up [2,3]. At the same time, prohibitive mask costs have become a persuasive force to ASIC vendors considering a transition to FPGA-based solutions, which sits well with their traditional needs for quick prototyping and rapid turnaround. Yet, the power problem in FPGAs is one of the most challenging issues to tackle due to the native requirement of programmability, and is undoubtedly the single biggest obstacle in its penetration of the mobile market. With static power ready to overtake dynamic power at the 28nm node and below, architectural and EDA-level enhancements are necessary if FPGAs are to remain a competitive option.

To some extent, combined efforts in the form of novel circuit design techniques and process technology advancements have helped to keep static power

O.C.S. Choy et al. (Eds.): ARC 2012, LNCS 7199, pp. 174–186, 2012.

manageable in the last decade. Some examples of the latter are high-K metal gate and MVCMOS technology. MVCMOS in particular is comparatively easier to deploy in ASICs because circuit slacks are known during the design phase, and involves but a choice of cells in the technology library used. Such is not the case in FPGAs, where critical path(s) cannot be determined until a design has been implemented.

However, FPGAs hold the key of an interesting concept - back-bias programmability. The use of reverse back bias (RBB) to adjust transistor V_T and hence reduce leakage power without compromising circuit speed has shown some promise in recent years [4,5], and has been adopted by the industry for several years now [6]. With SOI processes steadily maturing, such a design paradigm looks set to continue.

Existing works today study the possibilities surrounding having dual-V_T / V_{DD} LUTs or clusters. [7] suggested a technology mapping algorithm and clustering algorithm for mapping to dual-V_T logic clusters; [8] looks at tuning V_T from the placement step onwards. [9] suggested a mixed V_T/VDD track that showed some sacrifice to timing. A low power dual-V_{DD}-based routing switch is proposed in [10], but it is clear that the area overhead involved is large since significant circuitry is introduced per mux.

In this work, we propose a generic, RBB-programmable switch box architecture in addition to the more commonly presented dual-V_T LUT fabric. A novel self-checking routing architecture is proposed to take advantage of this true dual-V_T fabric. Compared to the baseline dual-V_T flow, the switch box advancement alone is shown to yield an average of 17.44% in leakage power savings, and with the full EDA flow, an average 29.65% in total power savings is observed.

The rest of this paper is organized as follows. We first introduce our dual-V_T switch box and LUT architecture in Section 2. In Section 3, we discuss the challenges of routing with switch boxes with dual-V_T capability, and describe an algorithm to exploit this architecture. Further leakage power mitigation strategies are presented in Section 4. Experimental results are presented in Section 5. Finally, we conclude this paper and discuss future works in Section 6 and 7.

2 Architecture

2.1 RBB Switch Box

The architectural focus in our work is the RBB switch box enhancement. We adopt a unidirectional single driver interconnect architecture representative of today's FPGAs [11,12]. A switch box will be used where connections between wires, or between a logic block output and wire, is required. Signals from interconnect wires drop off to logic block inputs via connection boxes. Figure 1 below depicts the driving structure.

The back bias option is available at the granularity of the switch box, meaning all connections utilizing any mux in a particular switch box will be subject to the

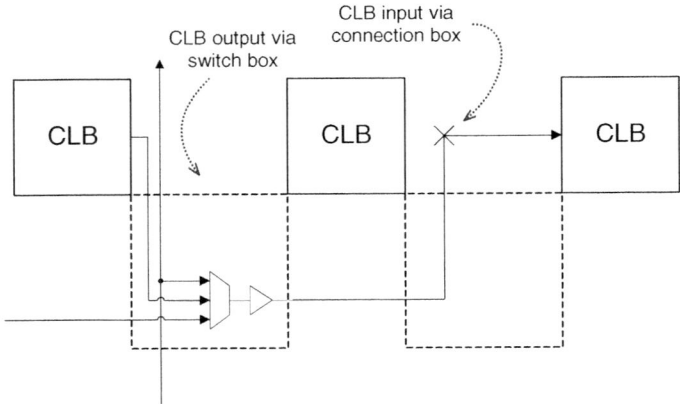

Fig. 1. Unidirectional single driver architecture. Wire-to-wire and output-to-wire connections are made via switch boxes; wire-to-input connections are made via connection boxes.

delay assigned by the V_T level of that switch box. Figure 2 describes this scheme. For wires longer than length-1, the wire feeds through intermediate switch boxes and are not subject to these delays. However, if a signal drops off at any of these intermediate points, then it will be subject to the delay of the associated switch box. This gives the router the flexibility to "skip" past switch boxes of different V_T levels.

This enhancement is simple, elegant, and architecturally agnostic in the sense that it is applicable to any connectivity structure including channel width. In addition, such an implementation incurs a minimal overhead of just one SRAM cell and mux per switch box (limited circuitry may be needed for distributing the negative back bias voltage). Clearly, this degree of freedom in delay must be factored in the timing driven router, which we will discuss later.

2.2 RBB Logic Block

In addition to the switch box, we implement a dual-V_T logic block architecture with granularity at the cluster level as shown in Figure 3 below. Such a design gives us the ability to also reclaim slack on non-critical routes by slowing down clusters along the routes, further reducing static power.

3 Routing Architecture

3.1 Dual-V_T Pathfinder Algorithm

In order to take advantage of dual-V_T in the switch boxes, critical path nets must be segregated from non-critical path nets, since shared use will result

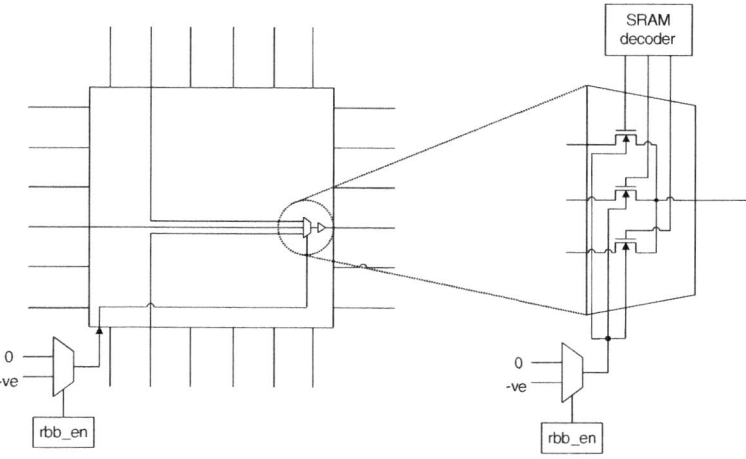

Fig. 2. Our RBB Switch Box Architecture. Each routing switch comprises a 3-input NMOS pass transistor and buffer. A negative back bias voltage is supplied into each pass transistor when in high-V_T mode.

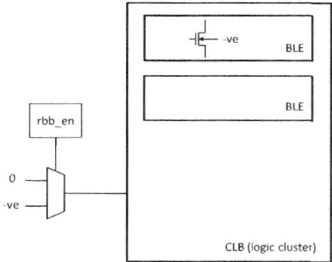

Fig. 3. Our RBB Logic Cluster Architecture

in the inability to tune switch box V_T without compromising circuit speed. To achieve this, the router must be intelligent enough to identify the criticality of all nets both upfront and dynamically.

Here, we focus on optimizing for power in timing-driven routing. Our routing algorithm is based on the Pathfinder congestion negotiation algorithm, but with intelligence injected surrounding criticality. In the original version of this algorithm [13], wavefront expansion is performed based on upstream and expected downstream cost of the net in question until all sinks are reached. Assuming all nets are routable, timing analysis is then performed the slack for each source-sink connection, which is then used in the next routing iteration to resolve congestion by prioritizing paths with little or no slack. With each routing iteration, the previous routing is ripped up and rerouted; in the first iteration, every connection is routed as critical, even if congestion occurs, and by some n iteration all congestion is resolved and a routed design is obtained.

It is not sufficient to simply have nets with low criticality avoid low-V_T switch boxes used by the critical net. This is because such an avoidance scheme will cause non-critical nets to extend and possibly become more critical than the "real" critical nets. The algorithm would then optimize this falsely critical net in the next routing iteration, resulting in indefinitely extended routes. Such a scenario is depicted in Figure 4. Originally, the non-critical path (in green) can use SB_2 to get to its sink at CLB_7. However, because SB_2 has been designated low-V_T, it needs to route a further distance through SB_4 and SB_5. If this route extends beyond the critical path, it will be recognized as the critical path in the next iteration, and so on.

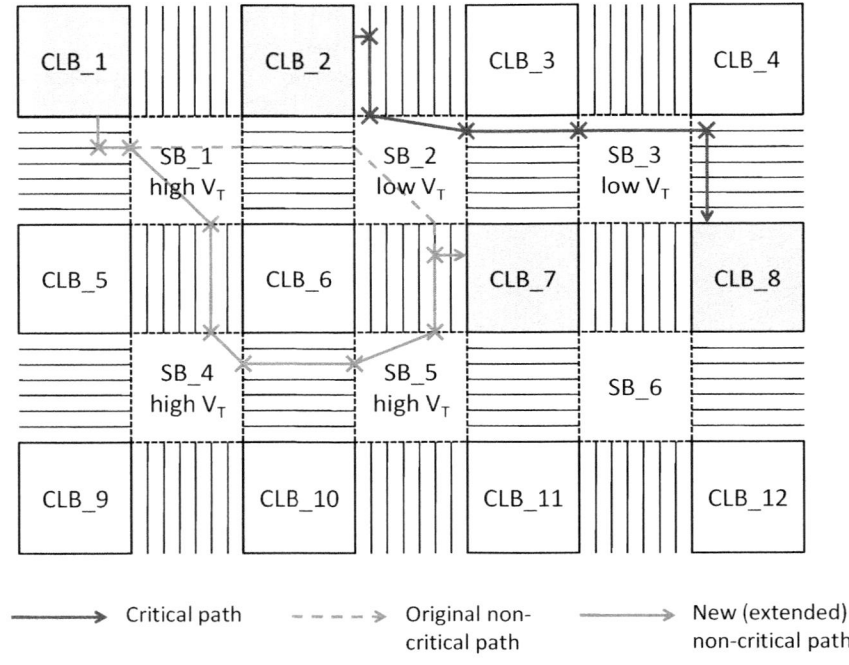

Fig. 4. Route extension due to switch box avoidance scheme

To deal with this problem, we honor the criticality evaluated in the previous iteration. After each routing iteration, the max delay of every routed net is stored. In the following iteration, every net is routed as non-critical (explained next); if the delay exceeds that of the previous iteration within a threshold margin, the net is ripped up and re-routed as critical. When routing a critical net, wave expansion occurs normally, with switch boxes spanning the route marked as low-V_T. When routing a non-critical net, low-V_T switch boxes are pruned away, with switch boxes spannning the route marked as high-V_T.

```
// PriorityQueue stores nodes in the current wave expansion sorted on total_cost
function dual_vt_timing_driven_route () {
  for (all nets i and sinks j) set Crit(i,j) = MaxCrit;
  while (overused resources exist) {
    foreach (net i) {
      update base costs for net i;
      timing_driven_route_net (i, false);
      if (not routable or (delay > prev_iter_delay±margin))
        timing_driven_route_net (i, true);
      store switch box locations and VT for this route;
    }
    update historical costs for all n;
    perform timing analysis and update Crit(i,j);
  }
}  // end single routing iteration

function timing_driven_route_net (net, route_as_critical) {
  rip up routing tree and update congestion cost;
  foreach (sink in decreasing Crit(i,j)) {
    while (not sink) {  // start wave expansion
      pop lowest cost node m from PriorityQueue;
      if (best path to m) {
        update path_cost(m) and total_cost(m);
        for all fanout nodes n of m {
          compute upstream cost;
          if (not route_as_critical) {
            if (n is on LVT switch box) { skip n };
            set switch boxes used to HVT;
          }
          else { set switch boxes used to LVT };
          add n to PriorityQueue;
        }
      }
    }  // end wave expansion
    update congestion costs and routing tree delay;
    for (all expanded nodes n) set path_cost(n) and total_cost(n) to ∞;
  }
}
```

Fig. 5. The dual-V_T switch box pathfinder routing algorithm

For path costing, the Elmore model is used but with the intrinsic delay associated with a high-V_T switch factored. When expanding into a wire, we prioritize longer wires by lowering the associated downstream cost if it stays within the bounding box; this will encourage the algorithm to use less low-V_T switch boxes, as well as guide it to "skip" past switch boxes of a different V_T level. In Figure 6 below, the high-V_T switch box SB_1 can "skip" through an low-V_T switch box SB_2 using a length-2 wire.

The full routing algorithm, which we call the *dual-V_T switch box pathfinder routing algorithm*, is shown in the pseudocode in Figure 5. For consistency, we keep to similar terminologies used in [13].

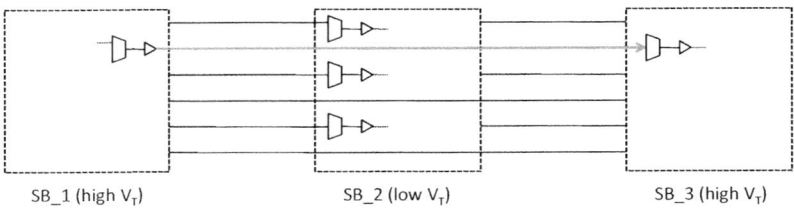

SB_1 (high V_T)   SB_2 (low V_T)   SB_3 (high V_T)

Fig. 6. Non-critical connection skipping through an low-V_T switch box

4   Further Leakage Power Mitigation Strategies

4.1   Slack Reclamation

Upon completion of routing, there may still be slack left in some nets. In most cases, the above routing architecture will introduces some amount of slack to the non-critical paths. We want to take advantage of these slack paths to further reduce leakage power, which can be significant in total. We do this by setting clusters along the slack paths to high-V_T i.e. RBB on, thereby reclaiming slack. We characterize delay numbers in high-V_T mode using SPICE simulations.

We make the observation that a typical net comprises a driver and several sinks. To reclaim slack, we perform a backwards breadth-first traversal of the timing graph and, where sufficient slack exists, set the LUT to high-V_T (if the edge in question corresponds to a LUT). Required times and slack of the parent nodes are then re-evaluated and upwards traversal continues, terminating when insufficient slack is available for reclamation i.e. slack available is less than the delay of a high-V_T LUT but more than that of a low-V_T LUT.

Because the RBB option is available only at the cluster level, clusters having LUTs of both V_T levels are considered illegal. To satisfy this constraint, a cluster sweep is performed to revert high-V_T LUTs back to low-V_T in such cases; this is so as to honor the circuit critical path. On completion of the process, a full timing analysis is then performed on the timing graph to update all net timing information.

4.2   Unused Resources

In addition, all unused switch boxes and LUTs are set to high-V_T in order to further reduce leakage. While the effect of this is relatively limited in our experimental flow (described below) due to VPR implementing the minimum array size required to realize a particular circuit, such an approach is expected to be highly relevant to the industry since real FPGAs are of a fixed array size and the tendency for leftover unused logic can be quite high.

5   Experimental Methodology and Results

An overview of our architectural evaluation framework is presented in Figure 7 below. In order to perform power estimation, we leveraged the power model for VPR 5.0 [14] developed by Poon and Jamieson [15,16,14]. Although the power estimation framework does not provide figures exact to SPICE simulation, it has nonetheless been proven to produce results with good fidelity [15]. We integrate our routing architecture into VPR 5.0, which we will call the Dual-V_T (DVT)-VPR for convenience.

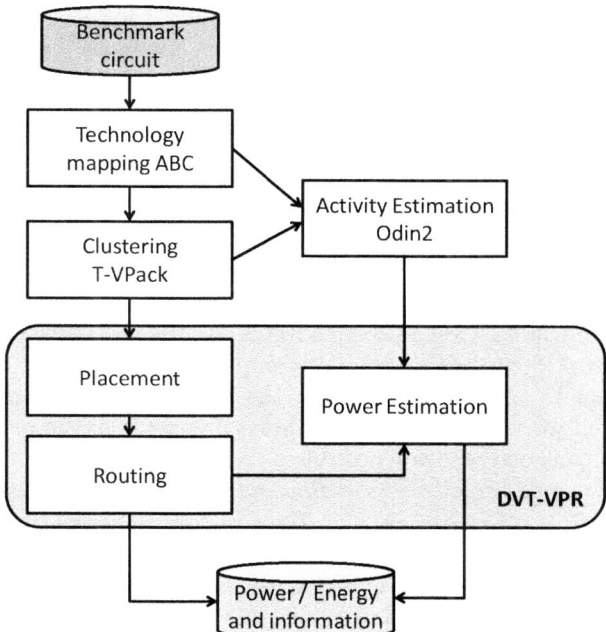

Fig. 7. Experimentation Flow. Our routing architecture resides within the routing step in DVT-VPR.

In the first stage, we take the benchmark circuit through ABC [17,18], a publicly available FPGA technology mapping tool. The tool is efficient at generating mapped circuits with low LUT count, in turn translating to both dynamic and leakage power savings.

Next, the technology-mapped blif generated from ABC is fed into T-VPack for timing-driven packing, again an efficient tool for minimizing cluster utilization. The output net file from T-VPack is then input into the activity estimation tool (or ACE) in Odin2, which is the first part of the power estimation framework described above. The ACE tool generates the activity and function files necessary for power estimation in DVT-VPR. The netlist file generated by T-VPack is passed into DVT-VPR where our routing architecture and slack reclamation framework reside. Finally, the output files from ACE are consumed by the second part of the power estimation tool in VPR for dynamic and static power calculations. We modify the tool to perform calculations for both cases of our full dual-V_T switch box and LUT architecture, as well as the native homogeneous V_T architecture, for results comparison.

In order to obtain figures representative of today's process nodes, an architecture file was generated for the IBM_CMS10LPE 65nm process node. HSPICE simulations showed an average of $2\times$ increase in leakage power versus the 0.18um node. For wire distribution, we created a frequency spread of $4\times$, $2\times$ and $1\times$ for length-1, length-2 and length-4 wires respectively, with no switch box nor connection box depopulation. Preliminary experiments showed that a reasonable spread of different wire lengths was important as the ability to "skip" switch boxes of different V_T levels was critical to the performance of our routing algorithm, with wire RC showing strong influence as well.

We picked the Wilton switch box architecture for use in our experiments. LUT input and cluster sizes are set to 4 and 10 respectively. For low-V_T levels, we designed to 0.41v and 0.37v for NMOS and PMOS respectively; for high-V_T, we designed to 0.53v and 0.48v for NMOS and PMOS respectively. The same low and high-V_T levels hold for both switch boxes and LUTs.

In our experiments, 19 MCNC benchmarks circuits were run through the evaluation framework described above. We compare the percentage savings offered by our full dual-V_T architecture against the native single V_T architecture. Because no related work on switch box architectures exist in the public domain, a comparison on this end was not possible.

We compare three broad metrics: *Routing Leakage Power Dissipation*, *Logic Block Leakage Power Dissipation*, and *Total Energy Consumption*. The first two metrics are directly relevant to our architectural enhancements. For the third metric, we choose to report energy since we want to avoid favoring cases where power is reduced simply due to slow clocks [15]. We have verified that in all cases critical path stays very nearly the same between our architecture and the single V_T architecture, and hence report only power-related metrics here.

A few key observations can be made from Table 1 below. Firstly, our routing architecture performs very consistently ($\sim$17%) in yielding leakage power savings. We believe this is due in large to the wavefront expansion algorithm and the manner in which tracks are widened as required according to circuit size. Logic block leakage power, however, vary greatly depending on the circuit in question and does not demonstrate correlation to circuit size. The second noteworthy point is that logic block leakage power savings (39.4%) average approximately twice that of routing leakage power savings (17.44%), which we already consider to be significant. This is due in part to unused logic blocks, whose V_T level were initialized to high in order to further reduce leakage power dissipation. In contrast, less switch boxes have had their V_T levels set this way since routing resource utilization does not scale linearly to logic block utilization (a well-known problem). In terms of total energy consumption, our framework yields an average of 29.65% savings.

Table 1. Results for dual-V_T switch box and logic cluster architecture versus baseline single-V_T architecture

Testcase	Routing Leakage Pow (W)	Routing Leakage Pow /w RBB (W)	Routing Leakage Pow %age Savings	LB Leakage Pow (W)	LB Leakage Pow /w RBB (W)	LB Leakage Pow %age Savings	Total Energy (J)	Total Energy /w RBB (J)	Total Energy %age Savings
alu4	0.01544	0.01273	17.58%	0.05470	0.03694	32.47%	9.39E-10	7.55E-10	19.55%
apex2	0.02136	0.01760	17.57%	0.07535	0.04736	37.15%	1.41E-09	1.07E-09	24.44%
apex4	0.02211	0.01822	17.59%	0.07439	0.04361	41.38%	1.31E-09	9.07E-10	30.58%
bigkey	0.00904	0.00745	17.60%	0.26465	0.12304	53.51%	1.93E-09	1.02E-09	47.21%
clma	0.07297	0.06014	17.59%	0.24247	0.15483	36.14%	7.28E-09	5.27E-09	27.66%
des	0.01739	0.01433	17.58%	0.39079	0.17669	54.79%	4.06E-09	2.21E-09	45.61%
diffeq	0.00566	0.00470	17.03%	0.05171	0.03252	37.12%	7.94E-10	5.72E-10	27.92%
dsip	0.01498	0.01235	17.59%	0.27426	0.12668	53.81%	1.86E-09	9.87E-10	46.85%
elliptic	0.02067	0.01714	17.11%	0.12816	0.07757	39.48%	2.45E-09	1.70E-09	30.49%
ex5p	0.01766	0.01456	17.56%	0.06199	0.03620	41.60%	9.23E-10	6.52E-10	29.30%
frisc	0.03020	0.02509	16.92%	0.12571	0.08098	35.58%	3.36E-09	2.44E-09	27.20%
misex3	0.01475	0.01216	17.57%	0.06779	0.04117	39.27%	1.09E-09	7.97E-10	26.54%
pdc	0.06707	0.05529	17.57%	0.20751	0.12583	39.36%	5.00E-09	3.47E-09	30.59%
s298	0.01290	0.01063	17.56%	0.04965	0.03207	35.41%	9.00E-10	6.41E-10	28.82%
s38417	0.01930	0.01599	17.15%	0.16043	0.10852	32.35%	2.33E-09	1.77E-09	24.00%
s38584.1	0.03634	0.02995	17.59%	0.17119	0.11767	31.26%	2.63E-09	2.04E-09	22.31%
seq	0.02154	0.01776	17.56%	0.08009	0.04906	38.75%	1.35E-09	1.02E-09	24.47%
spla	0.04017	0.03328	17.15%	0.17378	0.10316	40.64%	3.55E-09	2.43E-09	31.45%
tseng	0.00511	0.00421	17.58%	0.03165	0.02263	28.52%	5.37E-10	4.39E-10	18.30%
AVERAGE			17.44%			39.40%			29.65%

A good indicator of how well our routing architecture performs is the ratio of high-V_T switch boxes set *during the routing phase*, versus the total number of switch boxes used to implement the route. This is shown in Table 2 below.

Table 2. Ratio of high-V_T switch boxes set during routing versus total number of switch boxes used to implement the route

Testcase	# high-VT SBs	# low-VT SBs	Ratio of high-VT SBs / total SBs used in routing
alu4	70	76	0.479
apex2	79	89	0.470
apex4	55	88	0.385
bigkey	105	119	0.469
clma	224	304	0.424
des	139	149	0.483
diffeq	58	62	0.483
dsip	104	120	0.464
elliptic	114	141	0.447
ex5p	58	62	0.483
frisc	143	145	0.497
misex3	66	77	0.462
pdc	161	238	0.404
s298	60	60	0.500
s38417	199	200	0.499
s38584.1	194	246	0.441
seq	84	84	0.500
spla	144	179	0.446
tseng	42	57	0.424

6   Conclusion

In this paper, we presented a true dual-V_T architecture that supports RBB in both switch boxes and LUTs, as well as a routing algorithm to exploit such an architecture. To our knowledge, this is the first work that explores RBB at the switch box level, and has as well yielded promising results. In addition, the slack reclamation method presented ties in well with the proposed routing architecture to further exploit the RBB option for leakage power mitigation.

When compared against the baseline single V_T architecture, our proposed architecture saw an average routing leakage power savings of 17.44%, an average logic block leakage power savings of 39.4%, and an average of 29.65% in total energy savings. These results make a strong case for our architecture, and shows promise in tackling the critical need for leakage power mitigation in process nodes of the future.

7   Future Work

Because reverse back bias capability at the switch box level was not well-explored previously, we expect this architectural enhancement to introduce further algorithmic possibilities as well as constraints in the domain of dual-V_T routing. In addition, this work has yet to consider routing when V_T levels of clusters are already known - a flow that must be re-looked when V_T levels of LUTs are inferred at the technology mapping or clustering abstractions. Lastly, this routing architecture will require major enhancements in order to handle heterogenous FPGAs with complex blocks representative of FPGAs that exist in the market today.

Acknowledgment. This research is supported under Singapore A*STAR SERC Grant No 1122804010.

References

1. Lamoureux, J., Luk, W.: An Overview of Low-Power Techniques for Field-Programmable Gate Arrays. In: NASA/ESA Conference on Adaptive Hardware and Systems, pp. 338–345 (2008)
2. Sakurai, T.: Perspectives on power-aware electronics. In: IEEE International Solid-State Circuits Conference, Digest of Technical Papers, ISSCC 2003, vol. 1, pp. 26–29 (2003)
3. Roy, K., Mukhopadhyay, S., Mahmoodi-Meimand, H.: Leakage current mechanisms and leakage reduction techniques in deep-submicrometer CMOS circuits. Proceedings of the IEEE 91, 305–327 (2003)
4. Usami, K., Horowitz, M.: Clustered voltage scaling technique for low-power design. In: Proceedings of the 1995 International Symposium on Low Power Design, ISLPED 1995, pp. 3–8. ACM, New York (1995)
5. Rahman, A., Polavarapuv, V.: Evaluation of low-leakage design techniques for Field Programmable Gate Arrays. In: Proceedings of the 2004 ACM/SIGDA 12th International Symposium on Field Programmable Gate Arrays, FPGA 2004, pp. 23–30. ACM, New York (2004)
6. Lewis, D., Ahmed, E., Cashman, D., Vanderhoek, T., Lane, C., Lee, A., Pan, P.: Architectural enhancements in Stratix-III and Stratix-IV. In: Proceeding of the ACM/SIGDA International Symposium on Field Programmable Gate Arrays, FPGA 2009, pp. 33–42. ACM, New York (2009)
7. Chen, D., Cong, J., Dong, C., He, L., Li, F., Peng, C.-C.: Technology Mapping and Clustering for FPGA Architectures With Dual Supply Voltages. IEEE Transactions on Computer-Aided Design of Integrated Circuits and Systems 29, 1709–1722 (2010)
8. Kawanami, T., Hioki, M., Nagase, H., Tsutsumi, T., Nakagawa, T., Sekigawa, T., Koike, H.: Preliminary Evaluation of Flex Power FPGA: A Power Reconfigurable Architecture with Fine Granularity. IEICE Transactions on Information and Systems, 2004–2010 (2004)
9. Mondal, S., Memik, S.: A Low Power FPGA Routing Architecture. In: IEEE International Symposium on Circuits and Systems, ISCAS 2005, vol. 2, pp. 1222–1225 (May 2005)
10. Anderson, J.H., Najm, F.N.: A novel low-power FPGA routing switch. In: IEEE Custom Integrated Circuits Conference, pp. 719–722 (2004)
11. Lewis, D., Betz, V., Jefferson, D., Lee, A., Lane, C., Leventis, P., Marquardt, S., McClintock, C., Pedersen, B., Powell, G., Reddy, S., Wysocki, C., Cliff, R., Rose, J.: The Stratix routing and logic architecture. In: Proceedings of the 2003 ACM/SIGDA Eleventh International Symposium on Field Programmable Gate Arrays, FPGA 2003, pp. 12–20. ACM, New York (2003)

12. Lemieux, G., Lee, E., Tom, M., Yu, A.: Directional and single-driver wires in FPGA interconnect. In: Proceedings of IEEE International Conference on Field-Programmable Technology, 2004, pp. 41–48 (December 2004)
13. Betz, V., Rose, J., Marquardt, A.: Architecture and CAD for Deep-Submicron FPGAs. Kluwer Academic Publishers, Norwell (1999)
14. Jamieson, P., Luk, W., Wilton, S., Constantinides, G.: An energy and power consumption analysis of FPGA routing architectures. In: International Conference on Field-Programmable Technology, FPT 2009, pp. 324–327 (December 2009)
15. Poon, K.K.W., Wilton, S.J.E., Yan, A.: A Detailed Power Model for Field-Programmable Gate Arrays. ACM Trans. Des. Autom. Electron. Syst. 10, 279–302 (2005)
16. Jamieson, P., Kent, K.B., Gharibian, F., Shannon, L.: Odin II - An Open-Source Verilog HDL Synthesis Tool for CAD Research. In: Annual IEEE Symposium on Field-Programmable Custom Computing Machines, pp. 149–156 (2010)
17. Mishchenko, A., et al.: ABC: A System for Sequential Synthesis and Verification (2009), http://www.eecs.berkeley.edu/alanmi/abc
18. Mishchenko, A., Chatterjee, S., Brayton, R.K.: Improvements to Technology Mapping for LUT-Based FPGAs. IEEE Transactions on Computer-Aided Design of Integrated Circuits and Systems 26(2), 240–253 (2007)

Multi-level Customisation Framework for Curve Based Monte Carlo Financial Simulations

Qiwei Jin[1], Diwei Dong[2], Anson H.T. Tse[1], Gary C.T. Chow[1],
David B. Thomas[3], Wayne Luk[1], and Stephen Weston[4]

[1] Department of Computing, Imperial College London
[2] Department of Mathematics, Imperial College London
[3] Department of Electrical and Electronic Engineering, Imperial College London
[4] Credit Quantitative Research, J.P. Morgan, London

Abstract. One of the main challenges when accelerating financial applications using reconfigurable hardware is the management of design complexity. This paper proposes a multi-level customisation framework for automatic generation of complex yet highly efficient curve based financial Monte Carlo simulators on reconfigurable hardware. By identifying multiple levels of functional specialisations and the optimal data format for the Monte Carlo simulation, we allow different levels of programmability in our framework to retain good performance and support multiple applications. Designs targeting a Virtex-6 SX475T FPGA generated by our framework are about 40 times faster than single-core software implementations on an i7-870 quad-core CPU at 2.93 GHz; they are over 10 times faster and 20 times more energy efficient than 4-core implementations on the same i7-870 quad-core CPU, and are over three times more energy efficient and 36% faster than a highly optimised implementation on an NVIDIA Tesla C2070 GPU at 1.15 GHz. In addition, our framework is platform independent and can be extended to support CPU and GPU applications.

1 Introduction

Numerical methods such as Monte Carlo simulations play an important role in the finance industry, as complex mathematical models without closed form solutions are created to accommodate the growing complexity of financial products. Interest rate modelling is one of the most important fields in mathematical finance research to price fixed income products. In the past two decades this field has evolved from modelling a single instantaneous interest rate [8] to modelling the dynamics of an entire forward rate curve [7]. Modelling each curve has a complexity of $\mathcal{O}(n^2)$ in the number of time-steps, compared to the conventional single-point modelling (such as stock option payoff evaluation) which has a complexity of $\mathcal{O}(n)$. In a large financial institution where overnight sensitivity tests and risk management are vital and required by regulators, curve based Monte Carlo modelling consumes over 30% of the total computational capacity on the corporate compute grid. With computational requirements doubling every year,

O.C.S. Choy et al. (Eds.): ARC 2012, LNCS 7199, pp. 187–201, 2012.

hardware accelerators such as FPGAs and GPUs are increasingly being used to offload computationally demanding tasks from CPUs, in order to improve performance while reducing power consumption and data center space.

This paper proposes a customisable Monte Carlo framework for the automated generation of highly efficient curve based payoff evaluation accelerator, based on the Heath-Jarrow-Morton (HJM) mathematical framework. The main contributions are:

– a flexible Monte Carlo framework with multiple levels of functional specialisations which can be used to generate FPGA solutions for different applications without using a soft processor. The framework is designed to be platform independent and easily extendible to support CPU and GPU implementations (Section 3);
– a domain specific language to enable automatic generation of application-specific components and to support architecture specialisation to a particular application (Section 4);
– a process to identify the optimal floating point data format on target reconfigurable hardware for our architecture (Section 4);
– an evaluation of the proposed framework by comparing processing speed and energy efficiency to general purpose processors and graphics processing units over three case studies (Section 5).

2   Background

FPGAs are increasingly being used for acceleration of Monte Carlo models used in financial simulations. For instance, a platform independent domain specific language has been invented to produce optimised pipelined designs with thread level parallelism for Monte Carlo simulations from a high level abstraction [15]; an FPGA-based stream accelerator with higher performance than GPUs and Cell processors has been proposed for evaluating European options [13]; an architecture with a pipelined datapath and an on-chip instruction processor has been reported for speeding up the Brace, Gatarek and Musiela (BGM) interest rate model for derivatives evaluation [20]; an American option valuator using least-squares Monte Carlo method has been implemented [17]; a control variate Monte Carlo design for Asian options is presented [18], and a successful FPGA project in industry has been reported for collateralised default obligation (CDO) pricing [19]. However, most of the existing work seeks optimisations and generalisations for single-point simulations, while the more complex implementations usually involve a less efficient FPGA-based softcore to handle general control functions [20]. Moreover, a highly optimised complex hardware design is usually less flexible, hence problematic when changes occur frequently. The appropriate balance of performance and programmability of designs remains a challenging problem. We use the Heath-Jarrow-Morton mathematical framework to illustrate our approach to design space exploration for Monte Carlo designs with complex control.

Algorithm 1. HJM Monte Carlo Algorithm: a Single Path

Input: $f(0,T)$ = initial forward curve, σ = volatility model
Output: $f(t,T)$ = forward surface
1: **for** t=0 to t_{max} **do**
2:     **for** T'=0 to T'_{max} **do**
3:         **Calculate Drift**: obtain $\sigma(t,T)$ and get $\mu(t-\delta t, t+T')$ using Equation 2

4:         **Update forward Surface**: get $f(t, t+T')$ using Equation 1
5:         **Price Derivative State 1**: Use $f(t,t+T')$ to price the target derivative
6:     **end for**
7:     **Price Derivative State 2**: Use result from State 1 to price the target derivative
8: **end for**

The Heath-Jarrow-Morton (HJM) Framework [7] is a general framework for modelling instantaneous forward interest rate curve. It differs from short rate models in the way that it models the full dynamics of the entire forward interest rate curve, as opposed to a single point on the curve which is the short rate $r(t)$. The equation of the framework is shown in Equation 1:

$$df(t,T) = \mu(t,T)dt + \sigma(t,T)^T dW(t) \tag{1}$$

$$\mu(t,T) = \sigma(t,T)^T \int_t^T \sigma(t,u)du \tag{2}$$

where $f(t,T)$ is the instantaneous forward rate at time T as seen from time t and $0 \leq t \leq T$; $\sigma(t,T)$ is the forward volatility column vector of size d, where d is the number of factors in the framework; $W(t)$ is a random variable under standard normal distribution. For convenience we call t the time and T' the time offset from time t, with $T = t + T'$, therefore $f(t,T) \equiv f(t, t+T')$.

It can be seen that along each Monte Carlo path, a surface constructed by $f(t,T)$ is generated. Figure 1 shows the evolution of the forward rate curve over time for an arbitrary path of a Monte Carlo simulation. A general Monte Carlo algorithm for the HJM model is shown in Algorithm 1.

From line 5 of Algorithm 1, the forward curve $f(t,T)$ is used as a basic building block to evaluate interest rate products. The HJM framework is flexible in two ways: (a) the user can choose which volatility model to use (line 3 in Algorithm 1) and (b) the payoff evaluation function differs for different financial products (lines 5 and 7 in Algorithm 1). Based on different assumptions and applications, different volatility functions $\sigma(t,T)$ can be chosen. Table 3 shows some parameter settings for Equation 4 under different volatility models. Forward curves generated by the HJM framework are used to value different financial products. Table 4 shows a non-exhaustive list of valuation functions for different interest rate products.

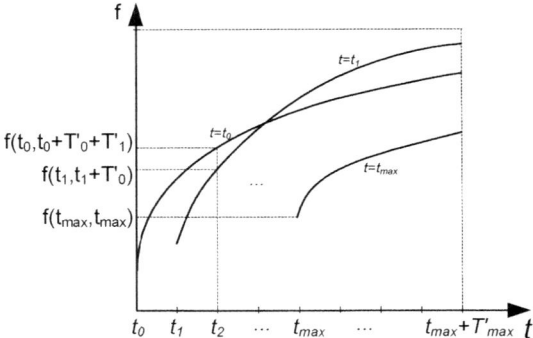

Fig. 1. The evolution of the forward rate curve from $t = 0$ to $t = t_{max}$ in one Monte Carlo path, giving $t_i = T_i = t_i + T'_{i-1}$

Table 1. Parameters in our framework

Model Parameters	
d	number of factors in the framework
t	the variable that tracks time in the model
T	another time in the future, given current time is t
T'	time offset from t to T, $T = t + T'$
$f(t,T)$	the instantaneous forward rate at time T, as seen from time t
$r(t)$	short rate at time t
$\sigma(t,T)$	forward volatility, a d-dimensional column vector
$W(t)$	d-dimensional standard random process

Statistical Test Parameters	
$\overline{X_1}$	mean of the reduced precision result
$\overline{X_2}$	mean of the "true" result
σ_1	standard deviation of the reduced precision result
σ_2	standard deviation of the "true" result
n_1, n_2	number of sampling in the simulation to get the reduced precision result and the "true" result
t	the t-statistic to test whether the population means are different
$d.f.$	degrees of freedom in significance testing
wE, wF	number of exponent bits and mantissa bits in a floating point number

3   Multi-level Customisation Framework

Figure 2 shows our proposed framework for the HJM model, which is independent of the choice of volatility structure and interest rate product. We define our framework based on a procedure for developing evaluators of financial product payoff, in which three levels of functional specialisations can be identified:

- **heavily specialised modules** do not change with applications and are platform dependent;
- **mediumly specialised modules** change occasionally with applications and can be platform dependent;
- **lightly specialised modules** are application dependent but platform independent.

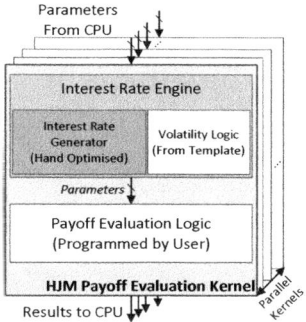

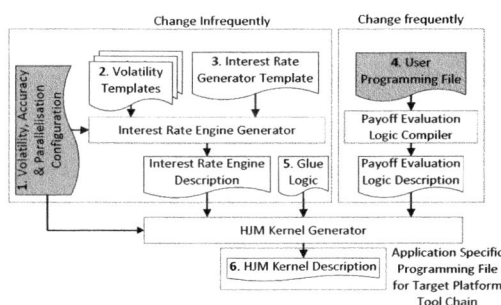

Fig. 2. Proposed framework for the HJM model, dark gray indicates stable part in the kernel, while white indicates flexible parts

Fig. 3. Proposed workflow for our Monte Carlo framework. Refer to Table 2 for details about the input and output files (numbered).

The procedure has two phases: in the **model developing phase** platform experts develop heavily specialised modules and define templates for mediumly specialised modules and optimise them for potential target platforms; in the **payoff evaluator developing phase** users choose a mediumly specialised module as a base component and a target platform, on which platform dependent financial product payoff evaluators are generated using a platform independent domain specific language and a special compiler. Since the user only programmes the platform independent lightly-specialised module in the framework, we have a clear separation of tasks in the financial product payoff evaluator development procedure. In addition, since we expect the model developing phase to be an one-off effort and the payoff evaluator developing phase to be a continuous effort thereafter, we have created an acceleration procedure in which platform dependent expertise is not required from application developers (users).

The main part of the framework is the HJM payoff evaluation kernel, which consists of three components: volatility logic (mediumly specialised), interest rate generator (heavily specialised) and payoff evaluation logic (lightly specialised). Volatility logic, corresponding to line 3 of Algorithm 1, is flexible in the model developing phase and it is stable in the payoff evaluator developing phase. Predefined templates are used to allow limited flexibility in volatility logic; this part is developed by collaboration between platform experts and users. Platform experts need to understand the user's requirements which are usually platform dependent. The interest rate generator, corresponding to line 4 of Algorithm 1, is stable by nature and can be developed by platform experts who also define the interface between the module and the payoff evaluation logic. On the other hand, the payoff evaluation logic is prone to change and we expect many instances of payoff evaluation logic to be created in the payoff evaluator developing phase over a long time. A platform independent domain specific language is used to allow non-experts to use the accelerated framework easily.

Table 2. Explanation of input and output files in our framework as illustrated in Figure 3

Idx[1]	Created By	Phase[2]	Specialisation[3]	P.D. [4]	Purpose
1	User	M	low	No	For non-expert users to target his/her design to a particular platform
2	User & Expert	M	Medium	Maybe	Optimised volatility model design
3	Expert	M	High	Yes	Optimised interest rate generator design
4	User	P	low	No	Payoff evaluation logic design without the need of knowing the underlying platform
5	Expert	M	high	Yes	Platform dependent glue logic, e.g. moving data around, etc.
6	Framework	P	high	Yes	Platform dependent programming file, e.g. VHDL, etc.

[1] These indices identity the six types of files in Figure 3
[2] The phase that creates the file. M stands for the model developing phase and P stands for the payoff evaluator developing phase
[3] Level of functional specialisation
[4] Whether the file is platform dependent

Table 3. Volatility structures used in the HJM framework

Volatility Structure	$\sigma(t,T)$	$\mu(t,T)$
Constant[1]	α	$\frac{1}{2}\alpha^2[T^2 - (T-t)^2]$
Exponential[1]	$\alpha e^{-\beta(T-t)}$	$\frac{\alpha^2}{\beta}(e^{-2\beta(T-t)} - e^{-\beta(T-t)})$
Stochastic[2]	$\widetilde{\sigma}(t,T)f(t,T)$	$\sigma(t,T)\int_t^T \sigma(t,u)du$

[1] α and β are calibrated model constants
[2] $\widetilde{\sigma}$ is a stochastic volatility process

Figure 3 shows our proposed workflow. The user begins the payoff evaluator developing phase by defining the choice of underlying platform, volatility model, accuracy requirement and parallelisation requirement in a configuration file. The choice of underlying platform defines whether the user wants the application to run on FPGA, CPU, GPU etc.; volatility model defines the interest rate engine; accuracy requirement defines word length of the datapath, and parallelisation determines the number of parallel datapaths in the system. Based on the configuration file, the interest rate engine generator combines an appropriate interest rate generator template and a volatility module template to produce an interest rate engine description. The engine description is a programming file that describes the target platform. The user writes domain specific programmes to utilise the interest rates generated by the engine and then builds appropriate designs to evaluate interest rate derivatives. The platform independent user programming file is compiled to a payoff evaluation logic description programming file for the target platform, by the payoff evaluation logic compiler. The HJM kernel generator combines the interest rate engine description and payoff evaluation logic description to produce a complete programming file, which is then used as input to the target platform tool chain to generate executables.

Table 4. Example interest rate products

Target Instrument	Payoff Evaluation Function
Bond	$B(t,T) = \exp\left(-\int_t^T f(t,u)du\right)$
Bond Option[1]	$(B(t,T) - K)^+$
CMS[2]	$Y(t,T) = \frac{1 - B(t,T)}{\sum_{a=t}^T B(t,a)}$
Swaption	$(Y(t,T) - K)^+ \sum_{a=t}^T B(t,a)$
CMS S.O.[3]	$(Y(t,T_1) - Y(t,T_2) - K)^+$

[1] $(x)^+ \equiv max(0,x)$
[2] Constant Maturity Swap
[3] CMS Spread Option

4   Application Specialisation Flow

In this section we discuss the specialisation process in our framework. We propose a "C" style control-based domain specific programming environment to demonstrate the programmability of our framework. The programming environment has the following assumptions:

- The programming environment provides a set of environment parameters P generated by its underlying framework at each iteration (one clock cycle for FPGAs, one for-loop iteration for CPUs, etc.), which can be utilised by the developer (user). This means that data are provided in a temporal manner as opposed to the conventional spatial manner. Instead of requesting a piece of desired data, the developer waits until the data are provided by the programming environment.
- Operator latency is implicit; results appear to be produced instantaneously. This allows the developer to use the framework without expertise in the target platform.
- The user can create model input variables, intermediate variables, accumulation logic, control logic and nothing else. The set of input variables V, once declared, is treated as a data environment, in other words $P' = P \cup V$.
- The user specifies outputs from intermediate variables, and output conditions.

The language is natively supported by CPU and GPU implementations and can be used to generate control and datapaths in hardware. We give a simplified definition of the grammar in Listing 1.1 in order to provide an overview of our domain specific language, it is not intended to be rigorous or comprehensive.

We now demonstrate the application specialisation process for reconfigurable hardware. To begin with, we map our language to the hardware architecture.

Listing 1.1. Simplified grammar for the domain specific language used in our framework. Note that the grammar is subject to extension and it is intended to show the capability of the language, hence it may neither be rigorous nor be comprehensive.

```
<configuration> ::= <statement>+
<statement> ::= <calc_statement>|<io_statement>
<calc_statement> ::= <ident> = <expression>
   | if ( <expression> ) { <calc_statement>+ }
       [else { <calc_statement>+ } ]?
<io_statement> ::= input ( <ident> )
   | output ( <expression> )
<expression> ::= <literal>
   |<unary_op> <expression>
   |<expression> <binary_op> <expression>
   |<func> ( <expression> [, <expression>]* )
<literal> ::= <env_literal> | <user_literal>
```

We assume $P = \{f_{i,j}, discount_i, dt, i, j\}$, $V = \{Imax, Jmax\}$ and $P' = P \cup V$, as shown in Figure 4, where i is the index for time step t, the incrementation of i depends on index j which is the index for time offset T'; $f_{i,j}$ is the discretised instantaneous forward rate at time T_j , as seen from time t_i; dt is the time difference between T_j and T_{j-1} or t_i and t_{i-1}; and $discount_i$ is the discount factor to present time. The top box in Figure 4 shows the programming environment in which one P' is provided in each clock cycle. The user relies on the programming environment to provide a correct set of parameters, and assumes that variable j counts inside each variable i. The bottom box in Figure 4 shows a fully pipelined design generated from the description in the top box. The n-buffer under the accumulator is to hide pipeline latency of the accumulator by keeping a history of n previous value. This effectively increases total pipeline latency of the datapath by n, however it allows full pipelining in the datapath without using low performance un-pipelined accumulator. Latency balancing buffers are omitted in the figures for simplicity. Figure 5 shows a possible extension based on Example 1, in which annuity is calculated based on prices of zero bonds maturing over a time period.

Reconfigurable hardware supports customised word length of its datapath in order to optimise hardware utilisation based on an accuracy requirement. Previous research focuses on fine-grained bitwidth optimisation, such as simulation [10], interval arithmetic [4], backward propagation analysis [6], affine arithmetic [12] and polynomial algebra [2]. However most of them are not straight forward for complex Monte Carlo problems where multiple levels of combinational logic consisting of floating point datapath and accumulators are combined with complex control-flow and feedback paths. We propose a purely statistical method to determine the optimal data format for reconfigurable hardware.

The accuracy of a financial instrument payoff calculated by a numerical method is usually affected by two main factors:

– Discretisation error: the error caused by transforming the model from a continuous mathematical space to a discretised computational space. In our case when the Monte Carlo method is used, the discretisation error comes from insufficient sampling of the underlying random source.

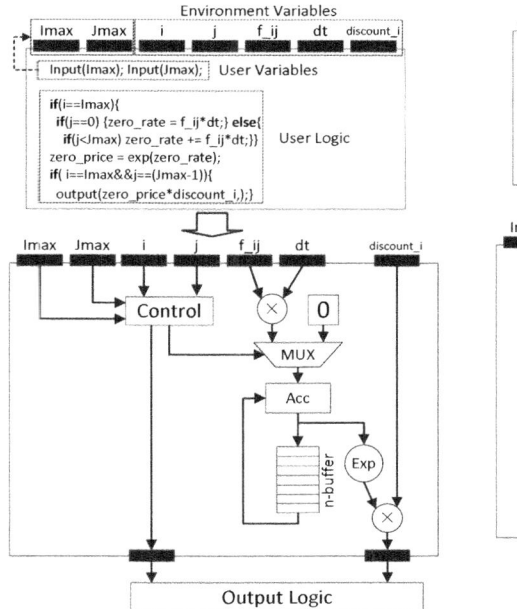

Fig. 4. Domain specific language Example 1

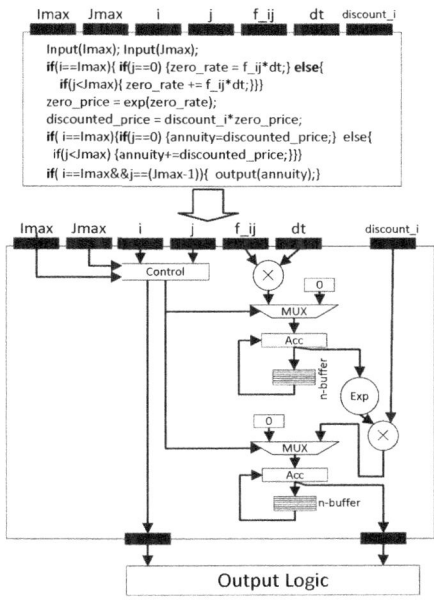

Fig. 5. Domain specific language Example 2, extending Example 1

- Finite precision error: the error caused by using number representations of insufficient accuracy. The error can be amplified or diminished by numerical operators in the datapath. In Monte Carlo simulations we expect the finite precision error to be a normally distributed random factor, according to the law of large numbers and the central limit theorem.

We therefore define the measure of accuracy to be the observed error due to the combination of discretisation error and finite precision error. Since Monte Carlo is a statistical method relying on the law of large numbers, we use Welch's t-test to assess the statistical significance of the error in the result [11]. The test determines whether there is any statistical evidence suggesting the Monte Carlo result is different from the "true result", which is the result calculated by a high precision datapath, e.g. double precision. We therefore set the null hypothesis to be that the Monte Carlo result and the true result are equal, assuming we know the true result and its standard deviation beforehand. We use Equation 3 to calculate the t-value and Equation 4 to calculate the degree of freedom ($d.f.$). These two values can then be used to obtain the p-value via the Students-t CDF. The definition of the variables are shown in Table 2. The experiment will run the Monte Carlo simulation using a customised floating point data format with wE bits of exponent and wF bits of mantissa. For the sake of simplicity from now on we define $wE = 8$ for all floating point number formats. We use the custom data format to build the datapath for a given Monte Carlo payoff evaluation simulation and run different experiments with n_1 starting from a smaller number and incrementing towards infinity. During the experiments we monitor the p-value, and once the p-value falls below a pre-selected statistically significant threshold (e.g. p=0.05 for 5% significance) the simulator is considered to have failed. If the test does not fail on the custom data format, we can conclude that the result from the custom datapath is not statistically different from the data format used to obtain the "true result".

$$t = \frac{\overline{X_1} - \overline{X_2}}{\sqrt{\sigma_1^2/n_1 + \sigma_2^2/n_2}} \tag{3}$$

$$d.f. = \frac{\left(\sigma_1^2/n_1 + \sigma_2^2/n_2\right)^2}{\left(\sigma_1^2/n_1\right)^2/(n_1 - 1) + \left(\sigma_2^2/n_2\right)^2/(n_2 - 1)} \tag{4}$$

5 Result

In this section we discuss the applications of our framework over three case studies: bond option, swaption, and CMS spread option (CMS S.O.). The details of these options are listed in Table 4.

We use the MaxWorkstation reconfigurable accelerating system from Maxeler Technologies to evaluate our framework. It has one MAX3 card with a Xilinx Virtex-6 SX475T FPGA. The card is connected to an Intel i7-870 CPU through a PCI express link with a measured bandwidth of 2 GB/s. The general purpose processor (GPP) in our comparison is a 4-core Intel i7-870 CPU running at 2.93 GHz.

We use the Intel Compiler (ICC) and the Intel Math Kernel Library for our software implementations. The SFMT random number generator and the Box-Muller transformation provided by Intel Vector Statistical Library (VSL) are used for random number generation. We have optimised the software implementations to the best of our knowledge, to ensure the comparisons are fair and accurate.

The FPGA implementations are generated based on: user programming files compiled automatically by our payoff evaluation logic compiler, and configuration files, volatility templates, glue logic and interest rate generator template written and optimised by hand. The files are assembled into a final design following the proposed workflow manually, while a fully automated system is under development. We use the MaxCompiler as our high level synthesis tool and our payoff evaluation logic compiler generates intermediate descriptions compatible with the MaxCompiler based on our domain specific language. We use one CPU core to drive the FPGA in our case studies. The payoff evaluation logic compiler is generated by ANTLR parser generator [1]. The hand-optimised interest rate generator consists of a LUT Optimised uniform random number generator [14], a wrapper to transform uniform random numbers to standard normal random numbers [16] and a floating point exponential operator [3]; other components are generated by Xilinx CoreGen.

We use Welch's t-test described in Section 4 to determine the optimal floating point number format to use on FPGA. The test is designed so that we have a

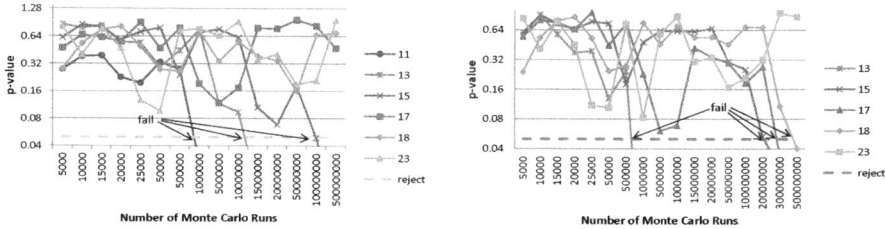

Fig. 6. p-value in log scale for Bond Option

Fig. 7. p-value in log scale for Swaption

set of applications A, let A_i ($i \in \mathbb{N}$) indicate the ith application in set A, and $A_{i,wF}$ indicate a variation of application A_i using a specific floating point data format with wF mantissa bits. We define a test result to be a tuple ($A_{i,wF}$, n), which is obtained from a Monte Carlo simulation of n paths using application $A_{i,wF}$. The test result is then compared to a reference result obtained from ($A_{i,53}, 10^9$), which is a double precision variation of A_i running one billion Monte Carlo paths. We assume that all reduced precision data formats under consideration have 8 exponent bits ($wE = 8$). We use Equation 3 to calculate the t-value and Equation 4 to calculate the degrees of freedom, from which the p-value can be obtained from standard t-distribution tables. Setting the null hypothesis to state that the result obtained from a reduced precision datapath is the same as the result obtained from a double precision datapath, if p-value is smaller than or equal to the significance level ($p = 0.05$), the reduced precision result is then rejected, since there is enough information to tell that the reduced precision result and the double precision result are from two different distributions. Otherwise the observation is consistent with the null hypothesis and we consider the reduced precision result to be not statistically different from the double precision result.

In our experiment we have $A = \{$ Bond, Bond Option, CMS, Swaption, CMS Spread Option$\}$, $8 \leq wF \leq 23$ and $5000 \leq n \leq 5 \times 10^8$. We use the MPFR library [5] to build reduced precision datapaths in order to carry out the experiments in a scalable way; however, because the calculations mirror those performed in hardware, the results also apply to the FPGA data-path. Due to space limitation we only discuss two representative cases: Bond Option and Swaption. Figure 6 shows different p-values of the bond option application with different number of bits for mantissa over various number of Monte Carlo runs. The data formats with $wF \leq 10$ are ignored as they fail the t-test when $n = 5000$. The 11-bit mantissa version fails when $n = 10^6$, which means there is no statistically significant evidence to tell the reduced precision result from the double precision result when $n < 10^6$. Therefore if the user only intends to run Monte Carlo simulations of $n < 10^6$ paths, he/she can get an answer not statistically significantly different from the double precision result by a reduced precision datapath. On the other hand, with a 17-bit mantissa we do not fail until 5×10^8 samples, which means the 17-bit version can produce a good enough result for $n < 5 \times 10^8$. Other variations all fail t-tests before $n = 5 \times 10^8$.

Figure 6 shows p-values for Swaption application, which is an extreme case where the 17-bit mantissa version fails t-test when $n = 3 \times 10^8$; it means that we need to increase the mantissa bits if n exceeds 3×10^8. However, this is the only application where the 18-bit mantissa version fails t-test. On the other hand, we don't see any 23-bit mantissa version fails any t-test during our experiments. In finance industry Monte Carlo simulations usually use $n = 5 \times 10^4$, which is well below the 3×10^8 threshold, so floating point numbers with 17 to 23 bit mantissas should be good enough to produce reliable results.

Table 5 shows a resource consumption comparison between double precision and reduced precision implementations. It can be seen that when double precision is used in the datapath, all implementations are bounded by Block RAM resource, since the designs require significant amounts of FIFO buffer to pipeline accumulators and to retime pipelines with long delay. We can only fit 2-3 double precision cores on the FPGA and utilise around 20% of the logical hardware resource. On the other hand, if we use reduced precision data format ($wE = 8, wF = 17$), we find Block RAM resource usage reduced by 15 to 20 times, and the design is now bounded by logic resources instead. This means that we can utilise more area on the FPGA to do computation and expect a higher throughput. The top clock frequencies also increase by about 1.4 times accordingly.

Table 6 contrasts GPP and GPU implementations with the FPGA implementations generated by our framework. Each FPGA implementation uses about 80% of the total logic resource available on the FPGA to avoid congestion in the place and route phase. The FPGA implementations are based on a reduced precision data format ($wE = 8, wF = 17$). The testing cases are Monte Carlo simulations of 100 million paths for GPP and FPGA, and an 89.6 million paths Monte Carlo simulation for GPU. The GPU testing case is designed to fit the GPU parallelism granularity to ensure fair comparison. It can be seen that the FPGA implementations are about 40 times faster than software implementations utilising one of the four CPU cores. They are about 10 times faster than the corresponding software implementations utilising all four CPU cores. It is not surprising to see that the FPGA CMS spread option implementation is the slowest, since it requires complex logic to sample two different sections on the forward curve, which implies larger kernels, slower clock frequency and fewer

Table 5. Resource Comparison: $wE = 8, wF = 53$ (double precision) and $wE = 8, wF = 17$ (reduced precision) on a Virtex-6 SX475T FPGA

	Bond Option		Swaption		CMS S.O.		Device
Num. Mantissa Bits	53	17	53	17	53	17	-
LUT (%)	6.2	**3.26**	7.95	**3.77**	11.64	**5.1**	297600
FF (%)	4.04	2.18	5.43	2.5	7.94	3.33	595200
BRAM (%)	**28.76**	1.88	**29.04**	1.88	**41.82**	2.02	1064
DSP (%)	6.55	1.39	7.04	1.49	8.09	1.74	2016
Clock Freq. (MHz)	195	270	185	265	170	230	-
Normalised Area	15x	1x	15x	1x	20x	1x	-
Normalised Freq.	1x	1.4x	1x	1.4x	1x	1.35x	-

Table 6. Comparison of MC simulations using double precision GPP(SW), reduced precision FPGA and single precision GPU

Device	Bond Option			Swaption		CMS S.O.[6]	
	SW[1]	FPGA	GPU[5]	SW	FPGA	SW	FPGA
Clock Freq. (MHz)	2930	160	1150	2930	150	2930	150
Num. of Cores	4	26	448	4	19	4	16
Num.Evaluations (B)[4]	177	177	154	177	177	177	177
Exe. Time (Seconds)	476	50.3	50.5	738	69.4	822	73.75
Power Consumption (W)[3]	183	87	240	184	87	184	85
Energy Efficiency[2]	2	40.5	12.7	1.3	29.3	1.3	28.2
Speed-up vs Single-Core[7]	4x	**44.8x**	32.8x	4x	**42.4x**	4x	**39.2x**
Speed-up vs Quad-Core[8]	1x	**11.2x**	8.2x	1x	**10.6x**	1x	**9.8x**
Normalised Energy	19.9x	1x	3.2x	22.5x	1x	24.1x	1x

[1] The software utilises all 4 physical cores by process level parallelism
[2] Measured in number of evaluations/second/Joule
[3] The idle power consumption of the system is 80W
[4] Number of point evaluations in the simulation, measured in billions of $f(t, T)$ calculation
[5] The benchmark GPU is an NVIDIA Tesla C2070 device
[6] CMS Spread Option
[7] Speedup against one core of a quad-core CPU
[8] Speedup against all four cores of a quad-core CPU

parallel kernels in the FPGA. The software implementation suffers less from the increase of complexity since the two samplings are independent of each other and the instructions can be efficiently pipelined.

We use an Ethernet-connected power measuring socket from Oslon electronics to measure average power consumption of the system, with a measuring resolution of 1 sample per second. As shown in Table 6, it is not surprising to see that FPGA implementations are generally about 20 times more energy efficient than software implementations, given that all power readings include idle power consumption of the system.

We now discuss our Graphics Processing Unit (GPU) benchmark to compare the FPGA implementations generated by our framework. The GPU is an NVIDIA Tesla C2070 device with 448 cores running at 1.15 GHz and has a peak double precision performance of 515 GFlops. The benchmark implementation on bond option is based on the standard parallel random number generator provided by CURAND Library and nvcc compiler with maximum optimisation flags turned on. The implementation is hand optimised so that access to off chip memory only occurs at the beginning and at the end of the kernel launch. We use warp level control to ensure the kernel only accesses on chip cache during the execution without any bank conflict or branch divergence. As shown in Table 6, the GPU implementation is about two times less energy efficient and the corresponding FPGA implementation is about 36% faster. Given the fact that both devices are using the 40nm technology, it can be seen that the FPGA implementations are gaining speed advantage and energy effciency from customisable data format, fully pipelined datapath and lower clock frequency.

It is difficult to make precise qualitative comparison between our approach and the traditional hand written approach, in terms of development time and quality of code. However, when compared with simple hand-written designs using a high-level programming language [9], which requires the user to write hundreds of lines of code, our automated approach requires less than ten lines of code (Figure 4).

6   Conclusion

This paper proposes an application independent Monte Carlo framework for interest rate derivatives payoff evaluations based on the HJM model. By identifying three levels of functional specialisations in the model, we allow a hand optimised component, a templated component and a programmable component in our framework, to retain good performance and to support multiple applications. The framework is designed to be platform independent and easily extendible to support CPU and GPU implementations. To specialise our framework to a particular application, we propose a domain specific language for the programmable component. We also propose a process for the FPGA platform to identify the optimal floating point data representation to ensure maximum utilisation of hardware resource. We have shown that, by adopting optimal number representation in the datapath, we can reduce the memory resource usage by 15 to 20 times, allowing better utilisation of logic resource.

The designs generated by our framework for a Xilinx Virtex-6 SX475T FPGA are generally about 40 times faster than a single-core implementation on a i7-870 quad-core CPU at 2.93 GHz, are over 10 times faster and 20 times more energy efficient than 4-core implementations on the same i7-870 quad-core CPU, and are three times more energy efficient and 36% faster than an NVIDIA Tesla C2070 GPU at 1.15 GHz.

Current and future work includes the following. First, explore effective automation of the proposed workflow while allowing user guidance where essential. Second, extend our framework to cover other numerical methods and other applications. Third, explore how advanced techniques, such as run-time reconfiguration, can further improve performance and energy efficiency.

Acknowledgment. The research leading to these results has received funding from UK EPSRC, Maxeler Technologies, J.P. Morgan and European Union Seventh Framework Programme under grant agreement number 248976 and 257906.

References

1. ANTLR, http://www.antlr.org/
2. Boland, D., Constantinides, G.: Automated precision analysis: A polynomial algebraic approach. In: IEEE Int. Symp. on Field-Programmable Custom Computing Machines (FCCM) (2010)

3. de Dinechin, F., Pasca, B.: Floating-point exponential functions for DSP-enabled FPGAs. In: Proc. Int. Conf. on Field-Programmable Technology (2010)
4. Fang, C.F., Rutenbar, R.A., Chen, T.: Fast, accurate static analysis for fixed-point finite-precision effects in DSP designs. In: Proc. Int. Conf. on Computer-Aided Design (2003)
5. Fousse, L., Hanrot, G., Lefèvre, V., Pélissier, P., Zimmermann, P.: Mpfr: A multiple-precision binary floating-point library with correct rounding. ACM Trans. Math. Softw. 33 (2007)
6. Gaffar, A.A., Mencer, O., Luk, W., Cheung, P.Y.K.: Unifying bit-width optimisation for fixed-point and floating-point designs. In: IEEE Symp. on Field-Programmable Custom Computing Machines (2004)
7. Heath, D., Jarrow, R., Morton, A.: Bond pricing and the term structure of interest rates: A new methodology for contingent claims valuation. Econometrica 60(1), 77–105 (1992)
8. Ho, T.S.Y., Lee, S.B.: Term structure movements and pricing interest rate contingent claims. Journal of Finance 41(5), 1011–1029 (1986)
9. Jin, Q., Thomas, D.B., Luk, W., Cope, B.: Exploring reconfigurable architectures for tree-based option pricing models. ACM Trans. Reconfigurable Technol. Syst. 2, 21:1–21:17 (2009)
10. Kum, K.I., Sung, W.: Combined word-length optimization and high-level synthesis of digital signal processing systems. IEEE Transactions on Computer-Aided Design of Integrated Circuits and Systems 20, 921–930 (2001)
11. Larsen, R.J., Marx, M.L.: An Introduction to Mathematical Statistics and Its Applications. Pearson Education (2011)
12. Lee, D.U., Gaffar, A., Cheung, R., Mencer, O., Luk, W., Constantinides, G.: Accuracy-guaranteed bit-width optimization. IEEE Transactions on Computer-Aided Design of Integrated Circuits and Systems 25, 1990–2000 (2006)
13. Morris, G., Aubury, M.: Design space exploration of the European option benchmark using Hyperstreams. In: Proc. Int. Conf. on Field Programmable Logic and Applications, pp. 5–10 (2007)
14. Thomas, D.B., Luk, W.: High quality uniform random number generation using LUT optimised state-transition matrices. J. VLSI Signal Process. Syst. 47, 77–92 (2007)
15. Thomas, D., Bower, J., Luk, W.: Automatic generation and optimisation of reconfigurable financial Monte-Carlo simulations. In: Proc. Int. Conf. on Application-Specific Systems, Architectures and Processors, pp. 685–689 (2007)
16. Thomas, D., Luk, W.: Non-uniform random number generation through piecewise linear approximations. In: Proc. Int. Conf. on Field Programmable Logic and Applications (2006)
17. Tian, X., Benkrid, K.: American option pricing on reconfigurable hardware using least-squares monte carlo method. In: Proc. Int. Conf. on Field-Programmable Technology, pp. 263 –270 (2009)
18. Tse, A.H., Thomas, D.B., Tsoi, K., Luk, W.: Reconfigurable control variate Monte-Carlo designs for pricing exotic options. In: Proc. Int. Conf. on Field Programmable Logic and Applications, pp. 364–367 (2010)
19. Weston, S., Spooner, J., Racanière, S., Mencer, O.: Rapid computation of value and risk for derivatives portfolios. Concurrency and Computation: Practice and Experience (to appear)
20. Zhang, G., Leong, P., Ho, C., Tsoi, K., Cheung, C., Lee, D.U., Cheung, R., Luk, W.: Reconfigurable acceleration for Monte-Carlo based financial simulation. In: Proc. IEEE Int. Conf. on Field-Programmable Technology, pp. 215–224 (2005)

A Low-Cost and High-Performance Virus Scanning Engine Using a Binary CAM Emulator and an MPU

Hiroki Nakahara[1], Tsutomu Sasao[2], and Munehiro Matsuura[2]

[1] Kagoshima University, Japan
[2] Kyushu Institute of Technology, Japan

Abstract. This paper shows a virus scanning engine using two-stage matching. In the first stage, a binary CAM emulator quickly detects a part of the virus pattern, while in the second stage, the MPU detects the full length of the virus pattern. The binary CAM emulator is realized by four index generation units (IGUs). The proposed system uses four off chip SRAMs and a small FPGA. Thus, the cost and the power consumption are lower than the TCAM-based system. The system loaded 1,290,617 ClamAV virus patterns. As for the area and throughput, this system outperforms existing FPGA-based implementations.

1 Introduction

1.1 Virus Scanning System

A **computer virus**[1] intends to damage computer systems. The growth of the Internet requires a high-speed virus scanning on an e-mail and a file servers. The throughput of the software-based virus scanning is at most tens of mega bits per second (Mbps) [16], which is too low. Thus, a hardware-based virus scanning is necessary. We consider a low-cost and high-performance virus scanning system shown in Fig. 1 for low-end users such as SOHO (small office and home office) and enterprise with the following features:

High throughput: The throughput is higher than that of servers (hundreds Mbps). It has a throughput with higher than one Gbps.

Low power and low cost: It uses a low-end (i.e., a small) FPGA and SRAMs[2], instead of a high-end FPGA and a TCAM. Table 1 shows that the TCAM dissipates much higher power than the SRAM. Although we can implement the CAM function on the FPGA [5,8], for the virus scanning, it requires excessive amount of resources for the FPGA.

Reconfigurable: It uses a memory-based realization rather than the random logic realization. Although the random logic realization on the FPGA is fast and compact, the time for place-and-route is longer than the periods for the virus pattern update. Some virus scanning software, e.g., Kaspersky [10], updates the virus data every hour.

---

[1] It is also called **a malware** (a composite word from <u>mal</u>icious soft<u>ware</u>). In this paper, a virus means a computer virus.

[2] As of Nov. 2011, the retail prices for semiconductor devices are as follows: a TCAM is hundreds USD (U.S. dollar); a high-end FPGA is more than ten thousand USD; a low-end FPGA is several USD; and an SRAM is tens USD [4].

O.C.S. Choy et al. (Eds.): ARC 2012, LNCS 7199, pp. 202–214, 2012.

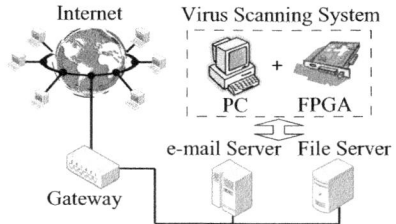

Fig. 1. Virus scanning system for an e-mail server and a file server

Table 1. Comparison of TCAM with SRAM (18Mbit chip) [9]

	TCAM	SRAM
Max. Freq. [MHz]	266	400
Power Dissipation [W]	12-15	≈ 0.1
# of transistors per a bit	16	6

1.2 Related Works

Our virus scanning engine uses two-stage matching to make the circuit compact [11]. Various two-stage matching implementations have been reported: A TCAM with a general purpose processor (MPU) [23]; a bit-partitioned Aho-Corasic DFA [20] with a special purpose MPU [1]; hash methods using cuckoo hashing [21]; parallel FIMMs with an MPU [13]; the parallel sieve method with an MPU [14]; and Bloom filter (PERG-Rx) [7].

1.3 Contributions of the Paper

Implementation of more than one million ClamAV virus patterns: We used a parallel sieve method.

High-level characterization of the bandwidth by the hardware and the software: We implement two-stage matching by the hardware and the software. We maximized the bandwidth by finding the optimal size of the hardware experimentally.

Comparison of various two-stage matching methods: We compare our method with various two-stage matching implementations with respect to throughput and area efficiency.

The rest of the paper is organized as follows: Chapter 2 introduces the virus scanning based on two-stage matching; Chapter 3 describes the binary CAM emulator for the FIMM; Chapter 4 shows the implementation results of the virus scanning engine; and Chapter 5 concludes the paper.

Table 2. Meta characters used in ClamAV

Meta Char	Meaning	Example
??	An arbitrary character	
*	Repetition of more than zero "??"	AA*BB={AABB,AA??BB, AA????BB,AA??????BB,···}
(AA|BB)	Set of characters	(AA|BB)={AA,BB}
{n-m}	Repetition of n or more than n "??" and m or less than m "??"	AA{1-2}BB={AA??BB, AA????BB}

Table 3. Virus patterns in ClamAV (version 0.96.5, December, 1st, 2010) and our implementation

Pattern type	#Patterns	Implementation	Realized
MD5 checksum	761,527	Hardware	Yes
Basic pattern	94,227	Hardware	Yes
Google safe browsing database	434,863	Hardware	Yes
Combination pattern	85	Software	No
Compression file analysis	106	Software	No
Total	1,290,808		

2   A Virus Scanning Based on Two-Stage Matching

2.1   Definitions

A **virus scanning** detects the virus on a **text** (executable codes or e-mails). A **pattern** is written by a **regular expression** consisting of **characters** and **meta characters**. A **pattern matching** is to detect variable-length patterns in the text. A character is represented by a pair of hexadecimal numbers. Table 2 shows the meta characters used in ClamAV. A **length** is the number of characters. A **subpattern** is a part of the pattern consisting characters only[3]. In this paper, k denotes the number of patterns, r denotes the length of a pattern, and m $(m \leq r)$ denotes the length of a subpattern.

2.2   ClamAV Virus Pattern

As of December 1st, 2010, ClamAV (version 0.96.5) contains 1,290,808 patterns [3]. Table 3 shows the pattern types, the number of patterns, and their detection methods. An **MD5 checksum pattern** is the MD5 hash value (128 bits) of the virus. It is detected by the hardware. A **basic pattern** is a **regular expression** of a part of the virus. It is detected by the hardware. A **Google safe browsing database pattern** is the MD5 hash value of the abnormal address obtained from the Google safe browsing API [6]. It is detected by the hardware. A **combination pattern** is a combination of basic patterns. It is detected by the logical operations of software such as "AND", "OR", and "NOT" of the basic patterns. A **compressed file analysis pattern** includes a file size, a file name, or header characteristics. Since the ClamAV committee announces that this pattern will be not supported, we do not implement this.

Fig. 2 shows the virus scanning system. Since the computing time for the Google safe browsing API and the basic pattern combination are significantly short, they are realized by software. The MD5 checksum generator is implemented by the commercial IP core [2]. Therefore, in this paper, $k = 1,290,617$ *patterns including the MD5 checksum pattern, the basic pattern, and the Google safe browsing database pattern* are realized by a **virus scanning engine** on the hardware (a small FPGA and SRAMs).

Example 2.1. *Table 4 shows an example of ClamAV patterns. For "W32.Gop", "736D74702E79656168" and "2D20474554204F49" are subpatterns.*   ∎

---

[3] However, a meta character "??" is permitted.

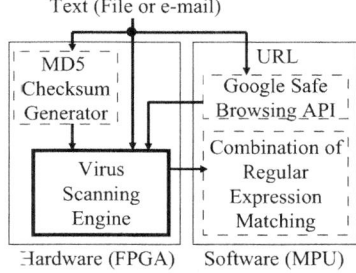

Fig. 2. Virus scanning system

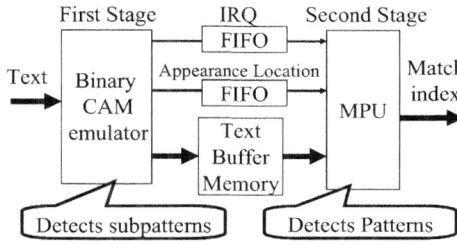

Fig. 3. Virus scanning engine using two-stage matching

Table 4. Examples of ClamAV patterns

Virus Name	Pattern
Trojan.DelY-3	64656C74726565{-1}2F(59|79)20633A5C2A2E2A
Trojan.MkDir.B	406D64202572616E646F6D25????676F746F2048
W32.Gop	736D74702E79656168*2D20474554204F49
Worm.Bagle-67	6840484048688D5B0090EB01EbEB0A5BA9ED46

2.3   Virus Scanning Engine Using Two-Stage Matching

A ClamAV pattern consists of subpatterns and meta characters representing the distance. To detect patterns, we use **two-stage matching**. Fig. 3 shows the virus scanning engine using two-stage matching. Since no subpattern contains meta characters, in the first stage, we use **a binary CAM emulator** to detect the subpattern. When a subpattern is detected, **the IRQ (interrupt request) signal** and **the appearance location** are sent to the MPU. Since the pattern contains meta characters, in the second stage, the embedded MPU performs PCRE (Perl compatible regular expression) [15] matching for the full length of the pattern. Since other subpatterns may be detected during the MPU operation, FIFOs are attached between the first stage and the second stage to store IRQ signals and appearance locations. Also, **a text buffer memory** is attached.

Example 2.2. *Fig. 4 shows an example of two-stage matching. First, at the appearance location "3", the first stage finds the subpattern "653D" (Fig. 4(1)). At this point, the*

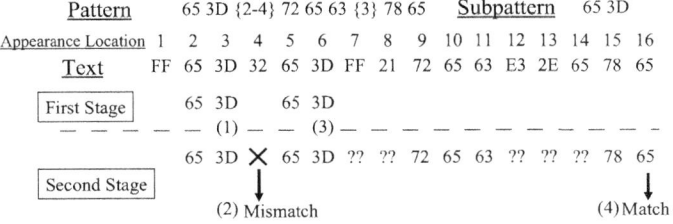

Fig. 4. Example of two-stage matching

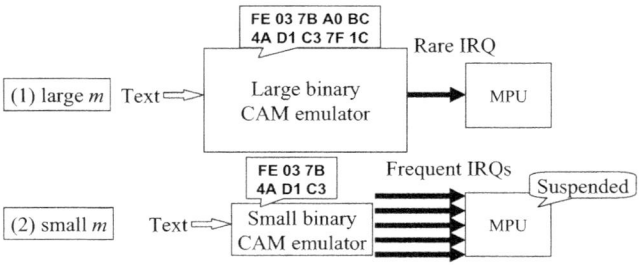

Fig. 5. Relation between the subpattern length m and the number of IRQs

second stage finds mismatch (Fig. 4(2)). Next, at the appearance location "6", the first stage finds the subpattern "653D" (Fig. 4(3)). Finally, the second stage detects the pattern (Fig. 4(4)).   ■

2.4 Subpattern Length m

For ClamAV, since most patterns are MD5 checksums or MD5 hash values consisting 16 characters (128 bits)[4], m is at most 16. Let k be the number of subpatterns with length m to be stored to the binary CAM emulator, then the **subpattern detection probability** $P(m)$ is $\frac{k}{m2^8}$ [5]. When m is large, since $P(m)$ is small, the IRQ signal rarely occurs[6]. However, the size of the binary CAM emulator becomes large (Fig. 5(1)). On the other hand, when m is small, the binary CAM emulator becomes small. Since $P(m)$ is large, the IRQ signal frequently occurs (Fig. 5(2)). In this case, the binary CAM emulator is suspended until the MPU finishes the operation, so that the system throughput decreases. Thus, to minimize the size of the binary CAM emulator, we must find the minimum m that does not suspend the MPU.

Problem 2.1. *Let k be the number of subpatterns with length m to be stored to the binary CAM emulator, T_{MPU} be the processing time for the regular expression matching by the MPU; $P(m) = \frac{k}{m2^8}$ be the subpattern detection probability; and T_{bCAMe} be the operation time of the binary CAM emulator to shift characters. Obtain the minimum m that satisfies the condition:*

$$\frac{T_{bCAMe}}{P(m)} \gg T_{MPU}. \tag{1}$$

$\frac{1}{P(m)}$ denotes the average distance of appearance locations, and $\frac{T_{FIMM}}{P(m)}$ denotes the **average IRQ period**. Here, we assume that subpatterns are uniformly distributed. The actual value of m is obtained experimentally in Section 4.1.

---

[4] For the basic patterns consisting of more than 16 characters, we extract the first 16 characters.

[5] When the distribution of the characters in the subpatterns is uniform.

[6] For a subpattern shared by multiple patterns, the second stage using the PCRE library detects the multiple patterns.

3   Binary CAM Emulator Using Four Index Generation Units

3.1   Index Generation Function

Definition 3.1. *[18] A mapping $F(X) : B^n \rightarrow \{0, 1, \ldots, k\}$, is an* **index generation function with weight** k, *where $F(a_i) = i$ $(i = 1, 2, \ldots, k)$ for k different* **registered vectors**, *and $F = 0$ for other $(2^n - k)$ non-registered vectors, and $a_i \in B^n$ $(i = 1, 2, \ldots, k)$. In other words, an index generation function produces unique indices ranging from 1 to k for k different registered vectors, and produces 0 for other vectors.*

Table 5. An example of an index generation function

x_1	x_2	x_3	x_4	x_5	x_6	f
0	0	0	0	1	0	1
0	1	0	0	1	0	2
0	0	1	0	1	0	3
0	0	1	1	1	0	4
0	0	0	0	0	1	5
1	1	1	0	1	1	6
0	1	0	1	1	1	7

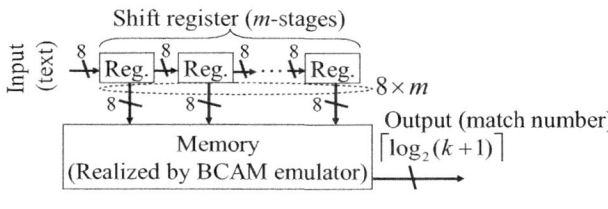

Fig. 6. Finite Input Memory Machine (FIMM)

Example 3.3. *Table 5 shows an example of an index generation function, where $n = 6$ and $k = 7$.* ∎

In a virus scanning, a registered vector corresponds to a subpattern of a virus pattern, while an index corresponds to the unique number for each subpattern.

3.2   Finite Input Memory Machine to Detect a Subpattern

Fig. 6 shows **a finite input memory machine (FIMM)** [12] that accepts k subpatterns with length m. In Fig. 6, *Reg* denotes an 8-bit parallel-in parallel-out shift register. The m-stage shift register stores the past m inputs, and the memory produces the match number. Let M_{FIMM} be the size of the memory [7] of the FIMM, then, we have $M_{FIMM} = 2^{8m} \lceil log_2(k + 1) \rceil$. Thus, a single-memory implementation is impractical for a large m.

3.3   Index Generation Unit for FIMM

In this paper, to realize the FIMM compactly, we use multiple index generation units (IGUs) [19].

Let $\hat{f}(Y_1, X_2)$ be the function whose variables $X_1 = (x_1, x_2, \ldots, x_p)$ are replaced by $Y_1 = (y_1, y_2, \ldots, y_p)$, where $y_i = x_i \oplus x_j$, $x_i \in \{X_1\}$, $x_j \in \{X_2\}$, and $p \geq$

---

[7] Since the amount of memory of the state variables for the shift register is much smaller than that for the output functions, when we calculate the memory size, we neglect it.

Table 6. Decomposition chart for $f(X_1, X_2)$

| | 0 0 0 0 1 1 1 1 x_3 |
| | 0 0 1 1 0 0 1 1 x_2 |
	0 1 0 1 0 1 0 1 x_1
000	0 0 0 0 0 0 0 0
001	0 0 0 0 0 0 0 0
010	1 0 2 0 3 0 0 0
011	0 0 0 0 4 0 0 0
100	5 0 0 0 0 0 0 0
101	0 0 0 0 0 0 0 0
110	0 0 0 0 0 0 0 6
111	0 0 7 0 0 0 0 0
x_6, x_5, x_4	

Table 7. Decomposition chart for $\hat{f}(Y_1, X_2)$

| | 0 0 0 0 1 1 1 1 y_3 |
| | 0 0 1 1 0 0 1 1 y_2 |
	0 1 0 1 0 1 0 1 y_1
000	0 0 0 0 0 0 0 0
001	0 0 0 0 0 0 0 0
010	2 0 1 0 0 0 3 0
011	0 0 4 0 0 0 0 0
100	0 5 0 0 0 0 0 0
101	0 0 0 0 0 0 0 0
110	0 0 0 0 6 0 0 0
111	0 0 0 0 0 7 0 0
x_6, x_5, x_4	

$\lceil \log_2(k+1) \rceil$. Table 6 shows a **decomposition chart** for the index generation function shown in Example 3.3. The columns labeled by $X_1 = (x_1, x_2, x_3)$ denotes **bound variables**, and rows labeled by $X_2 = (x_4, x_5, x_6)$ denotes **free variables**. The corresponding chart entry denotes the function value. Table 7 shows the decomposition chart for $\hat{f}(Y_1, X_2)$, where $Y_1 = (x_1 \oplus x_6, x_2 \oplus x_5, x_3 \oplus x_4)$, and the column labels denote $Y_1 = (y_1, y_2, y_3)$, and the row labels denote $X_2 = (x_4, x_5, x_6)$. When a column of a decomposition chart has two or more non-zero elements, it has a **collision**. The number of collisions is three in Table 6, while the number of collisions is only one in Table 7.

Table 8. Decomposition chart for $\hat{f}_1(Y_1, X_2)$

| | 0 0 0 0 1 1 1 1 y_3 |
| | 0 0 1 1 0 0 1 1 y_2 |
	0 1 0 1 0 1 0 1 y_1
000	0 0 0 0 0 0 0 0
001	0 0 0 0 0 0 0 0
010	2 0 1 0 0 0 3 0
011	0 0 0 0 0 0 0 0
100	0 5 0 0 0 0 0 0
101	0 0 0 0 0 0 0 0
110	0 0 0 0 6 0 0 0
111	0 0 0 0 0 7 0 0
x_6, x_5, x_4	

Table 9. Main memory for $\hat{h}(Y_1)$

y_3	0	0	0	0	1	1	1	1
y_2	0	0	1	1	0	0	1	1
y_1	0	1	0	1	0	1	0	1
$\hat{f}_1$	2	5	1	0	6	7	3	0

In Table 7, assume that the element '4' in the column (0,1,0) is realized by other IGU. By removing '4' from $\hat{f}$, we have $\hat{f}_1$ whose decomposition chart is shown in Table 8, where no collision occurs. Note that, we can represent the non-zero elements of $\hat{f}_1$ by the **main memory** $\hat{h}$ whose input is Y_1. Table 9 shows the function $\hat{h}(Y_1)$ of the main memory. The main memory realizes a mapping from a set of 2^p elements to a set of $k + 1$ elements. The output for the main memory does not always represent f, since $\hat{f}_1$ ignores X_2. Thus, we must check whether $\hat{f}_1$ is equal to f or not by using an auxiliary (AUX) memory. To do this, we compare the input X_2 with the output for the AUX memory by a **comparator**. The AUX memory stores the values of X_2 when the output of $\hat{f}_1(Y_1, X_2)$ is non-zero. Fig. 7 shows the **index generation unit (IGU)**. First, the **hash circuit** generates the transformed inputs Y_1 from the primary inputs (X_1, X_2), where $|X_1| = |Y_1|$. The detailed design method for the hash circuit is described in [18]. Second, the main memory finds the possible index corresponding to Y_1. Third, the AUX memory produces the corresponding inputs X_2' ($n - q$ bits, where $q = \lceil log_2(k + 1) \rceil$). Fourth, the comparator checks whether X_2' is equal to X_2 or not. Finally, the AND gates produce the correct value $\hat{f}(Y_1, X_2)$. We implement the main memory and the AUX memory (gray part in Fig. 7) by a single memory device with $|Y_1|$ ($= p\ bits$) inputs and $q + |X_2'|$ ($= n\ bits$) outputs.

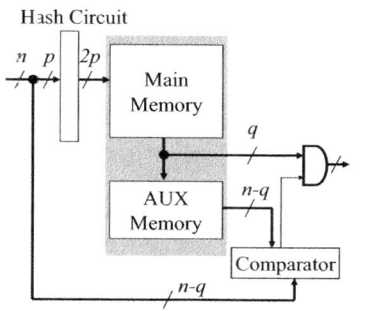

Fig. 7. Index generation unit (IGU) realizing the memory of the FIMM

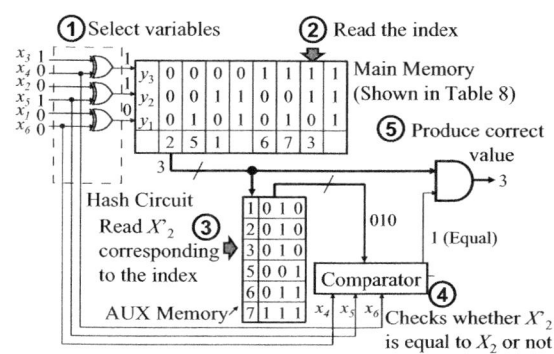

Fig. 8. Operation of IGU

Example 3.4. *Fig. 3.3 shows an example of operation of an IGU realizing $\hat{f}_1(Y_1, X_1)$ shown in Table 8.* ∎

Example 3.5. *When the decomposition chart shown in Table 8 is realized by a single memory, the memory size is $2^6 \times \lceil log_2(7 + 1) \rceil = 192$ (bits). On the other hand, the memory size for the IGU shown in Fig. 3.3 is $2^3 \times (3 + 3) = 48$ (bits). Hence, the IGU can reduce the memory size.* ∎

Table 10. Estimated value vs. experimental value for ClamAV 1,290,617 subpatterns stored in the standard parallel sieve method.

	Estimated		Experimental	
	p	Stored	p	Stored
IGU$_1$	21	963,815 (74.678%)	21	934,999
IGU$_2$	19	243,186 (18.842%)	19	303,310
IGU$_3$	17	61,816 (4.789%)	16	30,967
IGU$_4$	15	15,921 (1.233%)	15	16,056
IGU$_5$	13	4,195 (0.325%)	13	4,255
IGU$_6$	11	1,148 (0.089%)	11	638
IGU$_7$	10	416 (0.032%)	9	329
IGU$_8$	11	78 (remain)	6	63

Table 11. Estimated value vs. experimental value for ClamAV 1,290,617 subpatterns stored in the 4IGU

	Estimated		Experimental	
	p	Stored	p	Stored
IGU$_1$	21	963,815 (74.678%)	21	953,221
IGU$_2$	21	280,778 (21.755%)	21	311,943
IGU$_3$	21	45,028 (3.489%)	21	25,276
IGU$_4$	17	996 (remain)	16	177

3.4   Capability of the Index Generation Unit

The fraction of registered vectors realized by the IGU has been analyzed [17].

Theorem 3.1. *[17] Let f be an n-variable index generation function with weight k. Let the non-zero elements of f be uniformly distributed in the decomposition chart of f. Then, the fraction δ of registered vectors realized by the index generation unit (IGU) is given by $\delta \simeq \frac{1-e^{-\xi}}{\xi}$, where p denotes the number of inputs to the main memory, $k \leq 2^p$, and $\xi = \frac{k}{2^p}$.*

Example 3.6. *When $\frac{k}{2^p} = 1$, we have $\delta = 1 - e^{-1} \simeq 0.632$. In this case, the main memory realizes 63.2% of the registered vectors. Note that the hash circuit is used to make the function uniformly distributed.* ∎

Experimental results show that, by increasing the number of inputs p for the main memory, we can store virtually all vectors.

Conjecture 3.1. *[17] Consider a set of uniformly distributed index generation functions with weight k (≥ 7). If $p \geq \lceil log_2(k + 1) \rceil - 3$, then, more than 95% of the functions can be represented by an IGU with the main memory having p inputs.*

3.5 Realization of the Index Generation Function Using Parallel Sieve Method [14]

From Theorem 3.1 and Conjecture 3.1, we can estimate the number of registered vectors k stored in the main memory with p inputs. The parallel sieve method stores all the subpatterns in multiple IGUs.

Definition 3.2. The parallel sieve method *is an implementation of an index generation function using multiple IGUs. IGU_{i+1} is used to realize a part of the registered vectors not stored by $IGU_1, IGU_2, \ldots, IGU_i$. The OR gate in the output combines the indices to form a single output. In* **the standard parallel sieve method**, *the number of inputs to the main memory is chosen as $p_i = \lceil log_2(k_i + 1) \rceil$, where k_i denotes the number of registered vectors to be realized by IGU_j, $(j \geq i)$.*

Example 3.7. *Table 10 compares the numbers of estimated stored vectors with that for the experimental ones for ClamAV $k = 1,290,617$ subpatterns with length[8] $n = 40$. We can see that, the necessary number of IGUs is obtained from the given number of vectors k by using Theorem 3.1 and Conjecture 3.1. In this case, the total amount of memory is $\sum_{i=1}^{8} 2^{p_i} n = 13.33$ MBytes.* ∎

3.6 Realization of the Index Generation Function Using Four IGUs [18]

In this section, we show that most index generation functions can be realize with only four IGUs with the uniformed size. We call this **four IGUs method (4IGU)**.

Example 3.8. *Table 11 compares the estimated stored vectors with that for the experimental ones for ClamAV $k = 1,290,617$ subpatterns with length $n = 40$. By using Theorem 3.1 and Conjecture 3.1, we can show that, the 4IGU can store all given vectors. In this case, the total amount of memory is $2^p n \times 4 = 40$ MBytes.* ∎

---

[8] $n = 40$ is obtained experimentally in our implementation described in Section 4.1.

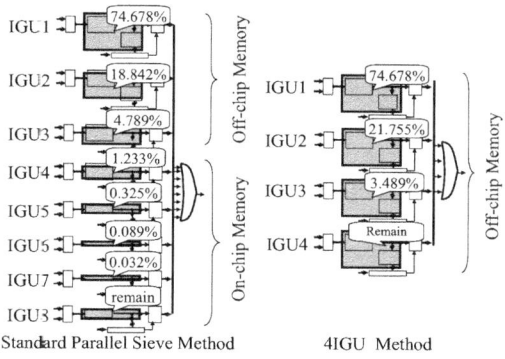

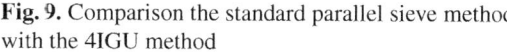

Standard Parallel Sieve Method   4IGU Method

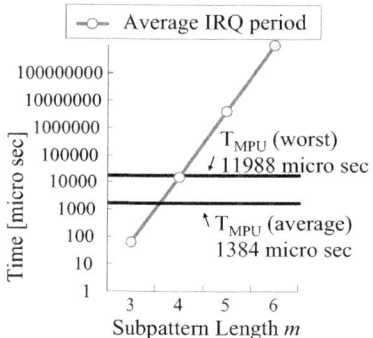

Fig. 9. Comparison the standard parallel sieve method with the 4IGU method

Fig. 10. Average and maximum operation times of MPU T_{MPU} and average IRQ period for different values of m

3.7 Discussion

Fig. 9 compares the standard parallel sieve method with the 4IGU method, when the number of registered vectors is 1,290,617 and $n = 40$. From theoretical analysis, as for the total amount of memory, the standard parallel sieve method (13.33 MBytes) requires less memory than the 4IGU method (40.00 MBytes). However, the 4IGU method is more suitable than the standard parallel sieve method for a small FPGA implementation;

1. The 4IGU is easy to update the registered vectors: The standard parallel sieve method requires many IGUs. This is inconvenient for the update of registered vectors.
2. The 4IGU uses off-chip memory only: The standard parallel sieve method requires many memories with different sizes. When we use the off-chip memory only, we have a problem since the FPGA has a limited number of pins. Also, if we use the on-chip memory only, the FPGA has a limited amount of on-chip memory. Although the standard parallel sieve method uses both on-chip and off-chip memories, it requires much on-chip resource on the FPGA.

So, the standard parallel sieve method is unsuitable for a small FPGA implementation. In Section 4.2, as for FPGA resources, we will show that the 4IGU method uses less resource than the standard parallel sieve method experimentally.

4   Experimental Results

4.1   Minimum Subpattern Length m

We obtained the minimum m that satisfies the relation (1). To obtain the subpattern detection probability $P(m)$, first, we implemented a cycle-accurate simulator for the 4IGU in C-language. Then, we scanned 2,963 cygwin executable codes. We assume that the 4IGU reads the data from the SRAM running at 400 MHz. Thus, we have

$T_{bCAMe} = \frac{1}{400} \times 10^6 \, \mu$ sec. We obtained the average operation time of the MPU (T_{MPU}) and the maximum T_{MPU} by matching 2,963 cygwin executable codes on the MicroBlaze [22] running at 100 MHz using the Perl Compatible Regular Expression library (PCRE) [15]. We used the hardware IRQ handler and the software context switch in the MicroBlaze. Fig. 10 shows the average T_{MPU}, the maximum T_{MPU}, and the average IRQ period $\frac{T_{bCAMe}}{P(m)}$ for different m. Since both the average T_{MPU} and the maximum T_{MPU} are smaller than $\frac{T_{bCAMe}}{P(m)}$, we chose $m = 5$ (40 bits) for implementation.

Table 12. Comparison with Other Methods

	#Pattern (#Char)	#LC	On-chip Mem [Bytes]	Th [Gbps]	#LC/ #Char	On-chip Mem/ #Char	Off-chip Memories
USC RegExp Controller(2006) [1]	1,316 (16,715)	41,787	768,819.2	1.40	2.4999	45.9957	SDRAM
Cuckoo Hashing (2007) [21]	4,748 (68,266)	2,982	142,848.0	2.20	0.0436	2.0925	SRAM
Parallel FIMMs (2009) [13]	65,536 (524,288)	77,304	1,048,576.0	1.59	19.3150	2.0000	None
Standard Parallel Sieve Method (2009) [14]	497,172 (3,977,376)	5,268	3,500,880.0	1.60	0.0013	0.8801	Three SRAMs
PERG-Rx (2009) [7]	85,625 (8,645,488)	42,809	387,072.0	1.30	0.0049	0.0447	SRAM
4IGU method (Proposed Method)	1,290,617 (42,461,299)	13,857	39,116.8	3.20	0.0003	0.0009	Four SRAMs

4.2 Implementation Results

We implemented a proposed virus scanning engine shown in Fig. 3 consisting of the 4IGU and the MicroBlaze (MPU) on the Inrevium Corp. PCI Express Evaluation Board (FPGA: Xilinx Inc., Virtex5 VLX50T-GB-R). We used four 16MBytes SRAMs running at 400 MHz for the 4IGU, and used one 512 MBytes SO-DIMM module running at 266 MHz for the MicroBlaze. The synthesis tool is the Xilinx ISE Design Suite ver. 11.1. In the implementation, the 4IGU used 6,279 logic cells (LCs); the MicroBlaze used 1,263 LCs; the DDR2-SDRAM controller used 6,324 LCs and 10 BRAMs; and the text buffer memory used 10 BRAMs. In total, the virus scanning engine used 13,857 LCs and 20 BRAMs. The 4IGU operated at 508.2 MHz, while the MicroBlaze operated at 100 MHz. Since we used four SRAMs running at 400 MHz, the 4IGU shifts 8 bits per one clock. Thus, the system throughput is $0.4 \times 8 = 3.2$ Gbps.

Table 12 compares various FPGA realizations. As for the throughput (Th), our system is 1.45-2.46 times higher. As for the LC requirement per a character (#LC/#Char), our system is 4.3 times lower than that for the standard parallel sieve method; and as for the on-chip memory requirement per a character (Mem/#Char), our system is 49.6 times lower than that for the PERG-Rx. This shows that our virus scanning engine is suitable for a small FPGA implementation. Although it requires four SRAMs, the cost for off-chip SRAMs is much lower than that for the high-end FPGA. Table 12 shows that our virus scanning engine is low-cost and high-performance.

5 Conclusion and Comments

This paper showed the virus scanning engine using two-stage matching. In the first stage, the 4IGU detects the subpatterns, while in the second stage, the MicroBlaze MPU detects the full length of patterns using PCRE library. Our system using Xilinx FPGA and four SRAMs stored 1,290,617 ClamAV virus patterns, and has the throughput of 3.2 Gbps. Experimental results showed that our virus scanning engine is suitable for a low-cost and high-performance system.

Our virus scanning engine has a vulnerability for the performance attack. When the attacker sends a sequence of stored subpatterns, the first stage generates an IRQ for every clock, and overflows the second stage. Kumar et al. [11] have proposed a method to protect against the performance attack. It attaches a flow counter to the FIFO in Fig. 3. When the value of the counter exceeds the threshold, the circuit detects the performance attack. Our virus scanning engine can incorporate the Kumar's method.

In our experiment, to find the optimum subpattern length m, we scanned cygwin executable codes. However, it is possible to use other binary codes. One candidate is Windows executable codes, since many commercial virus scanner scans them. Also, we implemented the interface with the hardware IRQ and the software context switch. Since the hardware context switch can switch the context quickly, it may increase system throughput, however, this also increases the amount of hardware. Considering practical simulation setup is the one of future work.

Acknowledgments. This research is supported in part by the grant of Regional Innovation Cluster Program (Global Type, 2nd Stage). Reviewer's comments were useful to improve the paper.

References

1. Baker, Z.K., Jung, H., Prasanna, V.K.: Regular expression software deceleration for intrusion detection systems. In: FPL 2006, pp. 28–30 (2006)
2. CAST inc., MD5 IP Core,
   http://www.cast-inc.com/ip-cores/encryption/md5/
3. ClamAV, http://www.clamav.net/
4. Digi-key Corp.,
   http://www.digikey.com/
5. Ditmar, J., Torkelsson, K., Jantsch, A.: A Dynamically Reconfigurable FPGA-Based Content Addressable Memory for Internet Protocol Characterization. In: Grünbacher, H., Hartenstein, R.W. (eds.) FPL 2000. LNCS, vol. 1896, pp. 19–28. Springer, Heidelberg (2000)
6. Google, Google Safe Browsing API,
   http://code.google.com/intl/ja/apis/safebrowsing/
7. Ho, J.T.L., Lemieux, G.G.F.: PERG-Rx: A hardware pattern-matching engine supporting limited regular expressions. In: FPGA 2009, pp. 257–260 (2009)
8. James-Roxby, P.B., Downs, D.J.: An efficient content-addressable memory implementation using dynamic routing. In: FCCM 2001, pp. 81–90 (2001)
9. Jiang, W., Wang, Q., Prasanna, V.K.: Beyond TCAMs: An SRAM-based parallel multi-pipeline architecture for terabit IP lookup. In: INFOCOM 2008, pp. 1786–1794 (2008)
10. Kaspersky, http://www.kaspersky.com/

11. Kumar, S., Chandrasekaran, B., Turner, J., Varghese, G.: Curing regular expressions matching algorithms from insomnia, amnesia, and acalculia. In: ANCS 2007, pp. 155–164 (2007)
12. Kohavi, Z.: Switching and Finite Automata Theory. McGraw-Hill Inc. (1979)
13. Nakahara, H., Sasao, T., Matsuura, M., Kawamura, Y.: A virus scanning engine using a parallel finite-input memory machine and MPUs. In: FPL 2009, pp. 635–639 (2009)
14. Nakahara, H., Sasao, T., Matsuura, M., Kawamura, Y.: The parallel sieve method for a virus scanning engine. In: DSD 2009, pp. 809–816 (2009)
15. PCRE: Perl compatible regular expressions, http://www.pcre.org/
16. Roan, H.C., Hawang, W.J., Dan Lo, C.T.: Shift-or circuit for efficient network intrusion detection pattern matching. In: FPL 2006, pp. 785–790 (2006)
17. Sasao, T.: Memory-Based Logic Synthesis. Springer, Heidelberg (2011)
18. Sasao, T., Matsuura, M., Nakahara, H.: A realization of index generation functions using modules of uniform sizes. In: IWLS 2010, June 18-20, pp. 201–208 (2010)
19. Sasao, T., Matsuura, M.: An implementation of an address generator using hash memories. In: DSD 2007, August 27-31, pp. 69–76 (2007)
20. Tan, L., Sherwood, T.: A high throughput string matching architecture for intrusion detection and prevention. In: ISCA 2005, pp. 112–122 (2005)
21. Thinh, T.N., Kittitornkun, S., Tomiyama, S.: Applying cuckoo hashing for FPGA-based pattern matching in NIDS/NIPS. In: ICFPT 2007, pp. 121–128 (2007)
22. Xilinx inc, MicroBlaze, http://www.xilinx.com/
23. Yu, F., Katz, R.H., Lakshman, T.V.: Gigabit rate packet pattern matching using TCAM. In: ICNP 2004, pp. 174–183 (2004)

Cost Effective Implementation of Flux Limiter Functions Using Partial Reconfiguration

Mohamad Sofian Abu Talip[1], Takayuki Akamine[1], Yasunori Osana[2],
Naoyuki Fujita[3], and Hideharu Amano[1]

[1] Graduate School of Science and Technology,
Keio University, Yokohama 223-8522 Japan
[2] Department of Electrical and Electronics Engineering
University of the Ryukyus, Okinawa 903-0213 Japan
[3] Aerospace Research and Development Directorate
Japan Aerospace Exploration Agency, Tokyo 182-8522 Japan
cfd@am.ics.keio.ac.jp

Abstract. Computational Fluid Dynamics (CFD) is used as a common design tool in aerospace industry. UPACS, a package for CFD is convenient for users, since a customized simulator can be built just by selecting required functions. The problem is its computation speed which is hard to be enhanced by using clusters due to its complex memory access patterns. As an economical solution, accelerators using FPGAs are hopeful candidates. However, the total scale of UPACS is too large to be implemented on small numbers of FPGAs. For cost efficient implementation, partial reconfiguration which can dynamically reconfigure only required functions is proposed in this paper. Here, MUSCL algorithm used frequently in UPACS is selected as a target. Partial reconfiguration is applied to the flux limiter functions (FLF) in MUSCL. Four FLFs are implemented for Turbulence MUSCL (TMUSCL) and eight FLFs are for Convection MUSCL (CMUSCL). All FLFs are developed independently and separated from the top MUSCL module. At start-up, only required FLFs are selected and deployed to the system without interfering the other modules. This implementation has successfully reduced the resource utilization by 44% to 63%. Total power consumption also reduced by 33%. Configuration speed is improved by 34-times faster as compared to fully reconfiguration method. All implemented functions achieved at least 17 times speed-up compared with the software implementation.

Keywords: CFD, FPGA, Scientific Computations, Reconfigurable Hardware, Partial Reconfiguration.

1 Introduction

The CFD has been used extensively in the design and optimization of fluid flow applications since many years ago. In aerospace industry, the CFD is utilized in design methodology for aircraft components such as jet engines and wings. It is a cost effective design tool whereas consists of intensive computational

O.C.S. Choy et al. (Eds.): ARC 2012, LNCS 7199, pp. 215–226, 2012.

and numerical analysis calculations. It presents methods to solve and analyze problems of the physical phenomena of fluids involving fluid flow on discrete space and time. Usually, software packages for the CFD with high accuracy are needed for aeronautical engineers as well as aerodynamics researchers.

UPACS (Unified Platform for Aerospace Computational Simulation) [1][2] developed by JAXA (Japan Aerospace Exploration Agency) is one of such CFD packages. Although it is a convenient tool for aerodynamics analysis, it sometimes takes several days or weeks when an analytical area grows large [3]. This is mainly caused by low parallelism accompanied with pointer links and complicated memory access pattern. Cluster computing or GPU which makes use of high degree of parallelism is not an efficient solution.

Reconfigurable systems using FPGAs have been utilized for acceleration of specific applications including informatics, digital image processing and others. Although the early reconfigurable systems did not focus on large scale numerical scientific application, the use of FPGAs for such area has been growing remarkably because of the rapid performance improvement of modern FPGAs with a large number of embedded multipliers and BlockRAM modules. Although some researches using FPGAs achieved significant speed-up ratio to the software [4][5], targets were simple programs rather than practical software packages. Our previous researches [6] tried to implement core subroutines in UPACS which accompany complicated memory access into FPGAs. Although the performance can be improved, it is found that the target requires too vast resources to implement on a small number of FPGAs. Since UPACS consists of various kinds of solvers, all of them are not needed to solve a target application. Here, we propose a system which can replace the required functions by making the best use of the partial reconfiguration provided in recent FPGAs.

The rest of this paper is organized as follows. Section 2 discusses related work. Section 3 is for explanation regards to UPACS package. The target subroutines and MUSCL algorithm are explained. Section 4 is about partial reconfiguration technology, and Section 5 describes the design and implementation in this work. Then following to Section 6 for evaluation, Section 7 will summarize this work with conclusion.

2   Related Work

In recent years, researches have been exerted in the area of CFD algorithm implementation using FPGAs. In this field, Andres et al. [5] and Sano et al. [7] reported the result for FPGA accelerations. However, their implementations are not for practical software packages. Another is for implementation of FPGA-based flow solver based on the systolic architecture for CFD [8]. This work proposed a systolic algorithm for the fractional-step method employing the central difference schemes. Although good results are obtained, their implementation is based on 32-bit single precision which is not suitable for UPACS.

Partial reconfiguration technology has attracted many researchers in this field. Recently, this technology was applied to secure content delivery system [9]. In the computer security applications field, partial reconfiguration is applied in AES algorithm implementation [10]. Another research has been done on an aerospace application using partial reconfiguration. LaMeres et al. [11] designed and prototyped the computing architecture which dynamically reconfigures depending on the environment. Another work has been done on the framework for a highly reliable fault tolerant system using partial reconfiguration in spaces applications [12]. However, none of them are in the CFD applications. Our trial is the first implementation example of the CFD on FPGAs with partial reconfiguration.

3   UPACS

UPACS is a CFD package to simulate compressible flow using multi-block grids. It gives researchers an easy way to run large scale simulations. It has been developed as a common aerospace CFD equipping with flexibility, scalability and portability since 1998. The application is written in FORTRAN 90 with the MPI interface. UPACS supports Euler, Navier-Stokes and Reynolds Averaged Navier-Stokes equations as governing equations. By choosing solvers, users can execute simulations on their parallel systems without any code tuning. Users also can select desired solutions and determine the number of process by setting parameters. In order to run a simulation, users just prepare a parameter file and grid data files. In this study, we focus on MUSCL scheme, since the routine which uses MUSCL from turbulence model to calculate residual occupies about 70% of total execution time. This percentage will grow up more than 90% as grid size increases [13].

3.1   MUSCL Algorithm

MUSCL (*Monotone Upstream-centered Schemes for Conservation Laws*) is a method to improve the accuracy and was introduced in a paper by Bram van Leer in 1979. It provides highly accurate numerical solutions for a given system. In UPACS, MUSCL is used in the turbulence model (TMUSCL) and the convection term (CMUSCL) calculation. It extrapolates cell surface values from cell center values shown in formula (1) to (4) and Figure 1.

$$q'_{i+1/2} = (q_{i+1} - q_i)/(\Delta_{i+1} + \Delta_i) \tag{1}$$

$$q'_{i-1/2} = (q_i - q_{i-1})/(\Delta_i + \Delta_{i-1}) \tag{2}$$

$$r = (q'_{i+1/2})/(q'_{i-1/2}) \tag{3}$$

$$q_{i\pm1/2} \cong q_i \pm \phi(r)\Delta_i q'_{i-1/2} \tag{4}$$

In the equations, q_i is the cell center value, Δ_i represents the distance between cell center and cell surface, $q_{1/2}$ is the cell surface value, and $\phi(r)$ is the flux limiter function (FLF). i in the formulas indicates the direction which can be extended to three dimensions. In addition, q_i consists of five physical values, and there are data dependency between them. FLFs are used to suppress oscillation of values. Such oscillation often arises in simulating the field where values change rapidly with a high order difference scheme. Six FLFs are chosen and shown in equations below which is symmetry TMUSCL consist of *no limiter, van Albada, van Leer* and *minmod* limiter functions. On the other hand, 2nd-order CMUSCL consists of *no limiter, van Albada, van Leer, minmod* and *superbee* limiter functions. 3rd order CMUSCL consists of *no limiter, minmod* and *Hemker-Koren* limiter functions.

no limiter,
$$\phi(r) = 0.5 * (r + 1)$$

van Leer,
$$\phi(r) = \frac{(r + |r|)}{(1 + r + EPS)}$$

van Albada,
$$\phi(r) = \frac{(r^2 + r)}{(1 + r^2 + EPS)}$$

minmod,
$$\phi(r) = max[0, min(1, r)]$$

superbee,
$$\phi(r) = [0, min(2r, 1), min(r, 2)]$$

Hemker-Koren,
$$\phi(r) = \frac{(r + 2r^2)}{(2 - r + 2r^2)}$$

where r is the input value expressed as formula (3) and EPS is a machine epsilon.

4 Partial Reconfiguration

Since each MUSCL function has similar structure except FLFs, we can design a single MUSCL module with all FLFs for TMUSCL, 2nd order CMUSCL and 3rd order CMUSCL. However, it becomes a large hardware which cannot be implemented on a single FPGA. The straight forward way is designing three MUSCLs each of which has their own FLFs. Although this approach reduces the hardware, we must provide three independent designs. Our approach is to provide a single design whose FLF can be replaced by making the best use of partial reconfiguration. The total required hardware and power are minimized, since it provides only a single FLF required in the target application. When the execution of UPACS starts and the functions required for MUSCL is decided, an appropriate FLF module is loaded by using the partial reconfiguration while the other part of FPGA is remaining unaffected.

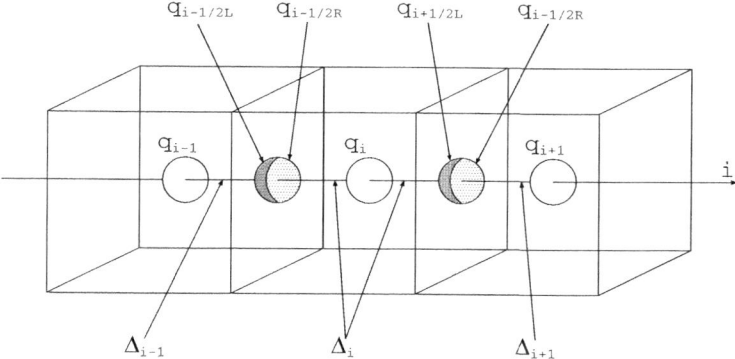

Fig. 1. MUSCL algorithm

Each FLF module has the same inputs and outputs, thus, it can be specified in the HDL description as the functional modules with the reconfigurable partition attribute in the description of MUSCL top module. Multiple instances corresponding to each FLF can be defined for such a single functional module. Software tools as NGDBuild, MAP and PAR detect the reconfigurable partition attribute on the instance and process it correctly.

5   Implementation

MUSCL algorithm is chosen as a top and static module. The FLF module is selected as a reconfigurable partition. The datapath can be obtained from dataflow representation of the algorithm shown in Figure 2. By inserting pipeline registers in the datapath, the fundamental structure of the pipeline is created.

All modules are implemented using IEEE754 standard 64-bit double precision floating-point arithmetic. Here, the floating-point computational module is based on the Xilinx Floating-Point Operator v5.0 incorporated into Xilinx ISE 12.4 software. The Floating-Point Operator v5.0 is an IP core for handling floating-point operations and it is configurable by the user from the CORE Generator tool. In order to generate high performance computation unit, the level of DSP48E usage is set to the maximum to get the desired output.

At one time, only one limiter function is used and employed in the FPGA. All limiter functions are synthesized separately with the top module. The top and reconfigurable module design are consisting of many arithmetic functions. The parameters used for each computing unit are shown in Table 1. Adder and Subtractor require 14 clock cycles per operation by using high speed mode. In addition, Multiplier takes 16 clock cycles with 11 DSP48E modules. The latency of Divider is set to be 57. Although it is possible to decrease the divider clock latency, it will severely degrade the clock frequency.

The circuit designs for all FLFs are shown in Figure 3. The smallest clock cycle is by *minmod* limiter function which only requires 2 clock cycles. The

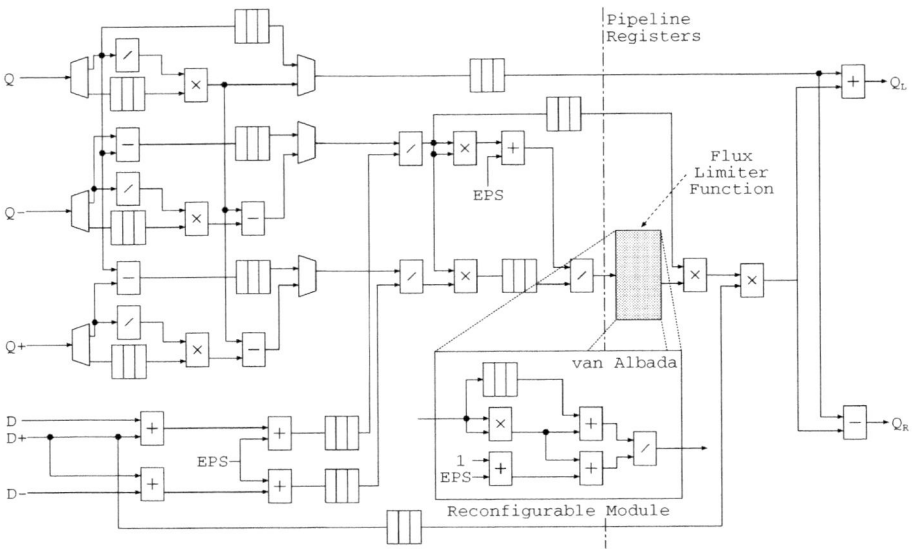

Fig. 2. MUSCL pipeline with van Albada limiter function

Table 1. Data of used computing units

Units	Latency	Registers	LUTs	DSP48E
Adder	14	947	797	3
Subtractor	14	947	798	3
Multiplier	16	483	362	11
Divider	57	5973	3261	0
Comparator	1	0	128	0

largest latency is by *Hemker-Koren* limiter function which requires 117 clock cycles to get result. *Van Albada* and *van Leer* limiter functions require 87 and 85 clock cycles, respectively. In these FLF modules, shift registers are used to synchronize the input value. Shift registers are 64-bit width and can take various clock cycle depth depending on the situation. Machine Epsilon (1×10^{-8}) and constant value 1.0 are also used in these FLFs modules. The rest are *minmod* and *superbee* limiter function. These two FLFs require comparator modules which are used for minimum and maximum value comparison.

6   Evaluation

In this section, evaluation results are shown based on consideration of the following three cases.

- *design-1:* One top module of MUSCL scheme with all FLFs.
- *design-2:* Three top modules only with the associate FLFs for TMUSCL, 2nd order CMUSCL and 3rd order CMUSCL.

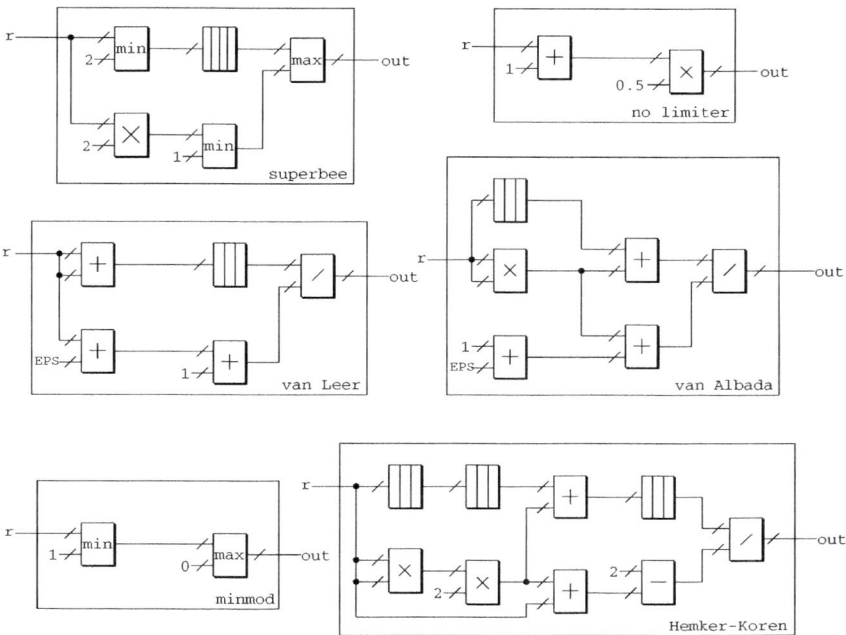

Fig. 3. Implemented flux limiter functions

- *design-3:* One top module of MUSCL scheme with partial reconfiguration FLFs. This is our proposed system.

Xilinx Virtex-6 XC6VLX240T FF1156 with speed grade -1 was selected as a target FPGA. All modules are described with Verilog HDL and simulated with Xilinx ISim Simulator. The modules are synthesized and used resources are measured using Xilinx ISE 12.4. Floor-planning, constraint entry and design rule checks (DRCs) are all accessed through the PlanAhead 12.4 software environment which supports a partial reconfiguration flow. In order to demonstrate that our system works on the real chip, Xilinx ML605 board is used with 200 MHz operating frequency.

6.1   Resources Utilization

The amount of used slice registers, slice LUTs and DSP48E are evaluated when the design is synthesized. The results for all three designs are shown in Figure 4 and Figure 5. This result shows that *design-3* has the lowest resource utilization compared to *design-1* and *design-2*. The resource utilization for *design-1* is the largest. The slice LUTs exceed 100% and so it cannot be implemented on a single chip.

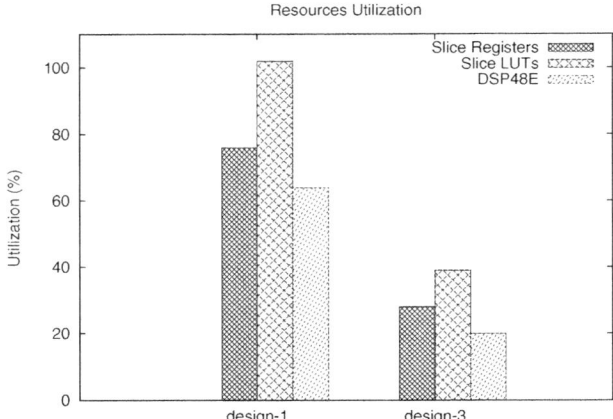

Fig. 4. Resource usage in *design-1* and *design-3*

6.2   Power Consumption

The result of total power consumption for all three designs are shown in Figure 6 and Figure 7. For *design-1*, Xilinx XPower Estimator(XPE) 13.3 is used since the design cannot be implement. It shows that *design-3* has the lowest power consumption compared to other two designs.

In *design-1*, the total power is increased with static power by unused limiter functions. In *design-3*, total power is only consumed by top MUSCL and the required limiter function. The power for *design-2* is less than that for *design-1*, but *design-3* is advantageous even when it is compared with *design-2*.

6.3   Configuration Time

The configuration time for full reconfiguration and partial reconfiguration are compared. In this case, only *design-2* and *design-3* are evaluated, since *design-1* cannot be implement on a single chip.

In the case of JTAG configuration, for Virtex-6 device, configuration time is given by:

$$configuration\ time = \frac{(2044 + bits\ in\ bitstream)}{TCK\ frequency}$$

where *bits in bitstream* is bit file size in bits and *TCK frequency* is maximum configuration TCK clock frequency. 2044 is the total clock cycles needed before and after programming the bitstream to FPGA.

In full reconfiguration, each total bitstream size is 9,017 KB. Based on the above formula, configuration time is equal to 1.119 sec. On the other hand, bitstream size for each partial reconfiguration bit file for the 2nd order FLF is 255 KB. This means that the configuration time is 0.031 sec. In the case of 3rd order FLF, partial bitstream size is 266 KB and corresponding configuration

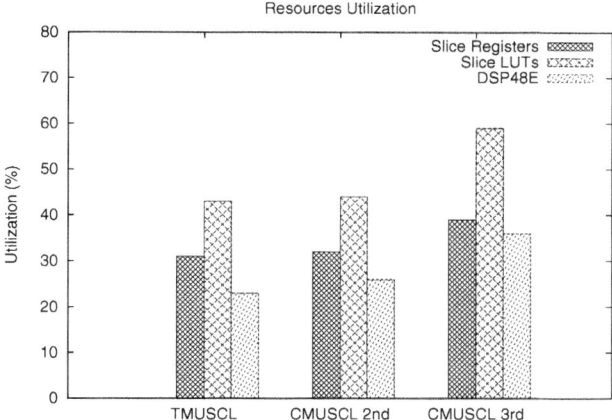

Fig. 5. Resource usage in *design-2*

time is 0.033 sec. In all means, the partial reconfiguration method accelerated the configuration speed by 34 times. In other words, execution time is not so degraded compared with *design-2* even if the FLFs are switched dynamically.

6.4   Performance

MUSCL is implemented with pipelined structure and the clock cycles are measured. Total clock cycles for MUSCL with each FLF is shown in Table 2. The number of clock cycles is corresponding for solving one iteration. In TMUSCL, *van Albada* is the largest, and it takes 290 clock cycles. In CMUSCL, *Hemker-Koren* requires 320 clock cycles to get the result.

In the target application, full reconfiguration for MUSCL will be performed once. After that, the desired limiter functions that want to be used is uploaded using partial reconfiguration. Since configuration time of the reconfigurable module is small, total execution time is not so much affected. If one limiter function is loaded, it will be used till the calculation is finished. The next limiter functions to be used is decided by the users. During calculations, it is not allowed to swap limiter functions dynamically in the system.

The execution time in MUSCL with partial reconfigurable FLFs is compared with the execution time by software. In software, MUSCL is executed by Core 2 Duo 2.4 GHz with Linux Kernel 2.6.18 operating system. The compiler used is GNU Fortran 4.1.2. The execution time to solve 100x100x100 cells iterative calculation is measured by using *call cpu_time* in Fortran 90 language and the 3rd order *Hemker-Koren* is selected for comparison, since it has the largest clock cycles. In software, the execution time took 0.08399 sec, while it takes 320 clock cycles to finish one iterative calculations in FPGA. Adding the time for I/O sending the data sequentially, it take 1,000,320 clock cycles to finish the 100^3 cells simulation. Since the operating frequency in FPGA is 200 MHz, the total execution time is 5.0016×10^{-3} sec. That is, by execution of CMUSCL in FPGA, about 17 times acceleration is expected.

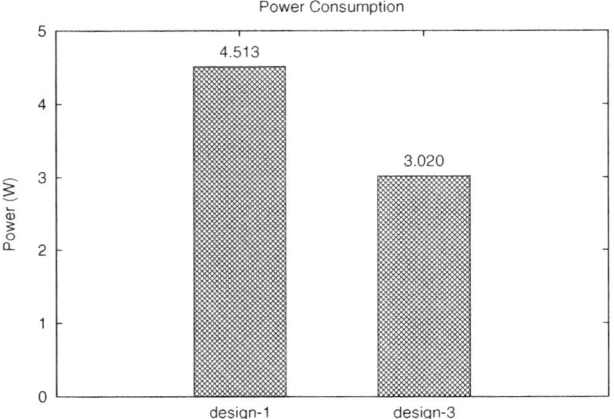

Fig. 6. Total on-chip power for *design-1* and *design-3*

Table 2. Clock-cycle in MUSCL

TMUSCL

Flux Limiter Function	# Clock-cycle
no limiter	233
van Albada	290
van Leer	288
minmod	204

CMUSCL

Flux Limiter Function	# Clock-cycle
no limiter 2nd	233
van Albada 2nd	290
van Leer 2nd	288
minmod 2nd	204
superbee 2nd	222
no limiter 3rd	233
minmod 3rd	204
Hemker-Koren 3rd	320

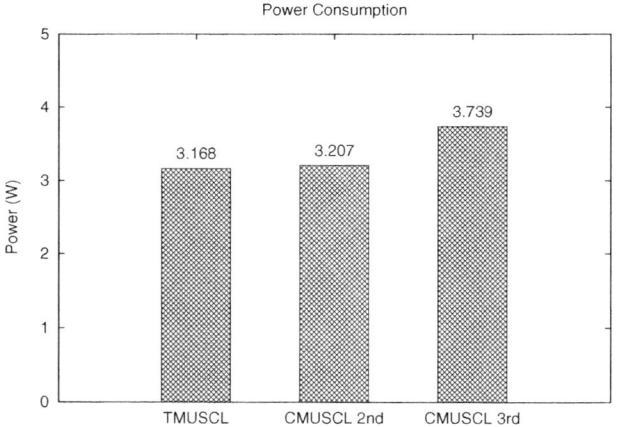

Fig. 7. Total on-chip power for *design-2*

7 Conclusion

This paper presents MUSCL algorithm implementation using partial reconfiguration platform for reducing required hardware resource and power consumption. This implementation has successfully reduced the resource utilization by 44% to 63%. Also, it reduced the power consumption by 33%.

Using partial reconfiguration, the time for configuration is 0.033 sec at maximum. When we provide only a single FPGA, and replace FLFs on demand for computation of TMUSCL, 2nd-order CMUSCL and 3rd-oder CMUSCL, the configuration time becomes an overhead. Although it won't occupy a large part of total UPACS execution time, we must evaluate its impact. It is depending on the structure and scheduling of the reconfiguration system with multiple-FPGAs; for example FLOPS-2D [6] for solving the total UPACS package. Our final goal is building such systems using partial reconfiguration techniques.

Acknowledgments. This work is supported in part by a Grant-in-Aid for the Global Center of Excellence for High-Level Global Cooperation for Leading-Edge Platform on Access Spaces from the Ministry of Education, Culture, Sport, Science and Technology in Japan.

References

1. Yamazaki, H., Enomoto, S., Yamamoto, K.: A Common CFD Platform UPACS. In: Valero, M., Joe, K., Kitsuregawa, M., Tanaka, H. (eds.) ISHPC 2000. LNCS, vol. 1940, pp. 182–190. Springer, Heidelberg (2000)
2. Takaki, R., Yamamoto, K., Yamane, T., Enomoto, S., Mukai, J.: The Development of the UPACS CFD Environment. In: Veidenbaum, A., Joe, K., Amano, H., Aiso, H. (eds.) ISHPC 2003. LNCS, vol. 2858, pp. 307–319. Springer, Heidelberg (2003)
3. Matsuo, Y., Tsuchiya, M., Aoki, M., Sueyasu, N., Inari, T., Yazawa, K.: Early Experience with Aerospace CFD at JAXA on the Fujitsu PRIMEPOWER HPC2500. In: Proceedings of the ACM/IEEE SC 2004 Conference on Supercomputing 2004, p. 11 (November 2004)
4. Smith, W.D., Schnore, A.R.: Towards an RCC-based accelerator for computational fluid dynamics applications. J. Supercomput. 30, 239–261 (2004)
5. Andres, E., Molina, M., Botella, G., del Barrio, A., Mendias, J.: Aerodynamics Analysis Acceleration through Reconfigurable Hardware. In: 2008 4th Southern Conference on Programmable Logic, pp. 105–110 (March 2008)
6. Morisita, H., Inakagata, K., Osana, Y., Fujita, N., Amano, H.: Implementation and evaluation of an arithmetic pipeline on FLOPS-2D: multi-FPGA system. SIGARCH Comput. Archit. News 38, 8–13 (2011)
7. Sano, K., Pell, O., Luk, W., Yamamoto, S.: FPGA-based Streaming Computation for Lattice Boltzmann Method. In: International Conference on Field-Programmable Technology, ICFPT 2007, pp. 233–236 (December 2007)
8. Sano, K., Iizuka, T., Yamamoto, S.: Systolic Architecture for Computational Fluid Dynamics on FPGAs. In: 15th Annual IEEE Symposium on Field-Programmable Custom Computing Machines, FCCM 2007, pp. 107–116 (April 2007)
9. Hori, Y., Yokoyama, H., Sakane, H., Toda, K.: A Secure Content Delivery System Based on a Partially Reconfigurable FPGA. IEICE - Trans. Inf. Syst. E91-D, 1398–1407 (2008)

10. Hori, Y., Satoh, A., Sakane, H., Toda, K.: Bitstream encryption and authentication with AES-GCM in dynamically reconfigurable systems. In: International Conference on Field Programmable Logic and Applications, FPL 2008, pp. 23–28 (September 2008)
11. LaMeres, B., Gauer, C.: Dynamic reconfigurable computing architecture for aerospace applications. In: 2009 IEEE Aerospace Conference, pp. 1–6 (March 2009)
12. Osterloh, B., Michalik, H., Habinc, S., Fiethe, B.: Dynamic Partial Reconfiguration in Space Applications. In: NASA/ESA Conference on Adaptive Hardware and Systems, AHS 2009, July 29-August 1, pp. 336–343 (2009)
13. Inakagata, K., Morishita, H., Osana, Y., Fujita, N., Amano, H.: Modularizing flux limiter functions for a Computational Fluid Dynamics accelerator on FPGAs. In: International Conference on Field Programmable Logic and Applications, FPL 2009, pp. 654–657 (September 2009)

Parallel Tempering MCMC Acceleration Using Reconfigurable Hardware

Grigorios Mingas and Christos-Savvas Bouganis

Department of Electrical & Electronic Engineering,
Imperial College London, Exhibition Road, London SW7 2BT, United Kingdom
{g.mingas10,christos-savvas.bouganis}@imperial.ac.uk

Abstract. Markov Chain Monte Carlo (MCMC) is a family of algorithms which is used to draw samples from arbitrary probability distributions in order to estimate - otherwise intractable - integrals. When the distribution is complex, simple MCMC becomes inefficient and advanced variations are employed. This paper proposes a novel FPGA architecture to accelerate Parallel Tempering, a computationally expensive, popular MCMC method, which is designed to sample from multimodal distributions. The proposed architecture can be used to sample from any distribution. Moreover, the work demonstrates that MCMC is robust to reductions in the arithmetic precision used to evaluate the sampling distribution and this robustness is exploited to improve the FPGA's performance. A 1072x speedup compared to software and a 3.84x speedup compared to a GPGPU implementation are achieved when performing Bayesian inference for a mixture model without any compromise on the quality of results, opening the way for the handling of previously intractable problems.

1 Introduction

Monte Carlo methods are a wide class of stochastic algorithms that rely on repeated generation of random numbers to solve problems like integration and optimization. By generating a large number of samples from the distribution of a variable of interest, Monte Carlo methods can draw conclusions about this variable and the system under study, without resorting to analytical or other numerical methods which are inefficient for many real applications. Monte Carlo is used in numerous fields ([13] provides an overview) but its core task in most cases is to solve the following problem:

Problem. Estimate the expectation of function $f(\mathbf{x})$ under $p(\mathbf{x})$, i.e. compute the following integral:

$$E_p[f(\mathbf{x})] = \int f(\mathbf{x})p(\mathbf{x})\mathbf{dx} \qquad (1)$$

where $\mathbf{x}$ is the random variable of interest and $p(\mathbf{x})$ is the probability distribution of $\mathbf{x}$. In Bayesian inference problems (e.g. machine learning, computational biology), $p(\mathbf{x})$ is usually the posterior distribution of the parameters of the model given the data. The function $f(\mathbf{x})$ is the function of interest. For instance, if a moment or tail probability of $p(\mathbf{x})$ is requested, $f(\mathbf{x})$ changes accordingly.

O.C.S. Choy et al. (Eds.): ARC 2012, LNCS 7199, pp. 227–238, 2012.

Monte Carlo methods draw independent samples from $p(\mathbf{x})$ (also known as the target distribution) and approximate the integral using the following sum:

$$\tilde{E}_p[f(\mathbf{x})] = \tfrac{1}{N} \sum_{i=1}^{N} f(\mathbf{x_i}) \tag{2}$$

where $\mathbf{x_i}$, $i \in \{1, ..., N\}$ are samples taken from $p(\mathbf{x})$.

Sampling independently from $p(\mathbf{x})$ is straightforward only when $p(\mathbf{x})$ has a simple form (e.g. Gaussian, Beta). For non-standard forms of $p(\mathbf{x})$, different approaches like Markov Chain Monte Carlo (MCMC) have to be used. MCMC draws dependent samples from $p(\mathbf{x})$ using a Markov sample chain [13]. The dependent samples can still be used to compute (2). This strategy can theoritically sample from any distribution. The transition kernel of the chain (which defines how each new sample is generated from the previous one) is crucial for the efficiency of the method. It must ensure rapid convergence to $p(\mathbf{x})$ and good mixing (fast movement around the support of $p(\mathbf{x})$). In cases of multimodal target distributions, simple kernels like the Metropolis kernel fail to do that, as they tend to get "stuck" in one of the modes [13].

Advanced MCMC methods have been proposed to sample from these distributions [9]. Here, the focus is on Parallel Tempering (PT) [8], a popular, representative population-based method which is used in Bayesian inference problems as well as in physics and polymer simulations with multimodal targets ([6] is an extensive survey of application areas). PT employs multiple Markov chains to enhance mixing and this makes it computationally intensive. A motivating example is [7], where runtimes of up to 14 days for calibrating a rainfall-runoff model are reported.

In this work, a novel hardware architecture which exploits the characteristics of modern FPGAs to accelerate PT is presented. The architecture is problem-independent; any target distribution can be sampled as long as the respective probability evaluation block is plugged in. Results show that a speedup of 460x compared to software is achieved when performing inference on mixture models. The way this result scales with the size of the problem and the available resources is also investigated. Moreover, the impact of the employed arithmetic precision to MCMC's quality of sampling is addressed for the first time, to the authors' knowledge. It is shown that large reductions in the employed precision of the most area-expensive part of the architecture (probability evaluation) are possible without compromising the accuracy of the estimates, as the error due to precision is lower than the variance of the approximation. This translates to a further speedup of 2.33x compared to the single-precision floating point version of the architecture, making the system 1072x faster than a CPU and up to 3.84x faster than a GPGPU implementation.

The rest of the paper is organized as follows: Section 2 gives a short review of recent research on MCMC acceleration. Section 3 presents PT. Section 4 proposes the hardware architecture and Section 5 describes the class of models used for evaluation. Section 6 presents implementation results and a comparison with existing CPU and GPGPU implementations. Section 7 concludes the paper.

2 Related Work

Lately, several studies on accelerating MCMC using hardware have appeared in the literature. The main problem with MCMC acceleration is its inherently sequential nature; generation of the next sample of the chain requires the previous one to be available. Research efforts focus on: 1) Computation of many chains with the same target distribution in parallel. 2) Acceleration of MCMC methods with natural parallelism. 3) Use of speculative methods to avoid stalls. 4) Parallelization of the operations inside every step of MCMC. 5) Separation of the problem into independent sub-problems and execution of separate MCMCs. Only the first three approaches are problem-independent.

In [2], a multi-FPGA architecture for learning Bayesian networks is described which massively parallelizes intra-chain calculations. Also, a small number of parallel chains are used to enhance mixing but no details are given on how much this strategy helps. [14] use FPGAs to accelerate inference in Markov Random Fields by splitting the problem into sub-problems and running many samplers in parallel. These works are not concerned with how to efficiently map MCMC methods on FPGAs, but rather on how to achieve problem-specific acceleration.

In [11], GPGPU implementations of PT and Sequential Monte Carlo (SMC) are presented and the achieved acceleration is encouraging. Section 6 compares their results to this work. [3] use a speculative strategy to accelerate MCMC on a multicore but the gains are limited. [12] demonstrate why inter-chain communications in PT can pose a significant overhead to a Tungsten cluster and propose optimizations to tackle the problem. Here, it is shown that this is not an issue when the proposed FPGA architecture is used.

In contrast to previous MCMC-related research on FPGAs, this work belongs to the second category described above; it is a study on the suitability of FPGAs to accelerate a class of MCMC methods (population-based MCMC) with natural parallelism. It proposes architectural choices and optimizations which simultaneously exploit the nature of these methods and the characteristics of FPGAs (deep pipelining, fast inter-circuit communication, custom precision). Other population-based methods [9,10] can also take advantage of the proposed architecture.

The idea of using custom arithmetic precision when implementing Monte Carlo methods in FPGAs has been investigated in the past [15,17] but this is the first work that examines MCMC in particular. Here, it is proposed that the probability evaluation's targeted precision should be treated in a different way than the precision of the rest of the MCMC operations.

3 Parallel Tempering

Parallel Tempering is a population-based method, i.e. it uses a population of Markov chains to improve mixing. These methods are the de-facto approach for sampling from multimodal targets. Each chain i samples from a different distribution $p_i(\mathbf{x})$, $i \in \{1, ..., M\}$. Distribution $p_1(\mathbf{x})$ is equal to the target $p(\mathbf{x})$ and the remaining distributions are smoothened versions of $p(\mathbf{x})$ (i.e. closer to the uniform distribution). Smoothing is defined by a parameter (the temperature) and distributions become smoother as i increases. If T_i is the temperature of distribution $p_i(\mathbf{x})$ (with $1 = T_1 < T_2 < ... < T_M$), then:

$$p_i(\mathbf{x}) = p(\mathbf{x})^{1/T_i}, i \in \{1, ..., M\} \tag{3}$$

The target distribution is the "coldest" distribution ($T_1 = 1$) and distributions get "hotter" for $i > 1$.

At time j, the state of PT comprises the samples $\{\mathbf{x}_1^{(j)}, \mathbf{x}_2^{(j)}, ..., \mathbf{x}_M^{(j)}\}$. PT updates all these samples independently (using separate transition kernels according to (3)). The hot chains move quickly in the space because their distributions are closer to uniform. Periodically, PT proposes sample exchanges between chains. These exchanges push samples from the hot chains to the colder ones and eventually to the coldest chain. The samples help the coldest chain escape from isolated modes, thus enhancing mixing. To compute summary statistics, only samples from the coldest chain are kept. Two kinds of operations are performed:

Update Operation. It generates a new sample given the previous one using a kernel. Here, a Metropolis kernel is employed: At time j and for chain i, a candidate sample $\mathbf{y}_i$ is drawn from a normal distribution centred around the previous sample $\mathbf{x}_i^{(j)}$. The candidate sample is accepted as the next sample ($\mathbf{x}_i^{(j+1)} = \mathbf{y}_i$) with probability $a(\mathbf{x}_i^{(j)}, \mathbf{y}_i)$:

$$a(\mathbf{x}_i^{(j)}, \mathbf{y}_i) = min\left(1, \frac{p_i(\mathbf{y}_i)}{p_i(\mathbf{x}_i^{(j)})}\right) \tag{4}$$

If the candidate is rejected, the previous sample $\mathbf{x}_i^{(j)}$ becomes the next sample ($\mathbf{x}_i^{(j+1)} = \mathbf{x}_i^{(j)}$). A global update comprises the update of all M chains.

Exchange Operation. It attempts to exchange samples between two chains. An exchange between chains q and r is accepted with probability $e(\mathbf{x}_q, \mathbf{x}_r)$ (the time step index j is omitted for clarity):

$$e(\mathbf{x}_q, \mathbf{x}_r) = min\left(1, \frac{p_q(\mathbf{x}_r)p_r(\mathbf{x}_q)}{p_q(\mathbf{x}_q)p_r(\mathbf{x}_r)}\right) \tag{5}$$

Many strategies have been proposed to exchange samples. Here, it was decided that performing exchanges only between neighbouring chains is the best way to maximize throughput (more in Section 4). A global exchange comprises exchanges between chains $(1, 2), (3, 4), ..., (M-1, M)$ or chains $(2, 3), (4, 5), ..., (M-2, M-1), (M, 1)$ (alternatively) and happens after every global update.

Figure 1 illustrates a simple case of PT. Normally, dozens or hundreds of chains are used, which can lead to long runtimes for difficult-to-compute targets.

4   System Architecture

4.1   Description

The tempered chains can run independently and only communicate during exchanges. The most computationally demanding task within each chain i is the

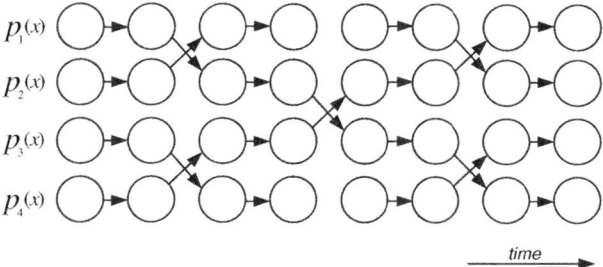

Fig. 1. Parallel Tempering updates and exchanges (four tempered chains)

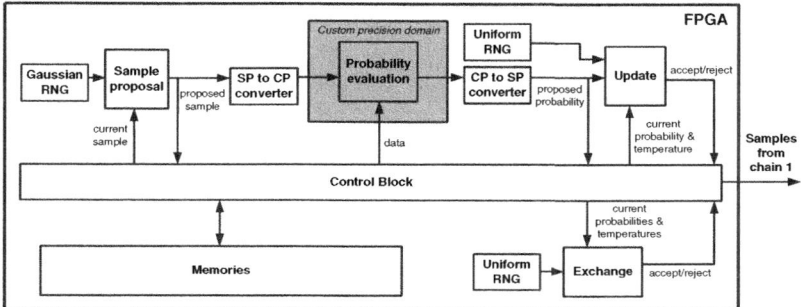

Fig. 2. Overview of the architecture

evaluation of the probability $p_i(\mathbf{y}_i)$ of the proposed sample $\mathbf{y}_i$. Due to the form of (3), this computation is the same for every chain (apart from the temperature and the proposed sample). To exploit this, the proposed architecture treats PT as a streaming application: One or more pipelines that implement the probability density are created and then fed with the independent chains. The temperature scaling is applied at a later stage. By keeping the pipelines fully utilized (using the multiple chains), the sampling throughput of PT is maximized.

Depending on the complexity of $p(\mathbf{x})$, there are two possible scenarios for the number of pipelines: 1) There are enough resources in the FPGA to fully parallelize the probability evaluation so that the pipeline can generate one probability per clock cycle. In this case, more pipelines can be instantiated to increase throughput, with the limit being the total resources of the FPGA. 2) There are not enough resources to fully parallelize the probability evaluation, therefore it can generate one probability per $C > 1$ clock cycles. Only one pipeline is used and the effort must be in optimizing the probability evaluation as much as possible to increase throughput. As this is the most realistic scenario given the complexity of real applications (e.g. large number of data in likelihoods), the remaining of this section focuses on this case.

Figure 2 illustrates the architecture of the system. The sample proposal block reads the current sample of every chain and generates a proposed sample, using numbers from a gaussian Random Number Generator (RNG) [16]. The probability evaluation block reads the proposed samples. Every C cycles, one

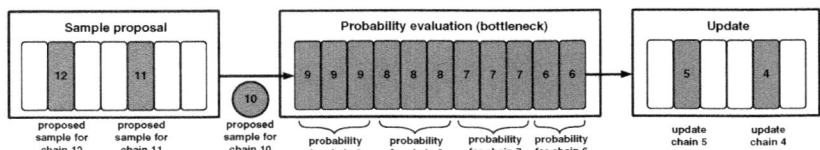

Fig. 3. Streaming through the sample proposal, probability evaluation and update pipelines at a specific time instance. Occupied stages are painted grey, unoccupied stages are painted white.

proposed probability is generated, the update block receives it (together with the current probability, the temperature and a uniform random number) and accepts or rejects the proposed sample using (4). This happens until all chains have been updated and then the sequence is repeated.

Similar to the probability evaluation block, all of the other modules are pipelined but they are under-utilized unless the probability evaluation block can generate one sample (or more) per cycle. Figure 3 demonstrates this; the stages of the pipeline occupied by each chain are visible. In this example, one probability value per $C = 3$ cycles is generated.

The exchange step is executed for a pair of chains in parallel to the above update operations. Every $2C$ cycles, the probabilities of the current samples of the chains, the temperatures and a uniform random number are used to implement (5). Exchanges are proposed between neighbouring chains and not randomly. This strategy was chosen to avoid stalls in the probability evaluation pipeline (chains 2, 3 are exchanged while chains 4, 5, etc are updated). Unlike CPU and GPGPU implementations [12,11], no communication between separate processors is necessary for the exchanges, due to the form of the architecture.

The rest of the design includes two uniform random number generators, precision converters to and from custom precision (see 4.2) and small Block RAMs for the storage of temperatures, samples and probabilities. A control block keeps track of which chain is inside which block and synchronizes memory operations.

The architecture is designed so that sampling from any $p(\mathbf{x})$ is possible. Only the appropriate probability evaluation block needs to be plugged in. The implementation of this block can be done with the help of libraries of floating point operators (e.g. FloPoCo [5]). The rest of the architecture is completely generic and does not change. In order to reduce the area consumption of the architecture and the dynamic range of the variables, probabilities are converted to logarithmic scale. This means that division and power operators needed to implement (4) and (5) are replaced by subtraction and multiplication operators which consume less area. More resources could be saved by "slowing down" the under-utilized modules when $C > 1$ but the gains are not significant and reconfiguration of the generic part (based on the value of C) would be necessary.

The throughput of the system (in samples per second from the coldest chain) is given by the following equation, assuming there are enough chains to fill the pipeline:

$$Throughput = \frac{clockrate}{CM} \qquad (6)$$

where *clockrate* is in Hz, M is the number of chains and C is the number of clock cycles between two consecutive probabilities generated by the probability evaluation block. Equation (6) is valid for any targeted problem and shows that the performance of the system can be maximized if the probability evaluation block takes full advantage of the FPGA's resources in order to minimize C. If more than one pipelines are used (first scenario above), $C = 1$ and the throughput in (6) is multiplied by the number of pipelines.

4.2   Using Custom Arithmetic Precision

Floating point arithmetic is used throughout the design but there are two precision domains. The first comprises the probability evaluation block. This part can be implemented in any precision to save resources (or increase throughput by parallelizing further) with the price of sampling from an altered distribution. The motivation to experiment with this approach was that in stochastic algorithms, it is possible that changes in precision are "hidden" behind randomness and affect results less than they would in a deterministic algorithm. Previous research has shown that MCMC's results can be robust when substituting the acceptance probability with an unbiased approximation [1]. No work has addressed the effect of limited precision to MCMC, though. Here, it was observed that even a large reduction of the first domain's precision will not affect the sampling quality (details in Section 6). The second precision domain includes the generic part of the system. This part always operates in single-precision floating point (double-precision can also be used). It is important to use high precision in order to preserve the convergence and mixing properties of MCMC and PT (which are mathematically proven for infinite precision). In other words, reducing the precision in the second domain means that sampling from any targeted distribution is not guaranteed and unexpected behaviour might occur, while reducing the precision only in the first domain guarantees correct sampling (from an altered but known distribution).

The use of two precision domains is also motivated by the fact that the generic part of the algorithm consumes a significantly lower amount of FPGA resources than the probability evaluation block for any non-trivial target distribution. Consequently, minimizing the area consumption of the probability evaluation block is the primary concern.

5   Bayesian Inference for Mixture Models

5.1   Description

Bayesian inference is a method of statistical inference used to draw conclusions about unobserved or unobservable quantities, given observed data [13]. A common setting is the following: Some data are given and a model with unknown parameters is believed to explain the data. The goal is to obtain the posterior distribution of the parameters given the data and calculate expectations under this posterior (see (1)). The initial belief on the values of the parameters is expressed by a prior distribution. MCMC is the most popular method used to solve this problem.

Mixture models are a powerful family of models used in numerous fields [4]. Multimodal posterior distributions often appear when performing Bayesian inference for these models. Hence, they are a representative case of problems that PT is used to solve.

To test the architecture's performance, a finite gaussian mixture model taken from [9] and [11] is used: A set of independent observations (data) $\mathbf{d} = d_{1:Q}$, where $d_q \in \Re$ for $q \in \{1, ..., Q\}$, is given. Each observation is distributed according to:

$$p(d_q|\mu_{1:k}, \sigma_{1:k}, w_{1:k-1}) = \sum_{i=1}^{k} w_i f(d_q|\mu_i, \sigma_i) \tag{7}$$

Here, f denotes the density of a univariate normal distribution, k is the number of mixture components and $\mu_{1:k}$, $\sigma_{1:k}$ and $w_{1:k-1}$ are the parameters of the model (means, variances and weights of components respectively).

A particular configuration of the model is used to compare this work with the implementations in [11]: $k = 4$, $\sigma_i = \sigma = 0.55$ and $w_i = w = 1/k$ for $i \in \{1, ..., k\}$. The posterior distribution of $\mu = \mu_{1:k}$ needs to be sampled. The prior distribution on μ is 4-dimensional uniform. The data $\mathbf{d} = d_{1:m}$ (with $m = 100$) are simulated using $\mu = (-3, 0, 3, 6)$. The likelihood function is given by:

$$p(\mathbf{d}|\mu) = \prod_{j=1}^{100} p(d_j|\mu, \sigma_{1:k}, w_{1:k-1}) \tag{8}$$

If $p(\mu)$ is the uniform prior, the posterior distribution for μ is given by:

$$p(\mu|\mathbf{d}) = p(\mathbf{d}|\mu)p(\mu) \tag{9}$$

The sampling distribution is multimodal (it admits 24 modes). The PT tempering schedule used is $T_i = (\frac{M}{M+1-i})^2$, where M is the number of chains.

5.2   Implementation of the Probability Evaluation Block

The target posterior (9) is implemented using pipelined floating point operators. The likelihood's 100 terms (each a 4-component mixture density) can be evaluated in parallel. Nevertheless, there are not enough resources in the targeted FPGA (see 6.1) to fully parallelize it and generate one probability per cycle (second scenario in 4.1). The throughput of the implementation is defined by the number of terms that can be evaluated in parallel (which affects C in (6)). This can vary depending on the operators' implementation and targeted precision. Moreover, if the complexity of the model changes the throughput will change. This is investigated in Section 6.

The 100 data of the problem are stored inside the FPGA and are read by the probability evaluation block. Each term's probability is converted to logarithmic scale so that the product in the likelihood is replaced by a sum. Although a particular configuration of the model is implemented here, different configurations and mixture models can be targeted using the same implementation principles.

Table 1. CPU (Xeon E5420) throughput in samples/sec [11] and speedup of FPGA (XC6VLX240T) and two GPGPUs (8800GT & GTX280) [11] vs CPU for different numbers of chains M. The likelihood is not parallelized in the GPGPUs.

Nbr. of chains (M)	8	32	128	512	2048	8192	32768	131072
CPU thr/put	8224.8	2056.2	514.0	128.5	32.1	8.0	2.0	0.5
LX240T speedup	92	368	460	460	460	460	460	460
8800GT speedup	1.1	4	17	60	168	230	268	279
GTX280 speedup	0.9	4	14	51	175	430	527	572

6   Results

6.1   Comparison to CPU and GPGPU Performance and Scalability

The architecture was implemented in VHDL and the target FPGA was a Virtex 6 XC6VLX240T, which has a high ratio of DSP-blocks/Slices (DSP blocks are needed for floating point operators). For a single-precision floating point datapath, the achieved frequency was 212 MHz (the critical path was inside the logarithmic operator). The design was tested for different values of tempered chains (M). The sampler visited all of the modes, which is the main goal.

The performance of the system was first compared to a CPU implementation of PT for the same target distribution [11]. The CPU code was written in C++ and ran on a Xeon E5420 (2.5 GHz). Table 1 shows the results.

A 460x speedup is achieved compared to software for $M > 40$. For $M \leq 40$ there are not enough chains to fill the pipeline and speedup drops (although it is still significant). This reveals the importance of keeping the pipeline fully occupied. This is easier with more computationally-intensive likelihoods. To illustrate this, Figure 4 shows how the speedup over software scales with the number of mixture components (k in (7)) for different FPGAs of the Virtex-6 family. Here, $M = 128$ and maximum utilization of the available resources is considered. For smaller problems (e.g. $k = 1$) no extra speedup is provided by increasing the size of the FPGA because of stalls in the pipeline. It is also observed that the speedup is not only sustainable for larger problems, but it also increases (for the same FPGA device). This is due to better utilization of resources and resource sharing by the synthesis tool when more components are used (e.g. full utilization of LUTs). Each FPGA's speedup converges to a maximum value defined by its available resources as utilization becomes better.

Comparisons were also made with the GPGPU implementations of PT in [11] (again for the same inference problem). The GPU code was written in CUDA and ran on an Nvidia 8800GT and an Nvidia GTX280 using single-precision. Table 1 shows the GPGPU and FPGA speedups over the CPU. It must be noted that the probability evaluation is not parallelized in the GPGPU implementations (each thread is assigned one chain). All the speedup comes from running many chains in parallel which is an ideal setting for a GPGPU. Nevertheless, in practice, dozens or hundreds of chains are enough for good mixing [9]. Indeed, the authors in [11] note that no improvement in mixing was observed for $M > 128$.

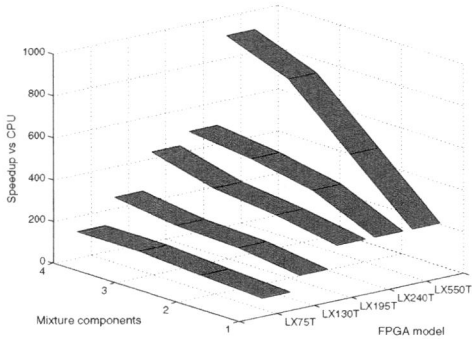

Fig. 4. Scaling of speedup over CPU with increasing problem size (number of mixture components) for different FPGAs of the Xilinx Virtex-6 family

A direct comparison with the GPGPUs' performance shows that the FPGA is faster than the 8800GT for all M and faster than the GTX280 for $M \leq 8192$. The maximum GPGPU speedups (279x and 572x respectively) are achieved only in the unrealistic case of thousands of employed chains (when the GPGPUs are fully utilized). No results are given in [11] on what the acceleration would be if fewer chains were used and the likelihood was parallelized.

6.2 Performance Evaluation under Custom Precision

Implementing the probability evaluation in reduced precision can provide a further speedup.Nevertheless, samples are taken from an altered distribution. To investigate the impact of this perturbation to the accuracy of sampling, two problems were examined: 1) A fully known mixture of 20 bivariate Gaussians (common test case in MCMC literature [10]) for which it is easy to measure the effect of precision to the output estimates (comparing to the known true values). 2) The more realistic inference problem described above. Here, the true values of estimates are unknown (this is why inference is performed) but it is known that e.g. means should be close to 1.5 [9]. The complexity of this problem allows for a valid throughput comparison to be made between implementations that employ different precisions. The probability evaluations were implemented for the following floating point precision configurations: (8,23), (8,19), (8,15), (8,11), (8,7), (8,5), and (8,3), where the first number represents the exponent bits and the second number represents the mantissa bits. The exponent bits were kept the same as in single precision to ensure adequate range.

For the first problem, Figure 5 illustrates the value of the mean estimator (first dimension) as the number of samples increases, for different precisions. The true value is also visible. The estimator remains accurate (within some variance) until a break-point is reached (precision (8,5)).

For the second problem, the speedup over the single-precision version was measured for all limited precision implementations. Ten runs of 10^6 samples were performed for each precision. The mean absolute error in the mean estimate over

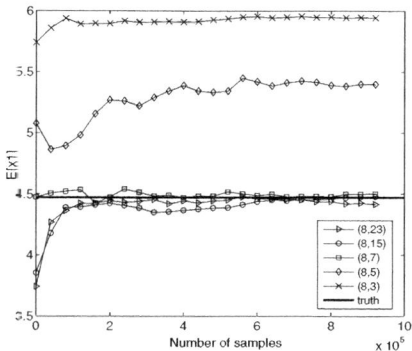

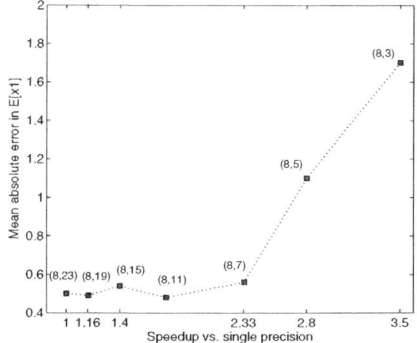

Fig. 5. 20-mode Gaussian target: Mean estimate (first dimension) for different precisions as the number of samples increases

Fig. 6. Mixture inference target: Mean absolute error in the mean estimate (first dimension) vs speedup over the single precision implementation

the 10 runs was calculated (taking 1.5 as the true value [9]). Figure 6 plots this error in the first dimension against the achieved speedup for each precision.

It can be observed that an extra speedup of up to 2.33x is provided by reducing precision without losing anything in sampling quality. This makes the system 1072x faster than software. This speedup is 3.84x and 1.87x higher than the maximum speedup of the 8800GT and GTX280 GPGPUs respectively.

These results demonstrate that the probability evaluation inside MCMC is indeed robust to precision perturbations in the sampling distribution. The error due to limited precision is smaller than the error due to the variance in the estimates until a break-point is reached.

7   Conclusion

This work presents a generic FPGA architecture for PT, a computationally expensive MCMC method. The characteristics of FPGAs and the nature of PT are exploited to maximize performance. A significant speedup compared to CPU and GPGPU implementations is achieved when doing inference in mixture models. The design is generic and can be used to sample from any target distribution. The work also demonstrates that MCMC is robust to the reduction of the arithmetic precision used to evaluate the sampling density. This implies that the flexibility of FPGAs to use custom precision can translate into significant gains in MCMC throughput, allowing for the tackling of previously intractable problems.

Future work includes the acceleration of other computationally demanding MCMC and SMC methods. A tool which could automate the generation of probability evaluation blocks is also under consideration.

References

1. Andrieu, C., Roberts, G.O.: The pseudo-marginal approach for efficient Monte Carlo computations. The Annals of Statistics 37(2), 697–725 (2009)
2. Asadi, N.B., Meng, T.H., Wong, W.H.: Reconfigurable computing for learning Bayesian networks. In: Proceedings of the 16th International ACM/SIGDA Symposium on Field Programmable Gate Arrays, FPGA 2008, pp. 203–211 (2008)
3. Byrd, J., Jarvis, S., Bhalerao, A.: Reducing the run-time of MCMC programs by multithreading on SMP architectures. In: IEEE International Symposium on Parallel and Distributed Processing, IPDPS 2008, pp. 1–8 (April 2008)
4. Chatzis, S.: A method for training finite mixture models under a fuzzy clustering principle. Fuzzy Sets and Systems 161(23), 3000–3013 (2010)
5. de Dinechin, F., Pasca, B.: Designing Custom Arithmetic Data Paths with FloPoCo. IEEE Design and Test of Computers 28, 18–27 (2011)
6. Earl, D.J., Deem, M.W.: Parallel tempering: Theory, applications, and new perspectives. Phys. Chem. Chem. Phys. 7, 3910–3916 (2005)
7. Fielding, M., Nott, D.J., Liong, S.Y.: Efficient MCMC Schemes for Computationally Expensive Posterior Distributions. Technometrics 53(1), 16–28 (2011)
8. Geyer, C.J.: Markov Chain Monte Carlo Maximum Likelihood. In: Proceedings of the 23rd Symposium on the Interface, Computing Science and Statistics, pp. 156–163 (1991)
9. Jasra, A., Stephens, D.A., Holmes, C.C.: On population-based simulation for static inference. Statistics and Computing, 263–279 (2007)
10. Kou, S.C., Zhou, Q., Wong, W.H.: Equi-energy sampler with applications in statistical inference and statistical mechanics. Ann. Statist. 34(4), 1581–1652 (2006)
11. Lee, A., Yau, C., Giles, M.B., Doucet, A., Holmes, C.C.: On the Utility of Graphics Cards to Perform Massively Parallel Simulation of Advanced Monte Carlo Methods. Journal of Computational and Graphical Statistics 19(4), 769–789 (2010)
12. Li, Y., Mascagni, M., Gorin, A.: A decentralized parallel implementation for parallel tempering algorithm. Parallel Comput. 35, 269–283 (2009)
13. Liu, J.S.: Monte Carlo strategies in scientific computing. Springer, Heidelberg (2001)
14. Mansinghka, V.K., Jonas, E.M., Tenenbaum, J.B.: Stochastic Digital Circuits for Probabilistic Inference. Technical Report MIT-CSAIL-TR-2008-069, Massachussets Institute of Technology (2008)
15. Saiprasert, C., Bouganis, C.-S., Constantinides, G.A.: Design of a Financial Application Driven Multivariate Gaussian Random Number Generator for an FPGA. In: Sirisuk, P., Morgan, F., El-Ghazawi, T., Amano, H. (eds.) ARC 2010. LNCS, vol. 5992, pp. 182–193. Springer, Heidelberg (2010)
16. Thomas, D.B., Luk, W., Leong, P.H., Villasenor, J.D.: Gaussian random number generators. ACM Comput. Surv. 39 (November 2007)
17. Tian, X., Bouganis, C.S.: A Run-Time Adaptive FPGA Architecture for Monte Carlo Simulations. In: 2011 International Conference on Field Programmable Logic and Applications (FPL), pp. 116–122 (September 2011)

A High Throughput FPGA-Based Implementation of the Lanczos Method for the Symmetric Extremal Eigenvalue Problem

Abid Rafique, Nachiket Kapre, and George A. Constantinides

Electrical and Electronic Engineering,
Imperial College London,
London SW7 2BT, UK
{a.rafique09,n.kapre,g.constantinides}@ic.ac.uk

Abstract. Iterative numerical algorithms with high memory bandwidth requirements but medium-size data sets (matrix size ∼ a few 100s) are highly appropriate for FPGA acceleration. This paper presents a streaming architecture comprising floating-point operators coupled with high-bandwidth on-chip memories for the Lanczos method, an iterative algorithm for symmetric eigenvalues computation. We show the Lanczos method can be specialized only for extremal eigenvalues computation and present an architecture which can achieve a sustained single precision floating-point performance of 175 GFLOPs on Virtex6-SX475T for a dense matrix of size 335×335. We perform a quantitative comparison with the parallel implementations of the Lanczos method using optimized Intel MKL and CUBLAS libraries for multi-core and GPU respectively. We find that for a range of matrices the FPGA implementation outperforms both multi-core and GPU; a speed up of 8.2-27.3× (13.4× geo. mean) over an Intel Xeon X5650 and 26.2-116× (52.8× geo. mean) over an Nvidia C2050 when FPGA is solving a single eigenvalue problem whereas a speed up of 41-520× (103× geo.mean) and 131-2220× (408× geo.mean) respectively when it is solving multiple eigenvalue problems.

1 Introduction

Recent trends have shown that the peak floating-point performance of the Field Programmable Gate Arrays (FPGAs) will significantly exceed that of the traditional processors [1]. We can accelerate scientific computations like the solution to systems of linear equations [2], [3] and [4] due to ever-increasing capacity of modern FPGAs in terms of floating point units and on-chip memory. The symmetric extremal eigenvalue problem is an important scientific computation involving dense linear algebra where one is interested in finding only the extremal eigenvalues of a $n \times n$ symmetric matrix. Unlike general eigenvalues computation which has a computational complexity of $\Theta(n^3)$, the extremal eigenvalues can be computed with much less computational complexity ($\Theta(n^2)$) [8]. Solving multiple independent extremal eigenvalue problems is common in semidefinite programming (SDP) solvers [6] where one has to find the extremal eigenvalues

O.C.S. Choy et al. (Eds.): ARC 2012, LNCS 7199, pp. 239–250, 2012.

of more than one symmetric matrix in each iteration and also in real-time eigenvalue based channel sensing for cognitive radios (IEEE 802.22) [7] where one has
to sense multiple channels simultaneously. Accelerating symmetric extremal
eigenvalues computation is of increasing importance in both cases. While, in
the former case, the goal is to reduce the overall runtime, in the latter case it
is desired to meet strict timing requirements which are in the range of a few
microseconds.

Existing FPGA-based eigensolvers [9], [10] and [11] compute all the eigenvalues of very small matrices by using the direct method of Jacobi which has a
computational complexity of $\Theta(n^3)$. We investigate a 2-stage iterative framework comprising the Lanczos method [5] followed by the bisection method [5]
which has an overall computational complexity of $\Theta(n^2)$.

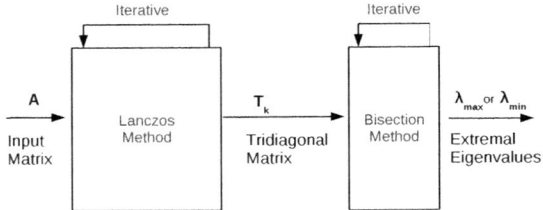

Fig. 1. Symmetric Extremal Eigenvalue Computation

The Lanczos method, like any other iterative numerical algorithm, is dominated by repeated matrix-vector multiplication which can be easily parallelized
using the FPGAs. We have noticed that with minimum modifications existing efficient architectures for matrix-vector multiplication in minimum residual
(MINRES) method [3] can be reused for the Lanczos method. We present a
streaming architecture comprising pipelined single-precision floating-point operators coupled with high-bandwidth on-chip memories leading to an architecture
with high throughput but also considerable latency. We exploit pipelining to
solve multiple independent extremal eigenvalue problems on the same architecture achieving an efficiency of almost 100% for higher order matrices. The key
contributions of this paper are thus:

- A specialized iterative framework for computing only the extremal eigenvalues of a dense symmetric matrix with a computational complexity of $\Theta(n^2)$.
- An architecture modified from [3] for accelerating multiple small to medium
  size symmetric eigenvalue problems.
- An FPGA implementation of the proposed architecture capable of a sustained performance of 175 GFLOPs on a 260 MHz Virtex6-SX475T for a
  maximum matrix of size 335 × 335.
- A quantitative comparison with an Intel Xeon X5650 and an Nvidia C2050
  GPU showing a speed up of 8.2-27.3× (13.4× geo. mean) and 26.2-116×
  (52.8× geo. mean) respectively when FPGA is solving a single eigenvalue
  problem whereas a speed up of 41-520× (103× geo.mean) and 131-2220×
  (408× geo.mean) when it is solving multiple eigenvalue problems.

2 Background

2.1 Symmetric Extremal Eigenvalue Problem

Symmetric eigenvalue computation is essential in many fields of science and engineering where one has to solve $Ax = \lambda x$ (A is an $n \times n$ symmetric matrix, λ is an eigenvalue and x is the corresponding $n \times 1$ eigenvector). In the particular case of the symmetric extremal eigenvalue problem, we are only interested in finding either $\lambda_{\max}$, $\lambda_{\min}$ or both eigenvalues. There are two main families of methods for solving the extremal eigenvalue problem: direct methods and iterative methods [8]. Direct methods compute eigenvalues in one shot, however, they incur a computation cost of $\Theta(n^3)$ and are more applicable when all the eigenvalues and the corresponding eigenvectors are required. While iterative methods only approximate the eigenvalues, their computational complexity is $\Theta(n^2)$ when only a few eigenvalues are desired and they are thus suitable for extremal eigenvalues computation. A flow is shown in Fig. 1 for the extremal eigenvalues computation comprising iterative Lanczos method followed by the bisection method.

Algorithm 1. Lanczos Method in Exact Arithmetic [5]

Require: Symmetric matrix $A \in \mathbb{R}^{n \times n}$, initial orthonormal Lanczos vector $q_0 \in \mathbb{R}^{n \times 1}$ and number of iterations k, $\beta_0 = 0$.
for $i = 1$ to k **do**

$$\overline{q}_i := Aq_{i-1} \qquad (lz1)$$
$$c_i := \overline{q}_i - \beta_{i-1}q_{i-2} \qquad (lz2)$$
$$\alpha_i := \overline{q}_i{}^T q_{i-1} \qquad (lz3)$$
$$d_i := c_i - \alpha_i q_{i-1} \qquad (lz4)$$
$$b := d_i{}^T d_i \qquad (lz5)$$
$$\beta_i := \sqrt{b} \qquad (lz6)$$
$$f := 1/\beta_i \qquad (lz7)$$
$$q_i := f d_i \qquad (lz8)$$

end for
return Tridiagonal matrix T_k containing β_i and α_i $i = 1, 2,..., k$

Algorithm 2. Bisection Method [5]

Require: α_i and β_i for $i = 1, 2, \dots . \ k$
a:= 0, b:= 0, $eps := 5.96 \times 10^{-8}$
for $i = 1$ to k **do**
   a := max(a , α_i - ($|\beta_i| + |\beta_{i-1}|$))
   b := max(b , α_i + ($|\beta_i| + |\beta_{i-1}|$))
end for
i := 1, q:= 1
while (|b-a| < eps(|a| + |b|)) **do**
   $\lambda := (a + b)/2$
   p := α_i - λ - β_i^2/q
   if (p > 0) **then**
      a := λ, i := 1, q := 1
   else if (i >= k) **then**
      b := λ, i := 1, q := 1
   else
      q := p, i := i + 1
   end if
end while
return λ

The Lanczos Method

The Lanczos method is an iterative Krylov Subspace method [5] which, starting from an initial $n \times 1$ q_0 vector, builds the subspace spanned by $K_k(A, q_0) = [q_0,$ $Aq_0, A^2q_0, \dots.., A^{k-1}q_0]$. It utilizes this subspace to approximate the eigenvectors and the corresponding eigenvalues of A. In order to find all the eigenvalues, A is generally reduced to a $n \times n$ tridiagonal matrix T [5] because there are efficient algorithms available for finding the eigenvalues of T. The main intuition behind the Lanczos method is that it generates a partial tridiagonal matrix T_k (see Algorithm 1) from A where the extremal eigenvalues of T_k are the optimal approximations of the extremal eigenvalues of A [8] from the subspace K_k.

Loss of orthogonality among the vectors is an inherent problem with the Lanczos method and often a costly step of re-orthogonalization is introduced [5]. However, investigation of the loss of orthogonality reveals it does not affect extremal eigenvalues [8] and therefore we do not need to perform re-orthogonalization. This significantly reduces the complexity of the Lanczos method and helps us designing an architecture highly specialized for extremal eigenvalues computation.

Bisection Method

The bisection method is an efficient method for finding the eigenvalues of a symmetric tridiagonal matrix T_k and it has a computational complexity of $\Theta(k)$ for extremal eigenvalue computation [8]. An extremal eigenvalue of the matrix T_k is computed by finding an extremal root of the polynomial.

$$p_k(\lambda) = \det(T_k - \lambda I). \tag{1}$$

The extremal root can be computed recursively from the roots of the polynomials $p_r(\lambda)$ where $0 \le r \le k$ (see Algorithm 2).

2.2   Sequential Runtime Analysis

We use sequential runtime analysis to find out the computationally intensive part of the flow shown in Fig. 1. We pick small to medium size matrices from SDPLIB [12], a collection of benchmarks for solving SDPs, and use Intel MKL library for sequential implementation on an Intel Xeon X5650. We show the runtime distribution in Fig. 2(a) and observe that it is the Lanczos method which takes most of the time reaching 99% for higher order matrices. On the other hand, the time taken by the bisection method is independent of the problem size as it only varies with the number of desired eigenvalues and their distribution [5]. We, therefore, focus our attention on parallelizing the Lanczos method.

The runtime distribution of the Lanczos method is plotted in Fig. 2(b) demonstrating that $lz1$ (matrix-vector multiplication) is the dominant operation which has a computational complexity of $\Theta(n^2)$. Hence our streaming architecture (see Section 3) shows how to use a parallel dot product circuit for accelerating this phase in a pipelined fashion.

2.3   Related Work

We briefly survey the existing FPGA-based eigensolvers. In Ahmedsaid *et al.* [9], Liu *et al.* [10] and Bravo *et al.* [11], the target applications involve Principal Component Analysis (PCA) where the matrix size does not usually go over 20 × 20. The direct method of Jacobi [5] and its variants are used for these small eigenvalue problems. The main reason behind using the Jacobi method is its inherent parallelism which can be exploited by systolic architectures requiring $\frac{n}{2}$ diagonal processors and $\frac{n(n-1)}{4}$ off-diagonal processors for a $n \times n$ matrix. Existing FPGA-based eigensolvers are not suitable for the extremal eigenvalues

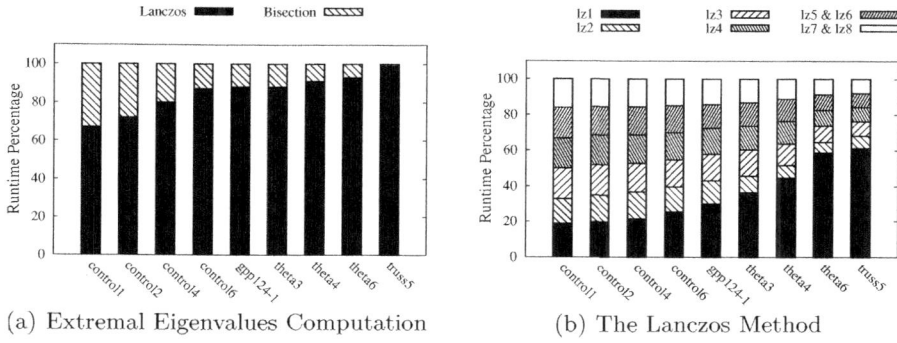

(a) Extremal Eigenvalues Computation   (b) The Lanczos Method

Fig. 2. Sequential Runtime Analysis

computation of matrices of our interest for two reasons. Firstly, they target very small matrices and are not resource efficient as the number of processors grows with $\Theta(n^2)$. Additionally, since the Jacobi method inherently computes all eigenvalues and eigenvectors, the approach utilized in these architectures is wasteful for computing only the extremal eigenvalues.

We propose an architecture based on the framework shown in Fig. 1 which is specialized for the extremal eigenvalues computation. Unlike previous approaches, the proposed architecture can address medium-size ($n \sim$ a few 100s) problems and is resource efficient as the number of floating-point units grows with $\Theta(n)$. Table 1 summarizes the previous work on eigenvalue computations on FPGA with the year, device, method, precision and the performance results.

Table 1. Comparison of FPGA-based Symmetric Eigenvalues Computation

Ref.	Year	Method	n	Device	Eigen-values	Freq. MHz	GFLOPs	Precision	Resources (asymptotic)
[9]	2003	Direct (Exact Jacobi)	8	Virtex-E	All	84.44	Not Reported	fixed point (16-bit)	$\Theta(n^2)$
[10]	2006	Direct (Approx. Jacobi)	8	Virtex-II	All	70	Not Reported	fixed point (16-bit)	$\Theta(n^2)$
[11]	2006	Direct (Exact Jacobi)	16	Virtex-II Pro	All	110	0.243	fixed point (18-bit)	$\Theta(n^2)$
This Paper	2011	Iterative (Lanczos Method)	335	Virtex-6	Extremal	260	175	floating point (32-bit)	$\Theta(n)$

3   Parallelizing the Lanczos Method on FPGAs

3.1   Parallelism Potential

We can identify the parallel potential in the Lanczos method from its dataflow graph shown in Fig. 3(a). We plot the number of floating-point operations per Lanczos iteration as well as the critical latency assuming ideal parallel hardware as a function of the matrix size in Fig. 3(b). We find out that the work grows with $\Theta(n^2)$ due to dominant matrix-vector multiplication ($lz1$) whereas the latency grows with $\Theta(\log(n))$ *i.e.* the latency of a single dot product circuit [3] (assuming there are n such dot product circuits working in parallel to perform matrix-vector multiplication). Thus the Lanczos method has a high degree of parallel potential ($\sim 10^4$ for large n).

We use **associative reformulation of computation** to implement single dot product circuit as a reduction tree [3] and perform matrix-vector multiplication in a pipelined fashion as n dot products where a new dot product is launched every clock cycle.

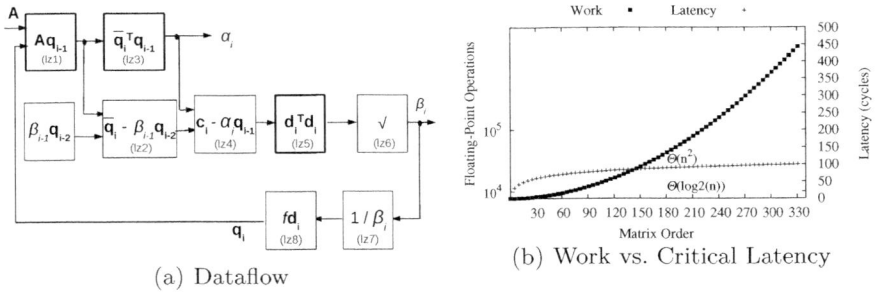

(a) Dataflow   (b) Work vs. Critical Latency

Fig. 3. Identifying Parallelism in the Lanczos Method

From the dataflow in Fig. 3(a), we can also observe **thread-level parallelism** as some of the operations may be performed in parallel *e.g.* ($lz2$) and ($lz3$). The operations ($lz2$), ($lz4$) and ($lz8$) can be unrolled completely with a latency of $\Theta(1)$ but since they contribute very little to the overall runtime of the system (see Section 2.2), we implement these sequentially.

We also use **pipeline parallelism** available in the architecture to solve multiple independent extremal eigenvalue problems arising in SDPs and eigenvalue based channel sensing while having the latency of solving a single extremal eigenvalue problem (see Section 3.3).

3.2   System Architecture

We present an architecture consisting of a parallelized Lanczos method coupled to a sequential architecture for the bisection method due to the latter's very low runtime contribution (see Section 2.2). We capture the high-level stream organization of the FPGA architecture in Fig 4.

The matrix A is loaded **only once** in the on-chip memory of the FPGA in a banked column fashion, and then the rows of A are streamed along with the Lanczos vector q_{i-1} to launch a new dot product in each clock cycle. We use deeply pipelined floating-point (FP) operators and aim to keep them busy all the time thus getting maximum throughput. The number of FP units is given by

$$\text{Total FP Units}(n) = 2n + 6. \qquad (2)$$

Referring to (2), $2n$ - 1 units are used for the dot product circuit whereas 7 FP units are used for other operations.

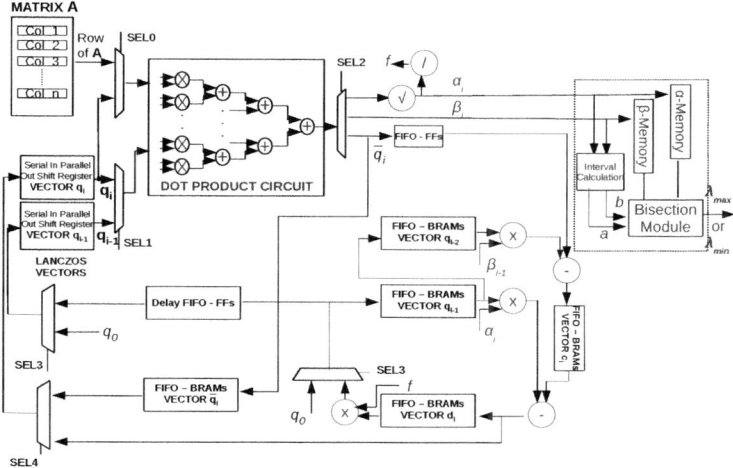

Fig. 4. Partial schematic for the implementation of the Lanczos method and the bisection method displaying main components including a dot product circuit module, FIFOs for storing Lanczos vectors, banked memory arrangement for matrix A, two memories for storing α_i and β_i and a Bisection Module

The Interval Calculation module computes the initial interval for the extremal eigenvalue using the Gershgorin circle theorem [5] and the Bisection Module computes the extremal eigenvalue in that interval in a sequential fashion as shown in Algorithm 2.

3.3   Solving Multiple Extremal Eigenvalue Problems

For solving a single extremal eigenvalue problem, the deeply pipelined nature of the dot product circuit in Fig. 4 leads to high throughput but also considerable latency. As a result, the pipeline will be underutilized if only single problem is solved, therefore, mismatch between throughput and latency is exploited to solve multiple independent extremal eigenvalue problems. The initiation interval of this circuit is $n + 2$ clock cycles (for $lz1$, $lz3$ and $lz5$) after which a new problem can be streamed into this circuit. The pipeline depth (P) of the circuit is given by (4) which indicates how many problems can be active in the pipeline at one time.

$$\text{Latency per iteration}(n) = 3n + k_1 \lceil \log_2 n \rceil + k_2. \tag{3}$$

$$\text{Pipeline Depth P}(n) = \left\lceil \frac{3n + k_1 \lceil \log_2 n \rceil + k_2}{n + 2} \right\rceil. \tag{4}$$

Referring to (3), the $3n$ comes from n cycles for ($lz1$) and $2n$ cycles for ($lz4$) and ($lz8$). The $\log_2 n$ term comes from the adder reduction tree and $k_1 = 36$ and $k_2 = 137$ derive from the latencies of the floating-point operators. We can see from (4) that the number of independent eigenvalue problems approaches to a constant value for large matrices (P $\rightarrow$ 5 as $n \rightarrow \infty$).

4   Methodology

The experimental setup for performance evaluation is summarized in Table 2 and dense matrices are extracted from SDPLIB [12] benchmarks shown in Table 3.

Table 2. Experimental Setup   **Table 3.** Benchmarks

Platform	Peak GFLOPs Single Precision	Compiler	Libraries	Timing
Intel Xeon X5650	127.8 [15]	gcc (4.4.3(-O3))	Intel MKL (10.2.4.032)	PAPI (4.1.1.0)
Nvidia GPU C2050	1050 [16]	nvcc	CUBLAS (3.2)	cudaEvent-Record()
Xilinx Virtex6-SX475T	450 [17]	Xilinx ISE (10.1)	Xilinx Coregen	ModelSim

Benchmark	n
control1	15
control2	30
control4	60
control6	90
gpp124-1	124
theta3	150
theta4	200
theta6	300
truss5	335

We implement the proposed architecture in VHDL and synthesize the circuit for Xilinx Virtex6-SX475T FPGA, a device with the largest number of DSP48Es and a large on-chip capacity. The placed and routed design has an operating frequency of 260 MHz. We find out that for a matrix of size 335×335, P is equal to 5 and we occupy nearly all the BRAMs available in the device. There is 50% utilization for the DSP48Es and 70% for the Slice LUTs and they show a linear increase as the number of floating-point units grows with $\Theta(n)$. Optimized Basic Linear Algebra Subroutine (BLAS) libraries are used for the multi-core and GPU implementations, an Intel MKL library for the multi-core and CUBLAS for the GPU. In the multi-core, the number of threads are set equal to the physical cores whereas in case of a GPU, the grid configuration is picked by CUBLAS automatically. We do not use multi-threading in the multi-core and GPU for solving multiple eigenvalues problem (see Section 6).

5   Results

We now present the performance achieved by our FPGA design, compare it with the multi-core and GPU and then discuss the underlying factors that explain our results.

5.1   FPGA Performance Evaluation

The peak and sustained single-precision floating-point performance of the FPGA is given by (5) and (6) respectively. For a matrix of size 335×335 and an operating frequency of 260 MHz, the peak performance of our design is 175 GFLOPs and sustained performance is 35 GFLOPs for a single problem and that the sustained performance approaches the peak performance when P problems are solved simultaneously as shown in Fig. 6(a). There is a linear increase in the performance with the problem size as the floating-point units grow with $\Theta(n)$.

$$\text{Peak Throughput} = \text{Total FP Units} = 2n + 6 \qquad \text{FLOPs/cycle}. \qquad (5)$$

$$\text{Sustained Throughput} = \frac{\text{P} \; (2n^2 + 8n)}{\text{P}(n+2) + \text{P} - 1} \; \text{FLOPs/cycle}. \qquad (6)$$

$$\text{Efficiency}(n) = \frac{\text{P}(2n^2 + 8n)}{\text{Total FP Units} \times (\text{P}(n+2) + \text{P} - 1)}. \qquad (7)$$

where $2n^2 + 8n$ represent the number of floating-point operations per Lanczos iteration. It is observed that even for low order matrices a high efficiency (70%) is achieved and the efficiency tends to 100% for large matrices. This is because the number of floating-point operators in dot product circuit grow linearly with n and by design the the dot product circuit remains busy.

5.2   Comparison with Multi-core and GPU

We choose Iterations/second of the Lanczos method as the criterion for performance comparison plotted in Fig 5(a). We can observe that the FPGA outperforms both multi-core and the GPU. The runtime percentage of each part of the Lanczos method is plotted in Fig. 5(b) for different architectures. We can see a decrease in the runtime of ($lz1$) for GPU and the FPGA because of the high parallelism available in this operation. The Lanczos method is memory-bound due to dominant matrix-vector multiplication ($lz1$) with an arithmetic intensity of 0.5 FLOPs per byte (n^2 x 4 bytes of data (single-precision), $2n^2$ FLOPs). It is for this reason the multi-core does not perform any better than single core for small matrices but show a speedup of 1.5× for large matrices as shown in 5(c). In the case of an FPGA, ($lz1$) is computed as n dot products where each new dot product is launched every clock cycle. Due to high on-chip memory bandwidth and streaming nature of the architecture, the overall design has much lower latency and high throughput. We get a speed up of 7.6-25.9× (12.5× geo. mean) using **associative reformulation of computation** and 1.04-1.22× (1.14× geo. mean) using **thread-level parallelism** with a combined speed up of 8.8-27.3× (13.4× geo. mean) for solving a single eigenvalue problem shown in Fig. 5(c). Using **pipeline parallelism** we additionally get a speed up of 4.3-19.1× (7.19× geo. mean) and, therefore deliver an overall speed up of 41-520× (103× geo. mean) when solving P independent eigenvalue problems shown in Fig. 5(c).

Although GPUs are highly efficient for dense linear algebra, we observe in Fig. 5(b) that the performance of GPU is even worse than the multi-core. This is due to medium-size data sets ($n \sim$ a few 100s) for which the GPU exhibits a performance less than 1 GFLOPs for BLAS 1 ($lz2$ to $lz8$) and BLAS 2 ($lz1$) operations [18]. Both BLAS 1 and BLAS 2 operations have very low arithmetic intensity to be exploited by multiple cores in the GPU. Additionally, we are using CUBLAS routines for matrix-vector multiplication which does not cache the matrix in the shared memory of the GPU and therefore the matrix is fetched repeatedly from off-chip memory in each iteration. When comparing

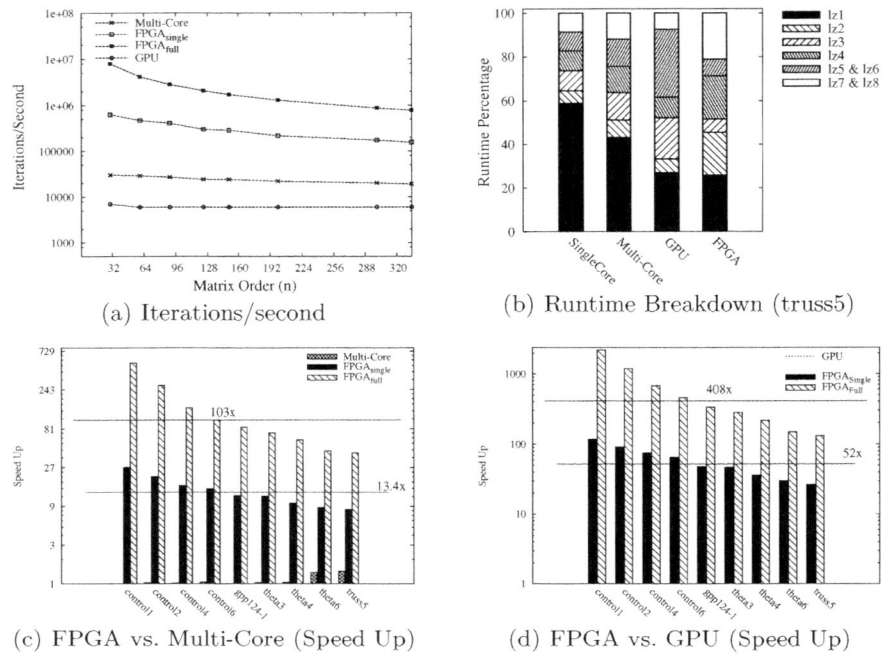

(a) Iterations/second

(b) Runtime Breakdown (truss5)

(c) FPGA vs. Multi-Core (Speed Up)

(d) FPGA vs. GPU (Speed Up)

Fig. 5. Performance Comparison ('single' is for 1 problem, 'full' is for P problems)

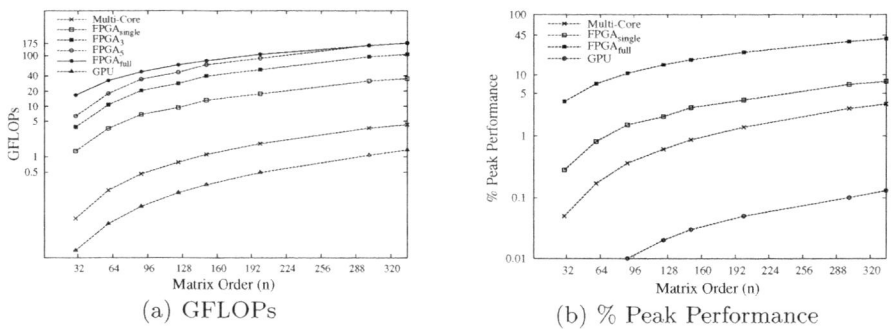

(a) GFLOPs

(b) % Peak Performance

Fig. 6. Raw Performance and Efficiency Comparison ('single' is for 1, 'full' is for P problems)

with our FPGA design, we get a speed up of 24.5-110.7× (49.4× geo. mean) using **associative reformulation of computation** and 1.04-1.22× (1.14× geo. mean) using **thread-level parallelism** with a combined speed up of 26.2-116×× (52.8× geo. mean) for solving a single eigenvalue problem shown in Fig. 5(d). Using **pipeline parallelism** we additionally get a speed up of 4.3-19.1× (7.19× geo. mean) and, therefore deliver an overall speed up of 131-2220× (408× geo. mean) when solving P independent eigenvalue problems shown in Fig. 5(d).

The raw performance of our FPGA design is compared with that of multi-core and GPU implementations in Fig. 6(a), and also their efficiency as a proportion of peak performance (see Table 2) is compared in Fig. 6(b). We can see for the maximum matrix size, the efficiency of the FPGA when solving single problem is approximately 7.79% whereas with P problems it increases to 38.9% of the peak performance. The efficiency of multi-core is around 3.34% and that of GPU is 0.13% and their efficiency increases with the problem size.

6   Future Work

We identify the following areas of research in this direction to further improve our results.

- We intend to further improve multi-core and GPU performance by solving multiple independent eigenvalue problems to hide memory latency.
- For small to medium matrices, we intend to have a customized GPU implementation of the Lanczos method where, like FPGA, the input matrix is explicitly loaded once in the shared memory and is reused for subsequent iterations. Similarly, we intend to consider I/O limitations in FPGA design.
- We are independently developing a BLAS library using the high level SCORE hardware compilation framework for stream computing [19]. We will exploit auto-tuning of implementation parameters to explore new architectures for the iterative numerical algorithms *e.g.* the Lanczos method.
- We would like to explore the algorithmic modifications in the Lanczos method for large-scale eigenvalue problems from different application areas where the matrix is fetched from off-chip memory in each iteration.

7   Conclusion

We present a pipelined streaming architecture coupled with high-bandwidth on-chip memories and demonstrate a sustained performance of 175 GFLOPs when solving multiple independent extremal eigenvalue problems. We show that the multi-core and GPU are underutilized for the medium-size data sets and achieve an efficiency of 3.34% and 0.13% respectively. Additionally, the dominant matrix-vector operation in the Lanczos method is memory-bound and has low arithmetic intensity (0.5 FLOPs/byte). On the other hand, the FPGA design exploits low latency high-bandwidth on-chip memories and the streaming computations to deliver a $41\times$ speed up over an Intel Xeon X5650 and $131\times$ over the Nvidia C2050 for a matrix of size 335×335. We therefore highlight iterative numerical algorithms with high memory bandwidth requirements but medium-size data sets as highly appropriate for FPGA acceleration.

References

1. Underwood, K.: FPGAs vs. CPUs: trends in peak floating-point performance. In: Proc. ACM/SIGDA 12th International Symposium on Field programmable Gate Arrays, pp. 171–180 (2004)

2. Lopes, A.R., Constantinides, G.A.: A High Throughput FPGA-Based Floating Point Conjugate Gradient Implementation. In: Woods, R., Compton, K., Bouganis, C., Diniz, P.C. (eds.) ARC 2008. LNCS, vol. 4943, pp. 75–86. Springer, Heidelberg (2008)

3. Boland, D., Constantinides, G.: An FPGA-based implementation of the MINRES algorithm. In: Proc. Field Programmable Logic and Applications, pp. 379–384 (2008)

4. Kapre, N., DeHon, A.: Parallelizing sparse Matrix Solve for SPICE circuit simulation using FPGAs. In: Proc. Field-Programmable Technology, pp. 190–198 (2009)

5. Golub, G.H., Van Loan, C.F.: Matrix Computations, 3rd edn. The Johns Hopkins University Press, Baltimore (1996)

6. Toh, K.C.: A note on the calculation of step-lengths in interior-point methods for semidefinite programming. J. Computational Optimization and Applications 21(3), 301–310 (1999)

7. Zeng, Y., Koh, C.L., Liang, Y.C.: Maximum eigenvalue detection: theory and application. In: Proc. IEEE International Conference on Communications, pp. 4160–4164 (2008)

8. Demmel, J.W.: Applied numerical linear algebra. Society for Industrial and Applied Mathematics, Philadelphia (1997)

9. Ahmedsaid, A., Amira, A.. Bouridane, A.: Improved SVD systolic array and implementation on FPGA. In: Proc. Field-Programmable Technology, pp. 35–42 (2003)

10. Liu, Y., Bouganis, C.S., Cheung, P.Y.K., Leong, P.H.W., Motley, S.J.: Hardware efficient architectures for eigenvalue computation. In: Proc. Design Automation & Test in Europe, p. 202 (2006)

11. Bravo, I., Jiménez, P., Mazo, M., Lázaro, J.L., Gardel, A.: Implementation in FPGAs of Jacobi method to solve the eigenvalue and eigenvector problem. In: Proc. Field Programmable Logic and Applications, pp. 1–4 (2006)

12. Brochers, B.: SDPLIB 1.2, a library of semidefinite programming test problems. Optimization Methods and Software 11(1-4), 683–690 (1999)

13. Intel Math Kernel Library 10.2.4.032 (2010), http://software.intel.com/en-us/articles/intel-mkl/

14. CUBLAS 3.2 (2010), http://developer.download.nvidia.com/compute/cuda/ 3_2_prod/toolkit/docs/CUBLAS_Library.pdf

15. Intel microprocessor export compliance metrics (2010), http://download.intel.com/support/processors/xeon/sb/xeon_5600.pdf

16. Nvidia Tesla C2050 (2010), http://www.nvidia.com/docs/IO/43395/ NV_DS_Tesla_C2050_C2070_jul10_lores.pdf

17. Sundararajan, P.: High Performance Computing using FPGAs (2010), http://www.xilinx.com/support/documentation/ white_papers/wp375_HPC_Using_FPGAs.pdf

18. Anzt, H., Hahn, T., Heuveline, V., Rocker, B.: GPU Accelerated Scientific Computing: Evaluation of the NVIDIA Fermi Architecture; Elementary Kernels and Linear Solvers, KIT (2010)

19. Caspi, E., Chu, M., Huang, R., Yeh, J., Wawrzynek, J., DeHon, A.: Stream computations organized for reconfigurable execution (SCORE). In: Proc. Field Programmable Logic and Applications, pp. 605–614 (2000)

Optimising Performance of Quadrature Methods with Reduced Precision

Anson H.T. Tse[1], Gary C.T. Chow[1], Qiwei Jin[1],
David B. Thomas[2], and Wayne Luk[1]

[1] Department of Computing, Imperial College London, UK
{htt08,cchow,qj04,wl}@doc.ic.ac.uk
[2] Department of Electrical and Electronic Engineering, Imperial College London, UK
d.thomas1@imperial.ac.uk

Abstract. This paper presents a generic precision optimisation methodology for quadrature computation targeting reconfigurable hardware to maximise performance at a given error tolerance level. The proposed methodology optimises performance by considering integration grid density versus mantissa size of floating-point operators. The optimisation provides the number of integration points and mantissa size with maximised throughput while meeting given error tolerance requirement. Three case studies show that the proposed reduced precision designs on a Virtex-6 SX475T FPGA are up to 6 times faster than comparable FPGA designs with double precision arithmetic. They are up to 15.1 times faster and 234.9 times more energy efficient than an i7-870 quad-core CPU, and are 1.2 times faster and 42.2 times more energy efficient than a Tesla C2070 GPU.

1 Introduction

Quadrature methods have been applied in different areas including pricing options [1], modeling credit risk [5], solving electromagnetic problems [14] and calculating photon distribution [8]. Using quadrature methods to price a single simple option is fast and can typically be performed in milliseconds on desktop computers. However, quadrature methods can become a computational bottleneck, for example, when a huge number of complex options are being revalued overnight under many different scenarios for risk management. Computational complexity also scales exponentially with the number of underlying assets, so accelerating multi-asset quadrature computation is a significant problem. Moreover, energy consumption of computation is a major concern when the computation is performed 24 hours a day, 7 days a week.

The ability to support customisable precision is an important advantage of reconfigurable hardware. Reduced precision floating-point operators usually have higher clock frequencies, consume fewer resources and offer a higher degree of parallelism for a given amount of resources compared with double precision operators.

O.C.S. Choy et al. (Eds.): ARC 2012, LNCS 7199, pp. 251–263, 2012.

The use of reduced precision affects the accuracy of the numerical results. However, with a higher throughput capacity using reduced precision, the integration grid spacing could be reduced which might actually increase accuracy. This paper introduces a novel optimisation methodology for determining the optimal combination of operator precision and integration grid spacing in order to maximize the performance of quadrature method on reconfigurable hardware. The major contributions of this paper include:

– optimisation modeling based on a step-by-step accuracy analysis and performance model. A discrete moving barrier option pricer is used as an example to graphically illustrate the analysis and to provide empirical evidence for the model (Section 3);
– a methodology and algorithms to determine the optimal mantissa bit-width and the integration grid density for a given integration problem by finding the Pareto frontier satisfying a given error tolerance level (Section 4);
– case studies of two financial applications and one benchmark quadrature problem using the proposed methodology, namely a discrete moving barrier option pricer, a 3-dimensional European option pricer, and a discontinuous integration benchmark (Section 5);
– performance comparison of the optimised FPGA implementation versus GPU and CPU. Our results show that the proposed approach increases performance by around 4 times, resulting in a total speed-up over double-precision software of 15.1 times while maintaining the accuracy. The optimised FPGA designs are 1.2 times faster and 42.2 times more energy efficient than comparable GPU designs (Section 6).

2   Background

There has been much interest in the use of accelerators such as FPGAs and GPUs for high performance computing. GPUs use the same type of floating-point number representation and operation as CPUs, namely IEEE-754 double precision and IEEE-754 single precision. Double precision has 53 bits of mantissa while single precision has 24 bits of mantissa. GPUs are shown to provide significant speedup over CPUs for many applications, especially when single precision is used [11]. For quadrature methods in option pricing, a GPU design using single precision running on NVIDIA Tesla C1060 demonstrated a speedup of 8.4 times while a Virtex-4 FPGA demonstrated a speed-up of 4.6 times over a CPU [20].

FPGAs provide customisable floating-point number operation which could be exploited to provide additional speedup. A mixed-precision methodology has shown to provide an additional performance gain of 7.3 times over an FPGA-accelerated collision detection algorithm [4]. Other works in bit-width optimisation aim to improve performance by using minimum precision in a data-path given a required output accuracy. One common approach is to develop an accuracy model which relates output accuracy to the precision of the data formats used in the data-path. The area and delay of data-paths with different precisions

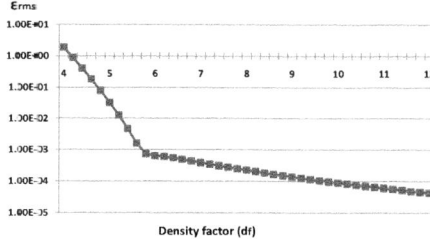
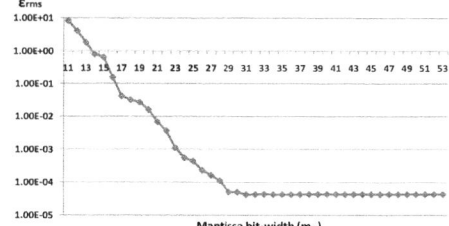

Fig. 1. The ϵ_{rms} for different d_f at $m_w=53$

Fig. 2. The ϵ_{rms} for different m_w at $d_f=12$

are modelled based on the accuracy model. The design with a minimum area-delay product can be obtained from the models. Common accuracy modeling approaches include simulation [10], interval arithmetic [6], backward propagation analysis [7], affine arithmetic [12] [13] [16] [17], SAT-Modulo theory [9] and polynomial algebra [3].

Our novel precision methodology presented in this paper is specialised for solving quadrature problems. The optimal design is determined by optimising both the spacing between integration grid points and the precision of floating-point operators, instead of considering only the precision only in other common approaches.

Let us now briefly introduce quadrature methods: numerical methods for approximating an integral by evaluating at a finite set of integration points and using a weighted sum of these values. There are many different methods of numerical integral evaluation. Two of the most common methods are based on the trapezoidal rule and Simpson's rule [19]:

Trapezoidal Rule:

$$\int_a^b f(y)dy \approx \frac{\delta y}{2}\{f(a) + 2f(a + \delta y) + 2f(a + 2\delta y) \cdots + 2f(b - \delta y) + f(b)\} \quad (1)$$

Simpson's Rule:

$$\int_a^b f(y)dy \approx \frac{\delta y}{3}\{f(a) + 4f(a + \delta y) + 2f(a + 2\delta y) + \cdots + 4f(b - \delta y) + f(b)\}$$
$$(2)$$

3   Optimisation Modeling

The proposed optimisation objective function is based on a step-by-step accuracy analysis and performance modeling. A barrier option pricer is used as an example to illustrate the relationship between accuracy, throughput, integration grid density and the precision of floating-point operations.

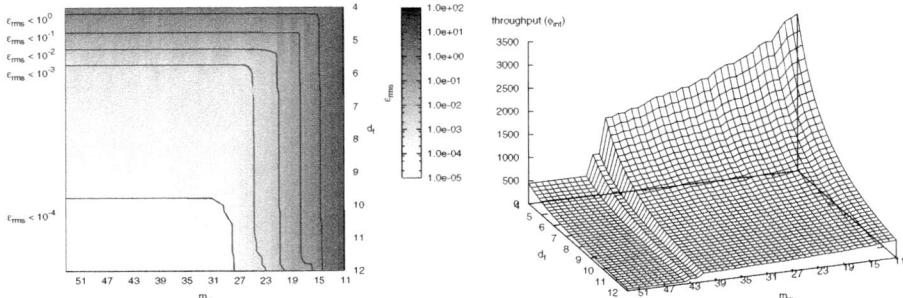

Fig. 3. The contour plot of ϵ_{rms} of barrier option pricer for different m_w and d_f **Fig. 4.** The aggregated FPGA throughput

3.1 Accuracy Analysis

There are two sources of error affecting the "accuracy" of the integration result, namely integration error ϵ_{int} and finite precision error ϵ_{fin}. The total error ϵ_{total} is a function of both error sources. Integration error ϵ_{int} is the error due to having a finite number of integration points within an integration interval. Finite precision error ϵ_{fin} is the error due to non-exact floating-point arithmetic. Floating-point number representation in computer has a finite significant bit-width. The rounding of the intermediate or final result leads to precision loss. We define grid density factor $\boldsymbol{d_f}$ as a variable which is inversely proportional to the integration grid spacing and we define $\boldsymbol{m_w}$ as the number of bits in the mantissa. Therefore, we have $\epsilon_{int}(d_f)$ and $\epsilon_{fin}(m_w)$ respectively to represent their relationships.

To measure $\epsilon_{total}(m_w, d_f)$, the root-mean-squared error $\boldsymbol{\epsilon_{rms}(m_w, d_f)}$ comparing with a set of reference results is used. The set of reference results are computed using a large value of m_w and d_f.

We investigate the result of $\epsilon_{rms}(m_w, d_f)$ by computing a portfolio of 30 barrier options using different mantissa bit-width and density factor. The computed option values are compared with a set of reference values using $m_w = 53$ (double precision) and $d_f = 20$. Fig. 1 shows the graph of $\epsilon_{rms}(53, d_f)$. We can see that the total error is decreasing with respect to d_f. Fig. 2 shows the graph of $\epsilon_{rms}(m_w, 12)$. This figure shows that with a sufficient large density factor, the total error of the result decreases with increasing mantissa bit-width. In addition, this figure also indicates that at $d_f = 12$, increasing mantissa bit-width for more than 33 would not increase the accuracy significantly. It is because ϵ_{total} is dominated by ϵ_{int} but not ϵ_{fin} after m_w reached 33. Therefore, using more than 33 bits of mantissa is consuming unnecessary resources.

Fig. 3 shows the contour plot of $\epsilon_{rms}(m_w, d_f)$ at different error levels for the barrier option pricer and provides an overview of the total error using different m_w and d_f combinations.

3.2   Performance Modeling

The performance of the system is defined with the following equation:

$$\phi_{int}(m_w, d_f) = \frac{\phi_{pt}(m_w)}{N_{pt}(d_f)} \tag{3}$$

ϕ_{int} is the throughput in aggregated integrations per second per FPGA, ϕ_{pt} is the throughput in aggregated number of integration points per second per FPGA and N_{pt} is the number of integration points per integration. Furthermore, we define p_L as the degree of parallelism (number of replicated cores) and $freq$ as the clock frequency of the FPGA. With multiple replicated and fully pipelined integration cores running in parallel, ϕ_{pt} is defined as:

$$\phi_{pt}(m_w) = p_L(m_w) \cdot freq \tag{4}$$

because each core can process one integration point per clock cycle. ϕ_{pt} and p_L is monotonically decreasing with m_w. A higher m_w leads to a larger core, so fewer cores will fit in the FPGA, reducing degree of parallelism p_L and lower aggregated integration points throughput ϕ_{pt}. ϕ_{pt} is also monotonically decreasing with d_f, as a higher d_f leads to more integration points per integration N_{pt} and fewer integrations could be computed per second. Therefore, we have the following inequalities:

$$\phi_{int}(m_{w_x}, d_f) \geq \phi_{int}(m_{w_y}, d_f), \forall m_{w_x} < m_{w_y} \tag{5}$$

$$\phi_{int}(m_w, d_{f_x}) \geq \phi_{int}(m_w, d_{f_y}), \forall d_{f_x} < d_{f_y} \tag{6}$$

Fig. 4 shows the 3D graph of aggregated FPGA throughput $\phi_{int}(m_w, d_f)$ of the barrier option pricer which is consistent with the above inequalities.

3.3   Optimisation Objective Equation

Our objective is to determine the set of (m_w, d_f) which produces the design with optimal performance while maintaining the same level of accuracy. We define ϵ_{tol} as error tolerance level. With the results from Equation 3 and 4, the following 2-dimensional optimisation problem can be formulated:

$$\max_{m_w, d_f} \left(\frac{p_L(m_w) \cdot freq}{N_{pt}(d_f)} \right), m_w \in \mathbb{Z}^+, d_f \in \mathbb{R}^+, \epsilon_{rms}(m_w, d_f) < \epsilon_{tol} \tag{7}$$

For example, Fig. 5 and Fig. 6 show the 3D plots of the optimisation result of barrier option pricer at $\epsilon_{tol} = 10^{-4}$ and $\epsilon_{tol} = 10^{-3}$ respectively by using the result of Fig. 3 and Fig. 4. We can see from the figures that the optimal aggregated throughputs are 350 and 1078 integrations per second. The corresponding (m_u, d_f) sets are (31,9.8) and (26,5.8).

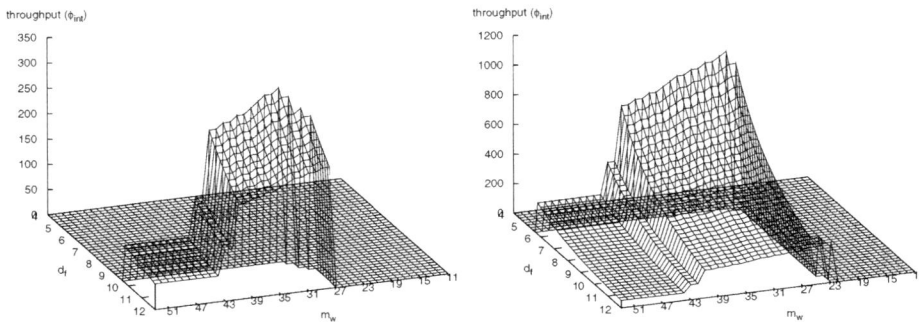

Fig. 5. The aggregated FPGA throughput satisfying $\epsilon_{rms}(m_w, d_f) < 10^{-4}$ **Fig. 6.** The aggregated FPGA throughput satisfying $\epsilon_{rms}(m_w, d_f) < 10^{-3}$

4   Optimisation Algorithm and Methodology

This section provides the algorithms and a systematic way to apply the precision optimisation technique for a quadrature problem. The optimisation algorithm uses the property that the throughput of the integration decreases monotonically with respect to both m_w and d_f as shown in inequalities (5) and (6). The optimal throughput will only occur at the Pareto frontier points (Pareto set **S**) of (m_w, d_f) satisfying $\epsilon_{rms} < \epsilon_{tol}$ and, therefore, it is not necessary to obtain the ϵ_{rms} values for all (m_w, d_f) combinations. Fig. 7 shows the Pareto frontier of a barrier option pricer and the corresponding throughput as an illustration.

The detailed steps of our proposed one-pass optimisation process are:

1. Prepare a set of sample inputs.
2. Evaluate the results of the sample inputs as reference values.
3. Apply Algorithm 1 to obtain a Pareto set **S**.
4. Apply Algorithm 2 on **S** to obtain the optimal ϕ_{int}.

In step 2, we will typically use double precision (m_w=53) and a sufficiently large d_f to obtain the reference values such that the reference values are known to be accurate. In step 4, the algorithm requires the values of function $N_{pt}(d_f)$ and $pL(m_w)$ in order to compute ϕ_{int}. The function $N_{pt}(d_f)$ could easily be determined with the knowledge of the integration problem. The parameters pL can be either obtained directly after the full FPGA implementation, or estimated using the resource usage of a single-core FPGA design. Fig. 8 shows our estimation of pL and the resource usage of a single-core barrier option pricer.

The whole optimisation process is completely automated in our case studies by designing the hardware implementation as a parametric template, with m_w and pL as parameters. The hardware implementations for different values of m_w are generated, placed and routed automatically from the template for the use of step 3 and 4.

Algorithm 1. Algorithm for obtaining Pareto set **S**

1: $S \leftarrow \emptyset$
2: **for** $m_w \in m_w^{min}..m_w^{max}$ **do**
3:     perform binary search for $\min d_f$ s.t $\epsilon_{rms}(m_w, d_f) < \epsilon_{tol}$
4:     **if** found **then**
5:         add tuple (m_w, d_f) to S
6:     **end if**
7: **end for**

Algorithm 2. Algorithm for determining the optimal precision and density factor

---

1: $\phi^{max} \leftarrow 0$
2: **for** $(m_w, d_f) \in$ **S do**
3:     **if** $\phi_{int}(m_w, d_f) > \phi^{max}$ **then**
4:         $\phi^{max} \leftarrow \phi_{int}(m_w, d_f)$
5:         $S_{optimal} \leftarrow (m_w, d_f)$
6:     **end if**
7: **end for**

---

5   Case Studies

The hardware architectures of two financial applications and one benchmark integration problem are designed. Simpson's rule is used in all three case studies. The optimal combination of (m_w, d_f) is determined using the optimisation methodology and algorithms as described in the previous two sections with $\epsilon_{tol} = 10^{-3}$. As the range of the floating-point numbers is known to be small, the exponent size of the floating-point operators is set to 8. The accumulation is performed in double precision ($m_w = 53$) to minimise the loss of accuracy due to insufficient dynamic range in the accumulator.

5.1   Discrete Moving Barrier Option Pricer

The first case study is the pricing of discrete barrier options, which is a real-world pricing problem for which there is no closed-form solution. The pricing equation of an barrier option using quadrature methods is derived from the Black and Scholes partial differential equation [2]. For an option with an underlying asset following geometric Brownian motion:

$$\frac{\partial V}{\partial t} + \frac{1}{2}\sigma^2 S^2 \frac{\partial^2 V}{\partial S^2} + (r - D_c)S\frac{\partial V}{\partial S} - rV = 0 \tag{8}$$

where $V(S, t)$ is the price of the option, S is the value of the underlying asset, t is time, r is risk-free interest rate, σ is volatility of the underlying asset, K is exercise price, and D_c is continuous dividend yield.

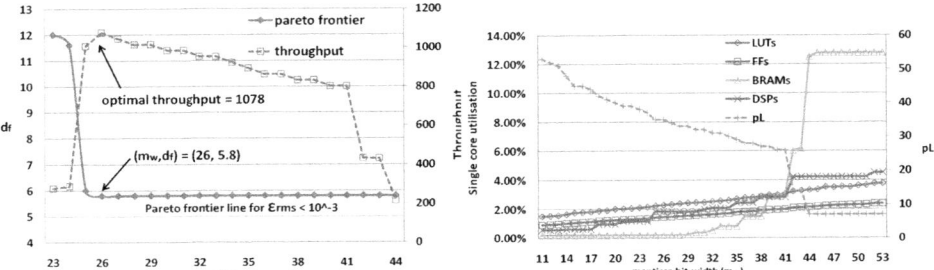

Fig. 7. The Pareto frontier line of barrier option pricer when $\epsilon_{tol} = 10^{-3}$

Fig. 8. pL estimation and the single core resource utilisaion of barrier option pricer

The following standard transformations

$$x = \log(S_t/K), \qquad y = \log(S_{t+\Delta t}/K)$$

give us the solution of $V(x,t)$ as:

$$V(x,t) = A(x) \int_{-\infty}^{+\infty} E(x,y)V(y, t + \Delta t)dy \qquad (9)$$

where

$$A(x) = \frac{1}{\sqrt{2\sigma^2 \pi \Delta t}} e^{(-kx/2)-(\sigma^2 k^2 \Delta t/8)-r\Delta t} \qquad (10)$$

$$E(x,y) = e^{(yC_2-(x-y)^2 C_1)}, \quad C_1 = \frac{1}{2\sigma^2 \Delta t}, \quad C_2 = \frac{2(r-D_c)-\sigma^2}{2\sigma^2} \qquad (11)$$

Since C_1 and C_2 will not change during the whole pricing process, they can be precomputed in software. Eq. (9) is the basic building block for quadrature option pricing. To price a down-and-out discrete moving barrier option with m time steps and B_m as the barrier price at time step m, we define the transformed position of b_m as:

$$b_m = log(B_m/K), \qquad (12)$$

then the option price V_m at time step m can be computed using the equation:

$$V_m(x, t_m) \approx A(x) \int_{y_{min_m}}^{y_{max_m}} E(x,y)V_{m+1}(y, t_{m+1})dy, \qquad (13)$$

where

$$y_{max_m} = x + 10\sigma \sqrt{t_{m+1} - t_m} \qquad (14)$$

$$y_{min_m} = \max(b_m, x - 10\sigma \sqrt{t_{m+1} - t_m}) \qquad (15)$$

The barrier option value is calculated iteratively backward from the expiry date to the present date as shown in Fig. 9. The main data-path for the hardware barrier core is shown in Fig. 10.

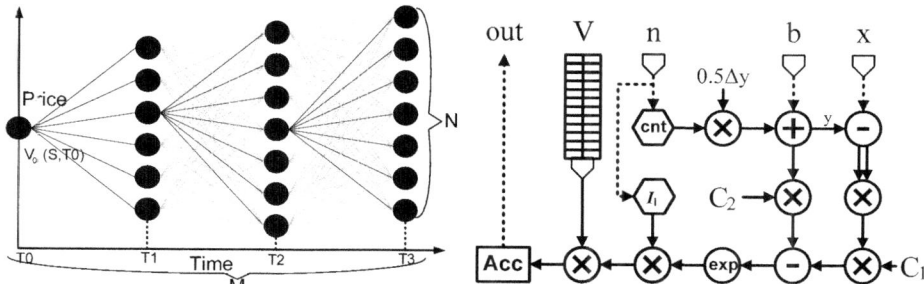

Fig. 9. The backward barrier option iteration process

Fig. 10. The hardware barrier option pricing core

As the change of price exhibits a Brownian motion, the value of y fluctuates proportional to $\sqrt{\Delta t}$. Therefore, the size of δy should also be defined proportional to $\sqrt{\Delta t}$. We define the grid density factor d_f as $\frac{\sqrt{\Delta t}}{\delta y}$. Using the methods from Section 4, the optimal (m_w, d_f) is found to be $(26, 5.8)$.

5.2   Multi-dimensional European Option pricer

The option pricing equation with multiple underlying assets using quadrature methods is based on the multi-asset version of Black and Scholes partial differential equation [1]:

$$\frac{\partial V}{\partial t} + \frac{1}{2}\sum_{i=1}^{d}\sum_{j=1}^{d}\sigma_i\sigma_j\rho_{ij}S_iS_j\frac{\partial^2 V}{\partial S_i\partial S_j} + \sum_{i=1}^{d}(r-D_i)S_i\frac{\partial V}{\partial S_i} - rV = 0 \qquad (16)$$

where r is the risk-free interest rate, d is the number of underlying assets, S_i are the underlying asset values, σ_i and D_i are the corresponding volatilities and dividend yields, and ρ_{ij} is the correlation coefficient between underlying asset values S_i and S_j. Note that $|\rho_{ij}| \leq 1$, $\rho_{ii} = 1$ and $\rho_{ij} = \rho_{ji}$. We make the logarithmic transformations

$$x_i = \log(S_i), \quad y_i = \log(S_i)$$

to be the chosen nodes at t and $t + \Delta t$. Let R be the matrix such that element $R(i,j) = \rho_{ij}$.The solution is:

$$V(x_1,\ldots,x_d,t) = C\int_{-\infty}^{+\infty}\ldots\int_{-\infty}^{+\infty}V(y_1,\ldots,y_d,t+\Delta t)$$

$$E(x_1,\ldots,x_d,y_i,\ldots,y_d)dy_1\ldots dy_d \qquad (17)$$

$$C = e^{-r\Delta t}(2\pi\Delta t)^{-n/2}(|R|)^{-1/2}(\sigma_1\sigma_2\ldots\sigma_d)^{-1}, \qquad (18)$$

$$E(x_1, \ldots, x_d, y_i, \ldots, y_d) = exp(-\frac{1}{2}\alpha^T R^{-1} \alpha), \tag{19}$$

$$\alpha_i = \frac{x_i - y_i + (r - D_i - \frac{\sigma_i^2}{2})\Delta t}{\sigma_i(\Delta t)^{1/2}} \tag{20}$$

We define the grid density factor d_f as $\frac{\sqrt{\Delta t}}{\delta y}$ such that it is inversely proportional to the grid spacing. The optimal (m_w, d_f) is found to be (20,23).

5.3   Genz's "Discontinuous" Benchmark Integral

Our last case study is Genz's "Discontinuous" benchmark multi-dimensional integral(21). It is a common test integral being used in evaluation of different numerical integration methods. In our tests we use $n = 4$ as the dimension and an integration domain of $[0, 1)^4$. Fully parallelised designs are used in our FPGA implementations and the data-paths can compute a single sample point per clock cycle, with constants c_i and w_i:

$$I = \int \int \cdots \int f_{dis}(x_1, x_2, \cdots x_n)dx_1 dx_2 \cdots dx_n \tag{21}$$

$$f_{dis} = \begin{cases} 0 & \text{if } x_0 > w_0 \text{ or } x_1 > w_1 \\ exp(\sum_{i=1}^{n}(c_i \times x_i)) & \text{otherwise} \end{cases} \tag{22}$$

In this problem, we define $d_f = N$ since its grid density should depends on the number of grid points only. The optimal (m_w, d_f) is found to be (11,96).

6   Result and Evaluation

We use the MaxWorkstation reconfigurable accelerator system from Maxeler Technologies for our evaluation. It has a MAX3424A card with a Xilinx Virtex-6 SX475T (XC6VSX475T) FPGA. The XC6VSX475T FPGA has a total of 297,600 LUTs, 595,200 FFs, 1,064 DSPs and 2,016 BRAMs. We set the target clock frequency at 100MHz ($freq$). The card is connected to an Intel i7-870 CPU through a PCI express link with a measured bandwidth of 2 GB/s. The Intel CPU has 4 physical cores.

The Intel Compiler (ICC) is used in our software implementations with optimisation flag -fast and SSE4.2 enabled. The software implementation is manually optimised in order to achieve the maximum throughput. Multiple processes are launched simultaneously in order to utilise all 4 physical cores of the quad-core i7-870 CPU.

For the FPGA implementations, we use the MaxCompiler as our development system, which adopts a streaming programming model similar to [15] and supports customisable data formats so that floating-point calculations can be performed with different mantissa bit-widths. The hardware implementations are synthesized, placed and routed using Xilinx 13.1 ISE.

Table 1. Comparison of different applications using i7-870 quad-core CPU, NVIDIA Tesla C2070 GPU, double precision XC6VSX475T FPGA and reduced precision optimised XC6VSX475T FPGA

arithmetic	Discrete barrier option			3D European option				Genz's benchmark		
	CPU	FPGA		CPU	GPU	FPGA		CPU	FPGA	
	double	double	optimised	double	double	double	optimised	double	double	optimised
clk freq. (GHz)	2.93	0.1	0.1	2.93	1.15	0.1	0.1	2.93	0.1	0.1
num. of cores	4	7	35	4	448	5	18	4	6	36
exec. time (sec.)	313	86.3	22.3	145	11.45	34.5	9.6	328.56	169.98	28.33
norm. speedup	1x	3.6x	**14.0x**	1x	12.7x	4.2x	**15.1x**	1x	1.9x	**11.6x**
opti. gain	-	1x	**3.9x**	-	-	1x	**3.6x**	-	1x	**6.0x**
APCC(W) ^{1,2}	89	13	16	69	117	4	5	81	4	4
AECC(J) ^{3}	27857.0	1121.9	356.8	10005.0	2026.7	138.1	48.0	26613.4	679.9	113.3
norm. energy	**78.1x**	3.1x	1x	**208.4x**	**42.2x**	2.9x	1x	**234.9x**	6x	1x

[1] APCC = run-time power consumption - idle power consumption.
[2] The idle power is $80W$ for FPGA and CPU system, and $154W$ for GPU system.
[3] AECC = APCC × execution time.
[4] In all applications, $\epsilon_{tol} = 10^{-3}$.

For the GPU performance result, we use NVIDIA Tesla C2070 GPU to measure the performance of our 3-dimensional European option pricer. The GPU has 448 cores running at 1.15 GHz and has a peak double precision performance of 515 GFlops.

The experiments are performed to compute a portfolio of 100 barrier options, a portfolio of 576 3D-European options, and a set of 1120 Genz's benchmark integrals.

6.1   Performance Comparison

Table 1 shows comparisons of the implementations running on a CPU with double precision arithmetic, an FPGA with double precision arithmetic, and an FPGA with optimised precision using our proposed methodology. The GPU result of the multi-dimensional European option pricer is also presented. The computed results of all designs are all optimised for $\epsilon_{tol} = 10^{-3}$ and have the same accuracy level. The measured execution time includes the data transfer time, which means the speedup figures are measured end-to-end.

Using the reduced precision optimisation techniques with XC6VSX475T FPGA, we achieve 3.6 to 6.0 times speedup gain over the original double precision FPGA designs. These optimised FPGA designs running on XC6VSX475T are 11.6 to 15.1 times faster than multi-threaded software designs running on a **quad-core** Intel i7-870, and 1.2 times faster than a GPU design running on a Tesla C2070.

6.2   Energy Comparison

We also compare the energy efficiency of the three applications on different devices. The average power consumption is measured using a remote power measuring socket from Oslon® electronics with an measuring interval of 1 second. Additional power consumption for computation (APCC) is defined as the power usage during the computation time (run-time power) minus the power usage at idle time (static power). In other words, APCC is the dynamic power consumption for that particular computation. Since the dynamic power consumption fluctuates a little, we take the average value of dynamic power to be the APCC. The additional energy consumption for computation (AECC) is defined by the following equation:

$$AECC = APCC \times Total\ Computational\ Time. \tag{23}$$

Therefore, AECC measures the actual additional energy consumed for that particular computation.

As shown in Table 1, the precision optimised FPGA designs demonstrate the greatest energy efficiency over both CPU and GPU. It is 78.1 - 234.9 times more energy efficient than an Intel i7-870 quad-core CPU, and 42.2 times more energy efficient than a Tesla C2070 GPU.

7   Conclusion

We presented a precision optimisation methodology for the generic quadrature method using reconfigurable hardware. Our novel methodology optimises the performance by considering both integration grid density and mantissa bit-width of the floating-point operators. Increasing the integration grid density reduces integration error but increases the required amount of computation, while increasing the mantissa bit-width improves precision but decreases the computation speed, due to reduced parallelism. Our proposed algorithm allows us to identify the optimal balance between the number of integration points and the precision of the floating-point operator, such that the throughput is maximised while the accuracy remains in a given error tolerance level.

Our three case studies demonstrate that using our proposed optimisation methodology, the reduced precision FPGA designs are up to 6 times faster than comparable FPGA designs with double precision arithmetic. They are up to 15.1 times faster and 234.9 times more energy efficient than an i7-870 quad-core CPU, and are 1.2 times faster and 42.2 times more energy efficient than a Tesla C2070 GPU.

Current and future work includes exploring the adaptive quadrature method on reconfigurable hardware [18]. We are also interested in extending the mantissa bit-width optimisation technique for other numerical methods.

Acknowledgment. The support of the Croucher Foundation, the UK Engineering and Physical Sciences Research Council, Maxeler, and Xilinx is gratefully acknowledged. The research leading to these results has received funding from the European Union Seventh Framework Programme under grant agreement number 248976 and 257906.

References

1. Andricopoulos, A.D., Widdicks, M., Newton, D.P., Duck, P.W.: Extending quadrature methods to value multi-asset and complex path dependent options. Journal of Financial Economics 83(2), 471–499 (2007)

2. Black, F., Scholes, M.S.: The pricing of options and corporate liabilities. Journal of Political Economy 81(3), 637–654 (1973)
3. Boland, D., Constantinides, G.: Automated precision analysis: A polynomial algebraic approach. In: Proc. IEEE Symposium on Field-Programmable Custom Computing Machines (FCCM), pp. 157–164 (2010)
4. Chow, G., Kwok, K., Luk, W., Leong, P.: Mixed precision processing in reconfigurable systems. In: Proc. IEEE Symposium on Field-Programmable Custom Computing Machines (FCCM), pp. 17–24 (May 2011)
5. Davis, M.H.A., Esparragoza-Rodriguez, J.C.: Large portfolio credit risk modeling. International Journal of Theoretical and Applied Finance 10(04), 653–678 (2007)
6. Fang, C.F., Rutenbar, R.A., Chen, T.: Fast, accurate static analysis for fixed-point finite-precision effects in DSP designs. In: IEEE/ACM international Conference on Computer-Aided Design, pp. 275–282 (2003)
7. Gaffar, A.A., Mencer, O., Luk, W., Cheung, P.Y.K.: Unifying bit-width optimisation for fixed-point and floating-point designs. In: FCCM, pp. 79–88 (2004)
8. Humphries, T., Celler, A., Trammer, M.: Improved numerical integration for analytical photon distribution calculation in spect. In: IEEE Symposium Conference on Nuclear Science, vol. 5, pp. 3548–3554 (2007)
9. Kinsman, A., Nicolici, N.: Finite precision bit-width allocation using SAT-Modulo theory. In: Proc. Design Automation and Test in Europe (DATE), pp. 1106–1111 (2009)
10. Kum, K.I., Sung, W.: Combined word-length optimization and high-level synthesis of digital signal processing systems, vol. 20(8), pp. 921–930 (2001)
11. Lee, A., Yau, C., Giles, M.B., Doucet, A., Holmes, C.C.: On the utility of graphics cards to perform massively parallel simulation of advanced Monte Carlo methods. Journal of Computational and Graphical Statistics, 769–789 (2010)
12. Lee, D.U., Gaffar, A.A., Cheung, R.C.C., Mencer, O., Luk, W., Constantinides, G.A.: Accuracy-guaranteed bit-width optimization. IEEE Trans. on CAD of Integrated Circuits and Systems 25(10), 1990–2000 (2006)
13. Lee, D.U., Gaffar, A.A., Mencer, O., Luk, W.: Minibit: bit-width optimization via affine arithmetic. In: DAC, pp. 837–840 (2005)
14. Masserey, A., Rappaz, J., Rozsnyo, R., Swierkosz, M.: Numerical integration of the three-dimensional green kernel for an electromagnetic problem. Journal of Computational Physics 205(1), 48–71 (2005)
15. Mencer, O.: ASC: a stream compiler for computing with FPGAs, vol. 25(9), pp. 1603–1617 (2006)
16. Osborne, W., Coutinho, J., Cheung, R., Luk, W., Mencer, O.: Instrumented multistage word-length optimization. In: Proc. International Conference on Field Programmable Technology (FPT), pp. 89–96 (2007)
17. Osborne, W.G., Cheung, R.C.C., Coutinho, J.G.F., Luk, W., Mencer, O.: Automatic accuracy-guaranteed bit-width optimization for fixed and floating-point systems. In: Proc. International Conference on Field Programmable Logic and Applications (FPL), pp. 617–620 (2007)
18. Rice, J.R.: A metalgorithm for adaptive quadrature. Journal of the ACM 22, 61–82 (1975)
19. Sueli, E., Mayers, D.F.: An Introduction to Numerical Analysis. Cambridge University Press (2006)
20. Tse, A.H.T., Thomas, D., Luk, W.: Design exploration of quadrature methods in option pricing. IEEE Transactions on Very Large Scale Integration (VLSI) Systems (2011) (accepted for publication)

Teaching Hardware/Software Codesign on a Reconfigurable Computing Platform

Markus Weinhardt

Osnabrück University of Applied Sciences, Osnabrück, Germany
mweinhardt@computer.org

Abstract. This paper reports on a practically oriented undergraduate course in Hardware/Software Codesign which uses an FPGA-based reconfigurable computing platform with a soft processor for analyzing and evaluating hardware/software trade-offs. The Altium Designer design flow was chosen for the practical lab exercises because it smoothly integrates HDL-based FPGA design with Embedded Programming. Furthermore, a "C to hardware" compiler allows to quickly migrate functionality from software to hardware. A complete hardware/software system was emulated on the Altium NanoBoard 3000XN. The board was also used for group projects ranging from image processing to digital audio and video processing.

Keywords: teaching, lecture, hardware/software codesign, soft processor, FPGA, Altium Designer, NanoBoard.

1 Introduction

This undergraduate course in Hardware/Software Codesign was designed for computer science, electrical engineering and mechatronics students at the Osnabrück University of Applied Sciences. It was held for the first time in the 2011 summer term. Like all courses at German Universities of Applied Sciences, this course stresses practical aspects. Therefore about half the course time consists of lectures, while the other half consists of lab exercises. Students study different target architectures as well as available models for specifying functionality and mapping the models to the target architectures. Two of the architectures - general-purpose processors and dedicated hardware - are also used in the practical exercises. At the end of the term, the students perform a two-week project in groups of two or three.

Using the Altium Designer [1] along with the FPGA-based NanoBoard 3000-XN [2], programs can be evaluated on the TSK3000A soft processor, a 32-bit MIPS-based RISC core, and on hardware (co)processors. The Altium "C to hardware" compiler *chc* implements a complete codesign system and thus enables quick hardware prototyping. Hardware/software trade-offs are easily analyzed.

The remainder of this paper is organized as follows: First, related work is reviewed. The next sections present the course organization and the lecture content while Section 5 reviews the practical exercises. Finally, Section 6 concludes the paper.

O.C.S. Choy et al. (Eds.): ARC 2012, LNCS 7199, pp. 264–275, 2012.

2   Related Work

There are many hardware/software codesign textbooks focusing on advanced synthesis and partitioning algorithms, e. g. the textbook by J. Teich and Chr. Haubelt [3] (in German). On the other hand, the new textbook by P. Schaumont [4] emphasizes the practical aspects of codesign and is therefore more suitable for an undergraduate course. The new course presented here was inspired by both by P. Schaumont's work at Virginia Tech [5] and by the codesign courses based on [3], e. g. [6]. Some aspects are also based on [7]. The lab exercises use some of the tutorials provided by Altium Ltd. for its Altium Designer [1].

3   Course Organization

This new, elective undergraduate course is recommended for second or third year students. Its prerequisites are the mandatory introductory programming and digital design courses which include lab exercises using C and VHDL, respectively. Having attended a course in computer architecture is useful, but not required. Hence all students have a working knowledge of C programming as well as some experience in HDL-based hardware design (simple combinatorial and synchronous circuits, FSM design etc.).

The course consists of 13 90-minute lectures, ten 90-minute lab sessions, and a two-week (full-time) end-of-term project. The following course materials are used: print-outs of the lecture slides, lab exercise descriptions, and tool tutorials. The students also have access to the books and scripts mentioned in Section 2, but no particular reading assignments were given. Some homework was given in the context of the lab exercises.

3.1   Learning Objectives

The learning objectives of this course are a) design, modelling and partitioning of HW/SW systems, b) automatic design generation (compilation and synthesis), c) evaluation of solutions by appropriate metrics, and d) implementing a HW/SW system in reconfigurable hardware. According to an evaluation performed at the end of the term, most students achieved these objectives. The practical lab exercises mainly dealt with objective d) which was the most interesting part for the students, cf. Section 6.

4   Lecture Content

The focus of this new course is on teaching the models used for specifying algorithms and the techniques for implementing them. This includes discussing target architectures ranging from standard processors to dedicated sequential hardware as well as methods and tools for mapping the models to heterogeneous architectures. The emphasis is on practically applicable, established methods rather than on the latest theoretical algorithms. The following sections summarize the chapters of the lecture.

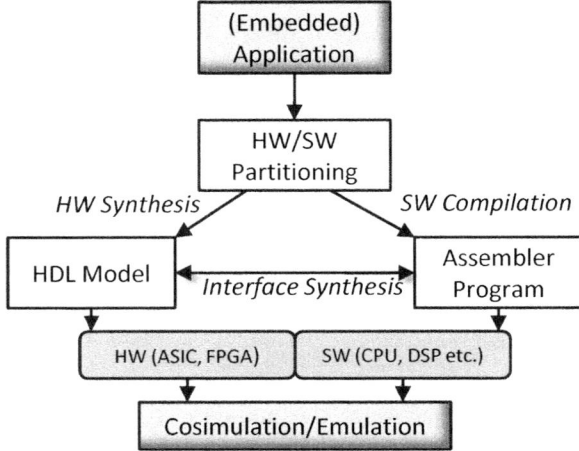

Fig. 1. Generic Codesign Flow

4.1   Introduction

First, a general introduction to the nature of hardware and software, i. e. their common properties and differences, and to system design is given. In this course, *incremental codesign* as defined in [5] is taught since it is more amenable to an undergraduate course and can be evaluated in practical lab exercises as described below in Sect. 5. In this approach, an application is first implemented in software on a standard processor and then incrementally optimized by hardware coprocessors.

4.2   System Design

The goals and constraints of system design - especially embedded design - are discussed and motivate the necessity of hardware/software *co*design as opposed to traditional system design. The general role of models and abstraction as well as a generic codesign flow, cf. Fig. 1, are introduced. The main synthesis tasks (allocation, scheduling and binding) are presented.

4.3   Target Architectures for Hardware/Software Systems

In this chapter of the lecture, the main implementation choices for algorithms are presented: dedicated sequential hardware and programmable processors. Furthermore, some special cases including micro-programmable architectures, von-Neumann and Harvard architectures, DSPs and ASIPs are introduced. Next, design methodologies - mainly ASICs and FPGAs - for digital circuits of any of the above-mentioned classes are covered. Finally, system implementation options ranging from board-level systems to systems-on-a-chip (SoCs) and configurable SoCs (CSoCs) are discussed.

4.4   Models

This chapter first introduces graphs, especially control-flow graphs (CFGs) and data-flow graphs (DFGs) as an important representation. These graphs are used in the discussion of the first class of models, sequential programs and processes. Besides single sequential programs, this class includes parallel processes with their communication and synchronization techniques. Here, hardware description languages (HDLs) are considered to be a special case of the parallel processes model with different semantics. The same is true for token-based data-flow models.

Another model more suitable for state-based interactive systems are finite state machines. It is shown that they can also be modeled by sequential programs or HDL programs.

The models are applied in a simple processor generation algorithm which generates a CFG from a C function, extends it to an FSM with data (FSMD), and finally synthesizes a datapath and a controller for it. The algorithm is based on [7, Section 2.4].

4.5   Hardware/Software Interfaces

Here, synchronization and communication issues are presented, especially the mutually exclusive coprocessor model vs. parallel processors (or processes) and blocking one-to-one communication vs. non-blocking communication with FI-FOs.

The main focus is on the Wishbone SoC bus [8] since it is an open standard which is also used by the Altium Designer [1] for the lab exercises. Wishbone is mainly used as a master/slave memory bus, but also supports multi-master systems and is useful for process to process communication, regardless of whether the processes are implemented as software or as hardware processors. Therefore data-flow models can be implemented by the Wishbone protocol as well.

4.6   Hardware/Software Performance Estimation and Partitioning

In this chapter the codesign flow is extended by hardware and software performance estimation methods to guide the design-space exploration, especially the HW/SW partitioning. Conceptually, a feedback path is added to the codesign flow presented in Fig. 1. Estimation methods and their accuracy are presented: analysis, simulation, emulation, rapid prototyping and profiling. The same metrics are used for software and hardware: performance (clock frequency, execution time, throughput), power consumption, and silicon area. The effect of hardware optimizations as e. g. operator sharing and pipelining on these metrics is demonstrated.

Finally, the estimates are used in partitioning methods. Since manual partitioning is still very common in practice and since the undergraduate audience of this course not only consists of computer science students, automatic partitioning algorithms (exact methods, greedy algorithms, and simulated annealing) are only briefly introduced.

4.7   Compilation, Code Generation and Synthesis

This chapter highlights the similarity of software compilation and hardware synthesis in the compiler frontend and the intermediate representations. Software register allocation and code generation are presented as synthesis problems with fixed resources, while hardware generation exploits all degrees of freedom of the design space.

The simple high-level synthesis algorithm presented in the chapter on models (cf. Sect. 4.4 above) is now elaborated. ASAP, ALAP and list scheduling are presented. The synthesis speed vs. area trade-off occurring during design space exploration is discussed. The implementation options (multi-cycle operators, operator chaining and sharing, and pipelining) and their impact on design metrics are presented. They are not only important for automatic synthesis systems, but also for manual RT-level HDL design as carried out in the lab exercises.

4.8   Reconfigurable Computing

The last part of the lecture gives a brief introduction to Reconfigurable Computing [9]. The use of FPGAs as target architectures, partial and run-time reconfiguration, and coarse-grain reconfigurable architectures [10] are discussed.

5   Practical Exercises

This section first introduces the Altium system used in this course. Then the lab exercises and projects are described.

5.1   Altium Designer and NanoBoard 3000

For the practical lab exercises, the design tool *Altium Designer* [1] and the Xilinx vendor tool *ISE* are used along with the *Altium NanoBoard 3000XN* [2], cf. Fig. 2.

Fig. 2. Altium NanoBoard 3000XN

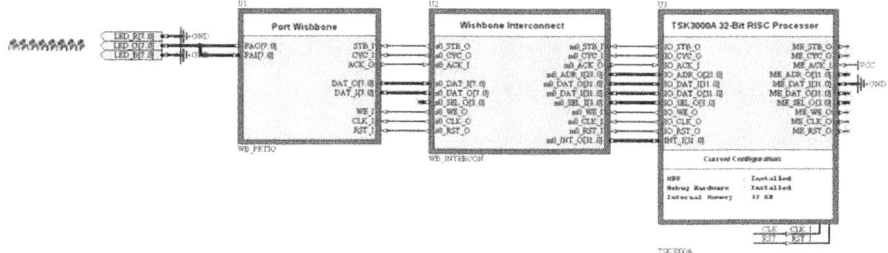

Fig. 3. Standard top-level schematics

Altium Designer is a complete IDE for FPGA design (schematic entry and HDL-based) and embedded design using soft processors including a C compiler and debugger. While many processors (including Xilinx' MicroBlaze) are supported, we chose to use Altium's own MIPS-based *TSK3000A* 32-bit RISC processor since it uses the open-standard Wishbone bus [8] for peripheral and memory connections. Since the Wishbone protocol is relatively simple, it can be directly implemented in VHDL or Verilog to synchronize manually designed custom hardware blocks with the processor.

The Designer is also well integrated with the NanoBoard. This combination allows the emulation of a complete HW/SW system consisting of a RISC processor and hardware coprocessors. The NanoBoard features a Xilinx Spartan 3AN FPGA and many peripheral devices including RGB-LEDs, buttons, switches, a touchscreen TFT color display (320 x 240 pixels), and a I2S stereo audio system with speakers. Furthermore, enough on-board memory (Flash, SRAM, SDRAM) and many interfaces (UART, SPI, USB, MIDI, IrDA, and an SVGA video output) are available. All components include hardware controllers and software drivers. They provide many opportunities for interesting student projects, cf. Section 5.3.

The top-level design is always entered as a schematic sheet in the Altium Designer. Figure 3 shows an example schematic with the TSK3000A processor, a Wishbone interconnect and a GPIO port component. On the left-hand side, the RGB color LEDs on the NanoBoard are connected to the port. By choosing this schematic component from a NanoBoard Peripheral Library, the respective constraint files are automatically generated. With a mouse-click, the design is automatically mapped to the FPGA on the NanoBoard and downloaded via USB. The Xilinx ISE tools are integrated in the Designer and called in the background.

However, schematic capture is not practical for complicated Wishbone systems with several interconnects, memories, peripherals and multi-master arbiters. For this purpose, Altium provides *OpenBus* documents which allow to connect a wishbone master interface to slave interfaces by simple arcs. Bus widths and memory or I/O addresses are set automatically. In Fig. 4, the TSK3000A on the top connects to a peripheral Wishbone interconnect on the left and to a memory interconnect on the right. The squares on the bottom left are peripherals like

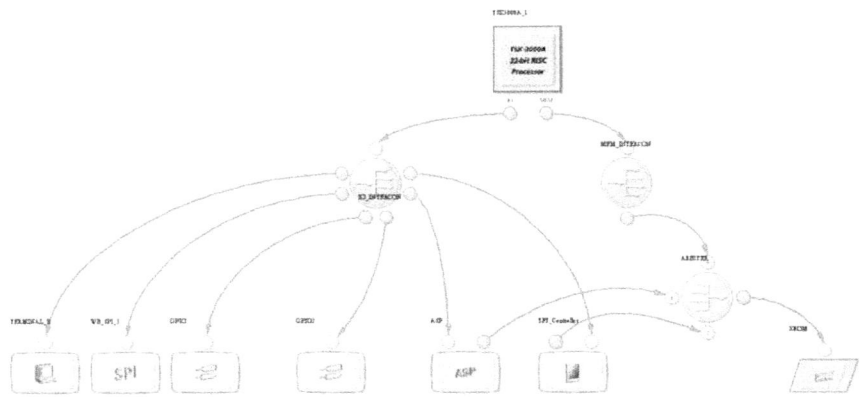

Fig. 4. OpenBus document

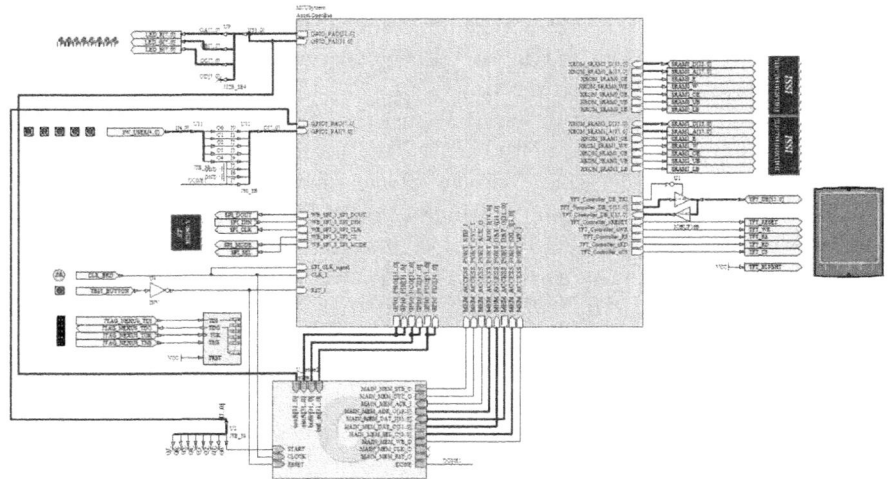

Fig. 5. Top-level schematic with OpenBus (top) and C Code (bottom) Symbols

GPIO, UART or SPI controllers. The parallelogram on the right is a RAM interface (connected to a multi-master arbiter).

The interface of an OpenBus document is exported to the top-level schematic and must be connected to the corresponding peripherals. Fig. 5 shows on the right-hand side two RAM chips and the TFT display connected to the OpenBus Symbol (box in the middle). The other peripherals are connected on the left-hand side.

The decisive reason for choosing the Altium tools in this course was the "C to HW compiler" *chc*. Though it is not a state-of-the-art, optimized high-level synthesis system, it proved very useful and quite stable for quick hardware prototyping. *chc* can be used in two modes as described in the following.

Application Specific Processor (ASP). This component is a generic hardware block which must be connected to the system (as shown in Fig. 4) if this mode is to be used. Then, any suitable functions in the processor's C code can be selected for hardware acceleration. The compiler synthesizes sequential hardware circuits for these C functions and includes them in the ASP block. The coprocessors are automatically called by the software. In this mode, the Altium Designer is a complete codesign system. Except for the manual selection of the functions to be accelerated, the entire codesign flow as shown in Fig. 1 is performed fully automatically. The ASP operates according to the coprocessor model, i. e. mutually exclusive to the processor. Nevertheless a considerable speedup above an order of magnitude could be observed for many applications by just selecting the hardware acceleration option (with a mouse-click) for suitable functions, cf. Table 1 below.[1]

C Code Symbols. In the other mode, a separate Code Symbol, i. e. a block in the top-level schematic, is created from a C function. The user can choose whether a combinational (single-cycle) or sequential (multi-cycle) circuit shall be synthesized. Such a symbol is shown on the bottom of Fig. 5. Just like other symbols generated from an OpenBus or from an HDL document, a C Code Symbol has an interface which must be connected at the top-level. The C function's input parameters are converted to input signals, and its output parameters (i. e. pointer parameters) are converted to output signals. Sequential circuits also contain start and stop signals for synchronization and allow some customizations like output registers. By setting the input and start registers from the processor over a GPIO port, these C Code Symbols can be controlled by software, but they operate as independent, parallel processors as taught in the lecture's Chapter 4. They may also have memory interfaces which result in Wishbone ports. By combining Wishbone ports of two C Code Symbols directly, even the data-flow model can be implemented.

5.2   Lab Exercises

Ten lab sessions are carried out over the course of a term. Some exercises expand over several sessions. The following sections summarize the lab with an emphasis on the *Image Rotation* assignment which illustrates the most important concepts presented in the lecture.

Using Altium Designer. In the first two lab sessions, the students work through given tutorials to familiarize themselves with the Altium Designer's top-level schematics, the open-bus documents, and embedded software development.

Models. The next session is used for a written assignment (homework) which explores the simple hardware generation algorithm and the data-flow model (cf. Section 4.4).

---

[1] Note that both the TSK3000A processor and all functions implemented in the ASP run at 50 MHz on the NanoBoard 3000XN.

```
void rotate_inner (uint16_t *pic_buf, uint16_t *tft_buf,
                   int sinA, int cosA) {
  int16_t x, y, dx, dy, xorig, yorig;
  uint16_t pixel;
  for (y=0; y<240; y++) // lines
    for (x=0; x<320; x++) { // columns
      dx = x-160; // centered coordinates
      dy = y-120;
      xorig = (dx*cosA>>8 + dy*sinA>>8) + 160;  // rotation
      yorig = (-dx*sinA>>8 + dy*cosA>>8) + 120; // kernel
      pixel = pic_buf[yorig*320 + xorig]; // read pixel value
      tft_buf[y*320 + x] = pixel; // write TFT buffer
    }
}
```

Fig. 6. Inner image rotation function

Image Rotation. An image rotation application is optimized over the next four lab sessions. It reads a 16-bpp RGB picture from Flash memory, transforms it by target-to-source mapping with a 2-D rotation kernel, and displays it on the NanoBoard's TFT panel.

The starting point of this incremental codesign exercise is a pure software implementation. The inner function rotate_inner shown in Fig. 6 only uses integer operations since the soft processor TSK3000A does not include a floating-point unit. Note that this version is about 10x faster than the original floating-point implementation.

Since *chc* uses function boundaries for HW/SW partitioning, the infrequent and expensive sine and cosine computations are performed in the calling outer function which remains in software. The values passed to rotate_inner are already shifted by eight bit and converted to integers. Hence rotate_inner can be automatically mapped to an ASP coprocessor. This results in a speedup of factor 22 at the expense of 27 % more hardware. Table 1 summarizes the hardware area (FPGA slices), the performance (clock cycle count for one call to rotate_inner), and the differences of the implemented versions.

For further optimization, the students map the rotation kernel to two dedicated hardware processors. As shown in Fig. 7, PROC_A reads the input pixels from pic_buf at the rotated position, and PROC_B writes them to the target position in tft_buf (last line in inner for-loop in Fig. 6). The pixel values are passed from PROC_A to PROC_B over a data-flow interface implemented with

Table 1. Image Rotation Implementation Summary

Implementation	HW area (slices)	HW overhead	Clock cycles	Speedup
Integer SW	3,060	-	16,980,560	-
ASP Coprocessor	3,888	27 %	769,774	22.1x
C Code Symbol & VHDL	3,740	22 %	669,610	25.3x

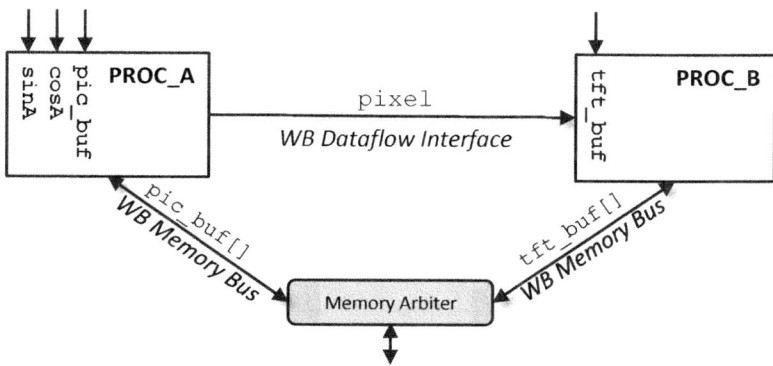

Fig. 7. Image rotation with two parallel hardware processors. For clarity, only the input registers, but no control signals are shown.

the Wishbone protocol. The two hardware processors execute in parallel and synchronize over the data channel. Additionally, both processors need to access the system memory over the memory arbiter. The only tasks remaining for the TSK3000A processor are overall synchronization and computing the sine and cosine values.

PROC_A and PROC_B could be implemented in C (as C Code Symbols) or as HDL blocks. In this exercise, PROC_A is implemented as a C Code Symbol with main memory access. Since PROC_B is relatively simple, is is chosen for manual VHDL implementation. Note that the TFT buffer is written in raster scan order. Therefore the for-loops for accessing tft_buf can be combined to a single loop over all pixels. Hence PROC_B executes the following code where each loop iteration reads a new pixel value from the data-flow interface:

```
for (p = 0; p<76800; p++)
    tft_buf[p] = pixel;
```

This code can be easily implemented as a pipelined VHDL design as shown in Fig. 8. It contains an address counter with an offset register for the TFT buffer's base address, a register for the pixel value, and two Wishbone interfaces: a slave interface (without address lines) for receiving the pixel values, and a master interface connected to the memory arbiter for writing the pixel values to the TFT buffer. The parallelization yields a 25 x speedup compared to the software implementation, cf. Table 1. Implementing the more complex PROC_A in VHDL as well would probably improve the speedup considerably. Surprisingly, despite containing two processors, the faster parallel implementation is also 4 % smaller than the ASP version. This is probably due to the overhead incurred by the automatic ASP generation.

Histogram Computation and Display. In the remaining lab sessions a design contest is performed: The computation and display of a gray image histogram on the TFT buffer has to be incrementally optimized. Now the students need to start from scratch by first implementing the application in software. Then, the design is optimized by moving as much functionality as possible to hardware, i. e. by generating FSMDs for the C code. The team with the fastest implementation wins the contest. This application lends itself to hardware implementation since the FPGA's Block RAM can be used for storing the histogram and the circuit can be pipelined. In the first contest, the winning student team achieved a 7.3-fold speedup for computing and displaying the histogram.

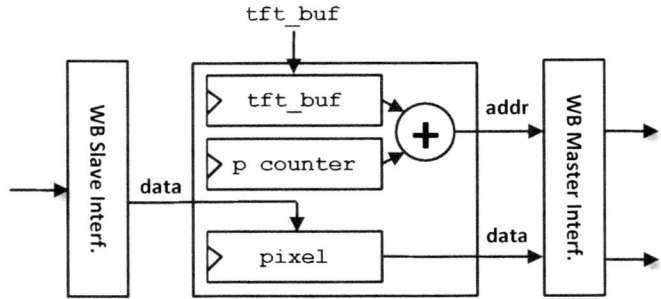

Fig. 8. Dedicated, manually designed hardware processor for PROC_B. For clarity, the controller and all control signals are omitted.

5.3   Group Projects

Finally, students perform two week end-of-term projects with individual assignments. They all use peripheral data sources and their drivers and include hardware-accelerated processing of the captured data. In the 2011 summer term, the following four projects were carried out:

- *Video Processing:* Capturing video frames from a PAL video camera (using an additional Video Peripheral Board) and displaying them on a SVGA monitor.
- *Audio Processing:* High-pass and low-pass FIR filtering on digitized audio (live or from a WAV file) and playing it on the NanoBoard's speakers.
- *Touchscreen Display:* Using the NanoBoard's touchscreen display for a small paint application and for selecting image regions for zooming using bilinear interpolation.
- *Infra-red Remote Control:* Using the NanoBoard's IrDA sensor to remotely control the display of a picture on a VGA monitor.

6   Conclusions

Illustrating important lecture topics in practical lab exercises was an important didactic goal of this course. Despite the complexity of the Altium Designer and the effort required to get accustomed to it, it proved to be very useful for this purpose. Since it implements a complete codesign flow, complex systems can be implemented quickly. As the students pointed out in the course evaluation, they liked the lab exercises and were impressed by the immediately visible benefits of hardware acceleration. Not surprisingly, the students did not like the theoretical parts of the lectures as much.

The theory presented in the lecture clearly distinguishes between the models for representing an application (parallel processes, data-flow etc.) and its implementation (software, dedicated hardware). This separation could also be maintained in the lab exercises.

In summary, the chosen course design proved successful and will be elaborated further in the future.

References

1. Altium Limited. Getting Started with the Altium Designer, http://www.altium.com
2. Altium Limited. Altium NanoBoard 3000 Series Data Sheet (2009), http://www.altium.com
3. Teich, J., Haubelt, C.: Digitale Hardware/Software-Systeme - Synthese und Optimierung, 2nd edn. Springer, Heidelberg (2007) (in German)
4. Schaumont, P.R.: A Practical Introduction to Hardware/Software Codesign. Springer, Heidelberg (2010)
5. Schaumont, P.: A senior-level course in hardware-software codesign. IEEE Transactions on Education 51(3) (August 2008)
6. Plessl, C.: Hardware/Software Codesign. Paderborn Center for Parallel Computing - Universität Paderborn. Lecture Notes (2010) (in German)
7. Vahid, F., Givargis, T.: Embedded System Design - A Unified Hardware/Software Introduction. John Wiley & Sons (2002)
8. Wishbone B4 - WISHBONE System-on-Chip (SoC) Interconnection Architecture for Portable IP Cores (2010), http://www.opencores.org
9. Bobda, C.: Introduction to Reconfigurable Computing. Springer, Heidelberg (2010)
10. Vassiliadis, S., Soudris, D. (eds.): Fine and Coarse-Grain Reconfigurable Computing. Springer, Heidelberg (2007)

Securely Sealing Multi-FPGA Systems

Tim Güneysu[1], Igor Markov[2], and André Weimerskirch[3]

[1] Horst Görtz Institute for IT-Security, Ruhr-University Bochum, Germany
[2] University of Michigan, 2260 Hayward St., Ann Arbor, MI 48109-2121
[3] ESCRYPT Inc, 315 E. Eisenhower Parkway, Ann Arbor, MI 48108

Abstract. The importance of hardware security of electronic systems is rapidly increasing due to (1) the increasing reliance of mass-produced and mission-critical systems on embedded electronics, and (2) the ever-growing supply chains that disentangle chip designers and manufacturers from OEMs. Our work shows how to dramatically reduce vulnerability to Trojan-horse injection and in-field component replacement. We propose methods to verify the authenticity and integrity of an FPGA configuration during startup and at runtime. We also developed efficient protocols for electronic sealing of a multi-FPGA system, which automatically enforces the system configuration detected upon power-up and bans further modifications.

1 Introduction

The proliferation of fake goods in the electronics industry is well documented. Between 2005 and 2008, US and Canadian authorities seized $78M worth of counterfeit Cisco hardware from China, including network modules, WAN interface cards, gigabit interface converters, and less expensive routers [8]. An even larger amount of fake networking hardware had previously been sold to customers, including financial institutions, universities, the FAA, the FBI and several branches of the US military. The Anti-Counterfeiting Task Force established by the Semiconductor Industry Association reports that "one company has seen fakes of 100 separate parts in three years".

Reportedly, the FBI is concerned that widely seen counterfeit equipment may be state-sponsored, to facilitate access to otherwise secure systems [2,8]. *IEEE Spectrum* pointed out that a Syrian air-defense radar may have been sabotaged during an Israeli bombing raid in September 2007 through a "kill-switch" planted by a European chipmaker [3]. With semiconductor manufacturing increasingly outsourced overseas, the DARPA-sponsored "Trust" program is addressing potential subversion of military electronics by seeking techniques to detect and disable such alterations. It ensures rigorous evaluation by funding work on concealing Trojan horses in ICs and identifying such Trojans.

Altering an IC often requires painstaking reverse engineering, but in some cases such alteration can be easy. For instance, the proposed "obligatory accreditation system for IT security products" in China [1] demands source code from hardware manufacturers, making reverse engineering unnecessary.

O.C.S. Choy et al. (Eds.): ARC 2012, LNCS 7199, pp. 276–289, 2012.

The challenges addressed in our work include (1) defeating Trojan horses, (2) component authentication in single- and multi-chip systems, and (3) countering unauthorized component replacement with deficient or compromised variants.

Contribution: Our proposal signficantly reduces the vulnerability of electronic systems by reducing the time interval when component replacement can be successful. It encompasses

- *Delayed logic design* via the use of FPGAs, which defeats many malicious alterations before system integration.
- *Chip integrity verification* required to prevent replacement of an existing chip.
- A protocol for *electronic sealing* of a multi-chip system that continually authenticates individual chips and prevents unauthorized replacement after the first power-up.

Outline: The remaining part of this paper is organized as follows. Section 2 covers our security objectives for secure (FPGA-based) hardware systems. Here we rely on security infrastructure available in recent FPGA devices, reviewed in Section 3. Section 4 outlines assumptions and requirements necessary to establish the methods and protocols proposed in Sections 5 and 6. Implementation details are discussed in Section 7, and concluding remarks are given in Section 8.

2   Security Objectives for Hardware Systems

The dramatic rise in chip piracy and concerns about subversion are due to the recent separation of design and manufacturing, traditionally performed by one company. Companies now tend to narrow their focus and fit into long supply chains that end with OEM system integrators. Convincing solutions to security challenges must account for this context.

Delayed Logic Design. It would be difficult to subvert a chip *before* its functionality is available to the attacker in any form — hardware or software. Therefore, *delaying logic design until after manufacturing and shipment* can dramatically reduce the time period during which a chip is vulnerable to replacement or alteration. Such delay is made possible by modern FPGA chips, which are sufficiently large, fast and cheap for many applications. Given their regular structure, blank FPGA chips can be tested quickly, after which a system integrator can program each chip with a precomputed trusted bit-stream.

Chip Integrity Verification. Along with ASICs and custom-designed chips, FPGA-based chips used in larger systems run the risk of being replaced by knock-offs or maliciously altered designs. Unfortunately, the low cost of FPGAs and the simplicity of FPGA design tools facilitates single and mass-produced knock-offs. However, such replacements are easier to detect because FPGA configurations are completely determined by discrete parameters (configuration bits). Therefore, one can compute a cryptographic hash of FPGA bit-streams and use this fingerprint to periodically authenticate the chip using a challenge-response protocol.

Electronic Sealing. Field-programming of component chips by a trusted system integrator defeats many replacement and Trojan-horse attacks performed *prior to system integration*. To guard against attacks *after system integration*, we use chips that report their own identity. The identity of each chip must be checked reliably, so that

- faking any part of the chip, such as communication circuits, would not allow passing identity checks.
- chips that lie about their identity (e.g., trying to replay overheard communications) do not pass the checks.

We address these challenges by several protocols for *electronically sealing* multi-chip systems. One option is for a dedicated hardware entity to periodically verify the identity of each FPGA by checking if it retains a shared secret. These checks can be performed between normal bus-level communications and would detect changes in a chip's identity.

3   State of the Art in FPGA Security

To detect chip tampering after start-up, our protocols for authenticating chip configurations use recent FPGA technology. We therefore review security features and techniques in recent FPGAs and in academic literature.

3.1   Security Features of Modern FPGAs

The introduction of bitstream encryption was the first feature that significantly improved FPGA security. Today, many (volatile) FPGAs support encrypted bitstreams to cryptographically protect configuration stored in an external memory – eliminating the threat of inspection and theft by unauthorized parties. Besides *confidentiality* of the Intellectual Property (IP) contained in the FPGA configuration, the installation of a secret key on each device can be also used as an effective tool to prevent *overbuilding* and *device cloning*. However, bitstream encryption does not solve all security issues. For example, attacks on the integrity of an FPGA configuration (which performs a security-related function) are countered by a non-cryptographic CRC checksum on most FPGAs, and CRC is easy to manipulate. Finally, some FPGA manufactures (such as Xilinx) install a device-specific identification number (ID) on their FPGAs with which FPGAs can be distinguished. For example, Xilinx' DeviceDNA is a 57-bit static device ID (of which effectively only 55-bit are used) that could be employed for device identification in cryptographic binding or sealing protocols. We classify modern FPGA devices as follows:

C1. FPGAs with authenticated encryption. Xilinx Virtex-6 FPGAs offer an AES-256 bitstream encryption and HMAC (based on a SHA-256 hash) function that can be used to ensure configuration confidentiality, authentication and integrity during power-up. Authentication/identification of multi-chip systems and (cryptographic) integrity checks at runtime are not supported.

C2. FPGAs with bitstream encryption only. Many high-performance FPGA (such as Xilinx Virtex II/4/5/6 FPGAs, larger Spartan-6, Altera Stratix II/III/IV/V, Cyclone III LS, Actel ProASIC3, LatticeECP) devices allow the use of encrypted bitstreams, mostly using AES-128 or AES-256 encryption. However, cryptographically strong authentication and integrity checks for the bitstream are not supported.

C3. FPGA without cryptographic features. Low-cost FPGA devices typically do not provide any cryptographic protection mechanisms for their configurations, except for an identification number (e.g., in Xilinx Spartan-3 A/AN devices). Since these devices do not provide any cryptographic trust anchor, an FPGA developer needs to include security features within the configuration bitstream. The security of this approach is bounded by the difficulty of reverse-engineerng the bitstream that contains the cryptographic secrets. Therefore, adapting our techniques to low-security FPGAs would require more work and incur a greater overhead.

3.2 Prior Academic Work

In [6, 21], the authors compiled a comprehensive list of security risks of FPGA-based systems. Further guidelines on trusted FPGAs can be found in [20, 18]. Several proposals perform bitstream authentication by extending the bitstream decryptor core within the FPGA's static configuration logic with an authentication function [5, 16]. Further work discusses the challenges of establishing and storing secret keys. Instead of plain memory cells that store the secret key, one can use Physically Unclonable Functions [15], which can be configured to derive cryptographic keys from chip-specific hardware fluctuations. For example, key establishment schemes based on (rather complex) PUF-based protocols were proposed in [19,9]. Keys can be established through public-key cryptography [10].

4   Threat Model, Assumptions and Requirements

Electronic hardware is produced and employed by several actors. The *Hardware Manufacturer* (HM) produces FPGA devices. The *Intellectual Property Owner* (IPO) owns application-specific designs, synthesizes them into configuration bitfiles and licenses for a fee, usually on a per-volume basis. The *System Integrator* (SI) embeds these designs in FPGA devices. The *End User* (EU) physically possesses the product, using it as intended or abusing it. The *Trustworthy Owner* (TO) owns the entire electronic system[1].

Threat Model. We assume that the IPO is trustworthy and seeks protection from design subversion. Our proposal relies on SI, also assumed trustworthy.

---

[1] The TO does not always run FPGAs devices. For instance, military systems are owned by the government but run by specific detachments.

Given that FPGAs are easy to program, SI and IPO may be the same entity. [2]
The EU may alter the system, and any malicious third party is included in the
EU group. The HM includes the entire development chain, and we distinguish
several cases in terms of trustworthyness.

The HM (or any part of the design and manufacturing chain) can introduce
Trojans, malicious programs, and backdoors in the FPGA. To defeat some of
these attacks, we assume that SI can randomly sample FPGAs chips from all
FPGAs produced, e.g., by purchasing them through proxies/anonymously. This
undermines targeted manipulation of FPGAs for use by the HM. Furthermore,
we assume that the SI *randomizes FPGA place-and-route*, so that each maps
FPGA differently, making it impossible to predict where each LUT/gate will
go in the FPGA (note that ASICs and custom-made chips cannot afford this
approach). Thus, HM's Trojans or malicious routines cannot connect to specific
internal signals of the chip. However, if the HM includes a general trigger (e.g.,
time-based), the issue will be detected by other users of the FPGA, very likely
before it can cause major damage to TO's systems. The HM may be able to inject a backdoor to read out the FPGA configuration. However, this issue is in the
domain of protection of intellectual property rather than our objective. Furthermore, our analysis assumes that HM already obtained the FPGA configuration
and can modify it maliciously.

The EU is able to add/remove one or several FPGA(s) to/from the system.
The added FPGAs may be under attacker's control. The EU is able to tap
into and alter the communication between FPGAs. The attacker is also able to
inject messages to the communication channel between FPGAs, but not probe
an FPGA or extract security credentials while the system is powered. When the
system is powered down, the attacker is not able to physically extract security
credentials in a short time period (say one hour). We assume that the attacker is
not able to replace the entire system (including all FPGAs) at once. We assume
that the TO regularly checks the system. For instance, one of the FPGAs might
be located in a physically secure compartment that is only accessible to the
TO and that regularly provides a status notification to the trustworthy TO.
Our proposed mechanisms will defeat all attackers that are located within the
described attacker model.

Further Assumptions and Requirements. The general *security objective*
pursued in our work is to prevent altered chips from successfully running in a
computer system. Therefore we propose cryptographic authentication and identification services for single and multi-chip systems. We rely on trustworthy
hardware infrastructure for authentication and on initialization at a physically-
secure facility by a trusted party. We also assume that each FPGA passes an
enrollment phase performed by a trusted party (e.g., the system integrator)
during which secrets are installed in the device or system. During system initialization in this environment, keys K_i for bitstream encryption are generated

---

[2] If FPGAs are shipped by an untrusted party, the receiver can check FPGA's integrity
   using proposed techniques. In this case, the initial receiver is included in the SI group
   and assumed trustworthy.

and loaded in the secure key store of each FPGA (either by programming eFuses or the battery-backed-up RAM). We assume that bitstreams are authenticated and that there is a mechanism in place to counter loading old versions (e.g., each bitstream version uses an individual bitstream encryption key). We further make the non-trivial assumption that CAD tools for FPGAs, used at the secure facility, are trusted and do not cause unintended side-effects [17]. Note that the possibility of subversion *before* initialization and enrollment, e.g., by injecting Trojan horses into the FPGA fabric, is inherently difficult since the FPGA configuration may be randomized at the last minute (the principle of *delayed logic design*) and multiple FPGA configurations, loaded one after another, can use the same logic elements.

Based on our assumptions, we now present mechanisms to integrate cryptographic configuration integrity checking and electronic sealing for FPGA devices of classes C1,C2. The availability of bitstream encryption in these two device classes can be regarded as basic trust anchor that enables the implementation of upper-layer security objectives on top (i.e., cryptographic authentication and integrity checks). Note that our proposals are solely based on symmetric cryptography that can be implemented in the fabric of an FPGA. This involves the standardized AES block cipher for encryption/decryption, an authentication function such as HMAC-SHA-256, and a method to distinguish FPGA devices (e.g., using DeviceDNA or PUFs). We further assume that these cryptographic standard primitives are sufficiently protected against implementation attacks, such as side-channel or fault-injection attacks.

5   Configuration Integrity Checking

Integrity checks of FPGA configurations (especially for security-critical component) are essential to hamper replacement attacks. We now present two possible methods to check the integrity of a single device beyond automatically provided CRC integrity tests (1) at startup time and (2) periodically during operation to detect Single Event Upsets (SEU) as well as a malicious tampering at runtime. Our proposal for (1) described in Section 5.1 is more lightweight, does not interfere with operations and resource requirements of the main application and only demands for a slightly larger external memory to provide the storage for a multi-boot FPGA configuration. The proposal (2) discussed in Section 5.2 performs periodical checks while the main application is running at the cost of augmenting the main application with relevant cryptographic functions (possibly requiring a larger FPGA device).

5.1   Integrity Check at System Startup

Since devices of class C1 already include a facility to authenticate FPGA configuration at startup, we focus on FPGA class C2, illustrated by a Xilinx Spartan-6 XC5SLX75. In particular, this device supports encrypted multi-boot configurations, which can be loaded in sequence. For devices that do not support multi-boot, a similar behavior can be achieved by using the partial reconfiguration of

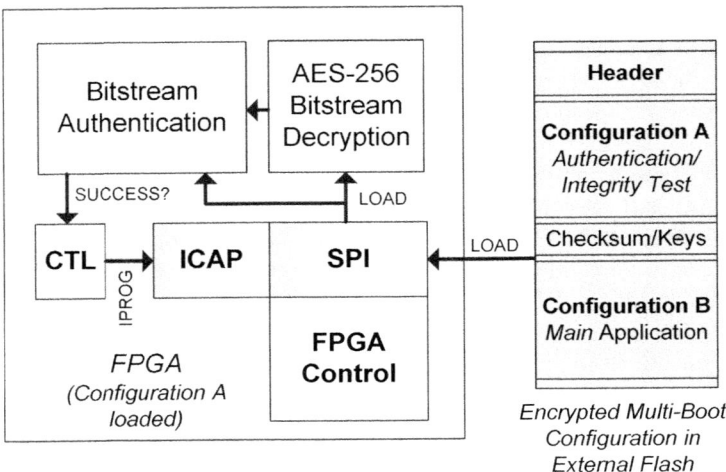

Fig. 1. Multi-boot configuration for bitstream authentication & integrity test

FPGAs and internal configuration interfaces such as Xilinx' Internal Configuration Access Port (ICAP).

The first configuration (A) contains a cryptographic authentication and decryption (and optionally an identification) function that directly decrypts and authenticates the multi-boot image (B) right after configuration. The authentication is based on standardized symmetric authentication mechanisms, such as MACs involving standardized block ciphers or keyed hash functions like HMAC. Note that the bitstream must be decrypted before authentication to prevent simple substitution attacks [5]. To this end, AES decryption engine is implemented in the fabric of the FPGA (additionally to the bitstream decryptor in the FPGA control logic which is not directly accessible to user logic). Secret keys and/or checksums required for authentication and integrity check can be stored in the configuration bitstream, which must be encrypted and inaccessible in decrypted form, so as to ensure cryptographic security. Upon passing the authentication and integrity test of the configuration image, configuration (A) issues a command (e.g., for Spartan-6 FPGAs, the IPROG command sent via ICAP) to load the second part of multi-boot bitstream (B) into the FPGA which contains the main application. Figure 1 illustrates the FPGA multi-boot configuration with configuration (A) currently loaded into the FPGA.

Configuration (A) can also be extended to perform security functions beyond authentication and integrity tests. For example, (A) can implement a PUF instead of or in addition to the DeviceDNA device identification function (see Section 6.1). It might be also beneficial to implement or derive a chip-specific secret value (e.g., obtained from a PUF or other complex secret function) in configuration (A) but actually use it in the main application (B) (e.g., to perform periodical integrity checks as described in Section 5.2). This requires passing a secret value K_c between these two FPGA configurations (preserving confidentiality) that are loaded one after the other on the same FPGA. An possible solution is to store a common global secret K_G in both encrypted configuration (A) and (B) that masks the derived secret value K_c from configuration (A) by xor using $c = K_G \oplus K_c$. The masked value c can then be stored temporarily off-chip until configuration (B) is loaded decrypting the off-chip secret via $K_c = K_G \oplus c$ again. Depending on the FPGA, it may also be possible to transfer the secret K_c on-chip between configurations. This can be done with read/write registers of an FPGA's control logic which remain unchanged during FPGA configuration. For example, 5×16-bit GENERAL and READBACK registers can be used (i) to store individual words $K_{c,i}$ (or masked c_i) of a temporary 80-bit secret in configuration A and (ii) read them back after loading configuration B.

5.2   Periodic Integrity Check at Runtime

To prevent attacks that are applied *during* system operation, the one-time configuration authentication at system startup presented in Section 5.1 is not sufficient. The solution presented in this Section applies to FPGAs of classes C1,C2 and is related to the proposal by Drimer [5] but our solution is counter-less and thus supports asynchronous authentication. Most devices of these two classes allow a readback of the currently used configuration using external and internal ports from the fabric. On many FPGAs (such as Spartan-6), a readback using internal ports remains possible even if bitstream encryption is used (using the ICAP interface) and also does not interrupt a continuous system operation. Thus, bitstream authentication can run in parallel to the main application. It can be periodically called to read the current FPGA configuration using the ICAP interface, verifying its integrity and authenticity (see Figure 2).

6   Electronic Sealing of Multi-chip Systems

Given a multi-chip systems, we want to prevent the injection of Trojan horses and replacement of individual components with knock-offs. Such tampering can be detected using mutual identification of individual chip-level components, performed within our proposed *electronic sealing* protocols. A generic solution to protect a single FPGA is provided by Altera's MAX II reference design [4] in which a CPLD is programmed to exchange cryptographic handshaking tokens with the FPGA device. However, this solution leaves unclear the storage of secret cryptographic key(s) and the applicability to multi-FPGA systems.

In this section, we propose three protocols for use with FPGAs of classes C1,C2 to enable electronic sealing based on an authenticated heartbeat for multi-FPGA systems[3] The first protocol (Section 6.1) employs a central chip or component to store cryptographic identifiers for all chips in the system, similar to Altera's solution [4] but more versatile. In Section 6.2, we further establish a

---

[3] While large FPGAs can already accommodate entire systems, multi-FPGA systems remain attractive in many cases, in part due to pricing of FPGA parts. For example, it is still cheaper to buy three largest Spartan-6 XC6SLX150 devices compared the cheapest, single Virtex-6 FPGA.

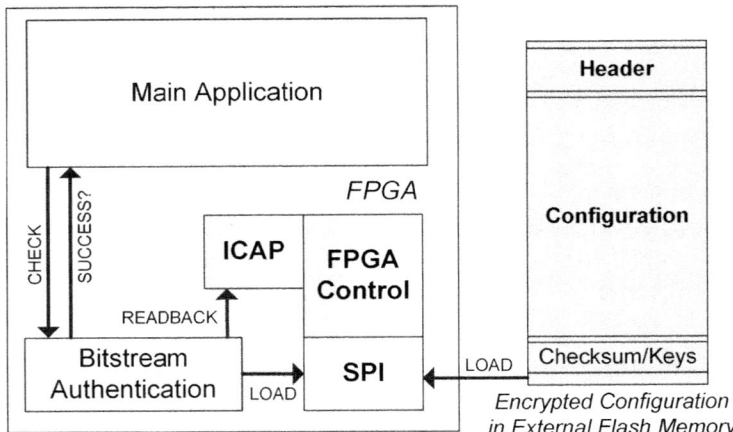

Fig. 2. Periodic integrity & authenticity checks of an FPGA configuration

decentralized method with which FPGAs perform a peer-to-peer authentication using a common global key without an additional security component. The third protocol (Section 6.3) performs electronic sealing in a ring topology without relying on a global key.

6.1 Symmetric Authentication and Central Security Module

For this protocol a central security module (CSM) is used to store individual keys K_i and identities ID_i of all deployed FPGAs. The ID_i of an FPGA can be derived using the DeviceDNA feature, if available. Alternatively, PUFs on FPGAs have evolved to a suitable method to derive device-specific identification numbers when no vendor support to distinguish devices is available. The individual (or global) secret keys K_i of each FPGA can be stored as encrypted part of the configuration in the system Flash or can be generated by another PUF. To reduce the number of logic resources occupied by secret key generation, a multi-boot configuration as shown in Section 5.1 can be used to generate secret keys beforehand in a separate configuration step. The CSM that manages all secrets can be either a CPLD located on-board, i.e., directly connected to the FPGAs via an internal bus, or it can be located at a remote back-end and connected via a network interface. The CSM needs to be initialized by a trusted party during system initialization where all keys K_i as well as the corresponding identifier ID_i for all FPGAs are stored in a permanent, internal key storage. The CSM's internal key storage must not be read nor overwritten externally. Updating or removing a key-identifier pair within the CSM is an optional feature but can be useful to allow later chip updates or replacements due to defects. This can be realized by authenticating the updating party against the CSM using a master-key after which overwriting (parts of) the key storage with external data is enabled for a limited amount of time.

Once the keys K_i have been stored within the CSM, a mutual authentication scheme is periodically initiated by the CSM at runtime as part of the normal system operation. This *authenticated heartbeat* phase draws on [5] and enables electronic sealing at system runtime as follows:

1. The CSM sends a random number R_1 to FPGA_i after a globally specified time interval.
2. The FPGA generates a random number R_2 and responds with $Enc_{K_i}(R_1, R_2, \text{ID}_{\text{CSM}})$, where ID_{CSM} denotes a target identifier of the CSM and $Enc_{K_i}(X, Y)$ denotes the encryption (e.g. AES-CBC) of X concatenated Y using key K_i.
3. The CSM first decrypts the message and checks if decrypted R_1 and ID_{CSM} is correct. Then, it extracts R_2 and sends the message $Enc_{K_i}(R_1, R_2, \text{ID}_{\text{FPGA}_i})$ to the FPGA, where $\text{ID}_{\text{FPGA}_i}$ denotes the target identifier of the FPGA.
4. The FPGA decrypts the message and checks R_2 and $\text{ID}_{\text{FPGA}_i}$.

After such a successful mutual authentication of both parties, both chips continue operation. If the CSM fails to authenticate an FPGA chip, it may permanently deactivate the entire system, broadcast a warning message, etc. Likewise, the system designer/integrator determines the appropriate response if an FPGA chip fails to authenticate the CSM, e.g., self-deactivation of the FPGA by erasing its bit-stream.

6.2 Pairwise Authentication

The following protocol does not rely on a CSM. Instead, all FPGAs use a global key K_G for mutual authentication using identifiers ID_i. The global key K_G can either stored directly in an encrypted part of the FPGA configuration or it can be realized as follows: during system initialization in a trusted environment, a PUF on each FPGA is used to derive a chip-specific secret key K_{PUF_i}. Then a global key K_G is selected randomly and a mask value M_i is computed for each FPGA i as $M_i = K_{\text{PUF}_i} \oplus K_G$. This mask value is stored (unencrypted) in permanent memory. Only by combining the correct secret K_{PUF_i} (obtained individually per device from the PUF) with the device-specific mask value, the global key can be recovered during system runtime: $K_G = M_i \oplus K_{\text{PUF}_i}$.

A single global key K_G allows efficient key deployment during initialization and requires only limited storage (a single key/mask). However, by extracting the global key from an FPGA, an adversary can replace any FPGA in the system.

After initialization by system integrator, every FPGA periodically invokes a mutual authentication process as part of the normal system operation. This *authenticated heartbeat* phase draws on [5] and encompasses the following steps:

1. FPGA_i sends a random number R_1 to FPGA_j, $i < j$ over a shared link using a multi-master communication protocol (for synchronization, arbitration and data collision detection).

2. FPGA_j generates a random number R_2 and responds with $Enc_{K_G}(R_1, R_2,$
   $\text{ID}_{\text{FPGA}_i})$, where $\text{ID}_{\text{FPGA}_i}$ denotes the target identifier of FPGA_i.
3. FPGA_i decrypts R_1 and $\text{ID}_{\text{FPGA}_i}$ and if they are correct, it responds with
   $Enc_{K_G}(R_1, R_2, \text{ID}_{\text{FPGA}_j})$, where $\text{ID}_{\text{FPGA}_j}$ denotes the target identifier of
   FPGA_j.
4. FPGA_j decrypts and checks R_2 and $\text{ID}_{\text{FPGA}_j}$.

The system designer/integrator determines the appropriate response in case an
FPGA fails authentication, e.g., an error message can be broadcast over the internal bus to prohibit communication with the FPGA that failed authentication.

6.3 Authentication Based on a Ring Topology

Compared to the protocol presented in Section 6.2, FPGAs are arranged in a ring
topology so that each FPGA only engages a symmetric authentication scheme
with its two nearest neighbors. Hence, this protocol does not require storing a
global key or a single individual key in each FPGA, but only the two individual
keys K_i and K_{i+1} with $i \in 0, ..., n-1$ are stored in each of the n FPGAs. These
keys can be stored or generated similarly as described in Section 6.2. Note that
extracting a pair of keys K_i and K_{i+1} from an FPGA does not, in itself, allow
faking another FPGA in the ring.

   The main advantage of this authentication scheme compared to the scheme
discussed in Section 6.2 is that only two individual keys K_i and K_{i+1} are stored
in every FPGA. Hence, an adversary is not able to replace an arbitrary FPGA
in the system after he has extracted the keys out of another FPGA. Further,
the entire FPGA ring can be authenticated by sequentially verifying every pair
of neighboring FPGAs.

7   Implementation Considerations

Our protocols and techniques draw on features common in modern FPGAs (e.g.,
JTAG TAP, ICAP, DeviceDNA), as well as standard cryptography available in
both academic literature and industrial IP portfolios. Our solution in Section 5
requires an additional core for bitstream decryption (AES-CBC) and authentication (e.g., HMAC as a standardized keyed hash function), implemented in the
programmable fabric. Similarly, electronic sealing requires encryption (AES) and
a device-specific identifier (based on the DeviceDNA feature or PUFs). Rather
than review well-known implementation details of state-of-the-art implementations, we cite relevant sources and provide an overview in Table 1. It is not our
intent to provide an exhaustive list, but rather to show feasibility of our proposals and limit implementation overhead, even for small FPGA devices of classes
C1,C2. For standard encryption and decryption, Drimer et al. describe small
and fast AES cores with different modes of operation (including authenticated
encryption) on Virtex-5 FPGAs [7]. Their smallest implementation requires 212
slices and 2 BRAMs using a fixed secret key. Logic slices in our reference FPGA

Table 1. Implementation cost (SLC = FPGA slices) and performance of required cryptographic primitives. Note that FPGA slices of Spartan-6 and Virtex-5 devices are very similar.

Primitive	Device	Resources	Throughput
AES [7]	Virtex-5	212 SLC/2 BRAM	1.7 GBit/s
HMAC/SHA-256 [12]	Spartan-6	110 SLC/1 BRAM	1.2 GBit/s
PUF (50 bit ID) [13]	Virtex-5	130 SLC	-

(Spartan-6) are quite similar to those on Virtex-5, and implementation results generally agree with those reported by Drimer et al. Optimized keyed hash functions such as HMAC-SHA-256 on FPGAs were described by McEvoy et al. in [14] and are also commercially available from Helion [12] taking 110 slices and 1 BRAM of a Spartan-6 FPGA. To implement the integrity check based on a multi-boot configuration and/or periodic runtime check described in Section 5, we combine the cryptographic primitives with an ICAP interface and a small-footprint Microblaze microprocessor soft core with fixed timer support which occupies 613 slices and 4 BRAMs on a Spartan-6. The complete solution requires less than 1000 Spartan-6 slices and 7 BRAMs. In a medium-sized Spartan-6 XC6SLX75 (see Section 5.1), this corresponds to a slice and BRAM utilization of 8.6% and 4.1%, respectively.

Protocols in Section 6 require fewer resources. To reliably distinguish FPGA devices (Section 6), one can use Xilinx DeviceDNA or any of FPGA-compatible PUF techniques [9, 13, 11]. Butterfly PUFs, for example, require 130 Virtex-5 slices to generate a 50-bit identifier [13]. Including overhead for control logic and the required encryption function [7], the resource consumption for electronic sealing is upper-bounded by 500 slices and 2 BRAMs (i.e., 4.3% of the slices and 1.2% of the BRAMs contained in the Spartan-6 XC6SLX75).

8   Conclusions

We proposed a comprehensive solution to guard against counterfeit integrated circuits in single- and multi-chip systems. In particular, *delayed logic design* in terms of FPGAs limits the time interval during which successful attacks can be mounted against a hardware system. Since modern FPGAs already provide bitstream encryption as a basic feature, we proposed in this work how to enable configuration authentication during system startup and runtime as well how to establish electronic sealing in multi-chip systems using only symmetric cryptography. We presented two reasonable techniques to verify the integrity and authenticity of FPGA configuration for devices that provide bitstream encryption. First, we proposed a multi-boot configuration that cryptographically verifies its own integrity before the actual main application is loaded. The second technique performs periodic configuration readback within the FPGA to prevent manipulations of security functions during runtime. A second major contribution deals with electronic sealing of multi-chip systems. We developed three efficient protocols based on a central security module, peer-to-peer- and ring-based communication that enable mutual authentication of system components to detect tampering or unauthorized replacement of protected devices. Finally, we evaluate the implementation overhead for common FPGA parts and show that it is moderate.

References

1. China to make foreign firms reveal secret info. Yomiuri Shimbun (September 2008), http://www.yomiuri.co.jp/dy/business/20080919TDY01306.htm
2. FBI Concerned About Implications of Counterfeit Cisco Gear. Slashdot (April 2008), http://hardware.slashdot.org/article.pl?sid=08/04/22/1317212
3. Adee, S.: The Hunt For The Kill Switch. IEEE Spectrum 45(5), 34–39 (2008)
4. Altera Corporation: FPGA Design Security Solution Using MAX II Devices. White Paper, ver. 1.0 (September 2004), http://www.altera.com/literature/wp/wp_m2dsgn.pdf
5. Drimer, S.: Authentication of FPGA Bitstreams: Why and How. In: Diniz, P.C., Marques, E., Bertels, K., Fernandes, M.M., Cardoso, J.M.P. (eds.) ARCS 2007. LNCS, vol. 4419, pp. 73–84. Springer, Heidelberg (2007)
6. Drimer, S.: Volatile FPGA design security – a survey (v0.96) (April 2008), http://www.cl.cam.ac.uk/~sd410/papers/fpga_security.pdf
7. Drimer, S., Güneysu, T., Paar, C.: DSPs, BRAMs, and a pinch of logic: Extended recipes for AES on FPGAs. ACM Trans. Reconfigurable Technol. Syst. 3, 1–27 (2010), http://doi.acm.org/10.1145/1661438.1661441
8. Gross, G.: US, Canadian agencies seize counterfeit Cisco gear. The Industry Standard (2008), http://slashdot.org/article.pl?sid=08/02/29/1642221
9. Guajardo, J., Kumar, S.S., Schrijen, G.-J., Tuyls, P.: FPGA Intrinsic PUFs and their Use for IP Protection. In: Paillier, P., Verbauwhede, I. (eds.) CHES 2007. LNCS, vol. 4727, pp. 63–80. Springer, Heidelberg (2007)
10. Güneysu, T., Möller, B., Paar, C.: Dynamic Intellectual Property Protection for Reconfigurable Devices. In: ICFPT 2007, pp. 169–176 (2007)
11. Güneysu, T.: Using Data Contention in Dual-ported Memories for Security Applications. Journal of Signal Processing Systems, 1–15 (December 30, 2010), doi:10.1007/s11265-010-0560-z
12. Helion Technology: Tiny Hash Core Family for Xilinx FPGA. Data Sheet (2010), http://www.heliontech.com/downloads/tiny_hash_xilinx_datasheet.pdf
13. Kumar, S., Guajardo, J., Maes, R., Schrijen, G., Tuyls, P.: Extended abstract: The butterfly PUF protecting IP on every FPGA. In: IEEE International Workshop on Hardware-Oriented Security and Trust (HOST 2008), pp. 67–70 (2008)
14. McEvoy, R.P., Crowe, F.M., Murphy, C.C., Marnane, W.P.: Optimisation of the SHA-2 family of hash functions on FPGAs. In: Emerging VLSI Technologies and Architectures (2006)
15. Pappu, R., Recht, B., Taylor, J., Gershenfeld, N.: Physical one-way functions. Science 297(5589), 2026–2030 (2002)
16. Parelkar, M.M.: FPGA security – bitstream authentication. Tech. rep., George Mason University (2005), http://ece.gmu.edu/courses/Crypto_resources/web_resources/theses/GMU_theses/Parelkar/Parelkar_Fall_2005.pdf

17. Roy, J.A., Koushanfar, F., Markov, I.L.: Extended abstract: Circuit CAD tools as a security threat. In: HOST, pp. 65–66 (2008)
18. Seamann, G.: FPGA bitstreams and open designs (April 2000), http://web.archive.org/web/20050831135514/ http://www.opencollector.org/news/Bitstream/
19. Simpson, E., Schaumont, P.: Offline Hardware/Software Authentication for Reconfigurable Platforms. In: Goubin, L., Matsui, M. (eds.) CHES 2006. LNCS, vol. 4249, pp. 311–323. Springer, Heidelberg (2006)
20. Trimberger, S.: Trusted design in FPGAs. In: Design Automation Conference (June 2007), http://videos.dac.com/44th/papers/1_2.pdf
21. Wollinger, T., Guajardo, J., Paar, C.: Security on FPGAs; state of the art implementation and attacks. In: ACM Trans. Embedded Comp. Sys., TECS (2004)

FPGA Paranoia: Testing Numerical Properties of FPGA Floating Point IP-Cores

Xuan You Tan, David Boland, and George A. Constantinides

Electrical and Electronic Engineering, Imperial College London,
London, SW7 2AZ, UK

Abstract. In the early days of computing, hardware platforms were developed independently and created their own conventions for floating point to suit their underlying hardware architecture, but this meant computer programmers had to understand these conventions when designing their algorithms, and adapt their algorithms when porting to new platforms. As a result, the IEEE-754-1985 standard was created to simplify design for computer programmers by ensuring that the same software will obtain the same results across all hardware platforms. While most computers largely adhere to the standard, sometimes corner cases can be missed. Paranoia is a test suite written by William Kahan in 1983, designed to discover obvious flaws in non-compliant floating point arithmetic. The Paranoia test suite continues to show errors and inconsistencies in modern computers and compiler libraries, and has recently found similar flaws in GPUs [1]. FPGAs have historically been used to create custom hardware designs, with a focus on performance for an application specific design, meaning such portability has not been an issue. However, transistor scaling has led to FPGAs with the potential for high floating point performance, and as such FPGA-based accelerators are increasingly adopting standard single or double precision cores within hardware accelerators for high-performance computing applications. As a result, this paper has created a framework to allow FPGA IP-cores to be tested against the Paranoia benchmark to ensure that FPGA IP-cores can been subjected to the same rigorous testing as their CPU equivalents. In this paper, we discuss this effort and provide compliance results for the main vendor and open source core generators.

Keywords: FPGA, Paranoia, IEEE 754 Floating Point Arithmetic.

1 Introduction

Since computers were first invented, a fundamental issue has been how to approximate the uncountably infinite set of real numbers with a finite representation. In general, the high performance and scientific computing community has settled on floating point representation. Initially, inconsistencies between a large number of available platforms each having their own definition of floating point resulted in differing results among various floating point libraries [2]. In 1977, Robert Stewart spearheaded the first standard for floating-point arithmetic, which would eventually become IEEE-754-1985 [2, 3].

O.C.S. Choy et al. (Eds.): ARC 2012, LNCS 7199, pp. 290–301, 2012.

Given that GPUs and FPGAs are increasingly being used in high performance computing due to their ability to exploit inherent parallelism in an algorithm [4,5], these devices should be subjected to the same degree of scrutiny so as to ensure any performance comparisons using a standard precision are fair and that non-compliance is both known and accounted for; we note that the well-known crash of the Ariane 5 satellite was a result of non-compliance with the IEEE 754 standard [6]. To this end, previously there has been some investigation into GPU floating point units [1]. In this paper, we develop a VHDL test suite that allows us to verify how well existing FPGA floating point operators conform to this standard and to ensure that any shortcomings are well documented for future FPGA floating point operator design.

2   Background

In this section, we first provide a basic background into floating point numbers and how they are defined using the IEEE standard, alongside some background into the field of hardware verification. We then introduce the main FPGA core generators that we test for IEEE compliance within our new framework.

2.1   Floating Point Representation

The general form of a floating point representation is given by equation (1), where s is a sign bit, R known as the radix (most commonly $R = 2$), e is the exponent, 'offset' is used to allow negative powers of the radix while keeping e non-negative in binary bit representation, and m is the mantissa [7].

$$(-1)^s \times R^{e-\text{offset}} \times 1.m \tag{1}$$

Given that floating point numbers map the infinite real number space onto a finite number of bits, certain errors must be present and tolerated. In floating point, there are three basic sources of error: rounding, underflow and overflow. Figure 1 presents a number line expressing the positive numbers for a "toy" binary floating point number system with a 2-bit exponent e which lies in the range $0 \leq e \leq 3$ (offset = 0), and 3-bit mantissa, and illustrates these errors. In this figure, numbers greater than 16 cannot be represented, showing overflow error; to reach larger numbers, a larger exponent is required. The potential round-off error is a function of the exponent, as seen in Figure 1, where the round-off error is guaranteed to be no more than 0.125 in the region $2 \leq x \leq 4$, but guaranteed to be no more than 0.5 in the region $8 \leq x \leq 16$. In the region $0 \leq x \leq 1$, no numbers can be represented and there is a large potential error compared to the neighbouring region; this is a result of underflow error.

FPGAs can implement any precision and have the ability to trade these errors for the performance and area of the circuit, but because of the increasing number of FPGA accelerators for scientific computing applications that adopt a standard representation [8], in this paper, we restrict to single precision results to focus on how closely existing FPGA IP-cores adhere to the IEEE floating point standards;

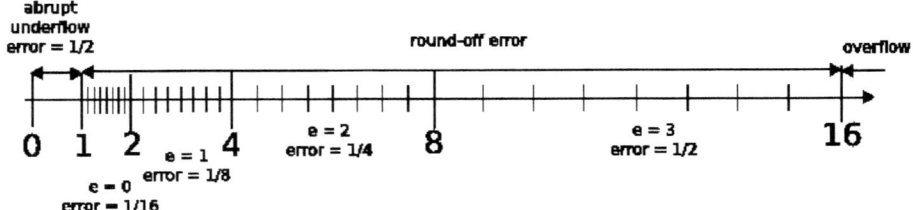

Fig. 1. Number line for an unsigned floating point representation where the exponent is 2 bits over the range $0 \leq e \leq 3$ and mantissa is 3 bits

we describe the main additional specifications within the IEEE 754 floating point standard in comparison to a basic floating point implementation in the following section.

2.2   The IEEE Standard

Rounding: Guard, Round and Sticky Bits. The IEEE-754 standard defines four rounding modes: "round to nearest even", "round towards $+\infty$" (ceil), "round towards $-\infty$" (floor), and "round to zero" (truncate) [9], with most software adopting the first mode. In order to ensure correct rounding, as defined in [10], additional bits are necessary within the internal floating point units. For example, suppose we were trying to compute the result of $16 - 15 = 1.000 \cdot 2^4 - 1.111 \cdot 2^3$. After normalisation, this becomes $(1.000 - 0.111) \cdot 2^4 = 0.001 \cdot 2^4 = 1.000 \cdot 2^1$. Even though the correct result is representable with three bits $(1.000 \cdot 2^0)$, the result returned is incorrect because a bit was lost during the right shift operation.

To ensure correct rounding, the IEEE Standard defines three bits additional bits to be suffixed to a floating point representation, namely the guard, round, and sticky bits. The guard and round bits are used as classic bits to locally increase the mantissa precision, after normalisation, while the sticky bit represents whether the result is exact, to ensure correct rounding for the basic arithmetic functions.

The IEEE Standard: Subnormal Numbers. Kahan proposed and helped standardise a representation called subnormal (or denormal) numbers, where if the exponent is all zeros, the "implied leading one" in equation (1) in the mantissa is turned into 0, changing the floating point representation to (2). This removes the "abrupt underflow" gap, seen in Figure 1, and ensures that the maximum rounding error does not increase when the number represented approaches 0 [11].

$$(-1)^s \times R^{-\text{offset}} \times 0.m \tag{2}$$

Exceptions and Flags. The standard defines five types of exception which should be flagged, and either create a default result or pass the an argument back to an exception handler; these are shown in Table 1.

Table 1. IEEE 754 exceptions and default values [10]

Exception	Default Result
overflow	$\pm\infty$
underflow	0 or denormal
divide by zero	$\begin{cases} \infty & \text{if } a \div 0, a \in \mathbb{R}^+ \\ -\infty & \text{if } a \div 0, a \in \mathbb{R}^- \\ \text{NAN} & \text{if } 0 \div 0 \end{cases}$
invalid	NAN
inexact	round(result)

Single and Double Precision. While the above specifications within the IEEE-754 floating point standard are defined across all precisions in radix-2 and radix-10 arithmetic, most users will only be aware of two specific precisions: single and double. Single precision consists of a sign bit, 8-bit exponent and 23-bit mantissa, double precision consists of a sign bit, 11-bit exponent and 52-bit mantissa. In our tests in Section 5, we only examine behaviour in IEEE-754 single precision arithmetic, which is often used in FPGA and GPU accelerators.

2.3   Hardware Test Suites

Aside from exhaustive testing across every possible input value, the only way to confirm that hardware performs exactly as specified is to perform some sort of formal verification of the hardware implementation [12,13,14]. However, such a process typically requires a lot of time and effort, which is unacceptable, especially when new algorithms that save time and area are being developed all the time. As such a more tractable approach is to create a test suite that identifies corner cases that are most likely to cause errors in the output, and test the hardware against these cases, alongside further random tests, to ensure it works as desired. In terms of floating point verification, the TestFloat [15], the IeeeCC754 test suite [16] and Paranoia [17] are three such test suites. In this project, we have chosen to focus on the latter, for it is the most well-known, as can be seen by its various translations – from its original BASIC program [17] into various languages, including Pascal [18] and C [19]. The popularity of Paranoia has ensured it is still used on modern CPU hardware to show flaws in many floating point arithmetic implementations [20], as well as to benchmark GPU floating point arithmetic [1], and for this reason, we wish to create the same level of scrutiny towards FPGA IP-cores.

2.4   Existing FPGA IP-Cores

FPGA manufacturers and developers have developed their own hardware designs that perform individual floating point operations. In this paper, we test the latest cores from the two major FPGA manufacturers Altera [21] and Xilinx [22], as well as the open source platform FloPoCo [23]. These cores typically offer a myriad of customisations exploiting the freedom of an FPGA to create specialised hardware, for example, the ability to tune variable widths of exponent and mantissa to obtain a superior hardware design to meet a designers specification, but also offer IEEE standard single and double precision cores. The specifications to which these cores adhere are detailed as follows:

- Altera Floating Point Megafunctions v11.0 (part of Quartus II v11.0 service pack 1) [21] only support round-to-nearest-even rounding mode, the default of IEEE-754-1985, and do not support subnormal numbers, flushing them to zero. However, there is support for exception signals for underflow and overflow.
- Xilinx DS816 Floating Point Operator v6.0 (part of Xilinx ISE v13.3) [22] supports round-to-nearest-even rounding mode, and both handshaking and exception signals for underflow or overflow are implemented.
- FloPoCo version 2.2.1 [23] has a special floating point format, with an additional two-bit prefix. The two bits are used only to signal exceptions, namely 00 for zero, 01 for normal numbers, 10 for infinities, and 11 for NaN. These differ from IEEE exception signals where zero (exponent = 00...00) or Infinity or NaN (exponent = 11...11), meaning FloPoCo cores can use these values to represent additional normal floating point numbers. FloPoCo also does not aim to support subnormal numbers.

3   Test Framework

The general framework for our approach is illustrated in Figure 2, using the example of Altera floating point units. In this framework, we create preprocessor and post-processor blocks and instantiate all the individual floating point operator cores. The preprocessor and post-processor blocks pass the input data and receive the output data from the desired core respectively, and additionally translate traditional floating point numbers in the testbench into the format desired by the floating point cores. For example, in the case of FloPoCo cores, we must translate the exception signals to and from their IEEE equivalents. This allows the testbench to be independent of all details of the hardware implementation.

While our framework is general enough to apply any tests to any hardware floating point cores, in our analysis, we focus only on Altera, Xilinx, and FloPoCo cores using the Paranoia benchmark. In the rest of this section, we detail the choices we have made to perform these tests.

3.1   Adapting Paranoia to FPGA Core Generators

Hardware Operators. In our implementation of Paranoia, as mentioned above, we instantiated individual floating point cores for operations whenever possible. We note however that using this methodology, we cannot test any more complex cores, such as the 3-Input Adder, Accumulator, or Multiply-Accumulator of the FloPoCo block. Instead, any complex expressions were handled by first breaking the operations into a two-input static single assignment form.

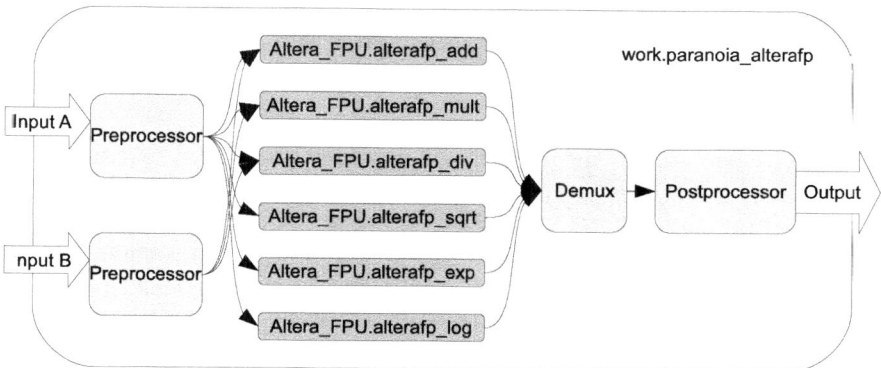

Fig. 2. Paranoia test framework as implemented with Altera IP-cores

Software functions. While we choose to use dedicated hardware operators whenever possible, the core generators are not capable of implementing every type of floating point operation required in Paranoia, so we implemented some operations, such as $floor(x)$, $\log_2(x)$ and $random(x)$, in software. Similarly, while no hardware core generator provides a specific exponentiation unit x^y, this function could be re-written as shown in (3), so we created a function that reads what is available from the hardware core generator and decides whether to implement it by multiplying a value initialised to 1 by the value x y times, or to use exponential and logarithm hardware blocks to approximate x^y; we note that if y is non-integer, it is only possible to apply the latter approach. Furthermore, given that neither approach would work in the case where $y = 0$, where the result must always be 1, this special case must be added to prevent the blocks failing the desired test.

$$z = x^y = e^{y \cdot \ln x} \tag{3}$$

As well as specific floating point operations, we also used software within our pre and post-processor blocks to simplify some basic operations. For example, while Altera and Xilinx provide a block to negate or find the absolute value of a float, this can be achieved cheaply by manipulating the sign bit, so we implement this directly. Furthermore, in the case of FloPoCo, two additional software changes had to be added in the pre and post-processor blocks. Firstly, because it does not have a subtract core, we had to first negate one of its inputs, and secondly it does not implement comparison, so for simplicity and speed we chose to uses the Altera compare core to perform comparisons for the results of operations from FloPoCo cores.

4   Paranoia on an FPGA

While the previous section described the overall framework to which one could apply any software testbench, in this section, we describe the set of tests taken from the paranoia benchmark, as well as any modifications that we made to these tests to make it suitable to test the desired hardware.

4.1   Basic Arithmetic

Listing 1.1 demonstrates the initial few lines of Paranoia, first defining the variables Zero as 0 and One as 1, from which most other floating point values are obtained through arithmetic operations on these two variables, and no other literals are used; we have recreated this style in our tests. Paranoia then runs several tests on basic arithmetic, for example, $3 \stackrel{?}{=} 2 + 1$. Particularly important is the zero comparison test, which tests if -0.0 is equal to 0.0, because if they are unequal, several later tests cannot be run. While FloPoCo has no compare core, as we mentioned in Section 3.1, meaning that it could not alone verify the difference between $+0$ and -0, we did add tests to ensure it created both positive and negative zero correctly. Eventually, more complex arithmetic tests are run.

```
Zero  =  0;
One  =  1;
Two  =  One  +  One;
TwoForty  =  Four  *  Five  *  Three  *  Four;
MinusOne  =  -One;
Half  =  One  /  Two;
```

Listing 1.1. paranoia.c(402-404,412-414) Initial tests

One set of arithmetic tests which we have removed are those that test for extra-precise sub-expressions, which are typically additional bits stored for intermediate results, because we have assumed throughout that the result is rounded before passing to the next; the subject of creating application specific fused data-paths on FPGAs that require additional internal bits to achieve equivalent results is a separate field [24, 25]. However, we do include Paranoia's tests that search for the presence of a guard, round and sticky bit in succession, to check that rounding is correct under several corner cases.

After tests for addition and subtraction, Paranoia tests for correct multiplication by evaluating if $X * Y \stackrel{?}{=} Y * X$ for several random values. Division is tested for several extreme values as described in the Paranoia benchmark, this includes values such as $\frac{1}{0}$ and $\frac{0}{0}$. We note that the latter tests should return exception signals which we aim to detect ($\pm\infty$ and/or NaN), as described in Section 2.2. Finally $\sqrt{x}$ is also tested for several corner case values as in the traditional version of Paranoia.

4.2   Exponentiation

Exponentiation (x^y) is tested using extreme values of x and y, as well as the value 0^0, which by convention should return 1 exactly, to enable compact representation of various series and sequences, especially polynomial or power series.

This is followed by a special test to throw up inaccuracies in the exponentiation function for non-integer values. In this test, the value e^2 is first computed in the reference precision by an iterative refinement process, then this value is compared against the evaluation of $x^{\frac{x+1}{x-1}}$ for several values close to 1, noting that these values should be almost equivalent given the result in (4). While these tests are performed as described in Paranoia, because none of the core generators create an exponentiation core, as we mentioned in Section 3.1, we replace this using the various alternatives; this enables us to perform additional multiplication tests, as well as implementing the desired function.

$$\lim_{x \to 1} x^{\frac{x+1}{x-1}} = e^2 \qquad (4)$$

4.3 Underflow and Overflow

Our tests for underflow and overflow are restricted to those which check that underflow and overflow are correctly flagged, as opposed to any handling of subnormals, because as mentioned in Section 2.4, subnormals are not supported by any of the core generators.

5 Results

We ran our hardware version of Paranoia on single precision (8-bit exponent, 23-bit mantissa) Altera v11.0, FloPoCo v2.2.1, and Xilinx v6.0 cores. Results were then compared with the results from a Intel Core i7 running single precision Paranoia compiled with gcc 4.4.3 (no errors). These tests revealed many differences between the FPGA floating point IP-cores and the Core i7 FPU, as summarised in Table 2. In this section, we highlight and discuss the differences detected between the FPGA IP-cores and the general purpose processor.

5.1 Basic Arithmetic

The Paranoia tests for basic arithmetic were in general satisfied, there were some differences from the IEEE 754 standard in the corner cases for division.

FloPoCo v2.2.1 Division by Zero. The IEEE 754 standard states that any value divided by zero should result in the exception signal $\pm\infty$ with the sign equal to the sign of the numerator, except in the case of $0 \div 0$, where the result should be signalled as NAN. Using the Paranoia benchmark, while the Xilinx and Altera blocks worked as expected, the FloPoCo block stated that $0 \div 0 = \infty$. While this could be argued to be a technicality, this incorrect exception signal could result in errors during future computations, for example when computing $e^{-(0 \div 0)}$.

Table 2. Success of FPGA IP-cores against Paranoia benchmark

Test Name	Altera v11.0	Flopoco v2.2.1	Xilinx v6.0
Basic Arithmetic			
Basic Arithmetic	☑	☑	☑
Division by Zero	☑	☒	☑
Add/Sub Rounding	☑	☑	☑
Multiplication Rounding	☑	☑	☑
Division Rounding	☒	☑	☑
Guard Digits	☑	☑	☑
Sticky Bit	☒	☑	☑
Sqrt Rounding	☑	☑	☑
Exponentiation			
x^y where $x, y \in \mathbb{Z}$	☑	☑	☑
$\lim_{x \to 1} x^{\frac{x+1}{x-1}} = e^2$	☒	☑	NI
Underflow and Overflow			
Thresholds	☑	☑	☑
PseudoZero	☑	☒	☑
X!=Z but X-Z=0	☑	☒	☑
Gradual Underflow	☒	☒	☒
☑	Passed this test		
☒	Did not pass this test		
NI	Not implemented in hardware		

Altera v11.0's Division Core Rounding. Altera's documentation states that the blocks adhere to round-to-nearest (even). However, the example of Table 3 shows that Altera calculates division differently to other cores. By performing the operation in double precision, one can confirm that it is the Altera core that rounds incorrectly. This also causes the Altera v11.0 cores to fail the Sticky Bit test, as seen in Table 2.

Table 3. Results after rounding for Paranoia's division test with various division cores

	Altera	FloPoCo	Xilinx	Intel
$\left(1.5 - 2^{-23}\right) \div \left(1 - 2^{-23}\right)$	1.5	1.5000001	1.5000001	1.5000001
3FBFFFFF÷3F7FFFFE	3FC00000	3FC00001	3FC00001	3FC00001
$\left(1.5 + 2^{-23}\right) \div \left(1 + 2^{-23}\right)$	1.4999999	1.5	1.5	1.5
3FC00001÷3F800001	3FBFFFFF	3FC00000	3FC00000	3FC00000

5.2 Exponentiation

As we mentioned in Section 3.1, none of the core generators create a hardware block to implement exponentiation, and as a result, we implemented this function using two methods. In the case where a value is raised to a positive integer power, this could be approximated using repeated multiplication, and similar to the previous tests for multiplication, this performed correctly for all cases, provided the special case for $0^0 = 1$ is added.

Exponentiation with Fractional Exponents in Altera v11.0's Logarithm Block. The previous test revealed no shortcomings with the logarithm and exponentiation cores for integer arguments. However, since $\frac{x+1}{x-1}$ is, in general, non-integer, because Xilinx core generator v6.0 does not support $\ln(x)$ and e^x, only Altera v12.0 and FloPoCo v2.2.1 can perform this test, which we implemented using the $x^y = e^{y \cdot \ln x}$ identity. Interestingly, this revealed a flaw in the Altera v11.0 logarithm core while calculating $\ln(0.99999994)$, as shown in Table 4.

Table 4. Arithmetic errors in Altera $\log(x)$ cores

	Altera	FloPoCo	IEEE Double
X	0.99999994 (0x3F7FFFFF)	0.99999994 (0x3F7FFFFF)	$1 - 2^{-24}$
ln(X)	-1.1641532e-10 (0xAF000000)	-5.9604645e-8 (0xB3800000)	-5.960464e-8

5.3   Underflow and Overflow

FloPoCo v2.2.1 and Subnormal Numbers. None of the core generators state that they support subnormal numbers, so unsurprisingly they do not pass related tests, such as those for gradual underflow. While Xilinx v6.0 and Altera v11.0 blocks simply flushed subnormal numbers to zero, interestingly, FloPoCo v2.2.1 contained some inconsistent subnormal evaluation. Firstly, when continually halving the value 1 to find the smallest representable value, FloPoCo returned 0x00000001. The fact that this number can be reached through repeated multiplications shows that subnormal numbers must be supported to some extent, because halving 0x00000001 would produce a number exactly between 0x00000001 and 0x00000000, although this implies the rounding mode is defaulted to round towards $+\infty$ as opposed to round-to-nearest even which requires the result to be even, i.e. 0x00000000. Furthermore, this number returns errors with division, for example (5) returns $+NaN$ instead of $+2.0$, and interestingly, this differs from its behaviour of division by zero described earlier, which always returns ∞.

$$Z = 0x00000001, \quad \frac{Z + Z}{Z} \tag{5}$$

6   Conclusion

This paper has presented a flexible framework to test hardware cores to which we modified the well-known Paranoia testbench to detect any flaws that modern FPGA IP-cores exhibit with respect to the IEEE 754 standard. By applying these tests, we have managed to highlight some limitations in current floating point core generators. Many users will be unaware of the current differences between fully IEEE compliant hardware and the current FPGA IP-cores, and we hope that documenting these differences allows suitable care to be taken when designing circuits using these cores.

We appreciate that in a custom computing world, in many applications, it is almost always worthwhile relaxing IEEE compliant specifications in favour of smaller or faster hardware, but we argue that prospective users must be aware of any such issues. By ensuring our community makes the same rigorous efforts as their general purpose computer counterparts, it is likely to provide trust that FPGAs are safe to use to accelerate applications and hopefully to gain more prospective users of FPGAs, and as such, the current framework will be made freely available to download from:

http://cas.ee.ic.ac.uk/people/dpb03/

References

1. Hillesland, K., Lastra, A.: GPU Floating-Point Paranoia (2004),
   http://www.cs.unc.edu/~ibr/projects/paranoia/gpu_paranoia.pdf
2. Kahan, W., Severance, C.: An interview with the old man of floating-point (1998),
   http://www.eng.auburn.edu/ agrawvd/COURSE/
   E6200_Fall07/READ/Kahan_Interview.pdf
3. IEEE, IEEE Standard for Binary Floating-Point Arithmetic, Std (1985)
4. Jones, A.: Supercomputing's future: Is it CPU or GPU? ZDNet UK / News and Analysis / Business of IT / IT Strategy (2010),
   http://www.zdnet.co.uk/news/it-strategy/2010/06/16/
   supercomputings-future-is-it-cpu-or-gpu-40089202
5. Gupta, S.: China's Investment In GPU Supercomputing Begins to Pay Off Big Time. NVIDIA Blog (2011), http://blogs.nvidia.com/2011/06/
   chinas-investment-in-gpu-supercomputing-begins-to-pay-off-big-time
6. Intel, "Intel and floating point". Cygnus Software (2006),
   http://www.intel.com/standards/floatingpoint.pdf
7. Kahan, W.: Lecture Notes on the Status of IEEE Standard 754 for Binary Floating-Point Arithmetic. University of California, Berkeley, Tech. Rep (1997),
   http://www.cs.berkeley.edu/~wkahan/ieee754status/IEEE754.PDF
8. Underwood, K.: FPGAs vs. CPUs: trends in peak floating-point performance. In: Proc. Int. Symp. on Field Programmable Gate Arrays, pp. 171–180 (2004)
9. IEEE, IEEE Standard for Floating-Point Arithmetic, IEEE Std. 754 (2008)
10. Goldberg, D.: What every computer scientist should know about floating-point arithmetic. ACM Computing Surveys (1991), http://download.oracle.com/
    docs/cd/E19957-01/806-3568/ncg_goldberg.html
11. Kahan, W.: A brief tutorial on gradual underflow (2005),
    http://www.cs.berkeley.edu/~wkahan/ARITH_17U.pdf
12. Beyer, S.: Putting it all together - formal verification of the VAMP. International Journal on Software Tools for Technology Transfer 8(4), 411–430 (2006)
13. Jacobi, C.: Formal verification of the VAMP floating point unit. Formal Methods in System Design 26(3), 227–266 (2005)

14. Kikkeri, N., Seidel, P.M.: An FPGA Implementation of a Fully Verified Double Precision IEEE Floating-Point Adder. In: IEEE International Conference on Application-specific Systems, Architectures and Processors, pp. 83–88 (2007)
15. Hauser, J.: Testfloat (2010),
    http://www.jhauser.us/arithmetic/TestFloat.html
16. Verdonk, B., Cuyt, A., Verschaeren, D.: A precision- and range-independent tool for testing floating-point arithmetic II: conversions. ACM Trans. Math. Softw. 27(1), 119–140 (2001)
17. Kahan, W.: Paranoia in BASIC (1983),
    http://netlib.org/paranoia/paranoia.b
18. Wichmann, B.A.: Paranoia in Pascal (1985),
    http://netlib.org/paranoia/paranoia.p
19. Sumner, T., Gay, D.: Paranoia in C (1986),
    http://netlib.org/paranoia/paranoia.c
20. Karpinski, R.: Paranoia - a floating point benchmark. Byte Magazine 10(2), 223–235 (1985)
21. Altera: Floating-Point Megafunctions User Guide (2011),
    http://www.altera.com/literature/ug/ug_altfp_mfug.pdf
22. Xilinx: LogiCore IP Floating-Point Operator v6.0 (2011),
    http://www.xilinx.com/support/documentation/ip_documentation/
    floating_point/v6_0/ds816_floating_point.pdf
23. de Dinechin, F.: FloPoCo, a generator of arithmetic cores for FPGAs (2010),
    http://flopoco.gforge.inria.fr/
24. de Dinechin, F., Pasca, B., Cret, O., Tudoran, R.: An FPGA-specific approach to floating-point accumulation and sum-of-products. In: Proc. Int. Conf. on Field-Programmable Technology, pp. 33–40 (2008)
25. Roldao Lopes, A., Constantinides, G.A.: A Fused Hybrid Floating-Point and Fixed-Point Dot-Product for FPGAs. In: Sirisuk, P., Morgan, F., El-Ghazawi, T., Amano, H. (eds.) ARC 2010. LNCS, vol. 5992, pp. 157–168. Springer, Heidelberg (2010)

High Performance Reconfigurable Architecture for Double Precision Floating Point Division

Manish Kumar Jaiswal and Ray C.C. Cheung

Department of Electronic Engineering,
City University of Hong Kong
mkjaiswal2@student.cityu.edu.hk, r.cheung@cityu.edu.hk

Abstract. Floating point arithmetic (FPA) are very crucial and critical domain for the hardware acceleration. FPA are widely used in the vast field of application. The division operation of the FPA is a very intensive operation, in terms of complexity, area requirement and performance speed. This paper presents an efficient FPGA implementation of double-precision FPA divisions on Virtex-2pro FPGA platform, for the ease of comparing with prior works. The proposed method is based on the method of binomial expansion, which uses look-up tables and partial block multipliers (PBM). Compared with previously reported work, the proposed design occupies smaller area (in terms of number slices, number of multipliers and the BRAM usage) with a higher performance gain and less latency. By using over 5 million unique random test cases, our results show that the proposed design gives an average error of less than 0.5 ULP (unit at last place), and a maximum error of 2 ULP without using any rounding scheme. However, rounding can also be added to the design to restore some accuracy at a slight cost in area.

Keywords: Floating point division, Partial Block Multiplication, Binomial Expansion, Reconfigurable Computing, Arithmetic, High Performance Computing.

1 Introduction

Floating point arithmetic is widely used in many scientific and signal processing applications [13,6,11]. Its huge dynamic range and convenient scaling of the number range provides an convenient platform for designers to realize their algorithms. However, implementing arithmetic operations for floating point numbers in hardware is very challenging. Among these operations (add, subtract, multiply, divide), division is generally the most difficult (inefficient) to implement in hardware. Division is a fairly common operation in many scientific and signal processing applications, so there is a need for efficient hardware implementations for division.

The IEEE-754 standard [9, 10] for floating point defines the format of the numbers, and also specifies various rounding modes that determine the accuracy of the result. For many signal processing, and graphics applications, it is

O.C.S. Choy et al. (Eds.): ARC 2012, LNCS 7199, pp. 302–313, 2012.

acceptable to trade off some accuracy [8] (in the least significant bit positions) for faster and better optimized implementations.

Many related work has been focusing on designing efficient division implementations. Generally speaking, this operation can be decomposed into two parts; first it takes the inverse of divisor and then multiplies with the dividend. Due to this issue, many hardware dividers focus on efficiently constructing the reciprocal of floating-point number. Different proposed architectures in the literature are based on Newton-Raphson method [12, 2], digit-recurrence method [12, 17, 2], seed-architecture [3], etc. Previous works include using huge look-up tables, along-with wider multipliers, which affect the area and performance.

The proposed method in this work is based on the well-known binomial-expansion, contains small look-up tables, and partial block-multipliers. It results in using smaller area, shorter delay, and correct up to required level (accuracy trade off). The method works properly for normalized numbers, and will also be extended to sub-normal numbers. All the exceptional cases are detected at input and output. The comparative study shows that our proposed architecture is able to achieve better and area-efficient hardware results over the prior works in the literature. We have used Xilinx ISE synthesis tool, ModelSim SE simulation tool, and Xilinx Virtex2-Pro X2VP30-7ff896 as our FPGA platform.

This paper is organized as follows. The next section is explaining our design approach. The Section 3 discusses the complete implementation with all required processing in floating point division operation. Section 4 has includes the implementation results and comparisons with previously reported implementations, and finally the paper has been concluded in the Section 5 with some possible proposed future work in Section 6.

2   Design Approach

The basis of our implementation is the well known binomial expansion method. The double precision floating point number is represented as,

$$\overbrace{Sign-bit}^{1-bit}\ \overbrace{exponent}^{11-bits}\ \overbrace{mantissa}^{52-bits}$$

In order to explain the floating point division in details, let x is dividend and Y is divisor. To obtain the resultant quotient Q, the following operation is required.

$$Q = \frac{X}{Y}$$

- Sign of the quotient is the XOR operation of the sign-bit of X and Y.
- The exponent of the quotient will be difference of the exponent of X and Y using a proper biasing.
- Mantissa of quotient is obtained by the division of the X-mantissa by the Y-mantissa.
- Finally, rounding and normalization of the mantissa division and adjustment of the output exponent are applied.

The sign and exponent manipulations are relatively trivial operations. The mantissa processing (division) is the most critical step in the this arithmetic operation. It has a major impact on the required area and performance speed. The present method performs this mantissa processing as below.

Let x represent the mantissa of X, and y represent mantissa of Y. Then their division result, let q, can be computed as follows,

$$q = \frac{x}{y} = x \times \frac{1}{y} = x \times \frac{1}{a_1 + a_2} = x \times (a_1 + a_2)^{-1}$$

We have divided the denominator mantissa in two parts, m-bit a_1 and remaining as a_2. a_1 is used to fetch some pre-calculated data from a look-up table.

Now, we get

$$(a_1 + a_2)^{-1} = a_1^{-1} - a_1^{-2}.a_2 + a_1^{-3}.a_2^2 - a_1^{-4}.a_2^3 + \cdots$$

As we are calculating with the decimal numbers, the content of each terms in the above equation will look like:

$$a_1^{-1} = 0.\ \overbrace{xxxxxxxx}^{full\ significant\ bits}$$

$$a_1^{-2}.a_2 = 0.\ \overbrace{00\cdots00}^{m-zero\ bits}\ \overbrace{xx\cdots xx}^{significant\ bits}$$

$$a_1^{-3}.a_2^2 = 0.\ \overbrace{00\cdots00}^{2m-zero\ bits}\ \overbrace{xx\cdots xx}^{significant\ bits}$$

$$a_1^{-4}.a_2^3 = 0.\ \overbrace{00\cdots00}^{3m-zero\ bits}\ \overbrace{xx\cdots xx}^{significant\ bits}$$

$$\cdots and\ so\ on$$

$$where\ m\ is\ the\ number\ of\ bits\ of\ a_1.$$

By inspecting the above terms, we can see that as we move towards higher order terms their contribution to the main result are diminishing. Only initial few terms mainly contribute to the final result (depends on the precision requirement). As a result, depending upon precision choices, we can select suitable number of terms for calculating $(a_1 + a_2)^{-1}$, based on the value of m.

For the present implementation, based on experiments over a large number of random test cases, seven terms (up to $a_1^{-7}.a_2^6$) have been taken for the purpose. The value of m we have chosen is eight. These values were selected based on available FPGA resources and precision requirement. We have further simplified the selected terms in such a way that helps use fewer hardware with low latency and good accuracy.

The simplification of all the selected terms are performed as below,

$$q = x \times [a_1^{-1} - a_1^{-1}\{(a_1^{-1}.a_2 - a_1^{-2}.a_2^2)(1 + a_1^{-2}.a_2^2 + a_1^{-4}.a_2^4)\}]$$
$$= x.a_1^{-1} - x.a_1^{-1}\{(a_1^{-1}.a_2 - a_1^{-2}.a_2^2)(1 + a_1^{-2}.a_2^2 + a_1^{-4}.a_2^4)\} \quad (1)$$

Though we can simplify the above equations even further, it will affect the area, latency and accuracy of the final result. The accuracy is affected due to the fact that floating point operations are not completely associative, i.e. $u(v + w)$ may not be exactly equal to $(uv + uw)$. This is mainly due to the finite number of bits used to represent the numbers.

In order to implement the eq.(1) for mantissa division processing, we need a set of multipliers along with some adder and subtractor. The sizes of the each operands in each multiplication terms of eq.(1) are quite large ($\geq$ 53-bit), we do need a large number of multiplier block on FPGA to implement all these multiplications. But, as we have seen above that most of the terms are associated with the leading zeros, we can effectively reduce some of the multiplier block. Another point is that, after all processing the desired output will need only 53-bit representation. In view on this, first, we will consider the Fig. [1] for block multiplication of two operands. In the multiplication, if we only need some of the most significant result bits, we can discard some of the lower order multiplier blocks (depends on the precision requirements). For example, if we do multiplication of two 51-bit operands using three block partitioning of 17-bit each, to get the only 51-bit MSB result, we can use only top 6 multiplier blocks. The error encountered from this case will be very minimal and will appear at most in the last bit of the 51-bit result. Thus, we have used this kind of optimization approach to perform all the multiplications of eq.(1). The details on this method is explained in details in the next section, along with all the required processing in the FPA division.

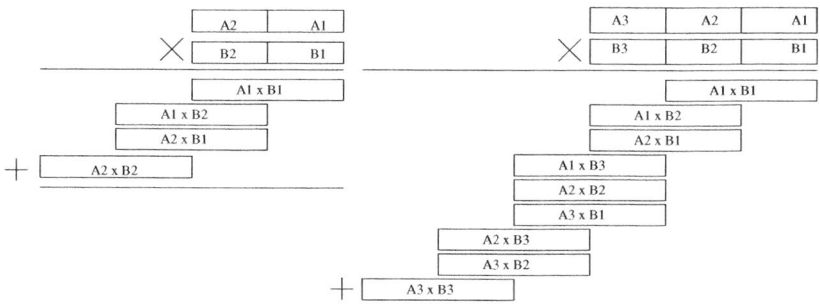

Fig. 1. Block multiplication using two and three blocks

3 Hardware Implementations of FPA Division

In this section, we have discussed the complete implementation of FPA division. Any floating point arithmetic operation generally works separately on the sign, exponent and mantissa part and finally combine them after rounding and normalization to get the final result. Similarly, we will perform the similar operations as follows.

The sign bit implementation of output quotient requires a very simple logic, and it is only the XOR operation between the input operands sign bits.

$$Sign\_out = Sign\_in1 \oplus Sign\_in2$$

The exponent computation of the output quotient is processed in two phases. In the initial phase, a temporary exponent is computed by taking the difference of the dividend exponent and divisor exponent, with proper BIAS adjusting. In the case of double precision floating point numbers the BIAS is equal to 1023, and generally it computed as $(2^{exp-1} - 1)$.

$$Exp\_out\_tmp = (Exp\_dividend - Bias) - (Exp\_divisor - Bias)$$
$$= Exp\_dividend - Exp\_divisor$$

Second phase of the exponent computation occurs after the normalization of the mantissa. In this phase, the temporary exponent is adjusted based on the normalization, and finally biased to produce the final exponent result.

Up to now, we have done with the simpler processing steps of the FPA division. Later part will include the complex processing of the mantissa division. The architecture for this purpose is shown in the Fig. [2]. This figure shows the analogous representation of the eq.(1).

As shown in the the Fig. [2], the very early computation involved is to divide the divisor mantissa in two parts (8-bit a_1 and 44-bit a_2). a1 has been used to fetch the pre-computed the inverse of the $1.a1$ (including the hidden bit of the mantissa). This pre-computed value has been obtained by using C-code, and the word size of this pre-computed data has been taken as 54-bit (found enough for the required precision). This data is then stored in a block memory (BRAM) available on the FPGA as a hard IP core. The address space of this BRAM is $2^8 = 256$. The latency of this BRAM is taken as one. The remaining processing involves mainly multiplication of intermediate terms, with some addition and subtraction. We have selected the size of the varying size of multipliers depending on the contribution of their terms in the final result. Also the block size of each multiplier has been selected as 17-bit due to the availability of 17-bit unsigned multiplier hard IP core on the Xilinx FPGA. It can be different depending on the resource availability. The size of the adder and subtractor has been taken relatively longer to save the precision, as loss occurs in these is more than that of multiplications. The details are as mentioned below.

Now, as soon as we receive the value of a_1 , we can get the pre-computed value of a_1^{-1} from the BRAM. The next step involves the computation of $x.a_1^{-1}$ and $a_1^{-1}.a_2$. For the computation of $x.a_1^{-1}$ we have used a 53-bit partial block multiplier (Fig. [3]), which used 6-multiplier block along with four 2x19 bit multipliers (implemented with logic slices) and a 2x2 multiplier (need four LUTs) with a latency of 6 stages. The size of this multiplier has been bigger (53-bit) than the others, because the output of this term mainly contribute to the final the result. Only 53-bit of the output result from this stage has been forwarded to the next stages. The computation of $a_1^{-1}.a_2$ is done by a 51-bit partial block

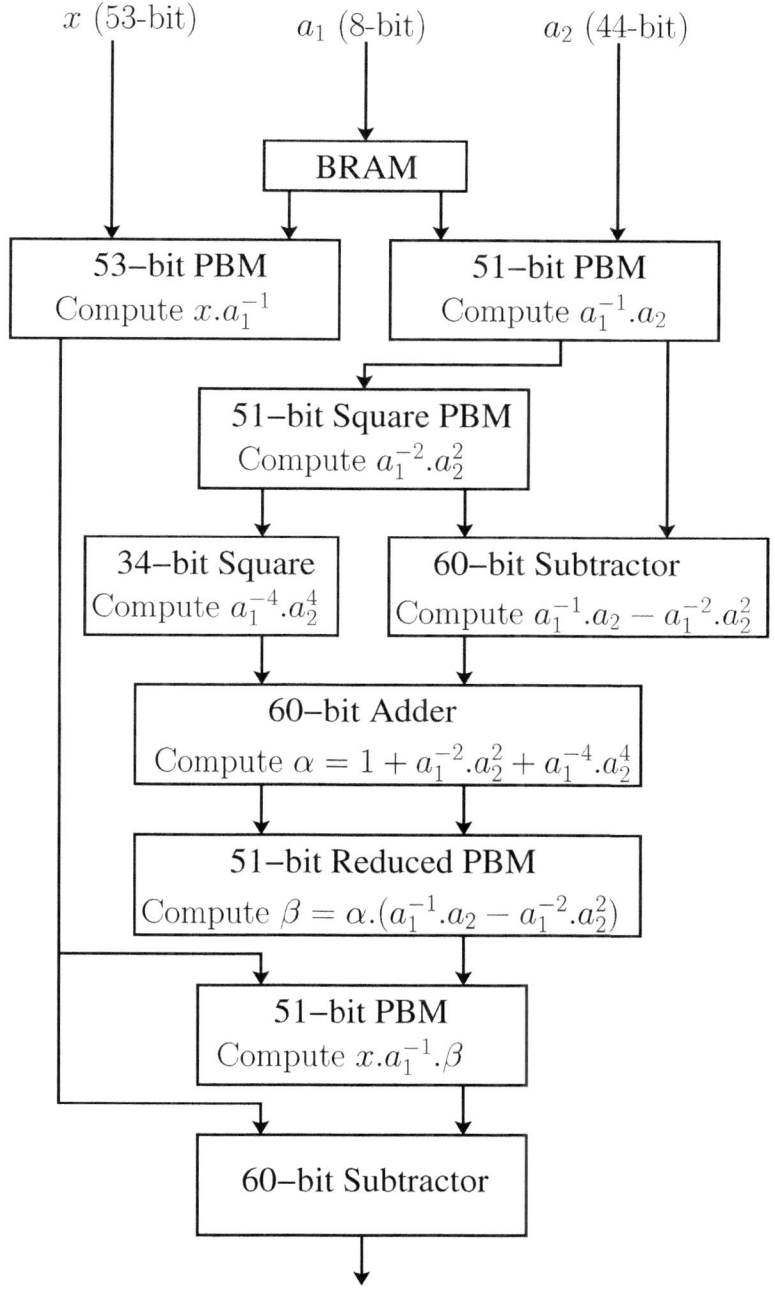

Fig. 2. Architecture of the Double Precision FPA Mantissa Division $(q = \frac{x}{y})$

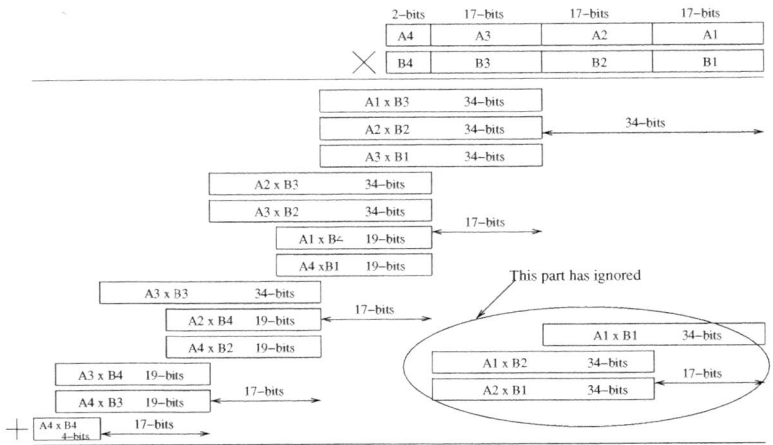

Fig. 3. 53-bit Partial Block Multiplication for $(x.a_1^{-1})$

multiplier, shown in Fig. [4]. This operation requires a 6-multiplier block, with a latency of 6-stages. This multiplier forward 51-bit result to next stage.

Next processing step is the computation of $a_1^{-2}.a_2^2$. This is the square of the previous stage output, and it has been computed by 51-bit partial block square multiplier, shown in Fig. [5]. This is mainly the 51-bit PBM multiplier, but due the special nature of the inputs (same input), here we have saved two more multiplier. This step requires only a 4-multiplier block, with a latency of 6-stages.

Further step computes two terms, $a_1^{-4}.a_2^4$ and $a_1^{-1}.a_2 - a_1^{-2}.a_2^2$. Since the term $a_1^4.a_2^4$ effectively contains 32-bit leading zero, and very few parts of it actually

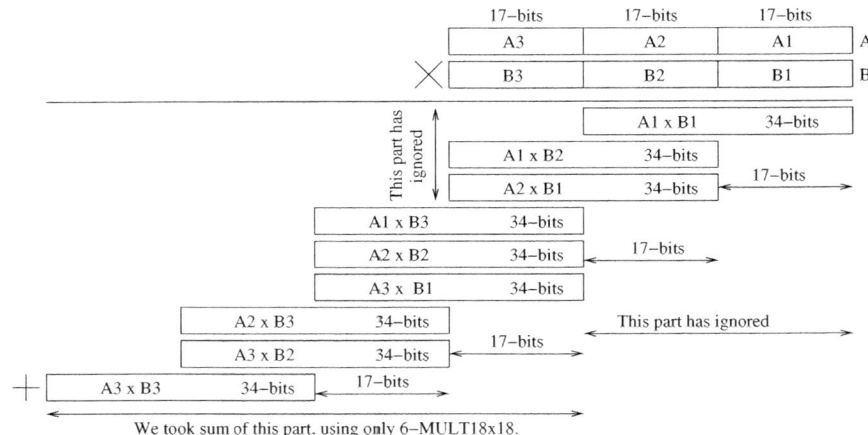

Fig. 4. 51-bit Partial Block Multiplication for $(a_1^{-1}.a_2$ and final stage multiplication)

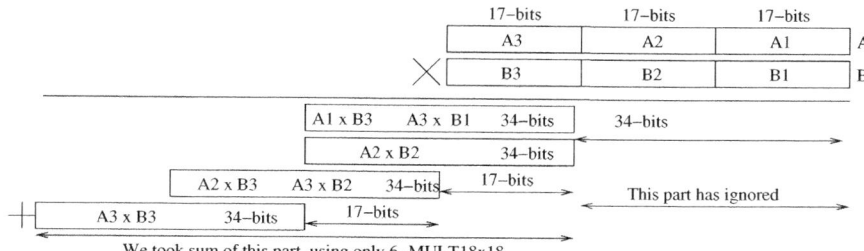

Fig. 5. 51-bit Partial Block Square Multiplication for $(a_1^{-2}.a_2^2)$

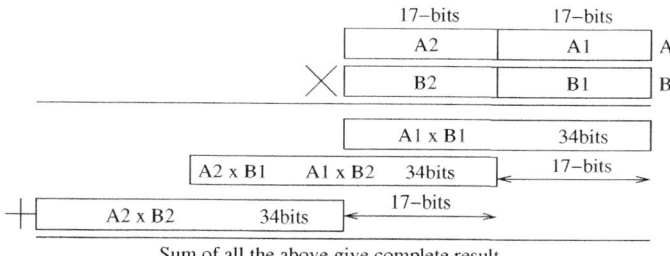

Sum of all the above give complete result

Fig. 6. 34-bit Square Block Multiplication for $(a_1^{-4}.a_2^4)$

contribute to the main result, we then compute it using a 34-bit square block multiplication (full multiplication Fig [6]). This multiplication uses a 4-multiplier blocks and has a latency of 5-stages. Term $a_1^{-1}.a2 - a_1^{-2}.a_2^2$ has been computed using a two stage 60-bit subtractor.

Next step uses a two-stage 60-bit adder to compute $1 + a_1^{-2}.a_2^2 + a_1^{-4}.a_2^4$. The output of this adder has a special nature. It is in the form of

$$1.\overbrace{00...00}^{15-bit}xxxxxxxx.....xxx$$

To exploit the availability of this term, in the next step multiplication, we use a 50-bit reduced partial block multiplier, which uses only a 3-multiplier block with a latency of 5-stages.

In next step we have computed the multiplication of $x.a_1^{-1}$ with the output of the last stage 50-bit reduced partial block multiplier. This multiplication has used a 51-bit partial block multiplier, which used 6-multiplier and has the latency of 6-stages. Finally, this stage output is subtracted from $x.a_1^{-1}$ to get the final mantissa division result. The complete mantissa processing needs 28-multiplier blocks and one BRAM.

After completing the mantissa computation, we normalize it to get it back in proper formatting and then adjusted the exponent accordingly to finalize the output floating point quotient.

Table 1. Hardware utilization and performance for Design On Virtex-2pro

Latency	Slices	LUT	FF	MULT18x18	BRAM	Freq(MHz)
36	2097	1974	3502	28	1	275

4   Results and Comparisons

This section has presented the complete implementation details of our proposed architecture of double precision floating point division. We have used a Virtex2-Pro FPGA chip for our implementations. The hardware implementation details are shown in Table [1]. Our proposed design is fully pipelined and has a latency of 36-stages. It uses 1974 LUTs, 3502 FFs, 28 Multiplier Block and 1-BRAM. The operating frequency of the design is clocked at 275 MHz. All the reported results are based on the post-PAR analysis from the Xilinx synthesis tool.

The accuracy information of the any floating point arithmetic operation is a general issue of consideration. This is due to the finite bit representation for a given standard, which the trivial issue of the rounding error. In similar context, proposed design has been validated over a 5-million unique random test cases. The average error found to be 1.0_0^{-16}, which is less than 0.5 ULP, whereas maximum error is found to be only 2 ULP. We have checked the literature and found that this level of accuracy is very suitable for a large set of applications [8]. Also, the current presented results are without applying any rounding. So, if we can add some rounding modules to the design, we expect to achieve even better accuracy results. The major objective of this work is to achieve the area and performance benefit, without damaging the precision requirement of the design.

Our comparison is mainly based around the Xilinx hardware resources. Even on this platform, many different division implementation are available with different speed-area-latency trade-offs. By using different instance we can obtain suitable trade-offs. Also, many design has reported the number of used multiplier and BRAM. Also, most of the available design has shown their implementation fully combinational or with very less latency, for them we have approximated

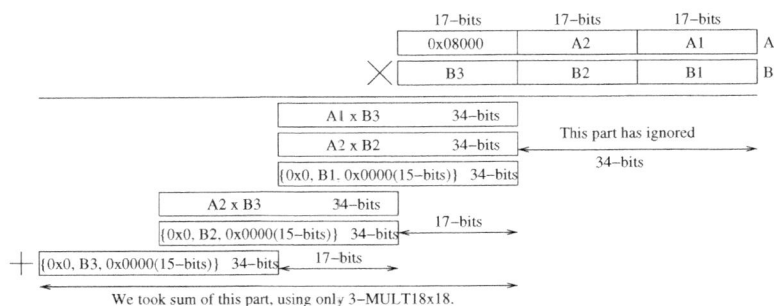

Fig. 7. 50-bit Reduced Partial Block Multiplication for (for $(a_1^{-1}.a_2 - a_1^{-2}.a_2^2) \times (1 + a_1^{-2}.a_2^2 + a_1^{-4}.a_2^4)$)

the hardware resources in terms of BRAM and MULT8x18. We have tried to put the available related work as much possible detailed for a better comparison.

Table [2] contains the comparison of our proposed design with the best available results. One of the most popular methods used for computing division is the Newton Raphson (NR) two-iterative procedure [12,2]. For double-precision it requires one look-up table in 15-bit address space, two 15×30 multiplication, two 30×60 multiplication and one 53×53 multiplication (equivalently 28 BRAM and 29 MULT18x18). The error performance of NR method with two iterations is discussed in [12], and it is minimum of $1.999999993 \times 2^{-55}$ and maximum of $1.284729483 \times 2^{-49}$, which is more than our method.

In [17], the authors have reported the floating-point division using SRT [1] division method on FPGA. In terms of performance, the pipelined approach is closest to our proposed implementation, but requires significantly more area (3245 slices and 14 BRAM for clock period of 6ns and latency of 47 cycles). Wang et al. [16] have presented a library for single precision floating-point operations. By extending it to double-precision, it requires $2^{27} \times 56 - bit$ storage in BRAM (impractical in available FPGA platforms) look-up table and 25-MULT18x18. [14] has shown the pipelined implementation with latency of 60, with a very small speed of 102 MHz with approximately 3000 Slices.

A low latency (30) pipelined implementation has been reported in the [15], but other design metrics are not much improved. This work has used digit by convergence method for their implementation. Authors have mentioned that they have used 6-steps for generating mantissa division result, and each steps used two multiplications. It has been mentioned that only last steps used full 54x54 bit multipliers (needs at least 2x9 = 18 MULT18x18), and other previous steps do not used full multiplication. So, it is not very clear that, how to achieve the total 32 MULT18x18 are being used in the paper, in all 6-steps, as minimum of 18 is being used in the last step only. Also, the existence of error is mentioned in the paper, but its magnitude details are not mentioned.

In [4] division of double precision floating point number has been performed using Goldschmidts algorithm, implemented on a Altera STRATIX-II FPGA platform. The area reported is large relatively compared to our proposed design (about 3500 ALMs, equivalent to about 4600 slices on a Virtex II [1], and has less performance and throughput.

Hemmert [7] and Xilinx [18] are the highly pipelined implementation. In [7], it shows their implementation on Virtex-4 with speed of 250 MHz, but latency (62) and required area (4100 slices) is larger, relatively. Similar situation is with Xilinx FPA division. In [5], the reported result of double precision FPA division has a latency of 32, with 4041 slices and 100 MHz speed. The number of BRAM and multiplier has not been reported, but mentioned that the look-up table with 213 address space (equivalent to 12 BRAM) with multiplier block has been used. We have shown the minimum of 16 MULT block for 53x53 bit multiplication, but actually it requires much more than this data.

---

[1] Sweeney, Robertson and Tocher - inventors of the algorithm.

Table 2. Comparison with other available designs

Method	Latency	MULT18x18	BRAM	Slices	Freq (MHz)
Newton-Raphson	-	29	28	-	-
Wang [17]	47	-	14	3245	166.6
Thakkar [14]	60	-	-	2920	102
Venishetti [15]	32	32	-	2653	216
Hemmert [7]	62	-	-	4100	250
Govindu [5]	32	16−	12	4041	100
Xilinx [18]	55	-	-	3721	173
Proposed	36	28	1	2097	275

In summary, the comparison results shown that the proposed module gives best performance, with less required latency and area. Proposed design is using less number of MULT18x18 and BRAM blocks.

5 Conclusions and Future Works

In this paper, we have presented an efficient architecture for implementation of double precision floating point division on FPGAs. The proposed modules achieve higher performance and area reduction, mainly in terms of number of multiplier blocks, number of block memory with less slices, when compared to other previously modules in the literature. Proposed design is able to fully pipelined and has the advantage of high performance with less required latency compared to the work in literatures. The error performance of the proposed design has been verified by using over 5 million unique random test case, which leads to an average error of 1.0×10^{-16} (which is less than 0.5 ULP error), with a maximum error of 2 ULP. The presented approach is able to achieve significant reductions in resources, with better performance gain and promising precision. The proposed work can further improve the parallelism by instantiating more floating point units on the device.

Future work includes the implementation of fully IEEE 754 compatible division, for instance, the addition of the denormal support, detection and generation of all exceptional signals and results accordingly. The major aim is to give more emphasis on the precision issue of the design and its improvement. Moreover, we are currently working on the theoretical evaluation and error analysis of the maximum error from the proposed architecture. It is important to optimize the proposed design by using different design metrics.

References

1. Altera: Stratix II vs. Virtex-4 Density Comparison. White Paper (2005), http://www.altera.com/literature/wp/wpstxiixlnx.pdf
2. Antelo, E., Lang, T., Montuschi, P., Nannarelli, A.: Low latency digit-recurrence reciprocal and square-root reciprocal algorithm and architecture. In: 17th IEEE Symposium on Computer Arithmetic, pp. 147–154 (June 2005)

3. Ercegovac, M., Muller, J., Tisserand, A.: Simple Seed Architectures for Reciprocal and Square Root Reciprocal. In: Conference Record of the Thirty-Ninth Asilomar Conference on Signals, Systems and Computers, pp. 1167–1171 (November 2005)
4. Goldberg, R., Even, G., Seidel, P.: An FPGA implementation of pipelined multiplicative division with IEEE Rounding. In: 15th Annual IEEE Symposium on Field-Programmable Custom Computing Machines (FCCM 2007), pp. 185–196 (April 2007)
5. Govindu, G., Choi, S., Prasanna, V.K.: Efficient Floating-Point Based Block LU Decomposition on FPGAs. In: Proceedings of the 11th Reconfigurable Architectures Workshop, New Mexico, USA (2004)
6. Guo, Z., Najjar, W., Vahid, F., Vissers, K.: A quantitative analysis of the speedup factors of FPGAs over processors. In: Proceedings of the 2004 ACM/SIGDA 12th International Symposium on Field Programmable Gate Arrays (FPGA 2004), pp. 162–170. ACM, New York (2004)
7. Hemmert, K.S., Underwood, K.D.: Floating-point divider design for fpgas. IEEE Trans. Very Large Scale Integr. Syst. 15, 115–118 (2007), http://dl.acm.org/citation.cfm?id=1553802.1553814
8. Hopf, J.: A parameterizable HandelC divider generator for FPGAs with embedded hardware multipliers. In: Proceedings of the 2004 IEEE International Conference on Field-Programmable Technology, pp. 355–358 (December 2004)
9. IEEE: IEEE standard for binary floating-point arithmetic. ANSI/IEEE Std 754- (August 1985)
10. IEEE: IEEE standard Floating-Point Arithmetic. IEEE Std 754-2008 pp. 1–58 (August 2008)
11. Jaiswal, M.K., Chandrachoodan, N.: FPGA Based High Performance and Scalable Block LU Decomposition Architecture. IEEE Transactions on Computers 99 (2011)
12. Montuschi, P., Ciminiera, L., Giustina, A.: Division unit with Newton-Raphson approximation and digit-by-digit refinement of the quotient. IEE Proceedings Computers and Digital Techniques 141(6), 317–324 (1994)
13. Parizi, H., Niktash, A., Kamalizad, A., Bagherzadeh, N.: A Reconfigurable Architecture for Wireless Communication Systems. In: Third International Conference on Information Technology: New Generations, pp. 250–255 (2006)
14. Thakkar, A.J., Ejnioui, A.: Pipelining of double precision floating point division and square root operations. In: Proceedings of the 44th Annual Southeast Regional Conference ACM-SE 44, pp. 488–493. ACM, New York (2006), http://doi.acm.org/10.1145/1185448.1185555
15. Venishetti, S.K., Akoglu, A.: Highly parallel fpga based ieee-754 compliant double-precision floating-point division. In: ERSA 2008, pp. 159–165 (2008)
16. Wang, X., Braganza, S., Leeser, M.: Advanced Components in the Variable Precision Floating-Point Library. In: 14th Annual IEEE Symposium on Field-Programmable Custom Computing Machines (FCCM 2006), pp. 249–258 (April 2006)
17. Wang, X., Nelson, B.: Tradeoffs of designing floating-point division and square root on Virtex FPGAs. In: 11th Annual IEEE Symposium on Field-Programmable Custom Computing Machines (FCCM 2003), pp. 195–203 (April 2003)
18. Xilinx: Xilinx Floating-Point IP Core, http://www.xilinx.com

A Modular-Based Assembly Framework
for Autonomous Reconfigurable Systems

Tannous Frangieh[1], Richard Stroop[1], Peter Athanas[1], and Teresa Cervero[2]

[1] Virginia Tech, Blacksburg VA 24061, USA
{tannous,blvninri,athanas}@vt.edu
[2] University of Las Palmas de Gran Canaria, E-35017, Las Palmas de GC, Spain
tcervero@iuma.ulpgc.es

Abstract. Configurable systems community has recognized the value of FPGAs in adaptable and scalable autonomous systems. While the underlying hardware framework for supporting run-time reconfiguration has existed for years, there have been negligibly few FPGA applications that have benefited from this. This is likely due to the reconfiguration model provided by the vendors and as such several alternative modes of assembly have been suggested, such as a tile-based assembly and a modular-based assembly. This paper proposes a framework based on the aforementioned modular-based assembly. The framework builds on TORC, an open-source C++ infrastructure and tool set for reconfigurable computing. A GNU Radio generated ZigBee demodulator is implemented using the proposed solution.

Keywords: Field-programmable Gate Array, Modular-Based Assembly, Dynamic Reconfiguration, Design Flow.

1   Introduction

For nearly two decades, several conceptual models have been created to facilitate development for adaptable and scalable autonomous systems, including *virtual hardware, hardware contexts, adaptive hardware*, and *adaptive fault recovery*. As the density of contemporary devices increased, FPGAs incorporated more computational units (CUs), justifying the need and potential usefulness of offline as well as online run-time reconfiguration. Recently, much theoretical and conceptual work has been presented on this topic, one vendor introduced finer-grain reconfiguration to its family of products [5] and the open-source community developed frameworks to support it [4]. Despite the effort, a chasm remains between theory and practice, and few applications adopted the process of run-time reconfiguration.

In real applications, an FPGA may be delegated several computational tasks and the computational demands of the tasks may be subject to change over the lifetime of the application. Moreover, as the application progresses in time, it can be advantageous to dynamically allocate resources as in software running on a multi-core processor. This is clearly apparent in, say, an embedded radio

O.C.S. Choy et al. (Eds.): ARC 2012, LNCS 7199, pp. 314–319, 2012.

application where factors such as radio link quality, modulation and demodulation schemes, carrier frequency, and channel conditions all may be factors that influence the optimal mix of run-time resources. The state of the art in FPGA flows however fails to address the computational needs of such applications, impeding the adoption and usability of such platform in various application domains. The work in [1] introduced a new paradigm of viewing FPGA designs and looks at reconfiguration from a different perspective that bridges the gap between finer grain reconfigurability, design flexibility and resource utilization. This work builds on the findings of [1] and presents a framework for modular-based assembly on FPGA systems.

The rest of the paper is organized as follows. Section 2 briefly summarizes the modular-based assembly model. Section 3 introduces the framework along with its different components. Section 4 presents the implementation results of a ZigBee demodulator using the proposed framework. Finally, in Section 5 we conclude and give directions into future work.

2   Modular-Based Assembly

Due to the fact that current partial reconfiguration models impose many design restrictions [3,5], including geometry, connectivity and relocation, the capability to arbitrarily assemble CUs at run-time is desirable. The slot-based PR model, in which CUs are based, assumes a fixed rectangular hole in an invariant design and fixed terminals around the periphery, with all variant computations requiring the same terminals and resources. However, the vast majority of signal processing applications fail to have such regular structures. Few deployed applications demonstrate benefit from this model of computation, and the Zig-Bee demodulator example presented in this work is no exception. In this work, we refer to *partial reconfiguration* as the process of modifying a portion of an FPGA configuration bitstream, and we do not restrict the process to online partial run-time reconfiguration.

Modular-based assembly allows higher freedom compared to current partial reconfiguration models, accommodating CUs of different shapes and resource requirements with flexible connectivity, making this model more general and appropriate for irregular topological application domains. In modular-based assembly, CUs (the modules) are fetched from a library of modules and accommodated within the FPGA. The modules are arranged on the device by means of a placer before a final routing stage stitches the design and a configuration bitstream is generated. Figure 1a illustrates the modular-based assembly model. This model was first demonstrated in the *Wires-on-Demand project* by Suris et. al [6], and it has been adapted into a more general implementation in this paper.

3   A Modular-Based Assembly Framework

Figure 1b presents a framework based on the modular-based assembly model. As the figure shows, the solution incorporates two main stages: a library building

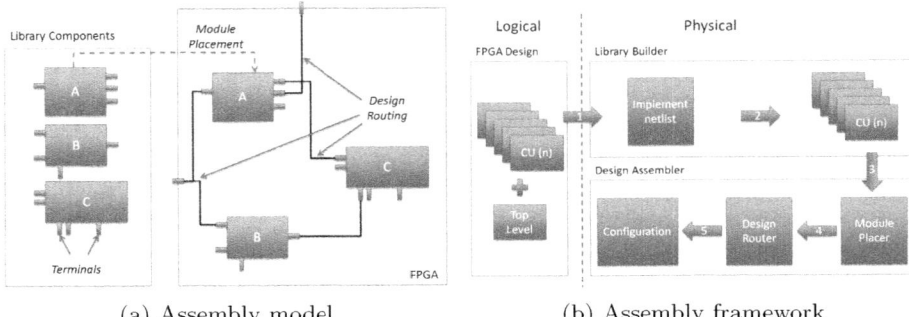

(a) Assembly model   (b) Assembly framework

Fig. 1. Modular-based assembly

stage and a design assembly stage. The assembly stage consists of a module placement step followed by a design routing step. Following is a description of each of the stages.

3.1 The Library Builder

An FPGA design starts with a design entry specification during which the hardware designer describes the system using a hardware description language such as VHDL or Verilog, a C-to-gates compiler such as Impulse C or Catapult C, or a graphical compiler such as LabVIEW FPGA. The description is then passed to a logical synthesis tool generating a netlist in terms of logic gates.

The library builder consumes CU netlists and generates a physical implementation for each of the input netlists. During physical implementation, the library builder fetches a netlist, maps it to the target FPGA, then places the resulting group of logic relative to a reference point on the target device. The resulting implementation is cached into a library holding physical representations of all CUs for later retrieval.

3.2 The Design Assembler

After the library builder processes the netlists of all CUs in a design, the design is assembled and all CU implementations are placed for the device and routed. A top level netlist of the design that describes the instanced CUs along with the connectivity information between them guides the assembler during placement and routing. After analyzing the top level netlist, the design assembler passes the list of design instanced CUs to the placer, and the corresponding connectivity information to the router. Details on the module placer and design router follows.

Module Placer. The module placer receives a list of CUs, then contacts the library builder for detailed information about each CU's physical implementation and resource usage; the physical implementation dictates the legal placements of a CU on an FPGA device. Every CU is assigned a priority based on its resource utilization, where a high priority indicates the use of scarce resources on the device. Following a decreasing order of priority, the placer fetches a CU and computes a random legal placement for the corresponding anchor point, avoiding resource conflicts with already placed logic. Due to the fact that all CU logic is placed relative to a reference point, it is sufficient to know the placement of a reference point to compute the location of any other resources in the group. The process continues until all CUs are placed or the placer fails to find a feasible solution.

Design Router. Once the design is placed, the design router traverses the connectivity list creating and routing the nets between all of the CUs' terminals. At the end of this stage a timing analysis step is performed against all design timing constraints to verify that the assembled design meets timing. The resulting design is passed to the vendor tools to generate a configuration for the target device.

3.3   Implementation Details

The suggested solution is general and one should be able to leverage any commercially available FPGA. However, due to the insight it provides to its tools and device architectures, Xilinx FPGAs were the choice of devices. That said, the framework leverages many of Xilinx's back-end tools while achieving its goal. In particular, the library builder uses Xilinx's *map* utility to implement the CUs' netlists, and the design assembler leverages *fpga_editor* and *par* utilities during placement and routing.

Moreover, the framework builds on the TORC framework [2] to augment the vendor tools with a C++ based suite of utilities that makes the proposed solution feasible. In particular, the library builder calls the developed *modularize* utility to group implemented logic into modules with relatively placed logic. The *module_placer* utility consumes the different CUs and randomly places them on an FPGA device. The placer code replicates the RPM grid (*generateRPMGrid*) used by Xilinx placement algorithms and leverages it when computing legal module placement. Finally, the design router takes advantage of the *connect_modules* utility to generate the logical nets between the placed CUs before they are routed.

4   Preliminary Results

To demonstrate the framework in action, a ZigBee demodulator was assembled using the GNU Radio framework with an XUPV5 FPGA board as the GNU Radio accelerator. GNU Radio is a tool for building open source software-defined radios. The tool works by taking generic signal processing blocks and tying them together in a flow graph that describes the input signals, all of the processing that occurs, and the outputs. GNU Radio lends itself to modular assembly because all of the signal processing blocks are modular. Traditionally, all signal processing occurred on a general purpose processor such as a CPU of a GNU

Radio host computer. The processing requirements to implement complex radio protocol standards however, could not be met by software running on a host machine. This problem is currently being addressed by adding accelerators, such as FPGAs, in the loop [7]. Using the modified GNU Radio framework from [7], capable of building custom FPGA hardware and piping computation to that FPGA, we built a demodulator for a computationally expensive protocol, ZigBee. The framework from [7] is also augmented to call our proposed modular-based assembly solution for FPGA implementations.

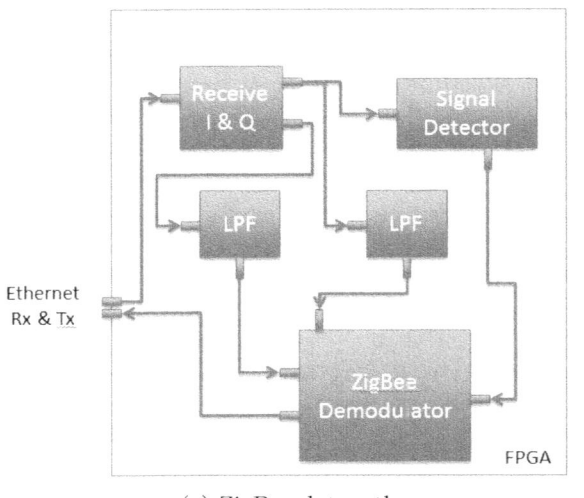
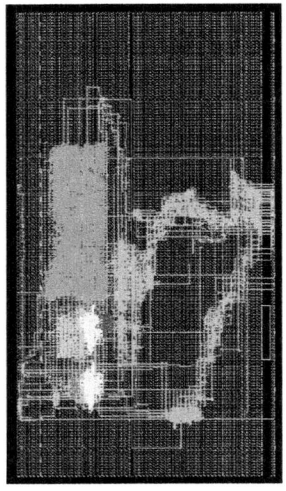

(a) ZigBee datapath

(b) ZigBee Virtex-5 implementation

Fig. 2. ZigBee demodulator

Although we have not built all of the signal processing blocks used by GNU Radio, the required blocks to decode the ZigBee protocol were generated. The datapath of the decoder consists of an interface to split the ZigBee signal into I and Q channels, a signal detector, two low pass filters and the ZigBee demodulator itself. The radio signal is digitized by a USRP2 device and is transmitted using a ZigBee transceiver module connected to a PC. Figure 2a shows the connectivity of a ZigBee demodulator design. When generating the datapath for the ZigBee demodulator, the netlist of the previously listed ZigBee modules along with the datapath connectivity was passed to our flow. Figure 2b shows an *FPGA Editor* screenshot of the output of the framework, implementing the demodulator. A configuration bitstream was generated for the implemented design and its operation was successfully verified. In the same figure, the ZigBee demodulator is highlighted in green, the two filters in yellow, the signal detector in red and the I & Q channels decoder in magenta.

5   Conclusion and Future Work

This paper presents an implementation of the modular-based assembly method proposed in [1]. The solution consists of a library builder that pre-compiles computational units in an application along with a design assembler that stitches the precomputed modules into a physical netlist before a device configuration bitstream is generated for it. Compared to the Xilinx PR flow, the proposed solution has proven to be flexible in terms of module shapes, the number of input and output terminals a module can have, and the ability to easily relocate logic on a device.

The authors are looking into extending the work in several directions. Firstly, although the random placer did the job for the tested design, enhancements to the placement algorithm are necessary as designs become more dense and timing critical. Secondly, the current implemented framework does not support the incremental changes mode highlighted by the authors of [1]. Such a feature is desirable to add further improvement on the flexibility of the solution. Finally, the authors are exploring bitstream processing alternatives that can be useful in autonomous embedded systems where running heavy weight tools is not usually an option.

References

1. Cervero, T., Frangieh, T., Athanas, P., Lopez, S., Sarmiento, R.: Scalable Models for Autonomous Self-Assembled Reconfigurable Systems. In: 2011 International Conference on Reconfigurable Computing and FPGAs, ReConFig (2011) (to appear)
2. Steiner, N., Wood, A., Shojaei, H., Couch, J., Athanas, P., French, M.: Torc: Towards an Open-Source Tool Flow. In: Nineteenth ACM/SIGDA International Symposium on Field-Programmable Gate Arrays (February 2011)
3. Xilinx: Early Access Partial Reconfiguration User Guide (UG208) (2006)
4. Sohanghpurwala, A., Athanas, P., Frangieh, T., Wood, A.: OpenPR: An Open-Source Partial-Reconfiguration Toolkit for Xilinx FPGAs. In: IPDPS Workshops, pp. 228–235 (May 2011)
5. Xilinx: Partial Reconfiguration User Guide (UG702) (2010)
6. Athanas, P., Bowen, J., Dunham, T., Patterson, C., Rice, J., Shelburne, M., Suris, J., Bucciero, M., Graf, J.: Wires on Demand: Run-Time Communication Synthesis for Reconfigurable Computing. In: International Conference on Field Programmable Logic and Applications, pp. 513–516 (2007)
7. Irick, C.: Enhancing GNU Radio for Hardware Accelerated Radio Design (Master's thesis), Retrieved from Virginia Tech Electronic Dissertations and Theses (URN etd-06072010-203946)

Constructing Cluster of Simple FPGA Boards
for Cryptologic Computations

Yarkin Doröz and Erkay Savaş

Sabanci University
Istanbul, Turkey
{yarkin,erkays}@sabanciuniv.edu

Abstract. In this paper, we propose an FPGA cluster infrastructure, which can be utilized in implementing cryptanalytic attacks and accelerating cryptographic operations. The cluster can be formed using simple and inexpensive, off-the-shelf FPGA boards featuring an FPGA device, local storage, CPLD, and network connection. Forming the cluster is simple and no effort for the hardware development is needed except for the hardware design for the actual computation. Using a soft-core processor on FPGA, we are able to configure FPGA devices dynamically and change their configuration on the fly from a remote computer. The softcore on FPGA can execute relatively complicated programs for mundane tasks unworthy of FPGA resources. Finally, we propose and implement a fast and efficient dynamic *configuration switch technique* that is shown to be useful especially in cryptanalytic applications. Our infrastructure provides a cost-effective alternative for formerly proposed cryptanalytic engines based on FPGA devices.

1 Introduction

Cryptographic operations usually contain high degree of parallelism, which favors repetitive instantiation of the same basic block for the cryptographic primitives. Thus, hardware-based cryptographic accelerators, harnessing the aforementioned parallelism, have become the focus of both industrial and academical interests in the last two decades.

Cryptanalytic studies aim to discover the strength of cryptographic algorithms against certain attack techniques, efficiency of which is determined by, to a large extent, amount of computational power available at affordable costs. As it is possible to make relatively accurate predictions (at least so far) for the increase in computational power and decrease in their associate costs in future (e.g. Moore's Law), we can provide some predictions for the future strength of certain cryptographic algorithms and their key lengths. Moreover, since increase in raw computational power does not necessarily lead to the same level of increase in our capacity for breaking ciphers, it is important to work on new architectures that will make an efficient use of the new *computing capabilities*.

Recent developments in FPGA technology, in terms of increased resources and declining costs, emphasize the configurable logic devices as the economic alternative for both cryptographic acceleration and cryptanalytic computations. Grasping this great potential, previous works in literature propose FPGA-based designs and architectures for both cryptographic acceleration [1,2] and cryptanalytic purposes [3,4,5].

O.C.S. Choy et al. (Eds.): ARC 2012, LNCS 7199, pp. 320–328, 2012.

Nowadays, many FPGAs can be configured to implement microprocessor cores that can handle mundane tasks, which are not performance bound and unworthy of valuable FPGA resources (e.g. TCP/IP communication). MicroBlaze, which is a soft processor core (*softcore* henceforth) by Xilinx and can be implemented even on inexpensive FP-GAs using the reconfigurable logic of FPGAs [6], can be utilized in this context.

In addition, FPGAs can be *dynamically* configured to implement multiple hardware designs. Relatively fast dynamical switching between configurations provides agility as well as flexibility to meet computational diversity of cryptologic applications. Moreover, the configuration files for multiple designs can be sent over a network.

This work uses Spartan-3E Starter Kit to form a so-called *FPGA cluster* for cryptologic purposes. Our approach differs from similar and the closest works in [3,4,5] in the sense that a super computer does from a server cluster. Our FPGA cluster can be formed using a host-PC acting as the *cluster head* and any off-the-shelf FPGA board featuring an FPGA, a network interface, local storage, and a simple CPLD.

The proposed cluster can be efficiently used for cryptanalytic purposes (e.g. exhaustive search). For certain cases, it can also be used as an accelerator to speedup the cryptographic applications. By supporting a fast, dynamic configuration switch, each FPGA board can combine the versatility of general-purpose computer with the parallel computing capability of hardware designs, even for FPGAs in the low-end of the cost spectrum. The software components we develop and denote as proxies running both in the cluster head and the softcore enables a transparent programing experience similar to the one provided by middleware for parallel programing and remote procedure call.

Outline of the paper is as follows. In Section 2, we introduce the architecture of the proposed FPGA cluster, employed FPGA boards and its components. We explain operational steps adopted for FPGA device and dynamic configuration switch technique in Section 3. Section 4 provides the details of the usage of the proposed cluster for cryptographic acceleration and cryptanalysis. Implementation details and experimental results are provided in Section 5. Finally, Section 6 concludes the paper.

2   Proposed Architecture for FPGA Cluster

The architectural overview of the FPGA cluster we use in our work is depicted in Figure 1. Since our architecture uses TCP/IP for communication, any FPGA board connected to the Internet can be a part of our cluster and individually accessed from anywhere in the network.

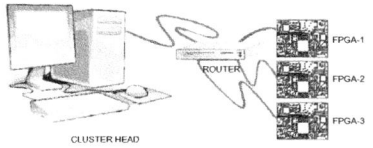

Fig. 1. General overview of the FPGA cluster

As pointed out earlier, our goal is to harness especially the computation power of inexpensive FPGA boards for the use in cryptologic applications. Therefore, we use Spartan-3E Starter Kit board, which is one of the basic equipment used in logic design courses. A Spartan-3E Starter Kit [7] is a board that consists of the following hardware components: i) volatile programmable unit (FPGA - XC3S500E), ii) a nonvolatile programmable unit (CPLD - XC2C64A), iii) 128 Mbit parallel flash memory, iv) 64 MB DDR SDRAM (MT46V32M16), v) Standard Microsystems LAN83C185 10/100 Ethernet physical layer (PHY) interface and vi) a RJ-45 connector. In Figure 2, we show how we utilize those components in our cluster.

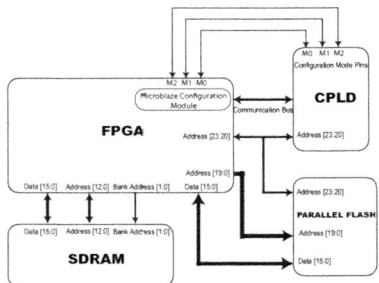

Fig. 2. Components of the FPGA board

For flexibity and transparency purposes, the proposed infrastructure is designed as a self-configuring system, which becomes ready for remote configuration once it is connected to the Internet. In addition, *runtime reconfigurability* allows to switch between 16 different configurations, which is controlled by the CPLD, dynamically.

3   Our Scheme and Its Operational Steps

Our scheme can be understood better if the following four key steps of its operation are explained in detail as follows:

Softcore Configuration: A state machine implemented in the non-volatile CPLD configures FPGA automatically using the configuration bit stream of the softcore stored in the parallel flash, when the device is turned on. Following the softcore configuration, a special program called *boot-loader* is executed by the softcore.

Execution of Boot-loader: The boot-loader is a small piece of code, which comes as a part of configuration file of the softcore and stored in internal Block RAM (BRAM) of the FPGA. It is responsible of moving the proxy code[1] from the parallel flash to the SDRAM since the latter is too large to fit in the internal BRAM.

Execution of Proxy for Implementing Client/Server Communication Model: To assign tasks, the cluster head communicates with FPGA boards using reliable TCP/IP protocols which are implemented by the proxy code on the softcore side. In our communication model, the cluster head and the softcore plays the roles of server and clients interchangeably.

Automatic, Remote Configuration of FPGA Device and Configuration Switch: The actual computations for specific tasks are performed by hardware implementations,

---

[1] The code of the main software application which is used to communicate with the cluster head.

optimized for the FPGA devices. Once the configuration file for a hardware implementation is available, the cluster head can send it through network to the FPGA devices. The proxy code running on the softcore is responsible of receiving the hardware configuration file and storing it in the parallel flash.

The configuration switch necessitates the execution of the following steps in this order: **i) Communication 1:** Input data is sent to the softcore and stored in parallel flash, **ii) Configuration switch 1:** Softcore removes itself from the FPGA and loads the hardware, **iii) Computation:** The hardware works on the task, and writes the results in the parallel flash, **iv) Configuration switch 2:** The hardware is removed and the softcore is loaded in the FPGA, **v) Communication 2:** The softcore reads the results from the parallel flash, and sends them to the cluster head.

Alternatively, especially for applications and FPGAs where the area overhead of the softcore is not important, the hardware design and the softcore can run simultaneously in FPGAs, which eliminates the need for configuration switch as described above. In subsequent sections, we give applications that benefit from the configuration switch.

4   Using FPGA Cluster for Acceleration of Cryptographic Computations and Cryptanalysis

A simple and inexpensive FPGA device such as Spartan-3 running at a low clock frequency of 119 MHz can perform an RSA exponentiation operation in about 8 ms using 1553 slices and 10 hardwired multipliers [1][2]. Similarly, the same FPGA device can achieve an encryption rate of 429 Mbps for the AES standard block cipher algorithm using only 103 slices at 161 MHz [8]. Since the FPGA device can realize more than one block of AES encryption engine, it is possible to reach much higher throughput values for encryption operation either using multi-message encryption techniques or a suitable working mode (e.g. counter mode). Therefore, using simple, inexpensive FPGA clusters can be cost-effective alternatives for accelerating cryptographic operations. However, cryptographic acceleration through a simple FPGA board may not be feasible if configuration switching is needed[3]. In Section 5, we provide a scenario where cryptographic acceleration may be possible even in the case of configuration switch. But, block cipher acceleration is always possible since the FPGA device can be shared between the softcore and the hardware.

Most cryptanalytic algorithms can be adjusted to alleviate the time overhead incurred in inter-process communication between the cluster head and the FPGA boards. Both designs in [4] for exhaustive key search and [5] for solving discrete logarithm problem (DLP) rely on a massively parallel computer of inexpensive FPGA devices as the computational work horse. Also, as stated in [5], certain computations in the Pollard's Rho

---

[2] Note that RSA timings for one signature operation vary between 0.15 ms and 8 ms on a PC depending on the processor (cf. http://bench.cr.yp.to/results-sign.html). In order to obtain acceleration over common PCs, a larger FPGA device that can accommodate more than one instance of crypto unit should be used. Otherwise, many FPGA boards will be needed to outperform PC implementations.

[3] Because of large resource consumptions some hardware designs cannot co-exist with the softcore (e.g. RSA).

method [9,10] for solving elliptic curve DLP (ECDLP) can be so adjusted to meet any bandwidth restriction between the cluster head and the FPGA boards.

For instance, in an exhaustive search for a AES key using the implementation in [8], one AES block (103 slices) can try approximately 3.3 million key candidates in one second. In a single computation task submitted to an FPGA, which takes about one minute, one additional AES block implemented on the FPGA resources gained by removing the softcore can try out an extra 200 million key candidates. This value commensurates with the number of AES instances that can fit in the space saved through removing the softcore. Since the communication between the cluster head and FPGA device is not intense (in fact only the key interval is needed to be communicated to the FPGA), overlapping communication and computation would not help. Therefore, in such cases it is always beneficial to apply the configuration switch.

5   Implementation and Experimental Results

In this section, we provide some implementation details and experimental results to evaluate the true potential of the proposed FPGA cluster for cryptologic computations. We start with the resources needed to implement the softcore in Spartan-3E (XC3S500E) device, which consumes 4,270 out of 9,312 (45%) 4-input LUTs and occupies 3,526 out of 4,656 (75%) slices. The utilization percentage for such a small FPGA device is relatively high and leaving limited configurable FPGA resources for hardware unit that will perform the actual computation. This is, in fact, one of the primary motivation for the scheme that will allow an efficient configuration switch between the softcore and the hardware unit.

In our experiments, we used a Linux-based PC (cluster head) and ASUS RT-N13U router in addition to three Spartan-3E Starter Kit boards. We used Verilog for all hardware designs and C/C++ language for software components on the softcore and the cluster head. The first experiment is intended to find out the efficiency of using the FPGA boards mainly for cryptographic acceleration if the hardware unit and the softcore cannot co-exist in the FPGA board and therefore, configuration switch is necessary. The experiment is performed as follows: the cluster head sends input values (e.g. messages to be encrypted or signed) to the FPGA device which are written in the parallel flash thereafter. After the transmission is completed, a configuration switch command is sent to the FPGA. Since we are interested only in the overhead the whole process creates, the hardware unit reads the data from the parallel flash first and then writes it back to it. Without doing anything else, it switches immediately back to the softcore configuration and the softcore sends the written data back to the cluster head.

The data exchanged between the cluster head and the FPGA are sent in different packet sizes (i.e. sizes of send/receive buffers in both sides). The timing values obtained through averaging for the first experiment are enumerated in rows 2-5 of Table 1. Timing overhead for handling 1 MB of data is about 27.31 s, on average. 1 MB of data, for example, means 8192 RSA operation (e.g. signature), where the modulus is 1024 bit. This results in an overhead of 3.33 ms per 1024-bit RSA operation. Considering that the state-of-the-art implementation of RSA for Spartan-3E in [1] executes the same operation in about 8 ms, this increases the effective time per RSA operation roughly by 37% percent, on average. Note that this overhead would be about 0.87 s for 1 KB data size, which is definitely not an acceptable performance for a cryptographic accelerator. In summary, our FPGA cluster may be useful in case the configuration switch is necessary only when we are able to group the input data in large chunks.

Table 1. Timing overhead (in seconds) for different data and packet sizes

Packet Size (B)	Storage Device	1 KB	10 KB	100 KB	1 MB
256	Parallel Flash	15.74	17.38	32.70	216.81
512	Parallel Flash	14.40	15.50	21.11	102.90
1024	Parallel Flash	13.65	14.33	16.77	72.73
1024(opt.^{4})	Parallel Flash	6.96	7.44	8.79	27.31
1024(opt.^{4})	SDRAM	0.27	0.35	1.06	7.81

In the second experiment, we measured the time to send and receive data of different sizes when configuration switch is not needed for the scenario where the cryptographic unit and the softcore fit in the FPGA device. The SDRAM can be used to store the data since there is no configuration switch that causes the SDRAM to miss refreshment cycles. The timing values for the second experiment are enumerated in the last row of Table 1 only for buffer size of 1024 B. As can be observed from the table, using the SDRAM rather than the parallel flash, decreases the total time by 19.50 s for 1 MB of data. However, the timing values in the last row should not really be considered as actual overhead since operations for sending/receiving data and writing/reading to/from the SDRAM can be overlapped with the actual cryptographic computation.

In the third experiment, we tried to measure the total overhead time when the data transfer is not intense and configuration switch can be used, which is typical mostly for cryptanalytic purposes. The cluster head sends a message of 32 B to the softcore, which contains the task description as well as the input parameters. After the task description and input parameters are received, two configuration switch operations occur to configure FPGA first with the hardware than with the softcore. We performed all steps except for the actual computation time of the task to determine the overhead in time. The timing results for one, two, and three FPGA boards are measured as 7.06 s, 7.09 s, and 7.14 s, respectively. These results show that we can multiply our computational power with minor overheads in time.

In the next experiment, we performed an exhaustive key search for PRESENT algorithm [11], which is a lightweight block cipher intended for embedded applications. The results for a single FPGA board are listed in Table 2. The maximum number of encryption engines that will fit in Spartan-3E is only 13. With configuration switch and communication costs included, we are able to test about 928 million keys in 61.76 s. The last row enumerates the experimental results when there is no configuration switch and the softcore and seven encryption engines run concurrently. This experiment demonstrate the advantage of configuration switch for exhaustive key search applications. Note that speed optimized, single-threaded C implementation of the PRESENT algorithm (cf.

---

[4] We optimized the execution times by adding cache to MicroBlaze and performing improvements in the software.

Table 2. Experimental results for exhaustive key search

Conf.	Area LUT + Slice	Max/Usable Freq. (MHz)	no of keys tried in $\approx 60s$
Single PRESENT	3% + 3%	187.37/NA	NA
13 PRESENT	74% + 99%	65.23/50	928,628,190 in 61.76 s
7 PRESENT + Softcore	83% + 99%	53.709/50	510,656,511 in 60.10 s

Table 3. Timing statistics (in seconds) for Pollard Rho's alg. on different number of FPGA boards

no of FPGA boards	no of runs	avg.	med.	max.	min.	stdev
3 (Spartan-3E500)[5]	36	927	849	2368	232	531
7 (Spartan-3E500)[5]	27	478	442	1074	223	216
5 (Spartan-3E500)+2(Spartan-3E1600)[6]	30	302	236	687	192	123

http://www.lightweightcrypto.org/present/) on a PC with an AMD 3.2 GHz quad-core processor and 4 GB RAM can try roughly 106 million keys in 62 s, which also demonstrates that acceleration of PRESENT algorithm is possible.

Finally, we implemented Pollard's Rho method [9,10] to compute discrete logarithms in elliptic curves over prime fields of odd characteristics. For elliptic curve arithmetic we used Huff model to take advantage of the fast explicit formulae for point additions on Huff curves [12]. The FPGA boards are used to find the distinguished points, which constitutes the most time-consuming part of the computation in Pollard's Rho method. Since a similar approach to the one in [4] is adopted, we only implemented point addition. The hardware implementation of the circuit to find the distinguished points (i.e. distinguished points-generating engine) consumes 50% of the total LUTs, 19% of slice flip-flops, and 5% of the block RAMs. In the experiments, we used an elliptic curve over a prime field where the prime is a 160-bit integer. The base point order is chosen as a 50-bit integer to demonstrate that the discrete logarithm can be computed within a reasonable amount of time using several FPGA boards. A single-threaded PC implementation on an AMD 3.2 GHz quad-core processor with 4 GB RAM completes the same task in about 6 minutes, on average, using NTL package [13].

In order to demonstrate that the time performance of the attack improves linearly with the number of FPGA boards (and the total number of distinguished point-generating engines), we conducted several experiments. Firstly, we optimized the distinguished point-generating engine to fit two instances of it in one FPGA device. Secondly, we employed different number of FPGA boards in our experiments. Using the same curve and the base point mentioned above, we solved different number of elliptic curve discrete logarithm problems (cf. the second column of Table 3) and enumerated the timing statistics in Table 3. As can be observed from the table, we can solve one elliptic curve discrete logarithm problem in about 5.03 minutes using seven FPGA boards (i.e. 22

---

[5] In these experiments, we performed the attack using three and seven boards of Spartan-3E500, each of which can fit two instances of distinguished points-generating engine.

[6] In this experiment, we performed the attack using two Spartan-3E1600, which can fit six instances of distinguished points-generating engine, along with five boards of Spartan-3E500.

instances of distinguished point-generating engine), on average and also outperform the PC based implementation[7].

6 Conclusion

The experiments demonstrate that the proposed FPGA cluster can be useful for both cryptographic acceleration and implementing cryptanalytic attacks. Dynamic configuration switch between the soft processor core and the hardware unit, proposed as among the foremost contributions of this work, proves to be useful especially in exhaustive search applications in cryptanalysis, where the need for interprocess communication is very limited (if not absent). Dynamic configuration switch can be useful even for more powerful FPGA devices since FPGA resources salvaged from the softcore can be put into effective use.

The proposed FPGA cluster offers advantages over PC-based implementations, when a single FPGA device can accommodate as many instances of the main computation unit as possible to take advantage of the parallelism the hardware implementations offer. While exhaustive search for simple algorithms such as PRESENT can be substantially accelerated, relatively heavy-weight algorithms such as RSA does not benefit from the cluster if only one instance of RSA circuit is implemented in one FPGA device. For acceleration of heavy-weight algorithms, either more advanced FPGA devices or a multitude of simple FPGA devices should be used. Naturally, price performance analysis of the FPGA cluster must be performed on the basis of the specific operation we are trying to accelerate.

References

1. Öksüzoglu, E., Savas, E.: Parametric, secure and compact implementation of rsa on fpga. In: Proceedings of the 2008 International Conference on Reconfigurable Computing and FPGAs, pp. 391–396. IEEE Computer Society, Washington, DC, USA (2008)
2. Le Masle, A., Luk, W., Eldredge, J., Carver, K.: Parametric Encryption Hardware Design. In: Sirisuk, P., Morgan, F., El-Ghazawi, T., Amano, H. (eds.) ARC 2010. LNCS, vol. 5992, pp. 68–79. Springer, Heidelberg (2010), doi:10.1007/978-3-642-12133-39
3. Kumar, S., Paar, C., Pelzl, J., Pfeiffer, G., Schimmler, M.: Copacobana a cost-optimized special-purpose hardware for code-breaking. In: FCCM, pp. 311–312. IEEE Computer Society (2006)
4. Güneysu, T., Paar, C., Pelzl, J.: Special-purpose hardware for solving the elliptic curve discrete logarithm problem. TRETS 1 (2008)
5. Güneysu, T., Paar, C., Pfeiffer, G., Schimmler, M.: Enhancing copacobana for advanced applications in cryptography and cryptanalysis. In: FPL, pp. 675–678. IEEE (2008)
6. Xilinx: MicroBlaze Soft Processor Core (2011),
   http://www.xilinx.com/tools/microblaze.htm
7. Xilinx: Spartan-3E Starter Kit (2011),
   http://www.xilinx.com/products/devkits/HW-SPAR3E-SK-US-G.htm
8. Helion: High Performance AES (Rijndael) cores for Xilinx FPGA (2011),
   http://www.heliontech.com/aes.htm

---

[7] We used Asus GIGAX1008B 8 Port 10/100 Layer2 Switch to connect seven FGPA boards.

9. Pollard, J.M.: Monte carlo methods for index computation   (mod p). Mathematics of Computation 32, 918–924 (1978)

10. Oorschot, P.C.V., Wiener, M.J.: Parallel collision search with cryptanalytic applications. Journal of Cryptology 12, 1–28 (1996)

11. Bogdanov, A., Knudsen, L.R., Leander, G., Paar, C., Poschmann, A., Robshaw, M.J.B., Seurin, Y., Vikkelsoe, C.: PRESENT: An Ultra-Lightweight Block Cipher. In: Paillier, P., Verbauwhede, I. (eds.) CHES 2007. LNCS, vol. 4727, pp. 450–466. Springer, Heidelberg (2007)

12. Joye, M., Tibouchi, M., Vergnaud, D.. Huff's model for elliptic curves. Cryptology ePrint Archive, Report 2010/383 (2010), http://eprint.iacr.org/

13. Shoup, V.: NTL: a library for doing number theory (2011), http://www.shoup.net/ntl/ (last accessed)

Reconfigurable Multicore Architecture for Dynamic Processor Reallocation

Annie Avakian, Natwar Agrawal, and Ranga Vemuri

School of Electronics and Computing Systems, University of Cincinnati
{avakiaam,agrawanr}@mail.uc.edu, vemurir@ucmail.uc.edu

Abstract. One of the challenges of multicore design is providing data quickly to all the processor cores running on a system. Recent proposals of hybrid and reconfigurable interconnect architectures try to take advantage of data locality to a certain extent by grouping processors that work on the same data. In this paper, we propose migrating processors instead of data to take advantage of data locality. This is realized by implementing a reconfigurable interconnect that allows reassignment of processor cores to different routers at runtime. We present the proposed architecture in detail, show a segmented hardware implementation of the proposed architecture, and discuss experimental results using PARSEC benchmark showing the performance gains of the proposed architecture. Our results show a gain in average L2 access time of up to 24% when implementing the proposed architecture compared to a hybrid architecture without reconfiguration. Finally we present area and performance data based on a detailed Verilog model and synthesis of the proposed architecture.

1 Introduction

One of the main challenges of multicore architecture is providing data as quickly as possible to all the cores. To address this issue, Network on Chip is gaining popularity due to its scalability and efficiency [1].

Different mapping strategies have been tested to reduce the overall access time. Foglia et al. in [2] show that the characteristics of the application running on a system along with the mapping protocol used, significantly effect the overall access time. Dybdahl and Stenstromr in [3] propose dynamically changing the amount of private cache that cores can utilize on a need basis.

Others have taken on a completely different approach altogether. They have proposed changes in the architecture to reduce cache access time. Das et al. [4] propose a hybrid Bus/Network architecture where eight processor cores are connected to a bus and the bus is connected to a router.

In our previous work [5], we proposed a reconfigurable architecture where the number of cores connected to a bus can be changed statically. The reconfiguration in this proposed architecture is limited and is statically done before the runtime of the application. In this paper, we propose a variation of that architecture where the mapping of cores to routers can be changed at runtime. To achieve this, we propose a hybrid bus-network architecture with reconfigurable interconnect, where the number of processor

O.C.S. Choy et al. (Eds.): ARC 2012, LNCS 7199, pp. 329–334, 2012.

cores attached to each bus is reconfigurable and is dependent on the needs of the active processes and applications executing on the system. This allows the reallocation of resources based on the needs of the executing applications.

This paper is organized as follows: Section 2 describes the proposed architecture and shows a segmented hardware implementation. Section 3 gives a detailed analysis of the benefits of the proposed method. Section 4 concludes.

2   Proposed Architecture

In order to dynamically assign cores to routers, two aspects need to be considered. The first is that more than one processor can be connected to a router at the same time, and the second is that the architecture allows dynamic reconfiguration. In this section, we present the proposed architecture and then show a segmented variation of the proposed architecture.

2.1   DyaReMA

DyaReMA allows the dynamic reassignment of processor cores based on the history of cache accesses. Processor cores that access remote data more frequently than the local data are reassigned to the remote router. Any processor core can be assigned to any router and processor assignments can be changed dynamically during runtime. DyaReMA is shown in Figure 1.

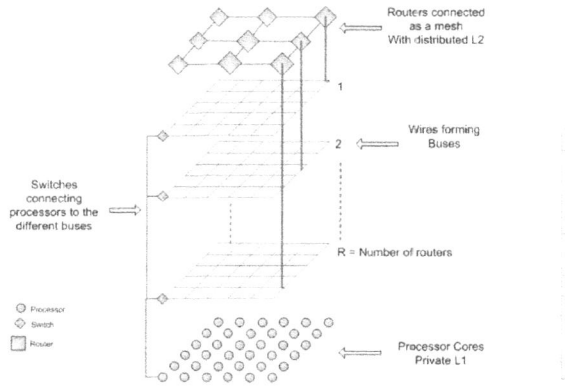
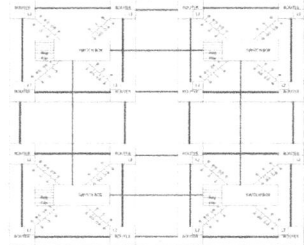

Fig. 1. Proposed Architecture   **Fig. 2.** 4x4 NoC Switchbox Architecture

1. *Packet Switched Layer.* In the figure, the squares at the top are the routers connected in a mesh. There are $k \times k = R$ routers. The last level cache (L2 in our case) is a dynamic NUCA and is distributed among the different routers. The request is moved from one router to the other using the XY routing algorithm.
2. *Set of Processors.* The circles at the bottom of the figure are the processors. There are $p \times p$ processors. The processors have private L1 cache banks.

3. *Circuit Switched Routing Layer.* The circuit switched routing layer is used to form buses that in turn connect to the routers. Since each router needs a dedicated bus, there are R routing layers. The processors connect to the routers by programmable switches. Every processing core has R programmable switches, and each switch is connected to one circuit switched routing layer.
4. *Programmable Switches.* The processors are connected to all the circuit switched routing layers by programmable switches. If the switch of a processor is *on* for layer j, that means the processor is connected to router j. Processors can be connected to one router at a time, therefore only one programmable switch of a processor can be *on* at one time.
5. *Router Bus Connectivity.* Each of the routing layers are connected to one router. These are assigned at design time and cannot be changed.

Distance Model. In order to ensure that our analysis takes into consideration the delays that the circuit might incur, we included distance calculation while analyzing the benchmarks. The distance between 2 processes is 1 unit time. In [6] it is stated that bus delay across 10mm is expected to be 12 clock cycles, meanwhile the new processors are around $140mm^2$ [7]. Therefore a one cycle delay between cores on the bus is a reasonable assumption in a regular architecture.

The distance between routers is calculated as $\frac{p-1}{r}$ where p is the number of processor cores on each row and r is the number of routers on each row. This ensures that the routers are equidistant. Therefore when calculating the number of hops, we add the bus distance between the core and the local router of the circuit switched layer and network hops needed to get to the remote router on the packet switched layer.

Processor Reallocation Policy. The processors are reallocated to different routers based on the history of memory accesses. In order to keep track of the data accessed, each processor has R counters where R is the number of routers in the system. The idea is to compare data accessed between the local cache and a remote one. If a processor core accessed a remote router more often than it accessed the local router, then that processor is a good candidate to be reassigned to the remote router.

But moving all the processor cores to their ideal location may result in all the cores being assigned to one router. Therefore in the proposed method, after moving a processor core (MP) and assigning it to the target router RT, if the number of cores on the target router reaches a certain threshold N, then another victim processor (VP) from the target router is moved to the router (RO) that hosted the moving processor core MP. The processor core that is chosen to be moved from RT is the one that is Least Recently Used.

2.2 DyaReMA with Reduced Number of Meshes

Having R number of meshes can be very costly. An alternative is to reduce the number of meshes to less than the number of routers. The number of meshes needed can range between 1 and R based on the characteristics of the applications for the target architecture. Routers can share the mesh, but this can limit the ability of the processors to connect to all routers.

If the number of meshes is less than R, then a routing algorithm needs to be used to find a path from the core to the target router on the available layers. If a path cannot be found due to other assignments, then a core cannot be reassigned to the router. Reducing the number of meshes available does reduce the area, but the reassignment time is increased since a path needs to be constructed between the core and the target router. On the other hand, having R meshes consumes more area, but reassignment is a one step process. Therefore, an analysis should be done on the importance of area versus timing for the target architecture to determine the number of meshes that should be available in the architecture.

2.3   Segmented DyaReMA

Ideally, all cores should be able to connect to any router. But with current technology, this can be very costly. Figure 2 shows a segmented architecture where cores can migrate to neighboring routers only. It is a 4x4 mesh NoC architecture with 128 cores. Some cores are *migrating cores* while others are *non-migrating*. Each 2x2 NoC has a switchbox that controls the migration of the cores. Migration happens only among those 4 routers, cores cannot be migrated to routers connected to different switchboxes.

The migrated masters on the bus are empty locations where the migrating masters (cores) can reside. The AHB bus signals of the migrating masters are multiplexed to drive the signal of the migrated master. Since the migrating master can occupy only one slot, the register file is used as the *select signal* of the multiplexer to determine which of the migrating cores from other nodes can migrate. The register file keeps track of the location of the migrated masters.

*Number of multiplexers = Number of migrating masters from each node * 4 * no of signals in the bus *2*
*Number of input for each multiplexer = Number of migrating master in a node * 4*

The protocol uses split transaction to grant the bus request to another core if the previous request cannot be served quickly. The AHB arbiter is responsible for assigning the control of the bus to the masters sitting on the bus.

3   Experimental Results and Analysis

3.1   DyaReMA Simulation Results

To verify reduction in access time when reassigning cores from one router to another, we simulated the architecture in Simics [8]. We used the benchmark suite PARSEC [9] since it was developed solely for multicore architectures.

The figures 3 and 4 show the results of the benchmarks having 64 and 128 cores. We used 3x3 and 4x4 routers respectively. Each core has a private L1 cache and the L2 cache is shared among the routers, so it is essentially divided into 9 or 16 cache banks.

The threshold number that is increasing from 4 to 16384 is the difference of data accessed between the local router and the remote routers before making a swap.

The figures show a significant improvement garnered from assigning processors to routers. As seen, there is a reduction of upto 24% of average hops required to access a

remote data. This is compared to the hybrid model that in itself has shown an improvement compared to a regular NoC model. The chosen threshold has a significant impact
on the output. In our experiments, a threshold beyond 256 has an adverse effect on the
64 core architecture, and a threshold larger than 2048 has an adverse effect on the 128
core architecture.

Of course the proposed architecture introduces a large overhead due to the bus layers. Since the proposed architecture is a hybrid architecture, the number of routers
needed for the 128 core architecture is 16 instead of 128. For a generic router of size
$0.3748mm^2$ in 90nm technology [10], the area savings is around $42mm^2$. For the bus
layers, the length of the bus needed is assumed to be 12*10mm to reach all the cores for
each layer since the cores are arranged approximately 11x11. In 90nm technology, wire
width of 3 lambda and spacing of 4 lambda, a 128 bit bus has an area of $4.8384\mu m^2$.
For 16 mesh layers the area needed is $77mm^2$. Therefore the area increase is around
$35mm^2$. If there are k metal layers, then the area increase due to the mesh layers is
reduced by a factor of k since each mesh can be assigned to a different metal layer.

3.2   Synthesis Models

To obtain realistic estimates of the area and performance of DyaReMA, we have developed a complete Verilog model of the Segmented DyaReMA explained in section
2.3 The developed model is highly parametrized. The components can be used to synthesize different architectures ranging from bus based, to NoC, to hybrid NoC, and
reconfigurable hybrid NoC architectures.

From the synthesis results, we observed that in the segmented DyaReMa architecture
shown in Section 2.3, five clock cycles are needed to access data found on the local
router. Meanwhile, on average, data obtained through the network with idle traffic takes
about 80 clock cycles. Therefore, migrating the core to a remote router gives sixteenfold
performance improvement. If the design with core migration has maximum operating
frequency less than that of the design without core migration due to the worst case
timing path added by the switch boxes, the bus can be pipelined. If a 5 stage pipeline is
added it will still give an improvement factor of 8.

We used Synopsis DC Compiler to obtain area. The gate count is calculated in terms
of NAND gate area for X1 drive strength which is 0.798.

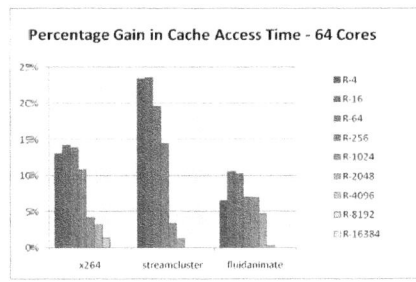
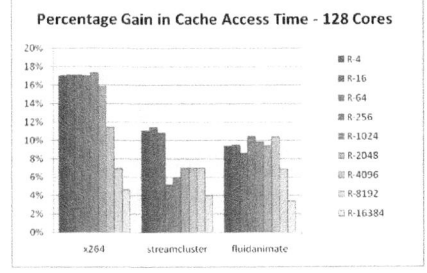

Fig. 3. Results for 64 Core   **Fig. 4.** Results for 128 Core

We synthesized 3 different architectures, NoC, hybrid architecture, and segmented DyaReMA. The results showed that a 2x2 NoC architecture with 4 processor cores has a gate count of $258K$ ($64.5k$ per core). A hybrid architecture with 2x2 routers and 8 processing cores per router has a gate count of $382K$ ($11.9K$ per core). A reconfigurable hybrid NoC with 2x2 routers and 7 processing cores has a gate count of $354K$ ($12.6K$ per core).

This shows that a hybrid architecture or a reconfigurable hybrid architecture have similar gate counts per processing unit, meanwhile a simple NoC architecture has a lot more overhead per core. Therefore the proposed reconfigurable architecture is a viable option to reduce cache access time.

4   Conclusion

The proposed method tries to reduce access time by reassigning cores to routers instead of or in addition to data migration. The architecture is a hybrid bus/network with reconfigurable interconnect. Our experimental results using Simics showed up to 24% improvement in average number of hops when accessing remote data. We also introduced a hardware implementation of a simplified version of the proposed architecture to show that the area penalty is not significant.

References

1. Duato, J., Yalamanchili, S., Lionel, N.: Interconnection Networks: An Engineering Approach. Morgan Kaufmann Publishers Inc., San Francisco (2002)
2. Foglia, P., Panicucci, F., Prete, C.A., Solinas, M.: Analysis of performance dependencies in nuca-based cmp systems. In: Symposium on Computer Architecture and High Performance Computing, pp. 49–56 (2009)
3. Dybdahl, H., Stenstrom, P.: An adaptive shared/private nuca cache partitioning scheme for chip multiprocessors. In: HPCA 2007: Proceedings of the 2007 IEEE 13th International Symposium on High Performance Computer Architecture, pp. 2–12. IEEE Computer Society, Washington, DC, USA (2007)
4. Das, R., Eachempati, S., Mishra, A.K., Narayanan, V., Das, C.R.: Design and evaluation of a hierarchical on-chip interconnect for next-generation cmps, pp. 175–186 (February 2009)
5. Avakian, A., Nafziger, J., Panda, A., Vemuri, R.: A reconfigurable architecture for multi-core systems. In: 2010 IEEE International Symposium on Parallel & Distributed Processing, Workshops and Phd Forum (IPDPSW), pp. 1–8. IEEE (2010)
6. http://www.itrs.net/
7. http://ark.intel.com/Product.aspx?id=37150
8. http://www.virtutech.com
9. Bienia, C., Kumar, S., Singh, J.P., Li, K.: The parsec benchmark suite: characterization and architectural implications. In: PACT 2008: Proceedings of the 17th International Conference on Parallel Architectures and Compilation Techniques, pp. 72–81. ACM, New York (2008)
10. Li, F., Nicopoulos, C., Richardson, T., Xie, Y., Narayanan, V., Kandemir, M.: Design and management of 3d chip multiprocessors using network-in-memory. SIGARCH Comput. Archit. News 34(2), 130–141 (2006)

Efficient Communication for FPGA Clusters

Stewart Denholm, Kuen Hung Tsoi, Peter Pietzuch, and Wayne Luk

Department of Computing, Imperial College London, UK
{swd10,khtsoi,prp,wl}@doc.ic.ac.uk

Abstract. Efficient communication between nodes is critical for achieving high performance in a computer cluster. Based on a dedicated inter-accelerator network, we enhance this communication with advanced networking functions, such as broadcasting and priority routing. This work enables decoupling user applications from physical network implementations, improving overall communication efficiency and modularity. A performance model is introduced taking into account application and platform specific parameters. Experiments are performed for various network configurations and application patterns. The results show up to a 55% reduction of communication time when employing our approach.

1 Introduction

Modern High Performance Computing (HPC) systems include heterogeneous hardware accelerators such as Field Programmable Gate Arrays (FPGAs.) There is usually no direct connection between these hardware accelerators and the cluster network. Gigabit Ethernet and the InfiniBand [1] network are two commonly employed communication technologies in HPC systems, as suggested by the Top500 supercomputer list [2]. Their involvement introduces significant overhead due to the data movement between the accelerators and the host memory.

To address this, HPC systems with heterogeneous accelerators are starting to incorporate direct inter-accelerator communications through dedicated connections. Figure 1 illustrates the idea of this inter-accelerator networking; the long, thick arrow shows a point-to-point (P2P) link. Similar configurations can be seen in existing FPGA based HPC systems [3, 6, 5]. Previous experiments indicate this helps improve the performance and scalability in applications [4].

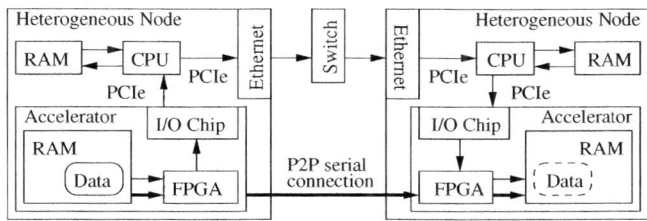

Fig. 1. Data transfer between accelerators in a heterogeneous cluster

O.C.S. Choy et al. (Eds.): ARC 2012, LNCS 7199, pp. 335–341, 2012.

The main objective of this work is to provide an efficient inter-FPGA communication framework without the need for centralised switching facilities. This can be achieved by supporting concurrent multi-destination addressing and by reducing redundant network traffic. The challenge lies in application-specific customisations, requiring the use of low level networking hardware. A parametrised user interface must be provided, as well as a model predicting performance gains.

The major contributions of this work include:

- A framework to support broadcasting and priority routing in an inter-FPGA P2P network. The data format, connection schemes, routing algorithms and architecture parameters can be customised for specific applications.
- A performance model for exploring the effects of various networking features and configurations. It provides an upper bound for expected performance and guides the decision making in each development stage by considering the customisable parameters.
- Experiments designed for measuring and evaluating the communication performance of the broadcast design. Results show an overall performance improvement of up to 55%, agreeing with the performance model estimation.

Various heterogeneous clusters equipped with FPGA-based accelerators have been reported in the last few years. The following presents several examples, and describes the differences between our work and that of others.

In the *sprit* cluster [6], there are 64 Xilinx ML410 evaluation boards connected via SATA cables, each channel of which provides up to 2.5Gbps bandwidth. The PowerPCs in the Virtex-4 FPGAs are used as the main controllers in the cluster. Previous experiments compare communication performance against physical factors, but it is unclear how the network is utilised at the application level.

The Axel cluster [4] utilises a 2D torus network via direct inter-FPGA connections. Networking functions are implemented in the FPGA fabric, avoiding software overhead in previous contributions. However, this work lacks advanced networking functions, such as broadcasting and priority routing.

The Maxeler platform includes a 10Gbps interface. Based on the original MaxRing technology [5], a CH2 connectivity expansion card is used to provide multiple channels with 10Gbps bandwidth. With this card, multiple nodes can be connected to form a larger ring, but other topolgies are not supported. Vendor specific APIs are used to control the data flow in the user application.

2   Broadcast Design

Without broadcasting, the user must send the same packet to each destination. This raises many issues. First, additional logic is needed to implement the multiple transmissions. Second, redundant packets occupy routing and queueing resources on all intermediate nodes. Third, addressing all the FPGAs in an application requires knowing the transmission path to each one; embedding this information in the application reduces the flexibility and scalability of the design.

Our broadcasting function addresses these issues without adversely affecting application performance. When encountering a broadcast packet, a router automatically duplicates it into the queues of all available outputs, storing a local copy if the packet originated at another node. Previously seen packets are discarded automatically. Following this cascading transmission method, packets are delivered to all participating accelerators regardless of the connection topology.

The implementation and performance evaluation of the framework is based on the network shown in Figure 2, but can be adapted to other topologies without any low level modifications. Each of the 16 compute nodes contain an AXM-XRC-5T2 board from Alpha-Data, interfaced to the host system through the PCIe bus. As suggested by Figure 1, the PCIe bus and Ethernet do not provide an efficient path for inter-FPGA communication. In the proposed framework, the RocketIO GTP serial communication resources in the Xilinx Virtex-5 FPGA are utilised as the main data communication channel. With the XRM-HSSDC2A I/C connectivity card, each FPGA accelerator is capable of sending and receiving data through four independent ports in full-duplex. Single channel InfiniBand cables, rated for 2.5Gbps, connect the accelerators to form a 2D torus. This hardware configuration is similar to the cluster in [3].

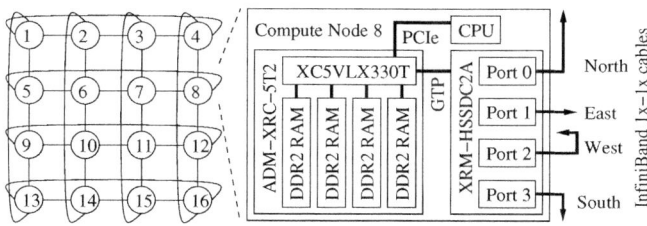

Fig. 2. A 2D torus network utilising P2P FPGA serial communication

3   Performance Model

Table 1 lists the parameters captured by our performance model. The platform specific parameters can be obtained from actual measurement and profiling on the target platform, or from the data specifications of the hardware components. The application specific parameters are obtained by extracting and abstracting the communication pattern of the target algorithm.

For a 1-to-all communication, the data from a single node must be sent to all other nodes to complete the process. The simplest model for the time T to send a packet from one node to another is:

$$T_{pkt} = p/B_l, \quad T_L = T_l + T_r + T_{pkt}, \quad T = (k-1) \times T_L + 2 \times T_a$$

where T_{pkt} is the time for transmitting a packet out of a hub, and T_L is the time for the packet to pass through a link. In a broadcasting scenario, the maximum number of links, $\hat{k}$, is used since that path will take the longest time to transmit. The value is dependent on the application and network topology. In our 16-node, 2D torus network, $\hat{k} = 4$ when the application is broadcasting to all nodes. The above analysis is modified as follows to represent 1-to-all communication:

$$T_P = \lceil d/p \rceil \times (T_L + T_a) + (\hat{k} - 1) \times T_L + T_a \tag{1}$$

Table 1. Parameters for network performance modelling

symbol	unit	meaning	typical value
		platform parameters	
p	bits	size of a packet	16 - 528
q		max. packets in a queue	64
ρ		error rate in link transmission	5%
B_l	Mbps	bandwidth of physical link	1600
T_l	μs	FPGA link transmission latency	0
T_r	μs	FPGA packet routing latency	0.57
T_a	μs	application to routing logic latency	0.13
		application parameters	
d	bits	total data size to be transferred	N/A
λ	s^{-1}	average packet rate	N/A
k		number of links along a path	N/A
$\tilde{k}$		average links per path	N/A
$\hat{k}$		maximum links per path	N/A

When a unicast packet is created, it will, on average, occupy $\tilde{k}$ number of slots in the queues along the path. For the duration of T', there will be $T' \times \lambda$ unicast packets created. For a cluster with N FPGA nodes and each node with four output queues, the network loading can be approximated as:

$$T_q = T_{pkt} \times (T' \times \lambda \times \tilde{k})/N/4 \tag{2}$$

When there is an error detected during packet transmission, the packet is automatically retransmitted within the link layer. Thus the effects of transmission errors in each node are independent and localised. The new link latency is:

$$T'_L = (T_L + T_q) \times (1 + \rho). \tag{3}$$

This new T'_L can be used in a more accurate approximation of the 1-to-all communication performance as:

$$T_{1-to-all} = \lceil d/p \rceil \times (T'_L + T_a) + (\hat{k} - 1) \times T'_L + T_a \tag{4}$$

4   Results

Our design is implemented within the CusComNet [4] framework on Xilinx Virtex-5 LX330T FPGAs. The throughput and latency of broadcast transmissions are measured and compared to CusComNet's unicast transmissions to multiple destinations. The InfiniBand cable line speed is set to 2Gbps due to observed instabilities above this value. Packet buffer sizes are set to 64 packets, each packet having a payload of 64 bytes. The 16-node cluster translates to address widths of 4 bits. The maximum number of packet identifiers is set to 8192 to ensure no two en-route packets will have the same identifier.

Our experiments are not designed to show the benefit of broadcast over multiple unicasts, but instead seek to determine the efficiency of the broadcast protocol, and whether the customisations have any detrimental effect.

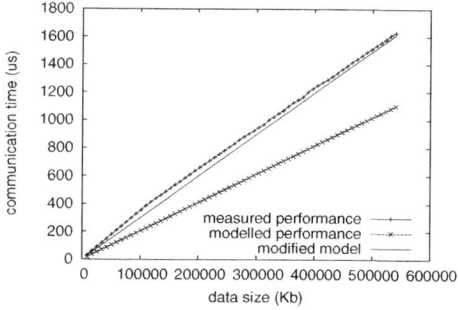

Fig. 3. Comparing measured and estimated performance in a 4-node network

Based on the model from Section 3, we measure the performance of 1-to-all broadcasting in a 4-node network comparing the communication times for various data sizes. $\hat{k}$ is set to 2 according to the network topology. The other platform specific parameters set to their typical values. Figure 3 compares the model to the observed results. The divergence may be due to the difference between the estimated T'_L and the actual link transmission time. Adding $0.5\mu s$ overhead to the T_L value, shown by the smooth line, matches the measured performance. We thus conclude, the model accurately represents of the system.

Figure 4(a) shows our implementation's improvement over multiple unicasts increases with data size, plateauing at around a 53% reduction in transmission time. As data sizes increase, packet buffers saturate and we can better compare the routing and packet handling of broadcast and unicast. Improvements are due to two factors: reduced buffer occupancy due to de-duplication of packets; and the use of the cascading packet routing algorithm. The latter provides benefit as the shortest path may not be the fastest due to packet congestion.

The question still remains as to whether these improvements are due to the efficient operation of the design or the inherent improvement of broadcast over multiple unicasts. Figure 4(b) shows the percentage speedup of our broadcast

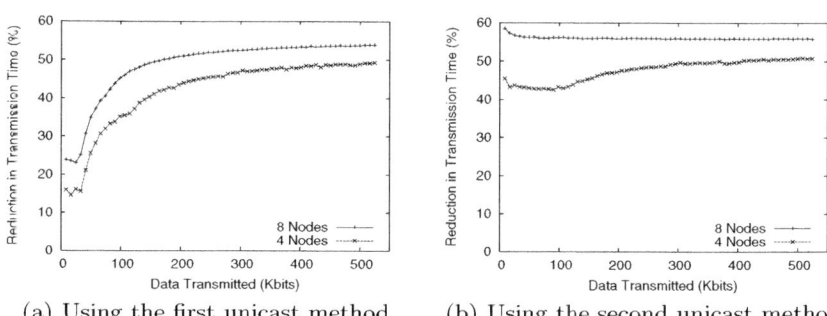

(a) Using the first unicast method   (b) Using the second unicast method

Fig. 4. Reduction in transmission time for broadcasting when implemented within CusComNet

implementation over a second unicast methodology, giving a similar result to Figure 4(a): about a $50 - 55\%$ speedup. The difference in speedup is most likely due to the first methodology's ability to utilise multiple output ports, thereby performing some operations in parallel and making use of additional buffer space.

When applied to different packet buffer depths in a 4-node cluster, Figure 5 shows our broadcast protocol's benefit is reduced when the packet buffers are not saturated. With larger data volumes, broadcast's reduction in total time versus multiple unicasts converges to around 50%. These results show our implementation does not have a negative impact on communication performance, and improves overall transmission times by $50 - 55\%$ for large data volumes.

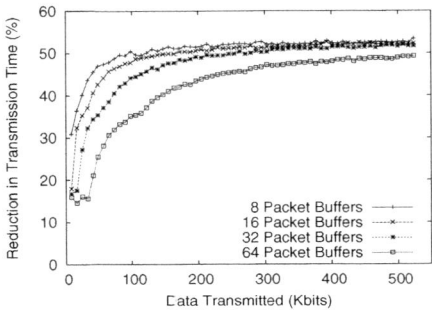

Fig. 5. Reduction in transmission time for broadcasting when using packet buffers of different sizes; using the first unicast methodology

5 Conclusion

This paper presents our customisable broadcasting framework. We outline the broadcast operation and develop a model to analyse its performance. Experiments show our broadcast implementation achieves up to a 55% reduction in transmission time when implemented within the CusComNet framework. We show our work benefits communications regardless of cluster size or packet buffer depths. We demonstrate a cascading broadcast routing algorithm that transmits data along all possible paths, and can therefore work with any network topology.

Acknowledgements. The support of Imperial College London Research Excellence Award, UK Engineering and Physical Sciences Research Council, Alpha Data, Maxeler, nVidia and Xilinx is gratefully acknowledged. The research leading to these results has received funding from the European Union Seventh Framework Programme under grant agreement number 248976 and 257906.

References

1. InfiniBand architecture specification release 1.2.1. White Paper (2010)
2. TOP 500 supercomputer sites (2010), http://www.top500.org/lists/2011/06
3. Baxter, R., et al.: Maxwell - a 64 FPGA supercomputer. In: Proc. Conference on Adaptive Hardware and Systems (AHS), pp. 287–294 (2007)

4. Denholm, S., Tsoi, K.H., Pietzuch, P., Luk, W.: CusComNet: A customisable network for reconfigurable heterogeneous clusters. In: Proc. IEEE Int. Conf. on Application-specific Systems, Architectures and Processors, ASAP (2011)
5. Lindtjrn, O., Clapp, R.G., Pell, O., Mencer, O., Flynn, M.J.: Surviving the end of scaling of traditional micro processors in HPC. IEEE HOT CHIPS 22 (2010)
6. Sass, R., et al.: Reconfigurable computing cluster (RCC) project: Investigating the feasibility of FPGA-based petascale computing. In: Proc. IEEE Symposium on Field-Programmable Custom Computing Machines (FCCM), pp. 127–140 (2007)

Performance Analysis of Reconfigurable Processors Using MVA Analysis

Ehsan Zadkhosh, Sepide Fatahi, and Mahmood Ahmadi

Department of Computer Engineering, Faculty of Engineering,
University of Razi, Kermanshah, Iran
{e.zadkhosh,m.ahmadi}@razi.ac.ir, fattahi.sepide@yahoo.com

Abstract. Collaboration of Reconfigurable processing elements in Grid Computing (CRGC) promises to provide both flexibility and performance to process computationally intensive tasks found in large applications. Reconfigurable computing provides much more flexibility than Application-Specific Integrated Circuits (ASICs) and much more performance than General-Purpose Processors (GPPs). GPPs, reconfigurable elements (RE) and hybrid (integration of GPPs and REs) elements are the main processing elements in the CRGC. In this paper, we propose closed queuing models for grid networks that incorporate the following processing elements: a GPP, a reconfigurable element (RE), and a hybrid element (combining a GPP with an RE). We examine two different models, one with feedback the other one without feedback. The performance metrics are the average response time and throughput. The proposed models are validated by take average response time and throughput of these models and simulation using OMNeTPP. Mean Value Analysis (MVA) is used to analytically compute the performance measures for these models. The comparison of the experimental (simulation) and analytical results suggest that the total average error for all the models with feedback and without feedback is less than 1.4% and 1.8%, respectively.

Keywords: Reconfigurable computing, queuing model, grid networks, mean value analysis (MVA).

1 Introduction

Reconfigurable computing has proven to be promising technology to increase the performance of certain algorithms in scientific and engineering applications in recent years. Any application of iterative nature such as image processing, digital signal processing, bioinformatics, cryptography and software defined radio etc; can be mapped on an FPGA by programming it with Hardware Descriptive Languages (HDLs). Performance modeling is a valuable tool to determine the performance and operating measures of a real world system. One of the significant analysis methods is the queuing modeling where a system can be viewed as a network of queues. A closed queuing network is one in which the flow of customers does not enter from outside, but is fixed within the network and keeps moving within the network. Items are served with a first-come-first-served (FCFS) discipline. Closed queuing networks are often more useful than their open counterparts because the infinite customer population assumption that is implicit

O.C.S. Choy et al. (Eds.): ARC 2012, LNCS 7199, pp. 342–349, 2012.

in open queuing networks is unrealistic. An appropriate queuing model for REs along with GPPs is essential for analytical performance modeling of an application in a computing grid. Traditionally, the grids utilize GPPs as their main processing elements. Because of incorporation of the REs in the grid network, there is need for appropriate models for these new processing elements to investigate the possibility of their utilization for compute intensive kernels of the grid applications. It is shown that mean queue sizes, mean waiting time, and throughputs in closed queuing networks can be computed recursively with MVA [8]. Apart from analytical modeling techniques, another widely used methodology to simulate it on various system configurations. The results of simulations can help in designing a system by saving a significant amount of time and resources. Simulation tools, therefore, must be sought to investigate the utilization of REs in grid networks. However, there is no specific simulation tool to study the behavior of REs in a grid network. All the traditional grid simulators do not include REs as grid resources. In this paper, we focus on these issues and provide the following: First a proposal of closed queuing models (with and without feedback) for the RE and hybrid processing elements in the grid network will be discussed. After that, we validated the proposed models as part of a large network and also study the performance of the network in terms of average response time and throughput of the processing elements in the grid using a multimedia processing application in our simulations. The remainder of the paper is organized as follows: Section 2 presents the related research in this area. In section 3 the proposed models for processing elements are presented. In Section 4, the performance analysis and simulation results of our queuing models are presented and compared. Finally, the conclusion and future work are provided in Section 5.

2   Related Work

In this section, we discuss some related work in the literature for the modeling and simulation of reconfigurable processors. In [6], an analytical model was proposed for partially reconfigurable processors using the queuing theory. The results show that the main limitation of such a system is the reconfiguration time. The model, however, does not take into account the modeling of memory modules which must be considered in real scenarios. In [9], an analytical performance model for a network of shared, heterogeneous nodes each containing a reconfigurable hardware was discussed and validated. In [11], The Collaboration of REs in Grid Computing (CRGC) by extending gridsim simulator for a general class of applications was proposed and simulated. In our previous work [7], we proposed an open queueing model using Jackson theorem for the GPP, RE and hybrid processing elements. In this paper, we propose theoretical queuing models of GPP, RE, and hybrid processors on a node level for grids using the closed queueing models and MVA analysis. Furthermore, we propose a simulation framework for these queuing models using OMNeTPP simulator.

3   Proposed Models for Processing Elements

In this section, we first introduce the GPP model with and without feedback. Subsequently, we describe our proposed queuing models for reconfigurable and hybrid processing elements. We assume that these processing elements are nodes of a large grid network and they can process submitted tasks according to their service rates. There is a constant population of n customers in the network. All customers in the networks have the same service demand distribution.

3.1   GPP Queuing Models

A closed queuing network for a general-purpose processor (GPP) without feedback is depicted in the Figure 1(b)(do not consider the dashed line and its label). This network consists of a Central Processing Unit (CPU) and a memory module, along with corresponding queue and single server [4]. μ_{GPP} and μ_m represent the service rates of CPU and memory module, respectively. The value of customer streams through different queues is λ. As no tasks leaves this network and all the tasks circulated in the same circuit we can write:

$$\lambda_{GPP} = \lambda_m = \lambda \tag{1}$$

Using MVA since both of the queues are identical we can drop the i index in the equations (1), (2) and (3). Starting from the initial value $N[0] = 0$, $M = 2$ (the number of queues) and k (the number of costumers) can vary from 1 to n. Therefore we have:

$$T[K] = (1 + N[K - 1])\frac{1}{\mu} \tag{2}$$

$$N[K] = \frac{K}{2} \tag{3}$$

$$\psi[K] = \frac{N[K]}{T[K]} \tag{4}$$

The probability of needing memory after being processed in CPU has been taken p_2 and equations (1), (2) and (3) should be used to compute the performance parameters. Figure 1(b)(with dashed line and its label), shows a closed queuing network with feedback if λ_D changed to $p_2.\lambda_D$.

3.2   Proposed Models for Reconfigurable Processing Elements

The proposed model without feedback for an RE is depicted in Figure 1(a)(do not consider the dashed line, its label, p_2s and $(1-p_2)$s. The reconfiguration module accepts the configuration tasks (bit-streams) and acts accordingly with a service rate μ_r, whereas the reconfigurable processor executes the incoming tasks with service rate μ_{RE}. Generally, an RE is configured to carry out parallel processing for multiple tasks and, therefore, can access multiple memory modules for input data. Consequently, the RE model should support n sub-modules of memory. Hence the proposed model supports n such memory sub-modules with service rate μ_{mi} ; i = 1,..., m, such that the sum of the service rates of these memory sub-modules is equal to the service rate of the reconfigurable processor, μ_{RE}. Based on our assumption that there are N tasks in the network and every N tasks need one reconfiguration and with respect to the values of customer streams through different queues (λ_D) the arrival rate of reconfigurable processor and reconfiguration module can be calculated as follow:

$$\lambda_{RE} = \left(\frac{N-1}{N}\right)\lambda_D \quad \lambda_r = \left(\frac{1}{N}\right)\lambda_D \tag{5}$$

Because of the fact that all the memory modules are considering the same, the λ_ms are equal to:

$$\lambda_{mi} = \frac{\lambda_D}{m}; i = 1, ..., m \qquad (6)$$

As mentioned in GPP, the model without feedback can be considered unrealistic. Because of this, the feedback model of RE have been proposed. The feedback with probability of $(1 - p_2)$ will just change the data stream of memories (λ_m) and the other data streams will remain unchanged as depicted in Figure 1(a) (the dashed line, its label, p_2s and $(1 - p_2)$s should be considered). The equations 1, 2 and 3 can be used for the computation of the performance parameters.

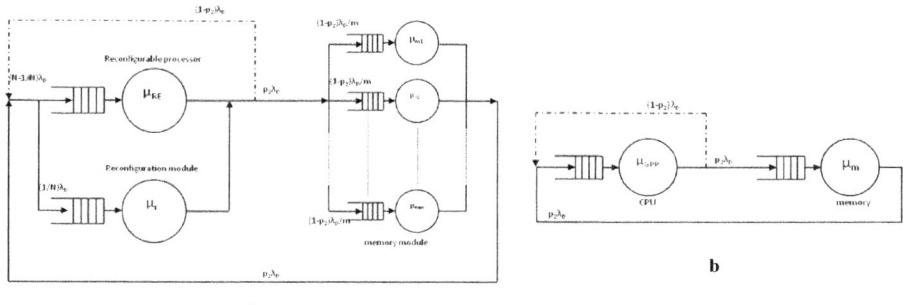

Fig. 1. (a)Closed queuing model with/without feedback for RE (b)Closed queuing model with/without feedback for a GPP

3.3 Proposed Model for a Hybrid Processing Element

The proposed model for a hybrid processing element without feedback, comprising GPP and RE is shown, on the module level, in Figure 2(do not consider dashed lines, their labels, p_2s and $(1 - p_2)$s). The feedback model for hybrid processing elements is depicted in Figure 2(the dashed lines, their labels, p_2s and $(1 - p_2)$s should be considered). As it can be noticed , some changes have happened in data streams in comparison to the model without feedback. Here the tasks after being processed in CPU and reconfigurable processor will back to the queue of using beginning point to get processed by CPU, reconfigurable processor and reconfiguration module. Where p_1 is the probability of the tasks for GPP then the arrival rate can be computed as follows:

$$\lambda_{CPU} = \lambda_m = p_1\lambda_D \quad \lambda_{RE} = (1 - p_1)\left(\frac{N - 1}{N}\lambda_D\right) \quad \lambda_r = (1 - p_1)\frac{\lambda_D}{N} \qquad (7)$$

The equations for this network are a combination of MVA equations for RE and GPP, with some differences.

4   Performance Evaluation and Experimental Results

The proposed models in Section 3 were validated by computing the average response time results, mean number of customers in each queue and throughput of the network,

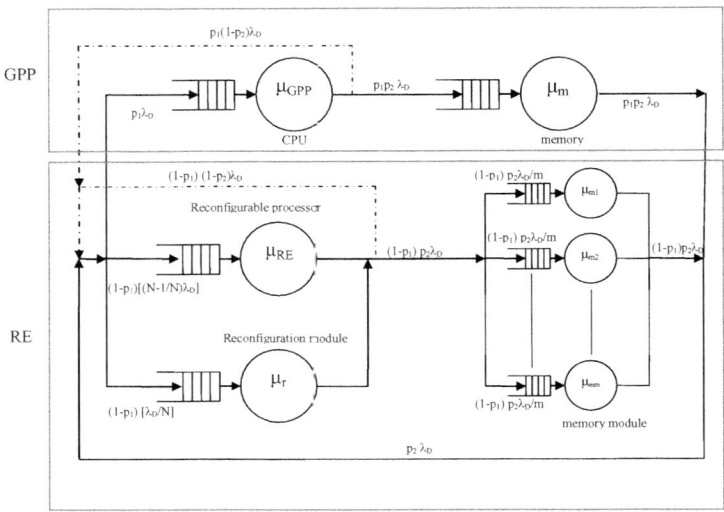

Fig. 2. Closed queuing model with/without feedback for hybrid processing element

using Maple v.14 and C programming language. Because of the recursion in MVA the maple results were so time consuming while the written C program for MVA was extremely fast. The simulation parameters used in our experiments are derived from the results presented in [12] for a large scale multimedia application with compute intensive kernels executed on the reconfigurable element and are provided in the Table 1. The service rate of GPP (μ_{GPP}) varies between 1 and 80, whereas the speedup of RE is taken as 5 as reported in [10]. Therefore, the service rate of RE was set to $5\mu_{GPP}$. Since the multimedia application in [10] uses 4 independent memory modules accessed in parallel, therefore the number of memory modules in RE is set to 4. In our experiments that for a fix number of customers (N), one reconfiguration is needed. Similarly, Table 1 also provides the details of different probability values used in both analysis and simulation models based on [3] and [10].

Table 1. The specification of the simulation environment

Specification	Value	Specification	Value
Service rate of GPP (μ_{GPP})	{1,...,80}	Speedup of RE	5
Service rate of RE (μ_{RE})	5 x μ_{GPP}	GPP memory bandwidth (μ_m)	μ_{GPP}
RE memory bandwidth (μ_{m_i})	μ_{RE}	Number of memory modules in RE	4
Service rate for reconfiguration (μ_r)	10	p_1 (Hybrid Element model only)	0.1
p_2 (in GPP, RE and Hybrid Element models)	0.6		

4.1   Result Discussion

We run our simulation experiment for different number of tasks (N). The simulations were performed for 200, 400, 600, 800 and 1000 tasks for each model. The output results were collected and analysed by using the output VEC files in OMNeTPP. The overall simulation response times for the all models were averaged out for the total number of tasks in each experiment, to compute average response time. The average response time of GPP with and without feedback computed analytically along with the results determined through simulation are depicted in Figures 3 (a) and 4 (a), respectively. Similarly, Figures 3 (b), 4 (b) and 3(c), 4(c) depict the same results for that of RE and hybrid element, respectively. From Figure 3, we can observe that the response time for the RE and hybrid processing elements in model without feedback is less than response time of the GPP. In addition, the difference of response time between RE and hybrid processing elements can be neglected. This is because the most part of the tasks are forwarded to the RE processing element as a individual part of hybrid processing element. Furthermore, we can observe that the simulation results and analytical results follow each other. The conditions in Figure 4 is similar to Figure 3. As we have seen the response time for the RE and hybrid processing elements in the model with feedback is less than the GPP. From Figures 3 and 4, we can observe that the behaviour of the all processing elements (GPP, RE, and hybrid) in the model with feedback and the model without feedback is similar. And as we expected, the throughput of RE and hybrid processing elements are about 5 times more than GPP. The results in Figures 5 (a) and (b) suggest that total average error for GPP, RE, and hybrid models without feedback for all task numbers is 1.16%, 2.02%, and 2.24%, respectively. Similarly the average error for GPP, RE, and hybrid models with feedback for all task numbers according to Figures 5 (a), and (b) is 0.69%, 1.59% and 1.9%, respectively. These percentage values of error were calculated by dividing total sum of error rates for each model by the respective task numbers. Finally, the total average error among the analysis and simulation results

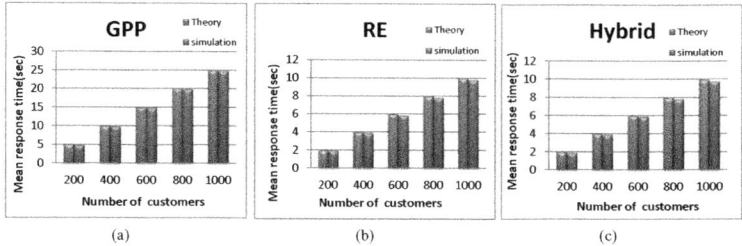

Fig. 3. Response time of MVA and simulation using no-feedback queuing models. (a) GPP (b) RE (c) Hybrid.

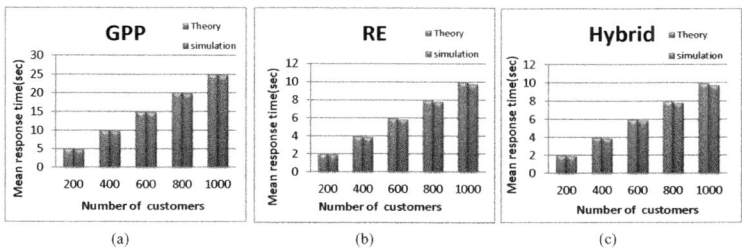

Fig. 4. Response of MVA and simulation using feedback queuing models. (a) GPP (b) RE (c) Hybrid.

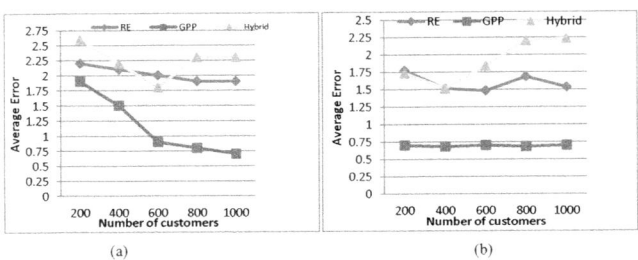

(a)   (b)

Fig. 5. (a) Average error (%) of no-feedback queuing models (GPP, RE, and hybrid). (b) Average error (%) of feedback queuing models (GPP, RE, and hybrid).

for all without feedback models was calculated as 1.8% and for feedback models it was 1.39%. The simulation results for average response time for all three models are in accordance with the average response time results computed analytically within a range of less than 3% relative error. This validates our proposed models for GPP, RE, and hybrid processing elements. The proposed models can be used to investigate the effect of reconfiguration time, number of reconfigurations of RE, and speedup factor on the overall response time of a grid system.

5   Conclusion

In this paper, we proposed closed queuing models using MVA analysis for the reconfigurable and hybrid processing elements in a grid network. The proposed models were validated using analytical and simulation results by taking average response time and throughput as validation metrics for these models. Based on the simulation and analytical results, the response time and throughput of the RE and hybrid processing elements to compared with GPP are improved. The models with feedback for the processing elements generated less error in comparison to the models without feedback. This is because, the models with feedback are more realistic. The simulation results suggest that the total average error for these models is less than 3%. The proposed models can be useful in implementing the real grid networks with RE (or hybrid element) as one of the high-performance processing elements. In our future work, we investigate the role of processing elements (type, numbers) and their network processing overhead in a grid system.

References

[1] Baldwin, R.O., Davis, N.J., Midkiff, S.F., Kobza, J.E.: Queueing Network Analysis: Concepts, Terminology, and Methods. Journal of Systems and Software 66(2), 99–117 (2003)
[2] Bhaskar, V.: A Closed Queuing Network Model with Multiple Servers for Multi-threaded Architecture. Computer Communication 31, 3078–3089 (2008)
[3] Bhaskar, V., Adjallah, K.H.: A Hybrid Open Queuing Network Model Approach for Multi-threaded Dataflow Architecture. Computer Communication 31(17), 4098–4106 (2008)
[4] Harrison, P.G., Patel, N.M.: Performance Modelling of Communication Networks and Computer Architectures. Addison-Wesley Longman Publishing Co., Inc. (1992)

[5] Hock, C., Hee, S.B.: Queueing Modelling Fundamentals with Applications in Communication Networks. John Wiley & Sons (2008)

[6] Lotfifar, F., Shahhoseini, H.S.: Performance Modeling of Partially Reconfigurable Computing Systems. In: Proceedings of the 2008 IEEE/ACS International Conference Computer Systems and Applications, pp. 94–99 (2008)

[7] Nadeem, M.F., Ahmadi, M., Nadeem, M., Wong, S.: Modeling and Simulation of Reconfigurable Processors in Grid Networks. In: International Conference on ReConFigurable Computing and FPGAs, ReConFig 2010, pp. 226–231 (December 2010)

[8] Reiser, M., Lavenberg, S.S.: Mean-value analysis of closed multichain queuing networks. Journal ACM 27 (April 1980)

[9] Smith, M., Peterson, G.D.: Parallel Application Performance on Shared High Performance Reconfigurable Computing resources. Performance Evaluation 60(1-4), 107–125 (2005)

[10] Tahir, M.A., Bouridane, A., Kurugollu, F., Amira, A.: Accelerating the Computation of GLCM and Haralick Texture Features on Reconfigurable Hardware. In: Proceedings of 5th International Conference on Image Processing, pp. 2857–2860 (2004)

[11] Wong, S., Ahmadi, M.: Reconfigurable Architectures in Collaborative Grid Computing: An Approach. In: Proceedings of the 2nd International Conference on Networks for Grid Applications, GridNets 2008 (2008)

PDPR: Fine-Grained Placement for Dynamic Partially Reconfigurable FPGAs[*]

Ruining He[1], Guoqiang Liang[1], Yuchun Ma[1], Yu Wang[2], and Jinian Bian[1]

[1] Dept. of Computer Science and Technology, Tsinghua University, Beijing, China
{myc,bianjn}@tsinghua.edu.cn
[2] Electronic Engineering Department, Tsinghua University, Beijing, China

Abstract. Dynamic Partial Reconfiguration (DPR) optimizes conventional FPGA application by providing additional benefits. However, considering the arbitrariness during manual floorplan and the limitation of local search when placement, it must be effective and promising if we combine the two stages to build a global optimization structure. In this paper, a novel thought for DPR FPGAs (PDPR) is proposed which tries to offer a one-stop floorplan and placement service. Experimental results show our approach can improve 32.8% on total wire length, 48.5% on reconfiguration cost, and 36.9% on congestion.

Keywords: Dynamic Partial Reconfiguration, Placement, frame.

1 Introduction

Dynamic Partially Reconfigurable (DPR) methodology switches system functionalities on-line by replacing only certain system components of the reconfigurable hardware. This methodology enhances traditional FPGA applications by reducing size, power, weight, and cost [1]. Though modern technology such as Xilinx' Virtex series in the field of FPGA has made DPR available for quite some time, designers are still suffering a great deal from current design methodologies.

Commonly used PR designs mainly follow Xilinx's Early-Access (EA) PR design flow, which requires that PR regions be manually defined in terms of shape, size, and physical location. This task is challenging since the designer is required of extensive PR design flow knowledge as well as low-level architectural details of the device. The manually trial-and-error process is not feasible since the design space grows exponentially with the number of PR regions. Additionally, the state-of-the-art design flow of module-based DPR systems optimizes the placement of each PR module separately. As recommended in Xilinx PR flow [1], the most demanding PR modules of each PR region should be chosen to finish the premier placement and routing with static logic. Then the design of static logic will be "invariable" for the other PR modules. After the architecture of the Static Logic and the pin locations of each PR region are fixed, the placement and routing of those remaining PR modules are implemented one after

---

[*] This work was supported in part by NSFC 61076035, 60876030 and 61106030 and National Science and Technology Major Project, 2010ZX01030-001-001-04.

O.C.S. Choy et al. (Eds.): ARC 2012, LNCS 7199, pp. 350–356, 2012.

another within their corresponding PR regions. Actually, the separated design process ignores the competitive relation between PR modules and the fixed static logic may not be fit for all the other PR modules. Therefore, the quality of the overall design cannot be guaranteed and the design flow may even fall flat in some cases.

Therefore, we integrated the coarse-grained layout optimization of PR regions with fine-grained placement inside PR regions which optimizes all PR modules simultaneously. Our approach makes the first attempt to combine the floorplan and placement of PR designs in this field and has the potential of achieving a thorough optimization. In this paper, the key contributions include:

- **Automatic layout optimization of Partial Reconfiguration regions.** Using our approach, PR regions can be determined and optimized automatically in terms of size, shape, and location.
- **Simultaneous optimization of Static Logic and all the Partial Reconfiguration modules.** Different from the sequential design used by traditional flow, static logic is no longer designed just for a specific group of PR modules but for the design as a whole. More preferable solutions can be achieved since we abandoned the local search.
- **Beneficial performance metrics for reconfiguration designs.** Not only are performance metrics such as wirelength, delay and congestion modeled for reconfiguration designs, but also reconfiguration cost and frame-based reconfiguration constraints are considered to fit practical needs.

Additionally, since layout solutions of static logic and PR modules can be exported separately, our approach can be merged into normal DPR design flow seamlessly, providing designers with an automatic tool to obtain better solutions.

2   Related Work

Some relevant work has been done focusing on floorplanning techniques for reconfigurable system designs. Early studies [2-5] formulated the floorplanning for DPR as a three-dimensional template placement problem in which PR modules are modeled as idealized fixed-size blocks and PR regions are assumed to be homogeneous areas. These assumptions make the approach hard to be applied in practical applications. Singhal and Bozorgzadeh [9] proposed a multi-layer floorplanner which merges the floorplanning of multiple designs and maximizes the overlap of their common components to achieve benefit from reuse. Banerjee, Sangtani, et al. [14] introduced a global floorplan generation method to obtain shared positions for common modules across sub-task instances. Yousuf et al. [8] introduced DAPR, a PR design flow which automates PR design's intricate design process. There are also many other studies [10-13]. However, due to the insulated placement of DPR designs, none of previous work can handle the simultaneous placement for both static logic and various PR modules in common regions.

The remainder of this paper is structured as follows. Section 3 formulates the problem for partially reconfigurable FPGA designs. Section 4 describes the overall optimization approach. The experimental results on benchmarks are given in section 5 and we conclude our current work and discuss future work in section 6.

3   Problem Formulation

In this paper, the target architecture for DPR is two-dimensional and fine-grained heterogeneous FPGA. The placement problem for reconfigurable FPGAs can be described as follows:

- Given a target FPGA architecture and its specific resource layout.
- Given a set of PR regions $PR = \{PR_1, PR_2, \ldots, PR_n\}$.
- Given a group of PR modules for each PR region. $M_i = \{m_{i,1}, m_{i,2}, \ldots, m_{i,c_i}\}$, $i \in [1, n]$. Each PR module requires a set of different computation resources.
- Given the Static Logic represented as M_s.
- Given the connection between fine-grained components in the form of netlist.

The objective of our optimization is: $Min\ \alpha^*WL + \beta^*TD + \gamma^*RC + \mu^* Cong$

WL represents wirelength estimation, TD means timing delay estimation of the critical path, RC denotes the estimation of reconfiguration cost, and $Cong$ indicates congestion estimation. $\alpha, \beta,\ \gamma$ and μ are coefficients to balance these objectives.

During the optimization process, several constraints should be considered:

- *Resource constraint*: Each PR region PR_i must satisfy the maximum resource requirement of every PR module $m_{i,j}$ in $M_i, i \in [1, n]$.
- *Reconfiguration constraint*: No frame sharing among PR regions is allowed, even if they hold its different pieces.
- *Overlap & No-overlap*: Different from traditional placement, components from different PR modules of a same module group are allowed to overlap with each other in this problem due to the time-division multiplexing of PR regions. But neither overlap between PR regions and Static Logic nor overlap between components from a same PR module is permitted.

4   Simulated Annealing Algorithm Framework

In this section, we present the Simulated Annealing framework of our approach. Based on VPR 5.0.2 [13], we revolutionize it to support the simultaneous floorplan and placement of DPR design. With multiple PR modules and PR regions, we need additional operations to generate new solutions in the SA-based exploration. Random moves during SA process can be classified into the following types:

- *Reshape of a PR region*: PR regions can be reshaped according to a given probability with constraints considered.
- *Transfer of a PR region*: PR regions can be moved on FPGA fabric according to a given probability with constraints considered.
- *Swap within a PR region*: Choose two grids of the same resource type in a PR region PR_i and choose a PR module $m_{i,k}$ in this region. And then we exchange the allocation of these two grids in $m_{i,k}$.
- *Swap within static logic*: Pair-wise exchange between grids in static logic can be performed in a similar way to VPR [10]. We also limit the swap region to the range [1, *maximum FPGA dimension*] and we update it according to equation (1).

$$range_{sl}^{new} = range_{sl}^{old} * (1 - 0.44 + R_{accept}^{old})$$ (1)

4.1 Cost Models

To achieve our optimization objective, a two-stage simulated annealing process is adopted. To obtain faster convergence in the first stage, three cost components including wirelength cost bb_cost_{DPR}, critical path delay cost td_cost, and reconfiguration delay cost rc_cost are modeled. In the second stage, we incorporate *non-linear congestion* cost nc_cost into our evaluation.

Reconfiguration Cost Model. Reconfiguration efficiency is one of the major issues deserving serious consideration when designing DPR systems. According to K. Papadimitriou et al. [7], the total reconfiguration time can be calculated by

$$RT = fs \times (fn + 1) \times 3.66 \times 10^{-3} ms \qquad (2)$$

where fs means the size of reconfigurable frame measured in bytes, while fn indicates the number of frames to be reconfigured in DPR design. In our model, we assign fs to be 164 bytes because we take the Virtex-4 as a case study.

Wirelength and Delay Model. In our model, for each PR region, we take the average value of wire length estimations of all PR modules in it as its wirelength estimation. And then we can get the total wirelength estimation bb_cost_{DPR} for the whole design.

$$bb\_cost_{pr}^{\ i} = (\textstyle\sum_{k=1}^{ci} bb\_cost_{pm}^{k})/c_i \qquad (3)$$

$$bb\_cost_{DPR} = bb\_cost_{SL} + \textstyle\sum_{i=1}^{n} bb\_cost_{pr}^{\ i} \qquad (4)$$

$bb\_cost_{pm}^{\ k}$ means the sum of the bounding box costs [10] of PR module $m_{i,k}$, and bb_cost_{SL} represents the wirelength estimation of static logic.

For critical path delay estimation, we estimate the critical path by the worst case of all the configurations of the DPR system. The timing cost is evaluated by

$$td\_cost = td_{SL} + \textstyle\sum_{i=1}^{n} max_{k=1}^{ci} td\_m_{i,k} \qquad (5)$$

where td_{SL} is the longest path delay within static logic and $td\_m_{i,k}$ is the longest path delay within PR module $m_{i,k}$ in PR region PR_i.

Congestion Relaxation. Based on the *non-linear congestion* model implemented by VPR 5.0.2 [13], congestion are classified into two types: Occ_{SL} caused by the routes of static logic and $Occ_{PR}^{i,k}$ caused by the interconnects between components in PR module $m_{i,k}$. The whole occupation value is calculated by

$$occupation_{m,n} = Occ_{SL} + \textstyle\sum_{i=1}^{n} max_{k=1}^{ci} Occ_{PR}^{i,k} \qquad (6)$$

Since placement solution generated in the early period of the SA process is far away from the final result, we postpone this task until the second stage of our algorithm to improve the congestion index.

4.2 Optimization of PR Region

Based on the amount all kinds of its required resources, we calculate the size of each PR region $Area_{pr}$ and then we generate the initial floorplan randomly. During the SA process, each PR region can be reshaped and transferred according to assigned probabilities.

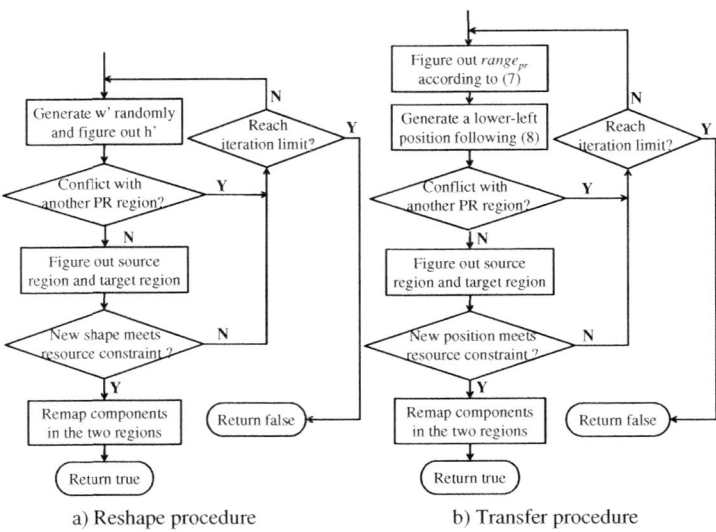

Fig. 1. Layout optimization procedure for PR regions

Reshape of PR Regions. For each PR region, we keep the coordinate of its lower left corner and we guarantee $height = \lceil Area_{pr}/width \rceil$ during the reshape process. When changing a PR region's shape, we just remap components from regions affected by this reshape. Fig.1 a) describes the detailed reshape process.

Transfer of PR regions. Taking the PR modules in a PR region as a cluster, the region can be transferred on the FPGA fabric. To make the moves to be local, we define a control parameter $range_{pr}$. Initially, $range_{pr}$ is set to be the size of the entire chip divided by the average area of PR regions. The value of $range_{pr}$ is then updated according to the following rule:

$$range_{pr} = range_{pr} * (0.56 + R_{accept}^{old}) \tag{7}$$

R_{accept}^{old} represents the fraction of attempted moves which were accepted in the previous Markov chain in the SA process. When transferring a PR region (a, b, w, h), we maintain its shape and just change the lower left coordinate to (a', b'), during which the following constraint must be satisfied:

$$|a' - a| \le range_{pr}, \ |b' - b| \le range_{pr} \tag{8}$$

Fig.1 b) shows the detailed process.

5 Experiments

To test our approach, basic VPR benchmarks are modified to construct PR modules. In our settings, we choose around 25%~40% components as reconfigurable blocks to compose several PR modules in each test case, and then these PR modules are grouped into PR regions. Each PR module consists of a set of components. During the construction, we try to follow the modular design and avoid connections between PR modules to the best of our ability. The reconfiguration module information is listed in Table 1. Taking *tseng* for instance, there are 1221 components and 1099 nets in total. We choose 315 components to construct 8 (i.e. 3+2+3) PR modules. VPR framework supports different FPGA architecture. In this paper, we simulate the structure of Xilinx Virtex-4.

Table 1. Reconfigurable test cases

Test cases	#Total components	#nets	# PR	# PM in each PR	#Total components in PM
tseng	1221	1099	3	[3,2,3]	315
alu4	1544	1536	4	[3,2,2,3]	640
disp	1796	1599	4	[3,2,3,4]	605
seq	1826	1791	3	[3,2,4]	550
s298	1941	1935	4	[3,3,4,4]	1000
elliptic	3849	3735	4	[4,2,3,5]	980
ex1010	4618	4608	5	[4,3,3,2,3]	1305

In this experiment, coefficients α, β, γ and μ in our cost function are assigned to the same value 1/4 to optimize four objectives equally. Experimental results of our approach and the simulated sequential process employed by industrial field are shown in Table 2. "*Cong*" represents congestion estimation and "*RC*" indicates reconfiguration cost. These results explain that with approximate 33% extra runtime, our approach reduces total wirelength by 32.8%, optimizes reconfiguration cost by 48.5%, and improves congestion situation by 36.9%.

Table 2. The Effects of Our Simultaneous Optimization Approach

Test case	Sequential Process					Our approach				
	WL	Delay	Cong	RC(e-6)	time(s)	WL	Delay	Cong	RC(e-6)	time(s)
tseng	32962	4.8172	6.353	43.217	43.27	21992	3.8675	2.9608	27.011	49.11
alu4	46687	8.1414	9.545	97.028	55.43	36413	8.9341	4.6616	73.829	77.17
dsip	51435	8.2646	21.198	175.270	82.01	49629	8.3706	14.7612	55.222	118.62
seq	64929	9.4725	14.218	90.072	74.86	40839	6.8788	5.01368	45.618	99.24
s298	40232	8.9093	3.849	112.245	77.86	26266	8.6388	4.81732	72.029	112.80
elliptic	231706	32.840	16.512	330.996	276.53	115893	21.8412	8.46771	82.233	356.11
ex1010	278818	39.955	18.388	247.881	378.65	140751	31.5018	11.8476	124.250	502.23
avg	1	1	1	1	1	0.6712	0.8661	0.6303	0.5141	1.3375

6 Conclusions and Future Work

Though DPR FPGAs have shown the potential to provide low cost and high performance designs, extensive manual floorplanning and inefficient placement due to the local search are still constraining the application of DPR technology. In this paper, a new placement approach is proposed which optimizes the layout of PR regions and designs all PR modules simultaneously. The proposed method not only makes the first attempt to combine floorplan and placement of DPR design in this field to build a global optimization structure, but also tries to provide an automatic tool which has the potential of lightening DPR designers' burdens in their daily work. The experimental results, which are based on a simulated Xilinx Virtex-4 implementation, show that our approach can improve the wirelength metric by 32.8%, reduce congestion by 36.9%, and optimize reconfiguration cost by 48.5%. Since DPR designs involve many other design issues such as partition pin allocation, routing and online task scheduling, etc., we will take into account these factors to make our algorithm more practical in our future work. Additionally, our approach will be applied on some practical design cases to further study its effects.

References

[1] Xilinx: Partial Reconfiguration User Guide (March 1, 2011)
[2] Bazargan, K., Kastner, R., et al.: Fast Template Placement for Reconfigurable Computing Systems. Presented at IEEE Design & Test of Computers, pp. 68–83 (2000)
[3] Ahmadinia, A., Teich, J.: Speeding up Online Placement for XILINX FPGAs by Reducing Configuration Overhead. In: Proc. VLSI-SOC, pp. 118–122 (2003)
[4] Walder, H., Steiger, C., et al.: Fast Online Task Placement on FPGAs: Free Space Partitioning and 2D-Hashing. In: Proc. IPDPS (2003)
[5] Ahmadinia, A., Bobda, C., et al.: A New Approach for On-line Placement on Reconfigurable Devices. In: Proc. IPDPS, pp. 134–140 (2004)
[6] Cheng, L., Wong, M.D.F.: Floorplan Design for Multi-Million Gate FPGAs. In: ICCAD, pp. 292–299 (2004)
[7] Papadimitriou, K., Dollas, A., et al.: Performance of Partial Reconfiguration in FPGA Systems: A Survey and a Cost Model. ACM Transactions on Reconfigurable Technology and Systems 4(4) (2011)
[8] Yousuf, S., Gordon-Ross, A.: DAPR: Design Automation for Partially Reconfigurable FPGAs. In: Proc. ERSA, pp. 97–103 (2010)
[9] Singhal, L., Bozorgzadeh, E.: Multi-layer Floorplanning on a Sequence of Reconfigurable Designs. In: FPL, pp. 1–8 (2006)
[10] Betz, V., Rose, J.: VPR: A New Packing, Placement and Routing Tool for FPGA Research. In: Glesner, M., Luk, W. (eds.) FPL 1997. LNCS, vol. 1304, pp. 213–222. Springer, Heidelberg (1997)
[11] Sankar, Y., Rose, J.: Trading quality for compile time: Ultra-fast placement for FPGAs. In: FPGA, pp. 157–166 (1999)
[12] Bian, H., Ling, A.C., et al.: Towards scalable placement for FPGAs. In: Proc. FPGA, pp. 147–156 (2010)
[13] Luu, J., Kuon, I., et al.: VPR 5.0: FPGA cad and architecture exploration tools with single-driver routing, heterogeneity and process scaling. In: FPGA, pp. 133–142 (2009)
[14] Banerjee, P., Sangtani, M., et al.: Floorplanning for Partially Reconfigurable FPGAs. Presented at IEEE Trans. on CAD of Integrated Circuits and Systems, pp. 8–17 (2011)

A Connection Router for the Dynamic Reconfiguration of FPGAs

Elias Vansteenkiste, Karel Bruneel, and Dirk Stroobandt

Ghent University, ELIS Department
Sint-Pietersnieuwstraat 41, 9000 Gent, Belgium
{Elias.Vansteenkiste,Karel.Bruneel,Dirk.Stroobandt}@UGent.be

Abstract. Dynamic Circuit Specialization (DCS) is a new FPGA CAD tool flow that uses Run-Time Reconfiguration to automatically specialize the FPGA configuration for a whole range of specific data values. DCS implementations are a factor 5 faster and need a factor 8 less LUTs compared to conventional implementations. We propose a novel routing algorithm for reconfigurable routing, called the Connection router. In contrast to TROUTE, another reconfiguration-aware router, our new router is fully automated and far more scalable.

Keywords: FPGA, Run-Time Reconfiguration, PATHFINDER, Dynamic Circuit Specialization (DCS) , CAD tool flow, Reconfigurable routing.

1 Introduction

Run-time reconfiguration (RTR) enables more efficient utilization of Field Programmable Gate Arrays (FPGA) by specializing an FPGA's functionality for the current problem specifics. This can be done by simply writing a specialized configuration in the FPGA's configuration memory. A specialized configuration uses fewer resources and can attain faster clock speeds than a generic implementation. The downside is the specialization overhead – the time needed to generate a specialized configuration and write it in the configuration memory. Generating a specialized configuration with a conventional FPGA tool flow can take in the order of minutes to hours, which is unacceptable for most applications.

In [3] the TLUT method has been developed. It is able to produce specialized configurations several orders of magnitude faster than a conventional FPGA tool flow, without sacrificing the quality (speed and area) of the specialized configurations. The method produces a specialized configuration in two steps. Off line, a parameterized configuration is created. This is a closed-form multi-valued Boolean function that expresses the FPGA configuration as a function of a set of parameter values. Online, this Boolean function is evaluated every time the parameter values change, in order to produce a specialized configuration. Since evaluating a closed-form Boolean function is a lot faster than running a conventional FPGA tool flow, the TLUT method greatly reduces the specialization overhead. E.g., the TLUT method can produce specialized FIR configurations (8-bit input, 8-bit coefficients and 128 taps) in only 1.3 ms, while the conventional method needs 35,634 ms.

O.C.S. Choy et al. (Eds.): ARC 2012, LNCS 7199, pp. 357–364, 2012.
© Springer-Verlag Berlin Heidelberg 2012

Parameterized configurations produced by the TLUT method only express the truth tables of LUTs as a function of the parameters. All routing between LUTs is fixed. This leads to good quality specialized configurations. However, it has been shown [4] that also expressing the routing bits as a function of the parameters (TCON method) leads to specialized configurations with an even better quality. The TCON method produces parameterized configurations starting from an RT level HDL description, using adapted versions of synthesis, technology mapping, placement and routing. Our research group is working on adapted algorithms for each of these steps, but in this paper we focus on the routing step.

In [4] a first reconfigurability-aware router, called TROUTE, is presented. Although TROUTE produces good quality results in a reasonable time, manual optimization of the input is needed. The new routing algorithm presented in this paper, solves this problem. It produces good quality results in a reasonable time, independent of the way the input problem is represented.

In the background section we describe the TROUTE algorithm and its limitations. The Connection router is presented in section 3 and the performance of the Connection router is discussed in section 4.

2   Background

2.1   Tunable Circuit

As explained in [4], the technology mapping step of the TCON method produces a *tunable circuit*. This is a circuit containing two types of functional blocks, Tunable LUTs (TLUT) and Tunable Connections (TCON). A TLUT is a LUT with the truth table bits expressed in terms of parameters. A TCON is a functional block, which has any number of input ports (set $\mathcal{I}$)) and any number of output ports (set $\mathcal{O}$). Every TCON has a connection function $\zeta_p : P' \to (\mathcal{O} \to \mathcal{I})$ that expresses how the output ports are connected to the input ports given a parameter value $p \in P'$. P' is the subset of $\{0,1\}^N$ that contains all possible parameter values. A TCON is an abstraction of reconfigurable interconnect between the LUTs.

In what follows we will use a TCON with the functionality of a 2×2 crossbar switch as example. This TCON has two inputs $\mathcal{I} = \{\hat{i}_0, \hat{i}_1\}$ and two outputs $\mathcal{O} = \{\hat{o}_0, \hat{o}_1\}$. A schematic of this TCON can be seen in Figure 1.

2.2   The TCON Routing Problem and TROUTE

The TCON routing problem is defined as follows. Given a tunable circuit containing TLUTs and TCONs and a physical location for each of the TLUTs, express the FPGA's routing bits as a Boolean function of the parameter inputs, so that the connections represented by the TCONs in the tunable circuit are realized for every possible parameter value in P'.

In [4] the TCON routing problem is solved by a reconfiguration-aware router, called TROUTE. TROUTE is based on the PATHFINDER algorithm. The available routing resources of the FPGA are represented in the routing resource

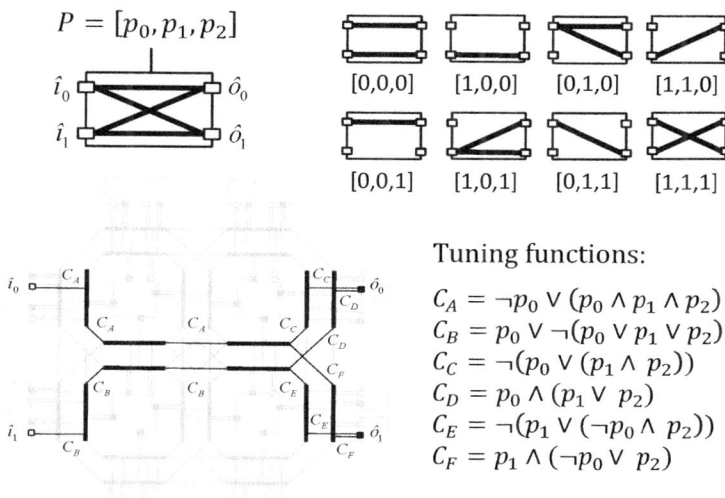

Fig. 1. TCON representation of a 2×2 crossbar switch (upper left) and the patterns and parameter values for which the patterns need to be activated (upper right). A possible implementation on a 2×2 FPGA after place and route (lower left) shows the TCON as a set of routing resources (wires and switches), where switches are controlled by Boolean functions of the parameter inputs, called tuning functions (lower right).

```
while (congestedResourcesExist()):
  for each TCON τ do:
    τ.ripUpRouting()
    routeTCON(τ)
    τ.resources().updateSharingCost()
  allResources().updateHistoryCost()
```

```
while (congestedResourcesExist()):
  for each connection ζ do:
    ζ.ripUpRouting()
    ζ.path = dijkstra(ζ.source, ζ.sink)
    ζ.resources().updateCongestionCost()
  allResources().updateHistoryCost()
```

Fig. 2. Pseudo code for the negotiated congestion loop of the TCON router

Fig. 3. Pseudo code for the negotiated congestion loop of the Connection router

graph (RRG), a directed graph where each node represents a routing wire on the FPGA and each arc represents a routing switch on the FPGA. In the same way as PATHFINDER tries to find disjoint subgraphs of the RRG for each of the nets in the input circuit, TROUTE tries to find disjoint subgraphs for each of the TCONs in the tunable circuit. Both algorithms do this iteratively by ripping up and rerouting nets or TCONs, respectively. The subgraphs are calculated independently of each other using a net or a TCON router, which tries to find a minimum cost subgraph[1] but does not explicitly force the subgraphs to be disjoint. In order to make the subgraphs disjoint, the cost of the routing resources is manipulated by a mechanism called negotiated congestion (see Figure 2). For more information on negotiated congestion we refer to [2,7].

---

[1] The subgraph cost equals the sum of the costs for all routing resources it contains.

In order to find a minimum cost subgraph that implements a TCON, TROUTE looks at a TCON as a set of connection patterns. The connection patterns of the 2×2 crossbar switch example are depicted in Figure 1 (upper right). TROUTE routes a TCON by routing each pattern separately. Nets that are part of the same routing pattern are active at the same time and thus have to be disjoint (in order to avoid short circuits). However, two nets that are part of different patterns are never activated at the same time and can thus share routing resources. This last property is used to minimize the routing cost of a TCON by maximizing the overlap among different patterns. The algorithm loops over all patterns of the TCON and stimulates overlap between patterns by setting the cost of previously used resources (for other patterns within the same TCON) to 0. Within a pattern, the algorithm loops over all nets in the current pattern and routes them using the net router. In order to keep the nets disjoint, the cost of previously used resources (for nets within the same pattern) is set to ∞. The negotiated congestion cost of a node is given by $c(n) = b(n) \cdot h(n) \cdot p(n)$, where $b(n)$, $h(n)$, and $p(n)$ are the base, history and present congestion cost.

2.3   Limitations of TROUTE

The TCON router avoids overlap between nets in the same pattern by setting the cost of the routing resources used by the already routed nets to ∞. This mechanism is called obstacle avoidance. It is well known that obstacle avoidance fails to find good quality solutions for complex circuits [7], due to the *enclosure problem*. The terminals of a net get enclosed by resources that are already used by other nets in the same pattern. Thus, when patterns become too complex the TCON router fails to find a routing graph. This is the first limitation. The second limitation is that the run time of the TCON router scales exponentially with the complexity of the TCON. In worst case scenario, the number of times that the Dijkstra algorithm needs to be invoked to (re)route a TCON with inputs $\mathcal{I}$ and outputs $\mathcal{O}$, is equal to $|\mathcal{I}||\mathcal{O}|(|\mathcal{I}| + 1)^{|\mathcal{O}|-1}$, which is clearly exponential in the number of outputs. The TCON of the 2×2 crossbar in Figure 1 has 8 patterns and needs 12 Dijkstra invocations. For a 4×4 crossbar the number of patterns increases to 624 patterns and the number of invocations to 2000.

In [4] these two issues were addressed by manually reducing the complexity of the input tunable circuit. This was done by splitting up larger TCONs into several smaller TCONs. E.g., a TCON representing a 4×4 crossbar was split into four 4:1 multiplexers. The patterns of these TCONs contain only one net, and thus the obstacle avoidance problem was avoided. Additionally, each TCON contains only four patterns, which greatly reduces the routing complexity. In the next section, we propose a new algorithm that is not dependent on the way the input tunable circuit is represented and thus solves the problems associated with TROUTE.

3   The Connection Router

In order to solve the problems of TROUTE, we developed a new routing algorithm, the Connection router. The Connection router uses a connection-based representation instead of the TCON-based representation for the reconfigurable routing in a tunable circuit. The connections in this representation are again associated to a connection condition, expressed in terms of the parameter inputs of the design. The condition is true for those parameter values that require the connection to be activated. The connection representation of the 2×2 crossbar switch example in Figure 1 is given by C_C for connection (i_0, o_0), C_F for (i_0, o_1), C_D for (i_1, o_0) and C_E for (i_1, o_1).

The pseudo code of the Connection router can be found in Figure 3. The negotiation loop of the Connection router will now rip up and reroute connections. Dijkstra's algorithm is used to calculate the lowest cost path between the source and the sink of the connections.

Connections are allowed to share resources, in contrast to nets/TCONs in PATHFINDER/TROUTE. Indeed, connections are allowed to overlap if they carry the same signal or if they are not active at the same time. Note that this complicates things for the negotiated congestion mechanism. To update the history $h(n)$ and the present congestion cost $p(n)$, the negotiated congestion mechanism needs to know how congested a routing node is. PATHFINDER/TROUTE simply counts the number of nets/TCONs that were sharing the node, but now things are more complicated. The Connection router needs to find a minimum partition of the connections that share the routing resource under consideration, so that each partition only contains connections that are allowed to overlap. This reduces to a so called minimum clique cover problem, which is NP-complete [6]. This problem needs to be solved in the inner loop of the routing algorithm and may lead to exuberant run-times. Therefore, the Connection router approximates the congestion and the legal sharing by only allowing overlap between connections that either share the same source or the same sink. Connections that share the same source carry the same signal and thus are allowed to overlap. Connections that share the same sink are allowed to overlap because they are never active at the same time, at least if we assume that the input to the router is a legal tunable circuit (no shorts). These simplified overlap rules allow a simplification of the minimum clique cover problem.

To compare the different overlap possibilities the connection router needs to accurately assess how a node used in a connection contributes to the cost of the complete solution. If a node is legally shared between several connections the cost should be divided, so that the sum of all the connection costs equals the cost of the complete solution. The cost of a node is thus given by:

$$c(n) = \frac{b(n) \cdot h(n) \cdot p(n)}{share(n)}, \tag{1}$$

where $share(n)$ is the number of connections that legally share the node n. Once the partitioning from the previous paragraph is performed, this number is equal to the cardinality of the partition the current connection is part of.

The algorithm described in this section solves both problems described in Section 2.3. The enclosure problem is solved because obstacle avoidance is not used anymore. The scalability problem is also greatly improved. To show this, we again calculate the worst-case number of Dijkstra invocations that are needed to route a TCON. A TCON with inputs $\mathcal{I}$ and outputs $\mathcal{O}$ will in worst case lead to $|\mathcal{I}||\mathcal{O}|$ different connections. This is also the number of Dijkstra invocations needed to route the TCON. To route a 4 by 4 crossbar, only 16 Dijkstra invocations are needed, compared to the 2000 Dijkstra invocations needed to route the crossbar using TROUTE.

4   Experiments and Results

To validate and compare the reconfiguration-aware routers, we used Multistage Interconnect Networks that are known as Clos Networks [5]. The connection router can handle every routing architecture that can be represented by an RRG.[2] Here we used a simple FPGA architecture[3] with logic blocks containing one 4-LUT and one flip-flop. The wire segments in the interconnection network only span one logic block. The architecture is specified by three parameters: the number of logic element columns (*cols*), the number of logic element rows (*rows*) and the number of wires in a routing channel (*W*).

Our Clos network uses 4×4 crossbar switches as building blocks. The TCON representation of one such switch' functionality needs 624 patterns. We can reduce this number to 16 by dividing the functionality over 4 TCONs, as described in section 2 (resulting in 4 patterns per TCON). The process of finding the perfect division of the functionality over different TCONs, such that the size of the TCON is acceptable and the patterns only contain one net, is difficult to automate. Nothing can be said about the existence of such representation. The Connection router avoids manual optimization, greatly reducing the design effort.

The goal of this experiment is to look at the possibilities of the Connection router and how they approach those of TROUTE, applied on a manually optimized representation of the tunable circuit. We compare three sizes, 16×16 (3 stages), 64×64 (5 stages) and 256×256 (7 stages). In our implementation the crossbar switches in the even stages are implemented using TLUTs and in the odd stages using reconfigurable routing. This results in a good balance between TLUTs and reconfigurable routing. We first tried to route the unmodified representation with TROUTE. These trials failed due to the previously mentioned (subsection 2.3) enclosure problem. Secondly we manually optimized the representation, as described in the previous paragraph, and routed again with TROUTE (these results are denoted *Troute**). In the last approach (*Con*) we used the Connection router to route the unmodified representation. The placement is done using an adapted version of the VPR routability-driven placer, called TPLACE (beyond the scope of this paper).

For each size we measured the number of wires and the minimum channel width (W_m). Table 1 shows the results. The parameters of the FPGA architecture and the number of LUTs for each size are also shown. As suggested in [1], we ensure low-stress place and route by choosing the number of LUTs in the FPGA

---

[2] For more information about RRG generation, see [1].

[3] A description of this architecture is provided with the VPR tool suite in `4lut_sanitized.arch`.

Table 1. Properties of six multi stage Clos network implementations. The numbers between parentheses are relative compared to the Troute* result.

Size	Type	Area		Architecture			
		LUTS	Wires	W_m	Cols	Rows	W
16	Troute*	16	456 (1.00)	6	8	8	7
	Con	16	428 (0.94)	5	8	8	7
64	Troute*	128	4178 (1.00)	11	18	18	13
	Con	128	4372 (1.04)	11	18	18	13
256	Troute*	768	24851 (1.00)	19	39	39	24
	Con	768	35229 (1.42)	20	39	39	24

architecture 20% larger than the number of LUTs in the circuit and the number of wires per channel 20% larger than W_m, the minimum channel width. We set the maximal routing iterations to 250 for both algorithms.

Con needs up to a factor 1.4 more wires than *Troute**. The Connection router has more freedom to share or not share resources, which leads to a larger search space. The chance to find a solution with more wires is higher. The Connection router is routability-driven. It stops when a solution is found for the given track width, there is no extra wire length optimization.

The routers are routability-driven, so in Figure 4 we compare the time needed to reach a solution for a given track width. The timing experiments are done using an Intel Core 2 processor running at 2.13 GHz with 2 GiB of memory running the Java HotSpot™ 64-Bit Server VM. The run-time of the Connection router is higher, due to the larger search space. This effect becomes more pronounced in case of the 256x256 network. Keep in mind that the Connection router is an automated process (no intervention of the designer is necessary), in contrast to TROUTE. The extra design time needed when using TROUTE is not accounted for in the charts. We assume the time to optimize the tunable circuit is higher than the run-time of the Connection router.

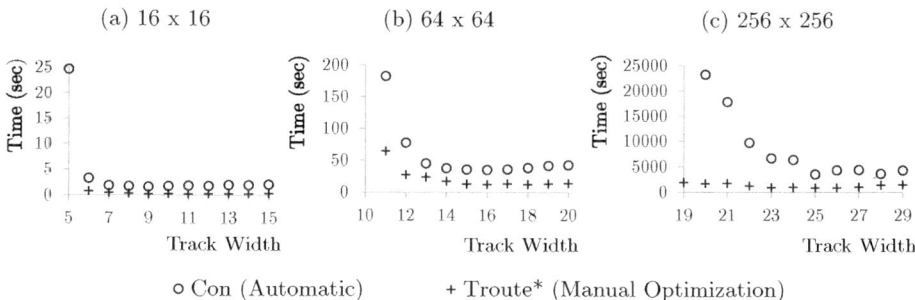

Fig. 4. Run-time to route Clos networks for a given track width. The connection router starts from a non-optimized and Troute from a manually optimized representation.

For the 16×16 network, the Connection router finds a solution with a smaller track width than TROUTE. This demonstrates that solutions with lower track widths are present in the solution space of the Connection router. For the 64×64 network, the Connection router and TROUTE have the same minimal track width. For the 256×256 network, the connection router does not find a solution for the minimal track width that TROUTE reaches, due to the larger search space. However, without the manual optimization, TROUTE would not even find a solution at all.

5 Conclusion and Future Work

In this paper we introduce a new reconfiguration-aware router, the Connection router. This algorithm is far more scalable than TROUTE, described in [4]. Starting from a non-optimized representation of a tunable circuit, the Connection router succeeds in routing representations that are unroutable for TROUTE. The quality of the routings produced by the Connection router approaches that of TROUTE, applied on a manual optimized representation. To achieve this, we use a connection-based representation for the reconfigurable routing.

There are many possibilities to improve the Connection router. We demonstrated that the Connection router can find solutions with lower track widths, but needs more time to find these solutions. In future research we will focus on improving the Connection router's efficiency and develop a wire length-driven and a timing-driven Connection router.

References

1. Betz, V., Rose, J., Marquardt, A.: Architecture and CAD for Deep-Submicron FP-GAs. Kluwer Academic Publishers, Norwell (1999)
2. Betz, V., Rose, J., Marquardt, A.: VPR: A New Packing, Placement and Routing Tool for FPGA Research. In: Proceedings of the 7th International Workshop on Field-Programmable Logic and Applications, pp. 213–222 (1997)
3. Bruneel, K., Abouella, F., Stroobandt, D.: TMAP: A Reconfigurability-aware FPGA Technology Mapper. In: Design, Automation and Test Europe (2009)
4. Bruneel, K., Stroobandt, D.: TROUTE: A Reconfigurability-Aware FPGA Router. In: Sirisuk, P., Morgan, F., El-Ghazawi, T., Amano, H. (eds.) ARC 2010. LNCS, vol. 5992, pp. 207–218. Springer, Heidelberg (2010)
5. Clos, C.: A Study of Non-blocking Switching Networks. The Bell System Technical Journal XXXII, 406–424 (1953)
6. Karp, K.: Reducibility Among Combinatorial Problems. In: Complexity of Computer Computations, pp. 85–103. Plenum Press (1972)
7. McMurchie, L., Ebeling, C.: PATHFINDER: A Negotiation-based Performance-driven Router for FPGAs. In: FPGA 1995, pp. 111–117 (1995)

R-NoC: An Efficient Packet-Switched Reconfigurable Networks-on-Chip

Hongbing Fan[1,*], Yue-Ang Chen[1], and Yu-Liang Wu[2,**]

[1] Wilfrid Laurier University, Waterloo, ON Canada N2L 3C5
hfan@wlu.ca
[2] The Chinese University of Hong Kong, Shatin, N.T., Hong Kong
ylw@cse.cuhk.edu.hk

Abstract. Networks-on-Chip (NoC) architectures have been proposed to replace the classical bus and point-to-point global interconnections for the next generation of multiple-core systems-on-a-chips. However, the one-to-one (unicast) based NoC communication paradigm is not efficient for one-to-many (multicast) communication requests, and the address based packet routing method lacks the capability to arrange routing globally for overall communication performance. To address these problems, we here propose a Reconfigurable NoC (R-NoC) architecture. The novelty of the R-NoC is that a structured virtual routing path can be established through the reconfiguration of routers so that packets are delivered fast along the pre-configured routing path. Load balance for overall communication performance can be achieved through the global arrangement of routing paths. In addition, custom network topology is proposed for specific set of applications to reduce the costs on area and power. Software simulations show that the structured data path approach has a significant performance improvement on multicast comparing with the traditional multiple unicast approach.

Keywords: Reconfigurable computing, packet-switching, NoC, SoC.

1 Introduction

Packet-switched Networks-on-Chip (NoC) architectures have been considered promising solutions for the global interconnection of the next generation of multiple-core systems-on-a-chip (SoC). Compared to the classical bus and point-to-point interconnection networks, the NoC solution provides a greater scalability in handling more processing elements (PE) and higher flexibility in handling various communication requests. Comprehensive research and practices on NoC have been carried out in the past decade [1], and many problems still remain open as presented in [7]. We consider the problems in communication paradigm and communication infrastructure, particularly on design problems in routing protocols, multicast communications, NoC router and network topology.

* Research partially supported by the NSERC, Canada.
** Research partially supported by RGC Earmarked Grant 2150500 and ITSP Grant 6902308, Hong Kong.

O.C.S. Choy et al. (Eds.): ARC 2012, LNCS 7199, pp. 365–371, 2012.
© Springer-Verlag Berlin Heidelberg 2012

Existing NoC communication paradigms are based on the approach of unicast communication scheme and local routing policy. That is, the fundamental communication functionality is to deliver a packet from a source network interface (NI) to a destination NI through routers, and local address-based routing polices are used to route a packet from one router to another. With the unicast scheme, a multicast communication request is served by a multiple unicast method, i.e. sending packets from the source to each destination one after another. As a result, it generates more data traffic and has a longer latency. The address-based routing approach cannot route packets along a pre-given path, and cannot balance traffic load globally to maximize overall communication performance.

On the other hand, the circuit-switched interconnection networks such as the routing networks in FPGAs [2] have advantages on multicast, latency, and global routing arrangement. For a multicast request, a dedicated data path (of tree topology) connecting the source to all destinations is first established through reconfiguring switches, followed by the simultaneous propagation of data signals from the source to all destinations. For a communication-ware application, routing paths can be computed and configured for all communication requests so as to improve the overall performance. However, the circuit-switched reconfigurable interconnection networks tend to have a high area and power cost [6]. In NoC architectures, communication resources are shared by different communication requests such increasing the routing capacity and reducing the area and power costs. To improve communication performance of packet switching, virtual circuit paths can be used with no-chip router support. The method of virtual circuit tree with on-chip router support for multicasting was proposed in [5], which provides a superior network performance across a variety of scenarios with lower overhead.

We propose the reconfigurable NoC (R-NoC) architecture, in which structured virtual routing paths can be established through the reconfiguration of routers for high performance communication requests, and load balance can be achieved globally through the arrangement of routing paths. This paper presents the initial investigations on R-NoC. Section 2 describes the architecture of R-NoC and protocols. Section 3 presents the design of reconfigurable routers and network topology. We developed a software system implementing the packet-switched reconfigurable interconnection network architecture. The software is used to simulate the behaviors of data communication along structured data paths, as well as a platform to development and execute distributed computing application running on multiple computers. The simulation and experimental results are described in Section 4, followed by conclusions in Section 5.

2   R-NoC Architecture and Protocols

The proposed R-NoC is for the global interconnection of multi-core SoCs as shown in Fig.1. The multi-core SoC architecture consists of heterogeneous processing element (PE) cores such as CPU, DSP modules, embedded memory blocks, etc. Each PE connects to the R-NoC through an NI. After mapping, an application uses a sub-group of the available PEs, which needs to be connected according to the communication requests defined by the application. The

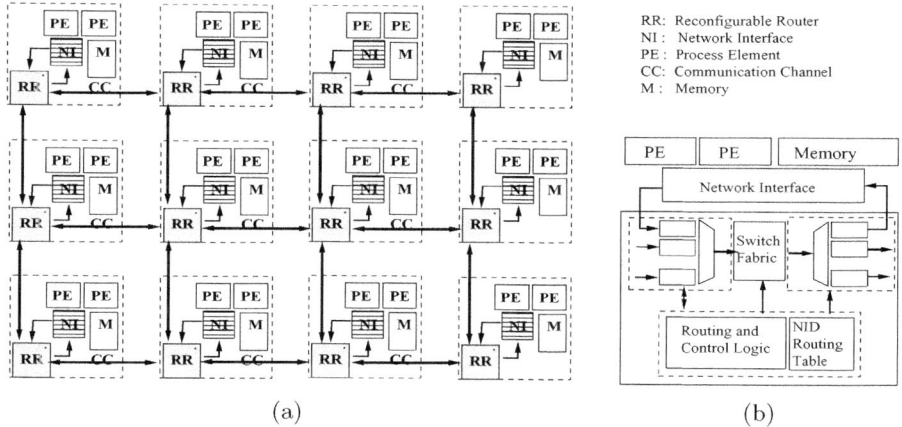

Fig. 1. (a) The architecture of reconfigurable networks-on-chip (b) Reconfigurable router

role of R-NoC is to provide an application specific communication network by configuring the R-NoC.

2.1   R-NoC Architecture Description

The main components of R-NoC are communication channels (or simply channels), NIs, and reconfigurable routers. A one-way channel has an outgoing buffer on one end and incoming buffer on the other end. A two-way channel has both outgoing and an incoming buffers on both ends. A packet in the outgoing buffer is transferred to the incoming buffer of the other end handled automatically by the channel. An NI is connected to a router by a two-way channel (Fig.1(a)), which handles the incoming/outgoing packets between the NI and its router. Two routers are joined by a two-way channel for packet forwarding in each direction. Each router has an unique address, and each outgoing buffer at a router has a channel ID. A packet is created at an NI by packing header and data from PEs; it is then added into the outgoing channel of the NI. An NI also picks and unpacks packets from its incoming channel, and passes the data to its PEs. A router picks up a packet from its incoming channel buffers, finds outgoing channels according to the routing information carried in the packet header and its routing policy, allocates outgoing channels, sets switch fabric, and finally puts the packet into the outgoing buffers. The address-based routing policy at a router returns an outgoing channel for given source and destination routers. In addition to the address-based routing, R-NoC uses an identity based routing policy which returns a list of outgoing channels according to a net identifer and routing table.

2.2   Structured Routing Path and Reconfiguration

The key feature of the R-NoC is the capability of building structured data path for fast data distribution. A structured routing path is a virtual circuit connecting a source router to a set of designation routers. Each routing path is assigned a net identifier (NID), which is used to identify the routing path. An NID routing table at each router is used to represent structured routing paths. An NID routing table is like a hash table with an NID as a hashing key and a list of outgoing channel IDs as values. E.g. entries $(nid_1; ch_1, ch_2)$, $(nid_2; ch_2, ch_3)$ in NID routing table at router r indicate that outgoing channels ch_1, ch_2 are on the routing path nid_1 at router r, and channels ch_2, ch_3 are on the routing path nid_2 at router r. Particularly, if $\{ch_1, ch_2\}$ contains an NI channel, then the NI is a destination; otherwise the router r is a relay.

A structured routing path is established by configuring the NID routing tables on the path. The configuration operations are done by reconfiguring packets. A configuring packet is a special type of packet carrying the address of targeted router and the data of NID routing table entries. A configuration packet is delivered by the address-based routing method. After arriving at the destination, the data will be inserted into the NID routing table.

2.3   R-NoC Protocols

The R-NoC protocols define the packet format, packet routing (address-based and NID-based) policy, and flow control. We use fixed length header and variable length data. The header consists of the fields: packet type, operation type, NID, source address, destination address, and data length. Data field follows if the data length is non-zero. Packet types are configuration type and data type. Operation types are adding (entry to routing table), removing (entry from routing table), clean (routing table), and reset (incoming and outgoing channels). The NID is used to identify both routing method and routing path. When the NID field is 0, it uses address-based routing, otherwise NID-based routing. When the NID field is non-zero, the routing control module looks up the NID routing table for the outgoing channels, then switches the packet to every outgoing buffer associated with the NID.

Flow control is done through the available buffer size registers which store the available buffer length of each outgoing buffer. After a packet is transported into the incoming buffer of the other side, the available buffer length register is updated to a new value. A packet can only be written into an outgoing buffer when the available length is bigger than the packet length. For NID routing, when all outgoing channels are writable, the packet will be written into the outgoing buffers associated with the NID. After a successful writing, the current packet will be removed from its incoming buffer; otherwise it either waits or moves to the next incoming buffer.

3   R-NoC Routers and Network Topology

The reconfigurable router is the core of the R-NoC. It is designed to implement the R-NoC protocols. Routers are connected by channels in a custom network topology for a group of applications. The network topology is routable for the applications and optimized for area and power efficiency.

3.1   Router Design

The R-NoC router contains incoming buffers, outgoing buffers, switch fabric, routing control logic, NID routing table, see Fig.1(b). For switch fabric, we propose to use a rearrangeable multi-level switch fabric, which is capable of one-to-many switching [4]. An array of two dimensional registers is used for the NID routing table. The width of an NID routing table is determined by the number of outgoing channels. The height is a design parameter to be chosen. For the routing control logic, we propose to add the following modules: (a) a reconfiguration module which handles the NID routing table operations, (b) an NID routing module which takes an NID as input and outputs a list of outgoing channels, (c) a channel allocation module which takes a list of outgoing channels, the length of the current packet, and available outgoing buffer lengthes as inputs, and produces a *writable* signal as an output, (d) a switch fabric controller which takes the list of outgoing channels and the *writable signal* as inputs and produces switch control signals as outputs, and (e) a feedback handling module which receives acknowledgement packets from children and produces a reply packet sent to a parent node.

3.2   R-NoC Topology Design and Routing

Given a routing specification (R, C), R is the set of routers and C is a set of routing requirements. Each routing requirement consists of a set of nets specified by communication requests after mapping. Each net represents a communication request (preferably with a high throughput demand), e.g, net $N = \{r_0, r_1, \ldots, r_t\}$ represents a multicast request from router r_0 to routers $r_1, \ldots, r_t$. A routing specification gives the interconnection requests for a given set of applications. The problem is to design a network topology such that it is able to route every given routing requirement and uses the least number of routers and channels, minimum buffer size and NID routing table size for area and power efficiency.

A two stage scheme for topology design was proposed in [3]. The first stage is to find an interconnection graph (only containing routers) that has routing solutions for all given connection requests. The second stage is to add intermediate routers to reduce the number of channels as a tradeoff. The same method has been used in topology designs for the circuit-switched interconnection networks [4].

The routing in a given topology is to find routing paths for all nets of a given routing requirement. This problem is similar to FPGA routing except that we deal with custom networks which usually have irregular topology. The mutlicast tree algorithms can be applied to solve this problem.

4   Software Simulation for R-NoC

To investigate the communication behaviors of the R-NoC architecture, we developed a software system to simulate the R-NoC architecture. The system comprises peer node and operating software. The peer node is a client/server program running on a computer, and plays the roles of both routers and NIs. Each peer node can make TCP/IP connection channel to some allowed peer nodes and each channel can be set an NID. The peer nodes together with the allowable connections form the topology of a custom network. The operating software is used to configure peer nodes to establish structured data paths using the allowable channels and to distribute data packets.

We tested the system with file distribution in serial (S) mode (multiple unicast) and parallel (P) mode (multicast along a structured data path). A node is set to send a file to one node at a time. The serial mode transfers the file along a tree in the depth-first order, thus only one node sends a file at a time, which has the nearly same time performance as the multiple unicast. The parallel mode allows multiple nodes to send file simultaneously. The underlying topology is a complete graph, i.e. each node is allowed to connect to another node and file transfer delay between any two nodes are the same. Table 1 show the experimental results for distributing a file of size 500K to n computers with $n = 12, 16, 20$ along a k-tree with $k = 1, 2, 3, 4, 5$. We see that the parallel mode along structured data paths is much faster than the serial mode. The improvement is mainly due to the parallelism which balances the load of nodes.

Table 1. Experimental results on file distribution along structured data path

n	k	S(sec)	P(S/P)	n	k	S(sec)	P (S/P)	n	k	S (sec)	P (S/P)
12	1	8.094	8.083(1.0)	16	1	10.943	11.042(1.0)	20	1	13.078	13.073(1.0)
12	2	7.802	2.443(3.2)	16	2	11.01	3.172(3.5)	20	2	14.177	3.984 (3.6)
12	3	7.948	1.641(4.8)	16	3	11.01	2.041(5.4)	20	3	13.448	2.906 (4.6)
12	4	7.802	1.969(4.0)	16	4	11.083	1.718(6.5)	20	4	12.713	2.281(5.6)
12	5	7.651	2 (3.8)	16	5	10.573	2.188(4.8)	20	5	12.771	2.177 (5.9)

5   Conclusions

We proposed the reconfigurable networks-on-chip architecture to address the multicast and global routing arrangement problems with the existing networks-on-chip architectures. We developed a software system to simulate the reconfigurable networks-on-chip architecture. Initial experiments on data distribution demonstrates a significant performance improvement for multicast and a high flexibility for global routing arrangement. The experimental investigation demonstrated the feasibility of the reconfigurable interconnection network architecture for both on-chip and office computing.

References

1. Bjerregaard, T., Mahadevan, S.: A survey of research and practices of network-on-chip. ACM Comput. Surv. 38(1) (2006)
2. Brown, S., Francis, R., Rose, J., Vranesic, Z.: Field Programmable Gate Arrays. Kluwer-Academic Publisher, Boston (1992)
3. Fan, H., Ernst, J., Wu, Y.-L.: Customized reconfigurable interconnection networks for multiple application socs. In: FPL, pp. 491–494 (2008)

4. Fan, H., Wu, Y.-L., Cheung, C.-C.: Design Automation for Reconfigurable Interconnection Networks. In: Sirisuk, P., Morgan, F., El-Ghazawi, T., Amano, H. (eds.) ARC 2010. LNCS, vol. 5992, pp. 244–256. Springer, Heidelberg (2010)
5. Jerger, N.D.E., Peh, L.-S., Lipasti, M.H.: Virtual circuit tree multicasting: A case for on-chip hardware multicast support. In: ISCA, pp. 229–240 (2008)
6. Lemieux, G., Lewis, D.: Design of Interconnection Networks for Programmable Logic. Kluwer-Academic Publisher, Boston (2003)
7. Marculescu, R., Ogras, Ü.Y., Peh, L.-S., Jerger, N.D.E., Hoskote, Y.V.: Outstanding Research Problems in NoC Design: System, Microarchitecture, and Circuit Perspectives. IEEE Trans. on CAD of Integrated Circuits and Systems 28(1), 3–21 (2009)

Novel Arithmetic Architecture for High Performance Implementation of SHA-3 Finalist Keccak on FPGA Platforms

Kashif Latif, M. Muzaffar Rao, Athar Mahboob, and Arshad Aziz

National University of Sciences and Technology (NUST) H-12 Islamabad, Pakistan
{kashif,mrao,athar}@pnec.edu.pk, arshad@nust.edu.pk

Abstract. We propose high speed architecture for Keccak using Look-Up Table (LUT) resources on FPGAs, to minimize area of Keccak data path and to reduce critical path lengths. This approach allows us to design Keccak data path with minimum resources and higher clock frequencies. We show our results in the form of chip area consumption, throughput and throughput per area. At this time, the design presented in this work is the highest in terms of throughput for any of SHA-3 candidates, achieving a figure of 13.67Gbps for Keccak-256 on Virtex 6. This can enable line rate operation for hashing on 10Gbps network interfaces.

Keywords: SHA-3, Keccak, Cryptographic Hash Functions, High Speed Encryption Hardware, FPGA, Reconfigurable Computing.

1   Introduction

Cryptographic hash algorithms are used in digital signatures, message authentication codes (MACs) and many other information security applications. Vulnerabilities found in a number of hash functions in recent years, including SHA-0, SHA-1, SHA-2, RIPEMD and MD5 led to the rendering of long-term security of these algorithms suspect [1-3]. To ensure the long-term robustness of applications that use hash functions National Institute of Standards and Technology (NIST) has announced a public competition in the Federal Register Notice published on November 2, 2007 [4] to develop a new cryptographic Hash algorithm called SHA-3. This competition is now in the final round with 5 candidates. Five short listed candidates are BLAKE, Grøstl, JH, Keccak and Skein. The tentative time-frame for the end of this competition and selection of official SHA-3 is in 4th quarter of 2012 [5].

This paper describes high throughput efficient hardware implementation of Keccak. The remainder of this paper is organized as follows. Section 2 gives brief description of Keccak. In section 3 we present the efficient hardware implementation of Keccak, elaborating our novel architectural approach using LUT resources. In section 4 we give the results of our work and compare it with the other reported efficient implementations of Keccak in section 5. Finally, we provide some conclusions in Section 6.

O.C.S. Choy et al. (Eds.): ARC 2012, LNCS 7199, pp. 372–378, 2012.

2   Brief Description of Keccak

Keccak is a family of sponge functions with members Keccak $[r, c]$ characterized by two parameters, bitrate r and capacity c. The sum $r + c$ determine the width of the Keccak-f permutation used in the sponge construction and is restricted to values in $\{25, 50, 100, 200, 400, 800, 1600\}$ [6]. For SHA-3 proposal Keccak team proposed the Keccak [1600] with different r and c values for each desired length of hash output [6]. The 1600-bit state of Keccak [1600] consists of 5x5 matrix of 64-bit words. Each compression step of Keccak consists of 24 rounds. Let us denote the state matrix with A. Each round then consists of following five steps:

$$C[x] = A[x, 0] \oplus A[x, 1] \oplus A[x, 2] \oplus A[x, 3] \oplus A[x, 4] \quad 0 \leq x \leq 4 \quad (1)$$

Theta (θ): $$D[x] = C[x - 1] \oplus ROT(C[x + 1], 1) \quad\quad\quad 0 \leq x \leq 4 \quad (2)$$

$$A[x, y] = A[x, y] \oplus D[x] \quad\quad\quad\quad\quad 0 \leq x, y \leq 4 \quad (3)$$

Rho (ρ) - Pi (π):$B[y, 2x + 3y] = ROT(A[x, y], r[x, y]) \quad\quad 0 \leq x, y \leq 4 \quad (4)$

Chi (χ): $$A[x, y] = B[x, y] \oplus ((NOT\ B[x + 1, y])\ AND\ B[x + 2, y])\ 0 \leq x, y \leq 4 \quad (5)$$

Iota (i): $$A[0,0] = A[0,0] \oplus RC \quad\quad\quad\quad\quad\quad\quad\quad\quad (6)$$

In above listed equations all operations within indices are done modulo 5. A denotes the complete permutation state array and $A[x, y]$ denotes a particular 64-bit word in that state. $B[x, y]$, $C[x]$ and $D[x]$ are intermediate variables. The symbol $\oplus$ denotes the bitwise XOR, NOT the bitwise complement and AND the bitwise AND operation. Finally, $ROT(W, r)$ denotes the bitwise cyclic shift operation, moving the bit at position i into position $i + r$ (modulo 64). The constants $r[x, y]$ and RC are cyclic shift offset and round constant respectively, and are defined in [6].

3   Implementation

We have implemented the 256-bit and 512-bit variants of Keccak on Xilinx Virtex 5 and Virtex 6 FPGAs. We have extensively used the Xilinx specific library resources in the design of Keccak data path. Xilinx LUT primitives are used to implement Keccak single round. This round then iterative number of times to achieve Keccak compression function. The use of primitives makes our design much efficient with minimum area, high speed and high throughput per area as compared to other reported work for Keccak.

3.1   Datapath of Keccak

The data path implemented for Keccak is shown in Fig. 1. The A_Reg represents the A matrix register, on which processing of Keccak algorithm takes place. Keccak data path is fully parameterized, such that the design may be synthesized for any value of r (bitrate) and c (capacity). For this reason, the width of each net is highlighted as r, c or $r + c$ in Fig. 1. The length of A_Reg also varies according to r and c and it is defined as $r + c$ (bits). For Keccak-256, r is specified as 1088-bits and c as 512-bits. For Keccak-512, r is specified as 576-bits and c as 1024-bits. Accordingly A_Reg

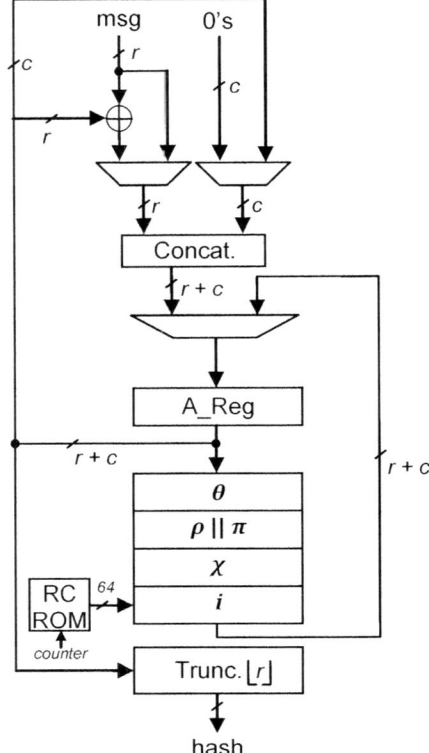

Fig. 1. Data path of Keccak

will be of 1600-bits. In beginning of every hash process **A_Reg** is initialized with all zeros. First message block is directly copied to **A_Reg** after concatenating it with c wide stream of 0's. The Concat block in Fig. 1 represents the concatenation operation. Compression function of Keccak consists of five steps. In Fig. 1 each step is denoted by the symbol as specified in Keccak specifications. These steps are θ, ρ, π, χ and i. We have combined these steps during implementation, wherever possible. We have implemented ρ and π as a single step. The round constants (RC) are stored in ROM using 24x64 bit single port distributed ROM. Respective round constant is addressed during each round using round number as ROM address.

3.2   Novel Arithmetic Architecture for Keccak Compression Function

Our novel arithmetic architecture for compression function of Keccak is now described. Keccak algorithm's compression function consists simple XOR, AND and NOT operations. These operations are implemented using LUT primitives from Xilinx specific libraries. Following are details of implementation of each step.

Theta (θ) Step: There are three equations in θ step. Equation (1) is implemented using LUT5 primitive for XOR logic as shown in Fig. 2(a). The INIT value in hexadecimal, shown under attributes in Fig. 2(a), configures the LUT to perform

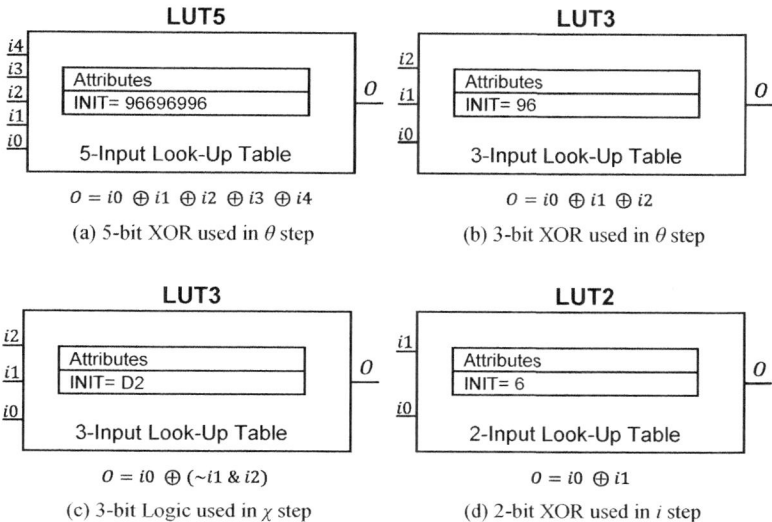

Fig. 2. LUT primitives from Xilinx Library used to implement Keccak's round steps

XOR operation at its inputs. The INIT value is derived by laying down the truth table for all possible combinations of LUT inputs. To XOR 5 64-bit operands of equation (1), LUT5 primitive is instantiated 64 times. For complete implementation of equation (1), 5x64 LUT5 are required. We can combine equation (2) with equation (3) as follows:

$$A[x,y] = A[x,y] \oplus C[x-1] \oplus ROT(C[x+1],1) \qquad 0 \leq x,y \leq 4 \qquad (7)$$

For implementation of equation (7), LUT3 primitive is used for XOR logic as shown in Fig. 2(b). The one bit rotation in last operand of equation (7) is implemented through rewiring. To implement the complete logic, 25x64 instantiations of LUT3 primitive are required.

Rho (ρ) and Pi (π) Steps: The ρ and π are permutations, which may be achieved through simple rewiring in hardware, at no resource cost. The cyclic shift constant $r[x,y]$ is fixed and known for each position of matrix A. It is also implemented by means of fixed rewiring.

Chi (χ) Step: In χ step three logical operations XOR, NOT and AND are used. These are implemented using LUT3 primitive as shown in Fig. 2(c). In order to accomplish the χ step, LUT3 with χ logic is instantiated 25x64 times.

Iota (i): The i step involves simple XOR of round constant with least significant 64 bits of A_Reg, i.e. $A[0,0]$. It is implemented using LUT2 primitive as shown in Fig. 2(d). LUT2 is instantiated 64 times for i step.

These five steps or a single round of Keccak algorithm are accomplished in one clock cycle. Therefore 24 clock cycles are required to complete 24 rounds of Keccak algorithm. After completion of 24 rounds on a message block, resulting r-bits of state of A_Reg are XORed with next message block and same round sequence is repeated again. This process continues till all message blocks are processed. At the end, state of **A_Reg** is truncated to the desired length of hash output.

4   Implementation Results

The design has been implemented on Xilinx Virtex 5 and Virtex 6. The resulting clock frequencies and area utilization after place and route are reported. Table 1 shows achieved area consumption ($Area$), clock frequency (F_{max}), throughput (TP) and throughput per area (TPA) for implemented designs. The $Block\ Size$ is the block size of message in bits and N_{clk} is the number of clock cycles required for hash of a single message block.

Table 1. Results for Keccak. F_{max} in MHz, $Area$ in Slices, TP in Gb/s and TPA in Mbps/Slice.

Device	N_{clk}	Keccak-256					Keccak-512			
		Block Size	F_{max}	$Area$	TP	TPA	Block Size	F_{max}	$Area$	TP	TPA
Virtex 6	24	1088	301.57	915	13.67	14.94	576	291.21	1015	6.99	6.89
Virtex 5	24	1088	275.56	1333	12.49	9.37	576	263.16	1197	6.32	5.28

5   Comparison with Previous Work

Table 2 shows the comparison of results with previously reported implementations in terms of throughput, area and throughput per area. E. Homsirikamol et al. [12] discussed and reported their results for various architectures of Keccak using

Table 2. Comparison of Keccak Implementations. F_{max} in MHz, $Area$ in Slices, TP in Gbps and TPA in Mbps/Slice

Author(s)	Device	Keccak-256				Keccak-512			
		F_{max}	$Area$	TP	TPA	F_{max}	$Area$	TP	TPA
This work	Virtex 6	301.57	**915**	**13.67**	**14.94**	291.21	**1015**	6.99	**6.89**
This work	Virtex 5	275.56	1333	12.49	**9.37**	263.16	**1197**	6.32	5.28
Keccak Team [6]	Virtex 5	122.00	1330	5.20	3.91	-	-	-	-
Strömbergson [7]	Spartan3A	85.00	3393	4.80	1.41	-	-	-	-
Strömbergson [7]	Virtex 5	118.00	1483	6.70	4.52	-	-	-	
Baldwin et al.[8]	Virtex 5	195.73	1971	6.26	3.17	195.73	1971	8.52	4.32
Matsuo et al. [9]	Virtex 5	205.00	1433	4.20	2.93	-	-	-	-
Akin et al. [10]	Spartan 3	81.40	2024	3.46	1.71	-	-	-	-
Akin et al. [10]	Virtex-II	136.60	2024	5.81	2.87	-	-	-	-
Akin et al. [10]	Virtex 4	142.90	2024	6.07	3.00		-	-	-
Kris Gaj et al. [11]	Virtex 5	238.38	1229	10.81	8.79	276.86	1236	6.64	5.37
E. Hom. et al. [12]	Virtex 6	-	1165	11.84	10.17	-	1231	7.23	5.87
E. Hom. et al. [12]	Virtex 5	-	1395	12.77	9.16	-	1220	6.56	5.37

pipelining, folding and loop unrolling approaches. For performance comparison, we considered the results of architecture based on basic iterative approach. However, our results in terms of throughput per area are exceeding all of their results. Our results for Virtex 6 and Virtex 5 are far ahead from all previously reported work in terms of throughput per area, except for Keccak-512 on Virtex 5. We show best results of our work in bold font in Table 2.

6   Conclusion

In this work we have presented high throughput hardware implementation of SHA-3 finalist: Keccak. Look-Up Table (LUT) resources on FPGAs are used to enhance the hardware performance of Keccak in terms of both speed and area. We reported the implementation results of Keccak-256 and Keccak-512 on Xilinx Virtex 6 and Virtex 5. We reported the performance figures of our implementation in terms of area, throughput and throughput per area and compared it with previously reported implementation results. Results achieved in this work are exceeding the implementations reported so far. We compared and contrasted the performance figures of Keccak-256 and Keccak-512 on Virtex 5 and Virtex 6. This work serves as performance investigation of Keccak on most up-to-date FPGAs. Moreover, our design can be used for latest gigabit wire speed communication networks such as 10Gbps Ethernet.

References

1. Xiaoyun Wang, X.L., Feng, D., Yu, H.: Collisions for hash functions MD4, MD5, HAVAL-128 and RIPEMD. Cryptology ePrint Archive, Report 2004/199, pp. 1–4 (2004), http://eprint.iacr.org/2004/199
2. Szydlo, M.: SHA-1 collisions can be found in 2^{63} operations. CryptoBytes Technical Newsletter (2005)
3. Stevens, M.: Fast collision attack on MD5. ePrint-2006-104, pp. 1–13 (2006), http://eprint.iacr.org/2006/104.pdf
4. Federal Register / Vol. 72, No. 212 / Friday, November 2 (2007), / Notices, http://csrc.nist.gov/groups/ST/hash/documents/FR_Notice_Nov07.pdf
5. National Institute of Standards and Technology (NIST): Cryptographic Hash Algorithm Competition, http://www.nist.gov/itl/csd/ct/
6. Bertoni, G., Daemen, J., Peeters, M., Assche, G.V.: The Keccak SHA-3 Submission version 3, pp. 1–14 (2011), http://keccak.noekeon.org/Keccak-submission-3.pdf
7. Strömbergson, J.: Implementation of the Keccak Hash Function in FPGA Devices, pp. 1–4 (2008), http://www.strombergson.com/files/Keccak_in_FPGAs.pdf
8. Baldwin, B., Hanley, N., Hamilton, M., Lu, L., Byrne, A., Neill, M., Marnane, W.P.: FPGA Implementations of the Round Two SHA-3 Candidates. In: 2nd SHA-3 Candidate Conference, Santa Barbara, August 23-24, pp. 1–18 (2010)

9. Matsuo, S., Knezevic, M., Schaumont, P., Verbauwhede, I., Satoh, A., Sakiyama, K., Ota, K.: How Can We Conduct Fair and Consistent Hardware Evaluation for SHA-3 Candidate? In: 2nd SHA-3 Candidate Conference, Santa Barbara, August 23-24, pp. 1–15 (2010)

10. Akin, A., Aysu, A., Ulusel, O.C., Savas, E.: Efficient Hardware Implementations of High Throughput SHA-3 Candidates Keccak, Luffa and Blue Midnight Wish for Single and Multi-Message Hashing. In: 2nd SHA-3 Candidate Conference, Santa Barbara, August 23-24, pp. 1–12 (2010)

11. Gaj, K., Homsirikamol, E., Rogawski, M.: Comprehensive Comparison of Hardware Performance of Fourteen Round 2 SHA-3 Candidates with 512-bit Outputs Using Field Programmable Gate Arrays. In: 2nd SHA-3 Candidate Conference, Santa Barbara, August 23-24, pp. 1–14 (2010)

12. Homsirikamol, E., Rogawski, M., Gaj, K.: Comparing Hardware Performance of Round 3 SHA-3 Candidates using Multiple Hardware Architectures in Xilinx and Altera FPGAs. In: ECRYPT II Hash Workshop 2011, Tallinn, Estonia, May 19-20, pp. 1–15 (2011)

CRAIS: A Crossbar Based Adaptive Interconnection Scheme

Chao Wang[1,2], Xi Li[1], Xuehai Zhou[1], and Xiaojing Feng[1,2]

[1] School of Computer Science, University of Science and Technology of China
[2] Suzhou Institute of Advanced Study, University of Science and Technology of China
{saintwc,bangyan}@mail.ustc.edu.cn
{llxx,xhzhou}@ustc.edu.cn

Abstract. This paper proposes a scheme of a crossbar based on-chip adaptive interconnection, named CRAIS. CRAIS utilizes crossbar to connect processors and IP cores in MPSoC. The interconnect topology of CRAIS can be dynamically reconfigured during execution. Empirical results on FPGA prototype demonstrated that CRAIS runs correctly with affordable hardware cost.

Keywords: Adaptive interconnect, crossbar, multi processor system on chip.

1   Introduction

Multiprocessor system-on-chip (MPSoC) has been regarded as one of the most promising architectures in the domain of very large scale integration (VLSI) systems. However, growing with computational complexity, on-chip data communication between processors has become the major bottleneck in MPSoC architecture [1].

In traditional SoC design, on-chip interconnection has primarily considered bus-based schemes for single processor architectures [2]. It has been long predicted that current bus-based architecture will run out of performance as SoC grows in complexity with more processing elements. In addition, the flexibility of bus-based architectures is constrained due to fixed data path interconnections [3].

To address this problem, past decades have witnessed the tremendous invasion of novel interconnection paradigms, including Networks on Chip (NoC), crossbar and ring-based interconnections. These approaches have been merged for designing scalable on-chip communication architectures, providing better structure and modularity. Of the state-of-art schemes, design flexibility of NoC is higher than other interconnection schemes, thus they are widely used in large-scale systems. However, for small scale MPSoC systems (which basically contain less than ten processors), crossbar based interconnection scheme is still popular due to its high performance.

In this paper, we describe CRAIS, a crossbar based adaptive interconnection scheme. We claim following contributions:

1) Adaptive interconnection with run-time configuration: we design and implement a hardware crossbar based interconnection module, which can be adapted automati-

O.C.S. Choy et al. (Eds.): ARC 2012, LNCS 7199, pp. 379–384, 2012.
© Springer-Verlag Berlin Heidelberg 2012

cally during task execution. Furthermore, tasks can be stored into buffers if they are not able to run immediately.

2) Prototype on FPGA development board. We take the effort to build a prototype on FPGA, and evaluate hardware logic resources consumed by CRAIS.

2   CRAIS Architecture

The system architecture is illustrated in Figure 1. The heterogeneous MPSoC platform consists of following components:

- Processor array: multiple processors are integrated to run control and user-interaction tasks. Each processor is connected to CRAIS through dual FIFO based links.
- IP core array: heterogeneous hardware IP cores (HWIP) are integrated into the platform to run specific tasks for hardware acceleration.
- CRAIS interconnection: all the function units (FUs, including processors and HWIP) are connected to CRAIS. Three major components are implemented inside CRAIS: first, a configuration controller is introduced to operate the configuration process. Second, a queue module shared by processors and IP cores is employed to buffer the tasks temporarily when task cannot run immediately. Finally, a semaphore is used for the synchronization.
- Peripherals. To support system debugging and verification, following peripherals are integrated: DDR DRAM controller, Ethernet controller, system ACE controller, UART, timer and interrupt controller.

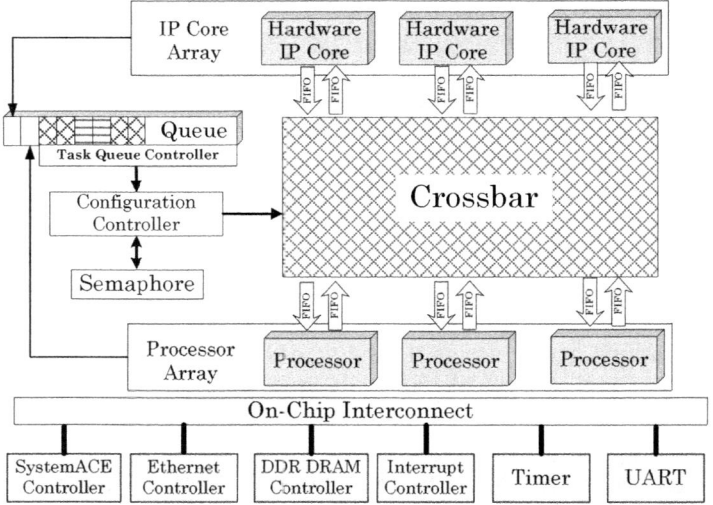

Fig. 1. Heterogeneous MPSoC Hardware Platform

2.1   Hardware Interconnection and Communication Protocol

In order to reduce the data transfer delay, we employ Xilinx FSL links between FUs and CRAIS. A FSL link provides a FIFO based peer to peer data path between master and slave modules. The read and write bus transactions can be directly called by specific instructions. In Xilinx Microblaze processor instruction set architecture (ISA), GET(get, nget, cget and ncget) and PUT(put ,nput, cput, ncput) instructions [4] are designed to operate data transfer between processor register files and FSL FIFO buffers. Similarly, all the IP cores are packaged into unified FSL based interface to be connected to CRAIS.

The processor and IP cores communicate with each other in a Master-Slave manner. When a task is distributed, processor acts as master. On the contrary, IP core plays a master role when results are returned in the end of execution.

In order to utilize FSL for run-time adaptation, the communication transaction is spited into two phases: configuration and data transfer. In this paper, we reuse the FSL signals from traditional bus communication protocol. The two-phase is described as follows:

- First, in configuration stage, the configuration activation request is sent through *FSL_M_Control* signal. The *FSL_M_Control* signal is reused to indicate whether current bus transaction is in configuration stage or data transfer stage. Simultaneously, *FSL_M_Data* interface is used to indicate the target hardware IP.
- After the requests are received, CRAIS should decide whether the task can be executed immediately. If the target function unit is idle, system will enter bus transfer stage for communication and execution.

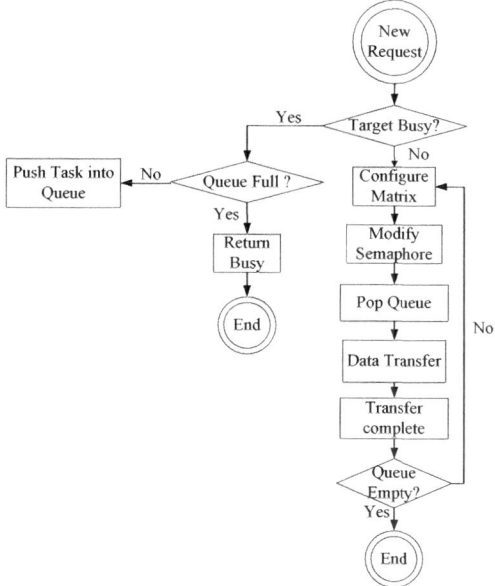

Fig. 2. Process flow of CRAIS adaptive interconnection

2.2   CRAIS Work Flow

Figure 2 outlines the specific process flow of adaptive interconnection algorithm, which is described in following steps:

Algorithm 1. Adaptive Interconnection Algorithm

1: A specific FU sends a task to CRAIS, indicating the target slave module.
2: On receiving the request, CRAIS checks the availability of slave FU: if Yes, then responses the acknowledgement signals to the master, and move to next Step. Otherwise, goto Step 5.
3: The configuration controller in CRAIS sets up the data paths between the master and slave FU, and updates the status of semaphore.
4: Data are transferred through FIFO and crossbar data path. In the end of the transmission, the execution will be started automatically. Meanwhile, goto Step 6.
5: If the target FU is busy, then all the new requests will be stored into the Queue module temporarily. If queue is full, no more requests are acceptable.
6: After the transmission of current task, the head task of the Queue will be released. Data paths are reconfigured according to the task information. Goto the Step 3 for configuration and data transfer process. If the Queue is empty, which means there are no more pending tasks in the system, the process will be terminated.

2.3   State Transfer

Figure 3 describes the state transfer diagram with following three states:

- When all the FUs are not busy, and the queue is empty, which means there are no tasks running in the system, therefore system is in IDLE state.
- When a new request arrives, CRAIS will enter BUSY state. The semaphore is set, and crossbar is configured.
- When a single request is finished, CRAIS turns into Free State. Here the queue model will be checked: if all tasks inside the queue are finished, go to IDLE State. Otherwise, go back to BUSY state. FREE State only takes for several cycles for checking the status.

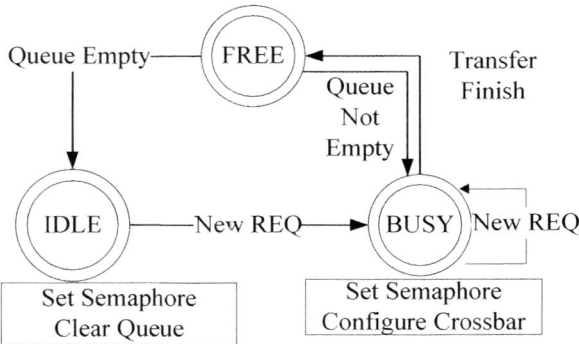

Fig. 3. State transfer chart

3   FPGA Prototype and Preliminary Results

3.1   FPGA Prototype

We built a prototype system on a state-of-art Xilinx Virtex-5 FPGA board and implemented IP cores from EEMBC Benchmarks: AES and IDCT modules. Along with the hardware modules, we also employ three Microblaze processors. Microblaze processor is a soft-core with PowerPC ISA, and also optimized for Xilinx FPGA implementations. The block diagram is presented in Figure 4.   At the time of writing this paper, the performance evaluation is still undergoing. We have verified the correctness and measured the hardware costs.

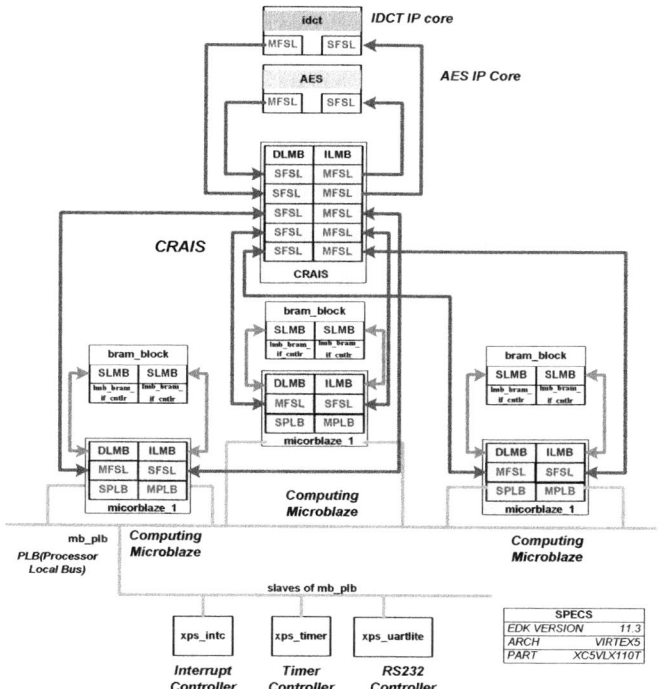

Fig. 4. Prototype system

3.2   Hardware Overheads

To evaluate hardware resources, we synthesized the system in Xilinx ISE and EDK tools with different widths of crossbar (8, 16, and 32).

Figure 5 depicts the hardware cost of CRAIS module with different data widths. When the data width is 64-bit, the module cannot be synthesized in the devices due to the limitation of IO blocks resources. The XC5VLX110T FPGA has only 640 IO blocks. When the data width is 64-bit, each connected block has at least 64×2=128 bits, excluding the request, control and status signals. For demonstration, we implemented 5 FUs, and then the total signal number is 128×5=640, which exceeds the limitation of FPGA device.

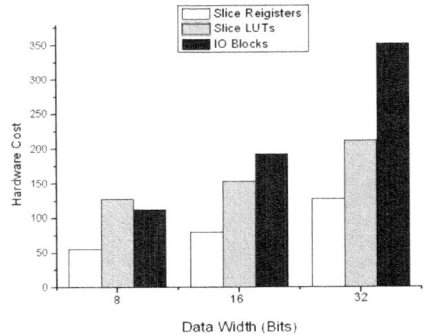

Fig. 5. Hardware cost for CRAIS module

4   Conclusion and Future Work

This paper describes a reconfigurable crossbar based on-chip interconnection scheme CRAIS, which not only regards processors and HWIP as function units, but also reconfigures the on-chip interconnections at run-time. Each FU is connected to CRAIS with a pair of peer-to-peer FIFO based links. We built a prototype system on FPGA and empirical results demonstrated that CRAIS works correctly with affordable hardware cost.

Acknowledgments. This research was supported by the National Science Foundation of China under grants No.60873221 and Jiangsu production-teaching-research joint innovation project No.BY2009128. We owe many thanks to the anonymous reviewers and editors for their valuable feedback and suggestions.

References

1. Benini, L., De Micheli, G.: Networks on chips: a new SoC paradigm. IEEE Computer 35(1), 70–78 (2002)
2. Wolf, W., Jerraya, A.A., Martin, G.: Multiprocessor System-on-Chip (MPSoC) Technology. IEEE Transactions on Computer-Aided Design of Integrated Circuits and Systems 27(10), 1701–1713 (2008)
3. Dally, W.J., Towles, B.: Route packets, not wires: on-chip interconnection networks. In: Proceedings of the 38th annual Design Automation Conference (DAC 2001), pp. 684–689. ACM, Las Vegas (2001)
4. Rosinger, H.P.: Connecting Customized IP to the MicroBlaze Soft Processor Using the Fast Simplex Link (FSL) Channel. Technical report, Xilinx Inc. (2004)

Author Index